Philippe Boisson

SAFETY AT SEA

POLICIES,

REGULATIONS &

INTERNATIONAL LAW

Translated from French
by Denis Mahaffey

Edition BUREAU VERITAS
PARIS

The views expressed in this book reflect the author's personal opinions, and Bureau Veritas is not responsible for them in any way.

EDITION BUREAU VERITAS - PARIS - 1999

I . S . B . N .   2-86413-020-3

SAFETY AT SEA

POLICIES,

REGULATIONS &

INTERNATIONAL LAW

To Julia, Hélène, Fanny and Martine.

PREFACE
by Mr. William A. O'Neil
Secretary-General
International Maritime Organization

IMO's mission is often summed up in the phrase "safer shipping and cleaner oceans". It is a task that never ends, because the technology of shipping is continually changing and IMO has to ensure that international standards are revised accordingly. This year will see a number of important developments taking place.

On 1st February the Global Maritime Distress and Safety System became fully effective - the culmination of a process that began a quarter of a century ago.

On 1st July requirements concerning vessel traffic services enter into force. A new regulation sets out when such schemes can be implemented. On the same day new measures to improve the safety of ro-ro passenger ships will become international law and new measures concerning the safety of bulk carriers will also become mandatory.

A month later, on 1 August, the waters of North Western Europe will become a "special area" under Annex I of the International Convention for the Prevention of Pollution from Ships, 1973, as modified by the Protocol of 1978 relating thereto (MARPOL 73/78).

Next year will see more changes being made and it is necessary to keep pace with what is happening. That is why this book is so significant. It helps to know why safety is so important - and what is being done to promote it.

William O'NEIL
Secretary-General, International Maritime Organization

ACKNOWLEDGEMENTS

Two decades separate this edition in English of my book on maritime safety policies, regulations and law from my doctoral thesis on the same subject. Twenty eventful years that have seen crucial changes in methods of accident prevention.

My work since 1981 in an international classification society has given me a vantage point from which to observe the day-to-day advances made by the maritime community in reducing accidents. I have also become aware of the difficulties that individuals and organisations experience in changing habits and attitudes, with the aim of achieving a more comprehensive grasp of safety concepts and, what is even more important, fostering a genuine safety culture in the shipping industry.

My references and analyses have been greatly enriched by the contacts and discussions I have enjoyed with those concerned with accident prevention. Indeed, it is the very wealth of such sources that has made the work of writing so lengthy and intricate. It is a topic on which every day brings new developments.

I would like to begin by thanking Mariane Harvey of the IMO library, and her whole team, who gave me much help with my research, for both the French and the English editions.

I am also most grateful to the experts and surveyors in the Marine Division of Bureau Veritas for their willingness to reread, comment and correct my manuscript, and in particular A. Seridji, J.F. Fauduet, H. Pinon, B. Godefroi, P. de Livois, F. Teissier, M. Lebrun, B. Dabouis, D. Beghin, C. Maillot, P. Ricou, A.M. Chauvel, L. Thubert, J.L. Cabaret, G. Tonnerre, M. Guyader and P. Frey. For this edition in English, I have also relied on the knowledge and skills of C. Gladish, R. Conibeer, C. Spencer, P. McOwan, J. Dickie and H. Champness.

I acknowledge the help I have received from extremely competent outside readers:
* Professor P. Bonassies of the Law Faculty of Aix-Marseilles University
* G. Fages, Elf Aquitaine, Paris
* Y. Rocquemont, Maritime Arbitrator, Paris
* M. Marshall, Technical Director, International Underwriting Association, London
* R. Sayer, Partner in Ince & Co, London
* R. Kohn, Head IMO Information Officer, London
* B. Farthing, Consultant Director, INTERCARGO, London
* J. Davis, Chairman of IMIF, London
* J. Bell, Permanent Secretary of IACS, London
* A. Blanco-Bazan, IMO Senior Legal Officer, London

* A. Popp, Senior General Counsel, Department of Justice, Canada
* E. Gold, Professor of Maritime Law, Dalhousie University, Halifax
* C. Horrocks, Secretary-General of ICS, London
* R. Bishop, Head of the Marine and Environmental Section, INTERTANKO, London
* J. Harrison, Group Legal Director, Lloyd's Register, London
* J. Parker, Secretary, Nautical Institute, London
* F. Wiswal, Attorney and Counsellor at Law, Proctor and Advocate in Admiralty, Vice-President CMI, Castine, USA
* J. Smith, IACS Permanent Representative to IMO, London
* R. Bradley, former Chief Executive of the United Kingdom Government's Marine Safety Agency, and Deputy General Manager of the Salvage Association, London
* R. Peckham, Head of Information Services, BRS, Paris
* R. Schiferli, Head of Secretariat and, N. Dofferhoff, Assistant Secretary, Paris MOU, The Hague
* T. Kruuse, Secretary-General, and P. Kent, Technical Representative, IALA, Saint Germain en Laye, France
* M. Gauthier, Senior Counsel, Transport Canada Legal Services, Ottawa
* J. Guy, Marine Consultant, Merlin Corporate Communications, Crawley, England.

I could not have wished for a better publisher than Bureau Veritas, with its worldwide reputation for risk prevention. I wish to express my warm gratitude to its Chairman, B. Renard, and B. Anne, Senior Vice-President of the Marine Division, for supporting the publication of this book.

I owe special thanks to Denis Mahaffey, who has collaborated for many years on Bureau Veritas publications in English, and who has coped splendidly with the challenge of translating my book to a very short deadline.

Finally, I wish to thank my family, friends and colleagues for their advice and encouragement during the six years that have gone into writing this book.

CONTENTS

LIST OF TABLES

ABBREVIATIONS

ABS	American Bureau of Shipping
ACDI	Annuaire Canadien de Droit International
ACOPS	Advisory Committee on Protection of the Sea
ADMA	Annuaire de Droit Maritime et Aérien
AFDI	Annuaire Français de Droit International
AFDM	Association Française du Droit Maritime
AIDI	Annuaire de l'Institut de Droit International
AISM	Association Internationale de Signalisation Maritime
AJIL	American Journal of International Law
AMRIE	Alliance of Maritime Regional Interests in Europe
ARPA	Automatic Radar Plotting Aids
ASLP	Archipelagic Sea Lane Passage
ATMA	Association Technique Maritime et Aéronautique
AUTF	Association des Utilisateurs de Transport de Fret
AWES	Association of European Shipbuilders and Shiprepairers
BAP	Best Achievable Protection (standards)
BCH Code	Bulk Chemical Code
BIMCO	Baltic and International Maritime Council
BOMM	Bulletin Officiel de la Marine Marchande
Bull.	Bulletin
BV	Bureau Veritas
Cass	Cour de Cassation
CAP	Condition Assessment Programme
CDI	Chemical Distribution Institute
CE	Conseil d'Etat
CEFIC	European Chemical Industry Council
CEFOR	Central Union of Marine Insurers
CENSA	Council of European and Japanese Shipowners Associations
CIRM	Comité International Radio-Maritime
CJTL	Columbia Journal of Transnational Law
CLC	Civil Liability for Oil Pollution Damage
CMI	Comité Maritime International
CNC	Centralised Navigation Control
COLREG	Collision Regulations
COPEREP	Committee of Permanent Representatives
COFR	Certificate of Financial Responsibility
COW	Crude Oil Washing
CSJWG	Classification Societies Joint Working Group

DMF	Droit Maritime Français
DNV	Det Norske Veritas
DOC	Document of Compliance
DSC	Dynamically Supported Craft
	Digital Selective Calling
dwt	Dead Weight Tonnage
ECDIS	Electronic Chart Display and Information System
ECJ	European Court of Justice of the European Communities
ECOSOC	Economic and Social Committee
ECS	Electronic Chart System
EEIG	European Economic Interest Group
EEZ	Exclusive Economic Zone
EMOM	Editions Maritimes et d'Outre-Mer
ENC	Electronic Navigation Chart
ENSTA	Ecole Nationale des Techniques Avancées
EPIRB	Emergency Position-Indicating Radio Beacon
ESP	Enhanced Survey Programme
EURACS	European Association of Classification Societies
EUROREP	European Vessel Reporting System
EWS	Early Warning Scheme
FAO	Food and Agriculture Organisation
FOC	Flag of Convenience
FSA	Formal Safety Assessment
FSI	Flag State Implementation
FTP	Fire Test Procedure
Gaz. Pal.	Gazette du Palais
GESAMP	Joint Group of Experts on the Scientific Aspects of Marine Pollution
GMDSS	Global Maritime Distress and Safety System
GNSS	Global Navigation Satellite System
GPG	General Policy Group
GPS	Global Positioning System
grt	Gross Registered Tonnage
HSC	High Speed Craft
IACS	International Association of Classification Societies
IAEA	International Atomic Energy Agency
IAIN	International Association of Institutes of Navigation
IALA	International Association of Lighthouse Authorities
IAPH	International Association of Ports and Harbours
IBC Code	International Bulk Chemical Code
IBJ	International Bulk Journal
ICAO	International Civil Aviation Organisation

ICC	International Chamber of Commerce
ICHCA	International Cargo Handling Coordination Association
ICJ	International Court of Justice
ICS	International Chamber of Shipping
IDIT	Institut de Droit International des Transports
IEC	International Electrotechnical Commission
IETM	Institut d'Economie des Transports Maritimes
IFSMA	International Federation of Shipmasters Associations
IFT	Institut Français du Pétrole
IGC Code	International Gas Carrier Code
IGO	Intergovernmental Organisation
IGOSS	Integrated Global Ocean Stations System
IGS	Inert Gas System
IHB	International Hydrographic Bureau
IHMA	International Harbour Masters Association
IHO	International Hydrographic Organisation
IJMCL	International Journal of Marine and Coastal Law
ILCQ	International and Comparative Law Quarterly
ILO	International Labour Organisation
ILU	Institute of London Underwriters
IMCO	Intergovernmental Maritime Consultative Organization
IMDG Code	International Maritime Dangerous Goods Code
IMIF	International Maritime Industries Forum
IMLI	International Maritime Law Institute
IMO	International Maritime Organization
IMPA	International Maritime Pilots Association
IMTM	Institut Méditerranéen des Transports Maritimes
INF Code	Irradiated Nuclear Fuels Code
INMARSAT	International Maritime Satellite Telecommunications Organisation
INTERCARGO	International Association of Dry Cargo Shipowners
INTERTANKO	International Association of Independent Tanker Owners
IOC	Intergovernmental Oceanographic Commission
IOPP	International Oil Pollution Prevention
ISF	International Shipping Federation
ISID	International Ship Information Databases
ISL	Institute of Shipping Economics and Logistics
ISM	International Safety Management
ISMA	International Ship Managers Association
ISO	International Organisation for Standardisation
IT	Information Technologies
ITF	International Transport Workers Federation
ITOPF	International Tanker Owners Pollution Federation
ITU	International Telecommunications Union
IUMI	International Union of Marine Insurance
JAMRI	Japanese Maritime Research Institute

JCP	Jurisclasseur Périodique (Semaine Juridique)
JDI (Clunet)	Journal de Droit International
JMC	Joint Maritime Commission
JMLC	Journal of Maritime Law and Commerce
JMM	Journal de la Marine Marchande
JO	Journal Officiel de la République Française
LL	Load Line
LMCLQ	Lloyd's Maritime and Commercial Law Quarterly
LMIS	Lloyd's Maritime Information Services
LNG	Liquefied Natural Gas
LOS	Law of the Sea
LPG	Liquefied Petroleum Gas
LRS	Lloyd's Register of Shipping
LSA	Lifesaving Appliances
LSI	Law of Sea Institute
MAIB	Marine Accident Investigation Branch
MARIS	Maritime Systems of the Future
MAREP	Marine Reporting Scheme
MARPOL	Marine Pollution
MEP	Member of the European Parliament
MEPC	Marine Environment Protection Committee
MER	Marine Engineer Review
MERSAR	Merchant Ship Search and Rescue Manual
MIF	Maritime Industries Forum
MOU	Memorandum of Understanding
MSC	Maritime Safety Committee
NAV	Safety of Navigation Subcommittee
NAVAREA	Navigation Area
NED	Notes et Etudes Documentaires
NGO	Non-Governmental Organisation
NLS	Noxious Liquid Substances
NMO	Norwegian Maritime Directorate
NPC	Navires Ports et Chantiers
NRC	National Research Council
NTM	Nouveautés Techniques Maritimes
NTSB	National Transportation Safety Board
NUMAST	National Union of Marine, Aviation and Shipping Transport Officers
NYIL	Netherlands Year Book of International Law
OBO	Oil/Bulk/Ore Carrier
OCIMF	Oil Companies International Marine Forum
ODIL	Ocean Development and International Law
OECD	Organisation for Economic Co-operation and Development

OJEC	Official Journal of the European Communities
OMBO	One-Man Bridge Operation
OMS	Office of Marine Safety
O/O	Oil/Ore Carrier
OPA	Oil Pollution Act
ORM	Operational Response Monitoring
OSPA	Oil Spill Prevention Act
P&I	Protection and Indemnity Club
PIANC	Permanent International Association of Navigation Congresses
PSC	Port State Control
PSSA	Particularly Sensitive Areas
PUF	Presse Universitaire de France
QSCS	Quality System Certification Scheme
RBDI	Revue Belge de Droit International
RCADI	Recueil des Cours de l'Académie de Droit International de La Haye
Rev. Dor	Revue de Droit Maritime Comparé
RGDIP	Revue Générale de Droit International Public
RINA	Royal Institute of Naval Architects
RIT	Revue Internationale du Travail
RJE	Revue Juridique de l'Environnement
RTSPB	Revue Technique du Service des Phares et Balises
SAR	Search and Rescue
SART	Survival Craft Radar Transponder
SBT	Segregated Ballast Tank
SENC	System Electronic Navigation Chart
SFDA	Société Française de Droit Aérien
SFDI	Société Française de Droit International
SIGTTO	Society of International Gas Tanker and Terminal Operators
SIRE	Ship Inspection Report Exchange
SHOM	Service Hydrographique et Océanographique de la Marine
SMCP	Standard Marine Communication Phases
SMS	Safety Management System
SNAME	American Society of Naval Architects and Marine Engineers
SMNV	Standard Marine Navigational Vocabulary
SOLAS	Safety of Life At Sea
SRS	Ship Reporting System
STCW	Standards of Training, Certification and Watchkeeping (for Seafarers)
SWATH	Small Waterplane Area Twin Hull
TOCA	Transfer of Class Agreement
TSM	Techniques et Sciences Municipales
TSS	Traffic Separation Scheme

UI	Unified Interpretation
ULCC	Ultra-Large Crude Carrier
UNCTAD	United Nations Conference on Trade and Development
UR	Unified Rule
USCG	United States Coast Guard
VDA	Voyage Data Recorder
VLCC	Very Large Crude Carrier
VDR	Voyage Data Recorder
VRP	Vessel Response Plan
VTMIS	Vessel Traffic Management Information System
VTS	Vessel Traffic Services
WHO	World Health Organisation
WMO	World Meteorological Organisation
WMU	World Maritime University
WWNWS	World-Wide Navigational Warning Service
WWRNS	World-Wide Radio Navigation System

CHAPTER 1

Safety at sea and prevention of accidents

I - GENERAL DEFINITIONS

• **Safety at sea**

1. - In the expressions "safety at sea" and "maritime safety", safety is both the material state resulting from the absence of exposure to danger, and the organisation of factors intended to create or perpetuate such a situation.

Three different concepts are distinguished by one legal authority in the use of the term in maritime law (1). These are health and safety, safety of navigation, and "state security", corresponding to the requirements of national defence.

At the present time, safety is regarded as one of the essential reasons for policing the marine environment, and as justification for the main departures from the principle of freedom of the seas. In this context, other commentators (2) have defined :
- safety of navigation, for the purpose of saving human life at sea and providing defence against perils of the sea, including heavy weather, collision, stranding or any other danger that may be encountered ;
- safety of trade, the aim of which is to protect a ship against dangers caused by unlawful acts, such as piracy, maritime fraud and barratry.

Safety of navigation being somewhat narrower in meaning, this book uses the expressions "maritime safety" and, more simply, "safety at sea".

• **Maritime risks**

2. - Unlike safety, the concept of risk is not easy to define. In the dictionaries, it is a synonym of danger, hazard, peril. In technical terms, risk is the consequence, in terms of cost, of an accident multiplied by the probability of its occurrence (risk = probability x consequence) (3). For lawyers, risk is the possibility of an event which may have damaging consequences.

The risks incurred by those engaged in an activity at sea, the ultimate hostile environment, are highly diversified, although they may be placed under two main headings (4) :
- personal risks, namely injuries and accidents suffered by those aboard ship; such events are the same as on shore, although their consequences may be increased by shipboard conditions ;
- collective risks peculiar to a ship, its cargo or conditions of navigation ; these can lead to accidents at sea, injurious events caused by the occurrence of fortuitous circumstances or negligent or deliberate acts (5).

---

(1) G. GIDEL : "Le droit international public de la mer". Tome III, Paris. Sirey 1934, 455.
(2) A.R. WERNER : "Traité de droit maritime général". Librairie Droz, Geneva 1964, 38-39.
(3) O. MALMHOLT : "First step in reducing accidents at sea. A risk inventory". Safety at Sea, May 1983, 46.
(4) ALBIACH and SMOL : "Traité du navire de commerce". Volume premier. E.N.S.T.A.. Paris, 1971, 7.
(5) R. RODIERE : "Traité général de droit maritime. Evénements de mer". Paris, Dalloz 1972, 11.

• **Casualties**

3. - Lloyd's Register of Shipping publishes lists of total casualties, in seven main categories :

- **Missing** : Ships of which no news is received after a reasonable period of time, so that their fate is undetermined ;

- **Fire** and **explosion** ;

- **Collision** : Ships which strike or are struck by another ship or ships, regardless of whether they are under way, anchored or moored ;

- **Contact** : Ships which strike a floating body (tree trunk, wreck, or platform, whether fixed or in tow) or fixed land installations (e.g. ports, bridges) ;

- **Wrecked/stranded** : Ships which involuntarily touch the sea bottom, not to be confused with deliberate grounding, producing the same effect ;

- **Loss** as a result of hull or machinery damage or failure ;

- **Foundering** : submersion of the ship as a result of heavy weather, springing of leaks or breaking in two, not as a consequence of any of the incidents listed above.

II - STATISTICAL ANALYSES OF SAFETY AT SEA

One way of assessing the level of safety at sea is to consult the many statistical sources available, usually produced by marine insurers or on their behalf.

• **Ship casualty statistics**

4. - These are the most numerous, cover the longest historical period and are generally the object of greatest media comment. They provide an analysis of world shipping losses in tonnage and number of ships, according to the criteria of geographical area, ship age, size, type and flag. Established on the same bases over several decades, they allow comparisons to be made over long periods. The two main sources as Lloyd's Register of Shipping (LRS) and the Institute of London Underwriters (ILU).

The LRS casualty review lists losses of all ships of more than 100 grt. Figures are based on actual losses, not constructive losses :
- constructive total losses are primarily ships accepted by insurers as beyond economic repair ;
- actual losses are mostly foundered, non-recoverable or destroyed ships, defined as such by insurers, not those scrapped by the owner for economic reasons, but which insurers might regard as recoverable.
    The ILU annual report contains a statistical appendix on ship and aircraft accidents. It takes account of all actual and constructive losses of ships of more than 500 grt, excepting war casualties.

The statistical sources of LRS and ILU are used widely by research institutes and other bodies concerned with safety at sea. The Institute of Mathematical Statistics & Operations Research (IMSOR), at the Technical University of Denmark, turned to ILU data to prepare an analysis of trends in marine losses and major casualties from 1984 to 1992 (6). In 1993, the Nautical Institute held an international conference on accident and loss prevention at sea (7).

Statistics available on the market do not claim to be exhaustive. These deficiencies are overcome by the authorities of leading maritime states, which possess their own means of analysis and synthesis. The Marine Accident Investigation Branch (MAIB), for example, supplies a report on British merchant ships involved in accidents. The Japan Maritime Research Institute (JAMRI) also issues regular studies, for example one on world and Japanese shipping casualties, published in 1993 (8).

• **Statistics on loss of life**
5. - These statistics throw a sharp light on the dangers that accompany activities at sea, but on the whole they remain quite inadequate. In the absence of worldwide databases on deaths and personal injuries suffered at sea, one has to rely on information issued by the private bodies referred to above.

LRS takes account only of passengers and seamen who have died or are missing in a total loss, not the huge numbers of accidents in the perilous seas of the Third World. The ILU surveys only loss of life caused by accidents to ships of more than 500 grt, whereas certain national sources reveal that most deaths and injuries occur on board small craft, particularly fishing boats and tugs (9). This shortage of internationally comparable data suggests that official figures could be multiplied by at least ten (10). Of course it is also possible to turn to the reports issued by flag administrations after an incident at sea, but the information they contain usually remains inconsistent and unequal in value, from one state to another.

• **Statistics on general average**
6. - Average has two very different meanings. It can refer to damage to a ship or its cargo, or to charges payable on a ship and its cargo, separately or jointly. Average is "general" when it involves contributions from those taking part in the maritime expedition, in other words the shipowner and the shipper.

Marine insurers have rather overlooked this survival of ancient times, a source of minor though complex claims. However, the system has very important implications for safety at sea: it is the bad shipowner, operating with old, substandard vessels, that totals the largest number of incidents. He is therefore likely to receive the largest amounts for general average from hull and cargo insurers.

(6) P. THYREGOD, B.F. NIELSEN : "Trends in marine losses and major casualties, 1984-1992". IMSOR Technical Report n° 8/1993. Denmark.
(7) The Nautical Institute : "Accidents and loss prevention at sea". International Conference and Workshops. London, Nov. 1993.
(8) JAMRI : "Analysis of World / Japan's shipping casualties and future prospects thereof". Report n° 47, November 1993, Tokyo, Japan.
(9) 1990 non-casualty-related deaths and injuries. US Coast Guard figures for all vessels in US waters. Lloyd's List, 16 Feb. 1994.
(10) "The Unknown Toll : the grim scandal of loss of life at sea". Lloyd's List, 16 Feb. 1994.
V. également R. GOSS : "The Future of Maritime Safety". 8th Chua Chor Teck Annual Memorial Lecture. Singapore, 12 Jan. 1994.

General average statistics also provide valuable information on the level of safety of world merchant shipping. Oddly enough, such information has become available only quite recently, thanks to the efforts of the International Union of Maritime Insurance (IUMI) and ILU, which since 1993 have gathered data on almost two thousand incidents.

These statistics show that the vast majority (at least 90 per cent) of the cases arise from ship operation, while the condition of the ship is responsible for only 50 per cent, and navigation for 30 per cent (cf figure 1).

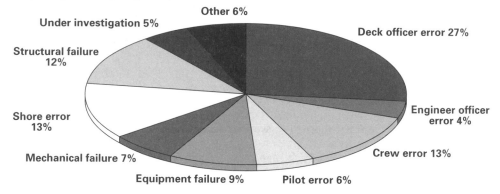

Figure 1 - Main causes of major claims
(Sources : UK P&I Club : Analysis of major claims 1993)

• **Compensation claim statistics**

7. - Another useful way of discovering the scale and origins of accidents is the statistical information provided by Protection and Indemnity (P&I) clubs, which cover the civil liability of shipowners.

The largest is the United Kingdom Mutual Steamship Assurance Association, which insures eight thousand ships, totalling 100 million gross tonnage, in other words a quarter of all world shipping. Since 1987, it has carried out a regular study of the average of 25 000 compensation claims it receives every year from its members. These statistics show the most frequent types of claims, their main causes, and predominant factors in the occurrence of accidents. They reveal that human error is the cause of more than 60 per cent of all accidents (cf figure 2) (11).

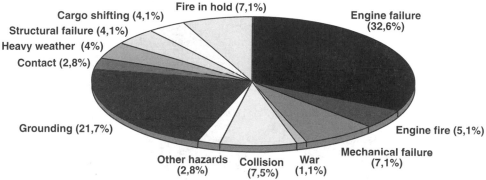

Figure 2 - The causes of General Average by number of claims *(Source : ILU Annual Report 1994, 12)*

(11) UK P and I Club : Analysis of major claims 1993, 12.

• Accidental oil spill statistics
8. - The final indicator of the level of safety at sea consists of statistics on accidental marine pollution. The most comprehensive studies in this respect have been carried out by the Joint Group of Experts on Scientific Aspects of Marine Pollution (GESAMP), an intergovernmental body set up by eight UN specialised agencies.

Other analyses are produced regularly by the International Tanker Owners Pollution Federation (ITOPF), and occasionally by certain non-governmental organisations such as the Advisory Committee on Protection of the Sea (ACOPS).

Statistics provide fuller general knowledge of accidents and their origins (12), although of course overall evaluations do not provide any opportunity for examining safety problems in detail. A factual investigation has to be made of every event, in order to discover the conditions under which it occurred. Such meticulous analysis is not always feasible, particularly when ships vanish at sea without trace.

III - RECURRENCE OF MAJOR MARITIME DISASTERS

Despite the technical progress achieved, the maritime community cannot claim the same level of safety at sea as in the air. The nature of the danger is too different, and its possible consequences remain formidable, despite the precautions that are taken (13). The history of shipping is punctuated by countless disasters, responsible for the deaths of thousands of people and large-scale ecological mishaps.

• Shipping accidents
9. - No period of history has been free of calamitous accidents at sea (cf figure 3). The most serious involve passenger transport, which was a fast-growing business throughout the 19th century. Three terrible events before the First World War were engraved on people's memories : the explosion of the *Sultana* in 1865 with 1 450 deaths, the foundering of the *Titanic* in 1912 with 1 501 deaths, and of the *Empress of Ireland* in 1914 with 1 270 deaths.

Since 1948, nearly all major maritime disasters have involved carferries and simple ferries used to carry passengers over short distances. There were 1 000 victims in the accident to the *Don Juan* in 1980, more than 4 400 in 1987 on the *Dona Paz*, and another 1 800 on the *Neptune* in 1993. Certain regions are particularly hazardous for shipping, such as the Philippines archipelago with its seven thousand islands. Since 1982, three thousand accidents have occurred in these waters, with an average six hundred fatalities every year (15). Philippines

(12) United Kingdom Mutual Steam Ship Assurance Association : Analysis of major claims, 1993, 12.
(13) P. CHAUVEAU : "Traité de droit maritime". Librairies Techniques, Paris 1958, 8.
(14)
- Otto MIELKE : "Les grandes catastrophes maritimes". Denoel, Paris 1958.
- K.C. BARNABY : "Some ship disasters and their causes". Hutchinson, London, 1968.
- Milton H. WATSON : "Disasters at sea. Every ocean-going passenger ship's catastrophe since 1900".
  Patrick Stephens, England, 1987.
- John MARRIOTT : "Disasters at sea". Hippocrene Books, Inc, New York, 1987.
- Edward T. GATES : "Maritime accidents. What went wrong ?" Gulf Shipping Company, Houston, 1989.
- Norman HOOKE : "Modern Shipping Disasters, 1963-1987". Lloyd's of London Press, London 1989.
- Charles HOCKING : "Dictionary of disasters at sea during the age of steam, 1824-1862".
  The London Stamp Exchange, London, 1989.
- Richard A. CAHILL : "Disasters at sea. Titanic to Exxon Valdez". Century, London, 1990.
(15) A. ALMAZAN : "Floating coffins shame". Lloyd's List, 1 March 1996.

sources say annual death tolls number tens of thousands. In general, it has been calculated that ten and a half thousand people died between 1983 and 1993 in shipwrecks occurring off the coasts of Third World countries (16).

Two recent disasters in European waters had worldwide repercussions. The capsizing of the *Herald of Free Enterprise* in March 1987 in the port of Zeebrugge, with the loss of 193 lives (17), and the sinking of the *Estonia* in September 1994 in the Baltic (18), with nearly 850 fatalities, induced the international community to engage in a far-reaching revision of the conditions of safety on ro-ro passenger ships.

Nowadays, lack of safety on board ships does not affect only people venturing out to sea. It also threatens coastal populations living near a port. There was the notorious case of the explosion of the *Mont Blanc* on 7 December 1917 in the Canadian port of Halifax, in which 1 900 people died, more than 9 000 were injured, and 6 000 were left homeless (19). In more recent times, a bulk carrier struck a pier in New Orleans in December 1996 on which a shopping mall had been built, injuring more than one hundred people (20).

• Oil spills and ecological disasters

10. - Another danger that threatens coastal populations is oil pollution caused by accidents to tankers. The fact that such spillage represents a small fraction of total damage to the ocean environment in volume should not hide the seriousness of such events. Massive, concentrated pollution of the coast can cause wide-scale ecological and economic damage to the area concerned. In thirteen years, for example, Brittany suffered six successive oil spills, the *Torrey Canyon* in 1967, the *Olympic Bravery* and the *Boehlen* in 1976, the *Amoco Cadiz* in 1978, the *Gino* in 1979 and the *Tanio* in 1980. Another ecological disaster that had a global impact was the pollution of the Alaskan coasts by the *Exxon Valdez* in 1989 (21), even though, in quantify of oil spilt, the accident came only thirty-fifth among the worst cases of oil pollution on record (22).

More recently, the *Aegean Sea*, the *Braer* and the *Sea Empress* accidents caused fairly limited pollution but, as with the *Exxon Valdez*, media repercussions were enormous.

Transport of toxic or potentially dangerous substances by sea constitutes yet another threat to the environment. Fortunately, few accidents have occurred in the last fifty years.

(16) J. MULRENAN : "Will Neptune be remembered?". Lloyd's List, 20 Fev. 1993.
(17) S. CRAINER : "Zeebrugge & learning from disaster". Herald Charitable Trust. London, 1993.
(18) Joint Accident Investigation Commission of Estonia, Finland and Sweden : "Final Report on the capsizing on 28 Sept. 1994 in the Baltic Sea of the Roro passengers vessel. MV *Estonia*". Helsinki, Edito Ltd, 1997.
(19) J.F. KITZ : "Shattered City. The Holifax explosion and the road to recovery". Nimbus Publishing Ltd, Halifax, 1989.
(20) D. OSLER : "100 injured as bulker hits US shipping mall»" Lloyd's List, 16 Dec. 1996.
(21)"Exxon Valdez, five years on". Lloyd's List, 24 March 1994.
(22) Y. SASAMURA : "Prevention and Control of Marine Pollution from Ship". 25th Annual Conference of the Law of the Sea Institute. Malmö, August 1991.

Figure 3 : Major disasters involving passenger ships in the 20th century

Number of casualties	Name of ship	Date	Place	Cause of accident
4200	DONA PAZ	1987	Sibuyan Sea, Philippines	Collision with oil tanker
1800	NEPTUNE	1993	Off Haiti, Caribbean	Overloading
1501	TITANIC	1912	Cape Race Newfoundland	Collision with iceberg
1012	EMPRESS OF IRELAND	1914	St Lawrence	Collision
1000	DON JUAN	1980	Tablas Strait (Philippines)	Collision
912	ESTONIA	1994	Baltic Sea	Shipwreck
450	TAMPOMAS II	1981	Java Sea	Shipwreck
448	SALEM EXPRESS	1991	Red Sea	Shipwreck
423	ADMIRAL NAKHIMOV	1986	Black Sea	Collision
300	DONA MARILYN	1988	Visayan Sea (Philippines)	
200	BINTANG	1988	Madura (Indonesia)	
193	HERALD OF FREE ENTERPRISE	1987	North Sea (Zeebrugge)	Capsize
158	SCANDINAVIAN STAR	1990	Skagerrak	Fire
150	HASAIL	1988	Bangladesh	
140	MOBY PRINCE	1991	Mediterranean Sea	Collision
134	MORRO CASTLE	1934	North Atlantic Ocean	Fire
128	LAKONIA	1963	North of Madeira	Fire

IV - EXPLAINING ACCIDENTS : FROM FATALISM TO CINDYNICS

It is not easy to accept the persistence with which maritime disasters recur, as the end of the Millennium approaches, with all its trappings of modernity. Scientific and technical progress, expected to solve nearly all our problems, appears to be making little headway as far as safety at sea is concerned. In the absence of overall solutions, prevention experts have produced several hypotheses and theories to explain accidents at sea

• **Fatalistic approach**

11. - The classic doctrine uses expressions like "maritime perils", an expression redolent with ideas of adventurousness and risk, but also of good luck. As Professor Chauveau puts it : "In the struggle that he has to wage against the elements that dominate him, the seaman, however experienced he may be, is never certain of emerging the winner. He cannot be instructed as to the best way of waging his combat : it is a question of opportunity or circumstance, which must be left to him to judge" (23).

The history of navigation itself goes part of the way to explaining this fatalistic attitude. The shipping trade, originally carried on by adventurers, developed against such a *laissez-faire*, liberal background that the many accidents of which bold navigators were victims were regarded as natural (24). This view of the unpredictability of the sea, however, was to be the foundation for one of the most original and longest-standing institutions of maritime law : limited liability.

• Deterministic approach

12. - Others reject the idea of chance, and lay two kinds of responsibility on technical factors. First, such factors are held responsible for the emergence of new dangers, arising from the increased draught, speed and size of modern ships. In addition, the inadequacy or failure of certain technical appliances on board ships remains a contributory factor in a number of accidents.

Most observers, however, consider that the fundamental causes of many disasters cannot be claimed to be purely technical. They consider that the perils of the sea create a situation in which the human factor takes priority

Whatever explanations are put forward, the deterministic approach cannot totally inform the phenomena involved. First, it provides an over-simplified explanation of an event, by giving excessive weight to certain technical or human factors. The corrective solutions that are proposed therefore necessarily remain incomplete. Accidents involving legal disputes nearly always give rise to a battle of experts, each insisting on his own point of view and interpreting the facts in the light of the interests he is defending. Technical objectivity has an uphill struggle to prevail (25). Finally, human error or technical failure produce catastrophic consequences only because the ship is afloat on such an unstable and shifting element. Few accidents are technical in origin: a number of unfavourable or aggravating factors so often combine to cause them.

• Systemic approach

13. - The unsatisfactory nature of traditional approaches has led to the appearance of new, more all-embracing methods of explaining accidents. Most of them make use of the theory of systems.

In this approach, an accident is not treated as the outcome of some act of God, or as a random occurrence or isolated technical event. It is seen as arising from the failure of a complex system, detailed analysis of which can reveal the sequence of events. All incidents caused by the various components of the system are examined with the closest attention and corrected, to prevent their recurrence (26).

This attitude goes beyond the purely technical circumstances of a disaster. It involves the development of a safety culture, a set of beliefs, standards, attitudes towards risks. Experience shows that the behaviour of human beings, their fears and beliefs, play a fundamental role in risk analysis and management, and in methods of dealing with crises and catastrophes (27).

(23) P. CHAUVEAU : op.cit, 8.
(24) DUCLAUX : "Réflexions sur le niveau actuel d'insécurité des navires". Jeune Marine n° 31. Jan-Fév. 1980, 8.
(25) D. DUCLOS : "Les catastrophes de la modernité". Le Monde, 9 juillet 1988, 2.
(26) B. TOFT, S. REYNOLDS : "Learning from Disasters. A Management Approach" - Butterworth Heineman, London 1994.
(27) J.P. DUFOUR : "L'accident qui sauve". Le Monde, 16 nov. 1994, 15.

In certain industrial sectors regarded as high-risk, particularly the nuclear industry, this approach has led to a new discipline : the science of dangers, or "cindynics", the purpose of which is to learn from disasters in order to analyse and control risks and deal with crisis situations (28).

• **Need for total approach**
14. - Can systemic and danger theories be applied to the facts of the maritime world ? The fragmented nature of the world maritime industry makes it a difficult subject for a total safety approach. However, there have been calls for the application of such an analytical method.

In 1981, the journal *Norwegian Maritime Research* published a study into the causal relationships of collisions and groundings, in which casualties were regarded as "a symptom of malfunction of the organising system which is responsible for coordination of all activities contributing to safety" (29). Every event was examined within a structured system comprising :
- the ship, itself incorporating three subsystems (technical, social and relational) ;
- the environment (sea, weather conditions, traffic) ;
- the maritime community (shipyards, international organisations, maritime authorities, educational system, health authorities, trade unions, shipowners, classification societies).

In 1994, Professor Goss, in an address on the future of safety at sea, also recommended a total approach, to study the possible effects of a change in maritime safety (30). Seven categories of interests are, he feels, concerned : people (crew, passengers), ships, cargoes, environmental effects (consumption, production, leisure), search and rescue, financial interests and operational factors, and other effects (coastal infrastructure, control, damage to marine structures).

In a study of global disasters (31), R.E. Allinson argues against a reductive conception of accidents, in which the responsibility for their occurrence is attributed to a single technical or human factor. He also suggests a more general approach to safety, placing emphasis on the ethical conduct of maritime undertakings.

The same approach is adopted by B. Toft and S. Reynolds, who see an accident as the failure of a complex system, requiring radical revision of inquiry and investigation mechanisms in order to draw lessons from disasters (32).

V - OUTLINE AND PLAN OF THIS STUDY

Early in 1976, when my initial research into safety at sea began, I already argued in favour of a total approach to this issue. In an earlier work published in 1980, I wrote that an accident must not be regarded as an isolated phenomenon, the causes of which are sought in order to act on them, but as the result, among other factors, of a complex system comprising individual passengers, seafarers, shipowners, ships and maritime craft, infrastructures, navigational aids and the environment.

(28) "Cindynics 94 : Risques et société". 2ème colloque international sur les sciences du danger. Paris, nov. 1994.
(29) K. DRAGER, S. KRISTIANSEN, J. KARLSEN, P. WIENCKE : "Cause relationship of collisions and groundings. Conclusions of statistical analysis". Norwegian Maritime Research n° 3, 1981, 22-32.
(30) R. GOSS : "The Future of Maritime Safety". op. cit. note 10.
(31) R.E. ALLINSON : "Global Disasters - Inquiries into management ethics". Prentice Hall, ISBN 0-13-145947-3.
(32) B. TOFT, S. REYNOLDS : "Learning from disasters". Butterworth - Heinemann, UK, 1994.

• Types of safety

15. - Three types of modifications can be made in the components of the complex system of maritime safety :
- preventive or primary safety actions, intended to prevent and eradicate accidents ;
- search, rescue and salvage or secondary safety actions, planned prior to an accident at sea, and intended to attenuate its consequences ;
- finally, compensatory or tertiary safety actions, intended to restore the functional situation of the various components of the system after an accident.

Reality often refuses to be pigeonholed into neat classifications and rigid categories. Safety at sea is no exception to this rule. The conditions of assistance at sea have a direct effect on prevention of accidents. The *Amoco Cadiz* disaster, for instance, led to a change in the salvage system, the traditional mechanisms of which provided no incentive for the salvage company to prevent any maritime pollution. The new 1989 Convention on salvage provides for the "safety net" system, encouraging the salvage firm to take preventive action, by reimbursing costs incurred in trying to avoid pollution, plus 15 per cent. In the same way, the conditions under which an individual bears liability could have positive or negative effects on his behaviour. A very strict regime, providing for removal of the traditional ceilings on maritime liabilities, could bring about a greater sense of responsibility among operators, as would seem to be proved by the new United States Oil Pollution Act.

• Importance of prevention

16. - Despite its limitations, this tripartite view of the problem remains useful from a methodological viewpoint, as a way of grasping the purposes of the maritime safety system. In this triple view, prevention of accidents is of capital importance for several reasons.

The effectiveness of certain techniques that contribute to secondary safety was called into question during oil tanker disasters. Whatever means of intervention are used (floating barriers, depollution craft), the fight against oil spills still remains a piecemeal matter. The accidents to the *Tanio* in Brittany and the *Exxon Valdez* in Alaska showed the very primitive nature of the ways of cleaning a polluted coast (brushes, hot water jets, shovels, mechanical diggers and civil engineering equipment).

Present mechanisms for compensation provide only partial reparation of the injury suffered, particularly in the event of major accidents.

The conditions under which merchant ships operate lend themselves to extreme dispersal of liabilities in the event of an accident, sometimes creating a legal maze (33). The case of the *Tanio* is a perfect example : this former French oil tanker, the *Lorraine*, belonged to a Swiss company, Locafrance International. It was bareboat chartered to the Malagasy oil transport company Petromad, after being sold in 1974 to the Panamanian company Cruz del Sol. The Société Française de Transports Pétroliers, a subsidiary of the Worms Group, was responsible for technical management of the *Tanio*, while its commercial management was entrusted to a Bordeaux firm, Socatra. At the time of the accident, the ship had been chartered by Elf Union, and subchartered by a British firm, Peninsular and Oriental, one of whose subsidiaries owned the cargo.

In general, maritime law provides for a limitation on the shipowner's liability. Victims have the greatest difficulty in breaking through this ceiling on compensation. Only successful claims against third parties that have contributed directly to the occurrence of the damage can make up the difference. This specific feature of maritime law is sometimes compounded by

---

(33) R. RODIERE : "Le naufrage de *l'Amoco Cadiz*" - Bull. des Transports, n° 1825, 17 mai 1978, n° 18, 240.

difficulties arising from company law practices, in particular the registration of a ship under a flag of convenience, or the creation of a separate company for each ship, creating a legal vacuum when liabilities are being investigated (34).

Finally, certain forms of pollution cause such enormous damage that no fair, complete compensation is possible. The total cost of the *Exxon Valdez* oil spill has been estimated at $10bn. By 1994, five years after the accident, fishermen had obtained only $287m, in other words barely 30 per cent of the $10bn quoted (35).

• Method of analysis

17. - In such an extensive area as the prevention of risks to shipping, any attempt at exhaustiveness would be vain. The intention of this book is to provide the most comprehensive answers possible to the kind of fundamental questions asked in the aftermath of a disaster like the *Amoco Cadiz* or the *Estonia*. Is it possible to prevent the occurrence of such tragedies ? Is the safety of seaborne transport deteriorating ? Is the level of safety sufficient ? Is the existing protective system suitable ? Is it not obsolete, out of date in the face of the vast changes in the modern world ?

In seeking solutions to the issue of better safety at sea, this book will study the preventive system as a whole, analyse its components, examine what it produces, namely the standards, procedures and rules of conduct that govern the behaviour of players in the maritime sector.

This approach is not without difficulty, because of the variety of the regulations that govern seaborne transport. The highly technical nature of the means deployed to build, operate and sail a ship means that they are the preserve of naval architects, engineers and scientific experts (36). Another difficulty is the strict legal approach needed to translate technical innovations into the language of law, and finally to apply recommended improvements uniformly and on a mandatory basis.

• Towards a total approach

18. - The narrowness of the standard-setting approach often masks the all-encompassing character of maritime safety. The value and effectiveness of a rule can be assessed only within its environment. It is the outcome of a complex system with multiple components: technical, economic, legal, media and political. The content of a standard, as well as the conditions for its enforcement, emerge from a careful interlinking of all these factors.

a) Technical aspects

19. - Maritime transport has benefitted from considerable advances in technology over the last century, affecting both naval architecture and navigation. These improvements have admittedly reduced some of the risks incurred by ships at sea, but they have also changed the nature of risks. Ships turn around more quickly, causing traffic congestion in certain maritime zones ; as ships have become increasingly reliable, upstream expertise has declined correspondingly. This has led to an under-evaluation of real transport risks, itself resulting in lightweight packaging, negligence in handling operations, and a lack of care in company logistics (37).

(34) Rapport de la commission d'enquête de l'Assemblée Nationale sur le naufrage de *l'Amoco Cadiz,* T.I. 69. On the compensation problems of the Amoco Cadiz oil spill Cf:
M. REMOND-GOUILLOUD : "Leçon d'un naufrage". Dalloz 1979 Chron. 133-138.
(35) "Fishermen secure $ 287 m for Exxon Valdez losses". Lloyd's List, 13 August 1994.
(36) J.P. GALLAND : "Expertises scientifiques et décisions publiques". Annales des Ponts et Chaussées n° 81, 1997, 32-38.
(37) Les entretiens de l'Assurance. Colloque de Paris, 1994, op. cit.

b) Economic aspects

20. - The shipping industry, battered by the recession since the mid-Seventies, offers a picture of ruthless competition. Serious overtonnaging, responsible for a steady decline in freight rates, has led operators to resort to every means to cut their operating costs. Use of old ships, trimming of maintenance costs to the strict minimum, and the recruitment of cheap labour to man them have been the main manifestations of this frantic search to save money. The crisis has affected the whole industry, creating commercial pressures that it is well-nigh impossible to reconcile with strict safety management (38).

The insecurity of maritime activities is financially draining, primarily for insurance companies, but also for the whole community. The cost of an accident becomes even greater if one takes account of loss of earnings, resulting from immobilisation of the ship, damage suffered by the cargo, total loss of the ship, death and bodily injuries suffered by seamen and passengers, and harm to the marine environment, which can reach astronomical levels for major ecological disasters.

The financial consequences of the *Exxon Valdez* accident are a clear illustration. While the damage to the ship and loss of part of its cargo, represented only US$46m, the related direct and indirect costs of the resulting oil spill were three hundred times greater : US$25m in court-imposed fines, US$500m to repair the injury suffered by organisations and private individuals, US$1bn to clear up the ecological effects, US$2.1bn to clean the Alaskan coasts, and US$5bn punitive damages.

One also has to add accruing interest charges of US$800 000 a day and estimated legal fees of US$100m for Exxon. The disaster will have cost more than US$10bn (39).

Ultimately, who pays for safety ? For certain economists, who take a very long-term view, it is the end consumer, the user of maritime transport, in other words passengers and seamen, and not the shipowner, nor the operator, nor the shipper or charterer, regarded as intermediaries (40). Hence the usefulness of a cost-benefit analysis of maritime safety rules.

c) Legal aspects

21. - Legal factors play a very important part in the functioning of the safety system. Seaborne transport, which is worldwide in extent, cannot be run on purely local or national rules. It requires universal standards which only states are in a position to agree and enforce on the international stage. This is why safety at sea involves so many different public law provisions. First, the law of the sea defines the rights and obligations of States with regard to ships in the various maritime zones : ports and inland waters, territorial waters, straits, exclusive economic zones, and the high seas. Treaty law applies, insofar as mandatory safety requirements are set out in multilateral conventions and treaties. Finally, environmental law includes aspects that govern prevention of accidental pollution and the fight against oil spills.

Maritime law, which determines legal relationships among private operators, also exerts a major influence. Attention has already been drawn to the possible consequences of liability mechanisms, and provisions for compensating victims of an accident or pollution, on the overall level of safety of maritime transport.

(38) Ph. BOISSON : "A la recherche d'une meilleure sécurité en mer". Le Monde Diplomatique. Dec. 1993, 22.
(39) F.W. WENTHER : *"Exxon Valdez*. The ten billion dollar bump in the night". LBA Section on Business Law. Marine and Transport Newsletter, April 1997, 11-14.
(40) R. GOSS : "The future of marine safety" op.cit. note 10.

d) Sociological aspects

22. - The weight of public opinion in determining the level of safety should not be underestimated, although it is very difficult to evaluate. As the end of the century approaches, there is general agreement that absolute safety does not exist, that risk is an integral part of transportation, and that an act of God and human error can outflank technical advances and preventive measures. But no-one is ready to accept that a damaged tanker should discharge its cargo of oil on to the coast, or that a passenger ship should go down with nearly a thousand people still on board. Public opinion refuses these modern-day cataclysms.

e) Media aspects

23. - The growth of the communications industry that is such a feature of today's world has distorted the collective perception of the dangers of navigation. Accidents are pounced upon by the audiovisual media which, because of satellite broadcasting, can show pictures of the event in real time on a global scale. The information, which almost becomes part of the entertainment industry, is fragmented and simplified for the needs of the general public, offering an unflattering view of shipping and safety, which is presented negatively, as a matter of mere passive precautions.

But despite this over-simplification, the media arouse the public conscience and often stimulate the standard-setting enthusiasm of the maritime community, in favour of better protection of men at sea and their environment. This is so true that one may wonder whether, without the dreadful images of oil-covered birds after the *Exxon Valdez* disaster, the Oil Pollution Act would have been brought on to the statute book in the United States, only eighteen months after the accident.

f) Political aspects

24. - Under pressure from public opinion, stirred up by the media, governments are forced to act quickly (41). The worst disasters give rise to major parliamentary debates in developed countries, voluminous investigation reports, and a myriad standardisation recommendations. The resulting series of measures is intended as much to prevent recurrence of the same type of event as to quieten the anxieties of worried politicians.

Certain commentators see this kind of legislation by disaster as disastrous legislation (42), adopted pragmatically in reaction to a specific accident, rather than the result of a comprehensive review of the whole problem. It has to be admitted, however, that most of the current regulation of safety has emerged from maritime disasters of the past. It is ultimately up to the state to set the acceptable level of risk for maritime transport, as for other activities. This has to take account of technical and economic constraints, but there are also political pressures on governments which have to be borne in mind.

(41) J. COWLEY : "The International Maritime Organisation and national administrations". Institute of Marine Engineers. London, 1989.
(42) Erik STENMARK. Interview in DNV Forum n° 1/93 "Legislation by disaster means disastrous legislation".

• **Contents of this study**

25. - This survey of maritime safety policies and law bears essentially on seaborne transport. This does not mean that accident prevention in relation to fishing, offshore operations or recreational sailing is less important or less topical. I have focussed on merchant shipping because it is the area in which regulations are the longest-standing, the densest, the most complex and the most international.

The value and effectiveness of such regulations and the safety policies that underlie them are assessed on three different levels : their foundations, their content and their implementation.

The first part of the book is devoted to the sources of international law on safety, its various public and private promoters, nationally and internationally, procedures for setting standards, rules and various legal instruments intended to prevent accidents occurring.

The second part deals with actual regulations, namely all the administrative and technical requirements, and forms of behaviour or conduct that ships are bound to observe. This part of the book engages a detailed analysis of the principal standards that govern the construction, equipment, operation and navigation of ships in the world. The development of regulations is presented for each type of vessel. The account illustrates the diversity as well as the deficiencies of the existing range of regulations.

The third part of the book turns to the crucial problem of now to enforce of legal provisions, and covers the establishment of powers of policing, surveillance, inspection and penalties in case of infringement. It will be seen that these powers remain the responsibility of governments, not international organisations, and that control of both shipping and navigation is shared among various authorities: flag States, port States and coastal States.

Finally, I try to make an overall assessment, and discern the main developments likely in safety at sea in the next century.

CHAPTER 2

The history of safety at sea

26. - Since the earliest times, the sea has always been synonymous with insecurity for those who venture on to it. "He that would sail without danger must never come on the main sea," as the proverb puts it.

This endemic absence of safety probably explains why early maritime trade was mainly the preserve of adventurers. The sea was associated with the idea of chance or fate, a concept still to be found in expressions such as "maritime perils". Seaborne transport developed in such a *laissez-faire* way that the many accidents of which bold navigators were victims were soon accepted as part of the natural course of things. As a leading contemporary professor of maritime law puts it, "The frailty of the human factor, in the face of the inexhaustible and indefinable sea, confers on the effort of navigation the character of a bold venture, which may succeed and prove quite profitable, but which can also fail and cause irreparable losses." (1)

The history of navigation since ancient times shows that the needs of safety came only gradually to the fore, in the wake of accidents and disasters, bringing about huge changes in the individual and collective behaviour of those engaged in maritime activities, who clung to ancient practices and habits.

I - INSECURITY AT SEA IN ANCIENT TIMES

27. - It might be thought that there were relatively few risks at sea in olden times, when craft of modest size. and few in number, using sails or oars as their mode of propulsion, never ventured far from the coast. In fact, the period was one of persistent insecurity, making sea voyages extremely hazardous. In addition to bad sea and weather conditions, piracy was rife throughout the Mediterranean. Ships were hard to handle and could so easily be tossed about by winds and currents. Shipwrecks, usually caused by storms, remained a frequent occurrence.

Until the end of the Roman Empire, seafarers were ill equipped to confront bad weather. Passengers and bulky cargoes were packed together on deck. Ships were loaded well beyond safety limits. Navigators knew little about winds. Derisory efforts were made to combat storms: the ship was bound round with ropes fore and aft, to prevent it splitting apart, and an anchor was dragged behind to slow down its progress (2).

Another method of dealing with imminent danger was to cast objects overboard: the cargo, rigging and even victuals were jettisoned to lighten the vessel. The decision was taken by the pilot, the ship's owner, or the most prominent or experienced passengers. The Romans

(1) A.R. WERNER : "Traité de droit maritime général". Librairie Droz, Genève 1964, 379.
(2) J.M. ANDRE and M.F. BASLEZ : "Voyager dans l'Antiquité". Fayard, Paris 1993, 441-442.

adopted their own interpretation of the practices of navigators from the island of Rhodes. The *Lex Rhodia de Jactu* stated that, if part of the cargo had to be jettisoned, the loss was to be borne by the owner of the ship and the owners of the cargo (3). This provision survives in modern maritime law, with the system of "general average".

One of the most effective preventive measures was a ban on sailing in winter, putting the seas out of bounds during the worst weather. The ban was not applied uniformly. In Rome, the period during which navigation was permitted lasted only from 27 May to 14 September. Certain calendars were even more restrictive, providing for a period of only fifty days starting at the summer equinox. The practice of laying-up in winter was justified mainly by meteorological conditions, particularly the dreadful storms. Cloudy skies often made it impossible to observe the stars, customarily used to determine the direction of the ship. The ban on sailing was accompanied in Roman law by an administrative penalty: no ship could leave port unless it held a *dimissorium*, a kind of sailing permit issued by the appropriate official (4).

Ultimately, the safety of a voyage rested on the shoulders of a single man, the pilot, the equivalent of the captain in ancient times. He bore technical responsibility for navigation, and the choice of the safest route and ports of call (5). However, his decisions were sometimes overridden by shipowners anxious to earn higher profits by sailing even in bad weather. Some ships took even greater risks than warships, and this explains the frequency with which shipwrecks occurred.

II - THE BEGINNINGS OF ACCIDENT PREVENTION IN THE MIDDLE AGES

28. - Conditions of navigation underwent very little significant change throughout the Middle Ages. Ships stayed in port in winter. Until the end of the 18th century, the Levantines sailed only from 5 May to 26 October (6). In the Baltic, maritime traffic was banned between Martinmas and Saint Peter's Day (22 February), on pain of confiscation of the cargo (7). Ships never went out of sight of the coast. Open-sea navigation was initiated in the Mediterranean from the 13th century, but not until the 15th century in the North. Hanseatic mariners found the position of their ships by using a sounding lead to measure the depth of the seabed at any point on their voyage (8).

Advances in ship safety did occur in the Middle Ages, with the implementation of the first preventive rules on loading. According to commentators, these originated in the *Lex Rhodia*. From the mid-13th century, the maritime authorities in large Mediterranean ports introduced very strict legislation on freeboard, in order to combat the abuses of unscrupulous shipowners and captains who overloaded their ships, at the risk of losing them, in order to earn more from the freight.

(3) J.M. PARDESSUS : "Collection des lois maritimes antérieures au XVIIIème siècle" 1er volume, Paris 1828-1845, 68-69.
(4) R. RODIERE : "Traité général de Droit Maritime". Dalloz 1976, Paris, Tome I 376.
(5) "A la recherche du droit maritime ancien dans la traduction biblique". Communications et mémoires de l'Académie de Marine n° 2 - 1992, 25.
(6) F. BRAUDEL : "La Méditerranée et le monde méditerranéen à l'époque de Philippe II". Armand Colin, Paris, 9ème édition 1990, 227.
(7) Ph. DOLLINGER : "La Hanse" (XIIè-XVIIème siècles). Aubier, Paris 1988, 181.
(8) R. FOSSAERT : "Le Monde au 21ème siècle. Une théorie du système mondial". Fayard, Paris 1991, 47.

The very first regulations appeared in Venice in 1255. They made it illegal to exceed the draught, marked on each ship by a cross. Similar provisions were to be found in Cagliari and Pisa at the same period, and also in Barcelona, in the decree issued by Iago de Aragon in 1258, and in the maritime statutes of Marseilles in 1284. The most elaborate regulations appeared in the 14th-century Genoese statutes.

In 1330, the maritime authorities in Genoa had already laid down not only very precise rules for calculating the maximum draught of certain ships, but also an inspection procedure and a whole range of penalties for anyone contravening the rules. The *Afficium Gazarie* appointed officials to measure ships in accordance with the rules in force, and attend to the affixing of irons to the hull, the precursors of loadlines. On every voyage, the captain or owner had to designate two of the merchants on board to keep watch on these iron markers. A system of guarantee payments and fines ensured that the law was applied strictly (9).

Despite these measures, shipwrecks remained a common occurrence in the Mediterranean, particularly during the winter season. A single storm, such as occurred in 1545 in the Adriatic, could sink fifty vessels (10). Northerners relied on repression: the Hanseatic League introduced very severe criminal legislation to discourage the most audacious adventurers. Measures applied mainly to the pilot, who was responsible for directing the ship. The *Sea Laws of Oleron* mention very stringent penalties for anyone failing in his duty. The captain, who exercised absolute authority on board, was empowered to cut off the luckless pilot's head if by ignorance he had endangered the cargo and the crew. In fact, these punishments were so barbarous that they were practically never applied (11).

III - POLICING OF NAVIGATION TO THE END OF THE 18th CENTURY

29. - As the modern age dawned, the growth of seaborne trade, marked by an increase in the number of ships, their greater speed and capacity, and the value of the property transported in them, provided an incentive for the introduction of policing methods among the major maritime nations.

Preventive rules became more generalised. A Spanish ordinance of 1563 required shipbuilders and owners to see to the perfect seaworthiness of their vessels, check the low water level, and lash the cargo securely (12). A Venetian law of 8 June 1569 prohibited shipowners from placing goods at certain places on the ship. In France, an edict on the Admiralty issued by the French king Henri III in March 1584 required maritime cities to oversee the abilities of ships' captains. The Marine Ordinance of August 1681 devoted a whole section to seamen and ships (13).

The most innovative measure consisted of stipulating ship surveys by the authorities in order to prevent accidents caused by the poor condition of a ship or inadequate equipment. Northern countries were the first to impose a system of surveys. The Recesses of the Diet of

(9) F. ATTOMA-PEPE : "Un aperçu du franc-bord des navires au Moyen Age". Bulletin Technique du Bureau Veritas, janvier 1976, 10-14.

(10) F. BRAUDEL : op. cit 228.

(11) Theses:
- H. LE PRAT : "Le pilotage en droit maritime français". Rennes 1963, 5.
- B. GONTIER : "Le pilotage maritime". Paris 1965, 6.

(12) J. MARIE and Ch. DILLY : "La sécurité maritime". Société d'éditions géographiques, maritimes et coloniales. Paris 1931, 7.

(13) B.M. EMERIGON : "Nouveau commentaire sur l'ordonnance de la Marine du mois d'août 1681". 2 vol. Ainé Noyon, Paris 1780.

the Hanseatic League of 1412, 1417 and 1447 contain references to this requirement. The Low Countries Ordinance of 1549 instituted a double survey, before and after loading of the cargo. The Genoese law of 1607 entrusted surveys to the "magnificent curators of the sea".

In France, organisation of the administrative supervision of shipping in ports dates back to Colbert's Naval Ordinance, which introduced the office of *huissier-visiteur*, or surveyor. A Royal declaration of 17 August 1779 completed these provisions by instituting the requirements of dual survey of ships, on the outward voyage and on the return trip. The most important text was adopted under the Revolution, with the Act of 9 August 1791 concerning navigational policing. This laid a strict obligation on captains of ships equipped for long voyages to solicit a survey before equipment and then before loading of the vessel. Inspections were carried out by surveyor-officers or surveyor-inspectors, consisting of certain navigators, builders or carpenters, appointed by the Commercial Courts, or by the local Mayor (14).

Despite these measures, risk prevention remained a very rudimentary matter. The safety of maritime trade was ensured mainly by introducing legislation to provide compensation and protection for the financial interests of shipowners. An original legal system was gradually established, based on the principle that the various parties with an interest in maritime transport had to bear their share of liability, and that only they were concerned with such problems (15). Several legal provisions met these requirements: joint ownership of ships, for instance, aimed at reducing hazards by sharing risks. Other mechanisms, such as bottomry, allowed their transfer (16). A third technique met with prompt success. It consisted of the involvement of a third party, the insurer, who took the place of the person normally bearing the risk (17). The events that led to accidents remained largely unknown and highly diversified, so that legislation to define the sharing of liabilities and repair of damage finally appeared as the most cogent solution and the most appropriate answer to the problem of insecurity (18).

IV - GROWTH OF INTERVENTIONISM IN THE 19th CENTURY

30. - The technological innovations that accompanied the Industrial Revolution encouraged the development of maritime transport during the 19th century. The most important developments were undoubtedly the introduction of steam-powered engines on board ships and the construction of iron and then steel hulls. These technical advances were accompanied, however, by an increase in risks at sea, corresponding to the greater number, size and speed of the vessels engaged in trade. Accident statistics reflect the acuteness of the problem: during the winter of 1820 alone, more than two thousand ships were wrecked in the North Sea, causing the deaths of twenty thousand people (19).

The principal attempts to achieve greater safety took place within a purely private framework: administrative supervision of shipping was regarded as a hindrance to free trade. There were fears of over-zealous states adopting excessively restrictive and invasive regulations, out of place in an industry subject to such fierce international competition. It was generally considered that the proper interest of the shipowner, who had committed all his wealth to the

(14) D. DANJON : "Traité de droit maritime". Librairie générale de Droit et de Jurisprudence, Paris 1910, 100 et suivantes.
(15) J. BONNECASE : "Le droit commercial maritime. Son particularisme. Son domaine d'application et sa méthode d'interprétation". Paris. Sirey 1931, 18.
(16) G. RIPERT : "Droit Maritime". Rousseau, Paris 1929, Tome 1, 83-84.
(17) L.A. BOITEUX : "La fortune de mer, le besoin de sécurité et les débuts de l'assurance maritime". Imprimerie Nationale, Paris 1968, 8-9.
(18) J. LE CLÈRE : "L'abordage en droit maritime et en droit fluvial". LGDJ, Paris 1955, 14.
(19) The Courrier, 5 mai 1822, quoted in Le Bureau Veritas 1828-1928, Edition du Centenaire, Paris 1928, 10.

acquisition of ships, ultimately represented the best guarantee of safety for all concerned. This *laissez-faire* attitude remained predominant through the first half of the 19th century, which saw the birth of the earliest classification societies. These purely private organisations made a fundamental contribution to the assessment of the safety of merchant ships by providing maritime insurers with accurate and regular information on the quality of shipping and ship equipment (cf chapter 6 below).

The middle of the century marked a decisive turning point on the issue of safety at sea, with the proliferation of preventive rules, increasingly introduced within an official framework. Two essential factors explain this growing state interventionism :
- Maritime transport was becoming a real industry, and so it was normal for the authorities to exercise their general policing powers, to monitor the safety conditions on board ships. This was in the interests of seamen, but also of the increasing numbers of other people who went on board ships. Gradually, industrial legislation affecting equipment, manpower and operating conditions were applied to the merchant navy ;
- The need to harmonise national rules, habits and customs in the area of navigation also helped reinforce the role of States, the only entities entitled under international law to sign agreements, treaties and other mandatory instruments.

State interventionism resulted in an extraordinary increase in the number of public law provisions relating to the safety of ships and navigation.

A - INCREASED CONTROL OF SHIPS

Two countries that displayed considerable transformations in preventive regulations and ship survey procedures were France and Britain.

1. Development of French regulations

31. - Promulgation of the 1808 Commercial Code did not make any fundamental changes in the previous system. It repeated provisions on surveys of departing ships laid down in 1779 and 1791 texts. These requirements concerning annual surveys were gradually extended to other vessels: steamships under the terms of an order of 17 January 1846, fishing craft and vessels engaged on home-trade navigation, under the Decree of 4 July 1853, ships carrying emigrants under the Act of 18 July 1860, steam packets under the Decree of 11 September 1896, and lifesaving equipment, under the Decree of 26 June 1903.

From 1870, legislation on the carriage of dangerous goods was introduced. Loading and unloading of such cargoes were regulated by a Decree of 2 September 1874.

Laws on merchant shipping, adopted on 29 January 1881 and 30 January 1893, and the Decree of 1st February 1893 reinforced inspection procedures. This Decree stipulated annual surveys of steamships by surveillance commissions instituted by the *Préfets* of territorial Departments, in the various ports involved in such navigation. A navigation licence was issued to the shipowner by the *Préfet*, after examining survey reports. Despite their complexity, surveys remained incomplete, and indeed certain ships were never inspected. Surveys were now periodic, and no longer coincided with a ship's voyages, so that they were less effective. They were confined to the strength and equipment of the vessel, and were concerned neither with the loading of the ship nor the abilities of the crew. There was also criticism of the impartiality of the surveyor captains, who were often indulgent towards substandard ships, particularly whenever they belonged to shipowners who were members of the commercial court to which the surveyors owed their appointment (20).

(20) LYON-CAEN and RENAULT : "Traité de droit commercial". LGDJ, Paris 1911, n° 549.

The whole system underwent far-reaching changes under the Act of 17 April 1907, completed by two Decrees on 20 and 21 September 1908. These measures introduced public health and safety rules on navigation. They covered every aspect of ship safety, building and preservation conditions, equipment and installations, conditions of loading and operation. The Act also set up a body of navigation inspectors responsible for carrying out ordinary and special departing surveys. Regarded as the basis of modern French regulations, these standard-setting and administrative provisions mark the final preeminence of state control of rules on maritime safety.

2. Establishment of British legislation

32. - Under the pressure of public opinion, disturbed by the recurrence of accidents at sea, British legislators, like those in France, sought to strengthen the safety of maritime transport. This interventionist attitude, however, came up against the resistance of traditional maritime circles, with little inclination to accept state interference in private business. Finally, interventionism was to win in gradual stages, culminating in the adoption of very detailed preventive regulations affecting the whole sector.

This trend began in 1836 with the appointment of a Parliamentary Select Committee to examine the causes of the steady increase in shipwrecks. The investigation drew attention to ten determining factors, including defective construction, inadequate equipment, imperfect state of repair, improper and excessive loading, incompetence of masters, drunkenness among officers and crew, and marine insurance which inclined shipowners to disregard safety. A first series of measures was introduced after the publication of the parliamentary report. In 1839, restrictions were placed on the transport of timber deck cargoes in the North Atlantic. In 1840 appeared the first rules on lights and traffic at sea. From 1846, passenger ships had to be inspected by officially approved surveyors.

The most important advance came with the Merchant Shipping Act of 1850. This legislation marked the real start of State action under the auspices of the Board of Trade, which had the task of monitoring, regulating and controlling all issues relating to merchant shipping, and more specifically the safety of ships and the working conditions of seamen, in order to correct the serious abuses that had been found. A bill passed in 1854 strengthened the powers of this government body. Also adopted was a whole series of technical provisions concerning safety equipment on wooden ships. The law also required iron ships to be fitted with a collision bulkhead and engine bulkheads. However, these measures had little effect, and an average of two thousand ships were lost annually. In 1867 alone, there were 1 313 shipwrecks causing the death of 2 340 British sailors and 137 passengers (21).

33. - In 1873, a Royal Commission was set up to investigate the claimed unseaworthiness of British vessels, particularly the conditions of loading. A member of Parliament, Samuel Plimsoll, made a number of observations, denouncing the scandal of "coffin ships". A year after the publication of his manifesto, Parliament adopted the Merchant Shipping Act of 1876, known as the "Plimsoll Act". This laid down new requirements, with criminal penalties for shipowners found guilty of operating ships that presented a risk for human life. The Board of Trade was for the first time authorised to detain substandard ships coming to take on cargoes in British ports.

The Plimsoll Act, which instituted draught of water marks, put an end to the dangerous practice of leaving the captain complete discretion as to loading. The new regulations banned bulk loading of grain, in order to prevent the cargo shifting, and grain in sacks as deck cargo.

---

(21) J.W. BULL : "An introduction to safety at sea". Brown, Son and Ferguson, Glasgow 1966, 16.

Any infringement warranted the arrest of the ship. The Act also required all merchant vessels of more than 80 tons to display a maximum loadline. Despite its very stringent provisions, the Plimsoll Act did not put an end to the scandal of shipwrecks. In 1882, more than three thousand seamen and three hundred and sixty passengers perished in more than 1,120 shipping accidents to British vessels.

Another Royal Commission was appointed in 1884, to try and end this dismal record. In its final report, published in 1887, the Commission recommended several improvements to the safety of steamships, which had gradually replaced sailing ships. In 1890, the Merchant Shipping Load Line Act laid down official rules for freeboard tables and calculations. These had been introduced five years earlier, on an experimental and purely voluntary basis, by the Board of Trade, which relied on the work of Lloyd's Register and Bureau Veritas to give them formal expression.

Up to the end of the century, the British legislative armoury was strengthened by many provisions, though without altering its fundamental mechanisms. The basic regulations, laid down in the 1894 Merchant Shipping Act, as amended by the Act of 21 December 1906, increased the seaworthiness and safety of ships, and health arrangements on board. Loadline requirements were applied to all vessels, including foreign ships visiting British ports.

Interventionism finally triumphed in all the major maritime nations, which followed the British model: Denmark with the Acts of 13 February 1890, 14 May 1909 and 3 January 1911, Sweden with the ordinance of 1st July 1898, Norway with the Acts of 13 February 1890, 14 May 1909 and 3 January 1911, 1st July 1898, Norway with the Acts of 9 June 1903, 3 October 1908, 24 April 1906, 8 August 1908 and 14 July 1909. On 7 June 1902, Germany promulgated an Act concerning seafarers. The Netherlands adopted a shipping bill on 1st July 1909. United States regulations on safety at sea were set out in the Seamen's Act of March 1915. Spain drew up measures similar to British legislation with its two Decrees of 18 January 1924 concerning safety on board ship and lifesaving appliances.

B - FIRST NAVIGATION RULES

34. - The 19th century also saw the first regulations on navigation at sea. Around 1840, with the earliest steamships, a number of nations became concerned about what steps could be taken to avoid collisions and shipwrecks. At the time, each of them acted separately. No ships carried navigation lights, except warships travelling in squadron by night. Whenever two vessels approached each other, it was customary to show one's presence by hoisting a flag or lighting a flare. British ships applied the signalling rules proposed by W.D. Evans, regarded as the father of present-day regulations.

The simplicity and effectiveness of British rules were appreciated by seamen in all countries, to such an extent that France, where maritime circles had long been calling for uniform legislation, signed an agreement in 1848 with Great Britain about the lighting of steamships. This was not exactly an international convention, but simply the acceptance of identical general rules in both countries (22). This first agreement met with resounding success, however, for its provisions were immediately copied and adopted by other leading maritime nations.

France and Britain subsequently signed other agreements, gradually setting up a proper maritime traffic policing force. An 1852 agreement covered signalling for sailing ships. In 1856, a series of rules on maritime signals established a communications guide containing 78 000 combinations of only eighteen flags (23). Another agreement in 1856 set standards for

---

(22) J. LORANCHET : "La nouvelle réglementation pour prévenir les abordages". JMM, 23 juillet 1953, 1417.
(23) G. GIDEL : "Le droit international public de la mer". Paris, Sirey, Tome I, 364.

navigation in fog, and in 1862 the first joint rules for routes at sea were laid down. In 1884, the two countries signed a treaty on lighting of fishing boats and special signals to be assigned to telegraph cable-laying ships.

All these rules were gradually introduced into French regulations on collision avoidance, with the Decrees of 28 May 1856, 19 September 1879, 1st September 1884 and 21 February 1897.

V - INTERNATIONALISATION OF REGULATIONS IN THE 20th CENTURY

35. - The quest for some uniformity of national rules and customs regarding safety at sea has intensified throughout the 20th century. But before going back over the main steps in this internationalisation of maritime law, it is worth summarising the causes of the trend.

A - REASONS FOR INTERNATIONALISATION

Several factors incited the major maritime nations to set up joint safety rules.

• Problem of the high seas
36. - The intention was to set the conditions for exercising the freedom of the high seas in the interests of the whole international community, and also to avoid anarchy leading to dangerous conditions for maritime navigation. The introduction of maritime traffic policing raised no problem in those parts of the sea that were the territorial waters of coastal countries, whose governments had full latitude to introduce whatever standards they pleased. The problem mainly involved the high seas, where the principle of freedom traditionally prevailed. It was very soon realised that it was in everyone's interest to agree on a minimum of rules to be respected, for both signals and traffic. These came to form the "common law of the sea", covering rules for navigation, rescue and collisions (24).

• Foreign ships in port
37. - In the early years of the century, every State laid down its own conditions for the control of ships in its ports. Three examples illustrate this regulatory and administrative diversity. In Britain, the 1906 Merchant Shipping Act officially applied loading and minimum loadline requirements to foreign ships. In France, the provisions of the 1907 Act on crews referred only to French ships, while those concerning surveys applied to both French and foreign vessels. The United States Seamen's Act of March 1915 applied to foreign ships sailing from American ports. But in practice, steamships not carrying passengers were exempted.

This range of provisions resulted in considerable uncertainty, for the navigational permits and seaworthiness certificates had no international validity. Confusion reigned, to the extent that ships visiting ports in several states were sometimes required to meet contradictory safety conditions.

• Regulation of competition
38. - Maritime trade has always been subject to fierce international competition. Repeated maritime disasters gradually convinced national legislators that economic rivalries, particularly as regard fleet operation, could endanger safety and bring this form of transport

(24) C.J. COLOMBOS : "The International Law of the Sea", London, Longmans 1967.

irretrievably into disrepute. It was realised that only an agreement among States, laying down minimum standards to be met by a particular ship performing a particular service, could offer a satisfactory long-term solution.

One example is freeboard legislation. Two identical vessels, but of different nationalities, frequently come into competition on the same route. If one of them is more heavily loaded than the other, the shipowner will earn a higher profit, but will expose his ships to greater dangers, and a correspondingly lower level of safety. If the same freeboard is displayed on the hulls of both ships, by means of a loadline, overloading will no longer be an acceptable commercial tactic. Internationally, the existence of a standard was more important than its content, for ultimately the intention was not to penalise states adopting strict regulation. It was also important to prevent less scrupulous countries from obtaining a competitive edge by introducing deliberately indulgent legislation.

B - STEPS IN INTERNATIONALISATION

39. - Accidents and major disasters encouraged States to cooperate in the search for safe, efficient maritime transport. This move towards internationalisation of the law took place in several stages. First came the uniformisation of local regulations, through bilateral treaties, agreements or understandings among the leading maritime nations. Next, these same nations were to hold international conferences, in order to set up genuinely universal rules. Finally, intergovernmental organisations were to take over and encourage the adoption of international instruments to regulate safety at sea and protection of the marine environment.

• **Diplomatic conferences and multilateral conventions**
40. - At the beginning of this century, the dogma of absolute freedom of competition reigned supreme. It was possible to build a ship more or less whatever way one liked, equip it with whatever instruments one liked, operate it according to whatever standards one liked, and sail it whatever way one liked on any seas. Only a few common navigational rules had emerged, following the holding of the first international conferences on the safety of maritime transport. On 28 July 1879, nineteen States adopted joint rules in London for an international signal code. On 1st September 1880, an international convention set the first rules for preventing collisions. On 28 July 1881 the first convention on health and safety for steam packet navigation was signed.

In 1889, a congress met in November in Washington DC, to draw up a proper code of the sea, covering rules on steering and sailing, lights and signals, and distress signals. This first major international maritime conference defined thirteen groups of regulatory principles, which were subsequently adopted and implemented by all the States, without giving rise to an official convention. The start of the 20th century saw the emergence of the first rules on wireless telegraphy, laid down by the Berlin Convention and rules of 3 November 1906. Two other basic conventions were signed in September 1910, one concerning collisions, the other lifesaving and assistance (26).

41. - When the transatlantic liner *Titanic* sank on 14 April 1912 off Newfoundland, after colliding with an iceberg, the event was followed by a spectacular acceleration in the standard-setting process. This appalling disaster had an enormous impact on public opinion, and encouraged realisation of the need for collective safety procedures. By July 1912, a wireless telegraphy conference, held in London, made intercommunication systems and radio

(25) Y. ROCQUEMONT : "La conférence de 1966 sur les lignes de charge". NTM 1967, 34.
(26) R. GOY : "La répartition des fréquences en matière de télécommunication". AFDI 1959, 572.

equipment on board ships compulsory. It also allocated certain wavelengths to ships and coastal stations, long-distance radiotelegrams and radiolighthouses. Its application was to be suspended during the First World War, but it came into force again in 1919.

The most important result of the loss of the *Titanic* was the first international conference on the safety of life at sea, held in London in January 1914 at the invitation of the British government. With great difficulty, this conference drafted an international agreement: the issue required a consensus which could be obtained only after interminable discussions on the various technical solutions proposed to reduce accidents. The first Convention on Safety of Life at Sea (SOLAS) was signed by only five states, but led to extensive application regulations in Britain, France, the United States and Scandinavia (27).

42. - The standard-setting process spread internationally between the Wars. The 1920 conference on the International Union of Electrical Communications revised the rules of the 1912 convention on wireless telegraphy, and the principles of the SOLAS Convention. Two other conferences, one in Washington in 1927 and the other in Madrid in 1931, finalised international regulations on radiocommunications.

A second conference on the safety of human life at sea took place in London in 1929, where a new SOLAS Convention was adopted, containing some sixty articles on ship construction, lifesaving equipment, fire prevention and fire fighting, wireless telegraphy equipment, navigation aids and rules to prevent collisions.

On 23 October 1930, three important texts, drafted in Lisbon under the auspices of the League of Nations, completed regulations on signalling at sea. The first text concerned maritime signals, the second was about manned lightships, and the third dealt with the characteristics of lighthouses and radiobeacons. Another agreement, reached in Geneva on 13 May 1936, harmonised the existing buoyage systems.

In the aftermath of the Second World War, international conferences on safety at sea proceeded to amend existing texts. On 10 June 1947, the Oslo Convention introduced a new registered tonnage system.

In 1948, the British government invited all the States that had signed the SOLAS Convention to attend an international conference, in order to revise the provisions on safety of life at sea. A new version was adopted in June by twenty-seven States, and came into effect on 19 November 1952.

• **The emerging role of international organisations**
43. - One might be tempted to believe that international law on safety at sea was established in the first part of the 20th century through the efforts of international organisations. Several of them did try to harmonise national rules.

The Comité Maritime International (CMI), set up in Antwerp in 1897 (28), contributed to the work of several diplomatic conferences. This purely private body, which brought together maritime law associations in Western countries, took part directly in the establishment of several texts relating to safety: collision in the 1910 Brussels Convention, and assistance and salvage at sea in 1910.

(27) GEOFFROY : "Les catastrophes maritimes et la récente conférence de Londres". Le Correspondant, 10 July 1914, 65.
(28) A. LILAR, C. VAN DEN BOSCH : "Le Comité Maritime International 1897-1972". CMI - Antwerp 1972.

Set up just after the First World War, the International Labour Organisation (ILO) fostered the introduction of specific regulations for working conditions at sea. In 1920, a convention was adopted on a minimum age for admission of employment as seamen on ships. In 1930, ILO also launched the first campaigns against flags of convenience (cf chapter 4 below).

Another organisation set up by the League of Nations and that played an important role in harmonising standards was the Temporary Transport and Communication Commission. It was responsible for the 1923 Geneva Convention on maritime port regimes. In London, a year later, two technical committees were set up within this agency, one to investigate the problems raised by unification of registered tonnage provisions, and the other to examine issues of maritime navigation, buoyage and lighting of coasts. These efforts culminated in the adoption of several international agreements at the Lisbon conference of 1930. The agency continued its work until 1939 (29).

44. - But on the whole, initiatives taken by international organisations were rather limited in the early part of the century. The whole period was dominated by the worldwide maritime supremacy of the United Kingdom. For a long time, the British fleet was the largest in the world, exerting considerable influence over principles and legal concepts (30). London was the favoured venue for major diplomatic conferences. The British government, sole depository of the SOLAS Conventions, thereby had control over the revisions of 1929 and 1948. British practice in fact inspired much of the work of international legislators, as regards both the equipment of ships and the rules of navigation. Certain observers went so far as to assert that the United Kingdom actually made up for institutional shortcomings on the international scene.

The post-Second World War period witnessed a gradual decline in British power and influence. 1948 marked a decisive turning point in the maritime history of nations when, on 6 March, a convention was signed in Geneva, setting up the International Maritime Consultative Organisation (IMCO), which was to assume responsibility for safety issues. From the Fifties, there was an increase in the numbers of international bodies and various commissions which had the task of reducing accidents at sea. Thereupon began the age of organisations, whose importance and influence were to grow steadily until the present day.

(29) SUDRE : "L'OMCI, institution spécialisée des Nations Unies". Thèse, Droit Montpellier 1973, Chapitre I, 3 à 13.
(30) C.P. SRIVASTAVA : "Towards Safer Shipping". Fair-play 19 May 1983.

PART ONE

SETTING SAFETY
STANDARDS

DIVERSITY OF SOURCES

45. - The most remarkable thing about maritime safety law is the diversity of its sources. This may be explained partly by the large number of promoters of regulations, acting internationally and nationally, and partly by the variety of ways in which accident prevention standards are established.

This multiplicity of standard-setting practices, which can be disconcerting for the non-expert, is a legacy of maritime history. Today, it also reflects the scale and complexity of the issues at stake.

Although States are now clearly the prime movers in efforts to improve safety at sea, their action is still closely scrutinised by the International Maritime Organization (cf chapter 3 below) and other intergovernmental institutions (chapter 4). Unlike the situation for other modes of transport, very important contributions have been made to safety at sea by private bodies (chapter 5) and more specifically classification societies (chapter 6).

Safety standards accordingly reflect three different realities. First, there are the technical rules adopted at an international level (chapter 7); the second group consists of purely national rules introduced in conformity with the provisions of the law of the sea (chapter 8); the third consists of unilateral measures that break with generally accepted standards (chapter 9).

CHAPTER 3

International Maritime Organization
(IMO)

46. - The International Maritime Organization today occupies a special position within the maritime community. This London-based organisation, which has 157 member States, employs three hundred officials and has an annual budget of nearly £18m, is the force behind nearly all the technical standards and legal rules for safety at sea and prevention of pollution by ships. Its priorities are reflected in its motto "Safer ships and cleaner oceans". The important part played by this institution in accident prevention is studied below in some detail: its specific characteristics (cf I below), structure (II), the nature of its activities (III), and the outlook for its future (IV).

I - IMO : CHARACTERISTICS AND SPECIFIC ROLE

47. - It was in the aftermath of the Second World War that the need was realised for an international body to deal exclusively with maritime issues (1).

Several factors encouraged States to strengthen international cooperation in the maritime sector : the recurrent accidents that made it vital to bring about a rapid improvement in the safety of seaborne transport; the need for greater uniformity in the rules and practice applied to maritime trade; the need to adopt new standards to cope with the thrust of new technologies applying to ships and their equipment, and the conditions of ocean navigation (2).

All these factors were taken into account by the Economic and Social Council of the United Nations (ECOSOC), when it decided to convene a United Nations maritime conference in Geneva from 19 February to 6 March 1948. This event culminated in a convention setting up the Intergovernmental Maritime Consultative Organisation (IMCO). This convention came into force on 17 March 1958. Under an amendment to this convention in May 1982, the institution was renamed the International Maritime Organisation (IMO).

The creation of IMO, with its specific characteristics, marked an important date in the evolvement of international maritime regulations.

(1) For some authors, the origins of IMO are in the 1926 Vienna Conference of the International Law Association. Cf K. SIMMONDS : "The International Maritime Organisation". Simmonds and Hill, London, 1994.
(2) H.B. SILVERSTEIN : "Superships and nation-states. The transnational politics of the Intergovernmental Maritime Consultative Organization". Westview Press, Colorado, 1978, 10-14.

A - SPECIALISED UNITED NATIONS AGENCY

48. - IMO comes into the category of "specialised agencies" provided for in article 57 of the United Nations Charter. Such entities are connected to the UN by agreements, the conditions of which are stipulated in article 63 of the Charter. The agreement on IMO was approved by the Resolution 204 of the UN Assembly on 18 November 1948, and by the IMO Assembly on 13 January 1959.

The status of specialised agency gives IMO legal and financial independence. It has its own management structure and budget, and enjoys certain privileges and immunities granted by the United Kingdom, on whose territory its headquarters are located.

B - INTERGOVERNMENTAL ORGANISATION

49. - IMO is an intergovernmental organisation (IGO) with 157 member States. There are two associate members, Hong Kong since 1967 and Macao since 1990 (3).

All IMO funding comes from States. The annual overall budget exceeds £18m (4). Contributions are calculated by a different formula from other UN agencies. The amount paid by each member States is based on two components : the tonnage of its merchant fleet (87.5 per cent), and its ability to pay (12.5 per cent) (5).

Table 4 shows a list of the top ten contributors and the size of their shipping fleets in 1997 (6). It shows that IMO is funded mainly by open registry countries like Panama, Liberia, Cyprus and the Bahamas. The United States, Japan and Northern European States, although they are a predominant force in world maritime trade, pay relatively smaller contributions. Such a situation is regarded as unfair by some members, who demand an overhaul of the system, to reflect the organisation's goals and real activity (7).

Table 4 - Top ten contributors to the IMO budget for 1997

Member States	£m	%	Number of ships	mgrt
1 Panama	2.49	13.59	6 188	21.128
2 Liberia	1.97	10.74	1 697	60.058
3 Japan	0.98	5.39	9 310	18.516
4 Greece	0.98	5.35	1 641	25.288
5 Cyprus	0.81	4.42	1 650	23.653
6 USA	0.76	4.19	5 260	11.788
7 Bahamas	0.77	4.24	4 221	25.523
8 Norway	0.70	3.85	715*	19.780*
9 Russian Federation	0.59	3.22	4 814	12.282
10 China	0.56	3.10	3 175	16.339

* Norway (NIS)

(3) IMO : "Basic facts about IMO". London, Jan. 1998.
(4) L36, 672, 200 for 1998-1999 in. "IMO cuts member fees by 5 %". Lloyd's List 12 Nov. 1997.
(5) "Transparency the key as O'Neil moves to change IMO's ways". Lloyd's List, 18 Nov. 1996.
(6) Basic facts about IMO and LRS : "World Fleet Statistics 1997". London, 1998.
(7) "Liberia seeks IMO cash rethink". Lloyd's List, 9 Dec. 1996.

The question has been raised whether a regional intergovernmental organisation can become an IMO member. A resolution of the European Parliament, adopted in 1994, suggested that the interests of European States should be advanced under the banner of a single EU representation (8). If such a proposal were accepted, subject of course to its political feasibility, IMO would function in a radically different way, with the formation of geopolitical groups representing different interests and regions of the world, like the Council of the UN Conference on Trade and Development (UNCTAD).

C - ORGANISATION WITH TECHNICAL POWERS

50. - Despite quite broad original goals, IMO has exercised its powers mainly in the technical field of maritime navigation (9).

These goals are defined in article 1 of the Convention of 6 March 1948 setting up the Organisation :
- "To provide machinery for cooperation among governments in the field of governmental regulation and practices relating to technical matters of all kinds affecting shipping engaged in international trade, to encourage and facilitate the general adoption of the highest practicable standards in matters concerning the maritime safety, efficiency of navigation and prevention and control of marine pollution from ships, and to deal with administrative and legal matters related to the purposes set out in this article ;
- "To encourage the removal of discriminatory action and unnecessary restrictions by governments affecting shipping (...) ;
- "To provide for the consideration by the Organisation of matters concerning unfair restrictive practices by shipping concerns (...)."

Only technical powers have been assumed to any extent by IMO, either on its own initiative, or at the request of other organisations (10). In addition, amendments to the constituent instrument, voted in 1975, have confirmed the new powers that IMO has assumed in practice (11), notably by institutionalising three specialised committees : the Legal Committee, the Marine Environment Protection Committee (MEPC), and the Technical Cooperation Committee.

This purely technical focus in the work of the Organisation, and its lack of interest in economic issues of concern to developing countries, were behind the decision in 1965 by the United Nations Conference on Trade and Development (UNCTAD) to set up its Committee on Shipping, which became active in 1967 (12).

In the last thirty years, IMO has gained a reputation for the establishment of technical safety standards. This success may be put down mainly to the efficiency of the structures to facilitate international communication and consensus.

(8) "EU urged to seek IMO member ship". Lloyd's List, 22 March 1994.
(9) IMO : Basic Documents Volume I. Convention of the International Marine Organisation. London, IMO, 1986.
(10) C. SRIVASTAVA : "Safer ships and cleaner oceans : thirty years' work of the International Maritime Organisation". Transport Reviews, 1989, vol. 9, n° 1, 45-47.
(11) J. DUTHEIL DE LA ROCHERE : "Une institution spécialisée renaissante. La nouvelle Organisation Maritime Internationale". AFDI, 1976, 454.
(12) W.H. LAMPE : "The 'New' International Maritime Organisation and its place in development of international maritime law" - Journal of Maritime Law and Commerce, vol. 14, n° 3, July 1983, 313.

II - IMO STRUCTURE

IMO comprises deliberative bodies, technical bodies and an administrative body.

A - ASSEMBLY

51. - As the governing body of the Organisation, the IMO Assembly comprises all member States. It meets once every two years in regular sessions, but can also hold extraordinary sessions if necessary.

Voting rules are the same for all IMO deliberative entities: every member has one vote, and decisions are taken either by a simple majority or by a qualified majority of two thirds of the members present, depending on the issue under debate.

A distinction should be made between the general powers of the Assembly and those attributed to it by the 1948 Convention.

The general powers of the Assembly concern the functioning of the Organisation, including election at each session of the President and Vice-Presidents of the Assembly (cf article 15a), establishment of rules of procedure (article 15b), election of members of the Council (article 15d), establishment of subsidiary bodies (article 16c), voting the budget (article 16g), and other financial powers (article 16h).

The Assembly also possesses special powers in relation to safety at sea, including the sole right "to recommend to members for adoption regulations and guidelines concerning maritime safety" (article 15j).

B - COUNCIL

52. - When IMO was set up in 1948, huge difficulties were involved in protecting the interests of traditional maritime nations, and setting a new balance between States supplying shipping services and those that used such services. Strong pressures were brought to bear by the service suppliers at the Conference, anxious that users might impose over-constricting and over-expensive standards on maritime transport, in the name of safety. The solution that was found was to assign most substantive powers to the IMO Council, and superintend its membership.

1. Broadening of Council membership

53. - Originally accused of being "a rich man's club" (13), the Council has become more democratic over the years, allowing a steadily increasing number of States to take part in the decision-making process.

The two initial selection criteria, namely the supply of international shipping services and an interest in international seaborne trade, were readjusted by a third factor guaranteeing fair geographical representation of Council membership. This trend was reflected in a considerable growth in the weight of the Third World on the Council, which was seen less and less as a club for the privileged.

---

(13) Linda Sue JOHNSON : "The International Maritime Organisation : a rich man's club". May 1985 in IMO Library, London.

At its 20th session in 1997, the Assembly elected thirty-two States to the Council, belonging to three categories :
- Eight shipowning States : China, United States, Russian Federation, Greece, Italy, Japan, Norway and the United Kingdom ;
- Eight chartering States : Germany, Argentina, Brazil, Canada, France, India, Netherlands, Sweden ;
- Sixteen States to ensure fair geographical representation: Algeria, Australia, Cyprus, Egypt, Finland, Indonesia, Liberia, Mexico, Panama, Philippines, Poland, Korea, Singapore, South Africa, Spain, Tunisia.

The Council is due to increase to forty members, when amendments to the IMO Convention adopted by means of resolution A.735 of 4 November 1993 come into force.

2. Council powers

54. - The Council meets whenever and wherever it wishes, as convened by its Chairman or at the request of at least four members (cf article 19).

In addition to the tasks involved in functioning of IMO (electing the Chairman, setting its rules of procedure, appointing the Secretary-General, making maritime recommendations), it receives recommendations and reports from the Maritime Safety Committee, which it transmits to the Assembly and, when it is not in session, to members for information, accompanied by its comments and recommendations (article 21b). It examines certain questions covered by a particular study by the Maritime Safety Committee (article 21c). It makes a report to each Assembly session on IMO activities (article 23). It can reach agreements with other organisations, subject to approval by the Assembly (article 25). Finally, except for maritime safety questions, the Council exercises all IMO functions between Assembly sessions (article 26).

C - MARITIME SAFETY COMMITTEE (MSC)

55. - Originally intended to be a restricted body, the Maritime Safety Committee (MSC) was the object of bitter controversy among states about control of its membership and functioning (14). Since 1978, when resolution A.315 came into effect, it has been open to all IMO members.

1. MSC specialised subcommittees

56. - The Maritime Safety Committee meets at least once a year, and on other occasions if at least five Committee members so wish. At each annual session, it elects its officers and adopts its rules of procedure. Since the 1974 amendment, a quorum is no longer required.

(14) Constitution of the Maritime Safety Committee of IMCO case (1960). ICJ Rep. 150 :
- CI. A. COLLIARD : "L'avis consultatif de la C.I.J. sur la composition du Comité de la sécurité maritime...". AFDI, VI, 1960, 338-361.
- L.F.E. GOLDIE : "Recognition and dual nationality. A problem of flags of convenience". The British Yearbook of International Law, 1963, vol. 39, 269-271.
- B. Mc CHESNEY : "Interpretation of convention for establishment of IMCO." AJIL, 1960, vol. 54, 884-894.
- R. PINTO : "L'affaire de la composition du Comité de la sécurité maritime de l'OMCI". JDI, 1961, n° 4,. 1190 and "Le droit des relations internationales". Payot. Paris, 1972, 183-185.
- ROSENNE : "La Cour Internationale de Justice en 1960". RGDIP, 1961, 507-517.
- K.R. SIMMONDS : "The constitution of the Maritime Safety Committee of IMCO.". ICLQ, 1963, vol. 12, 56-87.

In general, the MSC sets up a specialised subcommittee to deal with each major problem submitted to IMO. There are many such problems, because of the multiplicity and complexity of the issues under scrutiny. Nine subcommittees currently exist, on bulk liquids and gas ; carriage of dangerous goods, solid cargoes and containers; fire protection : radiocommunication, search and rescue ; safety of navigation; ship design and equipment, stability and loadlines and fishing vessels safety ; standards of training and watchkeeping, flag state implementation.

All IMO member States are invited to take part in the work of these subcommittees. In practice, the number of active delegations is very small. Subcommittees may set up working-groups, confined to a maximum of ten delegations, to study particular problems. These report back to the subcommittees on which they depend, and which communicate the reports to the MSC.

2. Scope of MSC powers

57. - The MSC is the highest technical body of IMO. Its functions are to consider any matter within the scope of the Organisation concerned with aids to navigation, construction and equipment of vessels, safe manning, rules for the prevention of collisions, handling of dangerous cargoes, maritime safety procedures and requirements, hydrographic information, logbooks and navigational records, marine casualty investigation, salvage and rescue, and any other matters directly affecting maritime safety (cf article 29a of the constituent charter).

The Committee is also responsible for taking all necessary steps to carry out assignments given to it under the terms of the convention setting up IMO, or tasks coming within its scope which may be assigned by or under any other international instrument and accepted by IMO (cf article 29b).

IMO members generally place considerable trust in the MSC, which provides them with a permanent decision-making body, capable of promoting efforts whenever circumstances require (15). The MSC can also adopt certain recommendations directly, particularly regarding traffic separation schemes and ship reporting systems (16).

D - LEGAL COMMITTEE

58. - The Legal Committee was set up in 1967, as a subsidiary body, to deal with the legal aspects of problems raised by the *Torrey Canyon* oil spill (17).

Responsible for examining any legal matters within the scope of IMO, the Legal Committee very quickly became the permanent body of the Council. Open to all IMO members, it operates in the same way as the MSC (18).

E - MARINE ENVIRONMENT PROTECTION COMMITTEE (MEPC)

59. - There are two reasons behind the creation of this committee early in 1974 : the growing importance of IMO activities connected with preventing pollution of the marine environment, following the *Torrey Canyon* disaster in 1967, and the impossibility of the MSC

(15) T. FUNDER : "IMO and its response to public challenges". IMO News, 1, 1998, VI-VIII.
(16) IMO. Resolution A.376, 14 November 1977.
(17) J.P. QUENEUDEC : "La remise en cause du droit de la mer". Colloque de Montpellier. Société Française pour le Droit International, 1972, Pedone, 16.
(18) G. IVANOV : "The role of IMO in the development of international maritime law". IMO News, 1, 1997, 21-26.

coping with any new tasks. The overall efficiency of IMO was considerably improved when this new permanent subsidiary body of the Assembly was established by Resolution A.297 of 23 November 1973 (19).

The MEPC was raised to full constitutional status in 1985. This Committee, which consists of all member States, is empowered to consider any matter within the scope of the Organisation concerned with prevention and control of pollution from ships. In particular it is concerned with the adoption and amendment of conventions and other regulations and measures to ensure their enforcement.

F - TECHNICAL COOPERATION COMMITTEE

60. - In setting up the Technical Cooperation Committee by Resolutions A.360 of 1975 and A.400 of 1977, IMO showed its determination to open the institution up to the concerns of the most underprivileged states and let them play a more active part in the decision-making process.

This Committee is open to all IMO members (cf new article 42). It meets at least once a year, elects its officers and adopts its rules of procedure (article 45). It submits its recommendations to the Council, and reports on its activities at each regular session of the Council (article 44).

Its function is to consider any matter within the scope of IMO concerned with the implementation of technical cooperation projects for which IMO is responsible, and any other aspects of technical cooperation related to IMO activities.

G - FACILITATION COMMITTEE

61. - The latest permanent subsidiary body is the Facilitation Committee, which emerged from a working group set up in 1968 to advise on implementation of the Facilitation Convention. The Council established it as a permanent body in 1972. Open to all member States, the Committee is intended to eliminate unnecessary paperwork and red tape in international shipping.

H - SECRETARIAT

62. - One of the most important bodies within IMO is its Secretariat. This comprises the Secretary-General and approximately three hundred technical and administrative staff based at IMO headquarters in London. This makes it one of the smallest agencies in the UN system.

The internal structure of the Secretariat consists of two large technical divisions, one dealing with problems of safety at sea, and the other with questions relating to the marine environment. There are four other divisions, for legal affairs and external relations, conferences, technical cooperation and administrative affairs.

In general, the Secretariat is responsible for IMO administration, and providing all the information needed for the work of other bodies. It attends to any tasks assigned to it by the constituent instrument, the Assembly, the Council and technical committees.

(19) "IMO. The first fifty years". IMO News, 1, 1998.
(20) "IMO healthy despite debts". lloyd's List, 2 August 1989.

There have been six different holders of the post of Secretary-General of IMO since 1958 : Ove Nielsen (Denmark) from 1959 to 1961, William Graham (United Kingdom), Acting Secretary-General from 1961 to 1963, Jean Roullier (France) from 1964 to 1967, Colin Goad (United Kingdom) from 1968 to 1973, Chandrika Prasad Srivastava (India) from 1974 to 1989, and William O'Neil (Canada) since 1990 (21).

The role of the Secretariat and the Secretary-General has evolved considerably since IMO was set up. In the early days, it remained quite modest: the Secretary-General was concerned only with administrative problems, staff management or relations with other United Nations agencies. There are several reasons for this low profile (22) : the close surveillance exercised by IMO members, the shortage of staff with advanced technical skills compared with member government expertise, and the lack of an executive role for the Secretariat. The arrival of C.P. Srivastava to head IMO gave a broader political dimension to the function of Secretary-General. As a citizen of a developing country, Mr Srivastava was behind the opening of IMO to the Third World. The personality of the current Secretary-General, William O'Neil, appointed on 1st January 1990, and reelected in 1993 and 1997 for a four-year period, has further enhanced the political nature of the post. His numerous declarations in favour of IMO being more ambitious in its goals, more directive towards its members, and more anticipatory and comprehensive in regard to the present major problems of safety at sea, have made the IMO Secretary-General one of the most important figures in the international maritime community (23).

III - IMO ACTIVITIES

IMO is engaged in three types of maritime safety functions.

A - STANDARD SETTING

63. - Article 2 of the 1948 Geneva Convention states the functions of IMO with regard to international legislation :

"a) (...) Consider and make recommendations upon matters" (coming within its scope);

b) Provide for the drafting of conventions, agreements, or other suitable instruments, and recommend these to governments and to intergovernmental organisations, and convene such conferences as may be necessary".

Under present international circumstances, and given the particular nature of the maritime world, so attached to the idea of freedom, IMO has to exercise its powers under difficult conditions. Despite these obstacles, it has achieved considerable results in setting standards, making the best use of the small amount of power left to it by States. It uses such powers to draw up draft conventions, and to formulate recommendations.

(21) "Basic facts about IMO". Focus on IMO, Jan. 1998, 3.
(22) R.I. McLAREN : "An evaluation of a secretariat's political role within the policy process of an international organization - The case of IMCO". Thesis, University of Pittsburgh, 1972.
(23) - B. BOX : "Builder of bridges" Seatrade Review, August 1993, 13-14.
- M. GREY : "Some self-auditing by the IMO Secretary General". BIMCO Bulletin, vol. 90, n° 3 - 95, 8-9.
- A. GUEST : "The high speed cop". The Baltic, Sept. 1997, 31-33.

1. IMO conventions

64. - Conventions and protocols are legal instruments which are binding on members. They lay down standards which all signatories undertake to incorporate in their national legal system. As soon as they come into force, all states that are parties to them must implement their requirements (24).

Since it first met in 1959, IMO has facilitated the adoption of forty conventions and protocols, nearly all of which are in force today. Most of them concern safety at sea and the prevention of marine pollution.

The main safety conventions contain provisions on the safety of human life at sea (SOLAS), loadlines (LL), special transport of passengers (STP), prevention of collisions (COLREG), container safety (CSC), training of seafarers (STCW), and search and rescue (SAR).

Convention on prevention of pollution (25) may be put under two headings : those that lay down technical standards aimed at improving the safety of certain types of ships, particularly oil tankers (OILPOL and MARPOL), and those that give powers to States to deal with the risk of pollution or incidents near its coasts (INTERVENTION and OPRC).

2. Codes, rules and recommendations

65. - Conventions are not the only instruments available to IMO in order to establish or change the rules of safety at sea. It possesses the power to "consider and make recommendations upon matters" coming within its scope (article 2a of the constituent instrument).

The Assembly, the MSC and the MEPC have adopted several hundred codes, sets of rules, guidelines, recommendations and resolutions. The terminological subtleties that lie behind these names have no legal consequences. By definition, the recommendations of international organisations are not legally enforceable (26). However, it should be noted that a number of safety codes and rules are incorporated in conventions by means of amendments, upon which they become binding on signatory states (27).

As already pointed out, IMO has issued very many different recommendations, which can be put under some main headings : ship construction, cargoes, ship operation, navigation, search and rescue at sea, radiocommunications, marine environment.

B - CONSULTATION ACTIVITIES

66. - Improvement of safety at sea is encouraged not only by the adoption of international conventions and recommendations, but also by the provision of "machinery for consultation among members and the exchange of information among governments" (article 2c of the constituent instrument). This has allowed a permanent consultation system to be set up.

(24) Th. MENSAH et Ch. ZIMMERLI : "L'activité réglementaire de l'OMCI". SFDI - Colloque de Toulouse. Pedone, Paris, 1975, 31-47.
(25) L. JUDA : "IMCO and the regulation of ocean pollution from ships". ICLQ, 1977, 558-584.
(26) M. VIRALLY : "La valeur juridique des recommandations des organisations internationales". AFDI, 1956, 66.
(27) C.E. HENRY : "The role of the International Marine Organisation in the enactment of international legislation. Thesis n° 387. University of Geneva, 1984.

IMO's status as a permanent fixed body encourages multilateral consultation among States (28). This privileged position allows it to offer the conditions necessary to any discussion among a number of governments. It also has the advantage of establishing contact, in a way obligatory, among experts from all maritime nations, thereby forging a consensus from their viewpoints (29).

The establishment of this global forum was originally met with scepticism on the part of traditional maritime circles, using the International Chamber of Shipping as their mouthpiece (30).

The main advantage of permanent institutional structures lies in the capacity to react immediately and trigger the standard-setting process without delay. Its continuity of operation allows the IMO Secretariat to regulate, select and communicate a considerable volume of information. This means that international maritime experts can meet at very short notice.

In practice, it has been found that IMO has considerably improved its speed of reaction to emergencies. When the *Torrey Canyon* was wrecked in March 1967, less than two months was needed for the Council to introduce the first antipollution measures (31).

Immediately after the *Amoco Cadiz* accident in March 1978, IMO recommended the installation of a dual control system for steering gear on board tankers. Since such equipment did not exist on the market, the maritime industry took three and a half years to find a technical solution to the problem. Amendments to the SOLAS Convention therefore could not be adopted until 20 November 1981, coming into force on 1st September 1984 (32).

The speed with which IMO can act was clearly illustrated at the time of the *Herald of Free Enterprise* disaster in March 1987. The MSC adopted the first amendments to the SOLAS Convention on 21 April 1988, and they came into force on 22 October 1989, under the tacit amendment procedure.

The *Estonia* disaster in September 1994 also led to an acceleration of the standard-setting process. In December of the same year, the MSC approved the Secretary-General's proposal to set up a group of experts to make a thorough urgent investigation of the safety of ro-ro ferries. Under the direction of an executive committee, the group submitted its report and conclusions in April 1995, for examination by the MSC the following month (33). Thanks to the efforts of an intersession meeting of the Committee at the beginning of October, a diplomatic conference met in November to adopt the amendments to the SOLAS Convention needed to prevent such a disaster from recurring (34).

The consultation and debating activities of IMO, involving both member States and international institutions, have tended to increase overall since 1959. This is the result of the function of memory or lookout performed by the London organisation. Its Secretariat, which sees to the continuity of general policy and staff, can permanently monitor decisions taken by other international bodies, and supply relevant information to technical committees and deliberative bodies. With these structures intended to foster communication and negotiation,

(28) D.W. McNEMAR : "The future role of international institutions" in "The future of the international legal order". Volume IV. The Structure of the International Environment. Cyril E. BLACH et Richard A. FALK. Princeton, N.J. 1972

(29) W. O'NEIL : "Celebrating years of success". Lloyd's List, 6 March 1998.

(30) Ch. HORROCKS : "Half a century of crucial regulation". Lloyd's List, 6 March 1998.

(31) R.H. M'GONIGLE et M.W. ZACHER : "Pollution, politics, and international law" University of California Press, 1978, 345.

(32) J. COWLEY : "The International Maritime Organisation and national administrations". The Institute of Marine Engineers. Lecture, 7 February 1989, London.

(33) "Agreement reached on RoRo Ferry Safety Measures". IMO News, 4-1995 and 1-1996, 3-6.

(34) SOLAS/CONF. 3/45, 29 November 1995.

IMO encourages the quest for the best solutions to any problem of safety at sea. It chooses the best method of reaching agreement on solutions acceptable to States, and on the form to be given to such agreements (35).

C - TECHNICAL COOPERATION

67. - In recent years, the characteristics of sea transport have changed enormously, with a huge rise in the number of States engaged in international maritime trade. Today, it is no longer enough to issue regulations: to be effective, a convention needs to be applied effectively and universally.

To ensure safety on board all ships, regardless of which flag they are flying, every State has to be provided with the means to observe the obligations it has entered into. Advice is enough for the richest nations; the poorest, with no spare resources, experience or competent staff, need special help. IMO has for many years provided this in the form of a technical assistance programme, which is nowadays one of the most important aspects of its activities.

1. Integrated Technical Cooperation Programme (ITCP)

68. - Since its creation, IMO has tried to provide help to new maritime States, usually developing countries with modest resources, very limited maritime experience, and no trained personnel. Today, the Integrated Technical Cooperation Programme enables IMO to offer the worldwide maritime community a whole range of assistance, consultancy or coordination services, for technical and legal issues within its scope (36).

The purpose of ITCP, drawn up on a regional basis, is to provide incentive for application of international regulations by transferring maritime skills and technologies. The relationship between assistance supplied under the terms of technical cooperation and the standardising functions of IMO provides a solid base for helping developing countries ratify and implement international conventions, by setting up their own technical management and training resources.

The programme covers the traditional areas of action of IMO: safety at sea, protection of the marine environment, maritime legislation and the related aspects of maritime transport and ports Every year the Technical Cooperation Committee issues a report on actions undertaken within the ITPC framework, for submission to all IMO bodies.

Integrated regional programmes contribute to the continuous development of ITPC and the performance of its activities.

The whole programme is drawn up by the IMO Technical Cooperation Division, which is also responsible for overseeing it. This Division also prepares regional programmes, sees to their coordination, establishes relations with donor countries, and formulates strategies for calling in contributions. It is not responsible for carrying projects into effect : this is the responsibility of the Maritime Safety, Legal Affairs and External Relations, and Marine Environment Divisions.

2. Importance of training

69. - Training is the most important aspect of the technical assistance provided by IMO. It is the shortage of qualified maritime experts, technical knowledge and infrastructures that on a day-to-day basis hinders the implementation of a uniform world maritime regime.

(35) G. PATTOFATTO : "Shaping the future of marine safety". Lloyd's List, 6 March 1998.
(36) IMO. Brochure on IMO's technical cooperation programme. London, 1994.

IMO has tried to overcome this deficiency by introducing modern teaching methods, so that developing countries can quickly train the necessary staff to a high level. One effect of this policy has been the opening of the World Maritime University (WMU) and the International Maritime Law Institute (IMLI).

a) World Maritime University

• Origin
70. - IMO adopted Resolution A.501, approving the creation of the University, in November 1981. The Secretary-General took only about fifteen months to carry out the project. Sweden provided a large cash contribution, the city of Malmö made the necessary buildings and equipment available, and the United Nations Development Programme (UNDP) provided additional finance. In February 1983, the agreement setting up the University was signed. It came into effect on 1st May, allowing training courses to begin by June.

• Goals
According to its constituent charter, the WMU is intended to be "the international maritime training institution for the training of senior specialist maritime personnel in various aspects of shipping and related fields (...) in furtherance of the purposes and objectives of the International Maritime Organisation".

The charter assigns three fundamental mandates to the University : offer concerned countries, mainly in the Third World, installations for high-calibre training of their maritime workers (teachers, administrators, inspectors, management cadres, experts in technical sciences of the sea, port managers, etc); help set up a team of internationally acknowledged experts including professors, lecturers and consultants, who will make their knowledge available to developing countries, in order to solve safety or pollution problems; finally, establish a uniform international surveyor training system.

• Organisation
The courses taught at the University last two years. They lead to a Master of Science degree in general maritime administration, maritime safety administration, maritime education, and technical management of shipping companies.

The University is run by a board of governors, under the chairmanship of the IMO Secretary-General. Teaching programmes and administration of the University are the responsibility of a rector, assisted by a vice-rector, and eight full-time professors. The team is completed by a roster of a hundred and fifty guest professors and lecturers, invited for periods to teach certain specialised subjects.

• Assessment
The educational success of the World Maritime University has been underlined on several occasions (37). Nearly a hundred students graduate every year. The WMU has been so successful with Third World nations that from 1985 a limited number of places were offered to students from industrialised maritime countries. Early in 1998, there were 1 400 WMU graduates from 130 countries.

A question mark remains, however, over stable long-term funding for the University, whose annual budget amounted to $7.5m in 1997 (38). Up to now, all funds have come from

(37) P.K. MENON : "The World Maritime University : an attempt to train specialist maritime personnel". Journal of Maritime Law and Commerce, vol. 17, N° 4, Oct 1986, p. 585-597.
(38) "WMU provides a network of maritime expertise". Lloyd's List, 6 March 1998.

voluntary contributions, mainly from the UNDP, Sweden and other Nordic countries. The gradual reduction in UNDP funding in the last five years has forced University leaders to look for other forms of financing (39).

b) International Maritime Law Institute

71. - The growing complexity of international conventions has in recent years proved one of the main obstacles to their implementation. This is largely due to the absence in developing countries of maritime lawyers and administrators with the right training and capacities to translate convention requirements into national legislation. IMO has tried to solve this problem by setting up the International Maritime Law Institute (IMLI) in Malta in 1989.

This Institute offers a one-year course to a maximum of twenty to twenty-five students each year. Like the WMU, the IMLI is directed by a board of governors. There is a very small administrative structure, comprising a director assisted by a deputy director, who call upon the skills of guest professors and lecturers.

Long-term financing is again a problem, since the IMLI budget depends entirely on voluntary contributions.

c) Other training initiatives

72. - Apart from the WMU in Malmö and the IMLI in Malta, three other training initiatives should be mentioned. The IMO International Maritime Academy in Trieste is largely financed by the Italian government. It offers students from developing countries an opportunity to attend seminars based on a range of model courses. Teaching is provided by a small permanent team, with guest lecturers.

Each year, IMO, in conjunction with the French government and the Port of Le Havre, organises a five-week course on port operation and management. This is provided free of charge to twenty senior port administration officials from Third World countries. Similar courses are given by Belgium and the Netherlands.

Finally, IMO has encouraged the creation of national networks of maritime training institutions in a number of underprivileged countries. Experience shows that this is an effective strategy for technical cooperation, allowing a broad exchange of experiences among maritime colleges throughout the world.

3. Technical cooperation funding

73. - IMO has no budget of its own with which to fund technical assistance programmes. Funds for this activity have fallen by 54 per cent over the last ten years (40). The UNDP, the main contributor in the past, has slashed its contribution, from $8m in 1988 to $1m in 1995.

There is an increasing gulf between the total amount of disbursements needed to finance various programmes and projects ($36.8m) and the sums allocated (barely $20.8m) (41).

(39) M. GREY : "University challenged by our industry's lack of support". Lloyd's List, 12 July 1995.
(40) IMO. Technical Cooperation Committee. Integrated Technical Cooperation Programme. Final Report on 1994, TC 41/5(a), 10 May 1998, paragraph 23.
(41) IMO, TC 40/3, October 1994.

In addition, the IMO technical cooperation programme depends on a very small number of major donors. The largest contributor in 1995 was Norway, and more than 70 per cent of the $7.1m came from only three donors : Norway, the World Bank Environmental Fund (GEF) and the UNDP. The donor base remains unstable, making any long-term assessment of viability difficult. Even though safety at sea is the prime concern of IMO, 52 per cent of the 1995 budget for technical cooperation was devoted to activities relating to protection of the marine environment, with expenditure on safety projects representing only 38.5 per cent of the total amount (42).

In general, the IMO programme is managed in an arbitrary way, which makes the future uncertain financially for certain extremely useful projects. This is the case, for example, of the World Maritime University, which in the last few years has had to reduce the number of entrants, for lack of funds (43).

On 26 June 1997, despite these inconsistencies, the Technical Cooperation Committee adopted a revised version of the ITCP. IMO has secured new funds of $4 050 200 for project activities for the period 1997-99. In addition, the Technical Cooperation Fund, built up by donations, provided $2 475 000 for the period 1996-97, and it will contribute $1 850 000 for 1998-99 project activities. For this same period, an additional £1m would be forthcoming from transferral to the TC Fund from the IMO Printing Fund.

New donors include the International Transport Workers Federation, which provided £1.5m for the period 1996-98 (44).

IV - DEVELOPMENT PROSPECTS

74. - Despite the advances in safety at sea achieved by IMO since it was set up, it is regularly the butt of severe and varied criticisms, particular of its standard-setting function. In the last twenty years, it has been accused of everything, and the opposite of everything : of having drawn up inadequate standards (45), which are no more than the lowest internationally acceptable common denominator (46) and on the other hand of producing too many regulations, which are too complicated, too difficult to implement, notably by developing countries (47); of acting in most cases after a disaster and too slowly (48), but sometimes of reacting too hastily (49) ; of failing to remove substandard ships from the world's seas (50), while denying it any possibility of action against States that turn a blind eye to the registration of such ships under their flags.

Although it refuses to be seen as a scapegoat (51) responsible for all the evils of the system, IMO's reputation and credibility have been damaged by the combination of several events on the international stage : the development of unilateral regulations (52), the gradual institutionalisation of port State controls (53) and the recurrence of accidents, like those affecting bulk carriers in the early Nineties (54).

(42) IMO, TC 42/2, May 1996.
(43) "IMO : seeking excellence through cooperation". World Maritime Day, 1996. IMO, London. (NB The class of 98 was a record high.)
(44) "TC programme seeks new resources". IMO News", 4, 1997, 21.
(45) "The nautical institute's challenge on the need for maritime safety enforcement". Lloyd's List, 21 May 1981.
(46) P. DOUGHTY : "Working to acceptable standards". The Motorship, Sept 1993, 59-61.
(47) J.SMITH : "The changing of the IMO". BIMCO Review 1994, 34-36.
(48) "Crime and punishment". Tradewinds, 2 April 1993.
(49) "ISF president attacks IMO over haste". Lloyd's List, 30 May 1991.
(50) "Challenge of IMO". Lloyd's List, 21 April 1992.
(51) "IMO refuses to be seen as international scapegoat". Lloyd's List, 21 July 1993.
(52) "IMO on trial". Lloyd's List, 29 May 1991.
(53) O. DIJXHOORN : "Port and shipping management : the role of IMO". Marine Policy, Sept 1993, 363-366.
(54) "IMO is plunged into safety crisis". Lloyd's List, 14 May 1991.

It has been criticised for two serious shortcomings. Despite its change of name in 1982, IMO has always remained a consultative body, which draws up and proposes solutions, but which has no power to have them adopted or applied. IMO has most signally been deficient in overseeing the implementation of regulations (55). Its members continue to remain free to perform the obligations they have accepted at an international level (56). No penalty is applied for ineffectiveness or failure to comply, so that safety performances remain very uneven, with casualty rates differing by a factor of 1 to 114 among different national fleets.

Some in fact deplore the fact that IMO has become a huge administrative machine, where political bureaucrats have gradually outnumbered technicians. For example, it has been estimated that every State had to produce more than 32 000 sheets of paper for every proposed rule change (57), while IMO admits that it produces about 15 million pages of documents every year (58). Such methods are not conducive to the adoption of safety rules that can be applied without delay to all world shipping. On the contrary, it generates a bureaucracy that represents a threat to safety (59).

It is in this politically difficult context , and against a background of worldwide economic crisis, that IMO is moving forward. It has set itself new goals, and is trying to find the means of attaining them.

A - NEW DIRECTIONS

The new directions followed by IMO since the early Eighties were influenced by two major events : the adoption of the United Nations Convention of 10 December 1982 on the Law of the Sea (UNCLOS), which came into force in November 1994, and the introduction by IMO of a strategic initiative to ensure better application of international standards (60).

1. Effects of new Convention on the Law of the Sea

75. - Although IMO is referred to by name in only one article of UNCLOS, it is clearly the organisation to which reference is made, particularly for any matters to do with the establishment of international rules on navigation and pollution (61).

An IMO Secretariat study of the effects of the LOS Convention set out to answer three fundamental questions : whether or not IMO treaties and other instruments should be revised or amended; whether IMO should undertake new tasks, or alter its current work programmes; whether it was necessary and useful to revise or establish new procedures or assume new roles that are needed, because of the provisions of UNCLOS concerning IMO (62).

The study examined in detail the aspects of the Convention that require action in each field covered by the three questions. Its conclusions were taken into account in the revision of existing conventions or the adoption of new regulations (63). IMO has remained very cautious about any new roles, considering the possibility of not assuming certain responsibilities assigned

(55) "IMO to be given new teeth". Seatrade Week, 4-10 June 1993.
(56) M. GREY : "Talking tougher, acting faster". BIMCO Review 1996, 107-110.
(57) "Atlantic death toll is highest since war". Sunday Times, 13 February 1994.
(58) "Secretary-General calls for mandatory training". Lloyd's List, 24 Sept 1987.
(59) "Bureaucracy, a threat to safety". Lloyd's List, 22 April 1989.
(60) K. HINDELL : "Strengthening the ship regulating regime". Maritime Policy Management, 1996, vol. 23, n° 4, 371-380.
(61) T. BUSHA : "The response of the International Maritime Organization to reference in the 1982 Convention to the competent international organization". Workshop of the Law Institute. Jan 1986. Jon Van Dyke, 1987.
(62) "Implications of the United Nations Convention on the Law of the Sea, 1982, for the International Maritime Organisation (IMO). Study by the Secretariat of IMO. LEG/MISC/1, 1987.
(63) V. ANDRIANOV : "The role of the International Maritime Organization in implementing the 1982 UNCLOS". Marine Policy, March 1990, 120-124.

by the Convention, and on the other hand of performing tasks not provided for in the new law of the sea. This attitude reflects the need for an international organisation to accept the obligations placed on it by a treaty, and particularly the decisive role played by its member states (64).

2. Strategy for application of standards

76. - IMO took an extremely important strategic decision in 1981, when it changed its emphasis from the development and adoption of new conventions or technical rules to the implementation of existing standards. This decision, contained in resolution A.500, involved a request to governments to redouble their efforts to ensure that existing measures were applied. It also provided a mandate for the future, affecting every aspect of IMO work.

To begin with, this new line of action resulted in a strengthening of technical cooperation and training (65). The IMO strategy took on a fresh dimension in the early Nineties, with the introduction of provisions to control the implementation of conventions. In this respect, 1993 was a key year, with the creation of the Subcommittee for Flag State Implementation (FSI), and World Maritime Day, devoted to this problem (cf chapter 23).

In the new relationship between IMO and its members, it is careful to avoid a heavy-handed approach, since it cannot dictate to them (66). Like a kind of watchdog (67), it is trying to make states aware of their responsibilities by trying to assess their efforts to comply with their obligations, rather than blaming them for inefficiency or powerlessness.

B - NEW RESOURCES

Does IMO possess resources commensurate with its new ambitions ? Are its structures appropriate to the control functions that states deign to assign it ? The solution depends on the resources made available to achieve these goals.

1. Renewed financial framework

77. - IMO went through an unprecedented financial crisis in the late Eighties, forcing it to make drastic cuts in its working budget (68). In 1989, unpaid membership fees amounted to almost £8m (69), forcing IMO to take a whole series of measures to make up the shortfall. These included staff reductions, a freeze on recruitment, and above all the obligation to cancel half the meetings scheduled that year, thereby seriously affecting its international credibility (70).

A temporary solution was found in 1991, when Resolution A.726 changed the system of funding: the amount of membership dues, 90 per cent of which depended on the size of the registered fleet, was reduced to 87.5 per cent, forcing industrialised countries to increase their contribution to the IMO budget (71). The problem was finally settled in 1992, when the two main contributors, Liberia and Panama, paid their arrears.

The crisis had consequences for the defaulters. In 1991, Liberia failed to win a seat on the Council (72), and in 1993 a group of thirteen countries were banned from voting, by virtue of article 56 of the constituent instrument (73).

(64) T. TREVES : "The role of universal international organizations in implementing the 1982 UN Law of the sea convention". 23rd Annual conference of the Law of the Sea Institute - Hawai, 1989.
(65) IMO : "Strategy for the development and implementation of maritime law". October 1989.
(66) "Patience the virtue of IMO's consensus manager". Lloyd's List, 15 Sept 1992.
(67) "IMO plea for new role as watchdog". Lloyd's List, 27 June 1995.
(68) "IMO cash crisis could halt meeting". Lloyd's List, 6 Dec 1988.
(69) "IMO healthy despite debts". Lloyd's List, 2 August 1989.
(70) "Tide of change leaves IMO floundering". Lloyd's List, 2 July 1989.
(71) "More to solve financial crisis at IMO". Lloyd's List, 31 Oct. 1991.
(72) "Liberia and Chile in IMO elections protest". Lloyd's List, 8 Nov 1991.
(73) "Liberia fails to win IMO Council place". Lloyd's List, 30 Oct 1993.

Any consideration of the long-term future of IMO must take account of this financial dimension: how ready are its members to pay for the services it performs ? The ways and means of its future action depend on the answer to this question.

2. More rational structure

78. - One possible way of reducing IMO costs is to rationalise its structure, to take account of the implementation of the goals to be attained. The question was put on the IMO agenda at the end of 1993, at the first joint session of the MSC and MEPC (74).

In Resolution A.777 of 4 November 1993, the Assembly recalled the terms of Resolution A.500, recommending that "proposals for new conventions or amendments to existing conventions be entertained only on the basis of clear and well-documented compelling need and having regard to the costs to the maritime industry and the burden on the legislative and administrative resources of member States". It also asked the committees to review their work methods and organisation of work, setting priorities for action. This demand for rationalisation was taken into account by joint MSC and MEPC guidelines, to ensure that they would perform their tasks efficiently, given the resources available to IMO (75).

This directive was amended in 1996 (76), to ensure better coordination of the work of subcommittees and greater efficiency in work programmes, with a preliminary assessment of new questions on the agenda, their general acceptance and the establishment of a list of priorities for such questions.

Even though they have been applied only recently, the new directives have already had beneficial effects (77). As certain writers point out (78), the fact remains that the definition of the doctrine of compelling need in the regulatory area is a complex subject, liable to controversy and a source of confusion, for the solutions depend on how one arbitrates among divergent or even contradictory interests.

3. New legal possibilities

79. - Recent new provisions have given IMO a more active role in the effective implementation of international regulations.

For example, the new STCW Convention on the training and qualification of seafarers cuts the Gordian knot of sovereignty, behind which the signatories of a convention traditionally take refuge when they do not want to put a measure into effect (79).

Over and above discussions in progress at IMO on its structures and mode of operation, there is the problem of what position IMO should actually occupy within the international community. As will be seen in chapter 4, many governmental institutions are working to improve safety at sea. Clearly, some rationalisation in this area could make the international standard-setting system more effective.

---

(74) OMI, MSC 63/2/1, 10 Jan. 1994.
(75) Guidelines on the organisation and method of work of the Maritime Safety Committee and the Maritime Environment Protection Committee and their subsidiary bodies. MSC/Circ. 680 et MEPC/Circ. 297, 31 May 1995.
(76) Welcome Speech of the Secretary-General for the 66th session of MSC. MSC 66/24, 18 June 1996, 1-5.
(77) IMO. Application of the Committee's guidelines. Revision of the guidelines on the organisation and method of work of MSC and MEPC and their subsidiary bodies. Note by the MSC and MEPC Chairmen. MSC 67/18, 4 Oct. 1996.
(78) Aline de BIEVRE : "Defining doctrine of compelling need". Lloyd's List, 11 Nov. 1996.
(79) "STCW amendments have added teeth ". Lloyd's List, 2 Nov 1995.

CHAPTER 4

Intergovernmental organisations

80. - At the present time, intergovernmental organisations, within which only States hold the power of decision, are particularly concerned with the regulation of maritime transport. Even as regards safety at sea, IMO does not have a monopoly. Many other organisations are involved in adopting standards, collecting data or taking actions in order to prevent accidents and protect the marine environment. Their involvement in the development of international cooperation is tending to produce an institutional system with complex ramifications (1). This structural environment may be clarified by making a distinction between worldwide institutions (cf I below) and those with a more regional role (II).

I - WORLDWIDE ORGANISATIONS

Organisations working on a worldwide basis are normally classified under two headings: those attached directly to the United Nations system, and those set up by special convention, and known as "specialised agencies". Four of these are engaged in furthering safety at sea. They are IMO, examined in the previous chapter, the International Labour Organisation (ILO), the International Telecommunications Union (ITU) and the World Meteorological Organisation (WMO).

Two other bodies are the International Maritime Satellite Organisation (INMARSAT) and the International Hydrographic Organisation (IHO).

A - INTERNATIONAL LABOUR ORGANISATION (ILO)

81. - Set up just after the First World War, the International Labour Organisation now has more than 170 member States. It plays a leading part in regulating the working conditions of seafarers, and improving their living conditions.

1. ILO responsibilities in the maritime sector

The ILO possesses extremely wide-ranging powers in the maritime sector. They cover such areas as minimum age, medical examinations, medical care, conditions of employment, hours of work, wages, articles of agreement, repatriation, social security benefits, competency certificates for officers and ships' cooks, vocational training, shipboard and shoreside welfare facilities, prevention of occupational accidents, freedom of association, the right to collective bargaining and other subjects (2).

---

(1) Jan LOPUSKI : "La coopération internationale dans les affaires maritimes : la formation d'un système institutionnel". DMF 1979, 457.
(2) "ILO activities concerning the human element" in IMO. MSC 66/13/9, 29 March 1996.

In adopting international standards on maritime labour, the ILO has always exerted a major influence on safety at sea. Its efforts aim to prevent the individual risks to which seafarers are exposed, while its instruments have a direct or indirect effect on the factors that enable seafarers to carry out their activities with appropriate competency, fitness and motivation

2. Internal structure

82. - The ILO comprises three main internal bodies : the General Conference, the Governing Board, and the International Labour Office. This is the only UN agency to have a tripartite organisation, bringing together representatives of governments, employers and workers.

The General Conference generally meets once a year, to draw up conventions and recommendations.

The Governing Body, which meets three times a year, oversees the work of the Office and draws up the budget.

The International Labour Office constitutes the permanent secretariat, based in Geneva. It is headed by a Director-General, and is staffed by a workforce of about one and a half thousand. Its role is to prepare the work of the Conference and the Governing Body, and collect and publish information (3).

Maritime Conferences are held about once every ten years, the most recent taking place in Geneva in October 1996 (4). Between these Conferences, meetings are held of the Joint Maritime Commission (JMC). This body presents two originalities. First, it is a consultative body accountable to the Office, which prepares the standard-setting work of the ILO. Second, the commission is a bipartite body, comprising twenty members plus four deputies representing shipowners, and the same number to represent seafarers, as well as the President and a representative of the employers' and workers' groups of the Governing Body, one appointed by employers, and the other by seafarers. The shipowners' group is administered by the International Shipping Federation (ISF) and the seafarers' group by the International Transport Workers Federation (ITF).

3. ILO activities

a) International Seafarer's Code

83. - Most of the ILO's activities are to do with setting standards. The Maritime Conference, held ten times since 1920, has adopted thirty-six conventions on seafarers. All its conventions and the twenty-seven accompanying recommendations form the "International Seafarers' Code" (5).

Three aspects of safety at sea have been covered by ILO instruments: conditions of access to the seafaring profession, crew numbers, and minimum standards on board ships (6).

---

(3) B. FARTHING : "International Shipping". Lloyd's of London Press, 3rd Edition, London 1997, 80-81.
(4) The International Shipping Federation. The ISF Year 96/97. London, 1997.
(5) F. WOLF : "L'Organisation Internationale du Travail et la Convention des Nations-Unies sur le Droit du Travail". Rosenne Collection, Nijhoff, 1989.
(6) H. STORHAUG : "International maritime labour standards". Report of the ILO Regional Seminar, Maputo, Report of the ILO Regional Seminar, Maputo, Dec. 1993. ILO, Geneva, 1995, 41-45.

b) Cooperation and technical assistance

Apart from its standard-setting activities, the ILO collaborates actively with other international institutions on all issues of concern to seafarers. It participates with IMO on the Joint IMO/ILO Committee on the health of seafarers. It has also set up several cooperative structures with IMO: a joint group of experts on fatigue, a joint committee on training, and a special joint working group to investigate human factors involved in accidents at sea.

As part of its programme of technical assistance to developing countries, the ILO organises regular regional and national seminars on maritime labour standards. These concern training of ship inspectors, to check whether they comply with the relevant standards of the Organisation, particularly Convention 147 on minimum standards (7).

4. Original means of action

84. - In the regulatory field, the ILO is concerned with promoting improvement and harmonisation of working conditions in various States. This implies the adoption of comprehensive, precise and uniform international regulations, by means of conventions and recommendations. Unlike IMO, the ILO possesses certain powers of compulsion regarding enforcement of its conventions by States.

There are two main differences between ILO and IMO conventions.

- International labour conventions are implemented quickly and on a compulsory basis: article 19 par. 6 of the ILO constitution requires governments to submit both conventions and recommendations within twelve or in exceptional cases eighteen months, "to the authority or authorities within whose competence the latter lies, for the enactment of legislation or other action". The ILO has means of overseeing compliance with this obligation. Every member of the Organisation must report back to the Director-General of the ILO on the measures it has taken to implement provisions. In order to facilitate transmission of such information, the Governing Body sends each State a memorandum containing numerous questions on the translation of provisions adopted internationally into national legislation (8).
- Each State can adapt its implementation of conventions, but the process is supervised. Article 19.5d requires every State to take appropriate measures to enforce the provisions of conventions which have been ratified. The extensive powers of the Organisation mean that careful supervision of implementation of international law then begins, based on three procedures: submission and examination of annual reports from member States ; a claims procedure open to worker and employer trade associations (cf articles 24 and 25) and a complaints procedure, restricted to States that have ratified the convention (cf articles 26 to 34) (9).

Enforcement of conventions displays remarkable adaptability : ILO technical standards can be implemented in countries with very different economic, social and cultural systems, thanks to the flexible legislative techniques, which make allowance for unequal levels of development of States (10).

(7) D. APPAVE : "The ILO and its maritime activities". Ibid, 9-15.
(8) H. STORHAUG : "The ratification, implementation and supervision of international labour standards". Ibid, 16-21.
(9) ILO : "Maritime labour Conventions and Recommandations". Geneva, 1994, Introduction 3.
(10) M. VALTICOS et F. WOLF : "L'OIT et les pays en voie de développement : techniques d'élaboration et mise en oeuvre de normes universelles". Colloque SFDI. Aix en Provence, Pedone, 1974, 131-141.

B - INTERNATIONAL TELECOMMUNICATIONS UNION (ITU)

85. - Communications play a very special role in relation to safety at sea. In a critical situation, such as an accident or a ship going down, they become a decisive factor in saving human life. The International Telecommunications Union is an intergovernmental organisation which has introduced cooperation among national administrations and private companies that instal and operate telecommunications services throughout the world.

1. Aims

The ITU is a worldwide organisation within which the public and private sectors coordinate the development of telecommunications and the harmonisation of national telecommunications policies. The ITU adopts international regulations and treaties governing all terrestrial and space uses of the frequency spectrum as well as use of the geostationary satellite orbit, within which countries adopt their national legislation. It develops standards to promote the interconnection of telecommunication systems on a worldwide scale, regardless of the type of technology used. It also fosters the development of telecommunications in developing countries. Since the Atlantic City Conference in 1947, it has been the UN specialised telecommunications agency.

The ITU is first and foremost concerned with technical issues. It is the only international organisation with general knowledge of telecommunications questions, not only because its members represent government departments responsible for telecommunications, but also because the main global providers of telecommunications goods and services play a very active part in its work.

The ITU makes a fundamental contribution to radiocommunications, by ensuring the rational, effective and economical allotment of radio frequencies for all radiocommunication services, including those that use the geostationary satellite orbit. It also engages in research into radiocommunications, and coordinates efforts to remove harmful interference among radiocommunication stations in different countries.

The ITU also remains the reference body for formulating telecommunications standards throughout the world. Its recommendations concern technical problems of operation and charging rates. In the maritime sector, it shares responsibility with INMARSAT, which handles the worldwide mobile satellite communications service.

2. Structure

86. - The ITU functions with the following structure :
- Plenipotentiary Conference, which is the supreme authority of the Union, and which meets every four years.
- Council, which acts on behalf of the Plenipotentiary Conference, and which meets annually.
- World Conferences on international telecommunications.
- General Secretariat.
- Three Sectors : Radiocommunication, Telecommunication Standardisation, Telecommunication Development., each of which operates through a Bureau located at ITU headquarters, in addition to the General Secretariat (11).

---

(11) "The International Telecommunication Union". ITU, Geneva, July 1994.

C - INTERNATIONAL MARITIME SATELLITE TELECOMMUNICATIONS ORGANISATION (INMARSAT)

87. - The International Maritime Satellite Telecommunications Organisation, set up by IMO in 1976, is the intergovernmental organisation responsible for managing the world satellite communication network.

1. Background

There were two purposes behind the creation of INMARSAT. First of all, it was felt important to lay the foundations for inter-State cooperation on maritime space communications, based on non-discriminatory principles. It was also necessary to find a remedy for the increasing congestion of medium and high frequencies at sea. Only the use of satellites could improve the system of communication between ship and onshore stations providing radio cover.

The convention setting up INMARSAT and an Operating Agreement were adopted on 3 September 1976, and came into effect on 16 July 1979. The Organisation began operating in 1981 from its headquarters in London (13).

2. Aims and role of INMARSAT

88. - Under the terms of article 3 of the convention, the purpose of INMARSAT is "to establish the space facilities needed to improve maritime communications, thereby assisting in improving distress and safety of life at sea communications, the efficiency and management of ships, maritime public correspondence services, and radiodetermination capabilities" (14).

INMARSAT, as an intergovernmental organisation, had eighty-one member States in 1996 (15). Each State designates a national organisation, public or private, which signs the Operating Agreement. It must ensure that this organisation meets its responsibilities (cf article 4). Governments also contribute to funds, on the basis of a financial interest proportional to their respective stake in the Organisation (cf article 5) (16). The system has been devised to ensure that the most important users are the largest shareholders. In 1996, the United States held 23 per cent, United Kingdom 9.3 per cent, Japan 8 per cent, Norway 6.8 per cent, and Greece 5.4 per cent (17).

The Organisation consists of an Assembly, Council and Directorate, headed by a Director-General.

3. Activities

89. - The creation of INMARSAT as an independent organisation was a major step forward for maritime radiocommunications. For the first time, the maritime world was provided with a communication system exclusively reserved for it and designed to meet its specific needs. The INMARSAT system had advantages which terrestrial radiocommunications could not offer (18).

(12) ITU : "Strategic Plan 1995-1996. Geneva, 30 Nov. 1994.
(13) "How INMARSAT came into existence". Lloyd's List, 5 July 1989.
(14) A summary of IMO Conventions, in Focus on IMO, Han. 1997, 18.
(15) IMO Conventions, Status at 1st January 1998, in Focus on IMO.
(16) "INMARSAT is owned and funded by shareholding member states". Lloyd's List, 5 July 1989.
(17) "INMARSAT on a voyage into uncharted waters". Lloyd's List, 7 May, 1996.
(18) O. LUNDBERG : "Organizations. INMARSAT : improving maritime communications". Marine Policy, October 1984, 337-345.

Its usefulness remains undiminished. Commercially, it makes a considerable improvement in the quality of ship-to-shore communications, regardless of the mode used (radiotelephony, telex, fax, high-speed data transmission). It also guarantees confidentiality, something that is impossible with radioelectric messages. Finally, it is very simple to use. Its primary purpose, however, remains safety at sea. A ship can use the INMARSAT system to send a distress message with the certainty that it will be received. It can also receive help and medical advice, weather forecasts, navigational findings and warnings, as well as position reports (19).

4. Future development of INMARSAT

90. - The INMARSAT Convention has been amended three times. In 1985, INMARSAT was empowered to provide services to aircraft as well as ships. In 1989, a further extension to provide services to land-based vehicles was introduced. In 1994, several amendments altered the functions and structure of the organisation. One of these provided for a change of name, to the "International Mobile Satellite Organisation", the abbreviation remaining INMARSAT.

These changes reflect developments that have been in progress over the last decade, particularly the extension of its services to other modes of transport. Another reason is the need to adopt a more solid administrative structure, to ensure that the organisation will remain commercially viable in the longer term.

In May 1995, disturbed at these developments, IMO recalled the "obligation for INMARSAT to continue to provide maritime distress, safety and general communications services". In February 1996, the INMARSAT Assembly decided in any case that the future structure of the organisation should preserve its intergovernmental character, and that its Assembly should continue to be subject to inter-State regulatory oversight of certain basic principles and public service obligations applying to maritime communications (20).

In March 1996, the INMARSAT Council recommended the formation of two separate legal entities: a limited liability company registered under national law, and the intergovernmental organisation (21).

In April 1998, the INMARSAT Assembly approved amendments to the INMARSAT Convention and Operating Agreement, which took account of IMO's comments on the restructuring (22). Under the new structure, all INMARSAT business will be carried on by a national company subject to ongoing regulatory oversight by the IGO of the performance of certain public service obligations under a Public Services Agreement (23).

(19) L. BRÖDJE : "Satellite communications". Presentation for Seatrade Tanker Industry Convention, London, Feb. 1995.
(20) Outcome of the 11th session of the INMARSAT Assembly in IMO. MSC 66/10/2, 21 March 1996. Note by the International Mobile Satellite Organisation.
(21) IMO. MSC 67/21/1, 4 Oct. 1996.
(22) "IMO is set to back revamp of INMARSAT". Lloyd's List, 9 March 1998.
(23) IMO. Report of the MSC on the 69th session. MSC 69/22, 29 May 1998, 10.14 - 10.17.

D - WORLD METEOROLOGICAL ORGANISATION (WMO)

91. - The first international meteorological network was established in 1654 by Ferdinand II of Tuscany. In 1853, the first International Meteorological Conference held in Brussels adopted a set of standard instructions for meteorological observations at sea. In Vienna in 1873, the First International Meteorological Congress created the non-governmental International Meteorological Organisation, which in 1947 became the new intergovernmental World Meteorological Organisation (24).

1. Aims

92. - The WMO, of which 181 states and territories are members, is a specialised agency of the United Nations. Article 2 of the WMO Convention defines the purposes of the Organisation, which are "to facilitate worldwide cooperation in the establishment of networks of stations for the making of meteorological observations, (...) ; to promote the establishment and maintenance of systems for the rapid exchange of meteorological (...) information ; to promote standardisation of meteorological and related observations and to ensure the uniform publication of observations and statistics; to further the application of meteorology to aviation, shipping, water problems, agriculture and other human activities; to promote activities in operational hydrology (...) ; to encourage research and training in meteorology (...)" (25).

2. Internal structure

93. - The WMO consists of central and regional decision-making bodies, administrative and technical entities (26). Decision-making bodies are the World Meteorological Congress, which meets every four years, to define general policy, adopt the budget and the technical rules governing international meteorological practice.

The Executive Council meets annually to review WMO activities and implement programmes approved by the Congress.

Six regional associations (Africa, Asia, South America, North and Central America, South-West Pacific and Europe), comprising of WMO members, coordinate meteorological activities within their respective regions.

The only administrative body is the General Secretariat, based in Geneva. It acts as administrative, documentation and information centre for the WMO.

Finally, there are eight technical commissions, comprising experts designated by members, to study any matters coming within their areas of competence.

3. WMO activities

94. - The WMO is engaged in seven major scientific and technical programmes, three of which have an impact on safety at sea.

---

(24) World Meteorological Organization : "The WMO Achievement. 40 years in the service of international meteorology and hydrology". WMO, n° 729. Genève 1990, 5-10.
(25) World Meteorological Organisation Publication. Basic Document n° 15, Geneva, 1995.
(26) World Meteorological Organisation. Annual Report 1995. WMO n° 836, Geneva, 1996.

• **World Weather Watch Programme**

This cooperation system, set up in 1964, is intended to supply the meteorological and related geophysical information needed to provide effective assistance in each member country. It also comprises a tropical cyclone programme.

• **World Climate Programme**

This programme is intended to improve the understanding of climatic processes, through internationally coordinated research, and the monitoring of climatic variations or changes.

• **Atmospheric Research and Environmental Programme**

This programme is designed to stimulate research into changes in the composition of the atmosphere. It also comprises weather forecasting and tropical meteorology research.

In collaboration with the Intergovernmental Oceanographic Commission (IOC), the WMO has implemented an Integrated Global Ocean Stations System (IGOSS), with the aim of improving knowledge of interactions between ocean and atmosphere, in order to increase the safety of maritime activities (27).

E - INTERNATIONAL HYDROGRAPHIC ORGANISATION (IHO)

95. - International cooperation in the field of hydrography began with a conference held in Washington in 1899, and two others in St Petersburg in 1908 and 1912. In 1919, a Hydrographic Conference in London decided to create a permanent body, the International Hydrographic Bureau (IHB), which began its activities in 1921. Monaco provided premises for the headquarters. In 1970, an intergovernmental convention came into force, which changed the organisation's name and legal status, creating the International Hydrographic Organisation (IHO), while retaining the initials IHB to designate the Monegasque secretariat (28).

1. Structures

96. - The IHO is an intergovernmental organisation of a consultative and purely technical nature. It is not a UN agency, but works closely with several UN bodies, notably IMO and the Intergovernmental Oceanographic Commission of UNESCO (29).

At present, there are sixty member states , with ten more pending (30). Member states are normally represented by their national hydrographer. The secretariat (IHB) currently employs twenty-one professional and administrative staff. These include a Directing Committee consisting of a President and two other Directors, who are elected at the five-yearly International Hydrographic Conference. All members have an equal voice in making technical decisions, both at the Conference and by correspondence between conferences (31).

(27) G. KULLENBERG, N. PHILIPPON-TULLOCH, A. TOLKATCHEV, A. ALEXIOU, Y. TREGLOS : "Cooperation between ILO and WMO". WMO Bulletin, vol. 44, n° 3, July 1995.
(28) A.J. KERR : "The IHO and its objectives". Paper used for the Maputo Conference, April 1995. IHO, Monaco, 1995.
(29) A.J. KERR : "The present day work of the International Hydrographic Organisation (IHO)". Sept. 1989, 5-7.
(30) IHO. Annual Report 1994. Part I General. 175-IV-1995, Monaco.
(31) IHO. Information paper n° 1. The International Hydrographic Organisation. S1/1902. Sept. 1992.

2. Aims and activities

97. - Under article 2 of the 1967 Convention, the IHO has four goals: coordination of the activities of national hydrogaphic offices ; the greatest possible uniformity in nautical charts and publications ; adoption of reliable and efficient methods of carrying out and exploiting hydrographic surveys ; and development of hydrographic sciences and techniques used in descriptive oceanography (32).

IHO Conferences have a multiple function. Most of them contribute to greater safety in maritime navigation (33). There have been several achievements, including progressive standardisation of marine charts (specifications, conventional symbols, characters and presentation) ; adoption of uniform standards for electronic charts ; training and technical assistance for hydrographic surveys ; compilation of nautical instructions, reproduction and printing equipment and processes, cartography and descriptive oceanography ; finally, issue of numerous publications, including the monthly *International Hydrographic Bulletin* in three languages, the *International Hydrographic Review*, the IHO annual directory, specifications for IHO maps and specialised technical documents (34).

F - OTHER INTERGOVERNMENTAL ORGANISATIONS

1. Specialised institutions

98. - Many intergovernmental organisations are involved in promoting greater safety at sea, including, in addition to those described above, the International Atomic Energy Agency (IAEA) and the IOC.

According to article 2 of its statutes (35), the aim of the IAEA is "to accelerate and enlarge the contribution of atomic energy to peace, health and prosperity throughout the world". The Agency has 122 member States, and wields considerable regulatory powers (36). It has issued safety standards on the transportation of fissile and radioactive materials (37). It has also helped IMO draw up technical requirements for the construction and equipment of nuclear-powered vessels (38).

The Intergovernmental Oceanographic Commission was set up by UNESCO to further international cooperation on scientific research into the oceans (39). The IOC has worked in close collaboration with IMO to establish the status and safety standards of ocean data acquisition systems and other devices used at sea to collect, store or transmit information on the marine environment (40).

(32) IHO : Basic Documents of the International Hydrographic Organisation. Convention on the IHO, Monaco, November 1992.
(33) A. KERR : "The International Hydrographic Organisation. New trends to its programmes". Dutch Cartography Journal 1994/1995.
(34) "The International Hydrographic Organisation in 1995". IAEA Bulletin 1996/2, 20-25.
(35) International Atomic Energy Agency : Statute amended up to 28 December 1989, Vienna, June 1990, n° 89-05761.
(36) IAEA : "Highlights of activities 95". Vienna, 1995.
(37) IAEA : "Transport of radioactive material". Vienna 1992 - IAEA/PI/A.2E 92 04 899.
(38) R. PEDROZO : "Transport of nuclear cargoes by sea". Journal of Maritime Law and Commerce, Vol. 28, n° 2, April 1997, 207-236.
(39) UNESCO : Manuel de la Commission Océanographique Intergouvernementale. Partie I. Statut et autres textes officiels, Paris, Edition révisée 1989, IOC/INF-785.
(40) IMO. Approval of the recommendations of the MSC on marking of oceanographic stations. Res. A.50(III), 18 Oct. 1963.

2. Research bodies

99. - In addition to the standard-setting activities of international institutions, work is also done by research bodies with a special status. An example is the Joint Group of Experts on the Scientific Aspects of Marine Pollution (GESAMP). This consultative body, which brings together technical experts from seven intergovernmental organisations (WMO, FAO, UNESCO, IAEA, WHO, UNEP and IMO), undertakes numerous investigations of marine pollutants, recommends solutions for their control, and publishes regular reports on the state of pollution of the marine environment (41).

3. Economic organisations

Certain organisations have filled the gap left by IMO in the economic sector, particularly UNCTAD and, on a more regional level, OECD.

• United Nations Conference on Trade and Development (UNCTAD)

100. - UNCTAD is a permanent body of the General Assembly of the United Nations, with 171 member States. It is concerned with all aspects of trade and development. Very close to Third World concerns, this organisation was the scene of sharp North-South confrontation and standoff during the Seventies. In particular, it has tried to define international relations in a way more favourable to developing countries which work together within the Group of 77 (a misnomer for over 130 such countries) An informal agreement reached with IMO in 1965 divided areas of competence between the two organisations, helping reduce sources of conflict and duplication of efforts.

As part of its concern with shipping, UNCTAD has tried to deal with flags of convenience, by adopting its 1986 Convention on conditions for the registration of ships (cf chapter 21 below) (42).

Today, UNCTAD has given up its insistence on controversial issues, and has embraced the dominant free market economic order. This is reflected in a considerable reorganisation of internal structures, with the setting-up of four new standing committees and five *ad hoc* working groups. One of these, the Committee on Developing Services Sectors, combines shipping and insurance matters (43).

• Organisation for Economic Cooperation and Development (OECD)

101. - Another intergovernmental economic organisation plays an important part within a more restricted geographical framework. With twenty-three members, consisting of nineteen European states plus Canada, the United States, Japan, Australia, New Zealand and Mexico, OECD policies are intended, among other aims, "to contribute to the expansion of world trade on a multilateral, non-discriminatory basis in accordance with international obligations" (cf article 1of the Convention of 14 December 1960).

---

(41) GESAMP : "Impact of oil and related chemicals and wastes on the marine environment". Reports and Studies n°50 London, 1993.
(42) E. GOLD : "International maritime law in transition. New challenges for education and training". Marine Policy, July 1989, 187-189.
(43) "UNCTAD broadens its maritime horizons". Lloyd's List, 21 April 1992.

The OECD has a Maritime Transport Committee, whilst at an earlier period it took vigorous action against flags of convenience. It has since 1992 focussed on substandard ships (44), with investigation of the competitive advantages derived by certain shipowners from their failure to observe current regulations and international standards (45), and possible actions to combat substandard shipping by involving players other than owners (46).

II - REGIONAL ORGANISATIONS

102. - The increasing importance of regional organisations in the promotion of safety at sea is undoubtedly one of the major new trends of the late 20th century. Technical maritime regulations were long the prerogative of a few intergovernmental organisations, perfectly integrated in the UN system, and benefitting from the enlightened counsel of many non-governmental organisations. This traditional way of setting standards now tends to be replaced by other mechanisms, operating within a more restricted geographical framework. The emergence of the European Union on the international maritime scene is a good illustration of this recent trend.

Europe clearly has an inbuilt concern for the safety of seaborne transport. Surrounded by thirteen different seas, it is naturally concerned with protecting its fifteen thousand kilometres of coastline. It is also one of the world's leading trading areas, and most of this trade is carried by sea : the figure reaches about 90 per cent for trade with third countries, and 35 per cent for intra-EU traffic (47).

The repeated occurrence of major disasters at sea in European waters in the early Nineties generated a political determination to strengthen regional maritime safety. The *Scandinavian Star*, the *Braer*, the *Estonia* and more recently the *Sea Empress* aroused strong reaction in the public and among politicians in the various States of the Union.

Both EU institutions and other European bodies (48) are currently engaged in a variety of actions, integrated into a common policy on safe seas which, to be fully comprehensible, needs to be set against its historical background.

A - CONSTRUCTION OF EU STRATEGY

103. - For many year the European Community took little, if any, action regarding the prevention of accidents at sea. The adoption of a common policy has changed this. Brussels has moved from an application strategy to a strategy of regulatory initiatives, and finally to an emphasis on the economic aspects of safety.

---

(44) OECD urges crackdown on substandard vessels". Lloyd's List, 30 May 1994.
(45) "Competitive advantages obtained by some shipowners as a result of non-observance of applicable international rules and standards". OECD/GD (96) 4, Paris, 1996.
(46) Revised paper on possible actions to combat substandard shipping by involving players other than the shipowner in the shipping market". OECD General Working Party of the Maritime Transport Committee, March 1998.
(47) European Communities. Economic and Social Committee. "Opinion on the Communication from the Commission on a common policy on safe seas". TRA/225. Brussels, 24 Nov. 1993.
(48) V. POWER : "EC Shipping Law". Lloyd's of London Press Ltd 1992, Chp. 20. The EC and Safety at Sea, 489-499.

1. Application strategy

104. - It was in the aftermath of the *Amoco Cadiz* disaster that Europe for the first time displayed concern for the safety issue. The EEC took action in two areas, by advising member states to ratify relevant international conventions (cf chapter 24), and encouraging early implementation of certain preventive measures. On 21 December 1978, two Directives were adopted : 79/115 concerning piloting of vessels by deep-sea pilots in the North Sea and English Channel (49) and 79/116 concerning minimum requirements for certain tankers entering or leaving Community ports (50).

The loss of the *Tanio* in 1980 led France to convene a regional conference on the safety of seaborne transport, with the aim of making new equipment compulsory on board ships, and in particular ensuring that port states enforced standards. This initiative led to the Paris Memorandum, signed by the maritime authorities of fourteen European countries on 26 January 1982 (cf chapter 25).

Two major passenger ferry disasters that occurred in Europe, the *Herald of Free Enterprise* in 1987 and the *Scandinavian Star* in 1990, led the Council of Ministers to adopt a Resolution on passenger ferry safety on 19 June 1990 (51).

2. Regulatory strategy

105. - The signing of the Maastricht Treaty in 1991 offered the European Union, as the Community now became, a legal opportunity to change its strategy and take initiatives to prevent accidents. The Treaty gave the Council for the first time the right to introduce "measures to improve transport safety" (cf article 75c as amended). Safety requirements theoretically were the concern of the Union exclusively to the extent that they affected, for example, the free circulation of vehicles or transport services. But it could also be concluded that, under the principle of subsidiarity, certain measures could be taken at another level. Amendment of article 75 confirmed that, even in the absence of exclusive competence, the safety of transport should be covered by the EU wherever it could take effective action.

These legal grounds enabled the Commission to draft two fundamental documents, which constitute current EU policy on the issue. These were the White Paper of 2 December 1992 on future development of a common transport policy, and the Communication of 24 February 1993 on a common policy on safe seas. Furtherance of this policy gathered pace following a series of accidents in 1993 and 1994.

a) Consequences of the Braer disaster

The oil pollution caused by the *Aegean Sea*, and initially even more seriously by the *Braer*, led to the publication in February 1993 of the important Commission Communication, "A common policy on safe seas" (52).

(49) OJ L33 of 8 Feb. 1979, 32.
(50) OJ L33 of 8 Feb. 1979, 33. See also Amendment published in OJ L315, 11 Dec. 1979, 16.
(51) OJ C206, 18 August, 3.
(52) Commission of European Communities. COM (93) 66. Brussels, 24 February 1993.

Acting under the pressure of public opinion, the Council of Ministers adopted the first measures during the second half of 1993 (53) including Directive 93/75 of 13 September that year concerning minimum requirements for vessels bound for or leaving Community ports and carrying dangerous or polluting goods (54).

b) *Consequences of the* Sherbro *accident*

Following several accidents during the Winter of 1993-94, including the loss of containers loaded with pesticides from the *Sherbro* in the Gulf of Gascony, the European Parliament passed three resolutions (55), concerning maritime safety on 20 January 1994, disasters in the North Sea on 10 February, and a common maritime policy on 11 February.

On 24 January 1994, Transport and Environment Ministers reached agreement on fresh action to reinforce safety at sea and prevent pollution. The main measures involved the passage of ships carrying dangerous products in EU waters that were ecologically sensitive or carried dense traffic (56).

In July 1994, new European Council initiatives (57) resulted in the adoption of three texts (58). These were Regulation no. 2978/94 of 27 November 1994, on the implementation of IMO Resolution A.747 on application of tonnage measurements of ballast spaces in segregated ballast oil tankers ; Council Directive 94/54/CE of 22 November 1994, on common rules and standards for ship inspection and survey organisations authorised to carry out inspection and survey of ships and relevant activities of maritime administrations ; Council Directive 94/58/CE of the same date on the minimum level of training of seafarers.

c) *Consequences of the* Estonia *disaster*

The loss of the *Estonia*, which caused 850 deaths in the Baltic at the end of September 1994, led the European Union further to strengthen measures related to safety at sea.

On 19 June 1995, the Council adopted Directive 95/21CE concerning the enforcement, in respect of shipping using Community ports and sailing in the waters under the jurisdiction of the member states, of international standards for ship safety, pollution prevention and shipboard living and working conditions. This was the Port State Control Directive, which came into effect on 1st July 1996 (60).

(53) "EC moves on sea safety". Lloyd's List, 10 June 1993.
(54) OJ L247, 5 Oct. 1993, 19-27.
(55) European Parliament Resolution on Maritime Safety. Extract of the meeting of January 20, 1994, in IMO Doc MSC 63/19/1 and MSC 63/19/1 Add. 1.
(56) Proposal for a Council Directive concerning the setting-up of a European vessel reporting system in the maritime zones of Community Member States, 17 December 1993. COM (93) 647 Final. OJ C22 of 26 Jan. 1994.
- European Parliament Opinion. OJ C128, 9 May 1994.
- Amended proposal COM (94) 220 Final. OJ C193, 16 July 1994.
- ESC Opinion. OJ C295, 22 Oct. 1994.
Cf also : "Safety warning for Europe". Lloyd's List, 24 March 1994.
(57) "EU agrees rebate plan". Lloyd's List, 14 June 1994.
(58) OJ, M319 of 12 December 1994, 1-20-28.
(59) "EU to intensify pressure on IMO over ro-ro safety". Lloyd's List, 22 Novembre 1994.
JMM, 25 novembre 1994, 3057 et 2 décembre 1994, 3131
(60) OJ, L157, 7 July 1995, 1-19.

Meeting after the SOLAS conference on the safety of car ferries, the Council stated its satisfaction with the results achieved by IMO in relation to damage stability standards. It reiterated its determination to keep the number of bilateral agreements on more stringent standards to a minimum, the ideal being to achieve a single regional multilateral agreement (61). The EU also adopted Regulation 3051/95 of 8 December 1995, which brought forward to 1st July 1996 the date of application of the ISM Code to ro-ro ferries (62).

In April 1996, under pressure from France, the European Commission began to examine navigation conditions in the Mediterranean, in order to enforce the same safety standards for ro-ro passenger ferries throughout Europe (63).

On 17 June 1996, in the teeth of strong resistance from Greece, the Council decided, subject to approval by the Parliament, that safety standards for international voyages should also apply to vessels of equal size engaged in national coastal transport (64).

3. An economic approach to safety

106. - In July 1995, the Commission of the European Communities updated its action programme on the common transport policy for the period 1995-2000 (65). On 13 March 1996, it made its intentions clear by approving two Communications with implications for safety at sea. One, drawn up by the Directorate General for Industry, is entitled "Shaping of Europe's maritime future". The other, entitled "A new approach to maritime strategy", and commonly referred to as the Kinnock Report (66). came from the Directorate General for Transport (67). This new approach is economic, with safety seen, not as the end in itself of a European policy, but as an aspect of a legal and financial framework that will avoid unfair competition for Community shipping (68).

This strategy integrates safety policies and regulations into the quest for greater competitiveness for the maritime industry (69). Brussels considers that problems arise less fom a lack of regulation than from shortcomings in the enforcement of standards and penalties for infringing them. What is needed is to remove any financial benefits arising from failure to observe regulations, by combining flag state and port state controls to the greatest effect (70).

These objectives were solemnly reaffirmed during the "Quality shipping" campaign, inaugurated by Neil Kinnock (71) and at the Lisbon Conference on 4 June 1998 (72) and the joint EC/UK Seminar in London on 14 December 1998 (cf Chapter 24 below).

(61) JMM, 15 Dec. 1995, 3159 et Europc transport, décembre 1995, II, 13-14.
(62) OJ, L320, 30 Dec. 1995, 14.
(63) "EU probes ferry stability in Med". Lloyd's List, 3 April 1996.
(64) OJ, Vol. 40/C 293, 26 Sept. 1997.
(65) European Communities. COM (95) 302 Final. Brussels, 12 July 1995.
(66) COM (96) 81, Final, 13 March 1996.
(67) COM (96) 84, 13 March 1996.
(68) "Europe plots shipping strategy based on quality and cooperation". Lloyd's List, 14 March 1996.
(69) A. DE BIEVRE : "Safe shipping in Europe and the mariners ". Seaways", Sept. 1996, 23-25.
(70) R. MURRAY : "Chance to grasp lifeline for European shipping". Lloyd's List, 19 June 1996.
(71) "Too many put profit abore safety". Lloyd's List, 17 Nov. 1997.
(72) "Kinnock in call to enforce safety rules". Lloyd's List, 5 June 1998.

B - EU MARITIME SAFETY PROMOTION BODIES

1. EU institutions

The European Union comprises the Commission, the Council of Ministers, the European Parliament and the Economic and Social Committee (ECOSOC) and the European Court of Justice (73).

• European Commission
107. - The Commission, which sits in Brussels, is headed by a President and nineteen Commissioners from member States, appointed since 1995 for a period of five years. It has a threefold function: to draft regulations, implement the treaties that govern the Union, ensure that institutional decisions are carried out, and manage the budget and all EU funds. The Commission is divided into twenty Directorates. The Transport Directorate (DG VII) is currently headed by Neil Kinnock, of the United Kingdom. It comprises a unit dedicated to maritime safety issues (74).

• Council of Ministers
108.- This is the only EU institution to represent member States directly. In fact, it is not a single body, but a number of councils consisting of leading national government representatives, usually the appropriate ministers from each member state.

The Council presidency is a revolving function, assumed by each of the fifteen member States for six months in succession. The Council is assisted by working groups, which carry out preliminary discussions of Commission proposals before the Council takes a decision. The most important of these groups is the Committee of Permanent Representatives (COREPER), comprising member States' permanent representatives in Brussels. The Council has no power to initiate projects. Its role is to consider proposals submitted by the Commission, after prior consultation of the European Parliament and the Economic & Social Committee.

Under the Rome Treaty, only the Council and the Commission are authorised to issue legal instruments, which belong to one of four categories :
- Regulations are general in application, and are binding in their entirety and directly applicable in all member states ;
- Directives are also binding, but the form and method are left to each member state ;
- Decisions are binding only on the State or person to whom it is addressed ;
- Recommendations and opinions are not legally binding on member States.

• European Parliament
109. - The European Parliament, which sits in Strasbourg, consists of 636 individual members (MEPs), elected directly in their countries by universal suffrage for a period of five years.

The Parliament's role is mainly advisory and supervisory. It does not have any actual legislative functions, but has to be consulted on the most important proposals of the Commission before they are adopted by the Council. It also has a certain oversight of the Commission and Council, which must reply to questions from members of Parliament.

The Parliament votes resolutions on subjects it regards as important. A very large number of resolutions concern safety at sea, most of them arising from maritime disasters.

(73) V. POWER : "EC shipping law". Lloyd's of London Press 1992, London, 65-82.
(74) "EC's man with a mission for safer seas". Lloyd's List, 27 February 1993.

• **Economic and Social Committee (ECOSOC)**

110. - ECOSOC differs from other EU institutions in that it has no power to take decisions binding on member States. Its role is purely consultative. Consisting of professionals and representatives of the business world, ECOSOC issues non-political judgements and expert opinions on topics under discussion. It must be consulted before any decision is taken on a wide range of questions. It may also take the initiative in submitting proposals.

2. Other EU initiatives

Three other initiatives taken within the European Union framework are worth mentioning.

• **Maritime Industries Forum (MIF)**

111. - Launched in 1991 by European Commissioners M. Bangemann and K. van Miert, the Maritime Industries Forum represents the first serious attempt to implement a consistent maritime policy within the European Union (75).

The MIF comprises representatives of all the maritime industries (transport, shipbuilding, equipment, ports, fisheries and related industries and services), trade unions, research institutes, MEPs, ECOSOC, EU member states, the Commission and the European Free Trade Area (EFTA).

Its recommendations are in no way binding on EU institutions or States, which are merely asked to examine them and take the requisite action. The MIF is a structure for achieving pan-EU consensus, and its propositions provide an efficient decision-taking tool on a political level (76).

Safety at sea is one of the clear concerns of the MIF which, in its 1992 report to the Commission, recommended several steps aimed at preventing accidents. In 1994 it assessed the degree of implementation of EU recommendations on the issue, and the need to modify them (77). Its latest sessions emphasise mainly the coordination of research and development programmes and human resources policies (78).

• **Alliance of Maritime Regional Interests in Europe (AMRIE)**

112. - The Alliance of Maritime Regional Interests in Europe is the result of an initiative taken by the European Parliament, to bring together all those interested in the future of maritime regions of the EU. The long-term objective is to establish a maritime strategy, recognising the massive contribution made to the prosperity of the EU by maritime activities (79).

In practical terms, AMRIE provides liaison and coordination for the EU Commission, maritime groups in the Parliament, the MIF and the Conference of Peripheral Maritime Regions (80).

(75) COM (91) 335 final, 20 Sept. 1991. "New challenges for maritimes industries".
(76) P. LEONARD : "L'Europe et la mer". Annales 1992 de l'IMTM, Marseille, 148.
(77) Marine Industries Forum. "Progress report on actions and initiatives taken relating to the work of the Maritime Industry Forum". Rotterdam 20-21 June 1994.
(78) Marine Industries Forum : "Fifth Report to the Commission". 7th Plenary Session. Marseilles, July 1996, 1620/08.
(79) AMRIE. Fourth high-level conference of Maritime Regions in Europe . Nantes, 23 and 24 Nov. 1995.
(80) "AMRIE wins widespread EU backing". Lloyd's List, 2 Dec. 1993.

AMRIE, which is made up of institutions, organisations and individuals from EU member States, has an office in Northern England and a secretariat in Brussels. It is managed by a Steering Group, and operates through four specialist working groups, which act as experts within the organisation (81). One of these is concerned with the quality of shipping.

Safety at sea and protection of the environment are among the leading concerns of AMRIE, which in 1994 focussed its efforts on eliminating substandard ships, and in 1995 on the human factor and crew qualification, as well as databases for ship inspection status. AMRIE also initiated the Maritime Information Society (MARIS) project. Early in 1996, AMRIE began to promote FEMAR, a political initiative on the use of information technologies to improve maritime teaching and training systems (82).

• Maritime systems of the future

113. - The "Maritime Systems of the Future" Task Force, set up in 1995 by three European Commissioners, has the role of coordinating all maritime R&D programmes. For the European maritime industry, the Task Force is a single interface and contact point helping coordinate Commission policy and programmes (83).

Five priorities have so far been identified (84), namely MARIS, competitive engineering and production in shipbuilding (application of information technologies), safe and environmentally friendly maritime transport systems, efficient maritime transport, and responsible and optimal exploitation of marine resources.

3. European regional agreements

114. - One of the first European agreements on maritime safety was the 1982 Memorandum of Understanding on Port State Control (cf chapter 27).

Following accidents in the Channel and the North Sea at the end of 1993, France took the initiative in convening the transport ministers of the five coastal countries of the area, the United Kingdom, Belgium, the Netherlands, Germany and France. The first meeting, held in Paris on 26 January 1994, reflected their determination to combine forces and resources to strengthen safety in a zone where maritime traffic is among the heaviest in the world (85).

C - EU MARITIME SAFETY POLICY

115. - European policy, established by the Commission, was presented in a communication of 24 February 1993 entitled "A common policy on safe seas", already referred to (84). This eighty-page document analyses the main causes of accidents at sea, in order to identify areas requiring urgent action at international, Community, national, regional or local level. The outlines of this ambitious policy are not new. They already appeared in the White Paper on the development of a common transport policy, adopted in December 1992 (87).

---

(81) AMRIE : "Progress Report - Autumn 1995". Brussels, 9 Nov. 1995.

(82) AMRIE Newletter, N° 1, April 1996, Brussels.

(83) Prospection of the Task Force "Maritime Systems of the Future. A competitive marine industry for Europe". DG III/D. Brussels.

(84) EC DG III/D : "The Task Force : Maritime Systems of the Future". Interim Report, Brussels, 12 March 1996.

(85) JMM, 14 Jan. 1994 69 and Le Marin, 28 Jan. 1994, 7.

(86) COM (93) 66 Final already mentioned.

(87) "The future development of the common transport policy". COM (92) 494 Final. Brussels, 2 Dec. 1992.

In 1996, the Commission presented a policy update, in two documents entitled "A new approach to maritime strategy" (88) and "Shaping of Europe's maritime future", already referred to (89).

1. Common policy on safe seas

116. - The Commission approach is based on fundamental principles and an action programme.

a) Fundamental principles

Three principles underlie the approach. As far as possible, standards must be drawn up at international level. This is the only way of guaranteeing a high level of safety throughout the world, and preventing any distortion of competition among shipping companies. The Community makes its contribution at the level of enforcement of standards by States. It can develop a common approach to implementing IMO regulations by all ships operating in EU waters; a proper balance needs to be struck between flag States and port States. While it is the primary responsibility of flag States to ensure that their ships comply with international standards, port States can organise effective control of their actual application.

b) Action programme

Application of these principles results in a Community programme involving four main types of initiatives.

The first such initiative, concerning flag States, has to focus on the consistent implementation of IMO regulations by member States, and the application of international standards to ships not covered by international conventions.

Measures concerning port States are intended to ensure closer and more effective control of ships sailing in EU waters under any flag.

The development of maritime infrastructures is intended to provide waste management installations, navigational surveillance and aid systems in certain ecologically sensitive zones or those with high traffic volume.

Finally, other measures are designed to support IMO, so that it can strengthen its essential role in setting international standards.

The ambitious timetable set at the beginning of 1993 has been largely respected in practice, while following consultation procedures before the European Parliament and ECOSOC.

2. A new approach to maritime strategy

117. - The safety aspect of EU maritime policy was reexamined by the Commission and presented by the Kinnock Commission in March 1996 (91). It hinges on seven principles: compulsory application of IMO resolutions at EU level ; promotion within IMO of regulations on flag administrations responsible for ship registration and control ; definition of common registration principles within the EU ; adoption of a code of conduct on maritime trade ;

---

(88) COM (96) 81 Final, 13 March 1996.
(89) COM (96) 84, 13 March 1996.
(90) G. PLANT : "A European lawyer's view of the government response to the Donaldson Report". Marine Policy, vol. 19, n° 6, 455-457.
(91) N. KINNOCK : "Developments in EU Maritime Policy". BIMCO Review 1996, 61-65.

encouragement of operators to achieve high quality standards (tax incentives, differential harbour dues, etc) ; legislative action and financial penalties on shippers using substandard vessels ; finally, introduction of compulsory third party insurance before entering EU ports.

3. Shaping Europe's maritime future

118. - Presented by the Commission on the same date (92), the Communication "Shaping Europe's maritime future" tries to examine how EU industrial policy could help reinforce competitiveness. Proposals put forward include three measures aimed at improving safety and environmental protection.

• Development of information and telecommunication technologies
As part of the ESPRIT programme, the Commission is funding fifteen or so projects relating to information technologies specially devised for maritime industries.

The most important of these is the MARIS initiative, which was included among the eleven pilot schemes adopted by the Group of Seven (G7) in February 1995.

• Coordination of research and development activities
This coordination is provided by the "Maritime Systems of the Future" Task Force and by an MIF working group, which provides a single interface for R&D programmes.

Within the framework of the transport R&D programme, a score of projects are helping increase efficiency, safety and protection of the environment in the maritime sector.

• Training
The Commission has devised the LEONARDO programme for the implementation of an EU vocational training policy.

4. Quality shipping

119. - Launched by the Commission in November 1997, the Quality Shipping campaign is an attempt to take account of market mechanisms and adjust them, in order to reinforce safety (93). The argument is that there are still far too many operating practices in shipping that are driven by considerations of short-term profit, with little regard for the safety of human beings, the environment and vessels (94).

Six areas of intervention are identified: enforcement of international rules, focus on the human element, making passenger ships safer, protection from marine pollution by ships, ensuring safe traffic flows, and development of a research programme for quality of shipping.

D - GROWING REGIONALISATION OF MARITIME SAFETY

Presentation of the common transport policy caused some dismay in professional circles, which saw a risk of regionalisation of maritime safety policy (95). Since the adoption of a

---

(92) "Europe plans radical action on shipping". Lloyd's List, 14 March 1996.
(93) H. HARALAMBIDES : "Quality Shipping. Market mechanism for safer shipping and cleaner oceans". Erasmus Publishing, Rotterdam 1998, Introduction : a synthesis.
(94) European Commission. Directorate General for Transport. Brochure on Europe and Quality Shipping. Brussels, 1997.
(95) "Shipowners criticise EC safety policy". Lloyd's List, 11 Dec. 1992.

common policy on this issue, the European Union no longer acts as mere guarantor of the application of international conventions, but as a potential legislator, ready to remedy any shortcomings on the part of international organisations. It has a political and legislative system for this purpose, all it needs is fast, effective action.

1. Value of specific Community standards

120. - The legal possibility of setting specific new standards for safety at sea concerns flag states.

While recognising the fundamental importance of intergovernmental organisations in setting uniform global standards, the EU is aware of the current weakness of international regulations, which are subject to a number of hindrances (96). These inadequacies are seen to justify a "communitisation" of interventions, the only possible way of taking certain initiatives (97).

Theoretically, EU standards should be confined to exceptional cases in which IMO proves incapable of providing a solution that meets EU needs, and action is required to guarantee safety in European waters (98).

In this approach, ECOSOC remains fundamentally opposed to the introduction of specific Community standards, which would result in regionalisation of regulations. Priority, argues ECOSOC, should be given to international rules (99).

2. EU position within IMO

121. - IMO and the EU have had longstanding institutional relations. By 1974, a cooperation agreement was signed between the two organisations, and this was updated in 1983. It confers observer status on the Commission, so that the EU can attend all conferences and meetings organised by IMO (100).

Even if the EU acknowledges IMO as "the reference body" as far as standard-setting is concerned, it is keen to ensure that the IMO rule-making process proceeds along lines acceptable to European interests, particularly that regulations should in fact achieve their goals, and be adopted quickly.

Several schemes could be considered as ways of reinforcing links between the two organisations. To begun with, it might be possible to coordinate positions adopted by EU member States at IMO, when new regulations are being adopted or existing standards amended. At the next stage, it would be possible to consider the introduction of mechanisms enabling the EU to speak with a single voice at IMO. This would involve a transfer of competencies from member States to the Community regarding safety at sea, something that is legally possible under the Maastricht Treaty. The move would result in the formation of a European bloc at IMO, making it easier to identify priorities, formulate common propositions and organise coordinated support during bargaining phases. This would however encourage the development of other regional blocs, a situation IMO is anxious to avoid, bearing in mind the experience of UNCTAD'S Shipping Committee.

(96) V. POWER : "EC maritime policy. A lawyer's reaction". European Transport Law. Vol. XXXI n° 2 1996, 203-217.
(97) Communication of 24 Feb. 1993, paragraphs 30 and 31, p.16.
(98) Communication of 2 Dec. 1992, paragraphe 22.
(99) Opinion of 24 Nov. 1993, paragraph 3.4.3.
(100) W. BLONK : "Cooperation between the European Union and IMO". BIMCO Bulletin, June 1995, 26-29.

The problem was discussed at length by the Council of Ministers in 1993. A Gentlemen's Agreement was signed between the Commission and member States, under which they participate directly in negotiations, while cooperating with the EU to define a common position (101).

In the longer term, one could reexamine the observer status of the EU. Two reasons could lead Brussels to apply for membership of IMO (102). These are the completion of the internal market, and the implementation of a global policy on transport and the environment. This possibility of regional representation does not enjoy unanimous support. It has been received favourably by the European Parliament (103), but has aroused criticism from ECOSOC (104) and professional groups in general. Such groups complain that EU bodies lack the practical experience to assume such a role, and denounce the drawbacks that could arise from the formation of bloc voting within IMO. This is seen as leading to a politicisation of debates and the weakening of its effectiveness.

This is not the intention of the European Union at present. Indeed, it has several times expressed its determination not to take a harder line than IMO (105).

(101) Communication of 24 Feb. 1993, paragraphs 146 to 151.
(102) "EU urged to seek IMO membership". Lloyd's List, 22 March 1994.
(103) Opinion of 24 Nov. 1993, 7.2.1.
(104) "Regional roles". Lloyd's List, 5 Jan. 1994.
(105) "European Commission is not taking a harder line than IMO". Lloyd's List, Dec. 1997.

CHAPTER 5

Maritime industries

122. - The regulation of safety at sea is not the sole responsibility of States and intergovernmental organisations. Numerous groups, associations, whether public, semi-public or private bodies, representing the interests of the maritime world, share in drawing up such regulations. They form what are known as non-governmental organisations (NGOs). The UN has defined their status as follows "Any international organisation which is not established by intergovernmental agreement shall be considered as a non-governmental organisation for the purposes of these agreements" (1).

There is at least one NGO to look after the international representation of every component of the maritime industry - which comprises all businesses engaged any way in shipping and trade.

Unlike States, which pursue national aims, NGOs seek to view the broad economic picture and thereby advance the business interests of their members. They usually have a more international view of their activities than governments can afford to adopt. On the other hand, defending as they do private and sectoral interests, they sometimes make insuffusant allowance for the problems that confront intergovernmental organisations.

With their knowhow and professional skills, NGOs make a major contribution to the process of setting standards. Because of the administrative and technical complexity of the issues involved in safety at sea, their expertise is invaluable to promoters of regulations, who would find it hard to do without the advice and recommendations of naval engineers, maritime navigation experts and users of sea transport.

I - DIVERSITY OF NON-GOVERNMENTAL ORGANISATIONS

123. - It is their extraordinary diversity that characterises non-governmental maritime organisations. Eight sectors are concerned with the process of safety regulation: shipbuilders and equipment manufacturers ; shipping companies including shipowners, charterers, fleet operators and managers ; seafarers ; shippers and cargo owners ; insurers ; classification societies and standard-setting bodies ; port authorities ; and finally navigational aid services. There are transport and maritime navigation technicians, together with lawyers and ecologists, who have set up a large number of associations, concerned in varying degrees with accident prevention.

(1) Article 71, paragraph 8 of Council Res. 288 (X) of 27 February 1950.

A - SHIPBUILDERS AND EQUIPMENT MANUFACTURERS

1. Shipyards

124. - Shipbuilding yards belong to five large organisations: the American Shipbuilders Association (ASA), the Association of European Shipbuilders & Shiprepairers (AWES), the Korea Shipbuilders Association (KSA), the Shipbuilders Association of Japan (SAJ), and the Shipbuilders Council of America (SCA). Only AWES enjoys consultative status at IMO.

a) Association of European Shipbuilders and Shiprepairers (AWES)

AWES comprises fourteen national associations of shipowners based in Europe. In December 1994, AWES changed its name from Association of West European Shipbuilders to the present one, so that shiprepairers could become members, although it retained the same acronym, because it is so familiar worldwide. One of its principal goals is to remove substandard ships from world shipping fleets, and it supports any international initiatives on this issue.

AWES launches its own initiatives at IMO and the European Commission. Concerted action was taken with the other shipbuilders' associations in March 1995, by arguing for tougher ship survey and inspection standards throughout the world, and encouraging a policy of scrapping the oldest vessels (2).

b) Euroyard

In October 1992, five major European shipyards set up an economic interest group, in order to protect their technological advance in shipbuilding. Extensive technical collaboration among the five yards led to the development of the oil tanker project known as E3 ("European - Economic - Ecological").

Another goal of Euroyard is also to move against substandard ships, through representations to the European Commission (3).

c) Technical and scientific cooperation

Scientific and technical cooperation among shipbuilders, shiprepairers, naval architects and other related industries is being developed through various associations and learned societies. The best known are the International Ship and Offshore Structure Congress (ISSC) and the Tanker Structure Cooperative Forum (TSCF).

Founded in Glasgow, the ISSC, which meets every three years, brings together marine engineering professors, practising engineers and experts from various countries, engaged in research into structural strength and problems affecting ships and other maritime structures. It fosters discussion of subjects of common interest, the exchange of information on preliminary results, work in progress or planned on a national level. It also recommends new research projects, particularly when cooperation among countries is of special interest or when the need is recognised for a standardised procedure (4).

(2) AWES. Annual Report 1994-1995. Madrid 1995.
(3) "Euroyard attacks substandard ships". Lloyd's List, 29 Oct. 1992.
(4) 12th International Ship and Offshore Structure Congres. General information and membership. Canada, Sept. 1994.

The TSCF was set up in 1983 by a number of shipyards, shipowners and classification societies, to share members' knowledge and experience of the performance of the structures of tankers in service (5). In cooperation with other organisations, the Forum has issued several publications since 1986 on the assessment and maintenance of tanker ship structures (6).

2. Equipment manufacturers

125. - Several international organisations represent industries supplying ship equipment. The most importance include the International Lifesaving Appliance Manufacturers Association (ILAMA), the Association of European Manufacturers of Internal Combustion Engines (EUROMOT), the Institute of International Container Lessors (IICL), and the Comité International Radio-Maritime (CIRM).

CIRM was set up in Spain in 1928 by eight companies engaged in the supply of radio installations and equipment for maritime navigation. It currently has more than sixty members, from seventeen different countries. Its goal is to enhance the safety of human life at sea and the efficiency of seaborne transport, by fostering application of technology to navigation and maritime communications. This goal can be achieved only by detailed technical and operational cooperation among the industries and organisations concerned (7).

B - SHIPOWNERS AND SHIPOPERATORS

126. - A whole range of organisations represent the interests of shipowners and shipoperators internationally. A dozen NGOs enjoy consultative status at IMO (8). Some of them operate within more restricted frameworks, like the Council of European and Japanese Shipowners' Associations (CENSA) at OECD, or the European Community Shipowners' Associations (ECSA) within EU institutions. Others without any formal status exercise considerable influence.

Not all these bodies have the same political weight on the international scene. Some represent regional associations of shipowners, others cover only certain shipping groups. Only a few are involved with the issue of safety at sea.

Even if the number of organisations competent to deal with the question remains only six or seven, this very plurality presents several disadvantages (9). These include duplication of efforts, a piecemeal approach to problems, wastage of time and money, and inefficiency, particularly in managing the image of seaborne transport. Organisations representing shipping have great difficulty in "selling" the serious efforts that the majority of shipowners take to produce and maintain acceptable standards of practice (10).

Possible remedies include the idea of setting up a single, powerful international body to represent all the interests of maritime transporters, which would be able to react quickly to important issues. This opinion is not universally shared. Some consider that the maritime industry, a captive of its history, does not need to speak with a single voice. Although it may be possible at certain levels, it becomes unrealistic in other ways, because the interests of the various shipping groups may well diverge (11).

(5) Tanker Structure Cooperative Forum, 1992. Shipbuilders meeting. Proceedings. Introduction London, Oct. 1992.
(6) Tanker Structure Cooperative Forum in association with IACS. "Guidelines for the inspection and maintenance of double hull tanker structures". Witherby, London 1995.
(7) CIRM brochure : "Comité International Radio Maritime. The principal international association for maritime electronics companies". London, June 1995.
(8) A list of these organisations is given by IMO. Res. A.840 (20) adopted on 26 Nov. 1997.
(9) "Unity is strength". Lloyd's List, 19 August 1992.
(10) H. SOHMEN : "Shipping : what to do about an underrated industry". BIMCO Review 1995, 41-43.
(11) I. MIDDLETON : "A number of hats". Seatrade Review. December 1993, 6-7.

1. International Chamber of Shipping (ICS)

127. - The International Chamber of Shipping attaches the greatest importance to safety at sea (12). Created in London in 1921, ICS membership comprises forty-three associations of shipowners. ICS members account for about 50 per cent of the world shipping fleet (13).

The aim of ICS is to promote the interests of shipowners and operators in all matters of shipping policy and ship operations. To that end, ICS strives for a regulatory environment which supports safe shipping operations, protection of the environment and adherence to internationally adopted standards and procedures. It also encourages high standards of operation and the provision of high-quality and efficient shipping services (14). Based in London, ICS has a very slimmed-down administrative structure, provided by Maritime International Secretariat Services (MARISEC), a body set up jointly with the International Shipping Federation (15). The scale and variety of its members, and the nature of the issues dealt with, make ICS an umbrella organisation covering the whole international maritime transport industry (16).

ICS is active on three aspects of safety at sea :
- Much of the study and research it carries out is devoted to accident prevention.
- It issues numerous publications in the form of guides and manuals containing practical advice for shipping industries, and which provide an essential supplement to government regulations. Among the twenty-five works published by ICS, alone or in collaboration with other private bodies, several are directly concerned with safety at sea (17).
- One of the essential tasks of ICS is to represent and defend its members' interests at international organisations. From the beginning, it has been an energetic participant in SOLAS conferences and all IMO meetings, where it has enjoyed consultative status since 1961 (18). Its action focusses on the technical, operational and legal aspects of maritime transport projects (19).

2. International Shipping Federation (ISF)

128. - Set up in London in 1909, the International Shipping Federation is concerned principally with industrial relations relating to the working conditions and training of ship crews, in an attempt to advance the viewpoint of employers internationally. It brings together national shipowner associations from thirty countries, representing more than half the world tonnage of shipping (20).

Like the ICS, the ISF tries to represent its members at intergovernmental organisations. Since 1919 it has been helping prepare ILO international maritime conferences. It provides secretarial services for the shipowners' group, and defends their interests at the Joint Maritime Conference (21).

(12) "International Chamber of Shipping. A united forum in search of solutions". Lloyd's List, 24 A oril 1996.
(13) ICS. Annual Review 1996/1997. London 1997.
(14) ICS. Annual Review 1997/1998, 2. Statement of purpose.
(15) "Marisec shows the benefits of sharing". Lloyd's List, 24 April 1996.
(16) "Shipping getting feel-good factor". Lloyd's List, 24 April 1996.
(17) Cf. list of publication in ICS. Annual Review 1994/1995, 28.
(18) W. O'NEIL : "A call for further action". Commemorative publication of ICS, 1921-1996. London 1996, 8.
(19) ICS, 1921-1996, Relations with other organisations, op.cit. 31.
(20) "Notable milestone for the ISF". Lloyd's List, 24 April 1996.
(21) ISF : "The ISF Year. 1996/1997". London, 1998.

3. Baltic and International Maritime Council (BIMCO)

129. - The Baltic & International Maritime Council, set up in 1905, is one of the oldest associations of shipowners. 2 600 maritime companies from 108 countries belong to the Copenhagen-based organisation, and control a fleet of more than 400m tdw - over 55 per cent of the world fleet (22).

Its main goals are to unite shipowners and other persons and organisations connected with the shipping industry, take action on all shipping-related issues, act as spokesman for the industry, communicate useful information on any problems affecting the sector, and prepare and improve charterparties, by negotiations with other interested parties (23).

Because of its non-political role and the diversity of its membership, BIMCO has specialised in technical assistance to shipowners, while maintaining a view on the general issues debated at IMO and UNCTAD (24).

4. International Association of Independent Tanker Owners (INTERTANKO)

130. - Formed in 1971 to defend independent tanker owners against the majors, INTERTANKO represents the owners of over 1 900 tankers, totalling 170m tdw, approximately 74 per cent of the independent world tanker fleet. Its 264 member companies come from some forty-three countries worldwide. It also has 273 associate members (25).

Safety at sea is one of the principal concerns of Intertanko, which has chosen as its motto "For safe transport, cleaner seas and free competition".

INTERTANKO has had consultative status at IMO since 1979. It requires its members to class their ships with one of the members of the International Association of Classification Societies (IACS), and to be insured by a P&I Club (26). It publishes regular circulars on the safety of tankers, and specialised studies (27).

5. International Association of Dry Cargo Shipowners (INTERCARGO)

131. - INTERCARGO was set up in 1980 to advance the views of maritime carriers of solid goods. The association is based in London, and its membership consists of 185 shipowners, operators and managers from thirty-three countries, which control approximately 90m tdw of shipping (28).

Since the dry bulker casualties of the early Nineties, safety has become one of the major priorities of INTERCARGO. It has drawn up recommendations intended not only for shipowners but for all those concerned (29).

(22) F. FRANDSEN : "A forum for all". The Baltic, May 1997, 50-52.
(23) The BIMCO Handbook 1995. Rules of BIMCO as adopted at the general meeting in Singapore, June 1993, Rules 4, 64.
(24) Special report on BIMCO. "Major strides in twin tasks". Lloyd's List, 24 April 1991.
(25) INTERTANKO. The Chain of Responsability. Annual Report and Review 1997. London, 1998, 4.
(26) D. LUNDE : "Great expectation for tanker safety". The Baltic, May 1997, 54-58.
(27) INTERTANKO : "Systematic approaches to tanker accident Analysis - Lessons learnt". Discussion Paper, April 1998.
(28) B. FARTHING : "Safety through association". The Baltic, London. May 1997, 64-66.
(29) INTERCARGO. "Safety recommendations". London, 1991.

INTERCARGO has also carried out detailed analyses of accidents, giving greater force to its participation in the work of IMO (30). As a consultative member of the organisation since 1994, INTERCARGO puts forward the viewpoint of dry cargo shipowners (31), by seeking the right balance between the demands of safety and the operational requirements of their business (32).

6. International Maritime Industries Forum (IMIF)

132. - The International Maritime Industries Forum was founded in 1975, following publication of a report on the problems of the tanker industry, faced at that time with the devastating effects of surplus tanker capacity on world markets (33).

The aim of the Forum at present is to recreate a healthy commercial and financial climate in all sectors of the maritime industry.

IMIF, which has 130 members from twenty-five countries, has no formal constitution or structure. The unique feature of IMIF is that its membership embraces all players in the maritime industries: shipowners, shipbuilders, cargo owners, insurers, classification societies, lawyers, accountants, surveyors, even the ITF. Its aim therefore is to develop prosperity in all those sectors (34).

IMIF constantly draws attention to massive overtonnaging, with the surplus tonnage driving freight rates down, thereby depriving owners of additional income needed to meet the cost of safety, non-pollution and reasonable crew conditions; and creating conditions in which only substandard operators can make anything approaching a profit, while responsible owners languish in the appalling market (35).

7. International Ship Managers Association (ISMA)

133. - The International Ship Managers Association was founded in April 1991 by the world's five leading shipmanagement companies. Today, ISMA represents shipmanagers from sixteen countries, controlling a fleet of over 2 300 vessels (36).

Its goals are to establish universal quality standards for shipmanagement, identify shipmanagement clearly as a recognised sector of the shipping industry, act as spokesman for the shipmanagement industry, and provide a forum for exchange of information and experiences (37).

Membership of ISMA involves a commitment to introduce a quality management system that conforms to the ISMA Code of Ship Management Standards (38). This requirement is very strictly enforced, and in January 1997 all members were asked to be certified (39).

(30) "INTERCARGO analyses of dry bulker losses". IBJ, April 1994, 88-89.
(31) "Polemis. New chairman for INTERCARGO". IBJ, July 1994, 84-85.
(32) INTERCARGO Annual Review 1997/1998. London, 1998, 15. Future Priorities.
(33) M. GREY : "Is it time to find a new role for Cassandra ?" Lloyd's List, 30 sept. 1995.
(34) Presentation of IMIF. Document published by the Forum. London, July 1998.
(35) D. HUGHES : "An evangelist carrying the message of scrap-and-build". Shipping Times, 20 Feb. 1997.
(36) "ISMA AGM" in ISMA Focus, Oct. 1996, 1.
(37) ISMA. "A profile of the International Ship Managers'Association". London. Oct. 1996, 2-3.
(38) J. SPRUYT : "How goes it with ISMA ? It's all in the book". Lloyd's List, 19 Sept. 1994.
(39) "Members go as ISMA tightens up". Lloyd's List, 17 Jan. 1997.

C - SEAFARERS

Two organisations represent seafarers at IMO: the International Federation of Shipmasters Associations and the International Confederation of Free Trade Unions, itself represented by the International Transport Workers Federation.

1. International Federation of Shipmasters Associations (IFSMA)

134. - The International Federation of Shipmasters Association was set up in 1974, to unite shipmasters throughout the world into a single professional organisation. In 1995, more than 8 200 shipmasters from forty countries were affiliated to the Federation (40).

The Federation, based in London, is intended to uphold international standards of professional competence for seafarers, in order to ensure safe operational practices, prevent industrial accidents, and protect the marine environment as well as the safety of life and property (41).

As a consultative member of IMO since 1975, and with the statutory obligation to have its headquarters in proximity to those of IMO (42), IFSMA is one of its most fervent supporters. Its official motto is "Unity for safety at sea" (cf article 6 of the statutes), and IFSMA is concerned mainly with preventing shipping accidents, and with the human factor in such accidents (44).

2. International Transport Workers Federation (ITF)

135. - Founded in 1896 on the initiative of British seamen and dockers, the International Transport Workers Federation currently has some three million members belonging to four hundred different trade unions, in more than a hundred countries (45).

Since 1948, the ITF has gained a solid reputation in the fight against free registration abuses (46). It has used its consultative status at IMO and UNCTAD to launch an international campaign against the harmful consequences of flags of convenience on labour conditions (47). This single crusade is being modified to the extent that the campaign is now directed at all substandard owners and managers. It acknowledges that certain "flags of convenience" are among the very best administered flags.

Since 1981, shipowners who have signed collective agreements with the ITF pay money into the ITF Welfare Fund. This fund has been used to invest USD 60m in more than eight hundred projects. It has also backed the setting-up of a maritime safety research centre at Cardiff University, the creation of a professorship of education concerning the human factor at the World Maritime University, and a maritime expedition which located the wreck of the *Derbyshire* in the China Sea (48).

(40) R. CLIPSHAM : "The shipmaster's obsession with safety". Journal of the Honourable Company of Master Mariners. Autumn 94, 336.
(41) R. CLIPSHAM : "The shipmaster with mixed nationality crew. Human error and the control of emergencies". The Nautical Institute. Glasgow International Conference on Marine Safety Management, 29-30 March 1995.
(42) IFSMA - Statutes art. 2 in preamble, statutes and bye-laws. London 14, May 1995.
(43) IFSMA - Annual report and accounts 1995. 21st Annual General Assembly, London, 12-13 May 1995.
(44) JMM, 21 June 1996, 1534.
(45) J.Y. LEGOUAS : "International transport workers federation. L'action de ITF". JMM 15 July 1994, 1869.
(46) H. NORTHRUP, R. ROWAN : "The international transport worker's federation and flag of convenience shipping". University of Pennsylvania. N° 7 Multinational Union Studies, USA, 1983.
(47) D. COCKCROFT : "Beyond 2000. Some thoughts on the future of marine trade unionism". Maritime Policy Management, 1997, Vol. 24, n° 1, 3-8.
(48) "ITF applies research pressure". Lloyd's List, 17 jan. 1995.

3. The Nautical Institute

The Nautical Institute is an international professional body for qualified mariners whose principal aim is "to promote high standards of knowledge, qualification and competence amongst those in control of seagoing craft". This organisation does not enjoy consultative statuts at IMO but plays a important role in safety matters.

The Institute publishes a monthly Journal *Seaways*. It contains the Institutes confidential marine accident report's MARS, which covers near-miss incidents and potentially dangerous occurences.

D - SHIPPERS AND CARGO OWNERS

Not all shippers' associations have their interests represented internationally. Only a few sectors which are well organised have set up organisations to defend and promote the profession. These include the European Chemical Industry Council and the Oil Companies International Marine Forum.

1. European Chemical Industry Council (CEFIC)

136. - The European Council of Chemical Industry Federations was set up in 1972, to represent the European chemical industry. It comprises twenty-one national federations under the aegis of the Consultative Assembly of Members Federations (AFEM) and forty-nine industrial firms under the banner of the Consultative Assembly of Member Companies (ACOM).

The mission of CEFIC is to carry out scientific studies on behalf of the chemical industry, promote public trust in, and support for, the industry, act as spokesman for the industry at international and European institutions (49). Since its earliest days CEFIC has s played an active part in the establishment of regulations on international transport of dangerous goods. In the maritime sector, it has set up a Chemical Distribution Institute (CDI), to improve quality and safety for the transport of chemicals by sea (50).

2. Oil Companies International Marine Forum (OCIMF)

137. - The Oil Companies International Marine Forum was set up in London in April 1970 (51), in response to the public unease aroused by the escalation of the tanker fleet, and its perils, as exemplified by the *Torrey Canyon* disaster (52).

The over-riding aim of the OCIMF, which has a current membership of forty-two oil companies and groups throughout the world, is to promote safety and prevent pollution from ships and terminals (53).

The OCIMF is responsible for representing its members on government bodies and national and international organisations, including IMO (54), and EU institutions (55).

(49) CEFIC. Annual Report 1994. Brussels, 1995.
(50) "CDI : all systems go". Hazardous Cargo Bulletin, July 1995, 6-47.
(51) OCIMF : "Making headway for twenty-five years". London, 1995.
(52) M. GREY : "OCIMF, twenty five years on". BIMCO Bulletin Vol. 90 n° 6, 95.
(53) OCIMF. Annual Review. August 1997, Introduction to OCIMF, 6-7.
(54) Special issue on the 25th anniversary of the. Lloyd's List. OCIMF, 17 Nov. 1995.
(55) "EU lifts marine safety role". Lloyd's List, 17 Nov. 1995.

The Forum also sponsors and coordinates joint research projects under the direction of its members. Many of these have led to the publication of technical guidelines for the benefit of the industry (56).

Since its creation, the OCIMF has published more than forty codes of practice and guidelines covering a wide range of subjects, such as the operation of tanker ships and terminals, maintenance, anchoring procedures, firefighting, inspection of ships and clean seas plans. These guidelines, most of which are regarded as recommended industrial practice in their areas, are used widely as reference documents by standard-setting authorities (57).

In November 1993, the OCIMF introduced the Ship Inspection Report programme (SIRE), with the aim of promoting the safety of oil tankers and preventing pollution (cf chapter 24 below).

OCIMF policy is hostile to any unilateral or regional legislation. It argues for effective application of international conventions, which it sees as the prime responsibility of shipowners, flag states and classification societies. It emphasises the important role to be played by port states, charterers and insurers in preventing risks, and the fundamental role of IMO in drafting regulations (58).

E - INSURERS

Insurers are represented internationally by several organisations, the most important of which are the International Union of Marine Insurance and the International Group of P & I Clubs.

1. International Union of Marine Insurance (IUMI)

138. - The International Union of Marine Insurance, set up in 1874, comprises national associations of hull and cargo marine insurers. The Zurich-based association has fifty-one full members and three associate members (59).

The basic role of the IUMI is to "represent, safeguard and develop insurers' interests in marine and transport insurance". In fulfilling its mission, it advances the interests of the marine insurance business, fosters cooperation among national markets on marine issues, facilitates the exchange and dissemination of information on marine technology and insurance. Finally, it promotes cooperation with other international maritime organisations, particularly IMO, where it has consultative status (60).

Its very modest structure consists of a secretariat and a liaison office, provided by the Institute of London Underwriters (ILU).

The cornerstone of IUMI's activities is the Annual Conference, which takes place each September in a different host country. This event, which is the largest meeting of insurers in the world, offers an opportunity to hear presentations by technical committees of current research, analyse casualty statistics, discuss legal issues, and review new methods of transportation.

(56) "Solidly-based research toward operational standards should improve industry image". Lloyd's List, 17 Nov. 1995.
(57) List of publication in OCIMF. Annual Review 1997, 34.
(58) OCIMF. "Tanker safety and pollution prevention. The OCIMF view on the issues". September 1993, London.
(59) IUMI : Presentation brochure. Zurich, 1994.
(60) "The history of development of protecti and indemnity clubs". Report of advanced study group n° 109 of the Insurance Institute of London. 8 Jan. 1957.

Fundamentally, IUMI remains a debating chamber, and an organisation for research and collaboration. While the problems raised at conferences are very numerous and highly diverse, practical solutions, in the form of guidelines for national association or reports to be submitted to IMO, are not always available.

2. International Group of P & I Associations

139. - This organisation comprises a score of Protection and Indemnity Clubs throughout the world. These mutual insurance associations were set up in the mid-19th century by groups of shipowners, to cover the risks arising from maritime expeditions (61). At the present day, P & I clubs insure 90 per cent of world tonnage, covering the contractual liabilities of shipowners or charterers.

The Group is intended primarily to arrange collective insurance and reinsurance for its members. Under the Inter-Group Agreement (IGA), any claims exceeding US$ 5m are shared out over the whole tonnage insured by the pool, which acts as excess loss reinsurer for each Club. For claims over US$ 30m, the Group buys excess loss reinsurance on the reinsurance market up to a maximum of US$ 500m for pollution damage, with the possibility of offering US$ 200 additional cover for oil tankers (62). The IGA is currently under attack by Directorate General IV of the European Commission, for competition distortion (63).

The Group also represents its members at international organisations (64). It promotes the exchange of information on marine insurance issues. Regarded by certain commentators as "under-utilised", the Group could in coming years become more proactive within the maritime community (65).

F - REGULATORY ORGANISATIONS AND CLASSIFICATION SOCIETIES

For a long time, the only bodies to set standards for shipbuilding were classification societies. Their role and international structure are described in chapter 6 below. Since the early 20th century, they have faced competition in certain areas from other standard-setting institutions. At present, most of these institutions are grouped together in two international organisations, the International Electrotechnical Commission and the International Organisation for Standardisation.

1. International Electrotechnical Commission (IEC)

140. - Founded in 1906, the International Electrotechnical Commission comprises fifty National Committees, representing all the electrical industries in each country. The object of the IEC is "to promote international cooperation on all questions of standardisation such as verification of conformity to standards in the fields of electricity, electronics and related technologies, and thus to promote international understanding" (cf article 2 of the statutes).

(61) M. O'MALLEY : "Is there a future for the International Group?". BIMCO Review 1998, 158-160.
(62) "Clubs face a number of pressing issues". Lloyd's List, 4 June 1998.
(63) International Group of P and I Clubs Presentation Brochure. London, June 1995.
(64) "Kulukundis warns of threat to P and I system". Insurance Day, 14 Dec. 1995.
(65) The International Electrotechnical Commission (IEC)/Structures and Operation - IEC, Geneva, 2nd edition 1995.

The IEC has set up two hundred technical committees (TC) and seven hundred working groups, which draw up standards dealing with safety, performance, construction and installation of electrical equipment in all sectors of industry. More than three thousand international electrotechnical standards have been published in the IEC catalogue (66).

In the shipping sector, TC 18 is specially charged with standards for shipborne installations, and even provides IMO with help in establishing technical standards for this type of equipment. Another committee, TC 80, deals with maritime navigation and radiocommunication equipment and systems (67).

2. International Organisation for Standardisation (ISO)

141. - Geneva-based ISO is a worldwide federation of national standards bodies from 109 countries. Its aim is to promote the development of standardisation and related activities in the world, with a view to facilitating the international exchange of goods and services, and to developing cooperation in the spheres of intellectual, scientific, technological and economic activity. Its work consists of adopting international agreements, which are then published in international standards.

One of the purposes of standardisation is to improve health, safety and protection of the environment, as well as the reliability and quality of goods and services. Its activities cover all industrial operations. The technical work of ISO is highly decentralised, being carried out by some 2 700 technical committees, subcommittees and working groups. These comprise qualified representatives of industry, research institutes, government authorities, consumer bodies and international organisations (68).

Two of its technical committees are concerned with maritime safety issues :
- TC 8 on ships and marine technology has set standards for the component parts and elements of a ship ;
- TC 104 on freight containers has standardised the characteristics of such containers.

ISO's principal claim to fame is its development and publication of the ISO 9000 standards, acknowledged as the international benchmark for quality in a commercial context.

ISO maintains various technical relations with UN specialised agencies, several of which are involved in standard-setting activities. It has been a consultative member of IMO since the beginning.

G - PORTS, TERMINALS AND PORT SERVICES

Ports are represented by several international organisations. This institutional diversity corresponds to the multiple activities and interests involved. Safety is of particular concern to port establishments, specialised terminals, handling firms, harbourmasters and pilots.

(66) IEC Annual Report 1994, 6.
(67) ISO : "Compatible technology worldwide". Genève 1994.
(68) "IAPH faces up to global challenges". Lloyd's List, 7 July 1995.

1. International Association of Ports and Harbours (IAPH)

142. - The International Association of Ports and Harbours, with headquarters in Tokyo, comprises 389 port establishments of all sizes and types, in eighty-seven different countries (69).

The IAPH and the World Port Conference provide a forum to exchange information on a variety of topics that have an important impact on the port community. The aim is to strengthen economic, commercial, legal and administrative links among very different authorities: private, public, semi-public and government-run ports.

A consultative member of IMO since 1867, the IAPH organisation comprises twelve special committees focussing on safety, environmental and other issues.

2. Society of International Gas Tanker and Terminal Operators (SIGTTO)

143. - The Society of International Gas Tanker and Terminal Operators was, set up in 1978 to encourage cooperation among all those concerned with the safe and reliable operation of gas terminals and tankers. Safety is a vital factor in the activities of SIGTTO, the role of which is to serve as a forum for the exchange of technical information and experience, conduct studies and research relating to safety or protection of the environment in the transport and storage of liquefied gas, and represent the interests of the gas industry at international organisations, particularly IMO, where it has enjoyed consultative status since 1983.

SIGTTO, which has ninety-eight members, representing more than 80 per cent of LNG interests, and about 50 per cent of LPG interests (70), issues a large number of regular publications, based on its research, more specifically the principles of handling liquefied gas on ships and in terminals (71).

3. International Cargo Handling Coordination Association (ICHCA)

144. - Cargo handlers have an important part to play in the safe performance of loading and unloading operations, but also in promoting the safety of the ship itself. A large number of international regulations exist, issued by IMO or the ILO, together with a plethora of private standards. Harmonisation of the rules and practices of port handling professionals is a concern of ICHCA, which has published several practical safety guides on the various relevant regulations (72).

4. International Harbour Masters Association (IHMA)

145. - In June 1996, the European Harbour Masters Association (EHMA), anxious to obtain a better hearing at IMO and work more closely with it, set up the International Harbour Masters Association (73). Several specialised commissions of E/IHMA, consisting of 280 harbour masters including seventy from non-European countries, have adopted recommendations on ship safety, transport of dangerous goods, maritime traffic services, hydrography or reception of ships in difficulty (74).

(69) Society of International Gas Tanker and Terminal Operators. London, 1st May 1996.

(70) SIGTO : "Liquefied gas handling principles on ships and in terminals". Witherby, London 1996.

(71) M. COMPTON : "Health and safety standards for cargo-handlers worldwide". BIMCO Review 1996, 248-251.

(72) M.J. RIDGE : "President's Report to the sixth congress of the European Harbour Masters' Association". Reykjavik, Iceland, 17 June 1996. Document de l'EHMA. Bristol.

(73) IHMA : "An overview of the association". Bristol 1996.

(74) E. EDEN : "International Maritime Pilots' Association". The Nautical Institute Publication, 1994, 20.

5. International Maritime Pilots Association (IMPA)

146. - Founded in Kiel in 1970, the International Maritime Pilots Association consists of thirty-five pilots' organisations from twenty-nine countries. A major element in the work of IMPA has been the active promotion of the safety aspect of piloting, by making significant contributions to various IMO instruments, in particular carrying out much of the groundwork that led to Resolution A.578 on guidelines for vessel traffic services.

IMPA has also published various informative notes on technical matters affecting the pilot's profession, and mariners in general (75).

H - MARITIME NAVIGATION SERVICES

The term "maritime navigation services" applies to organisations engaged in the installation and proper functioning of navigation aids, including buoyage, meteorology and radio links, and to institutes of navigation contributing to the establishment of rules of navigation.

1. International Association of Lighthouse Authorities (IALA)

147. - The International Association of Lighthouse Authorities was set up in 1957, to provide a permanent framework for the International Lighthouse Conferences, which had been held since 1929 on the initiative of several countries (76). It has a total of 225 members, of more than eighty different nationalities.

IALA brings together navigation aids authorities, manufacturers and consultants, and offers them the opportunity to compare their experiences and achievements. Its objective is to foster the safe, economic and expeditious movements of vessels through improvement and harmonisation of aids to navigation and marine traffic management practices, or any other appropriate means (cf article 1 of the Constitution).

The most important technical activities of IALA are carried on in technical committees. These study topical issues, and submit their findings to the Council for adoption as recommendations. The main committees deal with maritime marking systems, radionavigation systems, maritime labour services, the reliability of aids to navigation and documentation on these aids. IALA publishes numerous works, the most important of which is the *International Dictionary of Aids to Marine Navigation*.

Its consultative status at IMO, granted in 1961, allows it to take an active part in all discussions on safety of navigation. The IALA has made a considerable contribution to introducing a uniform system of buoyage throughout the world and continues, within other organisations, to monitor new developments in the maritime signalling sector (77).

(75) Ch. VILLE : "33 years of International co-operation". IALA Publication, 1991.
(76) T. KRUUSE : "The role of IALA". IALA Bulletin, 1996/2, 6-7.
(77) "Participate in PIANC". Presentation Brochure published by the PIANC International Secretariat, Brussels.

2. Permanent International Association of Navigation Congresses (PIANC)

148. - The Permanent International Association of Navigation Congresses, founded in 1885, is the oldest international association concerned with the technical aspects of navigation. Its aim is to promote the maintenance and operation of both inland and ocean navigation, by fostering progress in the design, construction, improvement, maintenance and operation of inland and maritime waterways and ports, harbours and coastal zones (78).

Based in Brussels, the PIANC is a forum for discussion and technical cooperation, sponsored by the governments of thirty-eight countries, and by two international river commissions. Its membership comprises approximately two thousand individual members and six hundred corporate members concerned with promoting navigation (79).

The PIANC has achieved substantial results for safety at sea. Its initiatives include a scheme for deep-draught vessels in port zones, the safety of coastal navigation, the effects of the sea on marine structures, and maritime traffic movements in general (80). More recently, it has devoted research to maritime and river environments (81).

The PIANC publishes numerous technical works in French and English, and a regular bulletin in the Association's two working languages.

3. International Association of Institutes of Navigation (IAIN)

149. - Institutes of navigation have been set up in the leading maritime nations, with the aim of matching the possibilities offered by technicians with the needs expressed by navigators. Most such organisations remain private bodies benefitting from unofficial backing (82). A few, however, enjoy official status and are recognised by governments, like the Institut Français de Navigation in France or the Royal Institute of Navigation in Britain (83).

The International Association of Institutes of Navigation was created officially in 1975 by the institutes of navigation of Australia, France, Germany, Italy, Japan, the United Kingdom and the United States. Almost immediately, it obtained consultative status at IMO.

The objective of the IAIN is to unite national and multinational institutes and organisations engaged in fostering human activities at sea, in the air, in space and on land, and which may benefit from the development of the science and practice of navigation and related information techniques. The IAIN accordingly undertakes to foster cooperation and assistance among members, organise congresses and seminars, and maintain links with relevant international associations.

Based in London, the IAIN has fourteen members at present. It makes an active contribution to the promotion of an international institutional solution for the Global Navigation Satellite System (GNSS). It also encourages interoperability of infrastructures for navigation and communication systems, and their use by relevant groups on land, at sea, in the air and in space (84).

(78) PIANC, Presentation Leaflet, Brussels, 1995.
(79) JMM, 30 March 1972, 787.
(80) R. ENGLER : "PIANC and the environment". PIANC Bulletin n° 87 - 1995.
(81) L. OUDET : "L'autorité sur mer". JMM, 25 July 1968, 1552.
(82) P. SCHMITZ : "Aspects et développements de la radiolocalisation en navigation". JMM, 16 September 1965, 2083.
(83) IAIN. Information brochure. 1995, London.
(84) F. WISWALL : "Comité Maritime International. A brief structural history of the first century". CMI 1897-1997, Antwerp.

I. MISCELLANEOUS ORGANISATIONS WITH INFLUENCE ON MARITIME SAFETY

Many other non-governmental organisations reflecting economic, legal or ecological concerns participate more or less actively in setting maritime safety standards.

a) Legal associations

150. - Several legal associations enjoy consultative status at IMO. The oldest, the most important and the most involved in maritime issues is the Comité Maritime International (CMI). CMI was created in Antwerp in 1897 (85), and today it encompasses about fifty national maritime law associations. Its purpose is "to contribute by all appropriate means and activities to the unification of maritime law in all its aspects" (cf article 1 of the statutes) (86).
Although it specialises in questions of damage compensation and not prevention of risks, the CMI can still exert some influence on the behaviour of the different parties engaged in seaborne transport, through provisions for liability. An example was given recently with the establishment of a legal regime for classification societies (87) (cf chapters 6 and 22 below).

b) Environmental and nature conservation organisation

151. - There are more and more environmentalist and conservationist bodies, and they exert a growing influence on the environmental policies adopted by states and international organisations. Some of these grassroots organisations engage in active lobbying, which can even succeed in influencing the decisions taken by major industrial groups, through their increasing control of the media and public opinion.
Five organisations are represented at IMO. These are the International Union for Conservation of Nature and Natural Resources (IUCN), the Worldwide Fund for Nature (WWF), the Friends of the Earth International (FOEI), Greenpeace International and the Advisory Committee on Protection of the Sea (ACOPS). Most of their efforts focus on the Marine Environment Protection Committee (MEPC) and the Legal Committee, with varying degrees of effectiveness depending on the projects under discussion. Most of these organisations suffer from having too few members to keep a permanent presence at discussions, and from their incapacity to offer satisfactory solutions to the technical problems of seaborne transport. Two such associations deserve particular consideration: Greenpeace and ACOPS

• Greenpeace International
152. - Founded in Vancouver in 1971 by a group of militants on behalf of Indian minorities (88), Greenpeace within a few years became one of the most powerful organisations of its kind, with five million sympathisers of all nationalities. Its organisation employs

---

(85) A. Von ZIEGLER : The Comité Maritime International (CMI) : "The voyage from 1897 into the next millennium". Uniform Law Review 1997-4, 728-757. CMI Yearbook 1997. Constitution (1992). Antwerp - Dec. 1997..
(86) - "Study of issues re classification societies". BIMCO Bulletin, vol. 91 n° 2, 1996, 67-71.
- F. WISWALL : "Comité Maritime International : Study of issues regarding classification societies". BIMCO Review 1996, 150-152.
- CMI : "Joint working group on a study of issues re classification societies". Report, London, 10 March 1997 in. CMI 1996 Annuaire. Antwerp I. Documents for the century conference, 328-342.
(87) M. BROWN, J. MAY : "The Greenpeace story". Dorling Kindersley, 1989.
(88) IMO. C 64/28/Add. 1. LEG 63/9/Add. 1, 16 July 1990.

1 300 people in forty-three offices covering thirty countries. With its headquarters in Amsterdam, the movement also has major logistic resources, including a flotilla of about ten boats, and it uses the most advanced communication tools.

In its actions in favour of environmental protection, Greenpeace has no hesitation in exerting direct pressure on potential polluters, through its army of determined activists. Within intergovernmental organisations, it intervenes in a more moderate way. At IMO, it is an energetic defender of ecological interests during discussions of any environmentally sensitive conventions or regulations (89).

• ACOPS

The Advisory Committee on Protection of the Sea (ACOPS) occupies a special position among ecological organisations. It was set up in 1952 by a large number of foundations, governmental and intergovernmental organisations, private companies and individuals, to encourage international agreements on reducing oil pollution of the seas. Nowadays, its action has been extended to other sources of pollution, with the particular goal of investigating and quantifying marine pollution problems.

II - NGO CONTRIBUTION TO STANDARD SETTING

Maritime industries differ from other industrial sectors in that they make a major contribution to the standard-setting process, drawing up safety standards, and also playing an active part in the work of international organisations.

A - IMPORTANCE OF PRIVATE REGULATIONS ON SHIPPING

153. - The standard-setting work of NGOs is evidence of the importance of private regulations for shipping. It takes two different forms :

First, there are voluntary industrial standards, intended to promote safety, protect public health or the environment. ISO standards, OCIMF codes of practice or classification society Rules fall into this category. These regulations, drawn up and implemented by professionals, often cover areas neglected by public legislative and regulatory systems.

Recent years have seen the growth of private codes of conduct intended, not to lay down technical standards, but to regulate the behaviour and obligations of members of a profession. These codes usually aim to forestall government desires to regulate certain activities, and this explains their great popularity in countries with a *laissez-faire* tradition, such as the United States (90), the United Kingdom (91) or Australia (92). Even if for many industries the essential goal is to restore the image of an activity that has been tarnished by major scandals or constantly negative publicity (93), codes of conduct represent an important component of what lawyers refer to as "soft law".

---

(89) K. ARROW : "Business codes and economic efficiency". In BEAUCHAMP et BOWIE : "Ethical theory and business", 3rd ed. Prentice Hall, N.J., 1988, 135-137.
(90) A. PAGE : "Self-regulation and codes of practice". Journal of Business Law 1980, 24-30.
(91) J. MCKAY : "Classification of Australian corporate and industry-based codes of conduct". International Business Lawyer, Dec. 1994, 507-514.
(92) T. HEMPHILL : "Self-regulating industry behaviour : antitrust limitations and trade association codes of conduct". Journal of Business Ethics 11, 1992, p. 915-920. Kluwer Academic Publishers.
(93) JMM, 6 May 1948, 1481.

Before analysing the effects and legal value of these private regulations, it is important to examine the reasons for their frequency in the maritime safety sector.

1. Reasons for popularity of private regulations

154. - Several factors explain the proliferation of private rules and standards in the shipping industry. They reflect the attitudes of both public authorities and industrialists towards accident prevention.

The state was for long reluctant to intervene in the shipping sector. Throughout the 19th century, its interference in business and trade remained most unpopular, even where safety at sea was concerned. It was considered that maritime navigation should not be hindered by restrictive measures which would have had the effect, under the banner of safety, of driving traffic away, to other modes of transport with less concern for safety (94).

Shipping industrialists have always considered that safety issues are part of their fundamental responsibilities. Regulation of an activity by means of private initiatives is more effective than state intervention, provided that they are drawn up by professionals fully aware of their scope of application. The maritime industry has to be seen to discipline itself, if the government is not to intervene, perhaps in a more heavy-handed way than the industry would like (95).

These reasons illustrate the importance of the private regulation that today prevails in the maritime transport sector. Not everyone shares this liberal attitude. Some people consider that "shipping has been self-regulated for too long, and far too many historical practices are simply not acceptable in this modern age of technology, communication and environmental concern" (96). Beyond this argument, the real effects and value of private regulation require some examination.

2. Legal value of private regulations

155. - The legal value of private regulatory initiatives naturally depends on the legal system within which they are intended to operate. In the United States, where codes of conduct and private standards are far more widespread, case law remains divided on their effects (97).

Certain jurisdictions consider that private regulation cannot be better than state laws : an industry which supplies a service or manufactures a product tends to be less strict than a public authority on matters of safety, because of the economic cost involved in stringent standards. By virtue of this argument, courts attribute only a relative value to professional codes, which are regarded as minimum requirements that have to be observed in order to ensure integrity within an industry.

Other courts have a more complex attitude. They recognise that professional codes of practice are useful in establishing a standard or general industrial policy establishing the need for vigilance by the manufacturer of a product or supplier of a service, who is held liable for negligence.

(94) Ph. BOISSON : "Turning commercial initiatives into public benefits : can private initiatives effectively raise international standards?". 1995, Bermuda Conference.
(95) N. DOUGLAS : "Shipping needs regulation to be profitable and efficient". IMIF Seminar, 1995.
(96) J. MANTA : "The effect of private sector self-regulation or litigation". Metropolitan Corporate Council, July 1996, 14.
(97) K. ARROW. Op cit, 137.

In general, American case law remains very prudent about the validity and justification private regulations, on the grounds that one cannot expect miraculous transformations in human behaviour merely through strict and rigorous application of standards (98).

B - MARITIME INDUSTRY ACTION IN INTERNATIONAL ORGANISATIONS

156. - Grouped together in large national and international organisations, the representatives of each sector of industry attempt to defend their interests by influencing the decisions taken by states and international institutions. On the question of safety at sea, the maritime industries are concerned mainly to make their voice heard at IMO. Lobbying is not confined to IMO, however: it extends to all bodies involved in regulating maritime transport (99). It is not possible within the framework of this book to list all the initiatives taken by maritime industries at various international organisations. Consideration will be confined to the example of NGO action at IMO.

1. Forms of participation in IMO

157. - Non-governmental organisations occupy an increasingly important position at IMO, thanks to the granting of a special legal status. Article 62 of the convention 1948 allows the Organisation to "make suitable arrangements for consultation and cooperation with non-governmental international organization".

A more important factor is the consultative status conferred on certain organisations. This procedure enables IMO to obtain information or expert advice from NGOs with special expertise in one of the particular sectors of interest to IMO, and also to offer such organisations an opportunity to present their viewpoint to IMO (100).

2. NGO status

158. - Consultative status confers rights and obligations on NGOs.

There are few obligations : a consultative member simply has to support IMO activities by encouraging dissemination of its principles and proceedings. NGOs also have to inform the General Secretariat of any aspects of their activities that might be of interest to IMO, and grant IMO reciprocal privileges.

Privileges include receiving notice of the agenda of sessions of all IMO technical and deliberative bodies, the right to submit written statements, make verbal comments at such sessions, be represented by an observer at all sessions held by IMO entities, and receive of resolutions, recommendations and technical documents issued by IMO.

Finally NGOs may be invited by IMO to send observers to international conferences, to express their point of view and supply all relevant information to government delegations.

---

(98) R. STEINER : "Government, industry and public management of the seas in the 21st century". Marine Policy, Sept. 1993, 399-403.
(99) IMO. Basic Documents. Volume 1. Rules governing relationship with non-governmental international organizations, Rule 2.
(100) IMO. Res. A.840. Relations with non-governmental organizations. 26 Nov. 1997.

3. Conditions for granting of consultative status

159. - The NGO must be able to make a meaningful contribution to the work of IMO. Its activity must have a direct link to IMO goals: its aims and functions must be entirely in conformity to the spirit, functions and principles of IMO. Next, the NGO must have a permanent headquarters, a governing body, an executive agent authorised under the statutes to speak on behalf of its members. The IMO Council is responsible for examining applications. This is done only once a year, and is renewed two years after consideration of the initial application.

Council guidelines for the granting of consultative status have been introduced to supplement earlier provisions, setting additional conditions, including a criterion to determine whether an NGO makes a notable contribution to the work of IMO, the impossibility of granting consultative status to an NGO that already has access to IMO through another organisation, or if such a status could cause conflicts or obvious duplication. Finally, NGOs seeking consultative status must be genuinely international. This is gauged by the size of their membership, geographical origin and the nature of the interests they represent.

4. Withdrawal of consultative status

160. - The status of consultative member is not granted on a permanent basis. Before each session of the Assembly, the Council reexamines the list of NGO members, and decides in each individual case whether maintenance of consultative status is necessary and appropriate. It reports to the Assembly, which has to approve the list submitted by the Council.

Directives also define the procedure to be followed: by evaluating the contribution of each NGO, the Council has to take into consideration factors such as attendance by representatives at meetings, their effective participation (e.g. number and type of documents supplied).

5. Proliferation and growing influence of NGOs

161. - Despite the very strict conditions laid down by IMO for the granting and maintenance of consultative membership, there has been an extraordinary proliferation of NGOs at IMO. From barely a dozen in the early Sixties, they have grown to fifty-three today (101). At the same time, they are increasingly participating in major diplomatic conferences convened under IMO auspices : in 1966, at the London conference on loadlines, a single organisation, ICS, was allowed to take part in the debates. At present, diplomatic gatherings to adopt a new international instrument, or amend an existing one, are attended by nearly all NGOs.

Some commentators have tried to explain this success by the capability and technical knowhow of NGOs, and by the influence they exert on public opinion (102). Others consider that they help bring a more democratic element into decision taking . This seems to be accurate comment, in such a technical and complex area as safety at sea and protection of the environment.

(101) J. BARNES : "Non-governmental organizations. Increasing the global perspective". Marine Policy, April 1984, 171-184.
(102) R. SYBESMA-KNOL : "The status of observers in the United Nations". Vrije Universiteit Brussel. Kluwer Antwerp, 1981.

However, there are disadvantages in the current system : apart from the top-heaviness that results from the huge proliferation of NGOs on an international scale, their participation in international organisations is not without its financial effect on operating budgets. IMO showed its awareness of this problem by initiating a study of the issue in 1995.

Carried out by the Secretariat in liaison with technical committees, this study contains three items of information (103). To begin with, the benefits of consultative status are indeed mutual: NGOs gain advantage from attending IMO meetings, while IMO has the benefit of their expert advice. Second, deep differences remain within IMO on the costs involved in their participation, and the advisability of asking for a financial or other contribution. Finally, the revision process provided for in rule 10, already referred to, should determine the contribution made by NGOs to the work of IMO and the benefits they obtain. Similarly, withdrawal of consultative status should be treated in the same way and with the same strict approach as granting of such a status.

The problem remains on the table. IMO has so far avoided being the very first UN agency to break with tradition and ask for any contribution from the NGOs that take part in its work.

(103) IMO. Council 74th session. Agenda item 25(b). C 74/25(b)/Add.1, 9 March 1995.

CHAPTER 6

Classification societies

162. - Classification societies have a fundamental role to play in preventing accidents at sea, through their dual role in the classification and certification of ships (1) :
- Classification, as a completely private service performed by these societies, consists of issuing rules for the safety of ships, and performing surveys and inspections to ensure that these rules are being applied. The main purpose is to protect the ship as a piece of property, and the rules apply principally to the structural strength of the hull and the reliability of its essential machinery and equipment. The shipowner uses the certificate issued by the classification society to obtain insurance at reasonable cost ;
- The technical skills possessed by classification societies, and their international networks of surveyors, have led them to assume another, public service role. Under powers delegated by governments, they enforce the regulations contained in international conventions on safety at sea and protection of the environment. In this case, they carry out the necessary surveys and inspections, and deliver official certificates of conformity to such regulations. Like classification, this is a certification service, by which a ship's compliance with previously established requirements is formally stated.

Classification societies have a dual function with regard to safety at sea :
- They set standards, by issuing Rules and Guidance Notes stipulating technical requirements for ships (cf chapter 7 below) ;
- They perform surveys and inspections to check that ships comply with their own rules and with statutory regulations (cf chapter 22 below).

Classification societies, which came into existence in the early 19th century, are now among key players in the maritime safety system. Their attributions are constantly diversifying to provide a better response to the new challenges of preventing risks at sea. This chapter emphasises the importance of their role and actions, by considering the origins of classification (cf I below), IACS and organisation of the profession (II) and the future of classification societies (III).

I - ORIGIN AND DEVELOPMENT OF CLASSIFICATION SOCIETIES

163. - Historically, classification societies have seen a transformation of their functions within the maritime community. Originally set up by marine insurers as a way of assessing the quality of ships, they gradually became certification organisations, with the task of ensuring that ships conformed to private classification standards and public regulations on safety at sea (2).

(1) J. BELL : "The role of classification in marine safety". 9th Chua Chor Teck Annual Memorial Lecture. Singapore, 13 January 1995.
(2) Ph. BOISSON : "Classification societies and safety at sea. Back to basics to prepare for the future". Marine Policy 1994, 18(5), 363-377.

A - CREATION BY MARINE INSURERS

Classification societies were set up to meet the needs of marine insurers at the beginning of the 18th century. At the time, hull and cargo underwriters worked under very difficult conditions, deprived of any reliable data on which to base their premiums, any periodic statistics on shipwrecks, or any accurate information on ships. Their only recourse was to question shipmasters and seamen on the age and nautical qualities of vessels known to them.

They tended to meet in coffee houses and inns near harbours, where the social atmosphere lent itself to conversation and exchange of information. The most famous of these was the coffee house opened by Edward Lloyd in Tower Street in London, at the end of the 17th century. These premises provided a club frequented by everyone concerned with a sea voyage, including shipmasters, owners, insurance brokers and merchants.

The information that circulated by word of mouth was unreliable, however: assessments of ships varied depending on individual sources, no general picture at all being provided. Sometimes, information was distorted under the influence of unscrupulous shipowners. Sometimes, particularly in England, where "shipnakers" were active, goods insured well beyond their real value were shipped on old vessels which had very little chance of ever reaching their destination.

It was against this background that the first classification societies came into existence.

1. Lloyd's Register

164. - It was in 1760 that leading underwriters and brokers who belonged to Lloyd's Coffee House decided to set up a committee to publish a maritime register. This was intended to supply all the basic information on ships needing insurance, including their principal characteristics, but also other factors of use in assessing the risks to be insured (3).

The oldest edition of this Register still in existence dates from 1764. Later editions, in 1768 and 1775, were published under the auspices of Lloyd's Insurance and Brokerage Society. They soon became indispensable in the task of rating ships. The principal clients were insurers, and they were responsible for the title "Insurers' Register". It was also called the "Green book".

The introduction in 1797 of a new ship classification system, which discriminated against ships built in yards not situated on the River Thames, led shipowners to issue their own rival "New register of shipping" or "Red book" in 1794. However, the initiative was unsuccessful, and both registers joined forces in 1834 under the name of "Lloyd's Register of British and Foreign Shipping".

2. Bureau Veritas

165. - The immediate reason for the establishment of Bureau Veritas was the difficult position of marine insurers on the mainland of Europe.

An unprecedented succession of shipwrecks in the winter of 1821 bankrupted several of the large insurance companies installed in Paris. The subsequent bitter competition among the survivors reduced premiums to a disturbingly low level. It was in this disheartening economic climate that two insurers and a broker founded an "Office of information for marine insurers" in Antwerp, on 2 July 1828. It was renamed "Bureau Veritas" the following year.

(3) G. BLAKE : "Lloyd's Register of shipping 1760-1960". Lloyd's Register, London 1960.

This institution intended to be of use to all sectors of the maritime world, such as shipowners, charterers and seafarers. But its primary responsibility was to inform insurers "how to deal with their competitors, and particularly by preserving them from underwriting risks of bad ships". The first Bureau Veritas Register was published in 1829 as a French version of the Lloyd's Register : "Lloyd's Français". In 1832 the society moved to an address near the Paris Stock Exchange, where so many French insurers were in business (4).

3. American Bureau of Shipping

166. - The forerunner of the American Bureau of Shipping was the American Shipmasters' Association, set up in 1862 by John Divine Jones, President of the Atlantic Mutual Insurance Company, and head of nine other marine insurance companies. The original intention was to organise examinations and issue professional diplomas to masters and officers in the American merchant navy. A few years later, its role was extended to include the survey, rating and registration of merchant ships.

By the end of the 19th century, the society adopted its present name of American Bureau of Shipping (ABS). Its sole concern was to meet the needs of American marine insurance, and the Board of Managers consisted of insurers or those with insurance-related interests. It was not until 1902 that the first representatives of shipowners and shipbuilders were admitted to this managing body (5).

4. Det Norske Veritas

167. - In the early years of the 19th century, Norwegian mutual maritime insurance clubs were trying to develop procedures for classifying ships, in order to verify their constructional qualities. From 1850, closer cooperation among members of the profession showed the need for some harmonisation. In 1859, seven insurance clubs agreed to issue common shipbuilding rules, and decided to set up a classification society together to cater for the Norwegian market. It was founded officially in 1864, as Det Norske Veritas (DNV).

When the first Register appeared in 1865, its clients were not shipowners but underwriters. The statutes included an obligation for any ship insured by these clubs to be classed and surveyed by DNV. When the Arendal club, the most powerful in the country, joined the society in 1869, this considerably strengthened its financial standing, and it began its international expansion (6).

B - DEVELOPMENT OF CLASSIFICATION

168. - The societies were extremely successful in the second half of the 19th century. Classification brought appreciable economic benefits to marine insurers, for whom the high financial value of certain vessels represented a serious risk. Awareness of their actual condition made it possible to bring these risks under control. This method of risk management was based on the award of a "rating" to each ship.

(4) Le Bureau Veritas, Société Internationale de Classification de Navires et d'Aéronefs 1828-1928 - Edition du Centenaire, France (1928).
(5) - "The History of American Bureau of Shipping ABS", USA (1991). Reprint of 125th anniversary issue (1862-1987) with new section for 1988/91.
- S.G. STIANSEN : "The origins and present activities of ABS". Presentation at the American Institute of Marine Underwriters' Seminar on Marine Insurance Issues, 1985, New York, USA (May 1985).
- H.S. KEEFE : "An underwriter looks at classification societies". Presented at the American Institute of Marine Underwriters' Seminar on Marine Insurance Issues, 1985, New York, USA (May 1985).
(6) H.W. ANDERSEN and J.P. COLETT : "Anchor and Balance. Det Norske Veritas 1864-1989" - Cappelens Forlag, Norway, 1989.

Due to various factors, classification was to evolve gradually from this assignment of ratings towards certification. The process became irreversible with the simultaneous emergence of a number of economic, commercial, technical or political factors in the second half of the century.

1. Commercial and economic constraints

The first constraint on classification arose from market forces. Shipowners wanted "term ratings" that would be valid for a reasonably long period, delivered after a complete survey of a vessel or its construction. They wished to have information on what rating would be assigned to their ships prior to publication in the Register, while being certain that, unless something untoward happened, it would remain valid for a number of years.

2. Technical constraints

169. - The introduction of term ratings required fuller regulations and the introduction of a more uniform approach, a kind of universally recognised ship construction code.

Lloyd's Register published its first rules for wooden ships in 1835, Bureau Veritas in 1851, DNV in 1867 and ABS in 1870. For iron ships, the first Lloyd's Register rules came out in 1855, those of Bureau Veritas in 1858, those of DNV in 1871 and those of ABS in 1877.

The appearance of these rules had immediate consequences for classification societies:
- First, it led to a change in the recruitment of surveyors, as the former shipmasters with pragmatic knowledge of ships gave way gradually to merchant navy engineers and mechanics;
- Second, rules reached new clients, since shipyards could now undertake to deliver a ship with a given rating ;
- Finally, the very philosophy of classification changed. rules gradually became the obligatory reference for assessing ship safety, since conformity to their requirements was considered adequate guarantee of such an assessment.

3. Regulatory constraints

170. - The development of statutory services performed for national maritime authorities helped establish the logic of certification as a way forward for classification societies.

In the second half of the 19th century, the leading maritime nations little by little took over from private organisations in regulating some aspects of safety at sea. States coped with the complexities of inspecting ships by delegating appropriate survey powers to classification societies. Lloyd's Register and Bureau Veritas were the first to be thus empowered in 1890 by the United Kingdom Board of Trade to assign freeboard to British ships.

Ultimately, the abrupt changes that affected classification societies took place under powerful market pressures. The diversification of the societies' clientele occurred almost immediately after the introduction of the term rating.

One result of all these upheavals was that rating was finally superseded by the concept of "class" which, in the modern meaning of the term, is the term rating of a ship, in other words its inclusion in the Register under the particular conditions dictated by the rules.

II - IACS AND ORGANISATION OF THE PROFESSION

171. - Classification societies today are characterised by their number and diversity. They differ in size, with the smallest employing only a few surveyors concentrated in certain determined geographical regions, while the largest have a network of surveyors extending over all five continents. They also differ in their legal status, with paragovernmental agencies operating alongside foundations, non-profitmaking associations and private concerns.

However, it is not so much this diversity that is prejudicial to their function as their worldwide proliferation. In 1950 there were fewer than ten clearly identified societies engaged in classification. There are now more than fifty, many of whom do not meet the minimum conditions for performing their role properly. This has resulted in unpardonable inconsistencies in applying safety standards, at one time bringing discredit on the whole profession (7).

Aware of these difficulties, the largest classification societies have joined forces in the International Association of Classification Societies (IACS), and since the Nineties they have made strenuous efforts to regulate the work of classification. There is much at stake: apart from the control of a billion-dollar market in 1996 employing more than ten thousand people (8), the societies need to be given the chance of a more active role in improving the safety of ships.

Table 5 - Statistical profile of major classification societies
(Source : Lloyd's List 5 June 1998)

Class society	Tonnage classified (mgt)		Staff			Exclusive offices
	end 1996	end 1997	Technical office staff	Field surveyors	TOTAL	
American Bureau of Shipping (ABS)	94.07	95.12	332	618	1.548	171
Bureau Veritas (BV)	32.07	33.23	300	700	1.500	420
China Classification Society (CCS)	14.71	15.24	120	810	1.500	51
Croatian Register of Shipping (CRS)	2.56	2.34	49	42	130	10
Det Norske Veritas (DNV)	74.90	76.10	450	750	4.230	300
Germanisher Lloyd (GL)	23.70	26.60	800	460	1.600	145
Hellenic Register of Shipping (HRS)	5.69	5.80	25	85	155	15
Indian Register of Shipping (IRS)	5.79	6.43	85	50	135	11
Korean Register of Shipping (KRS)	15.32	17.35	130	180	434	29
Lloyd's Register of Shipping (LR)	103.20	104.80	860	1.700	4.694	280
Nippon Kaiji Kyokai (Class NK)	98.05	101.76	213	331	925	80
Polish Register of Shipping (PRS)	4.00	5.00	95	140	370	14
Registro Italiano Navale (RINA)	13.84	14.85	← 357 →		517	54

(7) Ph. BOISSON : "Safety at sea, politics and international law. The changing role of classification societies". Bulletin Technique du Bureau Veritas n° 1, March 1994, 57-75.
(8) "Class war - The battle heats up" - Tradewinds, 21 March 1997, 14.

A - ORIGIN AND DEVELOPMENT OF INTERNATIONAL COOPERATION

172. - Classification societies first began to cooperate following the 1930 Conference on Loadlines, which recognised the need for the societies to confer on achieving uniformity in calculating freeboard. Contacts first took the form of international conferences, then specialised working groups (9). Today, IACS is the main channel for such cooperation.

1. Creation of IACS

On 11 September 1969, seven classification societies set up the International Association of Classification Societies (IACS), which was granted consultative status at IMCO in October 1969 (10).

IACS currently has ten members. The seven founder members (ABS, Bureau Veritas, Germanischer Lloyd, Lloyd's Register of Shipping, the Japanese Register Nippon Kaiji Kyokai, Det Norske Veritas, Registro Italiano Navale) have been rejoined by the China Classification Society, the Korean Register of Shipping and the Russian Maritime Register of Shipping.

There are also three associate members, the Croatian Register of Shipping, the Indian Register of Shipping, and the Polish Register Polski Rejestr Statkow (11).

Altogether, IACS members class 95 per cent of world shipping in tonnage (about 400m gross tonnage), and 50 per cent in number of ships (about 40 000). They undertake more than half a million surveys a year in about 1 200 offices throughout the world, with more than 6 000 frontline surveyors (12).

The aims of IACS differ very little from those of IMO. Both are trying to promote the highest possible safety standards at sea and prevent marine pollution; both cooperate with competent international maritime organisations, and both maintain close cooperation with maritime industries worldwide (13).

2. European Association of Classification Societies (EURACS)

The European Association of Classification Societies, founded in 1979, comprises the four societies that have their headquarters in EU countries. Its aim is to work towards improving standards of safety at sea and the prevention of marine pollution, coordinate members' technical standards, and promote uniform interpretation of relevant international conventions (14). EURACS maintains special relations with EU bodies.

3. EEIG Unitas

Three societies, Bureau Veritas, Germanischer Lloyd and the Registro Italiano Navale, decided in April 1993 to set up Unitas, a European economic interest group (EEIG). The main purpose is to strengthen cooperation in three areas : research and development, surveyor retraining, and drafting of classification rules (15).

The first Rules hammered out by all three societies, and published early in 1995, concern high-speed craft.

(9) "Achievements 1968-1998". IACS Briefing n° 7, June 1998.
(10) IMO - Assembly - 6th Session - A VI/29 - 8 August 1969.
(11) Since its re-instatement in 1998. "IACS rethink on Polish society". Lloyd's List, 3rd June 1998.
(12) T-C. MATHIESEN : "The changing role of ship classification societies". SNAME Annual Meeting 97. Ohawa, 1997.
(13) IACS Charter as amended and agreed by the council at its 22nd meeting and 3 May 1989. Art. 1.
(14) EurACS leaflet.
(15) Ph. BOISSON : "Evolution of the total class concept". Safety at Sea International, March 1994, 24-28.

4. LAN Alliance or Super IACS

In March 1995, three of the leading classification societies, LRS, ABS and DNV, announced their intention to introduce eight immediate initiatives and carry out three studies to reinforce safety at sea (16). This plan of action, known as the "LAN" Alliance (17), was accompanied by a threat to implement these new provisions unilaterally at the end of 1995, unless IACS reacted affirmatively(18).

The move worried the profession. IACS had not been consulted beforehand, and this individual action detracted from IACS cohesion and credibility (19). Finally, many of the "get tough" initiatives were already under discussion within IACS, and on the point of being adopted and applied by all members. The matter was settled in June 1995, when the IACS Council adopted seven of the eight measures proposed by the LAN. Five came into force immediately, and two became effective on 1st January 1996 (20).

B - IACS STRUCTURE

173. - IACS is directed by a Council, with the assistance of a General Policy Group (GPG), a permanent Secretariat and working groups (21).

The Council is the governing body. It consists of a senior executive from each member society, and meets twice a year to set policy and general lines of action. Its powers include appointment of the Permanent Secretary, the Quality Secretary and the IACS representative at IMO. Another task is to study the recommendations and reports of working groups, and sign agreements on cooperation with other international organisations. The Council is headed by a Chairman, elected in rotation for a period of one year.

The GPG is a subsidiary body which deals with current IACS business between Council sessions. It comprises a representative of each member society and the permanent IACS representative at IMO, and its job is to monitor the activities and work programme of IMO, prepare Council decisions, supervise the working groups, and administer long-term IACS programmes, reviewing them annually, with priority given to new technologies and survey techniques.

There are about thirty working groups, set up by the Council as the need arises. They are in charge of the bulk of standard-setting work, preparing draft unified rules, drafting answers to requests from IMO, and working out unified interpretations of current international regulations.

The Secretariat, set up in London in 1991 (22), consists of a Permanent Secretary, the permanent representative to IMO, a Quality Secretary and a technical and administrative team of ten (23). Its role is to coordinate the action of the different members, improve IACS outside representation and communications, attend to effective operation of the Quality System Certification Scheme (QSCS), and ensure that IACS internal rules are being observed.

(16) "Class Society link in ship safety move". Lloyd's List, 29 March 1995. "Class societies get tough plan spurs many questions". Tradewinds, 31 March 1995. "Class Impressions". Fairplay, 6 April 1995.
(17) "New confidence, class confidence". Fairplay, 17 August 1995.
(18) "Gauntlet thrown down in class war". Lloyd's List, 29 March 1995.
(19) M. GREY : "Ecumenical attitude to class". Lloyd's List, 19 April 1995.
(20) "Classification Societies. A little discord brings worthwhile results". Shipping World and Shipbuilder, Sept. 1995, 6-12.
(21) J. BELL : "Classification in maritime safety". Marine Transport International, 1995, 11-13.
(22) "Bell to head new IACS secretariat". Lloyd's List, 28 April 1992.
(23) "IACS finds its feet, in London". Tradewinds, 25 August 1995.

C - IACS ORGANISATION

1. Conditions of admission to IACS

174. - IACS has set minimum standards for applicants for membership (24). There are five such conditions: active participation in an IACS working party for more than three years, thirty years' experience of classification, a classed fleet of at least 1 500 ocean-going ships of more than 100 gross tonnage, with an aggregate total of at least 8 million gross tonnage, a technical staff of two hundred surveyors in sole employ, and possession of a currently valid IACS quality system certificate of conformity.

Requirements are less stringent for associate membership : fifteen years' experience of classification, a classed fleet of at least 750 ships with a minimum of 2 million gross tonnage, a technical staff of at least 75 surveyors in sole employ, and the obligation to publish rules in English and a shipping Register.

No new member has joined IACS since 1988, when the Chinese and South Korean Registers were admitted. Two societies are at present planning to acquire associate membership: the Indonesian Bureau of Classification and the Hellenic Register (HRS) (25).

The intention of the Greek society, which has failed to meet the conditions for recognition by the European Commission (26) to apply to join IACS, has roused opposition within the Association, because of the high level of casualties among ships on its Register (27).

Failure to respect IACS rules can lead to temporary or permanent withdrawal of membership. Following an investigation of transfers of class to the Polish Register (28), the Council announced its temporary suspension in May 1997 (29), followed by its readmission as an associate member a year later. IACS thus displays its determination to accept no compromises on maritime safety (30).

2. Quality Assurance System Certification (QSCS)

175. - The development within IACS of a programme for the certification of members' quality assurance systems was considered unavoidable, in order to show pi oof of IACS determination to improve quality (31).

a) QSCS scope and requirements

QSCS covers all safety-related services supplied by societies, including both classification services and statutory services. It operates under the direction of the IACS Quality Secretary, assisted by independent auditors, and it is supervised by a Quality Committee, consisting of representatives of each member society.

QSCS requires a satisfactory initial audit of the quality system of each society, leading to the issue of a certificate of conformity. Audits began in early 1992, and by March 1994 initial three-year certificates had been issued to the eleven members of IACS. After this period, a complete new audit is needed for their renewal.

(24) IACS Procedures. London 1993. 1, Membership.
(25) "Hellenic Register to apply to join IACS". Lloyd's List, 12 June 1996.
(26) "HRS fails EU test". Fairplay, 28 May 1998.
(27) "Push for IACS membership". Seatrade Review, Jan. 1997.
(28) "Expansive Polish Register of Shipping comes under fire". Tradewinds, 21 March 1977.
(29) "IACS suspends polish register". Lloyd's List, 20 May 1997.
(30) "Rescue mission". Lloyd's List, 20 May 1997.
(31) D.W. SMITH : "IACS comes of age". Shipbuilding Technology International 1993, 127-128.

The quality of societies' work is assessed by reference to the stipulations of a certification programme. An annual audit is also required to maintain the validity of the certificate (32).

b) Improvements to QSCS

Several important changes have been made in the initial IACS programme (33). QSCS was progressively aligned with the requirements of standard ISO 9001 in 1994. The scope of intermediate audits and the number of sites to be audited have been increased. QSCS is not confined to a system of checking procedures. With the introduction of internal vertical audits, it is used to focus more closely on quality of services, from the request for services to issue of the requisite certificate. QSCS reference documents take account of IMO requirements, as defined in Resolution A.739, stipulating directives for the authorisation of organisations acting on behalf of the flag administration.

Action has also been taken to reinforce the independence of the system in relation to IACS members. In December 1995, an advisory group was set up to supply the Quality Committee and Council with an impartial opinion on the functioning of QSCS. This body, which became operational in March 1997 (34), consists of representatives of IMO and maritime industries concerned with classification (shipowner and insurance associations). In a report issued in 1996 by an IMO consultant (35), the QSCS programme was described as "substantially complete", compatible with Resolution A.739, and its present development was judged positive.

3. Internal rules

176. - IACS strives to improve its efficiency and credibility in the maritime world by applying very strict internal rules (36). Initiated in the early Nineties, these procedures were strengthened in 1995 on the initiative of the three societies already mentioned. All these measures resulted in a considerable drop in what was regarded as substandard shipping (cf chapter 24).

D - IACS AND IMPROVEMENTS IN SAFETY

177. - IACS can boast of possessing the most advanced experience and knowledge of hull structure and propulsion units. This technical credibility earns it a careful hearing in all international gatherings.

1. IACS participation in standard-setting process

To begin with, IACS performs a fundamental task in drawing up technical standards affecting safety. It attends to the development of unified requirements, while also making a substantial contribution to the work of IMO (37).

(32) IACS : "Quality System Certification Scheme. Quality System Requirements". Approved by IACS Council, June 1991.
(33) "IACS strenghthens its quality system certification scheme". Internat. Bulk Journal, Sept. 1995.
(34) "IACS advisory group set up". Lloyd's List, 20 March 1997.
(35) IMO. MSC 66/23/1, 1st March 1996, Annex.
(36) J. BELL : "Current developments in classification". BIMCO Review, 1996, 121-124.
(37) Ph. BOISSON : "The role of IACS and the prospects for classification". New Directions in Maritime Law. Canadian MLA Conference. Halifax, 2 June 1995.

a) Development of unified requirements

Unified Requirements and standards leading to each society incorporating the same standards remains very time-consuming, because of the technical complexity of world shipping. The formation of thirty or so working groups and *ad hoc* groups within IACS has helped speed up the process. Since 1968, more than 200 unified requirements have been adopted by IACS on the most widely varying subjects, such as minimum longitudinal ship strength standards, fire protection of engine rooms, or inert gas installations on oil tankers. Special effort has been made to improve the safety of bulk carriers (38) (cf chapter 12 below).

b) Contribution to IMO work

178. - The importance of the role of IMO in drawing up international regulations on maritime safety requires no further introduction. Since 1969, when IACS obtained the status of consultative member, the two organisations have pursued a very fruitful collaboration (39). There are two levels of such collaboration. Its observer status enables IACS to attend all IMO meetings and express its opinion on subjects within its scope. Accordingly, representatives of classification societies pay particular attention to discussions within the MSC; the MEPC and subcommittees of both these bodies. IACS also has a permanent representative at IMO, whose role is to inform members of current work and facilitate their participation in various IMO meetings. Such participation is very considerable: in 1994, it was estimated to be more than 245 man/weeks (40).

The IACS contribution to the work of IMO takes various forms. To begin with, it makes a series of comments on work performed by IMO, as when, in the aftermath of the *Estonia* disaster in 1994, it commented on the safety of ro-ro passenger ships. IACS can also submit texts to IMO, arising directly from its own unified requirements. The safety code for the construction and equipment of gas tankers, for example, incorporated many aspects stipulated for classification purposes.

2. IACS and implementation of regulations

179. - One of the basic problems of maritime technical regulations is their implementation by States. IACS makes a significant contribution in this respect.

In general, it can issue a unified requirement containing provisions from an international convention that has not yet come into effect, or an IMO resolution, (which by definition is not mandatory). This transposition of IMO provisions to the class framework helps reduce deadlines for enforcement of IMO instruments.

An example is the Enhanced Survey Programme (ESP) for oil tankers and bulk carriers, which was introduced by IACS in July 1993, two and a half years before the date on which the corresponding amendments to the SOLAS Convention came into force.

Another instance is the early application of the International Safety Management (ISM) Code, where IACS encouraged the early auditing and issuance of certificates. Acting in this way, ahead of regulations and following their adoption, classification societies exert a considerable influence on the progress of standard setting (41).

---

(38) J. BELL : "IACS, London and maritime safety". The Baltic London Focus. Sept. 1996, 62-63.

(39) "IACS and IMO. The essential relationship". IACS Briefing. N° 4 February 1997.

(40) M. BOND : "Hitting safety compliance head-on". Seatrade Review, Jan. 1996, 53-55.

(41) "Class closer to IMO". The Motor Ship, August 1997.

Finally, two decisive factors may be mentioned. IACS members make huge investments in R&D, to finance more than a hundred technical projects focussing on safety at sea (42). Equally considerable efforts are made to provide training (43). These initiatives are of course made necessary by the fast changes in regulations, but they also reflect the determination of classification societies to remain the dedicated technical reference for the maritime community.

III - CLASSIFICATION IN THE FUTURE : THE CHALLENGES OF THE THIRD MILLENNIUM

180. - Their distant origins and longevity could make classification societies believe themselves immutable, protected from the changes and ravages of time. Fortunately, they refrain from trumpeting any such certainty, or displaying over-confidence in a maritime sector that is undergoing drastic reorganisation. As the end of the century approaches, three factors form the backdrop against which the destiny of classification will be played out : the technological revolution, the risks of legal claims and how fees are to be paid. In addition to these three determining factors, there is the problem of short-term image. It is important to reinforce confidence in the institution by removing substandard ships from the world fleet (44).

A - TECHNOLOGICAL CHALLENGES

During the 20th century, classification societies have lost their privileged position within the safety system : they are no longer the only standard-setting authorities, and now have to share this function with states and international organisations. Their monopoly of ship surveying has been eroded by certain private initiatives, which have led to the establishment of networks of surveyors and maritime inspectors of all kinds on an international scale.

The maritime industry can no longer cope with such fragmentation, and it is suffering the drawbacks of a duplication of efforts that results in lost efficiency. The present safety system cannot function on any long-term basis without the help of an undisputed technical authority, capable of providing reliable information on the quality of seaborne transport, quite independently of any commercial, economic or political pressure.

This is precisely where classification societies have a card to play. Their strategy is now directed towards restoring classification to an essential place in the prevention of accidents at sea and protection of the environment. The battle will be waged mainly in the technical field, which constitutes their area of special skill. For the moment, two major trends seem to be emerging: sophistication of working methods, and a total safety approach.

(42) "$ 70 million a year. A class act". The Baltic, Jan. 1998, 37-38.
(43) Over $ 18 million a year an about 11000 man-weeks.
In J. BELL : "IACS-classification for the future". Shipping International Sept./Oct. 1997, 42-46.
(44) D. THOMAS : "IACS restoring faith". Lloyd's List Maritime Asia, Feb. 1993, 33-37.

1. Sophistication of working methods

a) Need for a proactive approach

181. - One of the principal criticisms levelled at classification is its absence of scientific basis. Rules on ship structure are nearly always falling behind requirements, resting as they do entirely on extrapolation from past experience. Previously, this scientific shortcoming was counterbalanced by an attitude of caution, according to which whatever is too strong cannot fail... This measured caution did not prevent the appearance of localised weaknesses, undetected and which could weaken the whole structure.

Lord Carver spoke out against this in his 1992 report: "the systems which have evolved over the last two centuries to enhance safety at sea are not conducted on a scientific basis ; and (...) there are new developments in technology affecting the design, construction and operation of ships which the regulators struggle to keep up with and constantly fall behind as technology develops" (45). The report recommends a system based on a formal safety assessment, the purposes of which would be set by agreement at IMO, and a safety case presented by the operator for each ship (46).

Classification societies initially had reservations about the feasibility of such an approach (47). Recently, they have begun to review their method of classification, to take account of the techniques of risk analysis (48), and incorporate continuous surveys into inspection procedures. This is possible only on three conditions :
- First, they need to adopt a total approach to safety at sea, based on the interdependence of the ship, personnel, operations and management (49) ;
- Next, they have to devise sophisticated analytical methods for real-time assessment of the state of the hull, equipment and installations (50) ;
- Finally, full partnership has to be created with the shipowner (51) ; who, because of his increased responsibilities, cannot make do with a simple client-supplier relationship ; this new dimension will restore to its full place the fundamental role of classification in preventing risks at sea.

b) New philosophies and modes of action

182. - The permanent will for improved safety in shipping has led classification societies to work out other philosophies and modes of action. Computer programmes have been designed to assess the state of the ship, and information systems are used to facilitate worldwide survey data transmission (52).

(45) Safety aspects of ship design and technology. Select Committee on Sciences and Technology, House of Lords, UK Feb. 1992, 11.1, 67.
(46) M. GREY : "The safety case - A new approach to safety". BIMCO Bulletin, 1/93, 18-20.
(47) J.G. BEAUMONT : "Safety case techniques for ships". Foundation for Science and Technology. Lecture at the Royal Society. London, 6 April 1993.
(48) A. SERIDJI : "New risk assessment and risk management techniques". Bulletin Technique du Bureau Veritas. N° 3, Nov. 1996, 45-74.
(49) "Det Norske Veritas : the total safety class". Lloyd's List, 30 Oct. 1997.
(50) "ShipRight is lauched". Fairplay, 19 Feb. 1998.
(51) "BV builds on active partnerships with owners". Lloyd's List, 5 June 1998.
(52) M. BOND : "Class at the touch of a button". Seatrade Review, Jan. 1997, 53-57.

• **Computer tools**

The development of information technologies has led classification societies to develop systems for modelling ship designs, and optimising their structure, so that they will be safer. ABS introduced its SafeHull in 1993 (53), LRS ShipRight in 1994 (54), DNV Nauticus Hull in 1995 (55), and Bureau VeritasVeriStar Hull in 1995 (56).

It is difficult today to imagine all the future consequences of mass use of computer tools in classification procedures. However, it may be safely assumed that classification of ships will move from a corrective to a preventive standpoint (57), with the twofold effect, first of reducing the standard-setting activities of classification societies (58), and second of bringing about a radical change in relations between shipbuilders and shipowners (59).

• **Information technologies**

In response to the challenges of the information age, leading classification societies have moved towards a new conception of data transmission processes (60). Systems such as SafeNet (61), Class Direct (62) or VeriStar Info (63) have been introduced, with the aim of improving the conditions under which surveyors operate, by standardising surveys. This has been made possible by the generalised use of laptop computers, which are becoming the essential working tools of a surveyor. Another advantage is to provide shipowners with online consultation facilities concerning the class status and real state of their vessels, thereby making fleet management easier.

These new communication methods will bring about far-reaching changes in the way classification societies work and organise themselves: the need to work within a network should lead to a redistribution of tasks and responsibilities within organisations operating on a global scale.

Another revolution is imminent in the world of classification : databases on the technical condition of a ship (64) and compliance with the ISM Code (65) would be made accessible to third parties with a legitimate interest, such as port states and insurers. This might be the most important change, introducing an attitude of information sharing and transparency within the maritime community (66), which for centuries has been secretive and even obsessed with confidentiality (67).

(53) "ABS charts the way in calculating ship safety". Lloyd's List, 9 sept. 1993.
(54) "ShipRight Design, construction and lifetime ship case procedures". 100 AI. N° 1. 1994, 4-7.
(55) "DNV introduces Nauticus Hull". Maritime Monitor, 21 March 1995.
(56) "BV lauches cost-cutting datasystem". Lloyd's List, 7 Dec. 1995.
(57) "Iarossi demands safety action". Lloyd's List, 16 March 1998.
(58) "Class solutions. Clever systems point the way". Fairplay, 5 Sept. 1996.
(59) "Classification societies. Computers rule, ok". Fairplay, 18 August 1994.
(60) P. de LIVOIS, A. SERIDJI, S. MELLO : "Classification societies in the information age". Bulletin Technique du Bureau Veritas. N° 2, July 1996, 5-18.
(61) "ABS system offers vessel technical data". Lloyd's List, 28 Sept. 1996.
(62) "LR goes global with new survey systems". Lloyd's List, 6 June 1997.
(63) L. MONNET : "Veristar Info, a new system of communication betwen Bureau Veritas and its clients". Bulletin Technique du Bureau Veritas, n° 2, July 1996, 35-39.
(64) "IACS to ease access to class information". Lloyd's List, 19 May 1995.
(65) "IACS database". Lloyd's List 27 Sept. 1996.
(66) "A new transparency". Seatrade Review, 21 March 1997.
(67) Ph. BOISSON : "Information technologies. New prospects for maritime transport". Bulletin Technique du Bureau Veritas. N° 2, July 1996, 3-4.

2. Total class concept

183. - What should be the boundaries of the action of classification societies ? The question is currently much discussed within the sector. Traditionalists remain true to a restrictive concept of class which, they feel, should be reserved exclusively for the establishment of rules on the design, structure and certain items of equipment of a ship (68). In contrast, reformers propose a total approach to classification, integrating the human factor and ship operational standards (69).

The increasing attention paid to the human factor in safety regulations has encouraged classification societies to argue for a total approach to safety (70) :
-   In 1992, DNV launched the New Classification Concept (NCC), incorporating the main IMO safety conventions in its rules (71).
-   In 1994, Bureau Veritas developed its Total Safety Concept, in order to offer the maritime industry all information on the ship: structural assessment, safety management certification by the shipowner, crew qualification and certification of operational standards (72).
-   In 1997, ABS published a Guidance Notes on the application of ergonomics to marine systems (73), examining a relatively small number of important features where design can contribute to the prevention of human-element accidents (74).

In such an approach of total class service, it is important to emphasise that the system that will prevail will have an impact on the image of classification societies, and on their legal and financial situation.

B - LEGAL ISSUES OF LIABILITY

184. - In the last few years the legal risks run by classification societies have increased significantly. The CMI is currently seeking solutions to these problems, the implications of which could imperil the very existence of classification societies.

1. Increase in legal risks

The last twenty years have seen a huge increase in the number of lawsuits against classification societies. Several factors explain this trend. The societies are easy prey for those seeking legal redress. Their dense international networks allow them to operate anywhere in the world, and therefore be sued before any national jurisdiction. Claimants are tempted to "go shopping", and choose the court which is most likely to award the most substantial financial damages. In this respect, US courts clearly offer the most tempting prospect.

Most societies cover themselves against third party liability by means of insurance. This extended solvency increases the risk of legal action, encouraging plaintiffs to seek reparation of their loss in what they see as the defendants' deep pockets. Oddly, the risk of legal action is intensified by the traditional mechanisms of maritime law, which provides the owner of a ship with a legal limit on his liability. In order to break through this ceiling on

(68) "What class societies do". Lloyd's Ship Manager, Feb. 1997, 3.
(69) "Back to basics". Fairplay , 17 August 1995, 34-35.
(70) "A total approach to safety at sea". Lloyd's List, 24 June 1996.
(71) "Det Norske takes step to simplify the rules". Lloyd's List, 9 July 1992.
(72) P. de LIVOIS : "Towards a global concept of safety at sea". Bulletin Technique du Bureau Veritas. N° 4, Dec. 1994, 5-14.
(73) "ABS backs the human approach". Lloyd's Ship Manager, Feb. 1998, 50.
(74) M. GREY : "Ergonomics - A secret of good design". Lloyd's List, 14 Jan. 1998.

compensation, insurers, charterers and victims of an accident at sea or oil pollution can sue third parties who are alleged to have contributed to the occurrence of the damage. Classification societies are particularly attractive third parties, because there is no limitation on their liabilities (75).

Classification societies play a more important role than in the past in ship safety. In legal terms, this role has been confirmed by the new rule 3-1 of chapter II-1 of the SOLAS Convention, amended in 1995, which makes classification mandatory (76). In addition, classification society services are no longer confined to technical assessment of the ship. With the enforcement of the ISM Code, they are increasingly involved in its management and daily operations. There is a danger that these new functions may expose them to a whole new battery of lawsuits brought by third parties, such as insurers and charterers (77).

Finally, it is clear than insurance is no panacea for legal dangers. Cover of the civil liability of classification societies is capped at a level that may vary depending on organisations. Under no circumstances can their insurance cover large disasters. The gigantic nature of potential claims reveals the frailty of insurance-based protection. If the societies that are striving to limit risks at sea are to have their long-term future preserved, other paths may need to be explored (78).

2. CMI initiatives

185. - CMI has realised the problem. Anxious to harmonise maritime rules and practice worldwide, it is trying to meet the legal concerns of classification societies, currently faced with a disturbing proliferation of claims and disputes. Since 1992, a Classification Society Joint Working Group (CSJWG), comprising representatives of IACS, maritime industries (ICS, ICCC, IGP&I, IUMI and OCIMF) and IMO, has met about fifteen times to seek solutions to the problem (79).

Two possibilities have been examined so far: one concerns classification society liability towards third parties, the other their liability towards their clients (80).

As regards tort, the CSJWG therefore thought of formulating "principles of conduct", which lay down relevant standards of performance for all classification societies, regardless of their status, and whether or not they belong to IACS. Covering classification and also statutory services, these principles provide a reference that allow a society's performance to be gauged in different cases. Observance of these standards furnishes a presumption that the society has not been negligent in performing its services. Following an accident, the claimant would need to show proof either that the society involved in the accident has not observed the principles of conduct, or that these principles were absolutely deficient. The group also considered an amendment to the 1976 LLMC Convention on the limitation of liability for maritime claims, in order to introduce a limitation on liability in favour of classification societies. This idea, which remains a long-term objective of the CSJWG, has not been taken up, because of the huge difficulties of revising international agreements.

---

(75) Ph. BOISSON : "Classification society liability : Maritime law principles must be requestion ?". Sydney II - Documents of the conference. Annuaire 1994 du CMI, 235-252.
(76) C. HOBBS : "Great strides forward by class societies". Lloyd's List, 19 March 1997.
(77) P. RODGERS : "Classification societies facing a whole new world of liabilities". Lloyd's List, 26 may 1997.
(78) F.L. WISWALL : "Responsabilities and liabilities of classification societies in the 21st century". Paper for the annual members' meeting of the Swedish Club, Gothenburg, 8 June 1995.
(79) "Societies under pressures". Lloyd's List, 24 Jan. 1997.
(80) "Joint Working Group on a study of issues re classification society". Report London, 10 March 1997. Annuaire 1996 du CMI. Antwerp I. Documents for the Centenary Conference, 328-342.

As regards contract law, CMI has drawn up a series of model clauses for inclusion in conventions signed with national administrations and private contracts with shipowners. These clauses, implementation of which is left to each classification society, set down the various obligations of the two parties and the resulting conditions of liability. More specifically, they provide for exclusion of any liability for indirect losses incurred by the shipowner (cf article 8) and a limit on compensation - two points on which CMI has not yet been able to reach agreement (81).

C - FINANCIAL INDEPENDENCE

1. Need for independence

186. - The sharpest criticism against classification societies has targetted the real conditions of their independence within the maritime community. Attention has been drawn successively to the legal status of some of them (82), the lack of representative character in their management structure (83), and their arrangements for remuneration. This last issue has probably raised the greatest argument in the last ten years. Some commentators consider that the present system, in which classification is remunerated by fees paid by clients is unsatisfactory, generating an "unanswerable conflict of interest" (84). Societies have to juggle two totally opposed requirements: inflexibility in enforcing safety standards, and flexibility, in the form of a degree of indulgence towards certain clients, particularly shipowners who class a large part of their fleet on the same register.

Another drawback is the confidentiality of information on the safety of ships. In their relations with shipowners, classification societies have a contractual obligation of confidentiality, which stops them divulging certain items of information to other parties (85). IACS recently adopted several measures to improve the transparency of classification operations. Since January 1996, certain technical information on class and statutory inspections has been available to entities with a legitimate interest in maintaining ship safety, such as flag States, port States and insurers (86). Since September 1996, a database on implementation of the ISM Code, containing a list of ships meeting ISM requirements, has been available on the Internet (87).

2. New ways of paying class fees

Several systems have been worked out to alter the system by which classification services are paid for. None of them has so far obtained sufficient support.

First, there was the idea of entrusting an international organisation such as IMO with the task of paying classification societies (88). This suggestion seems unrealistic, given the limited financial resources of such intergovernmental organisations and their priorities (89).

---

(81) F. WISWALL : "Classification societies issues considered by the Joint Working Group". The International Journal of Shipping Law, Part 4, Dec. 1997, 171-187.
(82) "Class societies and the market". Trade Winds, 12 June 1998.
(83) - R. GOSS : "IACS move a welcome one". Lloyd's List, 4 August 1995.
(84) J. PRESCOTT : "An unanswerable conflict of interest". Lloyd's List, 15 oct. 1987.
(85) Tor. MATHIESEN : "The classification society. A nucleus of future information sharing". Shipping 95, Stamford, 27th March 1995.
(86) "IACS to ease access to class information". MER, August 1995.
(87) "IACS database". Lloyd's List 27 Sept. 1996.
(88) "A vision for the future of classification". MER, October 1994.
(89) "IACS helps standing of classification societies". Lloyd's List, 6 June 1997.

Next, it was suggested that classification fees should be paid by flag States. This would mean combining statutory and classification requirements in a single set of rules, which is not currently the case. There are also practical problems in implementation, because of the very different standards of organisation of states and their national administrations.

A third solution would be a subscription system, paid by insurers and other parties concerned with information on the condition and safety of ships, such as shippers or bankers (90).

3. Back to basics

187. - This third hypothesis, probably the least utopian, in fact represents a return to the original system which was abandoned in 1836. It would have the advantage of putting a stop to the duplication of inspections and the worldwide proliferation of different networks of surveyors. However, two obstacles have to be overcome.

First, the insurance sector has serious reservations about again becoming the elected client of classification societies. These reservations are based on the difficulty of devising a payment system that could be incorporated into the framework of annually renewable insurance policies (91).

Next, a change would be needed in the nature and content of classification society services, in order to respond more accurately to the needs of their possible future clients. It is no longer a matter of offering Yes/No class, stating that a ship meets or fails to meet standards, but rather, as was originally the case, rating units in service, with differentiated classes, quantifying both technical and operational risks of all kinds - and this would be a preliminary to any sea voyage.

Ultimately, the question that arises is whether two activities, arising out of different logics and philosophies, are compatible, in other words whether an organisation can simultaneously certify a ship's conformity to various regulatory requirements, and assess its level of safety by assigning a differential rating.

4. An approach to differential classification

The appearance of programmes to assess the condition of ships may be the sign of a change in the way of approaching the job of classification. The Condition Assessment Programmes (CAP) introduced in the early Nineties, at the request of major tanker charterers, provide a rating system based on four levels. The CAP assesses the state of the ship by reference to two types of data: design factors and survey findings (93).

Although there is no unanimity within the maritime community (93), this purely voluntary technical assistance service has had some commercial success (94). In 1996, it was estimated that three hundred oil tankers, mainly old ships, amounting to 5 per cent of the world tanker fleet, had undergone a CAP (95). CAP methods and rating scales, developed in a disparate way by the major classification societies, were recently harmonised (96).

(90) "Class societies should not work for the owners". Lloyd's List, 12 Oct. 1996.
(91) "Lindfelt calls for classification restructure". Lloyd's List, 12 June 1995.
(92) "Vela gets tough on old tankers". Lloyd's List, 8 April 1994.
(93) "Classification societies are urged to drop CAPS". Lloyd's List, 12 March 1997.
(94) "CAP get good reception from owners". MER, Dec. 1997, 18.
(95) "CAP harmonisation. Top classification societies end confusion". Fairplay, 27 June 1996.
(96) Class societies to harmonise tanker rating schemes". Lloyd's List, 3 July 1996.

CONCLUSION : new goals for IACS

188. - Faced with the three major challenges, technical, legal and financial, that currently confront classification societies, what will be the role and contribution of IACS ? Are its present structure and organisation adequate to deal with its new role ?

First, it should be recognised that, since it was set up in 1968, IACS has consistently adapted to a changing environment. A major step was taken in the early Nineties, with the setting-up of the permanent Secretariat and the Quality System Certification Scheme. This overhaul of the IACS setup helped restore the credibility of classification. More than ever today, IACS is perceived as a unique repository of technical expertise on the issue of ship safety (97).

For the present, there is a lot of work in the pipeline. Cooperation needs to be reinforced among all members, particularly the smaller ones, in order to continue raising the level of quality. The increasingly numerous standards and rules need to be simplified and harmonised. A safety culture needs to be encouraged within the maritime industry. One thing has today become certain: IACS cannot reach its goals in the short and medium term unless it remains strong and well organised (98).

(97) "Class milestones". Lloyd's List, 8 June 1998.
(98) E. PAPALEPIS : "Strong and organised IACS viewed as important". Lloyd's List, 30 June 1998.

CHAPTER 7

International regulations

189. - The safety of shipping is at present governed principally by international rules and standards. As an integral part of international public law, they conform to its modes of production and implementation.

The world community consists of equal and sovereign States. This concept of sovereign equality is fundamental in understanding the mechanisms by which international law is established. Whereas countries see to compliance with their own national laws, there is no international legislative entity to exercise regulatory powers over States. Everything rests on the acceptance of common standards by each of them (1).

International regulations on safety at sea are no exception to this rule. A State is bound by standards generated at an international level only by virtue of its own commitment to them, and only to the extent of such a commitment. This readiness or acceptance may be expressed in different ways. The commonest is a treaty, negotiated on a multilateral basis.

This chapter is more specifically concerned with what the law of the sea refers to as "generally accepted" international rules, standards, regulations, procedures and practices. The 1982 Law of the Sea (LOS) Convention does not define these terms and expressions, the sense and special meaning of which remain difficult to determine (2).

One thing is certain : even though IMO is designated by name in only one article of the LOS Convention, it is implicitly acknowledged to be the proper body to draw up international regulations on safety at sea and protection of the marine environment (3). Its role is defined in article 2 of the 1948 Geneva Convention on the International Maritime Consultative Organization (IMCO), later known as the International Maritime Organization (IMO):

a) (...) "consider and make recommendations upon matters"(within its attributions) ;
b) provide for the drafting of conventions, agreements, or other suitable instruments, and recommend these to governments and to intergovernmental organisations, and convene such conferences as may be necessary".

Conventions and recommendations do not have the same value in international law. Only conventions are binding on States. This legal consequence can create difficulties for their adoption, enforcement or amendment (cf I below). Recommendations and other instruments not contained in conventions are more flexible, but can also raise problems regarding their exact legal bearing and practical effectiveness (II).

(1) J. COMBACAU and S.SUR : "Droit international public" - Montcrestien, Paris, 1993, 23.
(2) B. VUKAS : "Generally accepted international rules and standards". 23rd annual conference of the LOS Institute, 12-15 June 1989 on the theme : "Implementation of the Law of the Sea Convention through international institutions". A. Soons editeur, 405-421.
(3) - T. TREVES : "The role of universal international organizations in implementing the 1982 UN Law of the Sea Convention" in "Implementation of the Law of the Sea - op.cit" 14-37.
- On the relationship between IMO and the LOS Convention. See IMO, LEG/MISC/2, 6 Oct. 1997.

I - CONVENTIONS AND BINDING INTRUMENTS

190. - A convention is any type of international agreement concluded in written form between States, and legally binding on them, by virtue of the principle *pacta sunt servanda* ("agreements are to be honoured").

In IMO practice, three expressions are used for such instruments :
- "Convention" is the term for most of the treaties adopted under IMO auspices ;
- "Agreement" is confined rather to commitments with a more limited scope ;
- "Protocol" applies to instruments amending the provisions of a convention which has not yet come into force.

A - ADOPTION OF CONVENTIONS

Unlike other UN specialised agencies, IMO does not have the power to adopt international conventions. It may only recommend, incite or persuade States to adopt draft conventions. Only a diplomatic conference can create an instrument with mandatory force At this first stage in international legislation, IMO possesses major prerogatives during the preparation of international conferences, although almost no powers are left to it when they actually take place.

1. Preparatory work

a) Principal steps

191. - The procedure for preparing convention texts comprises four steps :
- Proposals for regulations are submitted to IMO, by a State or group of States, or by an international organisation. These proposals are generally drawn up by committees, which meet very frequently. But other approaches are possible, such as the formation of an *ad hoc* working group, or investigation by a specialised subcommittee.
- The working group or subcommittee examines the proposal, decides whether it is well-founded, submits it to its main technical committee, and to the deliberative bodies of IMO, namely the Assembly or the Council.
- Once authorisation has been given by the Assembly or the Council, as the case may be, the subcommittee or working group may move to the third step, of making a detailed examination of the question, and asking States and international organisations possessing consultative status at IMO for any relevant advice, opinions or information to help it complete its task.
- The final draft is sent to the Council or Assembly, which then takes a solemn decision in the form of a resolution, and calls a diplomatic conference, which all States are invited to attend, with a view to adopting the proposed provisions.

b) Importance of preparatory work

The time needed to draft a convention can vary considerably, depending as it does both on the complexity of the point at issue, and on the time needed to obtain a consensus. This can range from eight months (for the 1978 SOLAS and MARPOL protocols) to five years (for the 1978 STCW Convention).

The extent of this work should not be underestimated. IMO plays a vital role at this preliminary stage in lawmaking. Its duty is to define the guiding principles of the debate, and also to encourage the emergence of a consensus. Any excessive haste could be fatal to a draft convention. If the text is inadequately prepared, the whole diplomatic conference could end in failure, as happened at the 1984 conference on compensation for damage caused by dangerous goods (4).

2. Diplomatic conferences

192. - IMO convenes diplomatic conferences. These are sent to all IMO member States, and to UN members and specialised agencies. Open to all governments, these events have a global dimension. States are treated on an equal footing : they may be represented by delegations or by observers. Intergovernmental and non-governmental organisations are invited to send observers, in order to provide national delegations with technical advice.

Once convened by IMO, the conference becomes an international body in its own right. The conference remains in control of its own general organisation, even if it is held at IMO headquarters. It elects its own chairman and vice-chairmen, and sets up its commissions, the number of which depends on topics on the agenda. It decides on its own organisational rules. The text can then be examined and discussed, first at specialised level, and then at plenary session debates.

The draft text is sent to governments and invited organisations before the conference, so that they may submit their comments. When these have been considered, the text is amended, to produce a draft that will be acceptable to most of the States attending the conference. When the convention has been agreed, it is adopted by the conference, and registered with the Secretary-General of IMO, who sends out copies to governments for final acceptance.

Diplomatic conferences often witness bitter arguments among delegations. The technical precision of the standard can lose all objective significance if the vital interests of certain States are affected. Differences may arise either about the future content of regulations, or about their scope of application. In either case, technical discussions are overtaken by political and economic considerations (5).

Two methods have been adopted to settle these disagreements. One way is to examine in commission the amendments proposed by delegations, for every single regulation. After a great deal of political manoeuvring, *ad hoc* majorities emerge. Another method is to issue simple recommendations which governments are then free to adopt and adapt to suit them, alongside the binding regulations.

B - ENTRY INTO FORCE OF CONVENTIONS

193. - Adoption of a convention is only the first step in the standard-setting process. It does not guarantee that internationally accepted rules and standards will in fact come into effect. Two preconditions are necessary for them to become enforceable : first, each State has solemnly to declare its commitment and readiness to ratify the convention ; second, certain conditions laid down in the convention for its implementation must be met (6).

---

(4) Ph. BOISSON : "Marchandises dangereuses. L'OMI sur la voie d'une convention" - JMM, 3 May 1991, 1126-1128.
(5) Y. ROCQUEMONT : "Les travaux de la conférence de Londres de 1960 sur la sauvegarde de la vie humaine en mer" - NTM 1961, 42-47.
(6) "The Conventions and other treaty instruments adopted under the auspices of the International Maritime Organisation". Focus on IMO, April 1989.

1. Statement of commitment

The convention remains open for signature by States, normally for a twelve-month period. They may become parties to the convention by :
- signature without reservation as to ratification, acceptance or approval ;
- signature subject to ratification, acceptance or approval, followed by ratification, acceptance or approval ;
- accession.

Consent may be expressed by signature where the treaty provides that signature shall have effect. The intention of the State to give that effect to signature appears from the full powers of its representatives or was expressed during the negotiations (Vienna Convention on the Law of Treaties, 1969, Article 12.1).

A State may also sign a treaty "subject to ratification, acceptance or approval". In such a situation, signature does not signify the consent of a State to be bound by the treaty.

Most multilateral treaties contain a clause providing that a State may express its consent by signature subject to ratification. In such a situation signature must be followed up by the depositing of an instrument of ratification with the depositary of the treaty.

The words "acceptance" and "approval" basically mean the same as ratification, but they are less formal and non-technical and might be preferred by some States which could have constitutional difficulties with the term ratification.

Accession is the method used by a State to become a party to a treaty which it did not sign whilst the treaty was open for signature.

2. Specific conditions for enforcement

Each IMO convention sets is own conditions for enforcement. Usually, the deposit of a number of instruments with the Secretary-General constitutes the starting point for implementation deadlines. These enable signatory States to take all the necessary steps to incorporate international regulations into their national legal system.

The setting of preconditions for the enforcement of conventions is a complex operation: conditions must be flexible enough to ensure that the convention can come into force as quickly as possible, while on the other hand it must be ensured that a large majority of the world fleet will from the start apply the new rules. Safety standards are meaningless unless they are adopted universally.

These opposing considerations explain the compromise solutions generally adopted by diplomatic conferences, which impose a certain number of ratifications and a minimum total tonnage (cf table 6).

C - REVISION OF CONVENTIONS

194. - Maritime technologies are progressing apace, which means not only that new conventions need to be drawn up to take account of all the changes, but also that existing provisions need regular revision. This updating involves the amendment of existing conventions by means of protocols or amendments :
- the protocol method is generally used to amend instruments that have not yet come into force, or to change the provisions of an existing treaty which cannot be covered by the tacit amendment procedure (cf below) ;
- more commonly, amendments are added, for express or tacit acceptance.

Table 6 - Main IMO conventions on marine safety
(Sources : Focus on IMO Conventions. Status at 1st Jan. 1998)

Titre	Yer of adoption	Requirement for entry into force	Entry into force	Contracting Parties +% world tonnage
SOLAS Convention	1974	25 States whose combined merchant fleets are not less than 50 % of world gross tonnage	25 May 1980	137 + 98.27 %
SOLAS Protocol	1978	25 States whose combined merchant fleets are not less than 50 % of world gross tonnage	1 May 1981	90 + 91.96 %
SOLAS Procotol	1988	15 States + 50 % world gt	–	28 + 41.73%
LL Convention	1966	15 States including 7 with not less than 1 mgt	21 July 1968	141 + 98.19 %
LL Protocol	1988	15 States with 50 % world gt	–	28 + 41.61 %
COLREG Convention	1972	15 States with not less than 65 % world fleet in number of ships or gt of vessels of 100 gt and over	15 July 1977	131 + 96.20 %
STCW Convention	1978	25 States with not less than 59 % of world gt	28 April 1984	130 + 97.55 %
SAR Convention	1979	15 States	22 June 1985	56 + 49.11 %
Intervention Convention	1969	15 States	6 May 1975	72 + 66.59 %
MARPOL + Protocol	1973	15 States with not less than 50 % of world gt of merchant shipping	2 Oct. 1983	104 + 93.49 %
Protocol	1978	As above	2 Oct 1983	104 + 93.49 %
Annex I	1978	As above	2 Oct 1983	104 + 93.49 %
Annex II	1978	As above	6 April 1987	104 + 93.49 %
Annex III	1978	As above	1 July 1992	85 + 78.22 %
Annex IV	1978	As above	1 July 1992	70 + 41.47 %
Annex V	1978	As above	31 Dec. 1988	87 + 82.03 %

1. Express acceptance procedure

Most IMO conventions provide for two amendment procedures, one within IMO, the other involving an international conference. For example, article VIII of the 1974 SOLAS Convention indicates the two ways of amending non-technical parts of the text :

•**Amendments after consideration within IMO** (SOLAS article VIIIb)

Any amendment proposed by a contracting State is submitted to the MSC for examination. Amendments are adopted by a two thirds majority of the contracting States present and voting in the MSC, which is broadened for the purpose to include non-IMO members. Amendments are then communicated to all contracting governments for acceptance. They come into effect on the date on which they are accepted by two thirds of contracting governments.

• **Amendments after consideration by a conference** (SOLAS article VIIIc)

The proposed change must concurred in by an least one third of the contracting States.

In this case, IMO calls an international conference to consider changes. The amendment is adopted by a two thirds majority of the States present and voting.

The express acceptance procedure raised no problem in the past, when most internat-ional treaties were ratified by a relatively limited number of States. Unfortunately, it proved quite inadequate by the Sixties, with the huge increase in the number of newly independent countries and the corresponding rise in States which were parties to multilateral conventions, and whose express acceptance it proved almost impossible to obtain.

The SOLAS Convention of 1960, which contained this express acceptance procedure for its amendments, was amended in this way in 1966, 1967, 1968, 1969, 1971 and 1973. None of these amendments was able to meet the conditions needed to come into effect, namely express acceptance by two thirds of the parties In 1974, IMO was forced to draw up a new instrument, incorporating all the changes made in the initial text, and introducing a new amendment procedure (7).

2. Tacit acceptance procedure

195. - From 1972, faced with the multiplicity of new problems calling for an urgent solution, the pace of technical progress in the maritime sector, and the unwieldiness of procedures for revising its conventions, IMO introduced a tacit acceptance procedure into technical conventions adopted under its auspices (cf table 7).

Table 7 - Amendment procedures for IMO convention
(Source : IMO News, N° 4 1994)

CONVENTION		ADOPTION	VOTING RIGHTS	ACCEPTANCE
LL 66 TM 69	Articles Annex	CSM Assembly „	MSC members IMO members „	Explicit „
COLREG 72	Articles Rules	Conference MSC Assembly	Parties MSC members OMI + Parties	No provisions Tacit
CSC 72	Articles Annex	MCS Assembly „	MSC + Parties IMO + Parties „	Explicit „
MARPOL 73/78	Articles Annex Appendix	MEPC „ „	Only Parties „ „	Explicit Tacit/explicit Tacit
SOLAS 74 STCW 78 LL PROT 88 SFV 77/93 }	Articles Annex*	MCS „	Only Parties „	Explicit Tacit

* For SOLAS 74, amendments to chapter I are the same as for articles.

a) Definition

The principle is simple: instead of stipulating that an amendment comes into force after being accepted by two thirds of the contracting parties, the new procedure provides for it to come into effect on a given date, unless a certain number of contracting parties raise object-ions before that date.

As regards the 1974 SOLAS Convention, for instance, an amendment to its technical appendices, except for chapter I, containing general provisions, "shall be deemed to have

(7) Y. SASAMURA : "34 years of IMO". IMO News n° 4, 1993.

been accepted (...) at the end of two years from the date on which it is communicated to contracting governments for acceptance. (...) However, if within the specified period either more than one third of contracting governments, or contracting governments the combined merchant fleets of which constitute not less than 50 per cent of the gross tonnage of the world's merchant fleet notify the (...) Organisation that they object to the amendment, it shall be deemed not to have been accepted" (article VIIIb vi 2).

b) Advantages

The tacit acceptance procedure offers several advantages. The date of entry into force is known to all concerned as soon as the amendment is adopted. All parties to the convention are invited to the amendment conference, and in general IMO measures are adopted by consensus. Although the contracting governments are entitled to reject any amendment, in practice very few of them have done so. They cannot complain that decisions have been forced upon them. This procedure is generally confined to technical provisions, which are rather less controversial than regulations involving political or economic advantages. Tacit acceptance allows amendments to come into force with the necessary speed at an international level, something that is impossible when conventional procedures are adopted.

The tacit acceptance procedure has greatly hastened the amendment process. For instance, the amendments to the SOLAS convention adopted by IMO in April 1988, shortly after the *Herald of Free Enterprise* capsized, came into effect on 22 October 1989, barely a year and a half after their adoption, thanks to a special procedure reserved for specially urgent matters (8).

3. Accelerated amendment procedure

196. - IMO recently embarked on an attempt to reduce further the time needed for amendments to the SOLAS Convention to come into effect. Under the existing text, draft amendments must be circulated to governments six months prior to adoption, and cannot enter into force until at least eighteen months after such adoption.

At its 62nd session, the MSC agreed to a proposal by the Secretary-General to reduce these periods in exceptional cases. If the first circulation period could be shortened to three months, and the waiting period to twelve months, the lapse of time between publication of a text and its implementation would be cut from twenty-four to fifteen months. The MSC agreed that amendments to this effect could be brought into force by tacit acceptance. This decision aroused serious controversy at the SOLAS conference of May 1994 (9).

After lengthy debate, the conference finally adopted a recommendation on an accelerated procedure to be applied in exceptional circumstances. Resolution 4 States that a conference of contracting governments can reduce from twelve to six months the period that must elapse before an amendment to technical chapters of the SOLAS Convention is assumed to have been accepted (10).

4. Towards greater IMO involvement

The other solution to the problem of revising conventions would consist of conferring wider powers on IMO for the adoption and enforcement of amendments. This possibility already exists in other IGOs, like FAO, ILO and WHO (11).

---

(8) "Tacit vs. explicit acceptance" - IMO News, n° 3, 1994, 5.
(9) "US move brings IMO safety split". Lloyd's List, 19 May 1995.
(10) "A summary of IMO Conventions". Focus on IMO, Jan. 1997, 11-12.
(11) Th. MENSAH, Ch. ZIMMERLI : "L'activité réglementaire de l'OMCI", SFDI, Toulouse conference on establishing public international law. Pedone, Paris 1975, 94.

An initial response was provided in 1975 when the convention setting up IMO was amended : the new article 15l allows the Assembly to take decisions on convening an international conference, or "follow any other appropriate procedure for the adoption of international conventions or of amendments to any international conventions". Seen as important by some commentators (12), this power to choose procedures still fails to offer a solution to the fundamental problem of acceptance of treaty amendments by the States involved.

D - IMPLEMENTATION OF CONVENTIONS

197. - Implementation of international conventions is the responsibility of the States that have ratified them. This fundamental principle of international public law is subject in practice to numerous exceptions.

1. Legal principles

Conventions, agreements and protocols are subject to the common law principle of *pacta sunt servanda*, recalled in article 26 of the Vienna Convention on treaties, and according to which an effective treaty is binding on the parties and must be implemented by them in good faith.

Each convention defines the content and exact bearing of the obligations it contains. An example is article 1 of the 1974 SOLAS Convention, which lays down two requirements:

"a)   The contracting governments undertake to give effect to the provisions of the present Convention and the annex thereto, which shall constitute an integral part of the present Convention. (...)

b)   The contracting governments undertake to promulgate all laws, decrees, orders and regulations and to take all other steps which may be necessary to give the present Convention full and complete effect, so as to ensure that, from the point of view of safety of life, a ship is fit for the service to which it is intended."

On several occasions, the IMO Secretary-General has spoken out on the importance of national regulations : "IMO's standards must be effectively applied and that is possible only through legislation. Legislation is the key to success. The state must be behind our conventions" (13).

The obligation on contracting States is not only to incorporate convention provisions into their national legal system. It also involves ensuring that safety standards are observed clearly, precisely, adequately, and in harmony with the actions of other States. Effective application also requires the state to have an adequate legislative and regulatory apparatus, as well as a maritime authority with enough staff to oversee the enforcement of standards on board ships.

2. Practical difficulties

198. - In reality, States do not always comply properly with these obligations. The enforcement of international conventions on safety at sea raises many problems. Internation-

(12) J. DUTHEIL DE LA ROCHERE : "Une institution spécialisée renaissante : la nouvelle Organisation Maritime Internationale". AFDI, 1976, 454.
(13) "Legislation the key to success". Lloyd's List, 24 Sept. 1987.

al regulations take a very long time to be incorporated into the national legal system of each State, and enforcement regulations are too uneven and different (14).

a) Slow pace of regulatory process

Two problems need to be considered : the coming into effect of a convention, and its actual enforcement by a State that has ratified it.

• Implementation deadlines
Very few conventions come into effect immediately, unless, of course, their provisions are directly favourable to the signatories. On average, a period of five to seven years elapses between the date of adoption and the date of coming into force.

This fact cannot be explained totally by the extremely strict conditions of enforcement stipulated in certain conventions. Other factors contribute to the slowness of the standard-setting process. There are texts like the MARPOL Convention whose enforcement raises inextricable technical or financial problems. Internal procedures on treaty ratification differ significantly from one State to another, and some of them may be particularly lengthy and complicated. Ultimately, so much depends on a government's will, its political margin for manoeuvre, and the means of pressure on the authorities available to maritime industries.

IMO assumes all the technical and administrative tasks needed for proper functioning of conventions, by issuing certified true copies in other languages than the original text, receiving and communicating all instruments relating to the treaty, and depositing the convention with the UN Secretariat.

In addition to its role as depository of national instruments, the IMO Secretariat acts as a spur to action. It issues reminders about conventions and other instruments that are awaiting acceptance; it supplies information on measures to be taken by governments; it offers help to developing countries which have difficulty in meeting their obligations.

The number of acceptances by States has grown spectacularly in recent years : 491 between January 1959 and October 1973, and 386 from 1973 to 1977. The record for ratifications was broken in 1979, when 184 acceptance instruments were deposited in a single year (16).

• Deadlines for incorporation into national law
The coming into force of a convention does not necessarily imply its effective enforcement. Again, delays occur in transcribing international safety standards into national law. This phenomenon may be explained by a whole series of reasons, generally the same as for ratification of conventions.

The main factor at this stage is the capacity to mobilise the authorities responsible for issuing implementing orders and regulations. In certain cases it is the scarcity of civil servants that raises a problem; in others, on the contrary, it is bureaucracy that slows down the standardisation process. These administrative difficulties are sometimes compounded by pressures exerted by certain private interests to delay adoption of regulations (17).

(14) W. O'NEIL : "The quest for safety : the limits to regulations". The Wakeford Memorial Lecture. Southampton, 24 mars 1997.
(15) R.M. M'GONIGLE, M.W. ZACHER : "Pollution, politics and international law. Tanker at sea". University of California Press, Berkeley, 1979.
(16) IMO News, n° 1, 1980, 1-2.
(17) J.N. ARCHER : "Implementation and enforcement of IMCO Regulations". MER, Feb. 1979, 22.

b) Differences in enforcement of standards

199. - Theoretically, the application of a convention drafted under IMO auspices should result in uniformity of national legislations. This would seem all the more logical because international law on safety at sea is essentially technical, without too many political or diplomatic considerations.

But in fact, when international rules have been accepted, they are seldom immediately effective, in other words applied consistently and fully by States. There are often considerable differences in implementing measures.

• Translation difficulties

IMO conventions are translated into several languages. The text of the final instrument of a conference and accompanying documents are usually issued in originals in English, Chinese, Spanish, French and Russian. Official translations may be supplied in other languages such as German or Arabic.

The large number of languages involved, reflecting mainly political considerations, raises many practical difficulties. Not all translations are accurate: some may give rise to diverging interpretations of the same technical standard.

Other problems arise from the *de facto* preeminence of English, often used for tricky negotiations and difficult compromises. Certain concepts peculiar to common law, such as "jurisdiction", "control", "responsibility" and "liability", do not have equivalents in other languages (18).

• Equivalence procedure

This procedure allows each State leeway in transposing legal rules established at an international level, and facilitates very flexible application under national legal systems. The procedure is set out in most IMO technical conventions.

According to this procedure, any State that believes that an installation, material, device or appliance, or even a fitting on board a ship, is at least as effective as an installation, material or device stipulated in the convention, may replace one with the other, on condition that it notifies IMO, which informs other contracting governments of the changes made (19). This procedure, although it may be justified in practical terms, is bound to open the door to very wide diversification of standards.

• Application case law

Certain international safety regulations, such as the regulations for preventing collisions at sea, give rise to case law interpretations. Since there is no international maritime court or international case law, such interpretation are handed down by a judge who naturally reflects national interests (20).

Contradictions in case law decisions can occur in national law (21). The danger is even greater in international law. In his time, G. Ripert already asserted that "a written law cannot provide for every possibility. The same law, interpreted by judges conversant with national law, imbued with national traditions and habits, involving a particular legal technique, will look very different after a few years" (22).

(18) L. LUCCHINI, M. VOELCKEL : "Droit de la mer". Tome I, Pedone, Paris 1990, 104.
(19) SOLAS Convention. Chapter I, Part A, Regulation 5.
(20) J.P GOVARE : "Les difficultés d'application et d'adoption des conventions internationales". JMM, 13 Feb. 1947, 1417.
(21) R. RODIERE : "Traité général de droit maritime". Paris, Dalloz. Evénément de mer (1972), 49.
(22) G. RIPERT : "Droit Maritime". Rousseau, Paris, 4e ed. 1950-1953, Tome I, 98.

3. International monitoring of effective enforcement

200. - Differences in the enforcement of international technical regulations can raise serious problems for shipowners and shipyards. Compliance deadlines and the scope of the relevant rules will depend on the state under whose flag the ship sails, and the type of traffic in which it is engaged. There will be ships built with the same characteristics, but presenting different levels of safety.

It would be preferable to establish certain procedures intended to ensure uniform application of safety laws. Naturally, there can be no question of international control of observance of the law by a supranational body. Control remains in the hands of States, which react spontaneously as soon as their interests are hurt by violation of an international convention (23). However, certain forms of control have been introduced within international organisations (24). As regards maritime safety conventions, the initiative has been taken by the ILO and to a lesser degree by IMO (cf chapter 24 below).

II - RESOLUTIONS AND NON-BINDING INSTRUMENTS

201. - In addition to treaties and conventions, two other sources of regulation exist: resolutions passed by diplomatic conferences, and other instruments adopted by international organisations.

A - DIPLOMATIC CONFERENCE RESOLUTIONS

IMO Conventions on safety at sea and prevention of pollution comprise a large number of resolutions. Their number has tended to rise steeply in the last few years: the 1974 SOLAS Conference issued sixteen recommendations, the Conference on the safety of fishing vessels issued eleven, the Conference on tanker safety eighteen, and the STCW Conference twenty-three.

There are several reasons for this trend. To begin with, resolutions offer a way of reaching agreement on a controversial technical standard. Certain commentators, in fact, see them merely as "consolation offered by the victors to the vanquished" (25). Recommendations also offer many advantages: they contain an assortment of ideas expressed by participants and not included in the convention. Some of them give details of the bearing of rules subject to difficulties of interpretation, while other facilitate application of the convention by States, by drawing their attention to problems which, at the present stage of technology, require more detailed examination.

Unlike treaties, these instruments do not involve the principle of *pacta sunt servanda*. Forming part of what has been referred to as "soft law"(26), international conference resolutions nevertheless have a certain legal weight. They form part of virtual law, in the process of formation, imperfect, but presaging later development and commitments (27).

---

(23) M. VIRALLY : "L'Organisation Mondiale". Armand Colin, Paris 1972, 332.
(24) L. KOPELMANAS : "Le contrôle international" RCADI, 1950, II, 58.
(25) Y. ROCQUEMONT : *op.cit,* NTM 1961, 47.
(26) C.M. CHINKIN : "The challenge of soft law : Development and change in international law". ICLQ, 1989, 38, 850-866.
(27) R.J. DUPUY : "Droit déclaratoire et droit programmatoire : de la coutume sauvage à la soft law". Colloque SFDI sur l'élaboration du Droit International Public. Pedone, Paris 1975, 132-148.

B - INTERNATIONAL ORGANISATIONS RECOMMENDATIONS

202. - International organisations issue various recommendations, resolutions, guidelines and regulations intended to prevent accidents at sea. These instruments have legal consequences for States. Their authority depends very much on the powers conferred on the organisation by its founders (28). Three examples will illustrate the diversity of situations relating to with safety at sea: IMO, ILO and the European Union.

1. IMO recommendations

The constituent charter of IMO makes provision for several types of recommendations. The largest number concern maritime safety and protection of the marine environment.

a) Diversity of recommendations

Three IMO bodies exercise powers relating to safety at sea :

• **Assembly**
Article 15i of the 1948 Convention allows it to advise members to adopt regulations or amendments submitted to it by the MSC.
Article 15j entitles it "to recommend to members for adoption regulations and guidelines concerning maritime safety, the prevention and control of maritime pollution from ships (...) or amendments to such regulations and guidelines which have been referred to it".

• **MSC and MEPC**
Since Resolution A.736 of 1977, the MSC can adopt certain recommendations directly, particularly on the matter of traffic separation systems. Article 29 of the Convention mentions both "recommendations" and "guidelines". Articles 38 and 39 give the same powers to the MEPC.

IMO recommendations may be placed in one of three categories, depending on their content :
- codes and technical regulations, containing standards, inspection procedures, rules of conduct and studies covering every aspect of safety at sea ;
- interpretative resolutions, which do not create standards but provide comment and interpretations about existing standards ;
- guidelines, traditionally comprising those that simultaneously define goals to be achieved and the means of attaining them, as well as those that simply indicate the ultimate aim, while leaving each State free to choose the means (29).

b) Effectiveness and value of IMO recommendations

203. - The terminological subtleties behind the words "recommendations", "resolutions", "codes", "manuals", "practices" and "guidelines", make little difference legally speaking. By

---

(28) J. DAVIDOW, L. CHILES : "The United States and the issue of the binding or voluntary nature of international codes of conduct regarding restrictive business practices". The American Journal of International Law, Vol. 72, 1978, 247-271.
(29) IMO. Resolution A.358, 14 Nov. 1975.

definition, the recommendations of international organisations possess no element of legal compulsion : States are not bound to implement them. There is a merely moral obligation not to block their effects, and to examine their possible domestic consequences (30).

The absence of legal constraint that characterises recommendations can become a source of confusion and differences of opinion (31). Each government is simply invited to adopt and incorporate the resolution into its national legal system to the degree that it is possible and reasonable. In other words, the State remains in absolute control of the standard-setting process. It can either take all necessary measures to impart legal or regulatory force to the recommendation ; or it may regard it as a pious hope and take no action at all. It can freely amend or abrogate instruments introduced to implement the resolution. It may also interpret it as it sees fit, and remove any effectiveness it may have possessed.

Yet despite their lack of enforceability, IMO recommendations are useful in three ways:
- They can give legal weight to certain private rules or practices. Even if IMO does not take the initiative for certain safety standards, its intervention is needed to adapt them to existing legal provisions, or facilitate their practical implementation (32).
- A recommendation quite often precedes a future mandatory regulation. It may be the prelude to a subsequent amendment to a convention, in cases where it has been not been possible, for lack of time or absence of consensus, to insert certain provisions in the original text.
- The force of resolutions depends largely on the confidence inspired by the organisation promulgating them, and its moral authority. The prestige of IMO within the maritime world is such that governments can hardly ignore its recommendations. As the only universal organisation working to improve safety at sea, IMO, through the texts drawn up by its specialised technical bodies, provides a model, as a basis for national legislation (33).

2. ILO recommendations

204. - ILO recommendations take two forms. They are either new technical rules which may be covered by a convention, and which spell out an international line of conduct, or simple practical guidelines, drawn up by committees of experts, to complete or interpret current standards set by convention.

ILO resolutions, like those of IMO, have only limited legal bearing. Their non-compulsory nature reflects the role played by intergovernmental organisations on the international stage ; in seeking consensus and cooperation, rather than laying down and overseeing the law.

3. European Union - a particular case

205. - Unlike other intergovernmental institutions, the EU is a supranational organisation, the only one in the world to have decision-taking powers. Its different bodies can issue regulations, directives and decisions which are binding on member States (34).

(30) M. VIRALLY : "La valeur juridique des recommandations des organisations internationales". AFDI, 1956, 66.
(31) GRUCHALLA-WESIERSKI : "A Framework for under standing soft law". McGill L.J., 1984, 37.
(32) L. OUDET : "L'autorité sur mer". JMM, 25 juillet 1968, 1551.
(33) B. OBINNA OKERE : "L'OMCI". These, droit, Paris 1973, 347.
(34) J.L. SAURON : "L'application du droit de l'Union européenne en France". La Documentation française, Paris, 1995, 11-16.

III - PROBLEMS RAISED BY STANDARDS

206. - International regulations on safety at sea have now become hugely complex. This is because standards are diversified, voluminous and incomplete (35).

A - DIVERSITY OF SAFETY RULES

International rules on safety at sea are seen immediately to be very numerous and extremely diverse. This diversity may be noted on three different levels :
- Public regulations comprise both legal requirements and technical standards, both of which involve different procedures for their production, implementation or conversion. For example, an international convention may contain both imperative rules, which all party States must implement, and simple recommendations, which States comply with to varying degrees.
- Not all technical standards have the same value. Their legal force differs, depending on whether they are laid down by convention or by resolution. In the former case, the principle *pacta sunt servanda* applies ; in the latter, some flexibility is left to the judgement of each national legislator in their implementation.
- Finally, rules may be remarkably precise in technical terms, and at the same time extremely vague in legal terms. Texts are often corrected and adjusted to ensure the widest possible agreement. Certain provisions are so vague that they leave the issue of application almost completely open.

These shortcomings complicate proper understanding and uniform interpretation of the law : national legislators experience the greatest difficulty in adjusting the international standard to a national legal environment, where rules have to be formulated rigorously and accurately.

B - VOLUME OF REGULATIONS

207. - The sheer quantity of regulations makes them difficult for States to comprehend and enforce. There are two reasons for this : the technical complexity of the problems raised, and competition among regulators internationally.

1. Inflation in regulations

Safety standards are clearly becoming increasingly detailed. Regulations that are free of any compulsory character are more easily adopted internationally. Their originators therefore have no compunction about complicating them with a wealth of detail, to the extent that they become obscure and incomprehensible for those concerned.

The proliferation of international institutions responsible for improving safety at sea does nothing to encourage restraint in setting standards. IMO, which has faced competition in the past from the ILO and UNCTAD, now has to confront regional organisations, in order to impose universal standards. The EU adopts not just measures aimed at harmonising the implementation of existing conventions, but also mandatory directives on problems that are still not properly in focus on a global scale.

---

(35) Ph. BOISSON : "La problématique des normes". Annuaire de Droit Maritime et Océanique. Tome XVI - 1998 - Université de Nantes, 175-185.

There is also a tendency for private organisations to indulge in over-regulation, for fear of having their powers taken over by public legislators. This anxiety is reflected, for instance, in the changes in certain classification rules towards a more all-embracing approach to prevention.

2. Quickening pace of standard setting

208. - Another source of anxiety is the quickening pace of legal change. The great number of new problems calling for urgent solutions, the huge increase in the speed of technical progress at sea, and the inconvenience of traditional mechanisms for amending international conventions, encouraged IMO to introduce a procedure in 1972, described above, for tacit acceptance of amendments. This procedure, although convenient, does not have only benefits. Technical standards age very quickly, forcing IMO members to keep a close eye on technological innovations, in order to handle the necessary regulatory consequences. This lays a steadily increasing workload on these States within IMO. An example is the 66th session of the MSC, held in London in spring 1966, and which had to deal in two weeks with nearly two thousand pages of documents (36). The inevitable bottlenecks occurred at the translation, setting and printing stages, making it very difficult to keep to the timetable stipulated by the MSC.

At that session, several delegations complained about such malfunctions, stating that they were quite unable to cover all aspects of IMO activities, and therefore to play an effective part in the rule-making process. There was sharp criticism of the proliferation of correspondence groups and intersession groups, as well as the frequency of amendments to IMO instruments. In certain cases, saturation point has been reached, making it impossible for governments to enforce the standards adopted. The absurdity of the whole situation was illustrated by the fact that the United Kingdom submitted a document intended to provide a remedy to this very situation (37), while at the same time the British delegation was formulating thirteen fresh proposals for changes in regulations before the same committee !

C - LOOPHOLES IN REGULATIONS

209. - Only some of the world's eighty thousand ships meet international standards. Several criteria for implementation apply to every IMO instrument : a ship's commercial activity, type of navigation, registered tonnage and age.

1. Commercial activity

IMO conventions apply only to vessels engaged in commercial navigation. Traditionally, international regulations do not apply to warships and recreational craft not providing any commercial service.

Certain instruments may be more restricted in scope, excluding ships without means of mechanical propulsion, wooden ships built by primitive techniques (cf SOLAS Convention, rule 3a), vessels which "navigate exclusively in inland waters or in waters within, or closely adjacent to, sheltered waters or areas where port regulations apply" (article II of STCW Convention 1978).

(36) "Paper chase". Lloyd's List, 7 June 1996.
(37) IMO. MSC 66/22/1, 29 March 1996.

2. Type of navigation

According to Regulation 1 part A of the first chapter of the 1974 SOLAS Convention, "unless expressly provided otherwise, the present regulations apply only to ships engaged on international voyages".

Regulation 2d defines an international voyage as "a voyage from a country to which the present Convention applies to a port outside such country, or conversely".

Article VI(d) of the Convention recalls that "all matters which are not expressly provided for in the present Convention remain subject to the legislation of the contracting governments".

3. Registered tonnage

210. - A ship's tonnage is the internal volume of the ship measured in tons. There are two types of registered tonnage :
- The gross tonnage (grt) is the volume of the hull and superstructures, without any deduction. It provides a reference for the application of various administrative regulations concerning navigation, equipment, manning and crew qualifications ;
- The net tonnage (dwt) is the volume of spaces available to carry cargo. It is important mainly for fiscal purposes, being used by maritime administrations and ports to calculate dues and taxes to be charged (38).

Until the late Sixties, several systems for measuring tonnage coexisted. This diversity was much criticised,. For obvious reasons, shipowners tried every device to keep the registered tonnage of their ships as low as possible.

As soon as it came into existence, IMO set out to find a solution to the problem. In 1959, it set up a Tonnage Subcommittee responsible for seeking a path towards harmonisation. In 1963, it decided to convene an international conference to settle the whole issue. The conference, which took place in London in June 1969, ended with the signing of a convention on tonnage measurement of ships (TONNAGE Convention), laying down a simplified universal system for tonnaging merchant vessels engaged in international voyages. Because of the very stringent conditions of application, this Convention did not come into force until 18 July 1982 (39).

Tonnage is a very important factor for safety regulations. Each international convention sets thresholds for its provisions :
- 150 grt for Loadline regulations (article 5) ;
- 500 grt for SOLAS regulations (rule 3a) ;
- 150 grt for MARPOL regulations for oil tankers and 400 grt for other ships (appendix 1).

4. Age of ship

211. - Most IMO technical conventions contain a "grandfather clause", which exempts existing ships from major alterations in construction and equipment. This principle is now increasingly being questioned, in the name of safety.

---

(38) M. STOPFORD : "Maritime economics. Rontledge, London, 1993. Appendix 2, 386-389.
(39) IMO News n° 2, 1994, 1.

a) Grandfather clauses

First introduced in the SOLAS 74 Convention, the principle has been repeated in various forms in later versions. It now appears in article VIIIe of the Convention, and in article 16.6 of MARPOL 74. These instruments stipulated that, unless expressly stipulated to the contrary, any amendment affecting ship structure would apply only to ships built on or after the date on which the convention came into force.

The principle means that major technical alterations in shipbuilding techniques apply only to new ships. These are defined as "ships the keels of which are laid or which are at a similar stage of construction" (SOLAS Chapter I, Regulation 2k).

The same principle applies to ships undergoing "repairs, alterations and modifications of a major character" (SOLAS Chapter II-2, Regulation 1.3). For many years, the principle of non-retroactivity of new standards was justified in economic terms. The ageing of the world fleet and the occurrence of grave accidents at sea have swept such considerations aside (40).

Despite the financial burden laid on the maritime industry, changes were therefore made from 1992 in SOLAS and MARPOL Conventions, making major modifications in design compulsory for existing as well as new ships. Two changes were particularly targetted: the damage stability of ro-ro passenger ships, and double hulls for tanker ships.

b) IMO guidelines

Keen to offer some security for investments in the maritime sector, while trying to curtail the use of grandfather clauses, IMO introduced interim guidelines, in order to restrict systematic recourse to such exemptions (41). These guidelines provide a new approach to the improvement of safety and pollution prevention standards on board existing ships, when constructional arrangements are proposed for new vessels.

These guidelines, issued by the MSC and MEPC in a circular of 23 July 1996 (42), set out a strategy that should avoid undue discrepancies between standards applying to new ships and those applying to ships in service. This strategy is also intended to ensure, when such discrepancies could arise, that standards for existing ships are likewise improved to an acceptable extent.

The guidelines are primarily intended for IMO technical committees, to help in the complex decision-making process, when proposals for new requirements or amendments are being considered.

It has been decided that the guidelines would be applied on "an interim, case-by-case trial basis, so that experience may be gained on their application, and necessary modifications may be made when the need arises" (43). Despite these limitations, the guidelines should lead to a curtailment of grandfather clauses. This could result in a rejuvenation of the world fleet. Many existing vessels will no doubt be scrapped if the cost of upgrading them far exceeds the benefits to be expected by the shipowner.

(40) G. THOMPSON : "New and old Vessels - The grandfather clause". International Summit Safety at Sea. Oslo 9-10 April 1991.
(41) IMO. Report of the correspondance group on the application of grandfather clauses. MSC 65/21, 10 Feb. 1995.
(42) IMO. "Interim Guidelines for the systematic application of grandfather clauses". MSC/Circ. 765. MEPC/Circ. 315, 23 July 1996.
(43) IMO. MSC 66/24, 18 June 1996.

CONCLUSION : Search for global consensus

   212. - Lack of uniformity, imprecision, complexity and loopholes in regulations are a major problem facing the shipping community. It is even more difficult to remedy these shortcomings because they are connected with the transactional nature of standards, and the inadequacies of the worldwide system that produces them. Like other international laws, maritime safety standards are the product of a balance of forces. They emerge from a difficult compromise between the divergent or even contradictory interests of different States. Improvements in the safety of life at sea and protection of the marine environment are of course among the common concerns of all members of the international community. But for political, economic or strategic reasons, every nation has a different viewpoint, even if the legal obligation is the same for all.

   Ultimately, if these problems remain unsolved, and unless the defects are corrected, it is the whole international system that could break down. A powerful State or a regional organisation might then be tempted to impose its will on safety issues.

CHAPTER 8

National regulations

213. - The development of the system of conventions on safety at sea, which has accompanied the growth and action of international organisations, has not removed the regulatory powers of individual States. Most IMO technical conventions recall this fact. An example is given in article VId of the 1974 SOLAS Convention, which declares that "all matters which are not expressly provided for in the present Convention remain subject to the legislation of the contracting governments".

Even within its sphere, however, a State cannot do exactly as it pleases. It has to take account of the principles of international law. If it decides to regulate activities excluded from specialised conventions, it must base its provisions on the conditions or principles contained in such instruments (1). In addition, the law of the sea must be respected.

These provisions of the law of the sea do not necessarily impose restrictions, but rather divide up regulatory powers over maritime navigation between shipping States, which possess a large merchant fleet, and States threatened by the exercise of this activity. Their interests are radically different: shipping nations are very attached to the principle of freedom of the high seas, and want minimum restrictions on the expansion of shipping, while countries which are more anxious about their coastlines want to impose regulations to safeguard their natural resources and environment.

The law of the sea has tried to balance these contradictory interests, by providing for regulatory powers to be assigned in accordance with "territorialisation" of the different zones where the ship is located. Originally the main emphasis was put on freedom of navigation, as a vital factor in the expansion of international maritime trade.

The new law of the sea, as contained in the United Nation Law of the Sea (LOS) Convention, adopted in Montego Bay, Jamaica in December 1982, and which came into force on November 1994, redefines sovereign jurisdiction and freedom of action in key sea areas covered by this Convention (2).

It acknowledges the need for increased protection of the marine environment. This is the reason for the principle of "safer ships on cleaner seas" (3).

I - REGULATORY POWER ON THE HIGH SEAS

214. - *Res nullius*, belonging to noone: the high seas are characterised by freedom of navigation. No national power holds sway there, outside territorial waters. Only the flag

---

(1) Cf. Recommendations n° 2 of 1960 SOLAS Conference and 1966 Loadline Conference.
(2) A-L. MORGAN : "The New Law of the Sea : Rethinking the implications for sovereign jurisdiction and freedom of action". IMO 97, 1996, 59.
(3) E. GOLD : "International shipping and the new Law of the Sea : New directions for a traditional use ?" ODIL, Cf also : Colin de LA RUE and Ch. B. ANDERSON : "Shipping and the Environment". Lloyd's Press, 1998, Ch. 21. Vol. 20, 1989, 433-444.

State in which the ship is registered can exercise its sovereignty. Indeed, it has not only the right but the duty to assume responsibility for the ship it sends to sea (4).

A - FLAG STATE RESPONSIBILITIES

The LOS Convention lays an obligation on States to introduce measures in two areas affecting safety at sea : navigation and protection of the marine environment. The terms "measures" includes all legislative or regulatory instruments formulating legal requirements.

a) Safety of navigation

According to article 94.3 of the LOS Convention, "every State shall take such measures for ships flying its flag as are necessary to ensure safety at sea with regard, *inter alia*, to :
a) the construction, equipment and seaworthiness of ships ;
b) the manning of ships, labour conditions and the training of crews (...) ;
c) use of signals, the maintenance of communications and the prevention of collisions".

Article 94.4 indicates other measures to be taken, "to ensure :
a) that each ship (...) is surveyed by a qualified surveyor of ships, and has on board such charts, nautical publications and navigational equipment and instruments as are appropriate for the safety navigation of the ship ;
b) that each ship is in the charge of a master and officers who possess appropriate qualifications (...), and that the crew is appropriate in qualification and numbers for the type, size, machinery and equipment of the ship ;
c) that the master, officers and (...) the crew are fully conversant with and required to observe the applicable international regulations concerning the safety of life at sea, the prevention, reduction and control of marine pollution, and the maintenance of communications by radio".

b) Marine environment protection

Under the general principle stated in article 192 of the LOS Convention, according to which "States have the obligation to protect and preserve the marine environment", flag States possess new regulatory responsibilities. They have to adopt laws and regulations for the prevention, reduction and control of pollution of the marine environment from vessels flying their flag (cf article 211.2) ; they must also adopt laws and regulations and take other measures so that vessels flying their flag comply with requests for information from a coastal State, in the event of breaches committed within the exclusive economic zone (cf article 220.4).

B - CONDITIONS OF EXERCISE OF FLAG STATE RESPONSIBILITIES

215. - The regulatory activities of the flag State are subject to certain conditions defined in article 94.5 of the 1982 LOS Convention. In taking these measures, "each State is required to conform to generally accepted international regulations, procedures and practices; and to take any steps which may be necessary to secure their observance".

(4) BONASSIES : "La loi du pavillon et les conflits de droit maritime" - RCADI, 1969, III, 611.

The LOS Convention refers in turn to "standards, rules, recommended practices and procedures, regulations, instruments", which are all "international" and "applicable" or "generally accepted".

No official definition of these expressions exists, and there is much discussion of their meaning and bearing. Commentators acknowledge the important role that may be played by IMO and ILO in their formulation. Some consider that all these terms refer only to international conventions drawn up under the auspices of these two organisations, while others would extend them to include non-convention instruments, such as recommendations, provided that they are "generally accepted" (5).

C - JUSTIFICATIONS OF FLAG STATE RESPONSIBILITIES

216. - The regulatory powers of the flag State are justified both by practical necessities and by legal factors (cf chapter 21 below).

• **Practical necessities**
First of all, it is logical to attach a ship to a given State, which thereby becomes responsible for its safety. The needs of international navigation mean that the ship sails through zones subject to different sets of conditions. For it to operate safely, the requirements it has to comply with must remain the same, wherever it is. It therefore has to be attached to a single legal system. Those managing a ship must be able to conduct business without being harassed by every State. The simplest means of avoiding the confusion that would result from a complex overlapping of successive national powers consist of attaching each ship to a State, its nationality being given material expression by the flag it flies (6).

• **Freedom of high seas**
Another reason arises from the principle of the freedom of the high seas. This space, where the ships spends most of its time at sea, is *res nullius*, in other words no one's property. To put it another way, no territorial sovereignty can be exercised over it, only the individual powers of States in relation to the ships and appliances to be found there. To avoid anarchy and insecurity on the high seas, international law confers a legislative monopoly on the flag State. This provides a second argument for the nationality of ships (7).

The principle of the sole competency of the flag State applies of course only to the high seas. Elsewhere, territorial sovereignty regains its rights, and regulatory powers are shared between flag States and coastal States.

Whatever the grounds for the regulatory powers of the flag States, two kinds of penalties may be imposed. A ship guilty of infringing safety regulations established by its State of registry may be prosecuted in its courts. Second, the State's international liability may be claimed if a ship sailing under its flag commits a breach, and if the state has failed in its regulatory duty, for example if its legislative bodies have failed to issue safety rules. This theoretical possibility has in fact never arisen.

(5) B. VUKAS : "Generally accepted international rules and standards" in Implementation of the LOS Convention through International Institutions - 23rd conference of the Law of Sea Institute, LSI Honolulu, 1989.
(6) Cl. DEMAUREY : "La nationalité du navire de mer". Thesis, Zurich, 1957, 18.
(7) François-Michel FAY : "La nationalité des navires". RGDIP 1973, 1008.

II - EXCLUSIVE ECONOMIC ZONE

217. - The exclusive economic zone (EEZ), which consists of a 200 mile-deep strip between the coast and the high Seas, is the first maritime area where the powers of the flag State and the coastal State can clash.

In certain ways, the EEZ is like the high seas : article 58 of the LOS Convention grants all States freedom of navigation and overflight in the EEZ. Regulatory powers relating to the safety of ships are therefore exercised by the States whose flag they fly. But the coastal State also possesses certain rights in the EEZ. Article 56 stipulates that there is jurisdiction with regard to :

"i) the establishment and use of artificial islands, installations and structures ;

ii) marine scientific research ;

iii) the protection and preservation of the marine environment."

This particular legal system can be adopted by States wishing to improve safety within the zone.

A - REGULATORY POWERS OF COASTAL STATES

1. Safety of navigation

Within the EEZ, the coastal State has the sole right to proceed with the construction of artificial islands, installations and structures. or authorise and control their construction, operation and use. It has sole jurisdiction over them as regards safety regulations and other laws (cf article 60.2). However, it must comply with certain requirements: give due notice of their construction, and maintain permanent means of giving warning of their presence (cf article 60.3); remove abandoned or decommissioned installations in order to ensure safety of navigation, establish safety zones around artificial islands in which it may take appropriate measures (cf article 60.4). The coastal State may not construct artificial islands or establish safety zones "where interference could be caused to the use of recognised sea lanes essential to international navigation" (article 60.7). Finally, it must provide adequate information regarding the extent of safety zones and remaining parts of structures not entirely removed.

IMO plays an important role here: without its recommendation, or dispensation, the coastal State cannot establish safety zones exceeding 500 metres (8). If the State fails to observe IMO advice, it could be held liable in the event of an accident, for example if a ship collides with an artificial island (9).

IMO Resolution A.671 of 19 October 1989 laid down several rules for safety zones and safety of navigation around offshore installations and structures. These include the obligation for the coastal State to require operators to take adequate measures to prevent breaches of safety zones, and ask them to report actions by ships endangering safety within such zones.

(8) IMO : "Implications of the UNLOS Convention 1982 for the IMO". LEG/MISC/1, 15. 10 Feb. 1986.

(9) T. TREVES : "La participation de l'Organisation internationale compétente aux décisions de l'Etat côtier dans le nouveau droit de la mer". In Le droit international à l'heure de sa codification. Etudes en l'honneur de Roberto Ago, Milan Giuffre, 1987, 480.

2. Pollution prevention

218. - The regulatory powers of coastal States regarding the environment are exercised throughout their EEZ, and more specifically in protected maritime areas and ice-covered areas.

a) General regulatory powers

Article 211.5 of the LOS Convention entitles the coastal State to "adopt laws and regulations for the prevention, reduction and control of pollution from vessels conforming to and giving effect to generally accepted international rules and standards".

Such laws and regulations must be designed to minimise the risk of accidents likely to pollute the marine environment, such as the adoption of routeing systems (cf article 211.1). They must also stipulate "prompt notification to coastal States, whose coastline or related interests may be affected by incidents, including maritime casualties, which involve discharges or probability of discharges" (article 211.7).

b) Specially protected areas

219. - More than five hundred protected maritime areas have been set up by over a hundred countries throughout the world. These zones have been classified as such in order to preserve all or part of the environment they form. They comprise marine reserves, natural parks, protected sites, natural reserves and zoological reserves, such as the Great Barrier Reef in Australia, the Galapagos Islands, or the United States Channel Islands.

Protected maritime areas are designated nationally by governments, which must observe several international conventions in doing so.

• Particular areas

Article 211.6a of the 1982 LOS Convention gives coastal States the possibility of identifying particular and clearly defined areas within their EEZ, requiring the adoption of special mandatory measures to prevent pollution from ships, for recognised technical reasons relating to their oceanographical and ecological conditions, their utilisation or the protection of their resources, and the particular character of the traffic.

Whenever a coastal State considers that a particular area meets these criteria, it approaches the proper international organisation to obtain approval for special measures, more stringent than those provided for in international rules and standards or navigational practices.

• Special areas

The annexes to the MARPOL Convention 73/78 define certain parts of the sea as "special areas", depending on the type of pollution referred to in each annex. Such an area is "a sea area where, for recognised technical reasons in relation to its oceanographical and ecological conditions and to the particular nature of its traffic, the adoption of special mandatory methods for the prevention of sea pollution is required" (10).

Under the terms of the Convention, these special areas enjoy a higher level of protection than other maritime zones, notably there may be severer restrictions concerning discharge of polluting substances (11).

---

(10) MARPOL 73/78 Convention. Annex I, chapter I, Regulation 1.10. Annex II, Reg. 1.7. Annex II, Reg. 1.3.
(11) A. MERIALDI : "Legal restraints on navigation in marine specially protected areas". Study to be published by Kluwer International as a contribution to a book edited by Tullio Scovozzi concerning marine protected areas.

• **Particularly sensitive sea areas (PSSA)**

First mentioned in Resolution 9 of the 1978 Tanker Safety Conference, the expression "particularly sensitive sea area" refers to any "area which needs special protection through action by IMO because of its significance for recognised ecological or socioeconomic or scientific reasons and which may be vulnerable to environmental damage by maritime activities" (12).

Unlike special zones, these PSSAs do not have any special legal framework. They can only be identified, in order to establish them, and coastal States later decide which international provisions are needed to protect them. It is this double concern that is addressed by Resolution A.720 adopted by IMO on 6 November 1971, which enumerates all these relevant guidelines (13).

Apart from the instruments already mentioned, there are a number of regional conventions containing provisions for the establishment of protected maritime areas. Special protocols have been signed for "specially protected areas", within the framework of the UN programme for regional seas and related regional conventions. The first such protocol was adopted for the Mediterranean by the 1982 Barcelona Convention. Similar protocols were signed in 1985 for the East African region (14), and in 1989 for the Caribbean.

The legal system applying to protected maritime zones reflects the balance that international law has established between the interests of coastal States, anxious to preserve certain ecologically sensitive zones, and the needs of shipping states, which are opposed to unwarranted hindrances to navigation in certain parts of the EEZ. It also acknowledges the exclusive powers of the coastal State, while simultaneously subordinating the exercise of such prerogatives to international supervision (15).

c) Ice-covered areas

220. - According to article 234 of the LOS Convention, coastal States also have the right to adopt laws and regulations as a way of preventing pollution from ships in ice-covered areas within the limits of their EEZ. The first requirement stated in the Convention is the existence of particularly severe climatic conditions, and the presence of ice for most of the year, making navigation impossible or extremely dangerous. The next requirement is the need to prevent a serious risk of major harm to the ecological balance or its irreversible disturbance.

B - STATE PRACTICES

1. Extension of claims

221. - Certain States have given an extensive interpretation to the provisions of the new law of the sea. Their national legislation on the establishment of an EEZ contains prerogatives that go well beyond those recognised in the 1982 Convention (16). Two considerations justify such extension : regulation of maritime traffic and protection of the marine environment.

(12) A. BLANCO-BAZAN : "The IMO guidelines on Particularly Sensitive Sea Areas (PSSA). Their possible application to the protection of underwater cultural heritage". Marine Policy, Vol 20, 1996, n° 4, 343-349.
(13) G. PEET : "Particularly Sensitive Sea Areas - An overview of Relevant IMO documents". IJMCL, Vol 9, n° 4, 1994, 556-576.
H. RING-BOM : "Environmental protection and shipping - Prescriptive coastal State Jurisdiction in the 1990's". Maruis Nb 224. Nordisk Institut for Sjzett. Oslo, Dec. 1996.
(14) A. FALL : "Marine environmental protection under coastal States extended Jurisdiction in Africa". JMLC. Vol 27, n° 2, April 1996, 281-291.
(15) Th. A. CLINGAN : "Vessel-source pollution, problem of hazardous cargo, and port State jurisdiction". In International Navigation : Rocks and Shoals Ahead ? Workshop of the Law of the Sea Institute. Honolulu, Hawai. January 1986.
(16) R.W. SMITH : "Global maritime claims". ODIL, Vol 20, 1989, 83-103.

An example is the Deep Water Ports Act, amended in 1984, and which establishes United States jurisdiction, by a specific agreement with the flag state for every ship entering or docking in deepwater ports, and also when they are in the safety zone and are engaged in activities connected or potentially interfering with the use or operation of artificial islands outside territorial waters (17).

France was also one of the first maritime nations to give effect to the creation of a 200-mile exclusive economic zone around its coasts, in Act no. 76-655 of 16 July 1975 (18). Article 4 of this Act stipulates that the French authorities exercise prerogatives recognised by international law for the protection of the marine environment. Under such provisions, several regulations have been adopted to reinforce safety beyond territorial waters.

Following the *Amoco Cadiz* disaster, the decision was taken to control and keep traffic away from the coasts of Brittany (20). The Ushant traffic separation scheme today comprises six maritime sectors, which must be respected by all ships using these waters. Only the upward sea lane, five to eight miles from the island of Ushant, and part of the first separation area, lie in French territorial waters. The same applies to the Casquet scheme, only part of the upward lane of which is located within the twelve-mile zone.

2. Validity of safety regulations outside territorial waters

The proliferation of measures introduced by coastal States to control maritime traffic beyond their territorial waters raises the question of their validity under international law. Apart from the three cases already mentioned, of artificial islands, particular ecologically sensitive areas, and ice-covered areas, the LOS Convention remains silent about the establishment and operation of traffic separation schemes within the EEZ. Doubts have also been expressed about the conditions under which coastal States could act in this respect.

Certain commentators consider that the EEZ is a unique, *sui generis* zone, involving a legal system half-way between those of territorial waters and the high seas. According to article 38 of the LOS Convention, all States enjoy "the freedom (...) of navigation (...) and other internationally lawful uses of the sea related to these freedoms, such as those associated with the operations of ships (...), compatible with the other provisions of this Convention". Such uses include the installation and operation of traffic separation schemes, subject to compliance with international rules for the adoption or modification of such systems (20).

III - STRAITS

222. - There are more than two hundred and sixty straits in the world (21). Geographers use the expression to describe a narrow sea passage between two land masses, and lawyers are concerned mainly with its width. According to Gidel, a strait is "any natural passage between two coasts, not exceeding a certain width and providing communication between two parts of the sea" (22).

(17) Deep Water Ports Act 1974, 14. International Legal Material (1975), 153 et 33 U.S.C. 1518 (c).
(18) J.O. 16 July 1976, 4299 and DMF 1976, 634.
(19) JMM, 30 April 1981, 1007.
(20) G. PLANT : "International traffic separation schemes in the new law of the sea". Marine Policy, April 1985, 146.
(21) L.M. ALEXANDER : "Navigational restrictions within the new LOS context : geographical implications for the United States". Peace Dale, R.I. offshore consultants, 1986.
(22) G. GIDEL : "Droit de la Mer". Volume III, Paris, Sirey, 1934, 730.

The concentration of shipping within these narrow seaways, some of which are strategically vital as well as important for international trade, has warranted certain exceptions to the principle of freedom of navigation. Coastal states have tried to regulate the passage of ships by various measures, while trying to make the transit safer by installing navigational aids. The building of bridges between the two banks of certain straits, like the Lille Belt, Fionia and the Bosphorus, has created additional difficulties for maritime traffic and increased the risk of accidents (23).

A - CHANGES IN THE LAW OF THE SEA

The law of the sea has attempted to reconcile the diverging interests of flag States, anxious to preserve the mobility of their ships, and coastal States, in favour of greater safety. Since 1958, changes have begun to appear in the legal system applying to straits, tending to increase the protection of coastal States.

The 1958 Geneva Convention on territorial waters is not very explicit: article 16.4 merely prohibits the coastal State from preventing the innocent passage of foreign ships through national straits (24).

The principle of free passage should be set alongside the decision of the International Court of Justice of April 1949, in the case of the Straits of Corfu (25), which permits the innocent passage of warships: the coastal State is entitled to control navigation, but can neither prohibit it nor make it subject to authorisation (26).

Loopholes in international law have encouraged the development of national regulations which, in the name of safety at sea, have gradually placed restrictions on freedom of navigation (27).

The 1982 LOS Conference tried to resolve this dilemma by defining a new system for straits used by international shipping: transit passage (28).

B - CONCEPT OF TRANSIT PASSAGE

223. - The right of transit passage, defined in article 38 to 44 of the 1982 LOS Convention, applies only to straits "which are used for international navigation between one part of the high seas or an exclusive economic zone and another part of the high seas or an exclusive economic zone" (article 37).

---

(23) W. SCHACHTE : "International straits and navigational freedom". ODIL, Vol 24, April/June 1993, 179-195.

(24) - R. LAPIDOTH : "Les détroits en droit international". Pedone, Paris, 1972.

- D. MONTAZ : "L'évolution du droit de la mer, de la conférence de Genève de 1958 à celle de 1975". Droit de la mer, Institut des Hautes Etudes Internationales de Paris, Pedone, 1977, 67.

(25) P. EISEMANN, V. COUSSIRAT-COUSTERE, P. HUR : "Petit manuel de la jurisprudence de la Cour Internationale de Justice". Paris, Pedone, 1971, 17-26.

(26) J.P. BEURIER : "Droit international de la mer". Livre 2 de l'ouvrage Droits Maritimes. Tome I, Mer, Navires et Marins. Editions JurisService. Paris, 1995, 100.

(27) Cl. DOUAY : "Le casse-tête des détroits". Le Monde, 23 oct. 1973, 9.

(28) D. MONTAZ : "La question des détroits à la IIIème Conférence des Nations-Unies sur le droit de la mer". AFDI 1974, 847.

1. Coastal State

a) Coastal State rights on safety issues

According to article 42, States bordering straits may adopt laws and regulations on safety of navigation and regulation of maritime traffic through the strait, and on the prevention, reduction and control of pollution. Whenever safety in the strait requires, they may introduce sea lanes and traffic separation schemes.

These provisions have been applied to the Strait of Bonifacio, which is an international waterway. Because of their ecological importance, IMO Resolution A.670 recognises the need to protect the vulnerable coastlines of France and Italy in the vicinity of this maritime strait, used by laden oil tankers and ships carrying dangerous chemicals. Considering that such traffic had increased by more than 40 per cent since 1985, IMO Resolution A.766 of November 1993 recommended both coastal States to prohibit or at least strongly discourage the transit of such ships, sailing under the French or Italian flags.

• Policing powers

Article 233 gives the State bordering on a strait certain policing powers, in the event of breaches of safety regulations, whenever they might cause or threaten major damage to the marine environment.

The States lying on each side of the Straits of Malacca and Singapore, anxious to prevent pollution, have reached a joint interpretation of this provision, which has to be reconciled with the general ban on placing any obstacle in the way of exercise of the right of transit passage (cf chapter 9 below).

b) Coastal State obligations

In laying down traffic separation schemes, the coastal State must respect certain conditions stipulated in article 41 of the Convention. Such systems must "conform to generally accepted international regulations" (article 41.3). Before designating or replacing sea lanes, the coastal State must submit the proposal to the proper international organisation. IMO is entitled "to adopt only such sea lanes and traffic separation schemes as may be agreed with the States bordering the straits" (article 41.4). When such systems involve the waters of several coastal States, they have to cooperate "in formulating proposals in consultation with the competent international organisation" (article 41.5). Finally, the coastal State must give due publicity to any measures (cf article 41.2), by showing clearly on marine charts all sea lanes or traffic separation schemes (cf article 41.6). Such notification must be made through IMO (29).

In general, coastal State regulations must not involve any discrimination in form or in fact among foreign ships. Neither may they have the effect of "denying, hampering or impairing the right of transit passage" (article 42.2).

Finally, coastal States must cooperate with user States, first in the establishment and maintenance of safety and navigational aids and other installations intended to facilitate international shipping, and second for the prevention, reduction and control of pollution from ships (cf article 43). Such cooperation, to be obtained by agreement, is mainly technical. Examples of financial cooperation, with the exception of the Cape Spartel lighthouse for the Straits of Gibraltar, maintained at the joint expense of several States since 1965, unfortunately remain quite exceptional.

---

(29) B. OXMAN : "Environmental protection in archipelagic waters and international straits. The role of the International Maritime Organisation". IJMCL, Vol 10, n° 4, 1995, 467-481.

2. User States

224. - According to article 38 of the LOS Convention, States whose shipping uses straits have a right of unimpeded transit passage. This expression is taken to mean "the exercise (...) of the freedom of navigation and overflight solely for the purpose of continuous and expeditious transit (...)" or "for the purpose of entering, leaving or returning from a State bordering the strait".

During transit passage, ships must "comply with generally accepted international regulations, procedures and practices for safety at sea, including the international regulations for preventing collisions at sea" and with international regulations on prevention of pollution (article 39.2). They must also respect the laws and regulations of the coastal State (cf article 42.4), particularly sea lanes and traffic separation schemes (cf article 41.7). Finally, they have a duty to cooperate with the coastal State, to improve and facilitate navigation in the strait (cf article 43).

IV - ARCHIPELAGIC WATERS

225. - The archipelagic State is a new concept in the law of the sea, dealt with in part IV of the 1982 LOS Convention. According to article 46, an archipelago is a group of islands which "are so closely interrelated that such islands, waters and other natural features form an intrinsic geographical, economic and political entity, or which historically have been regarded as such".

Archipelagic waters represent a new *sui generis* maritime area, which lie between archipelagic territorial waters and the internal waters of the islands that make up the archipelagic State. Inside this area, two different regimes exist side by side: right of innocent passage, which may be suspended (cf article 52) and right of archipelagic sea lanes passage (ASLP) (cf article 53).

A - ARCHIPELAGIC STATE REGULATIONS

Archipelagic States may regulate maritime navigation within their archipelagic waters, in order to improve safety at sea and prevent pollution from ships.

1. Designation of sea lanes

The State may designate sea lanes to be used by ships passing through archipelagic waters. These sea lanes are defined by a series of continuous axis lines connecting the entry points to the exit points. During their passage, ships may not deviate by more than 25 nautical miles to either side of these lines, which therefore define a corridor 50 miles wide (cf article 53.5).

Sea lanes must comprise all normal passage routes used for international navigation. They must follow all normal navigational channels, "provided that duplication of routes of similar convenience between the same entry and exit points shall not be necessary" (article 53.4). This provision means that passage through straits situated in archipelago relies on the right of ASLP, not transit passage (30).

---

(30) R.J. DUPUY, D. VIGNES : "Traité du nouveau droit de la mer". Economia, Paris, 1985, 796.

2. Traffic separation schemes

The archipelagic State is also entitled to institute traffic separation schemes, to ensure the safe passage of ships using narrow channels within sea lanes.

Article 53 defines the conditions of procedures governing the establishment of such schemes. These schemes, which are to conform to generally accepted international regulations (cf article 53.8), must be adopted by IMO (cf article 53.9). The axis lines of sea lanes and traffic separation schemes must be shown clearly on charts (cf article 53.10).

3. Anti-pollution regulations

Finally, the State may regulate navigation in order to prevent pollution of archipelagic waters by ships. This right is subject to the same restrictions as those imposed on a coastal State regulating maritime traffic within its territorial waters (cf article 54).

B - NAVIGATION IN ARCHIPELAGIC WATERS

226. - Since most archipelagos are located on major international routes, maritime States have succeeded in limiting hindrances to navigation by obtaining the right of archipelagic sea lanes passage, similar to the right of transit passage in straits (31).

However, the regime requires ships to respect sea lanes and traffic separation schemes established by the archipelagic States (cf article 53.11). According to article 54, ships must comply with generally accepted international regulations, procedures and practices for safety at sea, including the international regulations for preventing collisions at sea.

If the archipelagic State takes no action, the right of passage may be exercised in accordance with article 53.12, "through the routes normally used for international navigation".

C - INDONESIAN ARCHIPELAGIC WATERS

Indonesia was the first State to test the effectiveness of the new procedures introduced by the Law of the Sea Convention. After consulting IMO in August 1996, the Indonesian government filed a proposition with IMO, to designate sea lanes for the passage of foreign ships and aircraft (32).

The Indonesian initiative was the first of its kind, and as such raised numerous queries from Australia, notably as regards the role of the International Civil Aviation Authority (ICAO), the exact significance of the term "adoption", and the need to establish special procedures for adoption (33). Since this question was being raised for the first time by IMO, the MSC decided at its 67th session in December 1996 to act with caution, and to send the matter for fuller examination to the Safety of Navigation Subcommittee (NAV) (34).

---

(31) G. PRIESTNALL : "The regimes of archipelagic sea lanes passage and straits transit passage - Similarities and differences". Maritime Studies, Sept.-Oct. 1997.

(32) IMO. MSC 67/7/2, 30 August1996.

(33) IMO. MSC 67/713, 5 Sept. 1996.

(34) IMO. MSC 67/7.30 - 7.41, 19 Dec. 1996.

V - TERRITORIAL SEA

227. - The territorial sea extends from the boundary of a State's internal waters to twelve miles from its the baselines. The coastal State has sovereignty over this approach zone, where it exercises certain legislative powers, particularly regarding safety at sea. To protect the interests of international trade, the law of the sea has achieved a compromise between the need to protect the coastal State and the needs of navigation, by establishing a particular regime for this zone : the right of innocent passage

This principle, originally a common law matter, was codified for the first time in article 2 of the 1921 Barcelona Convention on freedom of transit. It was reaffirmed and detailed in the 1958 Geneva Convention on territorial waters and the contiguous zone.

The *Torrey Canyon* disaster led to a change in the concept of innocent passage. In an attempt to protect the ocean environment, certain coastal States have shown a tendency to regulate more severely the passage of ships presenting a particular risk (35). This new attitude to the idea of innocent passage, put forward by Canada and numerous Third World countries, was partly confirmed in the 1982 LOS Convention - only partly, for the new law of the sea places very clear limits on the regulatory powers exercised by the coastal State.

A - RIGHT OF INNOCENT PASSAGE

1. Regulatory powers

a) Area of competency

228. - The issues on which a coastal State may pass laws and regulations are listed in article 21.1. They include safety of navigation and regulation of traffic, protection of navigational aids, preservation of the environment and prevention, reduction and control of pollution. Article 22.1 also allows the coastal State to designate sea lanes and to lay down traffic separation schemes, whenever the safety of navigation requires.

On the other hand, the coastal State cannot legislate on any issues affecting the intrinsic safety of a ship. Article 21.2 points out that "such laws and regulations shall not apply to the design, construction, manning or equipment of foreign ships unless they are giving effect to generally accepted international rules or standards".

b) Conditions of exercise of regulatory powers

In general, several limits are laid on the regulatory powers of the coastal State. It has to act with "proportionality or reasonableness" (36). This is based on the interpretation given to article 24.1a, which declares that the State must not "impose requirements on foreign ships which have the practical effect of denying or impairing the right of innocent passage". Article 24.1b recalls the importance of the principle of non-discrimination; and article 21.3 requires due publicity to be given to all such measures.

Article 22 adds further conditions on the issue of sea lanes and traffic separation schemes. Safety of navigation must require such measures. The coastal State must take account of objective factors such as the channels customarily used by international shipping, the special characteristics of certain ships and channels, and traffic density. It must also take account of

(35) G. MARIANI : "Le droit de la mer à la veille de la 3ème Conférence des Nations-Unies". Publications du CNEXO, 31.
(36) B. SMITH : "Innocent Passage as a rule of decision : Navigation v. Environmental Protection". CJTL, Vol 21, n° 1, 1982, 49-102.

the recommendations of the proper international organisation. Failure to do so could make the coastal State liable for claims in the event of any incident involving a sea lane. IMO enjoys a presumption of worldwide technical competency in this area (37). Finally, such systems must be given due publicity, and be shown clearly on charts.

2. Coastal State rights of protection

229. - Article 25.3 mentions the possibility of temporary suspension of the right of innocent passage in specified areas of a State's territorial sea, if such a measure proves essential to protect its security.

Article 25.1 allows the State to take the necessary steps to prevent any passage which is not innocent, defined in article 19.2 as any passage which is "prejudicial to the peace, good order or security of the coastal State". These rather general terms are expanded by the enumeration of twelve cases in which passage is not innocent. The list, which considerably limits the power of action of coastal States, still leaves the possibility of certain initiatives to protect the environment.

Article 19.1e, for example, allows action to be taken against ships engaged in "any other activity not having a direct bearing on passage".

B - SPECIAL REGULATIONS FOR CERTAIN SHIPS

230. - The 1982 LOS Convention allows coastal State powers to be extended with regard to certain ships regarded as presenting a special risk for the environment (38).

Article 22.2 stipulates that tanker ships, nuclear-powered ships, and ships carrying nuclear or other inherently dangerous or noxious substances may be required to confine their passage to designated sea lanes.

In addition, according to article 23, such ships must carry documents and observe special precautionary measures, established for such ships by international agreements. This is a reference the 1974 SOLAS Convention, chapter VIII of which is devoted to nuclear ships, and to IMO Resolution A.748 of 1993, which lays down safety rules for the conveyance of irradiated nuclear fuels, plutonium and high-level radioactive waste (commonly referred to as the "INF Code").

Enforcement of these provisions can raise practical difficulties for certain types of ships.

1. Nuclear-powered vessels

Legislation on navigation of nuclear-powered ships makes no distinction between conditions for passage through territorial waters and those for periods spent in port. A uniform solution is adopted for both situations.

2. INF carrier ships

The new provisions of the law of the sea appear inadequate to states that had banned trade in radioactive substances on their territory. Fifteen of them recently threatened to prohibit

(37) T. TREVES : op.cit, 478.
(38) E. WEINSTEIN : "The impact of regulation of transport of hazardous waste on freedom of navigation". IJMCL, Vol 9, n° 2, 1994, 141.

the passage through their territorial waters of the *Pacific Pintail*, a British nuclear fuel carrier. This cargo could be conveyed from France to Japan by several routes : through the Panama Canal, round Cape Horn off the coasts of Argentina and Chile, or round the Cape of Good Hope in South Africa.

Several States have submitted draft rules to IMO, aimed at preventing ships carrying INF materials from exercising rights of passage through territorial waters, because of the growing threat raised by such hazardous waste for coastal interests and the marine environment in general. The Solomon Islands (39) and Argentina (40) have called for requirements to be introduced ranging from prior consultation about the route to be taken to exclusion from certain routes in zones where retrieval would be impossible.

These proposals are currently the subject of sharp discussions, within the MSC and the Legal Committee of IMO. Several delegations consider that general exclusion is excessive and contrary to the provisions of the 1982 Convention. The only measures that would be acceptable would be appropriate routeing arrangements (41).

Faced with this international divergence of views, operators of ships conveying INF materials show a degree of caution in their choice of shipping routes. For example, the *Pacific Pintail* took care not to cross the territorial waters of States hostile to this type of trade (42), no doubt from a desire to avoid a blast of international protest about the transport of hazardous waste, but also because of a legal uncertainty that IMO has not yet managed to dissipate.

3. Oil tankers

231. - Following the *Amoco Cadiz* disaster, and therefore well before adoption of the new LOS Convention, France immediately applied the provisions under discussion at the time. Its circular of 24 March 1978 institutes very strict control of traffic in French territorial waters for all ships carrying hydrocarbons, with a ban on coming within seven miles of coasts, designation of port access channels, obligation to give prior notification.

These regulations comply fully with article 211.4 of the 1982 LOS Convention, which indicates that "coastal States may, in the exercise of their sovereignty within their territorial sea, adopt laws and regulations for the prevention, reduction and control of marine pollution from foreign vessels". However, they must not hamper innocent passage.

The situation is different for damaged oil tankers, which may be banned from access to territorial waters. Certain States like China go further, by extending this measure to foreign tankers more than twenty years old, even in a perfect state of seaworthiness (43).

VI - INTERNAL WATERS

232. - Article 8.1 of the 1982 LOS Convention stipulates that "waters on the landward side of the baseline of the territorial sea form part of the internal waters of the State". These consist of ports, roads, bays and inland seas.

A coastal State exercises full and complete sovereignty over this part of the maritime territory, with sole power to regulate shipping entering and using its ports (44).

(39) IMO. LEG 74/12, 19 July1996.
(40) IMO. LEG 74/12/1, 9 August 1996.
(41) IMO. LEG 74/13, 22 Oct 1996, 97-102.
(42) "Right of passage means open seas for waste". Lloyd's List, 2 March 1995.
(43) IMO. FSI 5/11/2, 14 Nov. 1996. National Rules banning older ships.
(44) V-D. DEGAN : "Internal waters". NYIL. Vol. 17, 1986, 3-44.

A - PORT ACCESS

1. The traditional regime of the right of access

For a long time, the principle of freedom of access of foreign ships to ports prevailed. This rule, justified mainly by economic factors connected with the growth of the shipping trade, was not accepted without a fight, going as it does against the territorial powers of coastal States over their internal waters (45).

a) Geneva Convention 1923

The principle of freedom of access was codified by the Convention on the regime of maritime ports, signed in Geneva in December 1923. Article 2 of the appended Statute provides for "equality of treatment with its own vessels, or those of any other State whatsoever, in the maritime ports situated under its sovereignty or authority, as regards freedom of access to the ports, the use of the port, and full enjoyment of its benefits as regards navigation and commercial operations which it affords to vessels, their cargoes and passengers".

The Geneva Convention, which came into effect on 26 July 1926, has been ratified by only thirty-five States, not including the United States or the countries of the former Soviet Union. Some commentators have deduced from this absence of consensus that one cannot assume any right of access to ports, unless expressly stipulated by convention (46). However, this Convention remains the reference text which guides general practice followed by States on this issue. In general, doctrine is very much divided on the principle of freedom of access. Most commentators seem to come out in favour of free admission (47), but refuse to assert the existence of a common-law right of access to ports, except for the purposes of taking refuge (48).

b) LOS Convention 1982

233. - Recognition of freedom of access does not mean that ships can do whatever they like. The law of the sea grants coastal and port States wide powers of regulation to protect safety of navigation and prevent pollution.

• Regulation of navigation
To begin with, article 25.2 of the 1982 LOS Convention allows the sovereign State to take any necessary measures to prevent breaches of the conditions to which admission of ships to its internal water is subject.

---

(45) R. LAUN : "Le régime international des ports". RCADI, 1926, 34.
(46) T. TREVES in J. DUPUY, D. VIGNES : "Traité du droit de la mer" op.cit. 781.
(47) - C.J. COLOMBOS : "Le droit international de la mer". Paris, Pedone, 1952, 109.
- A.V. LOWE : "The right of entry into maritime ports in international law". San Diego Law Review. Vol 14, April 1977, n° 3, 597-622.
- L. de LA FAYETTE : "Access to ports in international law". IJMCL. Vol II, n° 1, 1996, 1-22.
- L. LUCCHINI, M. VOELCKEL : "Droit de la Mer". Tome 2, Vol 2, Pedone, Paris 1996, 282.
- R. GOY : "La liberté d'accès au port des navires de commerce". ERM, 1993, n° 7, 263.
(48) - G. GIDEL : "Le droit international public de la mer. Les eaux intérieures". Paris, Sirey, Vol 2, 1932, 50.
- N. GUYEN QUOC DINH, P. DAILLER, A. PELLET : "Droit international public". LGDJ, Paris, 1994, 1060.

Under the Convention, very extensive powers are exercised by a coastal State, which may :
- decide which of its ports are open to international shipping ;
- subject to rules of non-discrimination and prior notification (49), close certain port installations temporarily, unless a ship is forced to take refuge because of an accident (50) ;
- regulate access conditions.

• **Prevention of pollution**

The right to ban access to ports is recognised in several IMO conventions on prevention of pollution. For instance, article VIbis.4 of the 1971 amendment to the 1954 Convention, concerning the arrangement of tanks and limits on their size, recognises that if a contracting State has clear grounds for believing that a tanker does not comply with the required specifications, it may deny access to its ports or territorial waters. A similar provision appears in article 5.3 of the MARPOL Convention 1973/78, though with certain restrictions.

The wreck of the *Amoco Cadiz* led the 1982 LOS Convention to reinforce the rights of protection of coastal States. Article 211.3 allows the coastal state to impose special conditions on foreign ships wishing to enter its internal waters. The same possibility is granted to States in a single region that wish to harmonise different policies on the issue. Several conditions govern exercise of this right, in order to prevent misuse. The measures taken by a coastal State must have the aim of preventing, reducing and controlling pollution of the marine environment, be given due publicity, and be communicated to the proper international organisation.

According to certain commentators, these conditions very much limit the regulatory powers of coastal States (51). They cannot lay down special requirements for admission to its ports, for ships registered in states with which it is already bound by international agreements, such as the SOLAS or MARPOL Conventions. This interpretation is in line with traditional doctrine, prohibiting a coastal State from setting more severe standards for a foreign ship in its internal waters, if they affect the internal order of the ship, an area that is within the exclusive attributions of the flag State (52).

c) Local safety regulations

234. - Policing of navigation in ports, roads, estuaries and rivers open to navigation is one of the special areas of concern of local safety regulations. These concern access to such areas and their use, and secondarily prevention of collisions.

The validity of local regulations in international law is recognised in Regulation 1b of the COLREG Convention of 1972, which declares that "nothing in these rules shall interfere with the operation of special rules made by an appropriate authority, for roadsteads, harbour, rivers, lakes or inland waterways connected with the high seas and navigable by seagoing vessels".

(49) L. CAVARE : "Le droit international positif". Tome II, 1969, Pedone, Paris, 802.
(50) F. CASTBERG : "Distinction entre les eaux territoriales et les eaux intérieures". AIDI 1954. Tome I, 113 et suivantes.
(51) M. VALENZUELA : "International maritime transportation : selected issues of the Law of the Sea". 23rd conference of the Law of Sea Institute, LSI Honolulu, 1989.
(52) P. BONASSIES : "La loi du pavillon et les conflits de droit maritime". RCADI, 1969, III, 616.

However, the rule applies only where general rules and local rules are in conflict with one another. If there is no such conflict, the equivalence between the two sets of regulations leaves Regulation 1b without effect, even though general rules are added to local rules (53).

2. Special admission conditions

Concern for safety has encouraged coastal States to adopt protective measures that represent departures from the general policy of freedom of access. Certain vessels, such as nuclear-powered ships or dangerous or polluting ships present exceptional risks that warrant the establishment of special admission conditions.

a) Admission of nuclear-powered ships

235. - This question is of merely academic interest, since there are no longer any nuclear-powered merchant ships operating in the world. The solutions worked out internationally are worth attention, however, for they could easily be transposed to other situations involving major technological hazards.

• **Prior authorisation**
In the absence of a universal convention, flag and coastal States have signed bilateral agreements, to allow nuclear-powered merchant ships to enter and use their ports (54).
The United States concluded several treaties concerning the nuclear-powered *Savannah*, with European States admitting this ship (55). A series of similar agreements was signed by the German government and host countries for the *Otto Hahn* (56). Most such agreements contain two types of provisions, preventive measures intended to avoid any incidents, and other curative measures, to settle problems of liability and compensation (57).
Exorbitant preventive powers are conferred on the coastal State. It can require submission of a very detailed safety file, the purpose of which is to supply maximum information and guarantees concerning the reliability of the ship. It also has discretionary powers to accept or refuse entry to ships, even if they comply in every way with SOLAS requirements for nuclear ships, set out in chapter 8. It is entitled to lay down additional conditions, special sea lanes for navigation, and it can require an impact study concerning the consequences of the ship's passage or possible accidents. Finally, when the ship stays in port, the host State retains the right to demand increased supervision (57).

(53) - C. Kenneth MAC GUFFIE : "Marsden's Collision at Sea". British Shipping Laws. London. Stevens and Sons Ldt, 1962, 590.
- John Wheller GRIFFIN : "Griffin on collision. The American Law of collision". Edward Brothers Inc. 1963.
- A.N. COCKCROFT et LAMEIJER : "A guide to the collision avoidance rules". London, Stanford maritime Ltd. 1977, 135.
(54) L. LUCCHINI et M. VOELCKEL : "Passage dans les eaux territoriales et séjour dans les ports, du navire à propulsion nucléaire". Droit nucléaire et Droit océanique. Economica, Paris, 1977, 9 à 60.
(55) V.R. KOVAR : "Les accords conclus au sujet du *Savannah* et la responsabilité civile des exploitants de navires nucléaires". AFDI 1965, 788.
(56) BOULANGER : "La Convention de Bruxelles de 1962 sur la responsabilité civile et les accords du *Otto Hahn*". Colloque Paris 1975. Centre d'études et de recherches de droit international. Paris I.
(57) - OECD Nuclear Energy Agency and International Atomic Energy. Agency Symposium on the safety of nuclear ships. Hamburg, 5-9, Dec. 1997. Processing - Session V - Port Entry Considerations, 397-500.
- E. JANSEN : "The IMO and the peaceful use of nuclear energy through the last 30 years". IMO, September 1989.

b) Admission of ships in distress

236. - Ships in distress traditionally enjoy the right to take refuge in the nearest port. This very ancient principle is currently questioned by coastal States anxious to protect their environment and the safety of coastal populations.

• Right of entry in distress

Inspired by humanitarian considerations, the right of entry in distress in fact has two aspects: a foreign ship can enter the internal waters of a coastal State and put into its ports; it also benefits from certain immunities from the jurisdiction of the host State, such as the possibility of disregarding access rules, or non-payment of certain dues (58).

This customary right remains rather vague. What is a state of distress ? How does it differ from simply being damaged ? Commentators agree on acknowledging that it may be regarded as involving *force majeure* or exceptional navigational circumstances.

Several international conventions deal with cases of *force majeure*, though without detailing the criteria of the state of distress, which continue to raise controversy. Under article 18.2 of the 1982 LOS Convention, for example, ships can enter and anchor in territorial waters if "they are incidental to ordinary navigation or are rendered necessary by *force majeure* or distress". Article IV of the 1974 SOLAS Convention also stipulates that "a ship which is not subject to the provisions of the present Convention at the time of its departure on any voyage shall not become subject (...) on account of any deviation from its intended voyage due to stress of weather or any other case of *force majeure*".

Another source of controversy is the bearing of the immunities granted to a ship in distress. In the case of the *MV Frontier*, a South African court of appeal considered that a ship whose unseaworthiness caused the situation of distress could not hope to benefit from any jurisdictional immunity (59).

• Refusal of access for dangerous or polluting ships

The right of entry in distress is no longer absolute, as it was in the time of sailing ships. The enormous increase in the size of ships, the dangerous character of the cargoes they transport, and the large quantities of fuel on board, have led coastal States to cast doubt on the right of access for ships in difficulty. Two arguments have been advanced: legitimate public health concerns for the population of the coastal State, and above all the need to protect the environment.

In the past, such a measure remained exceptional. Nowadays, there is a tendency to extend it to cover all vessels in difficulty, especially oil tankers and ships carrying toxic, polluting or explosive products. Examples have abounded over the last twenty years (60).

The problem of what are labelled "maritime lepers" or "flying Dutchmen" (61) remains topical, as shown by the case of the *Kurdistan*, for which security of US$50 million was demanded before it could enter a Canadian port (62). There was also the *Khark V*, an oil tanker damaged by fire, abandoned by its crew in December 1989 off the Moroccan coast, and which was banned from entering Moroccan and Spanish territorial waters, even though the oil spilling into the sea could have been stopped if the ship had been given shelter (63).

(58) M.S. Mc DOUGAL et W.T. BURKE : "The public order of the oceans. A contemporary international Law of the Sea". Yale University Press, New Haven/London, 1962, 110.
(59) D.J. DEVINE : "Ships in distress - a judicial contribution from the South Atlantic". Marine Policy, Vol 20, n° 3, 1996, 229-234.
(60) "Leper casualties need safe havens". Lloyd's List, 10 June 1991.
(61) G. KASOULIDES : "Vessels in distress. Safe havens for crippled tankers». Marine Policy, July 1987, 186.
(62) E. GOLD : "Marine salvage : toward a new regime". JMLC, vol 20, n° 4, oct. 1989, 492.
(63) T. IJLSTRA : "The Khark V accident : oil tanker accident and salvors". Marine Pollution Bulletin, Vol 21, n° 3, 1990, 112.

In addition to the obligation of assistance or the subordination of assistance to the orders of the coastal State, such events raise the question of such a State's responsibility in the case of a decision to refuse to admit ships in difficulty to its internal waters. This is an important aspect of safety at sea, which the law cannot settle once and for all, but which has to be settled administratively and politically on a case-by-case basis. It is easy to understand the completely justifiable reluctance of a coastal state to accept a potential source of pollution close to its shores or in its ports. On the other hand, a number of examples have shown that it is often wiser to admit a ship in difficulty, rather than refuse it access. In the end, it depends on what risk the coastal State is prepared to take, given the precautions that may reasonably be deployed for this type of operation.

• **Salvage and safe havens**
A major convention, to replace the Brussels Convention of 1910 on assistance and salvage at sea, was adopted under IMO auspices on 28 April 1989. It came into effect in July 1996, introducing new provisions for assistance to ships likely to cause marine pollution, and those which could become dangerous wrecks.

Article 14.2 of this Convention acknowledges the possibility of increasing the compensation payable to a salvor who has prevented or minimised damage to the environment by 30 per cent of the expenses incurred. This compensation may even rise to 10 per cent in certain circumstances.

Without waiting for the new Convention to come into force, British insurance companies, in agreement with the International Association of Ports & Harbours (IAPH), proposed a new standard contract, the "Lloyd's Open Form 1990" (LOF 90), which places an obligation on the parties to insert a pollution prevention clause. This contract thus gives a port admitting a ship in difficulty full latitude to organise its entry in such as way as to ensure that risks are reduced and under proper control. There are no general rules, and every port applies its own local regulations (64).

The most effective solution, of course, remains the creation of ports of refuge, or "safe havens", specially equipped to receive dangerous or polluting ships in difficulty. Disaffected drilling platforms or deepwater ports could offer interesting possibilities. The issue was debated in 1986 in the Legal Committee of IMO, though without any satisfactory solution emerging. During discussion of article 9, on cooperation among the contracting parties, certain delegations mentioned the possibility of requiring a coastal State to offer assistance to ships in difficulty. The IAPH refused to associate itself with any proposal that could force States to designate safe havens for ships in distress (65). Failing any overall international agreement on the issue, the problem persists. Only a few States have so far listed sites where polluting ships can take refuge.

c) Admission of substandard ships

237. - Can a coastal State refuse substandard ships access to its ports ? The development of databases on the condition of ships and the new possibilities offered by information technologies make such a measure feasible at present. For the moment, only the United States and the European Union have considered such a move.

In December 1994, the US Coast Guard announced that it was introducing preventive State control, by boarding potentially substandard ships at sea, rather than waiting for them to

(64) R. MAST : "Acceptance of incident ship in port". Maritime Transport International 1993, 71-76.
(65) LEG 56/9, par. 88 and 91. April 1986.

enter American ports. The USCG pointed out that a substandard ship was in violation of its right of innocent passage, by being prejudicial to the peace, good order and security of the coastal State (66).

EU Council Directive 95/21/EC of 19 June 1995 concerns the enforcement of international standards for ships safety, pollution prevention and on-board living and working conditions (PSC), to vessels using EU ports and sailing in the waters under the jurisdiction of the member States (67). Article 11 of this Directive contains very clear stipulations on this point. If the ship captain or shipowner refuses to bring the ship into conformity with international conventions, it is to be refused access to any EU port, until the owner has provided evidence of full compliance with requirements. For the ship to be effectively banned from EU ports, the proper authority in the member State that has discovered deficiencies is required to alert immediately the authorities in all other member States. However, if the ship becomes an even more serious threat, either for marine fauna or for the coasts or interests of a member State, it could be authorised to enter an EU port, provided that adequate measures have been taken to ensure safe entry, and that the shipowner has provided the surety required by the host State.

This ban on admission to EU ports has been criticised by certain commentators. In his report *Safer ships, cleaner seas*, Lord Donaldson considered such a draconian measure not the most effective way of eradicating substandard tonnage. Apart from the practical difficulties of carrying it into effect, an access ban could create even greater threats to the environment, especially when a damaged oil tanker caught in a storm does not quickly find refuge (68).

B - SHIPS IN PORT

238. - Once it has entered port, a ship is subject to the laws of the coastal State. There are no exceptions to this principle whenever safety is involved. It applies on several levels.

• Regulation of movements and mooring
The ship must comply with all port State regulations to prevent accidents, particularly policing of maritime movements in the port, towing and piloting obligations, orders to do with mooring, quayside lighting, and rules on handling potentially dangerous or toxic goods.

• Ship safety
The port State may also oversee application of international regulations on safety of life at sea, loadlines and pollution prevention. It is entitled to carry out surveys and inspections, and to immobilise at the quayside any ships presenting a danger for safety or the environment (69) (cf chapter 25 below).

(66) J.E. HARE : "Flag, coastal and Port State Control : closing the net on unseaworthy ship and their unscrupulous owners". Sea Changes. Institute of Marine Law New Letter, n° 16, 1994, 67.

(67) OJEC, n° 157/1, 7 July 1995.

(68) Report of Lord Donaldson's inquiry into the prevention of pollution from merchant shipping. London, HMSO, May 1994. Denial of the right to enter UK ports, 11.72, 152..

(69) Rapport des travaux sur l'immobilisation forcée du navire du fait du prince présenté par E. LANGAVANT, in Colloque de Bordeaux sur l'immobilisation forcée des navires, 20-22 octobre 1988. Presse Universitaire de Bordeaux, May 1990.

• **Protective measures**

Immobilisation in dock or in the roadstead can present serious risks for the safety of the port, and sometimes for the surrounding urban area, particularly when such ships are carrying dangerous goods or explosives. In such cases, there are absolutely no international restrictions on the prerogatives of the coastal State. Port authorities may demand the immediate departure of the ship or order it to be moved from one berth to another within the harbour area. They may also go on board to take any measures necessary to handle the ship if the crew refuses to comply (70).

VII - INTERNATIONAL CANALS

239. - Sea canals, located entirely on the territories of certain States, have a special regime, and are treated differently from internal waters (71). These are international communication routes linking two free maritime areas. Freedom of passage therefore has to be observed, despite the territorial sovereignty of the surrounding State. The main interoceanic canals, Suez, Panama and Kiel, are covered by conventions regulating the right of passage.

• **Suez Canal**

The regime of the Suez Canal was laid down in the Constantinople Convention of 1888, which established free navigation on the waterway. Its provisions were completed by the Canal Navigation Regulations and the Canal Authority Code, confirmed by an Egyptian law of 24 April 1957. These rules require Canal Authority instructions and circulars to conform to COLREG and SOLAS Conventions, as well as to Egyptian legislation. They are of the greatest importance, since they lay down technical conditions for ships admitted to the Canal and transit procedures.

The validity of some of these rules under international law has been questioned on several occasions, notably after the adoption of circular 33/84 of 13 March 1984 allowing the Canal Authority to refuse for two years the passage of any ship failing to submit declarations on dangerous cargoes. Circular 86/84 of 9 April 1984 instituted more detailed supervision of ships and certain installations, in addition to checks on cargoes and documents (72).

• **Panama Canal**

The regime for the Panama Canal is laid down in two bilateral treaties, signed on 7 September 1977 between Panama and the United States. These treaties, which abrogate the treaty of 18 November 1903, are due to expire on 31 December 1999. Freedom of passage for ships has been recognised since the Anglo-American treaty of 18 November 1901. These rules are largely inspired by the Suez Canal regime (73).

(70) A. VIALARD : "Les actions de l'Etat sur les navires étrangers relevant du droit civil et pénal". In Les prérogatives étatiques sur les navires étrangers, Université de Bordeaux, 1981.
(71) Y VAN DER MENSBRUGGHE : "Les canaux et les détroits dans le droit de la mer actuel" in Droit de la mer. Paris, Pedone 1977, 181-247.
(72) T.A. SINTSOVA : "The regime of navigation in the Suez Canal". Marine Policy, July 1988, 263-270.
(73) International Navigable Waterways. Report on the Symposium. Buenos Aires 30 Nov. - 4 Dec. 1970. UNITAR. New York, 1975.

• Kiel Canal

The Treaty of Versailles of 1919, which internationalised the Kiel Canal, recognised freedom of access and passage for all ships. However, since the canal remains an inland waterway, safety regulations for navigation depend entirely on the German authorities (74).

CONCLUSION : increasing curtailment of freedom of navigation

240. - The safety of navigation and preservation of the marine environment have become essential concepts of public order at sea. The new law of the sea, laid down in the 1982 LOS Convention, makes significant inroads into the traditional principle of free navigation. With succeeding disasters at sea, coastal States have imposed increasingly stringent restrictions on ships, by extending the areas subject to their territorial sovereignty, but more importantly by adopting restrictive regulations for all ships passing their coasts (75).

Increasing prominence is given to new theories that tend to restrict freedom of navigation. The latest comes from a Norwegian research programme, involving exploration of the idea of "risk zone". It is based on indexing oil tankers according to the risks they represent for the environment, on the basis of their age, flag and anti-pollution features. Ships with a low rating on this index would be forced to make long detours round certain sensitive zones (76).

For the moment, there has been no application of these proposals. Safety at sea is a collective concept, that obliges States to reach agreement. Effective exercise of their powers usually comes up against legal and economic obstacles that preclude them acting unilaterally.

(74) The Kiel Canal - 100th Anniversary. BIMCO Bulletin, vol. 90, n° 4 - 1995.
(75) A.L. MORGAN : "The new Law of the Sea : Rethinking the implication for sovereign jurisdiction and freedom of action". ODIL, 1996, 27, 5-29.
(76) "Norway explores risk zone idea". Lloyd's List, 29 June 1994.

CHAPTER 9

Unilateral regulations

241. - Since the beginning of the 20th century, nearly all international regulations and standards concerning safety at sea have emerged from a consensus achieved in the relations among States. Multilateral conventions lay down universally accepted regulations, and intergovernmental organisations adopt recommendations that cannot take effect unless member States agree.

This policy of consensus is at present increasingly called into question by the spread of unilateralist attitudes. International law defines this concept as the display of a State will to carry out certain legal acts, generating standards that form part of the legal system and produce limited effects (1).

Commentators have drawn attention to the special part played by unilateralism in the formation of the law of the sea (2). Safety is no stranger to this trend. Negotiation is increasingly giving way to blunt assertions of urgent new priorities. Every fresh disaster at sea calls into question the effectiveness of the traditional path of consensus. A State whose vital interests are affected or simply threatened demands well-nigh instantaneous action, to remedy shortcomings or plug loopholes in international regulations.

This chapter is concerned with these one-sided actions to improve safety provisions. Consideration will be given in turn to how and why there has been this development (cf I below), justifications and areas where such practices occur (II), and finally their consequences for the international regulatory system (III).

I - GROWTH OF UNILATERAL MEASURES

242. - A relatively rare phenomenon thirty years ago, unilateralism is at present tending to become commonplace in international law. There are several reasons for this worrying trend in the form of legislation.

---

(1) On the subject of unilateral action in international law :
- J. DEHAUSSY : Jurisclasseur de droit international, vol. I. Fasc. n°14.
"Les actes juridiques unilatéraux." J.D.I., 1965.
- E. SUY : "Les actes juridiques unilatéraux en droit international public". Paris, 1962.
- G VENTURINI : "La portée et les effets juridiques des attitudes et des actes unilatéraux". R.C.A.D.I., 1964, II, 347.
(2) On the law of the sea :
- L. LUCCHINI et M. VOELCKEL : "Les Etats de la mer. Le nationalisme maritime". Paris, La Documentation Française, 1979, 304 à 311.
- G. APOLLIS : "L'emprise maritime de l'Etat côtier". Paris, Pedone, 1981.

A - CAUSES OF UNILATERALISM

The causes arise both from inadequacies in the present system, and from the immediate interests of States faced with a maritime disaster.

1. Inadequacies of the international system

The recurrence of accidents at sea has several times drawn attention to weaknesses in the institutional regulatory system. These include the difficulty of achieving a global consensus, slowness in establishing and enforcing the resulting legal provisions, and deficiencies and uncertainties in the standards and regulations they contain.

Rightly or wrongly, intergovernmental organisations, and IMO in particular, have been held responsible for this situation. The main criticism is aimed at their bureaucratic struct-ures, and their powerlessness to have stricter new standards adopted or existing regulations enforced. The general discontent has fuelled a certain scepticism about the real effectiveness of the institutional system. It has also encouraged the emergence of certain individual initiat-ives to prevent threats coming from the sea.

2. Reaction to disasters at sea

A unilateral act nearly always emerges from a disaster at sea. Such events are now the subject of intense media attention, arousing powerful feelings among the public, which then exerts almost immediate pressure on politicians.

The suddenness of such disasters explains the hasty reactions of certain States. There is no time to hesitate and negotiate solutions in the quiet atmosphere of international gatherings. The public mood demands quick decisions, refusal of any compromise, the curt assertion of an attitude that meets its expectations.

B - FORMS OF UNILATERALISM

243. - Unilateral action on safety at sea often takes the form of regulations, in other words legal instruments emanating from national legislative or regulatory authorities. Enforcement of the measures that have been taken is accompanied by physical actions such as boarding, inspecting or detaining ships (3).

This determination to adopt regulations that go beyond general accepted international standards can have different aims, for example to activate a decision-taking process, or to correct the deficiencies of the existing system.

If the aim is to spur action, unilateral behaviour rarely goes beyond a threat, intended to exert pressure on organisations, either to speed up the implementation of internationally adopted provisions, or to launch amendments to current conventions. In this case, unilateral action usually takes the form of official declarations by one or more States, which are amply commented in the media.

If unilateral action is intended to remedy existing provisions, the State carries its threats into effect, and adopts its own regulations. It is no longer the regulatory process that is called into question, but the actual content of standards.

In either case, the unilateral action may be taken by a single State, or by several States adopting individual measures with a similar content.

(3) L. LUCCHINI and M. VOELCKEL : "Droit de la Mer". Tome I, Paris, Pedone, 1990, 52.

II - UNILATERAL ACTIONS : AREAS AND JUSTIFICATIONS

244. - Humanitarian or ecological considerations are the main arguments of States taking unilateral action on safety. The measures themselves are based on natural justice rather than on solid legal arguments.

A - SAFETY OF LIFE AT SEA

Regulations on passenger transport by sea have been one of the particular targets of unilateral State action.

1. Draft US regulations on cruise ship safety

The cruise industry has grown spectacularly in the United States in recent times (4). This form of tourism is provided by cruise liners belonging to American and Norwegian companies, but registered under other flags, to avoid United States tax, labour and safety laws. The specific nature of this industry, and its mass public, have led the United States to place ocean cruises under close surveillance. In this hypersensitive environment, the slightest incident takes on major proportions, and generates exaggerated reactions from political and administrative authorities.

a) Celebration *accident*

On 10 February 1989, the passenger ship *Celebration* collided with a small bulk carrier off the coast of Cuba. The cargo ship sank, with the loss of three crew members. None of the cruise passengers was injured or killed, yet the accident caused an uproar in the United States (5) : the National Transportation Safety Board (NTSB) immediately embarked on an investigation into the accident, and a major study of the safety of passenger ships operating in US waters.
It also called for an increase in inspections in American ports and a strengthening of the powers of the US Coast Guard (USCG). Pressure was also put on Congress to take legislative steps as soon as possible.

b) Threat of unilateral action

The bill examined by Congress was intended to introduce severer controls on cruise vessels in American ports, regardless of their country of registration. In other words, American safety standards were to be applied to foreign vessels. The risk of driving some operators away from American ports to Santo Domingo or elsewhere was considered, but failed to shake the determination of Congress to take action.
It required official approaches to the State Department by thirteen countries and the Council of European and Japanese National Shipowners Associations (CENSA) to halt the legislative process.
On the basis of a decision of the Supreme Court (McCullough v. Sociedad Nacional de Marineros de Honduras), CENSA succeeded in having the precedence of flag State law affirmed. It argued the harmful effects of unilateral American action.

---

(4) J. CHARLIER : "Petite géographie des croisières maritimes". JMM, 3 nov. 1995, 2757 et suivantes.
(5) M. SOBEY : " International cooperation in marine casualty investigation : an analysis of IMO Resolution A.613". Maritime Pol. MGMT, 1993, vol 20, n° 1, 3-39.

Withdrawal of the bill did not affect the determination of Congress to act to improve safety on cruise ships. In a survey published in April 1993, the General Accounting Office, an investigative arm of Congress, denounced the lax attitude of certain flag States to regulations, leading to inadequate safety information for passengers, lack of firefighting training for the crew, and other deficiencies (6). In June the same year, the NTSB asked the USCG to enforce existing regulations with the utmost rigour (7). In October 1994, it requested Congress to adopt regulations to improve the qualification of crew members and training in emergency situations (8). Following a spate of fires and groundings in 1995 in US waters (9), the USCG decided to set up a task force to carry out an exhaustive survey of the safety of cruise ships (10). The findings, published in October 1995, gave priority to control of human factors in preventing accidents, but they did not lead to any unilateral action by the United States against ships flying foreign flags.

2. British regulations on carferry safety

245. - Every year, some twenty-four million passengers use the ferries that run between the European mainland and the British Isles. The scale of cross-Channel traffic has led the United Kingdom to be particularly vigilant about safety, especially since the appalling disaster of the *Herald of Free Enterprise*.

a) Herald of Free Enterprise *accident*

On 6 March 1987, the *Herald of Free Enterprise*, a ro-ro passenger vessel on the route between Belgium and England capsized and sank shortly after leaving the port of Zeebrugge (11).

This accident, which caused the death of 193 passengers and crew members, most of them British, was a national tragedy for the United Kingdom. Public opinion and the media pointed to the inadequacy of safety regulations, and called upon the authorities to take urgent steps to prevent such a disaster recurring.

An official enquiry opened a few weeks after the accident (12), led with all deliberate speed by the chairman, Mr Justice Sheen : on 24 July, a fifty-page report was published. It established the causes of the accident and the division of responsibilities, pronounced sanctions against the guilty, and recommended certain preventive measures.

The chairman did not come to a decision about the design of ro-ro ferries, but he recommended immediate action on essential safety equipment for crossings (13).

b) British solutions

246. - In the aftermath of the tragedy, the United Kingdom asked IMO to act urgently to improve the safety of ro-ro passenger vessels. It submitted a series of measures, most of them based on the findings of the Sheen inquiry. These were examined immediately by IMO, which between April 1988 and April 1992 adopted four series of regulations that meant far-reaching changes in the 1974 SOLAS Convention (14).

(6) " Report slams cruiseship safety standards ". Lloyd's List, 20 April 1993.
(7) - " Cruiseship fire safety under attack ". Lloyd's List, 8 June 1993.
- " US revives cruises safety fears ". Lloyd's List, 21 August 1993.
(8) " Crews in the safety spotlight ". Lloyd's List, 31 Oct. 1994.
(9) " USCG orders cruiseship safety review ". Lloyd's List, 27 July 1995.
(10) " Safer cruiseships ". Lloyd's List, 1st August 1995.
(11) S. CRAINER : " Zeebrugge : Learning from disaster ". Herald Charible Trust, London, 1993.
(12) "Herald inquiry is told that lessons have to be learned". Lloyd's List, 28 April 1987.
(13) " The Inquiry recommandations ". Lloyd's List, 25 July 1997.
(14) " IMO and ro-ro safety ". Focus on IMO. Sept. 1995, 13-18.

• Ro-ro ferry stability

Simultaneously, the British government launched a research programme to assess the effectiveness of the measures undertaken. Research showed that new residual stability standards provided effective protection against sudden capsizing. However, it drew attention to the poor safety showing of ferries in service, incapable of remaining afloat after damage in waves one metre high or even less (15).

Once these results were known, the United Kingdom proposed that SOLAS amendments on damage stability, which had come into force in 1990 for all new ships, should be made mandatory for existing ro-ro passenger vessels, from 1st March 1993. This request was accompanied by a threat of unilateral action if no agreement were reached internationally on the issue (16).

• Refusal of exemption clauses

Apart from their substantial financial implications (17), the United Kingdom proposals set out to be legally radical, in prohibiting any exemption clauses. Such "grandfather clauses", which appear in all IMO conventions, make any new technical requirements of an instrument applicable only to new vessels. In the opinion of the British, this policy could no longer be tolerated, following the *Herald of Free Enterprise* accident.

c) Regionalisation of safety standards

247. - In Spring 1992 , in the face of British determination, the MSC examined how the new stability standards could be applied to existing ferries. Despite their radical nature, the British proposals received the support of enough IMO delegations, so that the MSC decided to apply SOLAS 1990, in more flexible form, to ferries in service. In order not to lay too heavy a financial burden on shipowners, however, a period of grace of eleven years was set, beginning on 1st October 1994, so that ships in service could be upgraded (18).

Realising that its deadlines could not be respected at IMO, the United Kingdom turned to its European partners to hasten the regulatory process (19). On 27 July 1993, a regional agreement was signed in London by fourteen European countries (Belgium, Denmark, France, Germany, Greece, Ireland, Italy, Luxembourg, Netherlands, Portugal, Spain, Sweden, Norway, United Kingdom). Under the terms of this agreement, the States concerned undertook to apply SOLAS 90 standards in accordance with a stricter overall timetable to all existing ro-ro passenger vessels providing services in the Western European zone, and including notably the Channel, the Iroise Sea and the North Sea (20)

The threat of unilateral United Kingdom action was therefore set aside, but at the cost of a two-tier approach to safety at sea : one for North-West European countries, and the other conducted by IMO for the rest of the world. The idea of regional standards was born, and its importance was confirmed a few months later, following the loss of the *Estonia*.

3. Norwegian regulations on safety of ro-ro passenger ships

248. - One of the most serious accidents in the history of navigation, in terms of fatalities, was the loss of the *Estonia*, which encouraged the emergence of new regional regulations to reinforce the safety of passenger ferries in the Northern European zone.

---

(15) D. FOXWELL : " Ro-ro study critises ferry standards ". Safety at Sea International, Dec. 1994, 7-8.
(16) " Britain ready to go it alone on ferry safety ". Lloyd's List, 25 Nov. 1992.
(17) IMO. "Passenger and crew safety on board ship". World Maritime Day, 1991.
(18) " Existing ro-ro fleet to be upgraded ". IMO News, n° 2 1992.
(19) " Europe acts on ro-ro standards ". Lloyd's List, 26 June 1993.
(20) "Agreement concerning the stability of existing RoRo passenger ships operating services to or from ports within a designated sea area of North West Europe". In IMO, MSC 64/3/1, Annex, 13 Sept. 1994.

a) Estonia *accident and its repercussions in Northern Europe*

On 27 September 1994, the carferry *Estonia*, registered in Estonia, left the port of Tallinn on the Baltic for Stockholm, with 989 passengers and thirty-two cars and lorries on board. During the night, the ship ran into very heavy weather. About one in the morning, the Finnish maritime authorities received a distress signal. Within a few minutes the *Estonia* foundered off the island of Utö, south-west of Finland. 138 people were rescued, but there were more than 850 deaths (21).

Following the disaster, Estonia, Finland and Sweden set up a tripartite commission of inquiry to look for the causes of the accident (22). It published its final report in December 1997. The nine experts believed that the accident was due to seawater on the car deck. Water had got in through the bow doors of the ship, following the loss of the bow visor, which exposed the internal access ramp to the pressure of the waves, weakening its locking mechanism. The carferry had capsized so quickly because of the enormous quantities of water that had flooded on to the car deck, stability being affected by the sloshing movements of the unstable liquid mass, which destroyed the ship's equilibrium. This had already happened to the *Herald of Free Enterprise* (23).

This tragedy in the Baltic rekindled controversy about the safety of carferries, particularly in Northern European countries, where this very popular form of transport is also an important component of the leisure and tourist industries.

Without awaiting the findings of the *Estonia* inquiry, certain Scandinavian countries took provisional steps to improve the safety of existing ferries (24).

b) *Norwegian action*

249. - In contrast to other Nordic countries, Norway showed a determination to act fast and decisively to improve the safety of carferries.

• Formation of Norwegian working group

Only a few days after the *Estonia* sank, and without awaiting an IMO initiative, Norway announced its intention to draw up new regulations for the survival capacity of existing ro-ro ferries: in future, all ships visiting Norwegian ports would have to comply with a new damage stability standard, ensuring that they would remain upright despite the presence of a certain quantity of water on their car deck (25). While hoping that the Scandinavian countries and the United Kingdom would share its point of view, Norway hinted at the threat of unilateral action, if no international agreement could be found (26).

• Absence of international consensus on minimum damage stability standard

Well before being endorsed by IMO, the Norwegian solution for strengthening the damage stability of ferries sparked a conflict on the international stage. The need for a ferry

(21) - Lloyd's List, 29 Sept. 1994, 30 Sept. 1994, 1 Oct. 1994.
See also :
- H. HONKA : " Questions on maritime safety and liability especially in view of the Estonia disaster ". Essay in honour of Hugo Tiberg. Off print Juristförlaget, Stockholm, 1996, 351-382.
(22) Agreement between the Republic of Estonia, the Republic of Finland and the Kingdom of Sweden regarding the M/S Estonia. 23 Feb. 1995. Tallin in IMO Doc. Circular Letter N° 1859, 1995.
(23) The Joint Accident Investigation Commission of Estonia, Finland and Sweden : " Final report on the capsizing on 28 September 1994 in the Baltic Sea of the ro-ro passenger vessel MV Estonia". Edita Ldt. Helsinki 1997.
(24) - " Ferry bow doors to be sealed ". Lloyd's List, 5 Oct. 1994.
- " French orders ferry safety inspections ". Lloyd's List, 6 Oct. 1994.
(25) " Norway ready to act alone on ro-ro safety ". Lloyd's List, 21 Oct. 1994.
(26) " Ro-ro legislation could go regional ". Tradewinds, 4 Nov. 1994.

to be able to remain afloat with 50 centimetres of water on its car deck would require the owner to undertake major structural modifications.

Southern European shipowners' associations balked at the Norwegian project, putting forward three types of arguments. Technically, such a move would create too great a gulf in relation to existing regulations. In practice, such a difference was not justified, since the final conclusions of the investigation commission had not been published. Finally, it would cause irreversible financial harm to the maritime transport industry and regions served by ferries (27).

• Regulations of 8 August 1995

In 1995, under very heavy pressure from public opinion, Norway finally decided to act on its own. On 8 August, the Norwegian Maritime Directorate (NMO) published new design standards for existing ro-ro passenger vessels. The regulations stipulated that, from 1st May 1997, all such ferries visiting Norwegian ports had to be capable of withstanding a depth of 50 centimetres of water on their car deck (28).

The Norwegian authorities justified the regulations of 8 August 1993 by pointing out that their content did not differ from the proposals of the group of IMO experts, and that it merely preempted the results of the SOLAS Conference. If this conference failed to achieve results, Norway would be forced to maintain its own requirements.

The benefits of a regional solution were also put forward. In the absence of internationally acceptable standards, regulations had to remain flexible, in order to take account of local operating conditions.

c) 1995 SOLAS Conference and the spread of regional agreements

250. - Two groups of countries argued fiercely at the SOLAS Conference held in November 1995 : the Northern camp, in which the United Kingdom stood with the Scandinavian countries, Germany and the Netherlands, and a more moderate group, led by France and comprising several Mediterranean countries as well as Poland and Russia (29). After ten days of sharp bargaining, it was decided to apply the SOLAS 90 standard to all existing ro-ro passenger vessels, in accordance with a precise timescale. A compromise was worked out under which bilateral or regional agreements could be concluded outside the SOLAS framework, in order to impose new damage stability standards (30).

This provision, contained in Resolution 14 of the Conference, and which marked a departure from the principle of universality of maritime safety regulations, helped avoid the spread of unilateral measures, which would have struck a fatal blow at the credibility and effectiveness of IMO. However, it opened the door to a regionalisation of regulations and a two-tier system of standards (31).

The European Union rushed to take action. By 8 December 1995, the EU Council of Transport Ministers accepted a Swedish proposition to call a regional conference as a way of improving the safety of carferries (32).

(27) M. NEUMEISTER : " Sécurité des ferries et enjeux économiques ". JMM, 14 mars 1995, 916-917.
(28) A. GUEST : " Tight deadlines as Norway jumps gun on ro-ro safety ". Lloyd's List, 9 Sept. 1995.
(29) - " Two-win IMO ". Lloyd's List, 22 Nov. 1995.
- " Two-tier IMO ". Lloyd's List, 25 Nov. 1995.
(30) J. PRESCOTT : " IMO fudges issue in battle for unity on ferry stability ". Lloyd's List, 18 Dec. 1995.
(31) " IMO disappointment ". Lloyd's List, 1 Dec. 1995.
(32) " EU ministers back ro-ro safety regime ". Lloyd's List, 9 Dec. 1995.

• **Stockholm agreement of February 1996**

On 27 and 28 February 1996, eighteen States, including eleven European Union countries, signed a Northern European regional agreement in Stockholm, laying down specific stability requirements for ro-ro passenger ships (33).

It applies to vessels operating only within the "Northern Europe" zone, extending from Cape Finisterre in Spain to the North of Norway and into the Baltic

The technical basis of the agreement rested on a Danish proposal, amending the regulation about 50 centimetres of water on the cardeck. This depth may be reduced in relation to the freeboard, after damage caused by a breach in the plating, and the significant height of waves in a particular operating zone. The Baltic was the subject of endless bargaining at the Conference, resulting in the fixing of areas with a lower significant wave height, and therefore lower requirements for ships.

Opened for ratification on 1st July 1996, the Stockholm Agreement concerns about a hundred ships. Structural reconstruction would cost an average of US$750 000 (34). To allow companies time to adapt, an enforcement timetable was worked out, extending from 1st April 1997 to 1st October 2002.

On 18 June 1996, EU Transport Ministers undertook to adopt Stockholm Agreement standards for all ships passing through the territorial waters of relevant EU member States (35).

• **Regionalisation of standards**

Regionalisation of safety standards for ferries has today become a reality (36). Following the Stockholm Agreement, the American Society of Naval Architects and Marine Engineers (SNAME) recommended that Resolution 14 of the SOLAS Conference of 1995 should apply to Canadian and United States ferries in service engaged on voyages between the two countries (37).

The fragmentation of regulations that results from a regional conception of safety could culminate in a two-tier prevention system, which it would be no simple matter to explain to users of seaborne transport. This is even more true because a quest for greater safety is not the sole consideration in drafting regional standards (38).

B - PROTECTION OF THE MARINE ENVIRONMENT

251. - Certain unilateral regulations propose to prevent the oil spills and other ecological mishaps that are particularly feared by coastal States.

1. Canadian legislation on prevention of pollution

The wreck of the oil tanker *Arrow* in February 1970, which polluted 300 kilometres of the coasts of Nova Scotia, led the Canadian parliament to pass a bill in June 1970 on prevention of pollution in Arctic waters (39), completed by an enabling decree of 2 August 1972 (40).

(33) " Ferry safety agreement for Europe ". Lloyd's List, 29 Feb. 1996.
(34) " Older ferries under the spotlight ". Lloyd's List, 29 Feb. 1996.
(35) Europe Transport, juin 1996, II, 18.
(36) " Regional Reality ". Lloyd's List, 17 July 1996.
(37) " Rule changes culminate in Stockholm Agreement ". Lloyd's List, 16 Nov. 1996.
(38) Louis BAUMARD : " Sécurité et stabilité d'une activité". Le Marin, 14 March 1997, 4.
(39) V. SHARP : " La prévention de l'Arctique canadien ". Ministère des Affaires étrangères. Déclarations et discours. 16 April 1970, n° 70/5, 5.
(40) New Directions of the law of the sea. Documents, vol. I, 1973.
Oceana Publications, New-York, 199-210.

These regulations provided for the establishment of sixteen control zones for safety of navigation, 100 miles in width, in which the Canadian government could impose specific regulations on ships, going well beyond generally accepted standards. These regulations cover navigation (compulsory pilotage, assistance by icebreakers), as well as the construction, equipment and operation of ships (41).

Backed up by numerous doctrinal theories (42), the Canadian unilateral approach was subsequently given legitimacy at the 1982 Conference on the Law of the Sea, with the concept of ice-covered zones (cf article 234 of the LOS Convention, and chapter 8 above).

At present, Canada appears to have given up the idea of unilateral measures to improve the safety of navigation. Since 1991, regional cooperation has been developing through the Arctic Environmental Protection Strategy (AEPS), and a global system for protection of this fragile zone has been introduced (43).

2. Control of navigation in the Strait of Malacca

252. - The case of the Strait of Malacca also arose from criticism of the traditional law of the sea, which fails to provide satisfactorily for the safety of coastal States. It poses the problem of sharing responsibilities between States and international organisations in setting new maritime navigation regulations.

a) Specific nature of the Malacca Strait

Less than 24 miles wide at its narrowest point, the Strait of Malacca forms a maritime passage of primary importance, used every day by more than six hundred ships. The Strait is of vital importance to Japan, since about 90 per cent of its oil supplies from the Persian Gulf are shipped through this route on thirty oil tankers of 200 000 tdw, each of which makes nine voyages a year. Any detour through the Strait of Lombok and Macassar would mean a loss of four days on every voyage, pushing up freight rates, to the serious disadvantage of Japanese industry (44).

The narrowness of the passage is not the only navigational difficulty : visibility is poor because of the frequent rainfall, and there is dense traffic between the ports of Sumatra and those on the Malaysian peninsula. The shores of the Strait are irregular, with islands inhabited by numerous fishing communities.

b) First coastal State initiatives

253. - The States bordering this passage (Indonesia, Malaysia and Singapore) adopted two joint Statements in turn, imposing unilateral regulation of navigation through the Strait (45).

(41) J.Y. MORIN : " Le progrès technique, la pollution et l'évolution récente du droit de la mer au Canada ". A.C.D.I., vol. VIII, 1970, 227.
(42) - J.A. BEESLEY : " The Canadian approach to international environment law ". A.C.D.I., vol. XI, 1973, 5.
- CI. EMANUELLI : " La pollution maritime et la notion de passage inoffensif ". A.C.D.I., vol XI, 1973, 15.
- E. GOLD : " Pollution of the sea and international law : a Canadian perspective ". Journal of Maritime Law and Commerce, 1971, 5.
- L. HENKIN : " Arctic antipollution : does Canada make or break international law ? " A.J.I.L. 1971, 131.
- A.D. PHARAND : " Innocent passage in the Arctic ". A.C.D.I., 1968, 6.
- R.S. REID : " The Canadian claim to sovereignty over the waters of Arctic ". A.C.D.I., 1974, 111.
(43) D. ROTHWELL : " International law and protection of the Arctic environment ". ICLQ, Vol 44, April 1995, 280-312.
(44) J. PRESCOTT : " Strait choices to end a catalogue of disasters ". Lloyd's List, 7 june 1995.
(45) P. TILLMAN : " Strait of Malacca and the Law of the Sea ". The Australian Law Journal, vol. 68, 1994, 885-898.

In the first of these statements, on 26 November 1971 in Kuala Lumpur, Malaysia and Indonesia asserted that the safety of shipping in the Strait was a matter within their control. The statement added that the Strait was situated in their territorial waters, henceforth extended to 20 miles, and therefore did not constitute an international waterway and was not subject to the right of innocent passage (46).

On 6 March 1972, the Indonesian Foreign Affairs Minister announced his intention to prohibit tankers of more than 2 000 tons from using the Strait, in order to prevent any risk of grounding and pollution (47).

A series of accidents between January 1975 and April 1976 caused very sharp reaction among the three States bordering on the Strait. In a second joint declaration issued on 24 February 1977, they laid down unilateral technical regulations for navigation (48).

On 19 March, the Malaysian government proposed to levy a charge on all ships using the Strait.

c) Solutions to the conflict

Between 1972 and 1977, the three Strait States engaged in a broad diplomatic offensive, in order to give international credibility to their arguments. Their action resulted in certain moves :
- at IMO, Resolution A.375 defined the conditions of navigation in the Straits of Malacca and Singapore ;
- at the 1982 LOS Conference, article 233 of the Convention covered guarantees for straits used for international navigation, the joint interpretation of which by the Strait States was not accepted unanimously by the major maritime nations (49).

d) Reemergence of safety problems and search for regional agreement

254. - The debate on the safety of the Straits of Malacca and Singapore was reignited in the early Nineties by a series of fatal accidents, the most spectacular of which were the *Royal Pacific* (50), the *Nagasaki Spirit* (51) and the *Evoikos* (52).

The chronic safety problems of navigation in the Malacca Strait, aggravated by the problem of piracy, encouraged coastal States to relaunch the diplomatic process, in order to achieve agreement.

In October 1992, Malaysia asked for the establishment of a better traffic separation scheme and proposed introducing toll charges for ships using the Strait (53). In 1994, Japan tried to preempt this initiative by announcing the possibility of funding safety efforts in the Strait (54).

In September 1995, discussions were held on the interpretation of article 43 of the LOS Convention and on definition of the terms "user States" and "cooperation" (55).

(46) Ch. ROUSSEAU : Chronique des faits internationaux. R.G.D.I.P. 1973, 271.
(47) V.S. MANI et S. BALUPARI : " Malacca strait and international law ". Indian Journal of International Law. Vol. 13 - n° 3, 455.
(48) A.F.D.I. 1977, 732-733, J.P. QUENEUDEC. Chronique du droit de la mer.
(49) H. CAMINOS : " The legal regime of straits in the 1982 United Nations Convention on the Law of the Sea ". RCADI, 1987, V, Tome 205, 171, note 394.
(50) " Four die as cruise ship sinks ". Lloyd's List, 24 August 1992.
(51) " Crewmen lost in Malacca collision ". Lloyd's List, 21 Sept. 1992.
(52) "Tankers collide off Singapore". Lloyd's List, 17 Oct. 1997.
(53) " Paid passage ". Lloyd's List, 8 June 1993.
(54) " Malacca strait gains high priority ". Lloyd's List, 18 Sept. 1995.
(55) " Malacca confusion over UN rule ". Lloyd's List, 5 Sept. 1995.

A conference held in Singapore in September 1996 on safety of navigation and control of pollution in the Straits of Malacca and Singapore put forward the idea of an international fund to combat pollution (56). The IMO Secretary-General considered that all users would have to make a contribution, including the maritime industry (57). So far, only Japan has provided technical and financial assistance, whereas other States in the zone, including South Korea, Taiwan and China/Hong Kong use the facilities without making any contribution (58).

The beginnings of a solution were recently found, with the adoption by IMO in May 1998 of a stringent new vessel traffic system, known as STRAITREP, for all merchant ships passing through the Straits of Malacca and Singapore (59).

3. US legislation on oil pollution

255. - The most important unilateral regulatory move, by its content and international repercussions, remains the Oil Pollution Act (OPA), passed by the United States in August 1991, and which came into permanent effect in December 1994. For the first time, a comprehensive response was provided to the problem of marine oil pollution, on the scale of a large country. Despite its scope and suddenness, the American initiative should not have surprised the international maritime community, preceded as it had been by numerous earlier legislative moves (60). Although a party to nearly all IMO conventions, and a leading partici-pant at most international conferences, the United States have always preferred to act alone when their vital interests are involved.

For example, following a series of tanker accidents between December 1976 and March 1977 in American waters, the United States hinted at the possibility of adopting unilateral regulations, in the absence of an international agreement in the near future. Under this threat, IMO immediately convened a diplomatic conference on tanker safety, which resulted in the signing of two protocols in February 1978, amending the SOLAS and MARPOL Conventions (61).

a) Origin of OPA : the Exxon Valdez accident

256. - In the night of 24 March 1989, the VLCC *Exxon Valdez*, flying the Liberian flag, left Alyeska oil terminal loaded with 1 264 155 barrels of crude oil. To avoid icebergs that had broken off from the Columbia Glacier, and were drifting in the traffic separation scheme area of Prince William Sound, the tanker decided to leave the sea lanes. The ship's captain, Captain Hazelwood, handed command of the ship to the Third Officer, Lieutenant Collins, who despite his lack of qualifications was to keep watch on the bridge.

Around midnight, following a navigational error, the *Exxon Valdez* ran aground on Bligh Reef, which tore away part of its hull. Approximately 70 per cent of the cargo, amounting to forty thousand tonnes of crude, spilt out into the Sound, one of the richest fishing grounds in North America (62). The very thick oil slick, seven thousand square kilometres in area,

(56) " Malaysia calls for spill fund boost ". Lloyd's List, 4 Sept. 1996.
(57) Conference on navigational safety and control of pollution in the straits of Malacca and Singapore. Singapore, 2 Sept. 1996. Keynote address by Mr William O'Neil. OMI Documentation on the Internet.
(58) " Strait talking ". Lloyd's List, 6 Sept. 1996.
(59) "Malacca monitoring endorsed by IMO". Lloyd's List, 23 May 1998.
(60) D. FITCH : " Unilateral action versus universal evolution of safety and environmental protection standards in maritime shipping of hazardous cargoes ". Harvard International Law Journal. Winter 1979, vol. 20, n° 1, 127-174.
(61) A. AYORINDE : " Inconsistencies between OPA 90 and MARPOL 73/78 : What is the effect on legal rights and obligations of the United States and other parties to MARPOL 73/78 ? ". Journal of Maritime Law and Commerce, Vol 25, n° 1, Jan. 1994.
(62) R. CAHILL : " Disasters at sea " Century. London, 1990, 206-214.

polluted nearly two thousand kilometres of coastline (63). A huge clean-up operation began in the summer of 1989, mobilising nearly eleven thousand people, eighty-five aircraft and helicopters, and fourteen hundred ships. The cost of the disaster was estimated to be US$15 billion (64).

Given huge prominence by the media and ecological movements, very powerful in the United States, the *Exxon Valdez* oil spill triggered a profound reaction in public opinion. The scale of the television coverage led the United States population to look at pollution with different eyes. The strongest pressure was exerted on the political system to ensure that the country would never experience a similar disaster. Aware of the seriousness of the problem, members of Congress acted fast and effectively. Seven Parliamentary Commissions were set up to draft comprehensive anti-pollution legislation. On 18 August 1990, barely eighteen months after the *Exxon Valdez* accident, the Oil Pollution Act (OPA) was passed.

b) Contents of OPA

257. - OPA comprises nine separate titles :
- Title I deals in general with issues of liability and compensation.
- Title II amends the numerous pollution laws.
- Title III establishes an international regime for oil prevention and removal.
- Title IV contains measures for prevention and restoration of polluted sites.
- Other titles cover such varied aspects as special provisions for Prince William Sound, research and development, retroactive amendments to oil spills from the Trans-Alaska pipeline, and finally Federal budget grants and amendments to the oil spill liability trust fund.

All these provisions form a coherent set of requirements, reflecting a total approach to pollution, embracing prevention, combat and compensation (65).

• Pollution prevention
The preventive regulations applying mainly to tankers are intended to improve safety in three areas : construction and equipment, operation, and navigation.

• Tanker construction and equipment
The most important regulation concerns the requirement for oil tankers to be fitted with a double hull and double bottom. For new ships or those that have undergone extensive conversions, the deadlines for conformity were 30 June 1990 (date of signature of a shipbuilding contract), and 1st January 1994 (delivery date). Tankers in service also have to be fitted with

(63) J. BURGER : "Oil spills", Rutgers University Press. New Brunswich, New Jersey, 1997, 47-78.
(64) See the Special Report in Lloyd's List, 24 March 1994 : "Exxon Valdez, Five years on".
(65) Text of OPA 90 in Congressional Record - House, August 1990, H6232-H6284.
- K. KETKAR : " Protection of marine resources. The US Oil Pollution Act of 1990 and the future of the maritime industry ". Marine Policy, 1995, vol. 19, n° 5, 391-400.
- Burlingham Underwood and Lord : Report on United States Oil Pollution Laws. Part I, II, III, New York, 1990.
- J. SHIRLEY : " Oil Pollution Act of 1990. An overview ". Haight, Gardner, Poor and Havens, New York, Oct. 1990.
- Watson, Farley and William : " A practical commentary on the Oil Pollution Act of 1990 ". New York, Oct. 1990.
- Hill, Betts and Nash : "The Oil Pollution Act of 1990 ". 1st Oct. 1990, New York.
- Industry Forum on pending oil spill legislation, New York City, 16 March 1990.
- State Bar Association Meeting, New York, 25 October 1990.
- Association Française du Droit Martime : " L'Oil Pollution Act américain de 1990 : ses incidences sur les intérêts maritimes français ". Paris, 7 Feb. 1991.

double hulls by deadlines that take account of the age of the ship, its tonnage and type of construction (single skin, double bottom or double hull already existing). By 2010 at the latest, all other single-skin ships will be denied access to American waters.

• Tanker operation
These regulations apply to the crew, and consumption of drugs or alcohol.

The USCG was given the task of periodically examining regulations applied by foreign States, particularly those relating to manning, crew training and qualification, and watchkeeping. In the event of an accident to a foreign ship, the USCG is to establish whether the flag State's standards are at least equivalent to US standards, or those accepted internationally by the United States, and whether they have actually been applied.

Very strict rules are also laid down concerning drug and alcohol abuse. Whenever two officers note that the captain is under the influence or drugs or alcohol, and is incapable of commanding the ship, the first mate can relieve him of his duties. All nautical certificates can now be withdrawn or suspended for any breach of onshore regulations concerning driving under the influence of alcohol or drugs.

• Tanker navigation
Requirements concerning towage and pilotage were also strengthened. The USCG designates areas where single-hull oil tankers of more than 5 000 gross tonnage have to be escorted by at least two tugs. It is also responsible for indicating particularly sensitive areas where use of a pilot is compulsory.

• Prevention of pollution
Any ship carrying oil in US waters, wherever it is registered, must have a vessel response plan (VRP), and be equipped with retrieval equipment. Plans must allow for an extreme case of spillage. Shipowners must ensure the availability of personnel and facilities to respond effectively to contingencies and stop discharge of the whole cargo, even in bad weather (66).

Although shipowners have had difficulties in preparing VRPs, the USCG managed to approve about 1 300 plans for six thousand ships

• Liability for compensation
The OPA finally put paid to one of the traditional principles of maritime law, namely the limitation on the shipowner's liability. While the new Act admitted the possibility of such a limitation on a Federal level, it left it to each State to set its own conditions. Most coastal States grasped the opportunity to introduce a legislative system providing for unlimited compensation for pollution damage, accompanied by compulsory insurance (68).

This obligatory insurance raised many difficulties, because of the immediate impossibility of finding adequate insurance on the world market to guarantee full payment of pollution damage. Only a few bodies accredited by the USCG succeeded in delivering certificates of financial responsibility (COFR) (69) by 28 December 1994.

(66) L. CRICK, Ch. CORBETT : " U.S. vessel response plans and contingency planning ". BIMCO Bulletin, vol. 91, n° 1, 1996, 13-17.
(67) - R. NORTH : " OPA 90 - an update ". BIMCO Bulletin. Vol 89, n° 3, 1994, 20-22
- J. GALLAGHER : "OPA 90 update 1996". BIMCO Bulletin. Vol 91, N° 1, 1996, 18-20.
(68) M. REMOND-GOUILLOUD : " Marées noires : Les Etats-Unis à l'assaut (l'Oil Pollution Act de 1990)". DMF 1991, 339-353.
(69) - H. BRYANT : " Specialist insurers offer real OPA solution for shipowners ". Lloyd's List, 21 June 96
- " Financial rules on pollution still spark strong feeling ". Lloyd's List, 28 June 1996.

d) Effects of OPA

258. - OPA has political, legal and financial implications.

• **Politically,** OPA is one of the main manifestations of unilateralism in international law since 1945. Apart from the demonstration of the United States ability to ignore the rest of the world, and the isolationism instanced by this introduction of their own environmental protection measures, OPA called into question the international consensus that IMO had been struggling to achieve (70).

By marking at least a provisional break with conventional mechanisms, the American initiative damaged the credibility of IMO, in its role as promoter of international regulations. It also eroded the monopoly on safety at sea that IMO had exercised since 1958.

IMO was for a while overtaken in the campaign to prevent and combat pollution. It tried subsequently to make up by sponsoring amendments to the MARPOL Convention, including Regulations 13f and 13g on double hulls and alternative structural protection systems. But despite the adoption of these new standards on 6 March 1992, the United States refused to give way (71).

• **Legally,** OPA also marked a break with the international regime of shipowner liability. The new liability limit it introduces, with the already quite high ceiling of US$10 million (cf tanker is over 3 000 gt), remains illusory, since this Federal provision can be removed by State laws, exacting astronomical amounts in compensation.

OPA opens the door to a perilous fragmentation of maritime law. It could spawn a myriad different systems, established by national lawmakers leading a crusade against polluters, and anxious to appease public opinion, unaware of the real conditions of seaborne transport (72).

Internally, OPA encouraged the adoption of very harsh local regulations by individual American States. More than half State Congresses have issued environmental protection regulations which go far beyond Federal provisions, or the requirements of international conventions to which the United States are party. Not only do these impose unlimited liability on the shipowner, and more stringent emergency plans, but they also introduce certain exorbitant protective measures (73).

The legislation introduced by the State of Washington is particularly eloquent. In 1991, the State Congress enacted the Oil Spill Prevention Act (OSPA), and charged the State Office of Marine Safety (OMS) with implementing the law, which applies to all ships of more than 30 gross tonnage (74). In December 1994, the OMS promulgated Best Achievable Protection (BAP) standards, empowering it to assess the effectiveness of preventive plans introduced by shipowners (75).

Far exceeding Federal requirements, BAP standards were challenged legally by INTERTANKO (76), then by the US Department of Justice (77). Congress had always refused

---

(70) M. BLACKBURNE, C. BROWN : "The US Oil Pollution Act. A unilateral step". Lloyd's List, 25 Jan. 1991.
(71) " MARPOL decision withheld ". Lloyd's List, 15 August 1992.
(72) " Reform lost in a maze of bureaucracy ". Lloyd's List, 26 Sept. 1996.
(73) " Myriad of tough US pollution laws facing tanker owners ". Lloyd's List, 5 Oct. 1992.
(74) A. FALL : " Les conflits de législations en matière de protection de l'environnement marin aux Etats-Unis. L'exemple de l'Etat de Washington ". Unpublished study. University of Washington. Seatle, 1994.
(75) L. CRICK : " The Washington State BAP standards : "A case study in aggressive tanker regulation ". Journal of Martime Law and Commerce, vol 27, n° 4, Oct. 1996, 641-646.
(76) J. BENNER : " When plural and singular collide ". BIMCO Review, 1996, 73-76.
(77) " US backs Intertanko appeal against state ". Lloyd's List, 12 May 1997.

to give any preference to Federal laws over State laws for political reasons (78), and the Federal Administration finally left it to an American judge to settle the issue. He decided partly in favour of the Federal legislators (79).

• **Financially,** OPA created new costs, which the maritime industry will have to bear. The main aspects are :
- Shipbuilding : a VLCC with a double hull costs 15 to 20 per cent more than a conventional tanker ;
- Maintenance and repair costs : 25 per cent more ;
- Operation : extra manpower has to be hired to upgrade to watchkeeping and manning standards ;
- Navigation : the obligation for single-hull tankers to be escorted by two ships when they pass laden through American waters will cost approximately US$57.7 million for the period 1995-2015 (80) ;
- Emergency plan : introduction of a VRP against pollution is likely to cost US$2.7 billion (81) ;
- Insurance : initially, only integrated shipping companies were able to benefit from the COFR, by self-insurance backed up by the financial muscle of major US oil companies (82); ultimately, independent shipowners could be driven off the market, because insurance clubs refuse to provide a guarantee (83).

4. Regulation of navigation in the Turkish Straits

259. - As the only passage between the Black Sea and the Mediterranean, the Bosphorus presents certain features that make navigation particularly dangerous. Traffic moves simultaneously in both directions, even though the passage narrows at certain points to less than 700 metres. Fog is frequent in this region, while traffic is dense: from 1st July 1994 to 1st November 1995, 58 948 ships passed through the Strait of Istanbul. 16 per cent of these were very large vessels, and 15 per cent of them were carrying dangerous cargoes (84). In addition to this heavy traffic, high-speed ferries shuttle between the two shores of the strait, while numerous fishing boats and small boats without any VHF radio dart about in all directions (85).

Repeated accidents, including the wreck of the *Nassia* in March 1994 (86), have on several occasions threatened the city of Istanbul and its population of ten million people. They also led Turkey to regulate shipping in the strait more strictly (87).

(78) L. RAMBUSCH : " OPA 90 : Evolution or revolution ". International Business Lawyer, Sept. 1996, 362-367.
(79) L.C. SAHATJIAN : "Washington's BAP regulations valid". Lloyd's List, 8 August 1998.
(80) " New OPA rule hits oil tankers ". Lloyd's List, 20 August 1994.
(81) " OPA 90 blow for owners ". Lloyd's List, 4 Feb. 1993.
(82) " OPA 90 could make US spills uninsurable". Lloyd's List, 30 Janv. 1995.
(83) " Certificates of Financial Responsibility under the US Oil Pollution Act ". BIMCO Special circular n° 5, 21 December 1994.
(84) IMO Assembly. First statement by the delegation of Turkey. 15 Nov. 1995. Committee II A./19/6(b)/2, Annex 4.
(85) " High collision toll near pilot stations ". Lloyd's List, 15 March 1994.
(86) " 30 feared dead after Bosphorus tanker collision ". Lloyd's List, 15 March 1994.
(87) N. AKTEN, S. USTAOGLU, R. KODOPHAN : " Marine casuaties in the Turkish straits and their implications for the environment ". Procedings of International Seminar on Maritime Safety and Environmental Protection. Istanbul, 1-4 nov. 1994, Itü Maritime Faculty.

a) Montreux Convention

The Turkish Straits are subject to special provisions laid down by the Montreux Convention of 1936, which stipulates the principle of "freedom of passage and navigation" (88).

Article 2 indicates that in peacetime merchant ships will be free to pass through the Straits by day or night, without formality. Pilotage and towage remain optional.

Article 3 provides for health inspections for ships entering the Straits from the Aegean or the Black Sea. There are no arrangements for vessel navigation monitoring (89).

b) Turkish regulations of 1st July 1994

260. - The accident to the *Nassia* led Turkey to take unilateral action. In April 1994, considering the straits as "internal waters over which Turkey possesses complete sovereignty and control" (90), the Turkish government issued new navigation regulations for all ships flying any flag and in transit through the straits. These purely national regulations provided among other things for temporary suspension of traffic in transit in both directions, and one-way routeing, to ensure a safe passage for large ships carrying dangerous cargoes which would be unable to observe the traffic separation scheme (91).

At the same time, Turkey submitted a plan for organising traffic in this area to IMO (92). This was amended by the MSC, which in May 1994 adopted a whole series of regulations on navigation in the Bosphorus, the Dardanelles and the Sea of Marmara (93). Turkey did not take its recommendations into account, and on 1st July applied its regulations in full, causing sharp protest from user States.

• Solution of the conflict

IMO and its Secretary-General engaged in intensive diplomatic action to find a solution to the conflict (94).

Resolution A.827 was adopted on 23 November 1995, confirming the adoption of new and amended routeing measures other than traffic separation schemes. It also confirms the adoption of regulations and recommendations on navigation in the Turkish Straits, "which are not intended in any way to affect or prejudice the rights of any ship using the straits under international law". But the IMO Resolution indicates also that "national regulations promulgated by the coastal State should be in total conformity with the same regulations and recommendations".

Turkey first refused to give in to IMO, and persisted in applying its own regulations. This resulted in traffic congestion in the approaches to the area, and considerable delays in passing through the straits (95).

---

(88) I. SOYSAL : " The 1936 Montreux Convention 60 years later ". In Turkish straits, New problems. News solutions. Isis, Istanbul July 1995, 1-9.
(89) E. CERRAHOGLU : " Bosphorus safety ". BIMCO Review, 1995, 213-217.
(90) G. AYBAY, N. ORAL : "Turkey and the right to regulate traffic through the Turkish Straits". Lloyd's List, 15 Oct. 1997.
(91) G. PLANT : "Halting tankers in the straits". Lloyd's List, 24 April 1996.
(92) G. PLANT : "Navigation regime in the Turkish Straits for merchant ships in peacetime". Marine Policy, vol. 20, n° 1, 15-27, 1996.
(93) IMO. Circular SN/Circ. 166, 1st June 1994.
(94) IMO Legal Committee. 71st session. Document presented by the Russian Delegation LEG 71/12/5, 5 August 1994.
(95) N. COCKCROFT : "Safety of navigation in the Turkish Straits". Seaways, May 1998, 15-16.

In July 1997, a change of government in Ankara led Turkey to adopt a more conciliatory position (96) and accept the IMO proposals. This readiness to seek a compromise resulted in the adoption of Resolution A.859 of 27 November 1997, which "welcomes the wish of all to cooperate on this issue".

A permanent solution to the conflict is at present being worked out, with the announcement by Turkey of the introduction in 2000 of a vessel traffic system for the Bosphorus (97).

III - EFFECTS OF UNILATERAL MEASURES

A - POSSIBLE OUTCOMES OF UNILATERAL ACTIONS

261. - Regardless of the grounds and motivations behind State initiatives, unilateral actions have definite repercussions on the international legal system. Two situations are to be considered:

• **Case 1 :** Unilateral measures are rejected unanimously by the whole community of nations.

In such circumstances, they place governments in a confrontational situation, the outcome of which depends on the balance of forces involved :
- Either the State sticks to its position and possesses the means of having its decisions respected. In this hypothesis, the unilateral regulations come into force. An example is the United States, the world's leading economic power, which is indifferent to the effects of an isolationist policy. Geographically remote from its competitors, large energy consumer, and therefore large potential importer of oil and gas, the country can impose its conditions on shippers. Prospects for international maritime regulations depend largely on the attitude of the United States (98).
- Or else the State has neither the will nor the power to impose its legislation on other States. Its claims are regarded as exorbitant, and have to be reduced to more reasonable levels in order to be acceptable. This is the case for States bordering on the Malacca Strait or Turkey for the Bosphorus and the Dardanelles.

• **Case 2** : Unilateral measures are taken into account by the international community.

Again, two hypotheses arise. If other States acknowledge the justification for the unilateral action and there is broad acceptance of the solutions proposed, the initiative can give rise to an international customary procedure (99). If the action is accepted only by a few States, the position is arguable. Some consider that the measure possesses "an irreversible aspect" (100). Others, in contrast, consider that the more or less proven consent of coastal States is powerless, in isolation, to confer any validity whatsoever At the very most, it may reinforce its effectiveness as needed (101).

In either case, unilateral action leads from a *de facto* to a *de jure* situation.

(96) "Turkey pledges action over Bosphorus safety". Lloyd's List, 16 July 1997.
(97) "Bosphorus traffic seeks solutions". Lloyd's List, 25 July 1998.
(98) S. STRANGE : " Who runs shipping ? ". International Affairs, vol. 52, n° 3, July 1976, 347-367.
(99) J.Y. MORIN : "Le progrès technique, la pollution et l'évolution récente du droit de la mer du Canada, particulièrement à l'égard de l'Arctique". A.C.D.I., 1970, 233.
(100) LUCCHINI and VOELCKEL : " Les Etats et la Mer ". Op.cit 310.
(101) G. APPOLIS : op. cit, 13.

B - DANGERS OF UNILATERALISM

262. - There have been frequent declarations about the dangers of unilateralism. Maritime safety regulations drawn up outside multilateral conventions signed within the framework of international organisations, become a source of legal uncertainty and arbitrariness (102). Because of the complexity of the motivations that lead to individual initiatives, there is always the risk of deviating from the goals (103).

Safety problems cannot be settled in a piecemeal way; nor can they apply to only part of the world. Prevention of ecological damage cannot make progress through unilateral actions: a coastal State wishing to protect its shores by banning ships that fail to meet its standards from its territorial sea would merely shift the problem elsewhere. Such ships would be encouraged to frequent the coastal waters of other countries, which would inevitably have to take similar measures. The result would be a proliferation of unilateral actions, more or less overlapping, and "protection would quickly become protectionism" (104).

Despite these inconsistencies, the last twenty years have seen a worrying spread of unilateralist behaviour on the international stage, based on the argument of better protection for people and the environment. Admittedly, they are often mere threats intended to strengthen a State's position in multilateral discussions: but the fact remains that this attitude is contagious, and can be adverse to the development of shipping.

(102) W. O'NEIL : "Toward 2000 : IMO's next decade. The 25th Blackadder Lecture, 4 Feb. 1991. The North East Coast Institution of Engineers and Shipbuilders. Vol. 107, Part 3, 1991, 75-80.
(103) JMM, 27 April 1978, 939.
(104) JMM, 26 May 1978, 1223.

PART TWO

MARINE SAFETY REGULATIONS, RULES AND STANDARDS

263. - The safety of seaborne transport can be ensured at three different stages :

- during construction of the ship and installation of its equipment ;
- in operation, once the ship is commissioned and until it is scrapped ;
- during periods of navigation.

Different sets of regulations, rules and standards come into play at each stage, and they are to be examined in this second part of the book. Such an approach should not suggest any excessive compartmentalisation of safety at sea. Obviously, the means of prevention deployed during construction of a ship have a direct impact on operating and navigational conditions, and *vice versa*. Only a total approach allows the effectiveness and relevance of the whole system to be assessed.

CHAPTER 10

Construction and equipment
of merchant ships

264. - Unlike aircraft, ships come in an enormous variety of forms. Various categories may be distinguished, depending on the materials from which they are built (wood, steel, composites), their form of propulsion (sail, propeller, waterjet, airscrew), their commercial use (cargo or passenger transport), and type of service (transport of passengers and cargo, fishing, recreation, scientific research, public service).

But whatever type of ship is involved, one quality is vital: an ability to navigate. This must exist from the moment the vessel enters the water, and be maintained until the day it is withdrawn from service. Lawyers speak of "seaworthiness", the capacity to go to sea with safety.

Technical experts have defined a series of criteria by which such seaworthiness may be guaranteed. These include the ship's strength, navigability and stability. Two types of knowledge are used in the shipbuilding trade: naval theory, which means studying the nautical qualities of the floating body, and all the factors that can affect such qualities; and naval architecture, which allows the whole vessel to be constructed in accordance with predrawn plans.

The variety of types of ships, marine craft and boats of all kinds has at the same time led to the extreme diversification of rules for accident prevention (1). Only an approach based on the particular and not the general can ensure effectiveness : standards are intentionally specific, to take account of the risks peculiar to certain cargoes (oil, liquefied gas, chemicals), the mode of propulsion and the type of loading (in bulk or packages).

Apart from specific safety rules, the most important of which will be examined in the chapters below devoted to passenger ships, oil tankers and bulk carriers, a general risk-prevention system applies to most merchant ships.

This general system is defined by two major IMO conventions, one concerning the safety of life at sea (SOLAS) and the other ship loadlines (LL). It also comprises classification society rules, which predated public standards and continue in parallel to them. Before discussing the content of present-day regulations, the prevention principles underlying such regulations will be examined.

---

(1) C.F. SPENCER : "Spencer on Ships". Square One Publications. Worcester, 1996.

I - PRINCIPLES OF PREVENTION OF RISKS AT SEA

265. - The safety of a ship at sea depends on how well it is protected against the dangers to which navigation exposes it. The most serious risks, those that imperil the ship and the life of its occupants, are :
- complete or partial structural failure, causing the ship to sink rapidly ;
- flooding, as a result of the hull being torn open, whether a vertical tear in the plating, caused by a collision, or a horizontal tear in the bottom, caused by the ship running aground or hitting an obstacle at the waterline level ;
- fire breaking out on board, leaving the crew bereft of any immediate outside help.

A - SHIP STRENGTH

266. - Two factors need to be taken into account in order to assess the strength of a ship's structure : the strength of the materials used, and structural fatigue.

The strength of the materials is investigated for two reasons. The scantlings of a newbuilding need to be established on a rational basis, and it must be ensured that a newbuilding of given dimensions can withstand tensile, compressive, shearing, torsional, bending and various other stresses.

In both cases, elementary safety rules require the load placed on the materials not to exceed the permitted load for that material. Deformations must remain below acceptable limits, decided on the basis of practical considerations (2).

The ship must also be built strongly enough to withstand the hydrostatic and hydrodynamic forces to which it is subject at sea. In calm water, a ship withstands both downward vertical forces exerted by its weight and cargo, and upward thrusts resulting from the Archimedes principle. In general, the thrust exceeds the weight in the centre, whereas the reverse is true at the ends, because of the more slender lines of the hull. In rough water, two situations may arise. When the ship is on the crest of a wave, the upward thrust decreases sharply at the ends and increases in the centre, generating a bending stress in the ship (it is said to be "hogging"). When it is in the trough of a wave, the thrust increases at the ends and decreases amidships (it is "sagging").

Naval architects designing ship hulls make allowance for fatigue stresses acting on the hull, by including various longitudinal components (deck, side plating, keelsons, keel, longitudinal bulkheads) and transverse components (ribs, floorplates, transverse bulkheads) (3).

B - BUOYANCY AND STABILITY

267. - The second safety rule is that the ship must possess the capacity to survive even if its hull has been damaged. This depends on two factors : buoyancy and stability.

Buoyancy is the result of the downward weight of the ship and the upward thrust reflecting the Archimedes principle. The balance results from the thrust equalling the weight of the volume of water displaced by the underwater part of the hull. Reserve buoyancy is always provided by the part of the hull not submerged.

---

(2) E. CHICOT : " Construction du navire de commerce". Editions Maritimes et Coloniales. Paris, 1960, 135.
(3) J. MARIE, Ch. DILLY : " Utilisation et sécurité du navire de commerce. Navigation maritime". Société d'Editions géographiques, maritimes et coloniales. Paris, 1949, 19.

Stability is the ability of the ship to keep upright and to withstand heeling. It is measured by a modulus, the minimum value of which depends on the size and type of ship. The stability rises in proportion to the width of the ship. However, there is a limit : if the rolling period is too short, it could cause abrupt lurches in bad weather, generating excessive fatigue on the structure, and possible loosening of cargo. Stability also varies in relation to loading, which itself changes during the voyage, depending on loading and unloading operations and fuel and water consumption.

The stability modulus on passenger ships has to be so high because the vessel must retain acceptable conditions of stability and listing even after damage. Drawing lessons from major disasters at sea, experts have defined two elementary conditions of survival of a damaged ship: first, it must continue to float in a stable way, so that navigation and life on board remain possible; second, it must retain minimum freeboard, in other words not lie excessively low in the water.

The main defence of the ship against shipping water lies in the existence of subdivisions, which form watertight compartments between them. Subdivision adds considerably to the ship's life expectancy, allowing it to await rescue or head for help.

Finally, a maximum loading limit has to be placed on the ship, to prevent the deck from being level with the water, and foundering because of the accidental shipment of extra weight. This limit is the freeboard, a height measured from an upper deck known as the freeboard deck, with a mark to show the difference of draught. This must never be under water. The freeboard deck is often the subdivision deck on a passenger ship, in other words the deck surmounting the watertight bulkheads. The freeboard provides a safety margin, by ensuring that a certain volume of hull always remains above water.

C - FIRE PROTECTION

268. - If an accident occurs at sea, the people on board cannot expect immediate help. Furthermore, there is very little room for retreat from the effects. Once attempts to take action are abandoned, the passengers on board often panic, further complicating the task of the rescuers. Fire, whether it breaks out on the high seas, near the coast or even in port, raises very serious dangers for those on board.

All merchant ships are now built from steel plates. This material heats rapidly, and is an excellent heat conductor, encouraging the fire to spread, despite the presence of structural protection against fire.

Ships inevitably carry combustible or flammable products or materials, including diesel oil, fuel oil for propulsion and auxiliary engines, compressed gas cylinders, lubricating oil, furnishings, woodwork, plastic floor coverings and carpets, paintwork. A defective electrical installation, simple carelessness on the part of a crew member, are enough to transform the ship into a blazing inferno in a very short space of time.

Another specifically maritime problem is how to evacuate the smoke and hot gases released during a fire. In the enclosed, confined spaces so typical on board ships, these flammable, explosive gases build up in the different compartments, creating turbulence which can affect all areas. The result is that, as soon as the source of the fire reaches a certain size, flames spread throughout the ship.

Finally, firefighting efforts can themselves endanger its stability. The presence of hundreds of tons of water used to fight the fire creates a liquid volume, the weight and movements of which very soon impart a marked list, which can even make the ship capsize (4).

For all these reasons, it has been found vital to apply specific rules to protect against fire aboard ship, and fight any that break out. Regulations have moved in two directions. At the building level, first, there is a choice of quality of materials, to eliminate flammable products, and by equipping the ship with means of detection and firefighting. At the operational level, firefighting equipment must be used by competent, specially trained crew members. The principal aim is to limit one of the main causes of accidents, the neglect of the most elementary safety precautions.

International organisations, States and classification societies have tried to prevent these three major risks by laying down technical regulations on the construction and equipment of merchant ships. These regulations form what may be called the general safety regime of the ship, defined by three fundamental texts: the SOLAS Convention on safety of life at sea, the Loadline Convention on freeboard, and classification society rules.

II - SOLAS CONVENTION AND STABILITY

269. - Of all the international conventions affecting safety at sea, the most important is the Convention on the safety of life at sea (SOLAS). It is also one of the oldest, since the first version of the text dates from 1914 (5).

A - GENERAL DESCRIPTION OF SOLAS REGULATIONS

The current version of the Convention, adopted in 1974, covers the three principal areas of safety at sea : construction and equipment, operation, and navigation.

The most stringent technical provisions concern passenger ships. They will be examined in the next chapter.

Cargo ships must respect general constructional and equipment standards contained in chapters II-1 and II-2 of the Convention.

Chapter II-1 contains constructional arrangements intended to reinforce the watertightness and stability of a ship (Part B), standards concerning machinery installations (Part C) and electrical installations (Part D), and finally additional requirements for machinery premises operated without the permanent presence of crew members (Part E).

Chapter II-2 enumerates constructional standards intended to prevent, detect and fight fire on board. Cargo ships must apply the provisions of Part A, which contains general considerations and fundamental principles, as well as those of Part C specially aimed at such ships.

(4) - J. SERAY : " La lutte contre le feu à bord des navires de commerce " Navires, Ports et Chantiers, nov 1972, 937.
- J. SERAY : " La sécurité incendie à bord des navires de commerce ". Navires, Ports et Chantiers, juillet 1970, 518-531.
(5) "SOLAS : the International Convention for the Safety of Life at Sea, 1974". Focus on IMO, Jan. 1997.

B - SHIP STABILITY

270. - Stability factors are so important for the general safety of a ship that they will be examined here in some detail. The problem cannot be settled merely by constructional arrangements; a ship's stability depends not only on its own features and design, but also on commercial operating conditions (6).

The SOLAS Convention contains a particular provision on intact stability : Regulation 22, which concerns information on the stability of passenger ships and cargo ships.

1. Principles of the SOLAS Convention : stability tests and file

Once building work is complete, every passenger ship, of whatever size, and any cargo ship at least 24 metres in length, must undergo a trial to determine its stability.

The findings of this trial are recorded in a stability file, which contains much information, including the general plan and tank plan, different curves, scheduled loading conditions in operation, and other technical data.

The stability file has two functions. It allows the maritime authorities to ensure that a ship can meet minimum stability standards in the case of normal loading. It also allows the captain to estimate the stability of his own ship for any unscheduled loading condit-ions not included in the loading manual.

If the ship undergoes any conversion that affects its stability, the file for the captain has to be amended accordingly, and a fresh stability trial carried out if necessary.

2. IMO recommendations

Regulation 22 of the SOLAS Convention refers to other texts adopted by IMO, which detail certain additional requirements. These include Resolutions A.167 and A.206, which lay down recommendations on intact stability, and MSC Circular no. 346, which defines a criterion for rolling and strong winds (meteorological criterion), applicable to the intact stability of all passenger ships and cargo ships more than 24 metres long.

III - LOAD LINE CONVENTION

271. - One of the most effective ways of improving the safety of ships consists of limiting their loaded draught, in other words the quantity of goods on board. In ancient times, many shipwrecks were caused by the greed of shipmasters, who overloaded their vessel in total disregard of safety.

Most authors consider that the first rules on minimum freeboard for merchant ships date from the British Act of 1875, and the vigorous campaigning of the English parliamentarian Samuel Plimsoll. Their origin is in fact much older than this. Regulations already existed in the Middle Ages (7), and in certain forms in more ancient times (8) (cf chapter 2 above).

Today the freeboard regulations are defined by the international Load Line Convention (LL) adopted on 5 April 1966 and which came into force on 21 July 1968.

(6) C. DUONG et M. HUTHER : " Comportement transversal du navire et stabilité ". N.T.M. 1975, 119.
(7) F. ATTOMA-PEPE : " Un aperçu des francs-bords des navires au Moyen-Age ". Bulletin Technique du Bureau Veritas. Janvier 1976. 10.
(8) R. JIMENEZ : " The evolution of the Load Line ". ABS- Surveyor, May 1976, 7-13.

A - GENERAL REMARKS ON FREEBOARD

1. Definitions

272. - Freeboard is demonstrated by a circle 300 mm in diameter, affixed to each side of the ship in the middle. It is intersected by a line passing through its centre, which indicates the limit of the laden draught of the ship. Freeboard is defined as the distance between the water level outside the ship and the top of the freeboard deck at mid-length.

Beside the freeboard disc are the loadlines, indicating the various submersion limits for the ship. There are six of these, corresponding to the maximum depth of the ship in the water, depending on seasons and maritime regions, as follows, starting at the top :
- Tropical Fresh Water Load Line marked TF ;
- Fresh Water Load Line in Summer marked F ;
- Tropical Load Line marked T ;
- Summer Load Line marked S, which passes through the centre of the ring ;
- Winter Load Line marked W ;
- Winter North Atlantic Load Line marked WNA.

Figure 8 - Freeboard disc and load lines

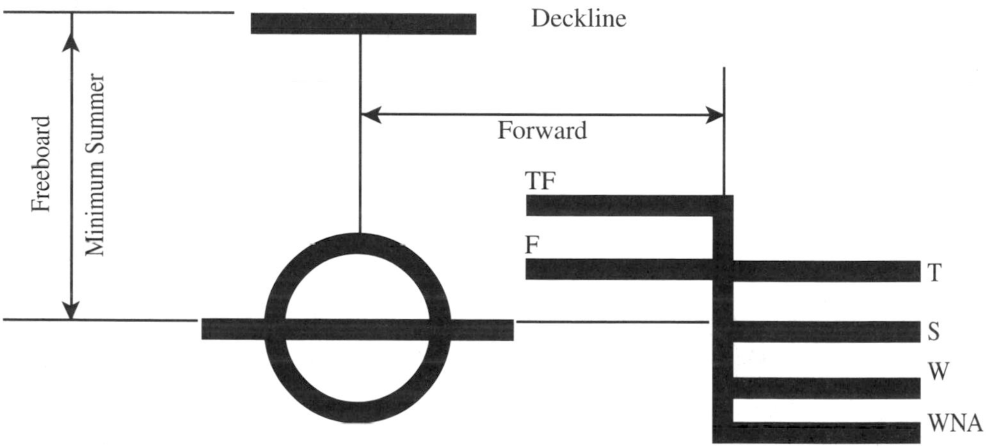

Finally, letters on each side of the disc indicate the name of the classification society that has assigned freeboard to the ship. Examples are BV for Bureau Veritas, LR for Lloyd's Register, and AB for American Bureau of Shipping.

2. Use and different types of freeboard

273. - What is the use of freeboard ? This fundamental feature for ship safety performs five main functions. The purpose is to provide a sufficient reserve of buoyancy, and ensure its maintenance under normal navigational conditions, particularly avoiding water from entering the holds when seawater covers exposed decks. Second, the freeboard protects crew members moving about or working on board, by providing a proper height of deck. Third, it guarantees that the hull will be strong enough to withstand the forces resulting from maximum settling in the water caused by the cargo. Fourthly, it provides sufficient intact stability. Finally, it ensures sufficient buoyancy and stability in case of damage. The first two such functions cover what technicians call the "geometric freeboard", the area covered by international loadline regulations.

The third function defines the "scantling freeboard". This requires the use of rules and calculations of materials strength, which since the end of the 19th century have been drawn up by classification societies.

The last two functions correspond to the "subdivision and stability freeboard", which is the concern of SOLAS regulations.

Freeboard rules are of the greatest economic importance in two ways : first, they require shipowners to observe a limit on the transport capacity of the ships on which their profit-earning capacity depends ; second, they have inevitable repercussions on shipbuilding techniques, which must meet requirements while keeping costs at a reasonable level (9).

B - CONTENT OF FREEBOARD REGULATIONS

274. - Assignment of a particular freeboard depends on several factors, some of which relate to the ship's constructional characteristics, notably the strength of the hull and its buoyancy in relation to the length of the vessel, the ratio of length to depth, shape and many other factors, such as superstructures, sheer (the curve imparted to decks to ensure that water will flow towards the midships area, and means of closure (doors, discharge ports, hatchways, scuppers). The purpose of all these provisions, referred to collectively as "conditions of assignment", is to ensure that structures situated below the freeboard deck are watertight.

Other factors are the type of cargo, the geographical area where the ship will be operating, and the season in which the voyage will take place.

Generally, the 1966 LL Convention differs from the previous version in permitting a reduction in the freeboard of large ships. Two provisions allow this reduction: Regulation 27, which distinguishes between tanker ships and others, and Annex II, concerning areas and seasonal periods, and various requirements for small craft (10).

1. Types of ships

275. - The main innovation of the 1966 LL Convention is the inclusion of freeboards, and buoyancy and intact stability regulations, in safety considerations. This has resulted in the division of ships into two types, A and B, defined in Regulation 27 of Chapter III. Regulation 26 of Chapter II lays down the special conditions for assigning freeboard to type A ships, allowing them to have lower freeboards than those of type B.

a) Definition of type A and B ships

According to Regulation 27.2, a type A ship is "one which is designed to carry only liquid cargoes in bulk, and in which cargo tanks have only small access openings closed by watertight gasketed covers". These ships are also characterised by "high integrity of the exposed deck" and "high degree of safety against flooding, resulting from the low permeability of loaded cargo spaces and the degree of subdivision usually provided".

This category includes all tank ships, particularly oil tankers, chemical and gas carriers, and incinerator ships.

(9) P. BLANC, R. SMOL : " La convention internationale sur les lignes de charge de 1966 et les principes du francbord ". Bulletin de l'ATMA. n° 67. Paris 1967, 715-731.
(10) F. PLAZA : " The International Convention on Load Lines, 1966 ". IMO, 9470Y.

According to Regulation 27.5, any ships that fail to meet the requirements above are regarded as type B ships. Certain type B ships, however, may be assigned a lower freeboard, if they comply with subdivision and intact stability criteria.

b) Freeboard tables

Regulation 28 of Chapter III contains tables showing basic freeboards before correction in relation to the length of the ship. There are two sorts of tables, for type A and for type B ships.

Freeboards are generally reduced in relation to the levels laid down in 1930. This reduction is especially clear for tankers, applying as it does to 85 per cent of all ships three hundred metres long. This appears logical, to the extent that tankers are very dependable as regards the perils of sea, and can quite safely navigate with sea washing over a deck.

The reduction in freeboard is smaller for other ships. Nevertheless, it results in an increase in deadweight, to the extent that openings in the decks and superstructures have to have proper protection. In order to guarantee uniform interpretation and application of the provisions of Regulation 27, IMO recommended states to adhere to certain requirements enumerated in Resolution 172 of 28 November 1968.

2. Zones, regions and seasonal periods

276. - The 1930 LL Convention set the maximum depths in the water to which a ship may be loaded, depending on the season of the year, and the part of the world. At the 1966 Conference, many exceptions to the classification based on meteorological data were requested and usually obtained. The new map of the regions, contained in Annex II of the Convention, shows quite clearly that the boundary lines of different zones have been drawn so that a particularly busy maritime route will be located entirely within one zone. Classification of a region as Summer or Winter seasonal zone rests on scientific considerations. However, as stated in the preamble to Annex II, "for practical reasons, some degree of relaxation has been found acceptable".

The 1966 LL Convention accordingly displays a kind of general shift from the old zones to a new classification, corresponding to a reduced freeboard. This is the case of the route followed by large oil tankers coming from the Persian Gulf and going round the Cape of Good Hope without putting in, to discharge their cargo in Western Europe : the route lies in the Summer seasonal zone the whole year round !

C - CHANGES TO THE 1966 CONVENTION

277. - Unlike other IMO technical conventions, the 1966 LL Convention does not include any tacit acceptance procedure for amendments. This explains the relative slowness of the revision process.

Five series of amendments have been adopted since 1971. So far, none of them has yet come into force, because of the small number of acceptances. The same is true of the Protocol of 11 November 1988, aimed at harmonising the requirements of the LL Convention on surveys and delivery of certificates with those of the SOLAS and MARPOL Conventions.

1. Need for thorough review

Although noone has seriously questioned the provisions of the 1966 LL Convention, it is nevertheless clear that freeboard regulations need review, to keep up with changes in marine technologies over the last thirty years. New types of craft have appeared, as well as multihulls, surface-effect ships and other high-speed craft. Considerable improvements have been made in welded hull construction. Past changes included steel hatch coversalready covered by the 1966 Convention instead of wood, machinery spaces located aft rather than amidships, for example (11). Finally, the appearance of new concepts and the facilities offered by information technology suggest that freeboard might be assigned on other bases than those adopted in 1930 and 1966.

Another campaign in favour of urgent review of freeboard rules was launched in October 1995 in the United Kingdom (12). Lord Donaldson, who led an investigation into the loss of the Derbyshire, emphasised the need to revise the provisions of the 1966 Convention, because of the numerous accidents to bulk carriers in recent years. He argued for provision to be made for the freak waves, 25 to 35 metres high, that ships can meet on certain seas around the world. This would require increasing the strength of hatch covers and other openings (13).

2. Future loadline convention

278. - In 1992, aware of the need for change, IMO, acting through its Stability, Loadlines and Fishing Boat Safety Committee (SLF), began a comprehensive overhaul of the 1966 Convention (14).

In December 1996, the MSC approved a plan (15) to terminate the work of revision in 1999, for the adoption of a new convention in the year 2000 (16). It is clear, however, that this deadline will have to be extended, because of the time needed for the working group to complete its review.

Table 9. Concept of the future LL regulations

(Sources IMO : SLF 39/7)

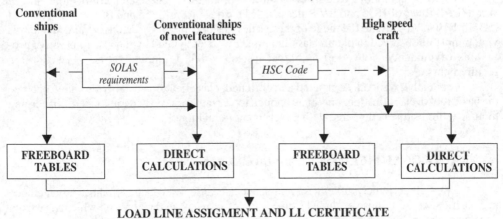

LOAD LINE ASSIGMENT AND LL CERTIFICATE

(11) Ph. ALMAN, W. CLEARY, M. DYER, J. PAULLING et N. SALVESEN : " The International Load Line convention : crossroads to the future ". Marine Technology. Oct. 1992, 233-248.
(12) " Lighter loads" . Lloyd's List, 27 Oct. 1995.
(13) " Donaldson urges load line rethink" . Lloyd's List, 26 Oct. 1995.
(14) IMO. SLF. 36/25, par. 22.3.3. et SLF 37/8, 7 July 1992.
(15) IMO. SLF 39/7. 10 June 1994.
(16) IMO. MSC/67/WP 10, 4 Dec. 1996, par. 8.8 & 8.9.

As shown in table 9, the future LL Convention will take account of three types of craft: conventional ships, those that present new features not covered by the provisions of the 1966 Convention, and finally the high-speed craft defined and regulated by the HSC Code. There are two possible approaches: retain the freeboard tables, subject to the necessary changes, or adopt a new approach based on use of the direct freeboard calculation method.

The planned technical amendments take account of the human factor, particularly "information to be supplied to the master" (Regulation 10), including a trim and stability booklet, loading manual, computer to calculate trim and stability, equipment for operational response monitoring (ORM) (17).

For conventional ships, the work of the subcommittee will probably involve a reduction in the freeboard of large ships and an increase for small ones (18).

During the revision process, the United Kingdom has proposed that these requirements should henceforth be incorporated in the SOLAS Convention, because of the influence of stability standards on the setting of freeboards (19). While acknowledging the advantages of combining the two instruments, the MSC is unwilling to decide for the moment, and has asked the SLF to study the advantages of merging the texts, and possible legal implications (20).

IV - CLASSIFICATION STANDARDS

279. - Classification societies were the original setters of safety standards. Long before states and international organisations became involved, these societies had drawn up technical rules for the structural strength of the ships they classed, and the reliability of machinery and equipment.

The first regulations date from the mid-19th century. These applied to ships built of wood (LRS Rules of 1835 and BV Rules of 1851), iron (LRS in 1855 and BV in 1858) or steel (BV in 1880). At present, the range of these rules has become far wider. Essential standards, which must be observed to obtain classification, are accompanied by the less imperative provisions of guidance notes and technical notes, which announce future classification requirements.

Gradually extended, completed and enriched, classification society rules have become the basic tool of classification, important enough to warrant some consideration here concerning their specific features compared with government regulations.

A - TRADITIONAL FIELD OF CLASSIFICATION

280. - It is extremely difficult for non-specialists to separate factors traditionally included in classification from those excluded from it. In any case, a list, the items on which vary from one society to another; is necessary to define the limits of rules.

(17) IMO. SLF 38/14, 21 Dec. 1993 & SLF 38/14/1, 21 Jan. 1994.
(18) IMO. SLF 38/8/1, 17 Dec. 1993.
(19) IMO. SLF 38/8/2, 5 Jan. 1994.
(20) IMO. MSC/66/24, 18 June 1996, par. 5.4 à 5.7, 24.

The main purpose of classification is to protect a ship for a given service and navigational notation as a piece of property. This is done by assessing the degree to which the various parts of the ship conform to a technical reference standard, namely the society rules. Their provisions are not primarily intended to ensure the safety of life at sea, which remains a State responsibility (21).

1. Points covered by classification rules

The two areas generally regulated by classification society rules are structural strength and watertight integrity of the ship's hull, and the safety and reliability of the propulsion and steering gear, as well as the auxiliary systems built into the ship "in order to establish and maintain basic conditions on board, thereby enabling the ship to operate in its intended service" (22).

Classification rules are drawn up with reference to the principles of naval architecture, marine engineering and other related subjects, and they apply to eight aspects of the ship (23): materials, structural strength, main and auxiliary machinery, control engineering systems, electrical installations, service or cargo installations, fire protection, detection and extinction, and more recently (since 1996) intact stability.

2. Points not covered by classification

Classification societies do not intervene in areas that are the sphere of shipowners, shipbuilders and national authorities. Classification accordingly generally excludes the choice of mode of propulsion, the power of the propulsion unit, ship operation standards (manning, crew qualification, equipment management, lifesaving appliances such as lifeboats and other craft, lifebelts and jackets), navigational aids (on-board equipment and instruments to facilitate navigation, such as radar, calculators, radio and IT equipment), equipment to ensure the safety of those on board, damage stability conditions, and finally pollution prevention and treatment installations.

B - ADAPTABILITY OF CLASSIFICATION RULES

281. - The fundamental characteristic of classification rules is their great facility to adapt to changes. Unlike the regulations laid down in international conventions, classification standards are constantly updated and amended.

1. Reasons for permanent updating

There are two sources of information that go to explain this remarkable adaptability: data drawn from events at sea, and innovations introduced by shipyards.

---

(21) Ph. BOISSON : " La classification et la certification des navires. Deux composantes fondamentales du système de sécurité maritime ". Renconter Air Mer, AFDM/SFDA. Paris, 21 février 1996.
(22) IACS. Internal Information n° 8 - Definition of Ship Classification, 1993.
(23) J.R.G. SMITH : " Classification as a statutory requirement by the year 2000 ". IMAS 11-13, Nov. 1992. Paper 7.
(24) P. BLANC : " Problèmes posés aux sociétés de classification par le développement des transports spécialisés ". NTM, 1964, 86.

Certain changes to rules result from the lessons drawn from maritime incidents and casualties. There is no difference on this point from national legislation, except for the speed with which societies can introduce amendments. Bureau Veritas, for instance, only a few months after the *Tanio* disaster in 1980, required certain oil tankers to have a loading gauge on the bridge.

Classification society requirements also reflect the specific needs of seaborne trade and the new technical possibilities offered by shipyards (24). The leading societies have set up a system of national and international committees, to help them seek the advice and opinions of all the professionals concerned, and facilitate communications within the maritime world.

2. Rule amendment procedures

Periodic revision of classification society rules takes the form of publication of yearly, half-yearly or even quarterly updates. Each society has discretionary powers to amend certain requirements, formulate new ones, change the conditions of application, authorise the application of provisions that it considers equivalent, given the particular features of a ship, equipment or installation (25).

Another procedure used by societies is the publication of guidance notes, the provisions of which are more flexible than those of the rules. Being by their nature more flexible, the recommendations contained in these documents can provide a basis for discussion with shipyards, which can propose equivalent measures, if they offer satisfactory technical arguments (26).

C - COMPETITION ON SAFETY STANDARDS

282. - What relationship exists between private classification standards and public safety standards ? While it is undeniable that private standards have advantages over public texts in the areas they have in common, their continued existence is partly threatened by changes in international regulations.

1. Authority of classification standards

Classification rules carry authority because of an extraordinary faculty for predicting future trends shown by the leading classification societies, which means that private standards are often ahead of public texts. These qualities are kept sharp by the very tough competition among the societies, on innovation, research and development. Unlike public authorities, which adopt a reactive demand in drafting standards, classification societies prefer to lead technical progress rather than trail behind it. Many of the rules contained in IMO conventions come directly from classification rules.

Commentators have drawn attention to the national and international bearing of classification, which "are absolute requirements for builders, owners and insurers". It has also been pointed out that, legally, classification rules "accepted willingly by all countries (...) were superior to positive laws" (27).

(25) V. ALBIACH et R. SMOL : " Traité des navires de commerce ". 5 vol. ENSTA, Paris, 1971, 26.
(26) JMM, 2 fév 1961, 229.
(27) G. RIPERT : " Droit Maritime ". Rousseau, Paris, 3 vol, 4e édition 1950-1953. Tome I, 282-284.

2. Recognition of classification

283. - Public regulations have always implicitly acknowledged the quality of classification standards for the design, construction and maintenance of ships.

The LL Convention of 1996 stipulates, for instance, that in order to receive the freeboard certificate, the ship must be of adequate strength. It considers that such a condition it met when the ship is built and maintained in conformity to the requirements of a classification society recognised by the flag authority (cf Annex I Regulation 1).

A similar provision is included in the SOLAS Convention for the issue of passenger ship safety certificates, and safety construction certificates for cargo ships of more than 500 gross tonnage. They require the materials and scantling of the ship's structure, boilers and other pressure vessels and their appurtenances, main and auxiliary machinery, electrical installations and other equipment, to be in all respects "in satisfactory condition and fit for the service for which it is intended". The only detailed rules that are regarded as authoritative and known internationally that cover these requirements are those of the classification societies (28).

IMO gave explicit recognition to classification in 1995, during the adoption of amendments concerning ship structure in the SOLAS Convention. The new Regulation 3-1 of Part A of Chapter II-1 states that ships are to be "designed, constructed and maintained in compliance with the structural, mechanical and electrical requirements of a recognised classification society".

This amended rule, proposed by the United States to avoid "the possible emergence of a variety of standards" and ensure consistency with the LL Convention (29), came into effect on 1st June 1998, making conformity to classification rules a statutory requirement (30).

The importance of this reference cannot be over-emphasised: it should allow classification societies to collaborate with IMO in creating design, constructional and equipment standards (31). There are also likely to be legal consequences regarding proof of the unseaworthiness of the ship and claims against classification societies, regarded as the ultimate guardian of statutory safety at sea (32). These new obligations could accompany recognition of a certain limitation of liability for third party claims, which until now has never been taken into account by national legislators.

3. Growth of public regulations

284. - Despite official recognition of classification societies, changes in regulations leave some doubt about the future of private safety standards. In the last century, rules were almost exclusively issued by classification societies. Today, they emerge largely from the requirements of international conventions, codes and recommendations drawn up by States under the auspices of IMO. It is not impossible that tomorrow they will be an entirely governmental or intergovernmental responsibility.

European Union initiatives are worth examining closely in this respect. Directive 96/98 on marine equipment was adopted by the EU Council of Ministers on 20 December 1996 (33).

(28) J.R. SMITH : " IACS and IMO, The essential relationship ". IACS Edition 3, 1st July 1998.
(29) - IMO. MSC 60/19/8, 14 Feb. 1992 ; FSI 2/INF-18, 26 Nov. 1993.
- IMO. Introduction of a standard for ship construction into SOLAS 74. MCS 64/21/5, 8 August 1994.
(30) " Class and statutory rules must work together ". Lloyd's Ship Manager, Feb. 1997, 65-67.
(31) A. DE BIEVRE : " The supremacy of class over statutory rules ". Lloyd's List, 3 Feb. 1997.
(32) A. DE BIEVRE : " Class authority given more legal clout". Lloyd's List, 6 June 1997.
(33) OJEC n° L 46/25, 17 Feb. 1997.

According to article 5.1, "Equipment (...) placed on board a Community ship on or after" 1st January 1999 "shall meet the applicable requirements of the international instruments referred to". Such equipment comprises all fixed appliances and installations on board ships, whether radar, navigational instruments or lifeboats.

Article 5.2 states that such conformity is "demonstrated solely in accordance with the relevant testing standards and conformity assessment procedures" consisting of a CE type examination or complete CE quality assurance. Equipment that meets conformity standards is to "have the mark affixed to it by the manufacturer or his authorised representative established within the Community" (article 11.1).

The Directive does not merely provide a framework for uniform, compulsory application of international testing standards : it requires organisations responsible for testing to meet common quality criteria. A compulsory audit every two years by the administration guarantees "that each notified body continues to comply with the criteria" (article 9.2).

Under the terms of article 7.1, the EU submits a request to IMO or, if appropriate, European standardisation organisations, asking for definition of detailed testing standards for relevant items of equipment, in other words those for which international texts have not yet provided any particular stipulations.

Ultimately, classification societies could be robbed of their standard-setting powers, if certain regional initiatives, like those of the EU, tend to spread. For the moment, they are entering into competition with other private standardisation organisations involved in the maritime sector, such as ISO (34). It will be up to IMO to see to it that such requirements do not duplicate the work of classification societies, traditionally competent in ship design and structure (35).

D - WHAT RULES FOR THE FUTURE ?

285. - One of the most important tasks of classification societies consists of defining the principles on which their ship classification rules will be based: certain bodies consider that rules should be highly sophisticated, in order to give designers a strict line of conduct to follow, whereas other believe that they should be simple and general, in order to leave designers a certain amount of freedom.

The introduction of new notations, to define scantlings by reference to direct calculations, has restarted discussions about what future rules could be like : elaborate or simple, general or based on direct calculations. To understand fully what is at stake, the traditional philosophy of classification needs to be recalled.

1. Philosophy of classification

The primary goal of classification rules is to provide calculation formulae and regulations, in order to define structural scantlings and standards of machinery equipment.

At Bureau Veritas, the calculation process is divided into three main phases. At the preliminary stage, the main characteristics of the future ship are determined (dimensions, service, capacity plans, hull lines, weight). Second, scantlings are established for longitudinal members and the primary structure. This is used to define the capacity of the structure, in other words its ability to withstand the loads to which it may be subject. The final phase

---

(34) IMO. Report of ISO/TC8 work programme submitted by ISO MEPC 41/4/1, 30 Dec. 1997.
(35) IMO. MSC 67/22, 19 Dec. 1996, par. 4.19-4.21, 20.

consists of an analysis of structural details, including those of machinery and outfit falling within the scope of classification.

2. New approach to classification

Considering that the use of regulatory formulae to calculate ship loads was a conservative method, certain societies have adopted a new, more refined approach, in order to improve structural design and the distribution of scantlings. This approach is based on direct calculation 17of the behaviour of external and internal pressures acting on it, evaluated in relation to forms, the distribution of the weights of the light ship, and loading cases. If it is accepted that struct-ural scantling must be based on the result of direct calculations, it might be concluded that rules are superfluous, since they are at the most a definition of appropriate analysis procedures and permitted stresses.

However, it is unlikely that rules could be stripped down in this way, for several reasons. First, the existence of certain rules remains necessary to determine the basic scantling and the scantling of components that are not covered by direct calculations, such as the superstruct-ures. Next, shipyards do not always have sufficient technical facilities to make such complex calculations, which require major information technology resources. Finally, the sphere covered by rules is very wide, dealing not only with structural problems but also with problems affecting propulsive units and ship equipment.

In fact, classification society rules, as they exist in their present form, would seem likely to remain for long a fundamental tool for classification societies, designers and builders.

CHAPTER 11

Safety of passenger ships

286. - The safety of passenger ships occupies a special place in international regulatory activity. There are several reasons for this. First, there is the specific economic context of seaborne passenger transport, and the nature and scale of the risks to which it is exposed. Second, such regulation has been in existence for so long, with the historical development of preventive standards. Finally, there is the highly diversified content of regulations, to adapt to the constraints of transport by sea.

According to Lloyd's Register, there were 2 828 passenger ships and 2 425 carferries in existence on 1st January 1998 (1). The size of this fleet reflects the varied expectations of an increasingly demanding clientele, using ships as a means of transport over short distances or for holiday cruises. The cruise industry displays amazing growth potential: the market is expected to reach ten million passengers by the year 2000 (2).

Passenger ships are relatively accident-free : the 218 accidents recorded in 1997 involved only one passenger/general cargo ship, two passenger/ro-ro cargo ships, and one passenger vessel (3). The risks faced by this type of seaborne transport should not be underestimated, however, A banal accident to a ship carrying a large number of people can turn into a terrible disaster. Since 1948, the most serious accidents, in terms of loss of human life, have involved carferries carrying passengers over short distances (4). The December 1987 collision between the *Dona Paz* and the Filipino oil tanker *Victor* caused the greatest maritime tragedy of all time, with some 4 400 casualties. A total of 10 500 people have died in the last ten years in accidents to passenger ships, mainly near the coasts of developing countries (5).

The first safety regulations for passenger ships appeared in the 19th century. This paralleled the growth of transatlantic voyages, needed to carry the huge numbers of emigrants to the New World (6). The frequency of appalling accidents, particularly the loss of the *Titanic* in 1912, which caused 1 501 deaths, led to the introduction of new safety regulations (7).

The Convention on safety of life at sea (SOLAS), adopted in 1914, was the first international effort to improve the safety of passenger transport. Its standards have continued to develop in the 20th century, with the adoption of new versions in 1928 ; 1948 and 1960 (8).

Current regulations on the safety of passenger ships are contained in the version of SOLAS adopted on 1st November 1974.

The 1974 SOLAS Convention came into force in May 1980. There have been numerous

(1) Lloyd's Register of Shipping : "World Fleet Statistics". 1997, London.
(2) Economist Intelligence Unit : The World Cruise Ship Industries in the 1990's.
(3) Lloyd's Register of Shipping : " World Casualty statistics ". 1997, London.
(4) " Worst Maritime Disasters ". Lloyd's List, 29 Sept. 1994.
(5) Jim MULRENAN : " Will Neptune be remembered ? ". Lloyd's List, 20 Feb. 1993.
(6) A.W. CROOK : " Safety of Passenger Ships " Lloyd's Register of Shipping, 1970,
(7) S. PAYNE : " Tightening the grip on passenger ship safety : the evolution of SOLAS ". The Naval Architect,
Oct. 1994, 482-487.
(8) IMO : 1991, J/4726.

amendments, in 1978, 1981, 1988, 1991, 1992, 1994, 1995, 1996 and 1997. These were necessary to provide for technical improvements in ship safety.

This chapter will examine in turn the general regulations of the SOLAS Convention applying to all types of passenger ships (cf I below), specific regulations for passenger ro-ros (II) and finally regulations on high-speed craft (III).

I - GENERAL SOLAS REGULATIONS

287. - These SOLAS regulations apply to all passenger ships of any tonnage engaged in international voyages.

Regulation 2 of chapter I of the Convention defines a passenger ship as "a ship which carries more than twelve passengers. A passenger is every person other than the master and the members of the crew or other persons employed or engaged in any capacity on board a ship on the business of that ship and a child under one year of age.

SOLAS regulations on construction, subdivision and stability, machinery and electrical installations may not apply to "passenger ships which are employed in special trades for the carriage of large number of special trade passengers, such as the pilgrim trade, on condition that such ships conform to :
- rules appended to the Special Trade Passenger Ship Agreement of 1971 ;
- rules appended to the Protocol on Space Requirements for Special Trade Passenger Ships of 1973".

This chapter examines only technical regulations on the construction and equipment of passenger ships contained in the first four chapters of the SOLAS Convention. Operating regulations are dealt with in chapter 16 below for the ISM Code and in chapter 19 below for navigational regulations.

Three recommendations recently adopted by IMO may also be consulted :
- Resolution A.792 of 23 November 1995 on safety culture in and around passenger ships ;
- Resolution A.796 of the same date on a decision-support system for masters of passenger ships ;
- Resolution A.857 of 17 November 1997 on combatting unsafe practices associated with the traffic in or transport of migrants by sea.

A - SUBDIVISION AND STABILITY

Regulations on subdivision and stability are set out in Chapter II-1, Part B of the SOLAS Convention.

1. Subdivision regulations

288. - Passenger ships are subdivided into watertight compartments so that, after a hypothetical accident to the hull, they will remain afloat in a stable position.

The degree of subdivision, measured by the maximum allowable distance between two adjacent bulkheads, varies depending on the length of the ship and the service in which it is engaged. The highest degree of subdivision applies to ships of the greatest length used to carry passengers (9).

---

(9) Bureau Veritas : " Safety of passengers and cruise vessels ". Technical Paper n° 388, revision 1, March 1997.

The SOLAS Convention gives empirical figures, from which the values of the factor of subdivision can be deduced from the length of the ship, and the service criterion assigned to it (cf Regulation 6).

The subdivision factor is always equal to 1, 1/2 , 1/3 or 1/4. The fact that it may never be greater than 1 means that the length of any compartment must never exceed the floodable length in its centre. This means that the ship's survival is ensured if only one of its compartments is flooded. Ships with a subdivision factor of less than 1/2 must survive with two adjacent compartments flooded. Factors 1/3 and 1/4 correspond to three or four compartments flooded.

Finally, SOLAS lays down various requirements concerning the watertightness of doors and openings (cf Regulations 17 and 18), decks, trunks, tunnels, duct keels and ventilators (cf Regulation 19), and bilge pumping arrangements (cf Regulation 21).

2. Stability regulations

289. - Damage stability standards are contained mainly in Regulation 8, which considers various hypotheses concerning flooding of the ship. Regulation 22 provides for the performance of a stability trial after completion and the establishment of a document stating the ship's precise stability characteristics under various operating conditions. A copy of this information is submitted to the flag State authorities for examination and approval.

Several recent disasters, such as the *Herald of Free Enterprise* in 1987, the *Royal Pacific* in 1992 and the *Estonia* in 1994, led IMO to carry out an in-depth review of subdivision and stability regulations (11). The next section of this chapter examines these changes, which concern mainly ro-ro pasenger ships.

B - FIRE PROTECTION

1. SOLAS 1974 regulations

290. - The basic principles that inspired the standards in the SOLAS Convention are listed in Regulation 2 of chapter II-2. These concern division of the ship into principal vertical sections by bulkheading possessing mechanical and thermal resistance, separation of accommodation from the rest of the ship by bulkheads with similar properties, restricted use of combustible materials, detection, location and extinction of any fire at the point where it has broken out, protection of exits and accesses to ensure more effective firefighting, possibility of rapid use of firefighting installations, and reduction of the risk of ignition of vapours released by cargoes (12).

These principles are supplemented by special regulations for passenger ships (cf Part B, Regulations 23 to 41-2).

2. Fires on the *Scandinavian Star* and *Moby Prince*

Two major disasters that led to major changes in existing regulations were the fires on board the *Scandinavian Star* and the *Moby Prince*.

A former cruise vessel, the *Scandinavian Star* had been making regular crossings between Norway and Denmark since 1989. Fire broke out in the night of 6 April 1990, causing

(10) " Rapid Pacific sinking revises stability issue ". Lloyd's List, 24 August 1992.
(11) W. O'NEIL : "Changes to passenger ship safety regulations adopted in recent years". IMO, 28 Oct. 1993.
(12) Ch. CUSHING : "Reducing risks ". Seatrade Review, March 1992, 175-179.

the deaths of 158 passengers, most of them Danish (13). The accident led to an official inquiry and a series of lawsuits in Denmark and the United States (14). A year later, almost to the day, fire on board the Iranian carferry *Moby Prince* near the port of Leghorn caused 144 fatalities (15).

3. Amendment of SOLAS Convention

291. - On 24 May 1991, IMO adopted a first series of amendments to chapter II-2 of the SOLAS Convention, with the aim of making passenger ships safe from fire. These amendments targetted large open spaces extending over more than three decks, like the *atria* so popular with cruise passengers.

In April 1992 a further series of measures applied more specifically to ships in service. It became compulsory to instal smoke detection and alarm systems (absent on board the *Scandinavian Star* with such disastrous consequences), and sprinkler devices for accommodation and service spaces, stairway enclosures and gangways. Other improvements involved emergency lighting, general alarm systems for critical situations and other means of communication.

In December 1992, the MSC adopted a third series of amendments applying to new ships, and involving automatic sprinkler, fire detection and alarm systems.

New standards defining the fire integrity of bulkheads and decks were introduced, like those applying to gangways and staircases. Such means must now be equipped with standby lighting, to enable passenÂers to identify all assembly points, and easily recognise escape routes (17).

4. Revision of chapter II-2

In October 1996, the Fire Protection Subcommittee of IMO undertook a complete revision of chapter II-2 of the SOLAS Convention.

The aim is to simplify regulations by putting technical provisions into separate codes. Several improvements have been planned (18), including the adoption of a code for application of fire test procedures (FTP), allowing administrations to approve products for installation on board ships, development of a new code of fire safety measures (19), implementation of risk analysis and formal safety assessment (FSA) methods for the amendment of these regulations.

The year 2000 has been set as the deadline for approval of the new chapter II-2, except for the FTP Code, which came into force on 1st July 1998 (20).

(13) "Are passengers ships safe?". Safety at Sea, April 1993, 23-26.
(14) David MOTT : " Tragedy could lead to improved safety on ferries ". Lloyd's List, 6 April 1991.
15) - "Ferry Inferno : 141 dead, one survivor". Lloyd's List, 12 April 1991.
- Ferry inferno still a mystery". Lloyd's List, 13 April 1991.
(16) W.S. HORRISON : "Current and future aims of IMO for passenger safety ". Superferry 92, February 1992.
(17) Ch. J. DORCHAK : " Statutory amendment influencing cruise vessels - 1994 ". Seatrade Cruise Shipping Convention - March 1994, Miami.
(18) IMO News, N° 4, 1996, 7.
(19) " Ferries become key issue as IMO reviews fire measures ". Lloyd's List, 30 Sept. 1996.
(20) " IMO delays fire safety moves ". Lloyd's List ,10 Oct. 1996.

C - LIFESAVING APPLIANCES AND ARRANGEMENTS

292. - The lifesaving appliances (LSA) now to be found on any seagoing ship play a fundamental role in safety, by keeping alive those that have abandoned ship. The successful rescue operations carried out on the *Jupiter* in October 1988 off Piraeus, in which 486 lives were saved (21), the *Oceanos* in August 1991 off South Africa (544 lives saved) (22), and the *Achille Lauro* in December 1994 off the Somalian coast (900 lives saved) (23), showed the importance of such equipment on board passenger ships.

International regulations on lifesaving appliances appear in chapter III of the 1974 SOLAS Convention, entirely revised by the MSC on 17 June 1983. These amendments came into force on 1st July 1986 and therefore apply to all new ships built after that date. Certain of these requirements also apply retrospectively to existing ships.

1. Lifeboats and liferafts

Regulation 41 requires all partially or totally enclosed lifeboats to be equipped with an engine. In addition, all totally enclosed boats must be self-righting. Passenger ships have to be provided with rescue boats on each side, in other words boats designed to rescue people in distress and to marshal craft (cf Regulation 20). Most passenger ships must carry partially or totally enclosed lifeboats on each side, able to accommodate fewer than 50 per cent of all the persons on board, with the remainder on liferafts under davits. Several provisions are intended to guarantee that all survival craft are kept in good condition, and can be used quickly in an emergency. According to Regulation 13, it must be possible to launch these craft even when the ship has a list of 20 degrees in either direction.

2. Means of communication

Traditional means of communication provided by radiotelegraph installations and radiobeacons are required to be replaced by the equipment provided for under the Global Maritime Distress and Safety System (GMDSS) (cf chapter 20 below).

3. Prevention of risk of hypothermia

Several regulations aim to reduce the threat of dangerous loss of body heat, or hypothermia. They concern individual lifsaving appliances, including immersion suits to reduce body-heat loss by a person in cold water, and thermal protective aids in the form of bags made from waterproof material with low thermal conductivity.

4. Location devices

Location devices are used to establish the position of survivors or lifeboats. The revised chapter III provides for new means in this area: certain lifebuoys are to be fitted with illuminated devices and automatic smoke emission devices. Lifejackets must be provided with lights and a whistle. Finally, there is provision for the use of retro-reflective materials.

In June 1996, a series of amendments completely changed chapter III, in order to take account of technological changes that have occurred since 1983. Most technical requirements have been transferred to a new international code on lifesaving appliances (LSA Code), for ships built on and after 1st July 1998.

---

(21) Lloyd's List, 24 Oct. 1988.
(22) Lloyd's List, 5 August 1991.
(23) - "Two die in Achille Lauro blaze". Lloyd's List, 1 Dec. 1994.
- "Weapon for the politicians". Lloyd's List, 1 Dec. 1994.

D - RADIO EQUIPMENT

293. - Radio equipment provisions, traditionally covered by chapter IV of the 1974 SOLAS Convention, have been amended in depth, with the introduction of the GMDSS.

Passenger ships also have to comply with the requirements of chapter V of the SOLAS Convention concerning safety of navigation, applicable to all merchant ships, regardless of their commercial functions and the type of voyage involved.

II - SAFETY OF PASSENGER RO-RO VESSELS

294. - Passenger ro-ro ships, or carferries, are used for voyages on short sea routes. Their internal structure is characterised by large vehicle decks, often occupying the whole length and width of the ship, in order to speed up loading and unloading of vehicles. A number of platform decks allow vehicles to embark on several levels. Their increasingly high superstructure houses decks for passenger amenities. Present ferries can carry several thousand passengers (24).

Ro-ros are now an integral part of the transport infrastructure in many countries, particularly in Europe. They provide an ideal form of transport for island States, and contribute to a country's transport system. For all these reasons, it is scarcely surprising that, despite a number of tragic accidents, there has never been any question of abandoning such ferries. However, two terrible accidents, to the *Herald of Free Enterprise* in 1987 and the *Estonia* in 1994, led to a far-reaching reform of SOLAS regulations for passenger ships (25).

Passenger ro-ros have been fiercely criticised for their lack of subdivision and poor stability. The very high centre of gravity and the absence of any subdivision of the vehicle decks can very quickly and irrecoverably compromise their stability. These vessels stand very high in the water, sometimes with twelve decks, carrying low-density cargoes.

The sea is kept out of the vehicle deck, which is a space without any transverse bulkheading, by a watertight ramp door at the stern, and by a bow door which, when shut, forms part of the outside plating. The space beneath the lowest vehicle deck, regarded as the subdivision deck, is divided up by watertight bulkheads, to meet SOLAS requirements.

Regulations are able to ensure the safety of these ferries provided that two conditions are met: the vehicle deck must not be flooded, and stowage of vehicles on the car deck is not affected by the ship heeling over in the event of damage (26).

A - CONSEQUENCES OF *HERALD OF FREE ENTERPRISE* ACCIDENT

295. - On 7 March 1987 the carferry *Herald of Free Enterprise* capsized shortly after leaving the Belgian port of Zeebrugge, and sank, causing the deaths of 193 passengers and crew members. The inquiry carried out by the United Kingdom attributed the accident to massive flooding of the vehicle deck through the bow doors, which had not been shut.

---

(24) Cf. special issue of Proceedings devoted to passengers vessels. US Coast Guards. Proceedings. Vol.45, n° 5, Sept/Oct. 1990, particularly R.L. MARKLE Jr : "Life saving systems", 45-49.
(25) "IMO and ro-ro safety". Focus on IMO, Sept. 1995.
(26) C. DUONG : " Present state of the question of safety of ro-ro ships ". Bureau Veritas, Nov. 1984.
- The Nautical Institute on Passenger ro-ro safety and vulnerability. Safety at Sea, May 1988, 21-24.

Following the disaster, the British government asked IMO to take emergency steps to make carferries safer. The British proposals, most of which were based on the results of the inquiry, were presented in four separate packages, involving amendments mainly to chapter II-1 of the SOLAS Convention.

1. Amendments of 21 April 1988

These amendments, which came into effect on 22 October 1988, concern Regulations 23 and 42 of the SOLAS Convention.

A new Regulation 23-2 requires installation on the navigation bridge of indicators for all vehicle loading doors, and a system for detecting infiltrations of water through these doors that could lead to major flooding. Ro-ro cargo spaces also have to be patrolled or monitored by television cameras capable of observing any undue movement of vehicles in heavy weather.

A new Regulation 42-1 deals with supplementary emergency lighting on board these ferries.

2. Amendments of 28 October 1988

Three new series of amendments were adopted in October 1988, to come into force on 29 Aril 1990.

The most important of these concerns Regulation 8 on stability in a damaged condit-ion. Devised well before the wreck of the *Herald of Free Enterprise*, this amendment is directly relevant to ro-ro safety and its adoption was therefore brought forward. Referred to as "SOLAS 90", this standard applies to ships built after 2 April 1990.

Regulation 8 has been considerably extended in scope : a ship's stability must make allowance for factors such as passengers crowding to one side of the ship, launching of survival craft also on one side, and wind pressure. The maximum angle of listing after flooding but before equalisation may not exceed 15 degrees.

A further amendment to Regulation 8 concerns intact rather than damage stability. Shipmasters must be supplied with the information needed to maintain adequate stability. After loading, and before departure, the master must determine the ship's trim and stability.

A new Regulation 20-1 requires cargo-loading doors to be locked shut before the ship begins a crossing, and remain closed until it is at its next ship berth.

Finally, an amendment to Regulation 22 requires passenger ships to undergo a lightweight survey every five years. This checks any changes in the ship's lightweight displacement and longitudinal centre of gravity. If variations are excessive, the ship must undergo a stability trial, and its stability file must be corrected accordingly.

3. Amendments of 11 April 1989

These amendments, which came into effect on 1st February 1992, change several regulations in chapter II-1, including those dealing with openings in watertight bulkheads on passenger ships. They have to be fitted with fast-closing sliding doors, controlled from the bridge. In general, all doors must be kept shut, except in exceptional circumstances.

4. Amendments of 1 April 1992

296. - A research programme established by the United Kingdom after the Zeebrugge disaster (27) cast doubt on the safety of ferries in service. They were judged to be incapable of remaining afloat after damage in waves only a metre high, or even less.

(27) N. THOMPSON : " Ro-ro - The crucial unsolved questions ". Lloyd's List, 4 March 1988.
- " DTp measures taken to improve ferry safety ". Safety at sea, May 1988, 25.

Under pressure from the British government, the MSC decided to introduce measures based on SOLAS 90 standards, in an effort to improve the stability of passenger ships (28).

Because of the huge financial burden that would have been placed on the maritime transport industry by strict application of these new measures, the MSC decided on an eleven-year period of grace from 1st October 1994, during which vessels built before 29 April 1990 would have to be upgraded to meet the new SOLAS requirements, referred to as "SOLAS 92".

The new regulation introduced by IMO was quite simple: a ship's survivability was assessed by a ratio A/Amax, based on a simplified probabilistic approach. Deadlines for upgrading ships to the SOLAS 92 standard depended on the percentage value obtained by this formula. For example, vessels for which the degree of compliance was only 70 per cent had to comply fully with the requirements not later than 1st October 1994. Table 10 shows the complete phase-in period and A/Amax values

**Table 10. Application of SOLAS 1992 stability requirements
to existing ro-ro passenger vessels**

Degree of compliance	Compliance
Less than 70%	1 October 1994
70% - less than 75%	1 October 1996
75% - less than 85%	1 October 1998
85% - less than 90%	1 October 2000
90% - less than 95%	1 October 2005

The implementation of these new regulations has led to extensive rejuvenation of the world fleet of ro-ro ships. In certain cases, the alterations that owners would have been forced to make were far too costly for old ships, with the result that a number of them have been scrapped and replaced by new tonnage (29).

B - CONSEQUENCES OF *ESTONIA* ACCIDENT

297. - On 28 September 1994, the passenger ro-ro *Estonia*, caught in a violent storm in the Baltic, capsized and sank in a few minutes, with the loss of more than 850 lives (30).

(28) - IMO News : "Existing ro-ro fleet to be upgraded " N° 2. 1992, 1.
(29) IMO News : " Passenger and crew safety on board ship ". Nᵒ 3, 1991, 3-14.
(30) On the Estonia accident :
The Joint Accident Investigation Commission of Estonia, Finland and Sweden. " Final Report on the capsizing on 28 September 1994 in the Baltic Sea of the ro-ro passenger vessel MV Estonia " - Edita, Helsinki 1997.

The scale of the disaster was so great, and the global repercussions so intense, that the whole issue of the safety of such ferries was reopened (31). The preliminary inquiry revealed that the outer bow door had been ripped off in the storm, letting massive quantities of water in. So much water accumulated on the vehicle deck that the ship lost its stability and suddenly capsized. The accident occurred during the night, while most of the passengers were asleep, and was so sudden that only 137 of them managed to escape before the ship sank beneath them.

The fact that the disaster once again involved a bow door and the presence of water on the vehicle deck raised numerous questions about the safety of ro-ro ships, how they were being operated, and even the very concept of this type of transport (32). IMO took the matter in hand by launching an urgent comprehensive reexamination of the problem (33).

1. Panel of experts

298. - On 4 October, a few days after the accident, the Secretary-General of IMO proposed to set up a panel of experts to examine various aspects of the safe construction and operation of ferries, and to submit recommendations to the MSC (34).

In December, the MSC approved the Secretary-General's suggestion (35), and formed a panel of twenty-two experts from various countries.

Their report, published in April 1995, was intended to inform the maritime community of all the requirements that might be introduced in coming years. It took the form of a comprehensive package of proposed amendments to the existing SOLAS, SAR and STCW Conventions, and the publication of new provisions containing IMO recommendations

Many of the measures involved technical aspects of the design and construction of ro-ros, and their stability and buoyancy. The panel was aware that some of them had serious implications for the operation of existing vessels, possibly forcing those that failed to conform to the new requirements out of service. Emphasis was also placed on the need to establish a culture focussing on safety in and around passenger ships (36).

The MSC examined the group's report and recommendations at its 65th session in May 1995. Because of the major changes they involved in existing regulations, the MSC decided to call an international conference on the safety of carferries in London at the end of that year (37).

2. SOLAS Conference of November 1995

299. - The diplomatic conference that took place in London from 20 to 29 November 1995, in a very tense atmosphere and under close media scrutiny, resulted in the amendment of numerous SOLAS regulations (38).

---

(31) H. HONKA : " Questions on maritime safety and liability, especially in view of the Estonia disaster ". Essays in honour of Hugo Tiberg, Offprint. Juristförlaget, Stockholm, 1996, 351-382.
(32) "Ferry design fault warning". Lloyd's List, 30 Sept. 1994.
(33) " Emergency safety panel set up by IMO ". Lloyd's List, 4 Nov. 1994.
(34)IMO. Safety of ro-ro ships. Note by the Secretary-General. MSC 64/3/4, 4 Oct. 1994.
(35) IMO. Report of the Maritime Safety Committee on its 64th session MSC 64/22, 22 Dec. 1994, par. 3.8-3.14.
(36) IMO. MSC. Ro-ro ferry safety.
- Report of the Panel of Experts on Ro-Ro Ferry Safety to the Steering Committee on Ro-Ro Ferry Safety. Note by the Chairman of the Panel of Experts. MSC 65/4/Rev. 1, 21 April 1995.
- Report of the Steering Committee on Ro-Ro Ferry Safety to the Maritime Safety Committee. MSC 65/4/7, 26 April 1995.
- Final Report of the Panel of Experts on Ro-Ro Ferry Safety. MSC 66/2/2/Add. 1, 1st Sept. 1995.
(37) "Major changes on the way for ro-ro ferry safety". IMO News, n° 2, 1995, 3-9.
(38) "Agreement reached on Ro-Ro Ferry Safety measures". IMO News n° 4, 1995 and n° 1, 1996, 3-6.

a) Stability regulations

The Conference achieved a significant improvement in damage stability standards for all existing ferries without incorporating the regional concept in the Convention. A new Regulation 8-1 requires all existing passenger ro-ros to comply fully with the SOLAS 90 standard, in accordance with a phase-in programme extending from 1st October 1998 for vessels complying with 85 per cent of requirements to 1st October 2005 for those meeting 97.5 per cent. A new Regulation 8-2, which contains special requirements for ferries carrying more than 400 passengers, is intended to phase out "one-compartment" ships or ensure that they can remain upright with two compartments flooded after an accident.

Requirements relating to a ship's survivability with 50 centimetres of water on the car decks were not included in the Convention. Many States, including France, considered that such requirements were unwarranted, that the very heavy investments involved provided no guarantee of preventing all the accidents to which ro-ro ships are prone (39). Additional research was needed to establish scientific bases for damage stability criteria (40).

France was strongly opposed to any regional approach, considering that the function of IMO was to establish universal regulations. Passenger safety should not be associated to regional criteria that were not fully justified technically, for this would mean accepting higher levels of risk in certain parts of the world. Finally, the adoption of regional standards would create a dangerous precedent, ending a global consensus and creating a serious hindrance to international trade by sea (41).

The Conference achieved a compromise by adopting a resolution permitting regional arrangements to be made on specific stability requirements. Certain States which had signed the SOLAS Convention could introduce stricter requirements for ro-ro passenger ships making regular scheduled voyages between designated ports in these States, having regard to prevailing sea and other local conditions. It was accepted that if these agreements contained specific stability requirements they should not exceed those specified in an annex to the resolution, particularly the criterion of 50 centimetres of water on the car deck (42).

b) Other amendments to SOLAS Convention

300. - The bitter arguments about stability issues overshadowed other, equally important amendments to the SOLAS Convention. The principal changes affecting existing car ferries from 1st July 1997 include the following :
- Regulation II-1/10 stipulates that the watertight door acting as vehicle loading/unloading ramp must not be subject to damage if the bow visor is damaged or detached ;
- Regulation II-1/15 states that remote-controlled doors must be shut before the voyage starts and remain shut during the crossing ;
- Regulation II-1/20 - 1/2/3 strengthens watertightness requirements for the car deck ;
- Regulation II-2/28-1 on escape routes ensures the rapid and orderly movement of passengers to assembly points ;
- Regulations amending chapter III on survival craft are based on the principle that a carferry is a proper ship, in which evacuation and lifesaving measures need to be reinforced, and the capacity to rescue shipwrecked people improved ;

---

(39) IMO. Proposal on ro-ro passenger ship survivability. SOLAS/CONF. 3/38, 24 Nov. 1995.
(40) IMO. Comments on the proposed draft SOLAS Amendments submitted by Italy. SOLAS/CONF. 3/9, 3 Oct. 1995.
(41) IMO. Document submitted by France. SOLAS/CONF. 3/25, 8 Nov. 1995.
(42) " IMO fudges issue in battle for unity on ferry stability ". Lloyd's List, 18 Dec. 1995.

- New provisions on radiocommunications also provide for the installation of a single-button distress panel to raise the alarm (cf Regulation IV/6) ;
- Finally, various amendments concern safety of navigation and transportation of cargoes (43).

3. Resolutions of 19th Assembly

301. - On 23 November 1995, the IMO Assembly voted five resolutions concerning the safety of ro-ro passenger ships (44) :

- A.792 on the development of a safety culture in and around passenger ships ;
- A.793 on the strength, and securing and locking arrangements, of shell doors (certain aspects of which were completed by IACS requirements) ;
- A.795 on navigational guidance and information schemes for ro-ro ferry operations ;
- A.796 on introduction of a decision-support system for shipmasters ;
- A.794 defining surveys and inspections for ro-ro passenger ships.

4. Stockholm European agreement

302. - In addition to IMO international regulations on carferries, there are now certain regional standards, under the Stockholm Agreement signed on 27 and 28 February 1996 by eighteen European States (cf chapter 9 above). Reached under the terms of the resolution voted at the 1995 SOLAS Conference, slightly amended, the Stockholm Agreement lays down specific stability requirements for ferries making regular scheduled international voyages between designated North-West European and Baltic ports, or to or from these ports. IMO acts as depository for this regional agreement (45).

In April 1998, a conference on safety at sea attended by nineteen European countries noted that all the recommendations of the commission of inquiry into the loss of the *Estonia* (46) had been taken into account in the international regulations that had emerged from the 1995 SOLAS Conference and the 1996 Stockholm Agreement, and that no further improvements would be considered in the short term.

5. EU initiatives

303. - Several recent surveys carried out in Europe have shown that carferries remain potentially dangerous (47) and that current safety standards are not being respected (48).

(43) J.F FAUDUET : "SOLAS Conference 1995 on the sefety of ro-ro passenger ships". Bulletin Technique du Bureau Veritas, n° 4, Dec. 1995, 21-34.
(44) "Five resolutions on ro-ro safety adopted". IMO News, n° 4 1995 and n° 1 1996, 13-22.
(45) - IMO. MSC 66/2/2/Add. 3, 27 March 1996.
- IMO. MSC 66/24, 18 June 1996, 2.12-2.13.
(46) "Why Estonia sank". Fairplay, 11th Dec. 1997.
(47) "Ro-Ro casualty record disastrous". Lloyd's List, 10 Jan. 1996.
(48) - "Risk of ro-ro capsize unacceptable, say MPs". Lloyd's List, 28 July 1995.
- "European ferry safcty questioned". Lloyd's List, 29 May 1998.

On 22 December 1994, in response to the *Estonia* disaster, the Council adopted a resolution for improving the safety of ro-ro passenger ferries (49). Its main objectives have been adressed by the following regulations :

• Council Regulation (EC) No 3051/95 of 8 December 1995 laying down the necessary provisions for the mandatory early application of the ISM Code to all ro-ro ferries operating regular services to or from ports in the European Community (50).

• Council Directive 98/18/EC of 17 March 1998 on safety rules and standards for passenger ships (51).

These regulations establish a common safety policy for carferries and high-speed passenger craft navigating regularly from or to EU ports, under whatever flag they sail. The Directive requires these ships, and more specifically those engaged on domestic voyages, to comply with SOLAS standards, harmonised interpretations of these by IMO, and classification standards specified by an approved organisation, It is compulsory to have a voyage data recorder (VDA) or "black box" on board, to record information in the event of an accident.

• Council Directive 98/4/EC of 18 June 1998 on the registration of persons sailing on board passenger ships operating to or from ports of the member States of the Community (52).

• Proposal for a Council Directive on conditions for the operation of regular ro-ro ferry and high-speed passenger craft services in the Community (53).

The Directive lays down a system of mandatory surveys which will provide a greater assurance of safe operation of these vessels and provides the right for member State to conduct, participate in or cooperate with any investigation of maritime casualties or incidents on these services (54).

Europe is not merely issuing regulations. Countries bordering on the Baltic, together with the United Kingdom, have set up a group known as the North-West European Research & Development Project, to establish a new damage stability rule framework based on probabilistic methods (55). As part of the BRITE EURAM programme, the EU is also funding a project entitled "Design for safety: an integrated approach to safer European ro-ro ferry design".

All this work will probably result in the next few years in new standards for the construction and equipment of passenger ro-ros.

(49) OJEC, C. 379, 31 Dec. 1994.
(50) OJEC, L 320, 31 Dec. 1995.
(51) - OJEC, L 144, 15 May 1998.
    - "EU planning tougher ferry safety rules". Lloyd's List, 19 Feb. 1998.
(52) - OJEC, L 188, 2 July 1998.
    - "Ferry firms must keep list of passengers". Lloyd' List, 30 Dec. 1998.
(53) - OJEC C 108, 7 April 1998 and C 384, 10 Dec 1998.
(54) A. DE BIEVRE : "Euro host State safety directive facing ro-ro ferry sector". Lloyd's List, 17 August 1998. See also Lloyd's Ship Manager, Oct. 1998, 69-70.
(55) "European safety study sent to IMO". Lloyd's List, 8 June 1996.

III - SAFETY OF HIGH-SPEED CRAFT (HSC)

304. - Transport of passengers at high speed has expanded rapidly in recent years, with the introduction of new types of maritime craft, including hovercraft, hydrofoils and jetfoils, airboats, small waterplane area twin hull (SWATH) craft and hydrojets.

These units, half-way between ships and aircraft, and also known as "dynamically supported craft" (DSC), differ from conventional vessels in their lightness and speed of movement. They usually travel at more than 30 knots, and quite a few of them can reach speeds of more than 60 knots. These special features have led to the establishment of specific safety regulations for such craft (56).

There have been few serious accidents involving high-speed craft in recent years, although they include three significant ones. On 15 December 1989, the *Apollo Jet Cat*, a catamaran operating between Hong Kong and Macao, lost control of its speed. It damaged six ships before crashing into a sea wall (57). In 1992, twenty-three passengers on the high-speed ferry *Royal Vancouver* were injured in a collision with the conventional ro-ro ferry *Queen of Saanich* off British Columbia (58). On 10 June 1996, four people were killed when the hydrofoil *Procida* hit a reef in the Bay of Naples (59).

The experimental nature of these craft means that strict application of existing regulations could have harmed their future development. For a long time, States merely issued recommendations (60).

A - DSC CODE 1977

IMO concerned itself with these units from 1967, by adopting a whole series of technical recommendations. These provisions, grouped together and supplemented by safety rules, were adopted by IMO on 14 November 1977 as a Code for Dynamically Supported Craft (DSC Code).

B - HSC CODE 1993

305. - The 1977 measures have been replaced by the High-Speed Craft (HSC) Code, now included in chapter X of the SOLAS Convention, under the title "Safety measures for high-speed craft" (61). This Code lays down design and construction standards for craft engaged in international transport. It also stipulates the equipment which should be provided,

---

(56) "Solving international ferry safety : the EU approach". The Naval Architect, April 1998, 3.
(57) "High Speed Safety". Coast Guard Magazine . July 1993, 26-27.
(58) C. JENMAN : " Lessons to be learned from the Apollo jet cat casualty in Hong Kong ". IMAS 91. High Speed Marine Transportation 11-13 Nov. 1991. Paper 25.
(59) " Canada crackdown on fast ferry rules urged ". Lloyd's List, 26 Nov. 1994.
(60) " Four die as fast ferry capsizes ". Lloyd's List, 11 June 1996.
(61) A. GRAHAM : " An overview on the implementation and development of safety standards ". RINA International Seminar on Safety for High-Speed Passenger Craft. The way ahead ". Paper n°1, RINA, London, May 1992.
(62) R. BURTON : "Swift rules for high speed craft". Safety at Sea International, Sept. 1992, 30-31.

as well as the conditions for their operation and maintenance. The main intention is to set safety levels equivalent to those required under the SOLAS and LL Conventions.

The HSC Code concerns two types of craft: "passenger craft which do not proceed in the course of their voyage more than four hours at operational speed from a place of refuge when fully laden; and cargo craft of 500 gross tonnage and upwards which do not proceed in the course of their voyage more than eight hours at operational speed from a place of refuge" (Regulation 2).

In order to ensure proper safety levels for high-speed craft, different principles have been introduced, particularly the requirement of an operating licence issued to the operator by the authorities, valid within a given geographical area, where means of communication, weather forecasting and adequate maintenance services are available. Many of these requirements are reminiscent of those applied to aircraft.

Classification of high-speed craft has also been the subject of a special procedure at Norske Veritas since 1960, Lloyd's Register since 1964, and Bureau Veritas since 1969. These societies are concerned mainly with the strength of the hull, buoyancy, and propulsive and electrical installations. In 1995, EEIG Unitas published comprehensive rules for high-speed craft, combining statutory requirements with classification standards (62).

(63) "EEIG Unitas publishes rules for high speed craft". Fast Ferry International, Jan.-Feb. 1995, 73.

CHAPTER 12

Safety of bulk carriers

306. - Dry bulk cargo transport by sea is being very closely monitored at present, not only because it is one of the most important sectors of the industry internationally, in terms of number of ships and volume of shipments, but above all because of there has been so much serious criticism of its safety performance.

In recent years the international maritime community has mobilised, to try and reduce accidents and loss of human life at sea. This chapter retraces these efforts, with particular attention to measures connected with ship structures. To illustrate the implications, and possible changes in current regulations, the essential features of this type of transport will first be touched on (1).

I - BULK CARGO SHIPPING

A - ECONOMIC AND TECHNICAL DATA

1. Volume of shipments

307. - Seaborne transport of bulk solids has expanded considerably in the last few years. According to the Institute of Shipping Economics & Logistics (ISL), 1 103 million tonnes of solid bulk cargoes were conveyed by sea in 1995, namely 23 per cent of world shipping trade. This represents 5 432 billion tonne-miles, namely 28 per cent of world trade, in second position just after hydrocarbons.

The total figure is made up mainly of 402 million tonnes of iron ore, 423 million tonnes of coal, 196 million tonnes of grain, 32 million tonnes of bauxite and 30 million tonnes of phosphate. Seaborne trade in all these products, except for grain, is rising steeply (2).

2. Composition of the world bulker fleet

Dry bulk cargoes are carried by four main types of dedicated ships, comprising 5 079 bulk dry carriers (in 1997), 242 combination carriers (0/0 and OBO), 157 self-discharging bulk dry carriers and 1 074 other more specialised bulk dry carriers (3).

---

(1) Cf bibliography on bulk carrier safety in the information sheet n° 25, 7 May 1998. IMO Library Information Services.
(2) Institute of Shipping Economics and Logistics : Shipping statistics and market review. World bulk fleet. N° 5, May 1997, Vol 41. Bremen, 9 and 36.
(3) Lloyd's Register. World Fleet Statistics, 1997, 9.

INTERCARGO has evaluated the world bulk fleet at 5 822 vessels of more than 10 000 tons. It distinguishes four types of such ships, according to size (4) :
- 3 106 handysize (10-35 000 dwt)
- 1 276 handymax (35-50 000 dwt)
- 979 panamax (50-80 000 dwt)
- 461 capesize (80 000 dwt and more)

B - CASUALTY STATISTICS

308. - Risks arising in connection with the shipment of bulk goods rose steeply in the late Eighties.

1. Bulker accidents

The repeated shipwrecks of large carriers, causing the deaths of hundreds of seafarers, has aroused considerable anxiety within the maritime community. This new awareness has emerged in three stages.

a) Wreck of the Derbyshire

309. - In September 1982, the combination carrier *Derbyshire* vanished under mysterious conditions 650 miles from the Bay of Tokyo, with the loss of forty-four people on board. This was one of the highest fatality rates ever to have been experienced by the British merchant navy. The event led to an official public inquiry, which opened only in October 1987 (5).

The conclusions to the report, published in January 1989, threw no light on the causes of the shipwreck (6). When the wreck was discovered in 1994, the British government decided to reopen the file (7). An assessment by Lord Donaldson in December 1995 (8) recommended sending an expedition to the site, to reexamine the reasons for the accident. This culminated in March 1998 in the publication of a report (9), which pointed out five factors which had led to the ship foundering, and made several suggestions on improving bulk carrier safety in general (10).

b) Series of accidents from 1980

310. - According to the Lloyd's Maritime Information Services (LMIS), there were 151 total losses of bulk carriers between September 1980 and August 1987, thirty-eight of them due to heavy weather. Accident rates for this type of shipping soared at the end of the

---

(4) INTERCARGO. Bulk carrier casualty report. Analysis of total loss and fatality statistics for dry bulk carriers 1990-1997. London, Sept. 1998.
(5) "Derbyshire - an end to the riddle ? ". Lloyd's List, 2 Oct. 1987.
(6) " Inquiry fails to resolve the riddle of the Derbyshire ". Lloyd's List, 24 Jan. 1989.
(7) " Derbyshire design under spotlight ". Lloyd's List, 5 Dec. 1995.
(8) Lord Donaldson's Assessment (Derbyshire). A report to the Secretary of State for Transport to assess what further work should be undertaken to identify the cause of the sinking of the MV Derbyshire. Dec. 1995. HMSO, London.
(9) Department of the Environment, Transport and the Regions (DETR) : M.V. Derbyshire Surveys. UK/EC Assessor's Report. A summary. London, March 1998.
(10) - Fairplay, 26th March 1998, 20-24.
- Lloyd's List, 13 March 1998.
- M. GREY : "Derbyshire expedition points to bulkship rule changes". BIMCO Bulletin. Vol. 93, n° 2, 1998.

Eighties : from May 1988 to April 1991, thirty-eight bulk carriers sank, causing 328 deaths and the loss of more than two million tons of cargo (11). In 1990 alone, there were 125 deaths and the loss of a million tons of goods in twenty-three accidents. 1991 was also a bad year, with 155 seafarers dying in twenty-eight accidents.

The trend was more encouraging in 1992 and 1993, but matters worsened again in 1994, with a 50 per cent increase in the number of fatalities and ships lost.

c) Accidents in 1997 and 1998

Two shipwrecks at the beginning of 1997, in which forty-five crewmen perished, were particularly disturbing to the maritime community. On 8 February, the *Leros Strength* was lost off the Norwegian coast (12). A few days later, another bulk carrier, the *Albion Two*, sank near the coast of Brittany (13).

Further accidents occurred early in 1998, including the loss of the *Flare* (14) and the *Fei Cui Hai*, with the death of fifty-two seamen. These accidents were attributed to failures in the structural integrity of older handysize bulkers.

2. Statistical analyses

311. - The numerous statistics available on bulker losses have been used to make detailed studies of the causes of accidents. Only the most important are examined here.

a) LMIS casualty database

LMIS statistics cover the loss of 425 bulk carriers between 1978 and 1997, which caused the deaths of 698 seamen. Certain conclusions can be drawn from analysis of the data :
- Trends in bulk carrier losses have not changed over the last twenty years. The public's expectations have changed, but the shipping industry's performance has not ;
- Weather is a dominant issue in bulk carrier safety: only 2 per cent of the lives were lost in good weather, while about two thirds were lost in storms and 5 per cent in hurricanes ;
- The average age of lost ships has edged up from seventeen to twenty-one years over the last two decades ;
- Heavy cargoes are dangerous, even those which have a low stowage density (16).

b) INTERCARGO studies

312. - INTERCARGO has carried out several studies of bulk carrier losses (17). The most recent, which involves the period 1990-97, reports 106 actual and constructive losses and 537 seafarers killed or missing (18). The study reveals a drop in casualties, drawing attention to the following factors :

(11) IMO. Report of the correspondence group on the safety of ship carrying solid bulk cargoes. MSC 65/INF.15, 31 March 1995, Annex 2.
(12) Lloyd's List, 10 Feb. and 14 Feb. 1997. Tradewinds 14 Feb. 1997.
(13) Lloyd's List 11, 17 and 19 March 1997. Tradewinds 14 and 21 March 1997.
(14) Lloyd's List, 19 Jan. 1998. - Tradewinds, 23 Jan. 1998.
(15) "Sinkings raise concerns over the integrity of handysizes". Lloyd's List, 23 Feb. 1998.
(16) - M. STOPFORD : "Bulk carriers in the dock or in dry dock". The Baltic, August 1998, 66-68.
- M. STOPFORD : "Bulk carriers - Safety by objectives". BIMCO Bulletin, vol. n° 3, 1998, 24-27.
(17) - MER, April 1994, 14-15.
- Maritime Monitor, April 11, 1995, 7.
(18) "Bulk carrier casualties reduced". Lloyd's List, 5 Sept. 1998.

- The main causes of accidents are taking water and plate failure (30 out of 106) ;
- The greatest loss of life was from bulk carriers that foundered due to plate failure (227 fatalities out of 637) ;
- The safety of capesize vessels over the last eight years has improved significantly ;
- The overall trend of losses of panamax vessels has also been downward ;
- Losses in the handymax size have followed a generally fixed pattern with one or two losses a year ;
- The handysize fleet has suffered the greatest number of ship losses compared with other types of bulk carriers, but the general trend of losses, as a percentage of the total handysize fleet, has been downward (19).

c) IACS database

313. - IACS has compiled a database from accident reports concerning all types of bulk carriers of more than 20 000 dwt that have suffered accidents attributable to structural failure (20).

Useful information has been drawn from this database, which covers 139 accidents occurring between 1980 and 1996 :
- 94 per cent of bulk carriers were at least 10 years old at the time of the accident, while 75 per cent were at least 15 years old ;
- 38 per cent of ships had alternate holds loaded, and 51 per cent were loaded homogeneously ;
- of the 82 single-hull bulkers that suffered accidents, 34 were carrying ire ore ; of 17 total losses, 11 had some holds empty, and of the 17 that suffered serious accidents, only 7 were loaded homogeneously.

II - HAZARDS OF DRY BULK CARGOES

314. - Transport of large quantities of solid goods by sea presents three major types of risks, connected with the actual nature of the cargoes, the state of the ship, and finally the conditions under which it is operated.

A - CARGO RISKS

Some products carried in bulk can be a source of danger, causing structural damage, capsizing, fire and explosion (21).

1. Structural damage

Contact with certain cargoes, particularly dense heavy products like iron ore, may subject a ship's hull to numerous stresses.

The over-concentration of weight on the inner bottom of the ship, or improper distribution among the different holds, can exert excessive strain on the ship's structure.

(19) INTERCARGO : Op. cit.
(20) IACS. Bulk carrier safety casualty statistical data. In Annex of a paper submitted at IMO. MSC 67/4/3, 1 Oct. 1996.
(21) "IMO and cargo safety". Focus on IMO, Jan. 1994.

Another problem is excessive stability, caused by incorrect loading. This can damage the hull because of the violent movements imparted to the ship by the sea. To avoid this sudden rolling, heavy products are often loaded into alternate holds, in order to raise the centre of gravity of the cargo. However, this can produce high shearing forces in the side shell (the full holds tend to sink in the water under the weight of the cargo, while the buoyancy of the empty ones tends to push them in the opposite direction,), and higher local stresses are generated in the frames, double bottoms and transverse bulkheads.

2. Capsizing

When it is not properly levelled or incorrectly distributed, cargo can shift during a voyage and cause loss of stability. The same problem can occur with certain cargoes that tend to liquefy as a result of vibrations and ship movements. This has been observed with small-grained products like coal or ore concentrates, particularly fines that are damp at the time of loading. The cargo becomes liquid, and slides or subsides to one side of the hold. This can cause the ship to heel, to the point where it may even capsize.

3. Fire and explosion

Certain bulk cargoes, like wood chips or coal, tend to heat spontaneously. Others, like iron obtained by direct reduction and iron concentrates, can cause spontaneous combustion. This produces a funnel effect, when empty spaces in the cargo encourage hot gases to rise, and cool air is sucked in below. This can contribute to the occurrence of a spontaneous combustion process, resulting in fire or explosion.

B - SHIP CONDITION

315. - A second risk factor is the condition of the ship and its degree of corrosion, which can affect structural integrity, and weaken the hull. Several aspects have to be taken into account.

1. Speed of corrosion

The corrosive nature of certain products often accelerates the process of structural deterioration. This applies to high-sulphur coal, the temperature of which can often reach 40°C, causing condensation on the side cooled by the seawater. This condensation mixes with the sulphur on the side shell and bulkheads, and runs over the lower parts of the hull at the foot of the side frames, where they are fixed to the hopper tanks. The loss of thickness, which often takes the form of corroded furrows, can in some cases be estimated at a millimetre a year in the foot brackets (22).

2. Domino effect

The most likely sequence of events resulting in the loss of a bulk carrier involves the following stages (23) :
- corrosion of frames and their attachment brackets, mainly the foot brackets ;
- concentration of such corrosion along the welds on the side plating (for frames) and on the lower stool (for the foot bracket); this happens because condensation, often acid because of the cargo, tends to run along this path ;

(22) D. ROBINSON : " Setting standards to improve bulker safety ". Safety at Sea. August 1993, 22-24.
(23) Bureau Veritas : " Safety of Bulk Carriers". International General Committee. 18th Council Meeting, 21st June 1995.

- loss of frame strength, intensified by the fact that foot brackets and frames are often damaged by discharging gear ;
- in bad weather, and also often when the ship is carrying a high-density cargo in alternate holds, stress levels on frames increase; depending on their condition, one of them may break away with a domino effect on all the others, followed by fracture of the side plating, usually along the top line of the lower stool ;
- flooding of the hold, or more than one if the fractures extend to adjacent sides, or if the transverse bulkheads, also weakened by the same corrosion, collapse or fracture ;
- foundering of the ship, either by snapping in two after buckling or tearing of the deck or bottom, if the ship failure moment is exceeded, or else by the bow sinking in the water and loss of longitudinal stability when the damage is confined to the forward holds (24).

3. Hatch cover strength

The inquiry into the loss of the *Derbyshire* has shown that bulkers suffer from fore end vulnerability and weak hatch covers, which make them particularly prone to damage by extreme sea conditions.

One very likely reason for at least some bulker losses is the combination of three factors: low freeboard, little fore end protection, and the very low capacity of cargo hatch covers to withstand green seas and wave impacts (25).

C - HANDLING METHODS

Ships carrying bulk goods, and particularly ore carriers and coalers, are subjected to excessive stresses and structural lesions caused by handling gear. This damage occurs during both loading and discharging (26).

1. Loading

316. - During loading , two factors contribute to damage: loading rates and loading sequences (27).

a) The speed of turnaround has forced ports to use equipment to speed up loading rates substantially. These rates can reach 18 000 tonnes an hour. Five minutes' inattention can therefore result in a 1 500 tonne error in the weight of cargo in a hold. It has been calculated that a 10 per cent weight error can generate a 35 per cent increase in the bending moment for a particular loading plan.

Indeed, pumps are often incapable of deballasting fast enough for loading. In this case, loading has to be suspended from time to time, in order to synchronise the two operations.

b) Loading sequences that are not properly established can have a deleterious effect. Unless they are strictly programmed, with checks on bending moments and shearing forces after every loading pass, the ship may be subjected to dangerous stresses. The best example is

(24) " Bulker flooding risks ". Safety at Sea International. August 1993 30-32.
(25) D. FAULKNER : "Hatch covers and bulker survivability". Seaways, April 1998, 14-16.
(26) "Cargo operations and improving bulker safety". BIMCO Bulletin. Vol. 90, n° 4, 1995, 14-16.
(27) " The structural price of port presures ". Lloyd's List, 17 Sept. 1991.

the *Trade Daring*, a 145 000 dwt bulk carrier which broke in two while being loaded with iron ore in Brazil.

In other cases, the ship leaves port while subjected to excessive stresses, and breaks in two as soon as sea conditions add any extra load (28). An Australian survey shows that most ships arrive at loading terminals without having examined any loading sequence (29).

2. Discharging

Handling gear used to discharge the cargo may cause localised structural damage. The grabs that pick up products in the hold can weigh up to 35 tonnes when unloaded, and they sometimes damage the ballast ceiling or frames (30). Bulldozers, used to scrape products from the corners of the holds to the centre, often start small cracks at the front of frame foot brackets. Finally, hydraulic equipment is used to clear ore or coal adhering to the walls or sloping areas, sometimes at a great height, and this can damage frames and bulkheads (31).

The damaged components "record" these repeated impacts, which add to the accumulated fatigue of the structure, and ultimately weaken the whole ship.

III - IMPROVED SAFETY OF BULK CARRIERS

317. - Most of the risks connected with transport of bulk cargoes are now known, even though preventive regulations do not have them completely under control. The origins of these provisions date back to the mid-Sixties. The standard-setting process quickened pace in 1990, when the safety of bulk carriers became a major source of concern for the international maritime community. Intergovernmental organisations, States and maritime industries reacted promptly to the increase in risks for this type of transport. Numerous actions were undertaken to improve the design and construction of ships, and their commercial operating conditions.

A - IMO ACTION

IMO was the first organisation to develop universal regulations for bulk carriers. Its efforts were first aimed at preventing cargo risks, after which it turned to structural safety and cargo handling (32).

1. Bulk Cargo Code of 1965

318. - IMO's first concern was with methods that would reduce the risks arising from the products carried in bulkers. At the request of the 1960 SOLAS Conference, it drew up the Code of safe practice for solid bulk cargoes (BC Code) (cf chapter 14 below).

(28) " Capsize bulker. A complex cocktail of stress ? ". Seatrade Review, Oct. 1994, 19-23.
(29) Bureau of Transport and Communications Economics : " Structural failure of large bulk ships ". Australian Goverment Publishing Service. Report 85. 1994.
(30) Ships of Shame Inquiry into Ship Safety. Parliament of the Commonwealth of Australia, Dec. 1992, 41-43.
(31) IACS : "Bulk carriers. Handle with care". London, 1997.
(32) "IMO and the safety of bulk carriers". Focus on IMO, Jan. 1998.

a) Cargoes concerned

The BC Code, first adopted in 1965, has been updated since then at regular intervals, by the IMO subcommittee on Containers and Cargoes. The latest version, dating from 1989, refers to three main types of cargoes :
- cargoes which may liquefy, mainly ore concentrates and certain types of coal ;
- materials possessing dangerous chemical properties, flammable solids, solids subject to spontaneous combustion, flammable solids that release gas in contact with water, toxic products, radioactive or corrosive substances ;
- all other materials that can present a particular risk when carried in bulk, such as clay, cement, iron ore, cast iron, sand and sugar, with the exception of grain, covered by other IMO regulations.

The BC Code explains the dangers associated with transport of certain types of bulk cargoes, gives guidance on various procedures to adopt, lists typical products shipped in bulk, gives information and advice on their properties and how they should be handled, and describes several test procedures which should be used to define the characteristic properties of cargoes.

b) Insertion in SOLAS Convention

Since 1991, the BC Code has been inserted into Chapter VI of the 1974 SOLAS Convention dealing with the safety of cargoes in general. Bulk goods, other than grain, are specially dealt with in two fundamental stipulations: Regulation 8 on the need for the captain to have information on the stability of his ship and the distribution of the cargo, and Regulation 7 on the importance of how certain cargoes are stowed.

Otherwise, the SOLAS Convention makes reference to the provisions of the BC Code. The 1991 amendments, which came into effect on 1st January 1994, give mandatory force as regulations to what had been adopted previously as a mere recommendation.

2. Interim measures in Resolution A.713

319. - The worrying increase in bulk carrier casualties in the late Eighties forced IMO to strengthen existing provisions.

In 1991, MSC Circular 531 warned operators against the dangers of cargoes shifting, and asked member governments to implement recommendations on stowage methods described in the BC Code. The circular also launched a feasibility study into voyage data recorders (VDR), more commonly known as "black boxes" (33).

IMO took a further step in November of the same year, by adopting Resolution A.713, which contains a series of interim measures to improve the safety of ships carrying solid bulk cargoes throughout the world. These concerned cargo handling operations, the stability of ships, detection of corrosion, and equipment to be installed on board to record structural stresses.

3. Resolution A.744 and the enhanced survey programme (ESP)

Quite aware of the role that classification societies play in this respect, IACS issued Unified Rule Z.10.2 concerning enhanced hull surveys of bulk carriers, which it has been applying uniformly since 1st July 1993. These rules led to the adoption of Resolution A.744 by IMO in November 1993, containing guidelines on the enhanced programme of inspections during surveys of bulk carriers and oil tankers.

(33) "Bulk carrier losses : feasibility study on voyage data recorders". IMO News, n° 2, 1991, 7-11.

4. 19th Assembly resolutions

320. - A succession of accidents in 1994 led IMO to consider further strengthening of regulations in this area (34).

At the end of 1994, the MSC decided to go ahead with an immediate sector survey of the safety of bulk carriers. A correspondence group was set up to investigate measures that could be introduced quickly in areas such as shipbuilding, equipment, surveys and operations (35).

Six principal areas of investigation were defined: survivability, design and constructional regulations, operating requirements, survey requirements, the ship-to-shore interface, and crew management and training.

States and maritime industries concerned with this problem formulated more than 180 proposals, which were examined by the group. However, it failed to accept any that were likely to have an immediate effect, and merely drew up recommendations (36). Despite the urgency of the situation, the MSC finally decided not to submit draft amendments to a SOLAS Conference dealing with the issue. It did present two draft resolutions, which were adopted on 23 November 1995 by the 19th IMO Assembly (37).

a) Resolution A.797 on safety of ships transporting solid bulk cargoes

321. - This resolution emphasises the need to take a number of interim measures until requirements and recommendations on the matter are prepared. Port states are accordingly asked to see to it that terminal operators use the ship-shore safety checklist during loading and unloading of dry bulk carriers. This list is defined in circular MSC 690 (38). Flag States are requested not to authorise single-hull ships of more than 20 000 dwt and more than ten years old to carry high-density cargoes such as ore, unless they conform to the enhanced survey programme. Shipowners are invited to apply a scheduled maintenance programme, and to have damage to hold structures caused during handling operations properly inspected and repaired. Finally, classification societies are asked to continue their research with shipbuilders, and set up a feedback system for survey practices, classification rules and design standards.

b) Resolution A.798 containing guidelines for the selection, application and maintenance of prevention systems of dedicated seawater ballast tanks

322. - This Resolution draws attention to the interdependence between the condition of the coating, survey regulations, and the importance of properly applied and maintained anticorrosion systems in seawater ballast tanks, which are especially vulnerable zones for the safety of a ship.

The MSC approved a new regulation for future inclusion in the SOLAS Convention, requiring such systems to be compulsory on board new oil tankers and bulk carriers. The Resolution provides guidelines to facilitate its implementation.

---

(34) "Bulker problem may be back, with a vengeance". Tradewinds, 4 Nov. 1994, 10-11.
(35) Terms of reference of the correspondence group on safety of ships carrying solid bulk cargoes. IMO. MSC 64/22 - Add 1. Annex 21, 5 Jan. 1995.
(36) Report of the correspondance group on the safety of ships carrying solid bulk cargoes. In IMO, MSC, 65/5, 31 March 1995.
(37) IMO News. N° 4, 1995 and N° 1, 1996, 7 to 17.
(38) " Bulk carrier safety clause ". BIMCO Bulletin, Vol 91, N° 4, 96, 41-43.

5. New SOLAS regulations

323. - These new regulations, drawn up by a working group on bulk carrier safety (39), and discussed at length by the MSC (40), were adopted at a conference held in London from 24 to 28 November 1997. They now form the new chapter XII of the SOLAS Convention, and are due to take effect on 1st July 1999 (41).

a) *Characteristics of regulations*

Four features characterise the new SOLAS regulations :

- They aim to increase the chances of survival of a damaged ship, starting from the principle that if it remains afloat, loss of human life can be avoided.
- They constitute what has been called "a second line of defence", to remedy shortcomings in ESP, revealed by the loss of the *Leros Strength* and *Albion Two* (42).
- They reflect one of the traditional spheres of classification societies: ship structural strength. During work on the SOLAS standards, the question arose as to whether classification rules guaranteed that a ship was strong enough to withstand static and dynamic loads, including those resulting from the movements of water in a flooded hold (43).
- They do not apply to all bulk carriers, but only to those carrying high-density solid cargoes. According to Regulation XII-1, the density limit is 1 t/m3 for new ships and 1.78 t/m3 for existing ships.

b) *Structural requirements*

• *Regulation XII-4 on damage stability*
324. - New bulk carriers at least 150 metres in length, and existing bulkers with a single side skin of the same size, must meet the damage stability requirements in order to survive the flooding of any cargo hold for new ships and the foremost hold for existing ships.

• *Regulation XII-5 on structural strength*
All new bulk carriers with a single side skin, carrying solid bulk cargoes with a density of at least 1 t/m3 and at least 150 metres long, must be strong enough to withstand flooding of any cargo hold under any relevant loading and ballast conditions, taking account of dynamic loads.

• *Regulation XII-6 on measures applicable to existing bulkers*
These provisions apply to bulk carriers carrying solid bulk cargoes with a density of at least 1.780 t/m3 and at least 150 metres long.

The transverse bulkhead between holds 1 and 2, and the double bottom of hold 1, must be strong enough to withstand flooding of hold 1. The Regulation makes provisions for distribution of loading or the possible reduction in deadweight.

(39) IMO. Safety of ships carrying solid bulk cargoes. Report of the working group. In MSC 66/WP.13, 31 May 1996.
(40) IMO. MSC 66/24, 18 June 1996, 18-23 ; MSC 67/22, 19 Dec. 1996, 15-20 ; MSC 68/23, 12 June 1997, 13-19.
(41) IMO. SOLAS/CONF. 4/25, 8 Dec. 1997.
(42) " Calm before decision ". The Motor Ship, June 1997, 47.
(43) J. ISBESTER : " Bulk carriers - a changing world ". Seaways, Sept. 1996, 45-49.

• *Regulation XII-7 on survey of the hold structure*
A bulk carrier more than 150 long and ten years old may not carry heavy cargoes unless it has undergone a periodical survey in accordance with ESP requirements, or all the cargo holds have been surveyed.

• *Regulation XII-8 on endorsement of the loading booklet*
Certain information is to be entered in the loading booklet of bulk carriers   There is also provision for marking the side shell of ships subject to loading restrictions.

• *Regulation XII-9 on special requirements*
Bulk carriers which cannot meet the requirements of Regulation XII-4 because of the design configuration of their cargo holds have to comply with special requirements on increasing the scope of annual surveys, bilge well high water-level alarm, information on hold flooding scenarii.

• *Regulation XII-10 on solid bulk cargo density declaration*
The density of cargoes with a declared density of 1.25 to 1.78 t/m3 must be checked.

• *Regulation XII-11 on loading instruments*
Every bulk carrier at least 150 metres long must be fitted with a loading instrument complying with the requirements of a classification society recognised by the administration. This will allow the captain to ensure that shear forces and bending moments do not exceed foot bracket limits during and after cargo handling.

6. 20th Assembly resolutions

325. - The second set of regulations on the safety of bulk carriers concerns the ship-shore interface (44). In 1997, IMO adopted two resolutions to provide solutions to this problem (45).
• **Resolution A.862 of November 1997 on the code of practice for the safe loading and unloading of bulk carriers.**
This Resolution contains recommendations for shipowners, masters, shippers, operators of bulk carriers, charterers and terminal operators on the safe handling, loading and discharging of solid bulk cargoes. It includes a ship-shore safety checklist to help ship and terminal personnel recognise potential problems by taking both parties step by step through procedures and requirements, from confirming whether the depth of water at the berth is adequate, to checking whether the terminal has been informed of the time required for the ship to prepare for sea on completion of cargo work (46).

• **Resolution A.866 of November 1997 on guidelines to ships' crews and terminal personnel for bulk carrier inspections**
This Resolution highlights the principal areas of bulk carriers that are likely to be susceptible to corrosion damage, in the form of a simple guide aimed at ships' crews and terminal operators.
The guidelines note that severe structural damage may be caused to bulk carriers by loading and discharging operations, including major damage which could endanger the ship's safety, or minor cracks that could develop into serious defects before the ship's next scheduled enhanced survey.

(44) M. LLOYD : "The bulk carrier and the port". Seaways, Feb. 1998, 21-23.
(45) IMO News. Assembly 20th session, N° 4, 1997, 26.
(46) " Long campaign ". Lloyd's List, 7 Sept. 1992.

The Resolution therefore recommends that terminal operators and members of the ship's crew should make their own regular inspections of cargo holds, ballast tanks and hatch covers, in order to detect damage and defects at an early stage.

B - ACTIONS BY MARITIME INDUSTRIES

1. Mobilisation of the private sector

326. - The worrying increase in accidents to bulk carriers in 1989-90 led to a general mobilisation in the private sector, in an effort to improve safety. Three of their initiatives are described here.

Shipowner associations developed a series of accident-prevention recommendations for their members. In 1992, the International Chamber of Shipping issued a Ship-Shore Checklist, to reinforce precautionary measures during loading or discharging operations (46). The same intentions led INTERCARGO to hold training and communication seminars from 1991. It has also carried out detailed accident studies and collaborated with IMO to amend existing standards (47).

At the same time, insurers set up or developed their own inspection systems. At the end of 1991, the Salvage Association began its first structural condition surveys, to analyse the structural integrity of ships, and more specifically the condition of the most vulnerable parts (48).

The International Cargo Handling Coordination Association (ICHCA), to which professional port terminal operators belong, has underlined their role, and the importance of the communication and cooperation to be developed with the shipmaster, to ensure proper performance of operations (49).

2. IACS and bulkers safety

327. - The largest number of actions were taken by the classification societies, which had been the first to raise the alarm. By Autumn 1990, some of them altered their research programmes accordingly, and set up working groups with shipyards and shipowners, to trace the origin of fractures on board large ships and work out corrective measures (50).

Bureau Veritas, which for a number of years had been carrying out extensive research into the structural strength of bulk carriers, began a large number of technical studies, some of which resulted in the amendment of Bureau Veritas Rules for the scantling of new ships in 1993 (51), and in March 1996 in the adoption of recommendations to avoid overloading of bulk carrier structures (52).

---

(47) " Safety of dry bulk carriers ". Document submitted by INTERCARGO. In IMO, MSC 64/19/7, 6 Oct. 1994.

(48) " Figures hide why bulk carrier sinkings are still a problem ". Lloyd's List, 14 August 1992.

(49) " Pressure grows for action on overloading/discharging practices ". International Bulk Journal, Dec. 1994, 99-101.

(50) " Bulker problems blamed on design ". Lloyd's List, 15 May 1991.

(51) - J.N. BABINET : " Bulk carrier structures : Bureau Veritas research and studies ". Bulletin Technique, N° 3, Nov. 1995, 31-45.

- J.N BABINET : " Bureau Veritas : specific rules to improve the safety of bulk carriers ". Bulletin Technique N° 3, Nov. 1995, 47-52.

(52) Bureau Veritas Recommendations to avoid overloading of bulk carrier structures. NI 402, DNC ROO E, March 1995.

The individual measures taken by each society could not have been fully effective without the intervention of the International Association of Classification Societies (IACS). Considering the issue of bulk carriers a priority, it mobilised its resources and technical skills in 1990, in a wide-ranging attempt to understand and control risks connected with the transport of bulk cargoes (53).

Its actions concern several areas, including studies, rules, publications, and other actions, carried out with the active participation of other international organisations (54).

a) Damage studies and analyses

328. - In 1990, IACS gave priority to analysing damage suffered by bulk carriers. The partial findings of this work, published in 1991, showed that corrosion or damage during cargo handling operations could cause serious damage to the side shell and internal structural components. Problem zones have been highlighted (cf figure 11).

11 - Typical bulk carrier cargo hold configuration
(Source : IACS)

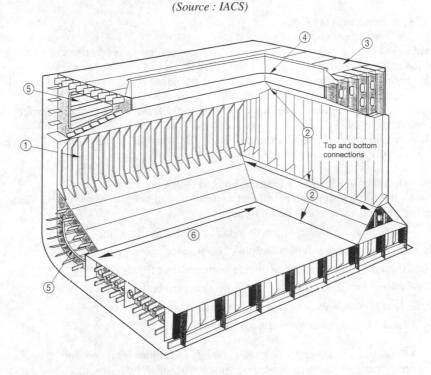

Problem areas to be given particular attention during inspections
1. Hold frame - connection to upper and lower wing tanks and side shell.
2. Boundaries of transverse bulkheads and bulkhead stools.
3. Cross deck structure.
4. Hatch corners/hatch coaming brackets.
5. Localised cracking and buckling of web frames and breakdown of coatings in water ballast tanks.
6. Inner bottom plating/hopper plating intersection.

(53) " Informed opinion is crucial for bulk carrier safety ". Lloyd's List, 19 August 1992.
(54) " Bulk carrier safety ". IACS Briefing, N° 5, Sept. 1997.

In June 1995, IACS launched a new research programme, this time intended to improve the safety and strength of new bulkers, and find practical solutions to reduce the risk of damage and loss to which the existing fleet is exposed. Between June and November 1995, several groups of experts, supervised by an IACS committee, carried out thorough technical studies, the conclusions of which were approved by the IACS Council in December (55).

A study of bulker accidents between 1980 and 1995 led IACS to focus its attention on single-hull ships more than 150 metres long and carrying heavy cargoes.

b) Rules

329. - One of the main functions of IACS is to harmonise its members' classification rules, by adopting Unified Rules (UR), and Uniform Interpretation standards (UI) for SOLAS regulations.

The studies referred to above provided the basis for major new regulations, which have been extended mainly since 1991 (56).

• **First measures (1991-95)**
The earliest provisions concerned :
- obligation for all new ships to have a corrosion-prevention protective coating in seawater ballast tanks (UR Z8 effective since July 1991) ;
- same type of protection for sides; shells and frames and for transverse bulkheads in new ship holds (UR Z9 effective since July 1993 ;
- requirements of minimum thickness for cargo hold frames in new bulk carriers (UR S12 effective since 1993) ;
- enhanced hull surveys for bulk carriers (UR Z10.2), which IACS has been applying uniformly since 1st July 1993 (cf chapter 22 below).

• **Decisions of 32nd IACS Council, London December 1995)**
Unified Rules were adopted for the strength of new bulk carrier hulls. Some of them cover the possibility of a hold being flooded :
- UR S17 on the longitudinal strength of hull girder after flooding ;
- UR S18 on the evaluation of scantling of corrugated transverse watertight bulkheads ;
- UR S20 on the shear strength of double bottoms after flooding ;
- UR S12 Rev. 1 on side structures of single side skin bulk carriers ;
- UR S21 on the evaluation of scantlings of cargo hold hatch covers ;
- UR S1 and S1A on loading conditions, manuals and instruments.

• **Measures affecting existing bulkers mainly conditions for inspection**
Stricter requirements concern enhanced surveys of side shell structures and hatch covers, during surveys carried out within the ESP framework since 1st January 1997. IACS has also speeded up application of ESP to bulk carriers which had not yet undergone a special survey by 1st January 1997, and completed these surveys by 1st January 1998 at the very latest (57).

(55) IMO. MSC 66/4/2, 1st March 1996.
(56) "Bulk carrier safety". Document submitted by IACS in IMO. MSC 65/5/1, 16 March 1995.
(57) "Bulk carriers : adressing the safety issues". The Baltic, March 1997, 57-60.

• **Decisions of 33rd IACS Council, Houston, May 1996**
Three new actions were taken to improve the safety of existing bulkers, namely advance completion of cargo hold surveys, strengthening of ESP, so that structural inspections will be more frequent and more detailed, and supply of new guidelines and information on loading (58).

• **Decisions of 34th IACS Council, London, December 1996**
330. - Following proposed amendments to the SOLAS Convention, prepared by the MSC in May 1996, IACS concentrated its efforts on existing bulkers. The problem was measures 1 and 2 in draft Regulations II-1/23-6 concerning the strength of transverse bulkheads and double bottoms in the event of a hold being flooded, making allowance for cargo and dynamic effects. These provisions required special examination and the drafting of suitable standards.

A working group drafted two standards for transport of heavy cargoes in existing bulk carriers more than 150 metres long, with vertically corrugated watertight transverse bulkheads and double bottoms. These proposals were submitted to the MSC but, without awaiting the conclusions of discussions at IMO, the 34th IACS Council decided in December 1996 to apply them to the transverse bulkheads between holds 1 and 2, and the double bottom of hold 1 on bulk carriers more than 150 metres long, transporting cargoes with a density of more than 1 t/m^3, in accordance with the following timetable (cf UR S19 and S22) :
- ships more than 10 years old on 1st July 1991 : not later than 1st July 2003 ;
- ships less than 10 years old on 1st July 1998 : upgrading not later than the due date of their third special survey (59).

This decision angered shipowners' associations, questioning its hastiness and the justification for the measures taken, both technically and economically (60). The *Leros Strength* and *Albion Two* accidents at the beginning of 1997 put an end to the argument, and provided evidence in favour of the position adopted by the classification societies (61).
At the 35th Council in Beijing in May 1997, IACS reaffirmed its determination to keep ahead of IMO decisions, while aligning its requirements with draft SOLAS amendments concerning definition of heavy cargoes (62).

(58) - " IACS approves bulker actions ". Lloyd's List, 28 May 1996.
- " A killing cure. Loading method may cause bulker losses ". Fairplay, 30 May 1996.
- " Regulators continue to target bulker safety ". Lloyd's Ship Manager, June 1996, 49-52.
(59) - " IACS acts over bulker safety ". Lloyd's List, 3 Dec. 1996.
- Bulker stress under the spotlight ". Lloyd's List, 3 Dec. 1996.
(60) - " Bulker owners fume over handling of safety changes ". Tradewinds, 6 Dec. 1996.
- " Are 100 000 seafarers risking their lives ? " Lloyd's List, 16 Dec. 1996.
- " Cost fears delay bulker safety agreement ". Tradewinds, 13 Dec. 1996.
- " Bulk safety move angers Greeks ". Lloyd's List, 8 Jan. 1997.
- " Storm clouds gather in bulk ". Lloyd's List, 10 Jan. 1997.
- " Bulk carrier stock ". Seatrade, Janv. 1997, 18-19.
- " Operator critises IACS bulker safety rules ". Lloyd's List, 12 Feb. 1998.
(61) - " No complacency ". Lloyd's List, 13 March 1997.
- " Gloves off in bulker debate ". Tradewinds, 21 March 1997.
(62) - " Toward consensus on bulker safety ". Lloyd's List, 6 June 1997.
- " IMO and IACS inch closer on safety ". Lloyd's List, 9 June 1997.

c) Specialised publications

331. - Analysis of damage to bulk carrier hulls provided a basis for two important IACS publications. In April 1992, IACS issued a brochure entitled "Bulk carriers: guidance and information to shipowners and operators" (63). This document presented a simplified account of contributory factors to structural hull failure and ship losses. It retraced the sequence of events leading to accidents and losses, and indicated the principal steps to be taken to reduce structural failures.

The second publication, in May 1994, was more ambitious. It bore the title "Bulk carriers: guidelines for surveys, assessment and repair of hull structure" (64). Intended to be a practical manual for the use of surveyors and other professionals, a hundred pages in length, and abundantly illustrated, it in fact supplements Unified Rules on ESP introduced by IACS in July 1993. It deals with ESP procedures and provides essential guidelines for their preparation and performance. It is particularly useful for other standard-setting authorities, shipowners and operators that have introduced examination and inspection schemes. The book also provides a quick illustrative source of reference for crews, flag authorities, port inspectors and repair yards.

Two other recent publications have been "Shipbuilding and repair quality standard"(SARQS) in 1996 (65), the first manual to offer a comprehensive guide to best practice in shipbuilding and repair, and "Guidelines and information on bulk cargo loading and discharging" in June 1997 (66).

In 1998, IACS published "Bulk carriers, handle with care" (67), a 24-page booklet which gives bulk terminal staff and ships' personnel a convenient guide to avoiding the risk to bulk carriers of excessive stress or damage from accidental overloading and other heavy cargo handling operations.

d) Early warning scheme

332. - In 1992, taking inspiration from practice in the air transport industry, IACS tried to set up an early warning scheme (EWS), in order to improve surveys and maintenance procedures, but also monitoring of the structures of large ships.

This scheme has a dual goal. The idea is to provide early warning of damage occurring on board ships, intended for IACS members, and allowing special monitoring of the damaged parts to be started. The scheme also comprises the establishment of a databank to encourage precise detection of certain forms of damage that could have serious structural consequences.

Despite practical difficulties of implementation, EWS has already led to an examination of the different types of damage to ship hulls. Each member society learning of serious incidents sends the appropriate IACS working group a detailed report, describing the damage, its possible causes, repairs carried out and suggested preventive measures.

(63) IACS . " Bulk carriers : guidance and information to shipowners and operators". London. April 1992.
(64) IACS : " Bulk carriers : guidelines for surveys, assessment and repair of hull structure ". London. July 1994.
(65) IACS. "Shipbuilding and repair quality standard". London, 1996.
(66) IACS : " Bulk carriers : guidance and information on bulk cargo loading and discharging". IACS. London, 1996.
(67) IACS. London, 1998.

CONCLUSION

333. - Action undertaken since 1991 by IACS, IMO and the whole maritime community to improve the safety of bulk carriers has already produced worthwhile results. These efforts should achieve full effectiveness in the years to come. It should be realised that such measures will have a significant economic impact on bulk transport. IACS has costed the new structural requirements for the 4 200 ships concerned, at between US$75 000 and 200 000 for each of them (68).

The efforts of regulators should not stop there. The safety of bulk carriers remains a priority for the maritime community as a whole (69), which will have to draw the necessary conclusions from accidents like that of the *Derbyshire* (70).

(68) " May day call over bulk carrier safety ". Financial Time, 8 May 1997.
(69) "Bulker safety to remain IMO priority". Lloyd's List, 23 May 1998.
(70) IMO. MSC 69/2/1, Add. 13 Feb. 1998 and MSC 69/22, 29 May 1998, 10.

CHAPTER 13

Safety of oil tankers

334. - Oil has been transported in bulk for more than a hundred years, in special ships with tanks that are an integral part of the actual hull. The first modern vessel to carry hydrocarbons in such tanks, instead of barrels, was the *Glückhauf*, built in England in 1886 and classed by Bureau Veritas (1). Over the succeeding century, remarkable technical developments in naval architecture have transformed the design and construction of oil tankers. However, despite these advances, complete control of the risks inherent in this type of transport has not yet been achieved.

Disastrous accidents provide regular reminders of the inadequacies of preventive measures. These repeated mishaps have given rise to much written comment (2), and partly explain the complexity and density of current regulations. This chapter is concerned with all such standards, which are intended to ensure both the safety of life and protection of the marine environment. The specific aspects of these regulations are best illustrated by first examining the technical and economic realities to which they apply.

I - REGULATORY CONTEXT

A - WORLD TANKER FLEET

335. - The world tanker fleet displays three fundamental features:

1. Cargo capacity

At the end of 1997, there were 6 933 oil tankers with a total capacity of 271 million dwt, representing 35.76 per cent of the total transport capacity of world shipping (3).

2. Ship size

336. - Even if the construction of very large crude carriers (VLCC) of more than 500 000 dwt was abandoned at the end of the Seventies for economic reasons, the world tanker fleet includes a large number of very high-tonnage vessels: 692 VLCCs of more than 234 000 dwt, including 25 in excess of 400 000 dwt.

Despite quite low casualty statistics (4), large oil tankers continue to arouse anxiety about their technical performance. There are five main areas of criticism :

(1) Bureau Veritas : Société internationale de classification de navires et d'aéronefs. Un siècle de construction navale - Edition du Centenaire, Paris, 1928, 85.
(2) - N. MOSTERT : " Supership ". Knopf, New York, 1974.
- P. BENQUET, Th. LAURENCEAU : " Pétroliers de la honte ". Edition n° 1, Paris, 1994.
- E. NALDER : " Tankers full of trouble ". Grove Press, New York, 1994.
(3) Lloyd's Register. World Fleet Statistics, 1997. London, 1998.
(4) " Tanker casualty rate lowest in 15 years ". IMO News, n° 4, 1992, 3.

• **Structural weakness**
In theory, large tankers are structurally designed to withstand the stresses that their weight exerts on each point of the hull under normal working conditions, namely when floating freely.

Nevertheless, a large ship is a fragile structure and is likely to remain so: a tanker 300 metres long made of 25 mm-thick steel plates corresponds to a model ship 3 metres long made of sheets of paper (5).

• **Lack of manoeuvrability**
The wreck of the *Torrey Canyon*, the *Olympic Bravery* and the *Amoco Cadiz* drew attention to the difficulties such large tankers had in manoeuvring. It has been suggested that this manoeuvrability seems to decrease further as tonnage increases, because of the deeper draught, the length of the stopping distance, and the inadequacy of the engines (6).

Other commentators, on the contrary, consider that size does not reduce manoeuvring capacity (7) and that, in practice, a large tanker does not rely on manoeuvres to avoid collision: foresight is an important aspect of safety (8).

• **Low buoyancy margin.**
This shortcoming, which characterises VLCCs in relation to other types of ships, is a serious handicap in the event of the ship running aground (9). In the case of the *Torrey Canyon*, the level of the sea was above the bow part of the upper deck by the second day, and the ship had already more or less lost its margin of buoyancy.

• **Anchoring and towing difficulties**
Several spectacular accidents, such as the *Amoco Cadiz* in 1978 and the *Braer* in 1993, have shown the limited possibilities of towing on the high seas in bad weather, and the gross inadequacy of anchoring systems for large ships in an emergency (10).

Finally large ships raise the problem of inspection. At a hearing of the House of Lords Select Committee inquiry in 1992, the Salvage Association underlined the practical limitations of inspection of the huge structures of a large ship. A VLCC, for instance, contains 50 000 square metres of exterior plate and 100 000 metres of main welding. Ultrasonic testing of the whole exterior plate would take 50 000 man-hours, inspecting the main welds for cracks would take 20 000 hours of visual examination, or 100 000 hours by magnetic particle inspection. The Salvage Association admitted that such ships were "virtually uninspectable" (11). At any rate, 100 per cent inspection is unachievable.

(5) H. LAURIN : " Protéger les navires c'est aussi protéger la mer ". Colloque Objectif Mer. Université Paris Sorbonne, 26-28 May 1983.
(6) J. ROPARS : " Au mépris de la prudence ". Le Monde, 25 April 1967, 14 et JMM, 27 April 1967, 910-911.
(7) J.B. HAMON : " A propos du naufrage du *Torrey Canyon* ". Le Monde, 9 May 1967, 11 and JMM, 11 May 1967, 1031.
(8) P. HUBERT : " La sécurité à bord des pétroliers ". La Revue maritime n° 304, June 1975, 704-774.
(9) M. ALBIACH : " Une augmentation du creux est propre à améliorer la flottabilité et le ballastage des pétroliers ". JMM, 25 May 1967, 1143-1144.
(10) - P. BRUCE : " Inadequacy of anchors in large ships ". Conference on mooring large ships. London 1979, Trans. Inst. Marine Engineers, C. 49, vol. 42.
- P. BRUCE : "Strandings put focus on adequacy of anchoring systems in large tankers". Lloyd's List, 9 March 1993.
(11) House of Lords. Select Committee on Science and Technology : " Safety aspects of ship design and technology ". 2nd Report, 14 Feb. 1992. London HMSO, 8, par. 3.17.

3. Ageing of large tankers

337. - In 1991, Lloyd's Register (12) reported that 192 of the estimated 386 VLCCs of more than 250 000 dwt were more than fifteen years old.

About 860 tankers representing 80 million dwt are due to undergo their fourth special survey (4SS) between 1996 and 2000. Age will not be a determining factor in the decision to scrap or overhaul them. A large number of economic, technical and regulatory aspects will be taken into consideration by owners (13). .

The accelerated ageing of the armada of large oil tankers is a familiar phenomenon, which has arisen mainly for economic reasons (14).

Age is a risk-increasing factor whenever it is linked to lack of proper maintenance and servicing.

Analysis of tanker casualties between 1991 and 1995 shows that more than 80 per cent of accidents involve ships more than 15 years old. In terms of tonnage over a longer period, 1985 to 1995, the age-group 15-19 years is the most dangerous. Table 12 shows the figures.

Table 12 - Age of tanker losses by number and tonnage
(Source : ILU. Casualty statistics 19967)

Age	Nb.	%	gt	%
0 - 4	1	1.4	551	0
5 - 9	2	2.8	148.445	11.7
10 - 14	4	5.5	22.677	1.8
15 - 19	18	25	569.409	45
20 - 24	30	41.7	458.434	36.3
25 and over	17	23.6	64.679	5.2
TOTAL	**72**	**100**	**1.264.195**	**100**

B - HAZARDS OF TRANSPORT OF OIL BY SEA

338. - Transport of oil by sea presents several kinds of risks, which may be put into two categories :
- internal : the cargo constitutes a potential hazard for the crew, in the event of fire or explosion ;
- external : the presence of large quantities of hydrocarbons in the tanks of an oil tanker in difficulty, or which has had an accident, represents a most serious threat for the environment; when the event occurs near the coast, the massive amounts of oil that may be released cause major damage to marine ecosystems.

(12) Lloyd's Register : World Fleet Statistics. London, 1997.
(13) " Owners dilemma over old tankers ". Ship Repair, Sept. 1995, 25.
(14) G. LOISEAU : " Le navire pétrolier de demain et la pollution ". Académie de Marine. Communications et mémoires, n° 2, Jan./Mar. 1992, 9-30.

1. Fires and explosions

These represent nearly half of all accidents. INTERTANKO recorded 500 serious tanker casualties in the period 1963 to 1996 (15) :
- 240 related to fire and explosion in the engine, accommodation and cargo compartments ;
- 60 due to grounding ;
- 70 involving collisions ;
- the remaining 130 caused by structural failures, loss of stability and/or foundering during rough weather conditions.

Fires and explosions are caused by the ignition of oil vapours. Explosions can be particularly deadly when they occur in port areas. The most serious accidents include :
- explosion of the Greek oil tanker *Spyros*, in dry dock in Singapore harbour in October 1978, causing 76 deaths (16) ;
- explosion of the French tanker *Betelgeuse* in January 1979 in the Irish port of Bantry Bay, causing 50 deaths (17) ;
- outbreak of fire and explosion on 31 December 1978 on board the Greek tanker *Andros Patria* off La Corunna, causing 30 deaths among the crew (18).

There have been other more recent accidents : the *Surf City* in February 1990 off Dubai (19), the *Indiana* in November 1992 in Singapore harbour (20), and the *Tpao* in Tuzla shipyard in February 1997 (21).

2. Oil spills

339. - Tanker cargoes are a potential danger not only for crew members but also for the environment. Although minimal amounts of hydrocarbons actually spill into the sea, and represent a very small part of total oil pollution of the world's oceans (cf Table 13), they give an extremely negative image of the maritime transport industry (22). Every oil slick, with its cortege of oil-covered birds, is now broadcast on every television channel in the world.

The International Tanker Owners Pollution Federation (ITOPF) has drawn up a table of the thirteen most serious cases of accidental pollution caused by hydrocarbon transport (cf Table 14). This classification does not include two recent groundings, of the *Sea Empress* in the port of Milford Haven in February 1996, in which 65 000 tonnes of crude oil were discharged (23), and of the *Diamond Grace* in July 1997 in Tokyo Bay, with 13 400 tonnes of crude spilt into the sea (24).

(15) INTERTANKO : "Systematic approaches to tanker accident analysis. Lessons learnt, Oslo, April 1998.
(16) JMM, 19 Oct. 1978, 2485.
(17) - JMM, 11 Jan. 1979, 58.
- B. TRENCH : " *Betelgeuse*, un an après le drame ". Le Marin, 11 Jan. 1980, 20.
- Conclusions de la commission d'enquête irlandaise et rapports des experts français au Ministre des Transports français. JMM, 7 Aug. 1980, 1910-1917.
(18) JMM, 4 Jan. 1979, 23.
(19) Lloyd's List, 6 April 1992.
(20) Lloyd's List, 28 Nov. 1992.
(21) Lloyd's List, 15 Feb. 1997.
(22) "Oil disasters spur industry to improve image". Lloyd's List, 6 May 1994.
(23) M. GREY : "Disaster command and control attacked". Lloyd's List, 18 July 1997.
(24) "Japan tackles its worst oil spill disaster". Lloyd's List, 3 July 1997.

Insurance claims on P&I clubs following oil spills represent only 15 per cent of total marine liability claims (26).

According to INTERTANKO (27), the number of oil spills over 700 tonnes averaged 24.2 a year during the period 1970-79. This was reduced to 8.9 a year during the period 1980-90, and has since fallen further, now representing less than 0.01 per cent of the total quantity of oil transported by sea every year.

Table 13 - Estimated inputs of petroleum hydrocarbons into the ocean due to marine transportation activities
(U.S. National Academy of Sciences)
(Sources : NRC (1985) ; IMO (1990).

	1981 (million tonnes)	1989 (million tonnes)
Tanker operations	0.7	0.159
Tanker accidents	0.4	0.114
Bilge and fuel oil discharges	0.3	0.253
Dry-docking	0.03	0.004
Marine terminals (including bunkering operations)	0.022	0.030
Non-tanker accidents	0.02	0.007
Scrapping of ships	–	0.003
TOTAL	**1.47**	**0.57**

Table 14 - Selected major oil spills
(Source ITOPF)

	Shipname	Year	Location	Oil lost (tonnes)
1	Atlantic Empress	1979	Off Tobago, West Indies	287 000
2	ABT Summer	1991	700 naut. miles off Angola	260 000
3	Castillo de Bellver	1983	Off Saldanha Bay, South Africa	252 000
4	Amoco Cadiz	1978	Off Brittany, France	223 000
5	Haven	1991	Genoa, Italy	144 000
6	Odyssey	1988	700 naut. miles off Nova Scotia, Canada	132 000
7	Torrey Canyon	1967	Scilly Isles, UK	119 000
8	Urquiola	1976	La Corunna, Spain	100 000
9	Hawaiian Patriot	1977	300 naut. miles off Honolulu	95 000
10	Independenta	1979	Bosphorus, Turkey	95 000
11	Jakob Maersk	1975	Oporto, Portugal	88 000
12	Braer	1993	Shetland Islands, UK	85 000
13	Khark 5	1989	120 naut. miles off Atlantic coast of Morocco	80 000

II - INTERNATIONAL REGULATIONS

340. - Risks connected with the seaborne transport of oil are covered by a plethora of international regulations for tanker ships. These have been drawn up in fits and starts, in abrupt reaction to major disasters at sea, imposing increasingly severe technical requirements on oil tankers. Despite their scale and diversity, these preventive standards, adopted by the international community under IMO auspices, do not deal with all aspects of safety, and the gaps are completed by national regulations and measures introduced by private industry.

A - APPLICATION OF SPECIFIC REGULATIONS FOR OIL TANKERS

Four series of events have marked the history of oil tanker regulations, and played a major role in their development.

1. *Torrey Canyon* and first efforts to reduce the consequences of accidents

341. - The first major oil spill in history was caused by a Liberian tanker, the *Torrey Canyon*, which ran aground off the coast of Cornwall near the Scilly Isles on 18 March 1967. The accident occurred in fine weather as a result of an navigational error. It caused serious pollution of large stretches of the British and French coastlines (27).

The event had extensive repercussions. For the first time, television and newspapers showed the whole world the black waves of oil contaminating holiday beaches, the slow deaths of thousands of seabirds coated with oil, the anger of fishermen whose livelihood was suddenly threatened, the powerlessness of the authorities to clean and restore the polluted areas. This desperate spectacle had a dramatic effect on public opinion and governments, making them aware of the danger represented by supertankers (28).

By revealing the inadequacies of international regulations, the *Torrey Canyon* disaster resulted in an overhaul of international maritime law and technical regulations, in an attempt to prevent accidents (29), reduce their environmental effects (30), and make arrangements for compensation for pollution damage (31).

(25) Lloyd's List, 22 Feb. 1996.
(26) " Spill acronyms and acrimony ". Insurance Day, 7 June 1995.
(27) - INTERTANKO. Op. cit, April 1998.
- United Kingdom, Secretary of State for Home Department . "Coastline Pollution : observations on the Report of the Select Committee on Science and Technology, Cmnd 3880, 1969.
- M. GREY : "Chain of events that heralded a new age of superspill". Lloyd's List, 18 March 1997.
(28) W. O'NEIL : "Disaster had dramatic effect on attitudes". Lloyd's List, 18 March 1997.
(29) M. KORKHILL : "Thirty years of upheaval for owners". Lloyd's List, 18 March 1997.
(30) - I. WHITE : "Three decades and still no miracle cure". Lloyd's List, 18 March 1997.
- "30 years on : what has happened since the *Torrey Canyon*". IMO News, n° 1, 1997, 11-18.
(31) - A. de BIEVRE : "IMO move has proved ground-breaking". Lloyd's List, 18 March 1997.
- IMCO. Conclusion of the Council on the actions to be taken on the problems brought to light by the loss of the *Torrey Canyon*. C/ES/III/5, 8 May 1967.

In terms of prevention, there was at the time no legal provision for avoiding or limiting the pollution caused by tanker accidents. The London Convention of 12 May 1954 for the Prevention of Pollution of the Sea by Oil (OILPOL) targetted only pollution arising from the operation of merchant ships. The amendments adopted in 1962 and 1969 provided no solution to the problem. It was not until 1971 that the first preventive measures were introduced.

a) 1971 amendments to OILPOL Convention

Immediately following the *Torrey Canyon* disaster, consideration was given to restricting the size of central and side tanks on tankers, in order to reduce possible oil spillage after an accident.

The project was discussed for several years at IMO and finally accepted by the MSC in March 1971, despite the reservations of numerous states. Its recommendations were partly confirmed by the Assembly in amendments to the 1954 OILPOL Convention, contained in Resolution A.246 of 15 October 1971 (32).

b) MARPOL Convention of 1973

342. - In 1969 the IMO Assembly, motivated partly by the *Torrey Canyon* accident, decided to organise an international conference with the aim of adopting a new convention. The conference met in London from 6 October to 2 November 1973, and ended with the signature of one of the most ambitious international treaties on marine pollution: the Convention for the Prevention of Pollution from Ships (MARPOL Convention).

Annex I to the Convention, devoted entirely to oil, places the accent mainly on preventing deliberate pollution, by placing new limits on the amount that may be discharged into the sea during routine operations, and banning the practice completely in certain zones.

Chapter III of Annex I, however, sets out a number of requirements aimed at reducing accidental pollution in the event of side or bottom damage to oil tankers (33).

2. VLCC explosions and action by private organisations

343. - Following the December 1969 explosion of three very large crude carriers, the *Marpessa*, the *Mactra* and the *Kong Haakon VII*, three organisations focussed their efforts on preventing such accidents.

The International Oil Tanker Terminal Safety Group (IOTTSG) carried out several experimental studies in 1970 into the dispersal of hydrocarbon vapours while oil tankers are being loaded. This work culminated in the issue of a safety guide, distributed to all shipowners by the Institute of Petroleum. Most provisions in this set of practical recommendations were subsequently taken up in classification society rules.

The International Chamber of Shipping (ICS) undertook more extensive work from 1970, when its Petroleum Committee set up a working party to study electrostatic charges as a cause of explosion in ship tanks during washing (34).

(32) R. Michael M'GONIGLE, M. ZACHER : "Pollution, politics and international law". University of California Press, 1979, 102-106.
(33) M. CORKHILL : "Marpol fine-tuning gets there in the end". Lloyd's List, 18 March 1997.
(34) "Tanker accidents learning by experience". Safety at Sea, April 1982, 16-20.

Three preliminary reports and a final report on oil tankers were published between September 1970 and October 1975. These documents pointed out the causes of accidents, and made recommendations for tanker and terminal personnel on the safe carriage and handling of crude oil and petroleum products on tankers and at terminals. The group's instructions were incorporated in the "International Safety Guide for Oil Tankers and Terminals", first published in 1978 and revised on numerous occasion since then (35).

At IACS, a specialised working group drew up two draft Unified Rules, one on cargo tank venting for petroleum tankers (36), and the other on inert gas generating installations on vessels carrying oil in bulk (37). These proposals were submitted in November 1971 to IMO, which incorporated them in its own regulations.

3. *Argo Merchant* and Tanker Safety and Pollution Prevention (TSPP) Conference of 1978

344. - In the Winter of 1976-77, there was a spate of fifteen accidents involving oil tankers off the coasts of the United States. The most spectacular was the wreck of the *Argo Merchant*, which foundered off Cape Cod on 15 December 1976, causing pollution of the fishing grounds of Georges Bank and the popular beaches of Massachusetts (38).

In a message to Congress on 18 March 1977, the American President presented a set of measures intended to improve the safety of oil tankers, emphasising the need for effective enforcement of standards, and announced a programme for all tanker ships to be boarded and examined by the United States Coast Guard (USCG) before entering American waters (39).

This action programme was submitted to IMO in April 1977 and examined by its technical committees in record time. Faced with the threat of unilateral measures, IMO decided to convene a diplomatic conference to amend existing tests. This Tanker Safety and Pollution Prevention (TSPP) Conference met in London in February 1978, and adopted two protocols to the 1974 SOLAS and 1973 MARPOL Conventions (40).

Barely a month after the TSPP Conference, one of the worst oil spills in history occurred in France, when the 230 000 dwt Liberian tanker *Amoco Cadiz* ran aground in heavy seas on 16 March 1978 on rocks off Porsall in Brittany. The accident was caused by damage to a rudder, and inadequate towing facilities. 400 kilometres of coastline were polluted, with disastrous consequences for ocean flora and fauna. Thousands of birds perished in this ecological cataclysm, which also had very serious economic repercussions for fishermen, oyster breeders and those in the tourist industry, all of whom had to stop every activity for several months (41).

Despite the progress achieved at the TSPP Conference, the *Amoco Cadiz* disaster showed that IMO still had much to do to increase the safety of tankers. This general pessimism was

---

(35) ICS, OCIMF, IAPH : "International Safety Guide for Oil Tankers and Terminals". Witherby and Co, London, 4th Edition 1996.
(36) IMCO : FP XII/4/3. 3 Nov. 1971.
(37) IMCO : FP XII/4/4. 3 Nov. 1971.
(38) IMO, Doc MSC 36/20/3. Note of the Government of the United States.
(39) A. POPP : " Recent development in tanker control in international law ". The Canadian Yearbook of International Law, 1980, vol. 18, 3.30.
(40) IMO. The International Conference on Tanker Safety and Pollution Prevention 1978. London.
(41) France :
- Sénat : rapport de la commission d'enquête, June, 1978, 13 à 52.
- Mission interministérielle de la Mer : " Le livre blanc sur l'affaire de l'*Amoco Cadiz* ". Paris, 1979.
- P. PHLIPONEAU : " La catastrophe de l'*Amoco Cadiz* ". La Revue Maritime, n° 338, July 1978, 2099-2106.
- J. DUMORTIER : " Réflexion sur la perte de l'*Amoco Cadiz* ". Jeune Marine, n° 27, Mar.-Apr. 1979, 10-11.

admittedly based on statistical evidence that was hardly to the credit of the oil industry: in 1979, the number of major oil spills of more than 5 000 barrels, which had remained around 25 a year throughout the decade, shot up to 36 (42).

4. *Exxon Valdez* and regulations on double hulls

345. - Eleven years later, almost to the day, another ecological disaster occurred, with the grounding of the *Exxon Valdez* in Prince William Sound in Alaska. Even though pollution was only a tenth of that caused by the *Amoco Cadiz*, this new oil spill, which received massive media attention, and damaged the beauty spots along the Alaskan coasts, had a drastic impact on American public opinion. Its legislative impact also had far-reaching implications. They began in the United States, with the adoption on 18 August 1990 of the Oil Pollution Act (cf chapter 9 above), and ended in 1992 with the amendment of the MARPOL Convention.

The standard-setting activities of IMO were given further impetus by two other accidents in April 1991: the collision between the *Agip Abruzzo* and the car ferry *Moby Prince* (43) and the explosion of the Cypriot tanker *Haven* off Genoa, which caused serious pollution on the Italian Riviera (44).

By July 1991, the Marine Environment Protection Committee (MEPC) of IMO proposed two major amendments to the MARPOL Convention (45), one concerning double hulls, and the other the introduction of an enhanced survey programme (ESP). These amendments were adopted by IMO in March 1992, and came into force on 6 July 1993.

All these measures still failed to put a complete stop to accidents, as evidenced by the *Braer* running aground in January 1993 off the Shetland Islands (46), and by the accident to the *Sea Empress* in February 1996 in the port of Milford Haven (47).

B - SPECIFIC TECHNICAL REGULATIONS

346. - Specific regulations for oil tankers appear in several IMO convention texts; They deal with three aspects of safety :
- design, construction and equipment, which are covered by the SOLAS and MARPOL Conventions ;
- operation, covered by the STCW Convention, several requirements of which refer expressly to those working on tankers, and by certain provisions of the SOLAS Convention on safety management (ISM Code) ;
- navigation, which is the concern of the COLREG Convention, containing special regulations for large ships whose draught makes them difficult to manoeuvre.

(42) IMO : "Cleaner oceans : the role of IMO in the 1990s. "World Maritime Day 1990, J/4434.
(43) Lloyd's List, 12 April - 26 April 1991.
(44) Lloyd's List, 15 April 1991, 9 Sept. 1992, 14 October 1992, 24 Nov. 1997.
(45) DREWRY : " Marine pollution and safer ships - Implications for the tanker industry ". Sept. 1992. London, 57-69.
(46) - Republic of Liberia. Bureau of Maritime Affairs. Report of investigation into the matter of the loss by grounding of the motor tanker *Braer* on the south coast of Shetland. 5 Jan. 1993. Monrovia, 17 Jan. 1994, Liberia.
- Marine Accident Investigation Branch : " Report of the chief inspector of marine accidents into the engine failure and subsequent grounding of the motor tanker *Braer* at Garths Ness, Shetland on 5 Jan. 1993 ". DOT London, 1993.
(47) - Marine Accident Investigation Branch. Interim Report into the *Sea Empress*. March 1996.
- Coast Guard Agency : " The *Sea Empress* incident : A report to the marine Pollution control unit ". Southampton 1997.
- " Department of Transport left exposed by the *Sea Empress* ". ENDS Report 253, Feb. 1996, 16-21.

1. Manoeuvrability and equipment

• SOLAS Protocol of 1978
347. - The 1978 TSPP Conference was the first to set technical standards for the equipment of large cargo ships (48) :
- all tanker ships of at least 10 000 gross tonnage must have two remote control systems for the steering gear, each operable separately from the navigating bridge :
- the main steering gear on new tankers of at least 10 000 gross tonnage must comprise two or more identical power units, and be capable of operating the rudder with one or more power units ;
- all ships of at least 10 000 gross tonnage and more have two radars, each capable of operating independently.

• SOLAS amendments of 1978
The wreck of the *Amoco Cadiz* led to strengthening of regulations. In November 1981, IMO adopted an amended version of Regulations 29 and 30 of the 1978 SOLAS Protocol concerning steering gear. The concept of duplication of steering gear control systems, so that in the event of a technical failure the ship can still be steered. These regulations came into force in September 1984.

• SOLAS amendments of December 1992
These concern construction requirements for new tankers built after 1st October 1994. A new Regulation 12-2 lays down requirements for access to spaces in the cargo area of oil tankers. New requirements were also added to Regulation 37 dealing with communication between the navigation bridge and machinery spaces.

• SOLAS amendments of May 1994
These amendments, which came into effect on 1st January 1996, contain two specific regulations for tanker ships :
- Regulation 15-1 requires all tankers of at least 10 000 dwt to be fitted with emergency towing arrangements fitted at both ends of the ship. Existing tankers must be fitted with a similar arrangement at the first scheduled dry-docking after 1st January 1996 but not later than 1st January 1999.
- Regulation 22 improves bridge navigation visibility for ships not less than 45 metres in length constructed on or after 1st July 1998.

2. Prevention of fires and explosions

348. - Fires and explosions are very serious risks on board crude and product carriers. Preventive measures are contained mainly in the SOLAS convention.

a) Fire prevention

Current regulations consist of the new part of chapter II-2 of the 1974 SOLAS Convention, which applies to all new tanker ships of at least 500 gross tonnage.

---

(48) IMO. SOLAS : the International Convention for the Safety of Life at Sea, 1974. In Focus on IMO, Jan. 1998.

Five fundamental principles underlie this new text :
- separation of accommodation from the rest of the ship by bulkheads possessing mechanical and heat-resistant properties ;
- protection of exits ;
- location and extinction of any fire at the point where it has broken out ;
- restricted use of combustible materials ;
- reduction of the risk of ignition of vapours released by cargoes.

The SOLAS Convention was amended by the 1978 Protocol on the safety of tankers. This amendment improves protection of cargo tanks (cf Regulation 60).

Two other major changes were made to the Convention in 1983 :
- Regulation 56 on the location and separation of spaces in tankers was completely rewritten, in order to include special provisions for combination carriers.
- Chapter III contains specific requirements for tankers, which must carry completely enclosed lifeboats equipped with a self-contained air support system, if the cargo could emit toxic gases. Lifeboats must also afford protection against fire for at least eight minutes, if the cargo is flammable.

b) Inert gas systems (IGS) and explosion prevention

Fire is not the only source of danger on board oil tankers. Under certain conditions, a single spark can cause an explosion, particularly when empty cargo tanks are filled with flammable gas. The normal way of preventing this is to fill the tanks with an inert gas. It is cleaned and then blown into the empty tanks, or into the space left above the oil in filled tanks.
The 1978 SOLAS Protocol contains most of the existing regulations on IGS, which is mandatory on board :
- new crude carriers and product carriers of at least 20 000 dwt :
- existing crude carriers of more than 20 000 dwt ;
- existing product carriers of at least 40 000 dwt and those of more than 20 000 dwt fitted with high-capacity washing machines.

Flag States may grant exemptions to existing crude carriers of 20 000 to 40 000 dwt, where it is considered unreasonable or impracticable to fit an IGS, and if such ships are not fitted with high-capacity washing machines. However, an IGS is always required when crude oil washing (COW) is used.

3. Prevention of oil spills

349. - The external safety of oil tankers has become as important as their internal safety. To quote an apt expression, "It is no longer the case only that a ship has to be protected against the sea, but that the sea also has to be protected against the ship" (49). Four structural measures that can help reduce the consequences of accidents are subdivision and stability provisions, limits on the size of tanks, defensive location of segregated ballast tanks, and construction of double-hull ships (50).

(49) M. REMOND-GOUILLOUD : in L'Oil Pollution Act Americain de 1990. Présentation du colloque de l'AFDM, Paris, 7 février 1991.
(50) IMO : "Preventing marine pollution. The environmental threat". In Focus on IMO, March 1998.

a) Subdivision and stability

Subdivision and stability requirements are intended to ensure that a ship will survive collision or grounding, in any loading conditions.

Regulation 25 of Annex I to the 1973 MARPOL Convention sets out precise requirements on this matter: tankers must be able to survive assumed side or bottom damage, to a degree which is specified on the basis of the ship's length. These requirements were considerably strengthened in 1984.

b) Tank size

The potential consequences of an accident increase with the individual volume of cargo tanks. It was therefore decided to limit the size of such tanks.

This measure is designed to achieve three purposes :
- limit the quantity of oil discharged into the sea after damage to a tank by collision or grounding ;
- limit the violence of any explosion ;
- increase the ship's buoyancy if several tanks are ripped open in an accident.

Restrictions on tank size are contained in Regulation 24 of Annex I to the MARPOL Convention. Sizes vary according to factors such as the arrangement of tanks, fitting of double bottoms, and installation of clean ballast tanks (CBT). On conventional tankers, centre tanks are limited to 30 000 cubic metres, and wing tanks to 15 000 cubic metres.

c) Defensive location of segregated ballast tanks (SBT)

350. - The segregated ballast system is an arrangement in which ballast water tanks and their accompanying lines and pumps are segregated from oil tanks and cargo installation on board the ship. In itself, this method is not intended to help prevent accidental pollution, but rather to reduce operational pollution.

It has been discovered, however, that careful positioning of SBTs may reduce the quantity of oil spilt into the sea after a collision or grounding, (51). This approach also helped reduce surplus tonnage, mainly the oldest ships, and thereby improve the general quality of the fleet.

Despite several shortcomings, this is the choice that was made at the TSPP Conference in 1978. A new Regulation 13E of Annex I to the MARPOL Protocol requires defensive location of segregated ballast spaces on board all new tankers of at least 20 000 dwt.

Another measure concerned the location of cargo tanks. The 1983 amendments to the MARPOL Convention banned the carriage of oil in the forepeak tank, the ship's most vulnerable point in the event of a collision (cf Regulation 14).

d) Double hull

351. - The double hull developed from the concept contained in Regulation 13E of the MARPOL Convention, in which a substantial thickness of void space should be placed between

(51) B. BOX : "Segretated ballast". Seatrade Review March 1994, 33.

the side and bottom, exposed to collisions and groundings, and the oil cargo. Regulation 13E protects about a third of the cargo, whereas a double hull provides total protection (52).

The MEPC inserted double-hull requirements in the MARPOL Convention in March 1992, in response to IMO Resolution A.675, seeking a reduction in the risk of marine pollution by oil (53). These requirements are contained in Regulation 13F, and refer only to new ships.

Unlike OPA, the MARPOL Convention allows for alternatives to the double hull. These different structural methods of cargo protection each have advantages and drawbacks. But whatever their effectiveness, implementation of the new regulations on double hulls will result in rejuvenation of the world tanker fleet.

• Regulation 13 of Annex I to MARPOL Convention

This Regulation takes account of two types of new ships :

- Oil tankers of at least 600 but less than 5 000 dwt must be fitted with double-bottom tanks. The capacity of each cargo tank is limited to 700 cubic metres, unless they are fitted with double hulls. New ships are tankers for which the building contract is placed after 6 July 1993, the keels of which are laid down on or after 6 January 1994, or which are delivered on or after 6 July 1996.

- Oil tankers of at least 5 000 dwt must be fitted with double bottoms and wing tanks extending the full depth of the ship's side. The regulation allows mid-deck height tankers with double-sided hulls, as a variant on the double-hull structure (54).

• Value of double hulls

352. - When double-hull requirements were included in safety regulations, a huge controversy sprang up within the maritime world for and against this type of protection (55). The discussion concerned both the economic (56) and technical (57) issues raised by double hulls in the construction, operation and inspection of oil tankers.

Certain drawbacks, particularly regarding stability, encouraged IMO to reexamine intact stability regulations for double-hull tankers in 1996 (58).

(52) Bureau Veritas : " Pétroliers à double coque. Effets sur la pollution des mers par les hydrocarbures ". Paris, Dec. 1991.

(53) - M. GREY : " IMO agrees new rules and design ". Lloyd's List, 13 March 1992.
- M. GREY : " The most important battle for cleaner safer seas still to come ". Lloyd's List, 18 March 1992.

(54) IMO. MARPOL 73/78. Focus on IMO, Oct. 1997.

(55) T. ALCOCK : "Ecology tankers and the Oil Pollution Act of 1990 : A history of efforts to require double hulls on oil tankers". Ecology Law Quarterly. Vol. 19, n° 1, 1992, 107-116.

(56) R. SCOTT BROWN, I. SAVAGE : "The economics of double-hulled tankers". Maritime Policy and Management, 1996, vol. 23, n° 2, 167-175.

(57) - W. MAGELSSEN : "Double hull, a political reality - for and against". BIMCO Bulletin, Vol. 91, n° 5, 1996, 37-43.
- Committee on Tank Vessel Design. Marine Board. Commission Engineering and Technical Systems. National Research Council : "Tanker spills - Prevention by design". National Academy Press, Washington D.C., 1991.

(58) - " Charterers reject double hulls ". Lloyd's List, 10 Feb. 1995.
- Ph. RANKINS : " Double trouble ". Lloyd's List, 24 March 1995.
- " Why some tankers sometimes tilt at terminals ". Marine Log. Nov. 1995, 40-41.
- " Vital operational questions face IMO stability experts ". Lloyd's List, 2 Sept. 1996.

15 - Double hull design with no longitudinal bulkheads
(Source : M. OSBORNE. Shell selected paper)

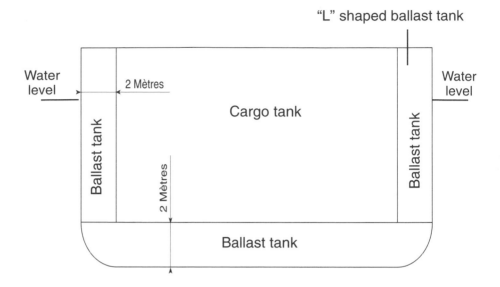

"L" shaped ballast tank

Water level

2 Mètres

Cargo tank

Ballast tank

2 Mètres

Ballast tank

Water level

Ballast tank

Ballast tank

• **Alternatives to double hulls**

In 1991, IMO carried out a major comparative study of the behaviour of double-hulled and mid-height deck tankers. This was funded by the oil and tanker industry.

The study produced the conclusion in January 1992 that both concepts could be regarded as equivalent, even if the effectiveness of each of them in preventing oil outflows is better or worse depending on circumstances (59).

This is why Regulation 13F admits other tanker design and construction methods, provided that they provide the same level of protection against pollution after collision or grounding, and are approved by the MEPC under IMO guidelines.

Two alternatives to double hulls have been developed, relying on the principles of horizontal subdivision of cargo spaces and the hydrostatic balance :

- the mid-deck tanker presented within the framework of the E3 ("European - Economic - Ecological") tanker project ;
- the Japanese mid-deck tanker (60).

The advantages of mid-deck tankers have failed to convince the American authorities which, under the terms of the OPA, will not recognise this technique as an alternative to

(59) IMO. Report of the IMO Comparative Study on Oil Tanker Design. MEPC 32/7/15, 17 Jan. 1992.
(60) " IMO set to back mid-deck design ". Lloyd's List, 18 Nov. 1992.
(61) "US builders double hull incentive call". Lloyd's List, 29 Jan. 1997.

double hulls. Refusing to acquire European or Japanese licences, American shipyards have put pressure on Congress to accept only the double-hull design (61).

16 - Mid-deck tanker design
(Source : Lloyd's List, 18 Nov. 1992)

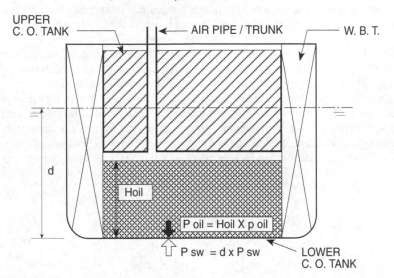

UPPER C. O. TANK — AIR PIPE / TRUNK — W. B. T.

d

Hoil

P oil = Hoil X p oil

⇧ P sw = d x P sw — LOWER C. O. TANK

• **Regulation 13G on double hulls for existing tankers**

353. - IMO has provided for progressive imposition of double hull requirements on existing ships, within the framework of a programme launched in 1995 (62).

According to Regulation 13G of Annex I of the MARPOL Convention, existing tankers must be fitted with a double hull not later than 30 years after their date of delivery. In addition, pre-MARPOL oil tankers built in the early Seventies must provide side or bottom protection to cover at least 30 per cent of the cargo tank area, not later than 25 years after their date of delivery.

Regulation 13G, which concerns crude carriers of more than 20 000 dwt, and product carriers of more than 30 000 dwt, allows other structural and operational variants, such as hydrostatic balance.

As a result of these new measures, most existing tanker ships in the world will have to be fitted with double hulls or scrapped. Many old tankers which cannot be retrofitted economically to meet the new standard will disappear. The MEPC has acknowledged this by adopting a resolution on the development of the ship-scrapping capacity to ensure smooth implementation of the MARPOL amendments. This resolution recommends states to take initiatives in cooperation with the shipbuilding industry and shipping industries, to develop scrapping facilities at a worldwide level, to promote research and development programmes and to provide technical assistance to developing countries anxious to develop their scrapping facilities (63)

(62) IMO : "Tanker safety : the work of the International Maritime Organisation". Focus on IMO, March 1996.
(63) IMO. Resolution MEPC.53 (32) adopted on 6 March 1992 in Annex 7 of the Report of the MEPC on its 32nd Session, MEPC 32/20, 24 March 1992.

CONCLUSION : Effectiveness of double hulls confirmed

354. - A study of double hulls (64) suggests that the effectiveness of this form of protection depends on three conditions. Oil tankers must be designed and built to high standards, operated by well-trained crews committed to their job, and maintained to higher standards than is apparent in some ships today. In this situation, the amount of oil outflows caused by the minor accidents that often occur within port limits will be reduced.

All those involved in the oil tanker industry must also become aware of the new types of problems that are bound to arise with double hulls, particularly as regards inspections and surveys. The oil industry, acting through the Tanker Structure Cooperative Forum, and classification societies, acting through IACS, have reacted promptly to this situation by publishing in 1995 "Guidelines for the inspection and maintenance of double hull tanker structures" (65). This 130-page document covers all the issues raised at present by the operation of this type of oil tanker: design, critical zones, structural failings, corrosion protection, need for accessibility for inspection and maintenance, structural surveys, maintenance and repair methods and programmes.

(64) Michael OSBORNE : "Double hull tankers - Are they the answer ?" Shell selected paper. London, 1994.
(65) Tanker Structure Cooperative Forum in association with IACS : "Guidelines for the inspection and maintenance of double hull tanker structures". Witherby and Co Ltd. London, 1995.

CHAPTER 14

Safety of cargoes

355. - Over the last hundred years, seaborne transport has undergone profound changes. From ancient times to the end of the 19th century, goods carried by sea were packed separately: grain in sacks, cotton in bales, liquids in drums or barrels. One of the most important technical innovations at sea was to use the ship's structures and hull as cargo containers.

Today, bulk transport in dedicated ships is the predominant form of the shipping trade. This mode of transport offers shippers certain benefits, particularly speed of loading and unloading, and therefore saves time. On the other hand it involves risks for those on board the ship and for the environment. These risks, which apply more particularly to ship structures, were discussed in chapters 11, 12 and 13 above.

The expansion of bulk transport has not eliminated packaged transport by sea, which has grown spectacularly in the last half century, with the success of containerisation and ro-ro handling.

Whether in bulk or in packaged form, goods on board a ship can serious endanger the ship and its crew, unless certain precautions are observed. This chapter analyses these dangers, and the measures taken to prevent and limit accidents. It focusses in turn on general provisions (I), and then specific provisions for certain cargoes (II), except toxic and dangerous goods, which are covered by the next chapter.

I - GENERAL REGULATIONS FOR CARGOES

356. - Because of the particular risks, for the ship and those on board, of transporting cargoes by sea, certain general precautions have to be taken on cargo ships.

Prior to 1991, these preventive measures were to be found in various IMO instruments, most of them adopted in the form of recommendations. The only compulsory measures concerned the carriage of grain, covered by chapter VI of the SOLAS Convention. In 1991, the MSC carried out a comprehensive review of this chapter, in order to cover all types of cargoes, in bulk, packages, unit loads, freight containers or vehicles, though excluding bulk gas and liquid cargoes (1).

The new requirements of the SOLAS Convention are based on two fundamental principles. The shipmaster remains responsible for the safety of the ship, its crew and cargo. Second, the shipper must provide him with full particulars on the cargo, far enough in advance to allow any precautions to be taken for the proper stowage and safe transport by the responsible officer (cf Regulation 2). This information must be confirmed in writing and on transport documents provided for the purpose, before the goods are loaded on board the ship.

---

(1) "IMO and Cargo Safety". Focus on IMO, Jan. 1994.

Chapter VI contains only nine regulations, but it is supported by a number of IMO codes and sets of regulations relating to safe transport of cargoes, particularly the Code of Safe Practice for Cargo Stowage and Securing and the Code of Safe Practice for Solid Bulk Cargoes (BC Code).

A - STOWAGE AND SECURING OF CARGOES

357. - A ship on waves is subjected to a whole series of longitudinal, vertical and predominantly transverse motions, resulting from rolling, pitching or momentary deviation off course. The forced generated by the resulting accelerations give rise to the majority of securing problems (cf diagram 27).

17 - Examples of a ship's motions at sea
(Source : International Organisation for Standardisation ISO 3874, 1988)

a) Rotational motions

b) Linear motions

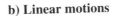

Brief sideways motion along slope
of the sea surface

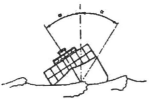

i) Roll

i) Sway

Brief, additional forward motion
along slope of sea surface

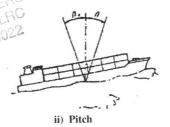

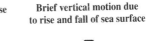

ii) Pitch

ii) Surge

Momentary deviation from projected course

Brief vertical motion due
to rise and fall of sea surface

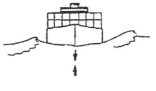

iii) Yaw

iii) Heave

1. Principles of the SOLAS Convention

Proper stowage and securing of cargoes are therefore extremely important for safety. This principle is recalled in Regulation 5 of chapter VI of the SOLAS Convention, particularly as regards goods carried on or below deck, which must be loaded and secured in such a way as to avoid damage or hazard to the ship and its crew, and to prevent any loss of cargo overboard.

The same applies to bulk cargoes. Regulation 7 emphasises the importance of trimming, and provides guidance on the use of tweendecks areas.

2. IMO recommendations

358. - To avoid the dangers arising from lack of precaution in stowing and securing cargoes, IMO has issued several guidelines in the form of Assembly resolutions or MSC circulars.

• **Resolution A.489 of 19 November 1981** (2) contains guidelines on safe storage and securing of cargo and other units in ships other than cellular container ships.

Cargo and other units include wheeled cargo, containers, flats, pallets, portable tanks, packaged units and vehicles, and parts of loading equipment which belong to the ship but are not fixed to it.

Administrations should ascertain that every ship is provided with a cargo securing manual appropriate to the characteristics of that ship and its intended service, The basic information to appear in the cargo securing manual is also indicated.

• **Resolution A.533 of 17 November 1983** (3) enumerates the elements to be taken into account when considering the safe stowage and securing of cargo units and vehicles in ships. Its purpose is to inform the various interested parties (shipbuilders, shipowners, shipmasters, port authorities, shippers, forwarding agents, road hauliers, stevedores and insurers) of the principal factors to be considered when designing and operating the ship or presenting the cargo unit or vehicle for shipment.

• **Circular MSC 385 of 8 January 1985** (4) recommends items to be included in the cargo securing manual. The object is to provide a uniform approach to the preparation of these manuals, their layout and content.

• **Resolution A.581 of 20 November 1985** (5) completes the recommendations of Resolution A.533 for securing cargoes. This is a crucial problem for ro-ro ships, because of their particular operating conditions.

Freight on such ships consists of a wide variety of goods, stowed in cargo units, vehicles or otherwise. Stowage of vehicles involves both the vehicle itself and the goods inside. If they are not stowed properly, the ship's stability may be seriously affected, resulting in accidents that cannot be predicted by the ship's crew.

(2) IMO Assembly. Resolutions and other decisions. 12th Session, 208-209.
(3) IMO Assembly. Resolutions and other decisions. 13th Session, 157-160.
(4) IMO. MSC/Circ. 385, 8 Jan. 1985.
(5) IMO Assembly. Resolutions and other decisions. 14th Session, 127-132.

Lashing is of the greatest importance on ro-ro ships. Because of the absence of bulkheads, one heavy package breaking away can loosen a whole cargo compartment. Lashing chains and slings are subject to variable loads; corrosion and excessive friction may make them wear out more quickly. Hauliers are responsible for securing goods inside vehicles, and this cannot be checked on board.

It is routine for the crew to resecure cargo units at sea, but the task may often be made more difficult and even dangerous by the unsatisfactory way loading operations have been performed by dockers.

Resolution A.581 aims to meet this problem by providing guidance on the securing and lashing of road vehicles carried on ro-ros. It applies to goods vehicles, semitrailers and articulated road trains with a maximum total mass of 45 tonnes, but not to coaches and buses. Guidelines concern securing points on the decks and on road vehicles, as well as lashing and stowage methods.

3. Code of safe practice for cargo stowage and securing

359. - All these recommendations are now included in a single code, adopted by the Assembly on 6 November 1991 in Resolution A.714, which was amended in 1994 and 1995 (7).

Rather than precise rules, this Code provides general and specific advice on the matter. It also suggests measures to be taken in heavy seas or if the cargo shifts.

The most important provisions include the requirement for ships to carry a cargo securing manual. This manual should define the characteristics of securing equipment on board and its conditions of use on various cargo units. It must also provide the master with information on forces acting on cargo units, and examples of securing methods to counterbalance such forces.

The IMO resolution provides for the manual to be established by a method accepted by the administration or approved by a classification society designated for that purpose. In 1994, for example, Bureau Veritas introduced the special mark "ACA", certifying that a ship has a stowage plan and securing equipment approved and inspected by Bureau Veritas (8).

Twelve annexes provide advice on stowing and securing specialised cargoes such as containers on deck, portable tanks, portable receptacles, wheel-based cargoes, heavy cargoes such as locomotives and transformers, coiled sheet steel, heavy metal products, anchor chains, metal scrap in bulk, flexible intermediate bulk containers (FIBCs), logs carried below deck, and unit loads (9).

Following incidents in December 1993 and January 1994, in which containers and dangerous goods were lost overboard, five European States asked IMO to make the CSS Code mandatory (10). The MSC took this request into account (11) and amendments to several regulations in chapters VI and VII of the SOLAS Convention were adopted in December 1994 (12).

(6) Rapport de la commission technique administrative française sur la sécurité des navires rouliers. N.P.C. July 1976, 466.
(7) IMO. Code of Safe Pratice for Cargo Stowage and Securing. London, 1992.
(8) Bureau Veritas : Securing of containers on board ship. NI 186. June 1984.
(9) J. KNOTT : " Lashing and securing of deck cargoes ". The Nautical Institute. London, 1994.
(10) IMO. Sub-Committee on containers and cargoes. Documents submitted by France. BC 33/5/6, BC 33/5/7, BC 33/5/8, 24 Jan. 1994.
(11) IMO. MSC 63/22/5. 18 Feb. 1994.
(12) " Cargo Stowage Code made mandatory ". IMO News n° 3, 1996.

A new Regulation VI.5.6 indicates that cargo securing manuals approved by the administration must be on board ships carrying transport units. Given the practical difficulties encountered by States and classification societies, IMO decided to postpone the application of the new provisions to 31 December 1997 (13). According to IACS, nearly 30 000 ships will need manuals, which can take three to twelve months to prepare, depending on the type of ships concerned (14). To help the work of shipowners and authorities responsible for approving the manuals, the IMO subcommittee for Carriage of Dangerous Goods, Solid Cargoes and Containers issued guidelines in the form of a circular, dated 18 February 1996.

B - SOLID BULK CARGOES

360. - The 1960 SOLAS Convention was the first to recognise the need for precautions when transporting bulk cargoes by sea, other than grain. This followed the wreck of the *Trevessa* (15).

The first Code of Safe Practice for Solid Bulk Cargoes (BC Code) was adopted by Assembly Resolution A.82 in 1965.

The BC Code has been updated regularly since then (15), and continues to be under revision by the Containers and Cargoes Subcommittee. Again, these are not formal rules, but recommendations, advice to governments, shipowners and masters. They propose an internationally accepted method of controlling the dangers likely to threaten the safety of ships carrying bulk cargoes (except for grain, which has its own provisions). The BC Code contains general measures applying to all types of cargoes, and also specific precautions for certain cargoes presenting particular dangers.

1. General precautions

The general precautions in the BC Code include the need to protect machinery and the ship's interior from dust, and to ensure that bilges and service lines are in good order and not damaged during loading and unloading. Attention is drawn to the fundamental importance of distributing the cargo properly throughout the whole ship, to ensure stability and avoid subjecting the structure to excessive stresses. For this purpose, the shipmaster must be in possession of full information so that he can organise the safe loading of his ship.

Levelling of the cargo is another major factor in limiting the risk of shifting. It also reduces oxidation, by restricting the area of cargo exposed to the atmosphere. The density of the cargo must also be taken into account. Iron ore, for example, should be loaded in the tank top on the ship.

The BC Code provides a list of regulations adopted by ILO for cargo handling operations. Some cargoes are subject to oxidation, which may result in the reduction of oxygen supply, the emission of toxic fumes, and self-heating. Dust may be a health hazard. Finally, certain cargoes may release flammable gases that could create a risk of explosion.

2. Particular precautions

361. - The BC Code contains specific provisions for several types of cargoes that present particular dangers.

(13) IMO. MSC 66/24, 18 June 1996, 9.27-9.34.
(14) IMO. MSC 66/9/2, 1 March 1996, Document submitted by IACS.
(15) IMO. Code of Safe Pratice for Solid Bulk Cargoes (BC Code). 1994 Edition. London.

a) Cargoes which may liquefy

Such cargoes comprise concentrates derived from copper, iron, manganese, nickel, lead, zinc ores and various pyrites, as well as coal fines, coal sludge and other substances. These materials present a latent risk of shifting: when loaded, they consist of relatively dry grains, but contain enough moisture to liquefy when compacted and subjected to vibration. The cargo becomes semi-fluid, and it may slide to one side when the ship rolls, and not return to its original position when the roll is in the other direction. In some cases, shifting of the cargo could impart a dangerous list to the ship, and finally cause it to capsize.

Several measures are needed to prevent these hazards. First, the master must be conversant with the properties of the materials to be loaded on board, and particularly the permitted humidity level. Various sampling and testing methods may be used to define the properties of cargoes, which should appear on a certificate given to the master before the goods are embarked.

b) Materials presenting chemical hazards

Appendix B of the BC Code contains a detailed list of substances possessing dangerous chemical properties. Some of these may be put in the category of dangerous goods when they are carried in packaged form, whereas others present risks only in bulk. Examples include wood chips, coal and iron, which could either cause rarefaction of oxygen in the ship's cargo spaces, or heat spontaneously.

Such materials must be separated carefully from other dangerous goods carried in packages or unit loads.

II - SPECIFIC REGULATIONS FOR CERTAIN CARGOES

362. - Special recommendations exist for three types of cargoes: timber carried on deck, grain and containers.

A - TIMBER ON DECK

1. Type of hazard

Timber is often carried on deck, where its presence in large quantities raises the ship's centre of gravity. Stability can also be affected adversely if deck cargoes absorb moisture during the voyage, or if water starts to freeze, causing ice to accumulate on deck. On the other hand, the ship's buoyancy is improved, and the timber provides extra protection of the deck against heavy seas.

2. 1966 Loadline Convention

The first regulations on safe transport of timber on deck were laid down in chapter IV of the 1966 LL Convention. These regulate the construction of the ship (cf Regulation 43) and stowage (cf Regulation 44). They provide for a particular way of calculating freeboard (cf Regulation 45), allowing it to be reduced, except in the North Atlantic Zone in Winter, where freezing can cause additional problems.

3. Code of safe practice for ships carrying timber deck cargoes, 1966

IMO Resolution A.287 of 20 November 1973 contained a very comprehensive Code of Safe Practice for Ships Carrying Timber Deck Cargoes (16). Like similar IMO documents this Code, amended in 1978 and 1990, is not mandatory. It is intended to provide guidance for national authorities called upon to implement all or any of its provisions.

The Code applies to all ships at least 24 metres in length. Timber deck cargoes are those carried on an uncovered part of the freeboard deck or superstructure deck. They include timber and sawn lumber, carried in bulk and in packages.

The Code covers cargo stowage and lashing, ship stability, height of the deck cargo and protection of the crew. An annex provides information on points such as establishment of stability curves and stability assessment by rolling period tests.

B - GRAIN TRANSPORT

363. - According to Regulation 2 of chapter 6 of the 1960 SOLAS Convention, the term "grain" comprises products which are all directly or indirectly foodstuffs, such as wheat, maize (corn), oats, barley, rye, rice, pulses and seeds.

1. Nature of hazard

Grain presents a serious hazard when carried in bulk by ship. Because of its particular properties, it tends to shift inside cargo spaces. Grain is quite fluid, and can slide easily under the effect of gravity. On board certain dedicated ships, known as "self-trimmers", the issue is resolved at the building stage by installing equipment that allows the grain by itself to occupy the whole volume of the hold. On board conventional cargo ships, the solution is to fill the holds as full as possible, to the point that the grain is in contact with the top panels of the holds. Natural compaction removes the air contained between the individual grains, and the cargo can lose more than 2 per cent of its volume within a few days. This reduction creates a space, allowing the whole mass of the grain to shift whenever the ship rolls and pitches.

2. Current regulations

Following the 1991 amendments and the revision of chapter VI of the 1974 SOLAS Convention, detailed provisions for grain transport have been removed from the text of the Convention, and incorporated in the International Code for the Safe Carriage of Grain in Bulk (International Grain Code) (17).

a) SOLAS regulations

Grain transport is at present regulated by part C of chapter VI of the SOLAS Convention, which now contains only two regulations, intended primarily to define the scope of the International Grain Code.

---

(16) IMO. Code of Safe Practice for Ships carrying Timber Deck Cargoes. London, 1992.
(17) IMO. International Code for the Safe Carriage of Grain in Bulk (International Grain Code). London, 1991.

b) International code for the safe carriage of grain in bulk

Unlike other IMO codes, implementation of these provisions is mandatory. The Code applies to all ships, including those of less than 500 gross tonnage.

The Code contains three fundamental regulations. First, calculations have to be made to demonstrate that the ship possesses sufficient intact stability throughout its voyage to ensure acceptable residual dynamic stability, allowing for the unfavourable effects of the heel caused by assumed movements of the cargo. Second, grain bulkheads or boards, used to reduce shifting, must meet the intact stability criterion, again allowing for the heel caused by assumed movements of grain inside the different compartments. Third, the minimum permitted stability for a grain ship must take account of the angle of heel caused by assumed shifting of the cargo, the residual righting force, and the initial metacentric height.

C - CONTAINER TRANSPORT

364. - Of all package cargoes, containers are by far the most numerous: more than 4.3 million of them travel every year by sea to all points of the globe.

This expansion of container transport in recent years has led several organisations, including IMO and ISO, to try and improve their safety and to set standards.

18 - World container ship fleet statistics
(Source : Lloyd's Register World Fleet Statistics, 1997)

TEU capacity	No	TEU capacity	Age
499 or less	395	110 195	13
500 - 1999	1132	1 321 898	11
2000 - 3999	506	1 439 523	8
4000 or over	154	714 080	3
TOTAL	**2 137**	**3 585 696**	**10**

1. IMO regulations

In 1972, IMO presided over the adoption of an International Convention for Safe Containers (CSC Convention). In collaboration with ILO, it has also issued a set of guidelines on loading cargoes in containers or vehicles.

a) CSC Convention

365. - The 1972 CSC Convention has two goals: one is to maintain a high level of safety in the transport and handling of containers, by providing acceptable test procedures and related strength requirements; the other is to facilitate international container transport by providing uniform international safety regulations, equally applicable to all modes of surface transport, with the aim of avoiding proliferation of divergent national safety regulations (18).

(18) IMO. : "International Convention for Safe Containers, 1972 (CSC), 1996 Edition, London. Foreword.

• Approval of containers

Containers used for international transport must be approved by the administration of a State which is party to the Convention (cf article III.2). The term "approval" means the decision by an administration that a design type of a container is safe within the terms of the Convention (cf article II.5).

According to article IV, every administration is to establish an effective procedure for the testing, inspection and approval of containers in accordance with the criteria laid down in Annex I to the Convention. The administration may entrust such operations to organisations duly authorised by it. Such organisations perform the lifting, rigidity and strength tests stipulated in Annex II to the Convention, and affix the compulsory safety approval plate to each container.

This plate shows that the container complies with CSC safety standards. It must be affixed at a readily visible place, where it would not be easily damaged, and displays relevant technical information (cf Annex I, Regulation 1).

Article V recognises the principle of reciprocal acceptance of safety-approved containers. "Approval under the authority of a contracting party, granted under the terms of the present Convention, shall be accepted by the other contracting parties for all purposes covered by the present Convention. It shall be regarded by the other contracting parties as having the same force as an approval issued by them."

Once fitted with their safety approval plate, containers may normally be used for commercial purposes, while remaining subject to minimum safety inspection formalities (cf article VI).

• Container maintenance

According to article IV.4, "every container shall be maintained in a safe condition". Regulation 2 of Annex I places this obligation on the owner of the container, who must "examine it or have it examined in accordance with the procedure prescribed or approved by the contracting party concerned, at intervals appropriate to operating conditions".

The time elapsing between the date of construction of the container and its first examination may not exceed five years, and subsequent examinations must be at intervals of not more than 30 months. However, the contracting party may approve a continuous examination programme if satisfied, on evidence submitted by the owner, that such a programme provides an equivalent standard of safety.

Certain organisations have defined the general procedure and particular conditions for approval, control and inspection of existing containers. Bureau Veritas has issued two sets of rules; for the homologation and inspection of containers (19) and for the classification and certification of containers (20).

• Container tests

Annex II to the Convention deals with safety aspects of the construction and testing of containers. It expressly requires the container to be subjected to various tests, corresponding to a set of safety standards, applicable to both land and maritime transport.

Because of the simplified procedure for amending these regulations, they are extremely flexible, allowing test procedures to be adapted quickly to the needs of world container traffic.

---

(19) Bureau Veritas. Rules for the homologation and inspection of containers. Paris, 1968, NI 140.
(20) Bureau Veritas. Rules for the classification and certification of freight containers. Paris, 1992, IND-IT 178.1.

b) IMO/ILO guidelines on loading of cargoes in containers

366. - The person responsible for loading and securing goods inside a container plays an essential role in safety. Shippers, forwarding agents, road or rail vehicle drivers, dockers, crews and reception staff rely on his skills and ability..

Any error or lack of precaution during packing could cause serious and costly damage to the goods being carried, and also cause grave accidents and physical injury during transport or handling of the container.

In the Seventies, IMO and ILO began to draw up training guidelines for the loading of cargoes in containers. These guidelines were published in 1978 in the form of a brief guide, which drew attention to the effects of pitching, rolling and other movements of a ship in bad weather on the content of containers. These make transport of containers by sea far more dangerous than on land.

The guidelines, revised in 1984, contain advice for those in charge of packing of cargoes in freight containers. These do not include tank containers or dry cargoes carried in intermediate bulk containers. In general, they consist of certain national regulations and specific recommendations from the container operator or carrier regarding the packing and securing of bulky or heavy items and the use of specialised containers, such as tank or refrigerated containers.

c) Rules for the stowage and securing of containers on board ships

367. - Containers must comply with regulations for safe stowage and securing of cargoes. Regulation 5 of the new chapter VI of the SOLAS Convention recalls that containers must not be loaded beyond the rating shown on the safety approval plate provided for in the CSC Convention.

The SOLAS Convention also refers back to the 1991 CSS Code, Annex I of which contains specific advice for containers carried on deck, on ships not specially designed or outfitted for this type of transport.

2. ISO standards

368. - ISO was concerned with containers from 1961. So far, a score of standards have been drawn up , mainly by technical committee ISO/TC 104 (Freight Containers), and are contained in a specialised code (21).

These standards involve classification, dimensions and ratings (cf ISO 668), specification and testing of series 1 freight containers (general cargo containers, thermal containers, tank containers, dry bulk containers, platform and platform-based containers) for general purposes (ISO 1496) and air/surface (intermodal) general-purpose containers (ISO 8323) handling and securing (ISO 3874); coding, identification and marking (ISO 6346), information related to containers on board vessels (ISO 9711) and container equipment data exchange (CEDEX) (ISO 9897).

Although they are not mandatory, ISO standards are applied throughout the world.

---

(21) International Organisation for Standardisation. ISO Standard Handbook Freight Containers 2nd Ed. UDC 621.869.88, 1992.

CHAPTER 15

Safety of transport of dangerous goods at sea

369. - Noone today would question the important implications of transport of dangerous goods by sea. Yet less than a hundred years ago, so few such products were carried by ship that no restrictions were considered necessary. In the post- Second World War period, the world economic situation was revolutionised by the booming petrochemical industry, and modernisation of the fleet of dedicated ships. This led to a huge increase in the amount of dangerous substances transported. Nowadays, according to IMO criteria, more than half the cargoes in the world may be regarded as dangerous, hazardous or harmful to the marine environment (1).

Such transport raises a general safety problem, of concern not only to shipping operators and users, but also to others not involved directly in transport. Urban populations living near port areas are the main potential victims of the explosion of a dangerous cargo; but coastal populations are also under threat from toxic waste in the sea.

Such threats are growing inexorably. As the world becomes increasingly industrialised, it generates ever more toxic and dangerous substances and waste. This is a general problem of society, of which this chapter deals only with the issue of transport of such substances by sea.

Discussion will focus in turn on the concept of dangerous goods (cf I below), risks connected with the conveyance of such cargoes by sea (II) and regulations to prevent accidents (III).

I - CATEGORISATION OF DANGEROUS GOODS

370. - More than five thousand dangerous substances have been identified throughout the world. In the absence of any uniform definitions and classification, it is no easy matter to regulate their transport by sea.

Several criteria may be used to classify dangerous goods :
- dangerous properties (e.g. flammability, toxicity, corrosiveness) ;
- risks faced by human beings and the environment ;
- mode of transport, with each of them assessing the dangers of a substance in a particular way, and consequently imposing specific requirements (2) ;
- mode of packaging used for their transport.

Maritime regulations distinguish four main categories of dangerous cargoes, described below.

---

(1) "IMO and dangerous goods at sea" in Focus on IMO, May 1996.
(2) Y. DE BOUVER : " La formation et l'information des participants aux transports de marchandises dangereuses ". European Transport Law. Vol. XXVI, n° 1 and 2, 1991, 40-83.

A. LIQUEFIED GAS

371. - An increasingly important source of energy, gas is also one of the most useful raw materials for the international petrochemical industry. There are two main types of liquefied gas: petroleum gas and natural gas.

Liquefied petroleum gas (LPG) is transported under pressure at atmospheric temperature, refrigerated at atmospheric pressure, or under pressure and semi-refrigerated. Dedicated LPG tankers are built to carry them (3).

Liquefied natural gas (LNG) is carried at a temperature of -165°C in special methane tankers (4).

B. LIQUID CHEMICALS IN BULK

372. - Liquid chemicals in bulk present four categories of dangers for the marine environment, as shown in the classification in Regulation 3 of Annex II to the MARPOL Convention. Category A comprises substances that would present a major hazard to either marine resources or human health, or cause serious harm to amenities or other legitimate uses of the sea, and therefore justify the application of stringent anti-pollution measures. Examples are cresols, naphthalene, lead tetraethyl or carbon sulphide. Category B comprises substances that would present less of a hazard, such as acrylonitrile, ethylene dichloride, carbon tetrachloride or phenol. Category C comprises substances that would present a minor hazard, but which still require special operational conditions, such as benzene, styrene, toluene or xylene. Category D comprises substances that would present a hazard, but which still require some attention to operational conditions, such as acetone, phosphoric acid or animal or vegetable oils.

Liquid chemicals in bulk are conveyed by dedicated vessels, cellular tanker ships designed specially to carry a large variety of products for different owners.

C. SOLID PRODUCTS IN BULK

373. - Several solid products in bulk can present serious risks during transport (5). They include a wide variety of substances, including pitch, coal, quicklime, petroleum coke, wood chips, organic waste, iron, ferrosilicon, aluminium slag, wood pulp pellets, sawdust and silicomanganese.

The dangers of some of these products result from their inherent physical and chemical properties. Others become dangerous only when they are carried in bulk. Such materials may dilute the oxygen content of the air in the cargo space or, like wood chips, be subject to spontaneous heating.

D. DANGEROUS GOODS IN PACKAGES

374. - Packaged dangerous goods constitute a very high proportion of this trade. A study carried out by CEDRE in 1989 (6) showed that only 10 per cent of the 2 000 chemicals on ships in the English Channel were carried in bulk. An average of 5 to 10 per cent of the

(3) Bureau Veritas : "Liquefied Gas Carriers". W5.5/DIVERS 2/LIQASBD. Doc.
(4) B. DABOUIS : " RAMS analysis of large membrane-type methane gas tankers". Bulletin Technique du Bureau Veritas, n°1, Sept. 1994, 35-74.
(5) "Deadly peril that lurks in safe cargo holds". Lloyd's List, 14 Sept. 1988.
(6) CEDRE : " Evaluation du trafic des produits chimiques sous forme conditionnée en Manche ". R 89.63 C. 1989.

boxes on a container vessel carry dangerous goods, and on some routes the figure can be as high as 20 per cent (7).

Dangerous goods are traditionally divided into nine classes of products :
Class 1 : Explosive substances and articles
Class 2 : Gases, compressed, liquefied or dissolved under pressure
Class 3 : Flammable liquids
Class 4 : Flammable solids, liable to spontaneous combustion, or which, in contact with water, emit flammable gases
Class 5 : Oxidizing substances (which provoke combustion) and organic peroxides which are subject to violent or explosive decomposition
Class 6 : Toxic and infectious substances
Class 7 : Radioactive materials
Class 8 : Corrosive substances
Class 9 : Miscellaneous dangerous substances and articles such as aerosols, some ammonium nitrate fertilisers, asbestos, safety matches and substances designed as "marine pollutants".

II - HAZARDS OF DANGEROUS GOODS

375. - The risks presented by seaborne transport of dangerous goods may be judged on two different levels, the individual and the collective. Certain products are a greater fire hazard for individuals than petroleum and similar flammable substances. They may also be a very dangerous health hazard, mainly because of the toxic effect of inhaling their vapours, swallowing them or absorbing them through the skin, and their corrosive effect on the skin. The main collective risks are fire and explosion, and marine pollution.

A - DANGERS TO HUMAN LIFE

1. Fires and explosions

Ships loaded with dangerous goods may explode. When such an accident occurs in port, near an area with a high population density, the consequences are nearly always cataclysmic. Maritime history has recorded several fearful disasters of this kind.

• *Mont Blanc*
This French ship of 3 000 gross tonnage was carrying 2 300 tonnes of picric acid and 3 000 tonnes of TNT in its holds, as well as numerous barrels of petrol, when it collided with another ship, the *Imo*, in the Canadian port of Halifax on 7 December 1917. This caused the most disastrous man-made explosion prior to the atom bomb. The blast flattened the port and half the city, followed by an enormous tidal wave that drowned the unfortunate survivors of the explosion. 3 000 people were killed, 9 000 injured and 6 000 left homeless (8).

---

(7) M. LE CAM : " Considérations sur les transports de produits chimiques en vrac ". NTM 1974, 87.
(8) - J. KITZ : " Shattered City. The Halifax explosion and the road to recovery ". Nimbus Publishing Ltd. Halifax, 1989.
- R. GHYS : " Influence of disasters and accidents on the legislation covering transport of dangerous goods ". European Transport Law, Vol. XXVI, n° 1-2, 1991, 3-25.

• *Fort Stikene*

The cargo ship *Fort Stikene* was carrying 1 400 tonnes of explosives when it entered Bombay harbour in April 1944. Earlier, in Karachi, it had taken on board a large cargo of cotton and several drums of oil, separated only by a thin tarpaulin. A discarded cigarette end was probably the cause of the apparently minor fire that broke out. Having experienced several similar incidents in previous months, the port authorities were slow to react. The two dreadful explosions that followed killed 1 250 people and destroyed about fifteen nearby ships.

• *Grandcamp*

The freighter *Grandcamp* was loading a cargo of ammonium nitrate in the port of Texas City in April 1947 when fire broke out on board. The inadequacy of the firefighting installations resulted in a first explosion, so violent that it brought down two aircraft flying overhead. The blast damaged the hold panels of another freighter, the *High Flyer*, a few hundred metres from the Grandcamp, causing a second explosion. There were 468 deaths.

• *Ocean Liberty*

Three months later, in July 1947, a similar sequence of events occurred in the port of Brest, on the *Ocean Liberty*, which was also carrying ammonium nitrate. The explosion was not so violent, but still killed 21 people.

2. Hazards of liquefied gas

376. - Growth in the seaborne transport of liquefied gas since 1975 has aroused much comment in France and the United States. In 1978, the American General Accounting Office published a bulky three-volume report on the safety of gas tankers, describing the main risks of accidents, and various preventive regulations (9). In June 1990, CEDRE issued a mini-guide to dealing with the risks associated with transport of methane, on the assumption of 10 000 tonnes of LNG (25 000 cubic metres) being spilt.

Fortunately, very few accidents have occurred since the introduction of liquefied gas tankers. In a document issued in 1992 (11), Lloyd's Register assessed the risks connected with seaborne transport of LNG, reporting that, of the 29 incidents between 1972 and 1991, none caused any bodily or ecological damage. These findings were confirmed in 1993 by a French study indicating that no loss of human life was recorded, nor any incident with consequences for outside parties, for 17 000 voyages worldwide, involving a total of 620 million tonnes (12). Quality of design and construction helped just prevent a disaster in June 1979, when the methane tanker *El Paso Paul Kayser* tore a 180-metre gash in its hull, as it ran aground on rocks near Gibraltar with 100 000 cubic metres of LNG in its tanks (13).

(9) General Accounting Office : " Liquefied energy cases safety ". EMD 78-28, July, 31, 1978.
See also a study of the U.S. Coast Guards published on 1st Feb. 1976 : " Liquefied natural gas : views and practices, policy and safety ". Department of Transportation, CG, 478, Washington.
(10) M. NEUMEISTER : " Méthanier : une bombe flottante ? " JMM, 12 Feb. 1993, 369-370
(11) Lloyd's Register : " Risk assessment review of the marine transportation of liquefied natural gas ". STD Report n° 3000 . Sept. 1992.
(12) A. GOY, G. ROLET : " La gestion des risques technologiques liés au transport maritime du GNL ". JMM, 11 June 1993, 1349-1351.
(13) JMM, 12 July 1979, 1732 ; 16 August 1979, 2021 ; 12 February 1993, 371-372.

B - MARINE ENVIRONMENT POLLUTION

377. - Pollution of the sea resulting from the explosion of seaborne noxious products raises an equally serious threat. Certain apparently trivial accidents can result in large-scale ecological disasters.

• *Taquari*

In 1971, the *Taquari* was wrecked near the coast of Uruguay, with iminoethane methyl isothiocyanate, 24 tonnes of mercury compounds and other toxic products in its tanks. Some time later, following a storm, the metal containers began to crack. In 1978, the appearance of a huge red tide forced the coastal populations to move inland. In addition to the powerful fumes, pollution resulted in the uncontrolled proliferation of seaweed, which killed the fish, marine animals, and later human beings that consumed it (14).

• *Carvat*

When the Yugoslav freighter *Carvat* was wrecked on 14 July 1974 in the Strait of Otranto, the Italian authorities remained anxious for two years. The ship was carrying sealed metal drums containing 250 tonnes of lead tetraethyl, an exceedingly toxic product. Fortunately, the wreck was lying in shallow water, and could be salvaged, at great expense, by the two states under threat. If the operation had failed, the ship's cargo would have turned the Adriatic into a biologically dead sea (15).

• *Sinbad*

In December 1979, the Iraqi ship *Sinbad*, caught in a violent storm off the coast of the Netherlands, lost 51 cylinder of chlorine gas overboard (16).

• *Dana Optima*

On 13 January 1984, during another storm in the North Sea, 39 containers and trailers carried as deck cargo on the *Dana Optima* were lost overboard. One of them contained 80 drums of a highly toxic material, dinosebum. 67 of them were recovered. Some of them were badly damaged, and had lost part of their contents. Danish and Dutch fishermen were advised not to fish in this area (16).

• *Ok Menga*

In June 1984, the *Ok Menga*, a barge loaded with 2 700 drums of sodium cyanate, capsized in rough seas off Papua New Guinea (16).

• *Mont Louis*

On 25 August 1984, the French ro-ro cargo ship *Mont Louis*, carrying a cargo of uranium hexafluoride (UF6), a highly radioactive product, was rammed by the ferry *Olau Britannia*, and sank off Ostend a few hours later. Fortunately, there were no victims, and the 18 drums were recovered within a few weeks (17).

(14) " Un Minamata au Brésil ". Le Monde 22 April 1979, p. 35 and RGDIP 1979, 137.
(15) RGDIP 1976, 1257-1259.
(16) IMO. CDG 44/15, 7 August 1992.
(17) - Le Marin, 1 Sept 1984 - JMM, 22 Sept. 1984, 2012 - Le Monde, 9-10 Sept. 1984, 13.
- " Mont-Louis : des faits, des lésions ". Revue Mer, Jan.-Feb. 1985, 4-13.

• *Santa Clara*
In January 1992, the Panamanian-flag container ship *Santa Clara* lost 21 containers carrying 441 drums of arsenic trioxide off the New Jersey coast (18).

• *British Trent*
On 3 May 1993, again near Ostend, the *British Trent* collided with the Panamanian freighter *Western Winner*. The British oil tanker, which was carrying 24 000 tonnes of petrol, 28 000 tonnes of diesel fuel, and 900 tonnes of heavy fuel oil, spilt part of its cargo into the North Sea. The accident caused 7 deaths and 27 injuries (19).

• **Pollution of French coastline in 1993**
In September 1993, during heavy weather in the Gulf of Gascony, a cargo ship lost several containers loaded with detonators and dynamite (20). On 8 December, the container ship *Sherbro* suffered a similar accident in the Channel. Following a storm, 88 containers filled with bags of pesticides fell overboard and a few weeks later caused massive pollution of the French coastline (21).

These events caused acute anxiety among coastal populations, and French public opinion reacted sharply to media coverage. There were two parliamentary reports on the safety of maritime transport (22).

Despite these cases, however, maritime accident statistics involving dangerous goods remain generally satisfactory, given the world volume of such goods carried. The reason is to be sought in the repeated preventive efforts of the whole maritime community.

III - REGULATIONS ON SEABORNE TRANSPORT OF DANGEROUS GOODS

378. - The regulations that currently govern seaborne transport of dangerous goods are complex, many in number, and difficult to read and understand. They comprise general rules that apply to all dangerous substances, carried in bulk or in packages, and specific standards for bulk liquid or dry cargoes.

All existing regulations may be divided into two categories, depending on their aims: safety of ships and those on board, and protection of the environment.

A - SAFETY REGULATIONS

These regulations are contained mainly in the 1974 SOLAS Convention, amended in 1983, which is supported by a number of international codes. There are also specific provisions on many different aspects of safety.

(18) - USCG : " Marine board of inquiry M/V Santa Clara I ". Washington DC, 18 May 1992, 16732/03 HQS 92.
- D. LEWIS : " In the eye of a storm ". Hazardous Cargo Bulletin, May 1993, 74-78.
(19) - Lloyd's List, 4 and 5 June 1993.
(20) Le Marin, 24 Dec. 1993.
(21) "Probe finds cause of Sherbro lost boxes". Lloyd's List, 31 May 1994.
(22) Sénat : " Transport maritime : plus de sécurité pour une mer et un littoral plus propres ". Rapport d'information n° 500, 13 June 1994.
Assemblée Nationale : " La sécurité maritime : un défi européen et mondial ". Rapport d'information n° 1482, 5 July 1994.

1. SOLAS Convention 1974

379. - Two chapters of this fundamental Convention on safety at sea are concerned here :
- Chapter VI, on the transport of cargoes which, because of the particular risks they present for ships or those on board them, may require special precautions.
- Chapter VII, entirely devoted to transport of dangerous goods, and divided into three parts:
  . Part A : Dangerous goods in packaged form or in solid form in bulk
  . Part B : Ships carrying liquid chemicals in bulk
  . Part C : Ships carrying liquefied gases in bulk

This chapter provides the necessary legal framework for the establishment of national and international regulations on dangerous goods.

Revised several times since 1974, chapter VII contains compulsory requirements for all cargo ships, including those of less than 500 gross tonnage (cf Regulation 1.1)

Regulation 1 of Part A of this chapter VII prohibits the carriage of dangerous goods by sea except when they are carried in accordance with the provisions of the SOLAS Convention, and requires each contracting government to issue detailed instructions on safe packing and stowage of dangerous goods, which must include the precautions necessary in relation to other cargo. The Convention also divides dangerous goods into nine classes, and refers to the detailed requirements of the IMDG Code (cf. below) and to the relevant sections of appendix B of the Code of Safe Practice for Sold Bulk Cargoes (BC Code).

2. International Maritime Dangerous Goods (IMDG) Code

380. - In 1956, a committee of experts on the transport of dangerous goods met in Geneva under United Nations auspices, with the triple brief of drawing up an exhaustive list of dangerous goods, defining a classification and labelling system, and providing for the conclusion of an international agreement to cover all modes of transport.

In 1961, IMO set up a working group to draft regulations, based on the classification and labelling systems established by the UN committee. In September 1965, the Assembly adopted Resolution A.81, approving an international maritime code for dangerous goods, and advised member governments to adopt and use it as a basis for their national regulations. Since 1970, the IMO Code has been published separately, as the International Maritime Dangerous Goods (IMDG) Code.

a) Presentation

The IMDG Code takes the form of a five-volume loose-leaf encyclopaedia. This allows the Code to be kept regularly updated, by inserting separate supplements, which contain all amendments. The 1995 edition incorporates all such amendments, including the most recent, which came into force on 1st July 1995.

The Code is intended for all professionals concerned with dangerous goods, including manufacturers, packers, shippers, forwarding agents and road, rail, river and maritime hauliers, as well as port authorities and warehousing and terminal companies.

b) Contents

381. - The IMDG Code is divided into three parts. Volume I contains the general introduction, stating the conditions of transport of dangerous goods ; designation, marking, labelling, placarding and documents needed for their dispatch. It is completed by Annex I, which contains recommendations on packing. Adopted by the MSC in 1984, these divide forms of packing into three groups, according to the degree of danger presented by different goods. They are intended for manufacturers of dangerous goods and of packagings for them, shippers and carriers, and the competent authorities.

The second part of the Code consists of volumes II, III and IV. They present the nine categories of dangerous goods in detail. Each category is preceded by an introduction with a description of the properties, characteristics and definitions of different goods. It also formulates detailed advice on their handling and transport. Each category is identified by a mark, label or leaflet label to be affixed to the packages. Datasheets issued for dangerous goods under the Code are all produced on the same model, summarising information on the goods in question: UN number, chemical formula, property or description, packaging group, remarks on packing, stowage, separation of materials, labels.

Volume V forms the third and last part of the IMDG Code. It contains emergency procedures for ships carrying dangerous goods (EmS), the medical first aid guide for use in accidents involving dangerous goods (MFAG), the BC Code, reporting procedures, IMO/ILO guidelines for packing cargo transport units, recommendations on the safe use of pesticides in ships, and other relevant recommendations issued by IMO.

c) Amendment of the IMDG Code

382. - In response to a constantly changing industry, IMO has made many changes to the IMDG Code since 1963, in both its presentation and its content. Amendments are made by the Dangerous Goods, Cargoes and Containers subcommittee (DSC), which updates the provisions of the Code, generally once a year. At each of these sessions, a series of amendments is drafted, involving the replacement of between a hundred and two hundred pages.

A new procedure adopted by MSC in 1991 laid down the principles for amending the Code. It makes a distinction between complete revisions of the Code, giving rise to a new edition every ten years, and other urgent substantial amendments, which may be adopted every two years, or ordinary amendments, every four years (23).

IMO is currently engaged in harmonising the IMDG Code with regulations for other modes of transport, at a frequency of two years (24), particularly the UN Committee recommendations ("Orange book") and ADR (European agreement on international transport of dangerous goods by road). This goal cannot be reached until 1st July 1999, when amendment 29 of the Code will take effect (25). Complete harmonisation will be achieved only in 2001, with reformatting of all three sets of regulations (26).

d) Universality of IMDG Code

There are three editions of the IMDG Code, in English, French and Spanish. The Code has also been translated completely or partially into other languages, to further universal application.

At present, it is applied in fifty countries, whose merchant fleets represent more than 83 per cent of the gross tonnage of world shipping. The legal system in each state determines

(23) "IMDG Code amendments agreed". IMO News, n° 3, 1996, 15.
(24) M. CORKHILL : "Reformatted IMDG Code for new dangerous goods area". BIMCO Bulletin, vol. 93, n° 2, 1998, 36-38.
(25) IMO. MSC 68/23, 12 June 1997, par. 10.9.
(26) " IMO dangerous goods experts request a period of transition ". Lloyd's List, 7 March 1997.

whether the Code is mandatory, or simply recommended. A state opting for this second solution in no way escapes its obligations under the SOLAS Convention. It simply has greater freedom in applying the provisions. On 3 December 1991, IMO Assembly Resolution A.716 recalled the fundamental importance of this document, and called upon governments to base their national regulations on the IMDG Code. Current initiatives to reformat the Code may offer IMO a chance to amend the SOLAS Convention, to make certain parts mandatory (27).

3. IGC Code

383. - The regulations adopted by IMO in 1975 are based on the rules issued by classification societies. Resolution A.238 contains a Code for the construction and equipment of ships carrying liquefied gases in bulk (GC Code), and Resolution A.329 contains recommendations for ships not covered by the GC Code (29).

Ships carrying liquefied gas in bulk, and built after 1st July 1986, are now covered by Part C of chapter VII of the 1974 SOLAS Convention. Those built earlier must meet the requirements of Resolutions A.328 and A.329.

The SOLAS regulations in fact refer to the International Code for the construction and equipment of ships carrying liquefied gases in bulk (IGC Code), adopted by Resolution MSC.5(48) on 17 June 1983.

This text takes account of technical advances. It requires dedicated ships to observe design and construction standards and provide outfitting to reduce the risks to which the ship, its crew and the environment are exposed. It rests on the principle of dividing ships into different types based on the dangers presented by the products carried (30).

4. MFAG

384. - The medical first aid guide for use in accidents involving dangerous goods (MFAG) provides information on how to deal with injuries resulting from such accidents. It was drawn up jointly by IMO, ILO and WHO.

Under the terms of the 1978 STCW Convention, the master, officers and crew of a ship that regularly carries chemicals must be informed of the general risks to which they are exposed, and the precautions to be taken. They must be conversant with safety regulations, and have learnt how to give first aid in the event of an accident.

5. Port safety rules

385. - Dangerous goods can present risks on land during transport, notably while being handled in port. To limit such risks, IMO Resolution A.289 of 20 November 1973 adopted a series of practical safety rules to provide port authorities or other relevant organisations with a model to be used in establishing safety standards and procedures for the safe storage and handling of dangerous cargoes. These recommendations define the responsibilities of port authorities and the principles of local regulations: prior notification of the arrival by sea of dangerous cargoes, manoeuvres and berthing of ships inside the port, unloading, inspections, storage, handling, and emergency procedures. The MSC amended these provisions in 1979 and 1995, and they are now contained in the Recommendations on the safe transport of dangerous cargoes and related activities in port areas (31).

(27) "Giving the dangerous goods rulebook sharper teech". Lloyd's List, 17 Feb. 1998.
(28) G. MASSAC : " La sécurité à bord des méthaniers ". La Revue Maritime, June 1975, 748.
(29) IMO : "Gas at sea". Focus on IMO, Oct. 1986.
(30) - IMO. International Code for the Construction and Equipment of Ships Carrying Liquefied Gases in Bulk. IGC Code, 1993 Edition. Cf also : - Bureau Veritas : "Gas Carrier Safety Handbook". 2nd Edition LLP, London 1997.
(31) IMO. MSC/Circ. 675, 30 Jan. 1995.

IMO refers to other regulations on handling and use of lifting gear: ILO Convention 32, the ILO Guide on safety and health in port work, and the Code of safe practice for handling of dangerous goods in packages/Cargo handling gear, recommended by the International Cargo Handling Coordination Association (ICHCA).

B - ENVIRONMENTAL PROTECTION REGULATIONS

386. - The main tool developed by IMO to prevent marine pollution by noxious substances is the 1973 MARPOL Convention, which covers all forms of pollution by ships (32) and is completed by various other regulations.

1. MARPOL Convention

Two technical annexes to the Convention stipulate preventive measures regarding chemicals: Annex II concerning noxious liquids carried in bulk and Annex III concerning harmful substances carried in packages or containers, portable tanks, road or rail tankers (33).

a) Annex II : Noxious liquids in bulk

Regulation 3 of Annex II divides noxious liquids into four categories, based on the risks for the environment. Each category corresponds to different discharge criteria, depending on the dangers for marine resources. Approximately 600 substances are listed in appendix II to this Annex.

Category A substances may be discharged only into reception installations. Discharge into the sea is permitted for other categories of substances, but only under strictly controlled conditions. In any case, no outflow of residues containing noxious substances is authorised less than 12 miles from the coast, and in water shallower than 25 metres. Even stricter conditions apply in the Baltic and Black Seas (cf Regulation 5).

Parties to the Convention must publish detailed requirements for the design, construction and operation of chemical carriers, respecting at least all the provisions of the BCH Code (cf Regulation 13).

Drawn up in the early Seventies, Annex II was to a great extent outdated by the time it took effect in October 1986. Its implementation raised enormous technical difficulties. IMO drew up several major amendments, which were adopted by the MEPC in December 1985.

For practical reasons, IMO decided that parties to the 1973-78 MARPOL Convention would have to comply with the provisions of the amended Annex II, from 7 April 1987.

In March 1996, the new IMO subcommittee on Bulk Liquids and Gas (BLG) undertook a complete review of Annexes I and II to the Convention, due to be completed in the year 2000 (34). These amendments will require the most hazardous chemicals to be carried in double-hull ships (35).

(32) IMO. "Chemicals at sea". Focus on IMO, June 1986.
(33) IMO. "MARPOL 73/78". Focus on IMO, October 1997.
(34) - " Bulk liquids and gases ". BIMCO Bulletin, Vol. 91, n° 2, 1996, 52-54.
- " Revising MARPOL for the next century ". Lloyd's List, 19 Dec. 1996.
(35) " Rules become more rigourous ". Lloyd's List, 17 June 1996.

b) Annex III : Noxious substances carried in packaged form

387. - Under the terms of this Annex, signatories must publish detailed standards for packing, marking, labelling, documentation, stowage, quantity limitations, exceptions and notifications to prevent or minimise pollution of the marine environment by harmful substances (cf Regulation 1.3).

Regulation 7 prohibits jettisoning into the sea of harmful substances carried in packaged form, except where necessary to ensure the safety of the ship or save life at sea.

Unlike Annexes I and II, Annex III is optional: governments ratifying the Convention may choose not to accept provisions relating to harmful substances in packaged form. In practice, several states have taken advantage of this opt-out, depriving the regulations of much of their effectiveness. Ratified by 78 countries representing 78 per cent of the tonnage of world shipping, Annex III came into force on 1st July 1992 (36).

2. IMDG Code

388. - IMO made a major amendment to the IMDG Code in 1985, in order to facilitate implementation of Annex III. The idea was to extend its bearing by incorporating provisions for the transport of substances or objects harmful to the marine environment and identified as "marine pollutants".

Annex III does not contain a list of substances involved, but defines "harmful substances" as those identified as marine pollutants in the IMDG code It also comprises an appendix stating the criteria for identifying marine pollutants (cf Regulation 1.1).

3. Bulk Chemical (BCH) Code

389. - The threats raised by ships carrying chemicals in bulk, to both human life and the marine environment, led to the first standard-setting initiatives on this subject. Classification societies (37) and port authorities (38) were the first to lay down safety regulations.

In January 1968, IMO decided to draw up a code of regulations to define criteria for the design, construction and equipment of chemical carriers. The Code for the construction and equipment of ships carrying dangerous chemicals in bulk (BCH Code) was adopted by Assembly Resolution A.212 in 1971. It applies to ships built on or after 12 April 1972.

a) Content of BCH Code

The BCH Code is based on the principle of classifying all chemicals on the basis of the dangers they present and, depending on such dangers, defining the type of ship to be used to carry them. The more dangerous the chemical, the higher must be the degree of protection of the cargo and the survivability of the ship..

The Code takes account of five major types of risks: cargo fire, health hazards, water pollution, atmospheric pollution and product reactivity.

The Code assigns a type of ship (I, II or III) for each of the listed products. These types correspond to decreasing danger criteria for each chemical.

Several provisions ensure protection of the ship in the event of collision or grounding. These include the position of the tanks in relation to the ship side shell, buoyancy and damage stability criteria, and limitation on the quantity of cargo carried in tanks.

(36) IMO New, N° 3, 1992, 1.
(37) - Ch. BARRAS : " Classification appraisal of chemical tankers ". Marichem Conference, Amsterdam, November 1995.
(38) OECD, IMO, UNEP : " Workshop on chemical safety in port areas ". Naantali, Finland, 18-21 Oct. 1993.

b) Amendments to BCH Code

The Code was drawn up in a hurry, and this explains many loopholes and imperfections. The MSC tried to correct these with no fewer than ten series of amendments adopted between 1972 and 1983, bringing about many improvements. In 1978, several measures were introduced in order to accelerate implementation of the Code and settle problems with existing ships. In 1980, criteria were defined for assessing the risks presented by bulk chemicals, and guidelines set for the uniform application of survival requirements. In 1983, IMO made the BCH Code mandatory, by incorporating it in the new chapter VII of the SOLAS Convention. Finally, in 1985, the MEPC inserted a new chapter in the BCH Code, containing new requirements on pollution (39).

4. IBC Code

390. - Another IMO measure on the same subject is the International Code for the construction and equipment of ships carrying dangerous chemicals in bulk (IBC Code). This Code, similar to the IGC Code for gas carriers, comprises the provisions of the ten series of amendments to the initial BCH Code, and other improvements.

In adopting the IBC Code in 1982, the MSC decided that it would apply only to new ships built on or after 12 July 1986, while existing ships would remain subject on a voluntary basis to the requirements of the original BCH Code. The IBC Code was incorporated into chapter VII of the SOLAS Convention and became mandatory. Regulation 10 of this chapter states that a chemical tanker ship must meet the requirements of the IBC Code.

Major amendments were made in 1985, in order to extend the scope of the Code to cover pollution (40).

5. International Nuclear Fuels (INF) Code

391. - The IMDG Code, which applies International Atomic Energy Agency (IAEA) regulations for the transport of radioactive materials, does not contain any standards for the design and equipment of ships carrying radioactive waste. To fill in this gap, IMO Resolution A.748 of 4 November 1993 (41) adopted the Code for the safe carriage of irradiated nuclear fuel, plutonium and high-level radioactive waste in flasks on board ships (INF Code). This initiative also corresponded to the intentions of paragraph 17.22 of Agenda 21 of the UN Conference in Rio (UNCED), which had encouraged IMO and IAEA to collaborate on this issue (42).

The INF Code applies to both new and existing ships, regardless of size, and including small vessels of less than 500 gross tonnage, carrying irradiated nuclear fuels, plutonium and high-level radioactive waste in approved flasks. These ships are divided into three classes, depending on the total quantity of radioactivity authorised on board. For each class, provisions exist for damage stability, fire protection, hold temperature control, structure, means of stowing the cargo, electricity supply, radioprotection equipment, training and emergency plans.

(39) IMO. BCH Code. Code for the Construction and Equipment of Ships Carrying Dangerous Chemicals in Bulk". 1993 Edition, London.

(40) IMO. IBC Code. International Code for the Construction and Equipment of Ships Carrying Dangerous Chemicals in Bulk including Index of Dangerous Chemicals carried in bulk. 1994 Edition, London.

(41) R. PED ROZO : "Transport of nuclear cargoes by sea". Journal of Maritime Law and Commerce, vol. 28, n° 2, April 1997, 207-236.

(42) " After Rio : What happened to Agenda 21 ? ". IMO News, n° 1, 1994, 10.

Amendment of the INF Code was undertaken in Resolution A.790 of 12 December 1995. In March 1996, the Secretary-General of IMO called a special consultative meeting of all entities concerned by the INF Code. Thirteen countries made a statement on the need to make application of the Code mandatory (43). The MSC considered and approved the proposal in June 1997, and asked the DSC subcommittee to prepare amendments to chapter VII of the SOLAS Convention (44).

The European Commission is attempting to make the requirements of the Code compulsory. In November 1996, it produced a draft directive aimed at incorporating the whole INF Code into EU legislation (45).

IV - SAFETY OBLIGATIONS FOR THE TRANSPORT OF DANGEROUS GOODS BY SEA

392. - Who is answerable for the safety obligations applying to transport of dangerous goods by sea ? According to international regulations, three particular protagonists are concerned : the shipper of the dangerous goods, the shipowner-operator, and the shipmaster and crew.

A - SHIPPER'S OBLIGATIONS

In general, the shipper must provide the master of the ship with appropriate information on the cargo sufficiently in advance of loading to enable the precautions which may be necessary for proper stowage and safe carriage of the cargo to be put into effect (cf SOLAS Convention, chapter VI, Part A, Regulation 2).

For dangerous goods, the shipper must supply several documents at the time of shipment: a shipping manifest giving essential information on the risks presented by the goods to be carried, a packing certificate for containers, or bill of lading for road vehicles, stating that the goods have been properly loaded and secured. Information supplied by the shipper must also comprise a signed certificate or statement showing that the goods have been correctly packaged (cf SOLAS Convention, Regulation VII.5).

According to the IMDG Code, section 12, shippers of dangerous goods in packages must use approved containers complying with the CSC Convention of 1972. These packagings must be strong and properly maintained. The Code also recommends a visual inspection of containers used to carry dangerous goods, to detect any damage, and not filling damaged containers.

B - SHIPOWNER-OPERATOR'S OBLIGATIONS

393. - Every ship carrying dangerous goods must be in possession of a list, a special bill of lading and/or a stowage plan, enumerating the goods on board and stating the place of stowage. Before departure, the port State is supplied with copies of these documents (cf SOLAS Regulation VII.5)

In the case of marine pollutants, the shipowner must keep on land a copy of the document stating the total quantity of each dangerous substance or article being carried, as well as

---

(43) " Meeting held on INF Code ". IMO News, n° 3, 1996, 17-18.
(44) IMO. MSC 68/23, 12 June 1997, 15.14 and 15.15.
(45) " Europe to enforce IMO nuclear code ". Lloyd's List, 16 Nov. 1996.

a description of the containers used for transport, and their locations (cf IMDG Code, general introduction to section 9).

Before accepting a cargo for transport, the owner must obtain all necessary information. The Code of safe practice for cargo stowage and securing recommends a special check that the various goods to be loaded are compatible with one another, or are adequately separated, that the cargo is suitable for transport on the ship, that the ship is fit to carry the cargo, and that the cargo is safely stowed and secured, in accordance with the IMO Code (cf Resolution A.714 of 6 November 1991).

C - MASTER'S AND CREW OBLIGATIONS

394. - There is one overriding principle in all regulations: the shipmaster remains responsible for the safety of his ship, the crew and its cargo. Certain recommendations concerning stowage and obligations as to notification follow on from this principle.

a) Stowage recommendations

The IMO Code makes various recommendations to the master. He should accept the cargo on board his ship only if he is satisfied that it can be transported in complete safety (cf section 1.5.3). He should be provided with appropriate information on the cargo to be carried, so that proper plans may be made for stowage, as regards both handling and transport (cf section 1.9.2).

The master must take great care in planning and supervising stowage and securing of the cargo, to prevent it sliding, tipping, racking or collapsing (cf section 2.2.1). He is also advised to attend closely to loading operations, and inspect stowage in port, and as much as practicable during the voyage (cf section 2.6). The master should ensure that the equipment needed to secure the cargo is on board the ship and in good working order (cf section 2.8). Finally, he is to refuse any cargo if the packing certificate for the container or vehicle is unavailable (cf section 2.9).

b) Obligations to report events at sea

These obligations are defined in a new Regulation 7.1 of chapter VII of the SOLAS Convention. If any event causes or might cause loss overboard of packages of dangerous goods, the master must immediately send the closest coastal State a report with all available details on the circumstances.

If the ship is abandoned, or when the report is incomplete or impossible to obtain, the owner, charterer, shipmanager, operator or their agent must assume the master's obligations as far as is practicable.

CONCLUSION : Harmful effects of optional regulations

395. - Three comments may be made in concluding this chapter.
1. Carriage of dangerous goods is covered by a large number of technical provisions, which are both precise and diversified. Nearly every substances has been regulated by the industry, within a standard-setting framework developed by international organisation, particularly IMO (46).

(46) E. GOLD : " Legal aspects of the transportation of dangerous goods at sea ". Marine Policy, July 1996, 185-191.

2. These provisions are also applied in widely varying ways. The reason is to be sought in the diverse nature of the regulations (47). Containers carrying dangerous goods are subject to compulsory technical regulations established by the SOLAS, MARPOL and CSC International Conventions, codes, guidelines, non-compulsory codes of practice adopted by IMO (IMDG Code), and purely private standards (ISO), implementation of which is left to the initiative of the transport industry.

3. This huge variety of references leaves States considerable freedom in applying regulations. This is the area of "soft law", recommendations, advice, optional provisions, giving priority to flexibility over strict application. The law is consequently incomplete and unfocussed, incapable of meeting the modern requirements of safety at sea and environmental protection.

Gaps in international law leave the door open to regional initiatives (48) and unilateral measures. As regards regulations, the European Union has no hesitation in making this soft law on safety at sea binding on member countries of the Union, by means of compulsory directives.

For example, the Directive of 13 September 1993, which came into force two years later, laid down regulations on minimum information to be supplied by shippers, owners and masters of ships carrying dangerous or polluting goods.

396. - Finally, a strengthening of port inspections is likely. Several inquiries now in progress have shown the need to improve inspection procedures :

- In 1990, an initial study carried out in German ports showed that of 2 910 containers inspected, 782 had defective markings, 219 packing certificates were not in line with regulations, 619 containers displayed loading errors. Furthermore, more than 75 per cent of the vehicles inspected showed deficiencies (49).
- Another study carried out by the US Coast Guard in 1993 provided similar findings: 25 per cent of intermodal freight containers moving through the ports of New York and Los Angeles failed to comply with standards (50).
- Spot checks on containers, under the term of MSC circular 694, which came into effect in June 1995, produced surprising results: of 885 containers in Sweden carrying dangerous goods, 43.3 per cent showed deficiencies, while the proportion was 45 per cent in Japan and 75 per cent in Canada (51).

Inspections may be stepped up under new provisions, such as the MARPOL Convention amendments, which since March 1996 have allowed port states to check the ability of crews to perform on-board procedures to prevent pollution, or the EU Directive which came into force in July 1996 concerning ways of targetting port inspections on ships regarded as dangerous.

---

(47) A. CHIRCOP : " The marine transportation of hazardous and dangerous goods in the law of the sea. An emerging regime ". Dalhousie Law Journal. Vol. 11, N° 2, March 1988, 612-638.
(48) M. GREY : " Dangerous goods by sea - recognizing the hazards". BIMCO Bulletin, Vol. 90, n° 1, Feb. 1994, 15-16.
(49) " That insecure feeling ". Hazardous Cargo Bulletin, Oct. 1992, 18-21.
(50) IMO. Sub Committee on the carriage of dangerous goods. " USCG container inspection program ". Submitted by the United States. CDG 45/INF 10, 19 Nov. 1993.
(51) " Dangerous box blunders set alarm bells ringing at IMO ". Lloyd's List, 6 May 1997.

CHAPTER 16

The human element
and safety management

397. - For more than twenty years, there has been general agreement on the overriding importance of the human factor in safety at sea (1). Official figures for shipping casualties, insurance reports and port authority observations already confirmed in 1975 that human error (2) was the principal cause of about 80 per cent of all accidents (3).

It might therefore be concluded that measures taken by the maritime community to prevent accidents would have targetted this factor. Nothing of the sort is true. The safety programmes implemented by international organisations, States and the maritime industry in general have devoted about 80 per cent of available resources to technical and technological solutions, leaving only 20 per cent for issues related to human beings (4).

This is an odd paradox of the maritime safety system, aware that the greatest improvements are available at a human level, but still concentrating on standards for ships and their equipment.

However important they may be, technological innovations have not prevented disasters at sea. Neither double hulls, nor high-tensile steels, nor sophisticated fire-prevention systems, nor shipboard electronics, can guarantee safety. In certain cases, it has even been found that technological advances may lead to increased risk of accident, because of the increased complexity of the man/machine interface. Safety remains a human issue, and a human solution has to be found to safety problems.

This chapter will deal with the fundamental role played by the human element in the occurrence and avoidance of accidents (cf I below). It will attempt to explain what is involved in the expression "human factors" in maritime transport (II). Finally, the solutions adopted by IMO, in particular the ISM Code, will be examined (III).

---

(1) " Optimum maritime safety demands a focus on people ". IMO. World Maritime Day 1997.
(2) U.S. Department of Commerce : "Human error in merchant marine safety". Maritime Transportation Research Board. Washington D.C., June 1976.
(3) " The industry and tanker accidents ". Safety at Sea, n° 129, Dec. 1979, 19-23.
(4) IMO. "Role of the human element in maritime casualties". Submitted by the United States. MSC 65/15/1. 10 Feb. 1995.

I - PERSISTENCE OF THE HUMAN FACTOR IN ACCIDENTS AT SEA

A - HUMAN FACTOR AS A CAUSE OF MARITIME DISASTERS

398. - The human factor has played a decisive role in four recent disasters in the history of navigation.

1. *Herald of Free Enterprise*

The tragic accident to the *Herald of Free Enterprise* on 6 March 1987, in which 195 people died, resulted in an official British inquiry, carried out by Lord Justice Sheen. Its report into the causes of the disaster was published on 24 July 1987 (5).

This report left no doubt about the cause of the disaster. The carferry was overloaded and no doubt ballasted in the bows when it left the port of Zeebrugge with its bow doors wide open. The water rushed unhindered into the vehicle deck, quickly destabilising and capsizing the ship.

Three men were accused of negligence. Captain David Lewry should have checked that all the proper procedures had been carried out before setting sail. The first officer, Leslie Sabel, failed to check that the sailor responsible for closing the bow doors was at his post before leaving the vehicle deck. This was the assistant bosun, Mark Stanley, who had fallen asleep in his cabin at the time of departure. Criticism was also levelled, without their responsibilities being involved directly, at assistant bosun T. Ayling, for having too narrow a view of his tasks, and the senior master John Kirby, who had not taken account of instructions issued by the company in 1984.

The inquiry also considered that the shipping company, Townsend Thoresen, was at fault at all levels, from the board of directors to management staff. The directors had never really understood their responsibilities for safety, while management had never really realised its duties. The company was run with a clear lack of professionalism, with a *laissez-faire* policy that had led to the rejection of several requests from shipmasters asking for the installation of safety equipment, and stricter supervision of the number of passenger and weight of the freight on board.

2. *Exxon Valdez*

399. - The biggest oil spill in United States history was caused by a series of operational and navigational errors committed on board the *Exxon Valdez*, which ran aground off the Alaskan coast on 24 March 1989.

Shortly after the tanker left the Alyeska terminal, Captain Joseph Hazelwood decided to move out of the compulsory traffic lanes in Prince William Sound, because of drift ice. He handed over control of the ship to a third mate unqualified to be in charge on the bridge. Following a navigational error, the *Exxon Valdez* ran aground on Bligh Reef, tearing its hull and spilling 40 000 tonnes of crude oil into the sea (6). Nine hours after the accident, the National Transport Safety Board (NTSB) carried out alcohol tests on the ship personnel. Results for Captain Hazelwood were over the limit (7).

---

(5) -Department of Transport : " Formal investigation on mv Herald of Free Enterprise ". Report of the Court n° 8674. London HMSO 1987.
- S. CRAINER : " Zeebrugge : Learning from disaster ". Herald Charible Trust, London, 1993.
See also Lloyd's List, 25 July 1987.
(6) R. CAHILL : " Disaster at sea. Titanic to Exxon Valdez ". Century, London 1990, 214-228.
(7) " Exxon sacks masters for alcohol abuse ". Lloyd's List, 1 April 1989.

During the inquiry carried out by the NTSB, the company Exxon Shipping stated that the oil spill was the result of a human error by the third officer Gregory Cousins, who had delayed bringing the ship back into the traffic lane. At the same hearing, the State of Alaska recognised that the accident was the outcome of human and organisational failure. Clearly, the captain had been negligent, but Exxon itself had also been very deficient in safety management on board the ship (8).

3. Scandinavian Star

400. - On 7 April 1990, the carferry *Scandinavian Star* was swept by fire shortly after it came into service on the route between Oslo and Frederikshavn. 158 people died in the accident, and criminal investigations were opened by the Danish public prosecutor. After twenty months' inquiries, three people were charged, the shipmaster Hugo Larsen, the operator O. Hansen, manager of the shipping company Da No Lines, and the shipowner H. Johansen (9).

In a lengthy report published in January 1991, an inquiry commission led by the Copenhagen maritime and commercial court concluded that the ferry was not operationally fit to carry passengers when brought into service on 1st April 1990. The master was criticised for abandoning ship, before doing everything in his power to save the passengers. More important, the inquiry revealed the numerous shortcomings of the shipping line, notably the mixed crew, recruited too quickly, unable to familiarise themselves with the ship in one week, and not having had time to carry out fire drill (10).

4. Braer

401. - On 5 January 1993, the tanker *Braer* ran aground and broke up on rocks in the Shetland Islands, releasing its cargo of 84 700 tonnes of oil into the sea. The accident led to the publication of three reports, published on 20 January 1994: two concerning the causes of the shipwreck, by the British Marine Accident Investigation Branch (MAIB) and the Liberian maritime administration, and the third by the British Marine Pollution Control Unit, on the oil pollution issue (11).

These documents aimed sharp criticism at the behaviour of the Greek shipmaster Alexandros Gelis who, according to the British report, had been guilty of several forms of negligence. He had failed in his duty to preserve the seaworthiness of his vessel by taking no steps to secure or jettison the pipes carried on deck. Neither had he opposed the fact that the whole crew had crowded on to the bridge, abandoning the main spaces, and in particular the engine room (12).

---

(8) National Transportation Safety Board Marine Accident Report : Grounding of the U.S. tankship Exxon Valdez on Bligh Reef, Prince William Sound, March 24, 1989. Washington DC, 31 July 1990.
(9) " Tragedy could lead to improved safety on ferries ". Lloyd's List, 6 April 1991.
(10) Norwegian Official Reports : The Scandinavian Star disaster of 7 April 1990. Main Report. Oslo. Government Printing Service, 1991.
(11) " Braer spill caused by series of failings ". Lloyd's List, 21 Jan. 1994.
(12) Department of Transport. Marine Accident Investigation Branch " Report of the chief inspector of Marine Accidents into the engine failure and subsequent grounding of the motor tanker Braer at Garths Ness, Shetland on 5 January 1993.

The report of the Liberian Bureau of Maritime Affairs emphasised the communication difficulties between the master and the Shetland Coast Guard concerning the need for towage. The grounding was not caused by a lack of professional competence, but by faulty reporting in the command chain, and by the inability to select priorities in the information available or examine the consequences of events (13).

Finally, certain commentators (14) consider that the shipowner could also be criticised for negligence in ship management practices and training of navigators, particularly officers.

B - RESEARCH INTO HUMAN FACTOR

402. - Since the early Nineties, there has been an amazing proliferation of reports and studies on the subject of the human factor. To allow these documents to be consulted, the USCG asked the United States National Technical Information Service in 1996 to develop a comprehensive database on the human element (15). The most important sources of information are mentioned below.

• United Kingdom DoT
In 1980, the British Department of Transport entrusted the first research into the influence of human factors in casualties in accidents to the Tavistock Institute of Human Relations (16), which issued its final report in 1988 (17). It revealed that 90 per cent of collisions and 75 per cent of fires and explosions occurring in the British merchant fleet between 1970 and 1979 were caused by human error.

The Marine Directorate of the Department of Transport used these findings as a basis for a general guide to the subject in 1991 (18).

• Australian DTC
The Australian Department of Transport & Communication reported in 1992 that almost three quarters of the accidents investigated over the previous ten years were due to human error, and only 25 per cent to mechanical or structural failures (19).

• USCG
In 1992, the United States Coast Guard launched a research programme into human factors in five areas: manning, qualifications and diplomas ; design of automatic systems; communication ; safety data and procedures ; organisational practices.

---

(13) Republic of Liberia. Bureau of Maritime Affairs. Report of investigation into the matter of the loss by grounding of the motor tanker Braer on the South coast of Shetlands. 5 Jan. 1993, Monrovia, 1994.

(14) D. STRATTON : " Shipboard management ; Human element and leadership ". FCIT, AMIQA, Cormacs Ltd, London, 1995.

(15) IMO. Role of the human element in maritime casualties. Report of the Correspondance Group. Submitted by the United States. MSC 67/12/3, 12 Sept. 1996.

(16) P.T. QUINN et S.M. SCOTT : " The human element in shipping casualties ". 4 volumes. The Tavistock Institute of Human Relations. London, July 1982.

(17) D.T. BRYANT, A. DE BIEVRE, M. DYER-SMITH : " The human element in shipping casualties, Phase II". The Tavistock Institute of Human Relations. London, August 1988

(18) D.T. BRYANT : " The human element in shipping casualties ". Marine Directorate, Department of Transport, HMSO, London, 1991.

(19) " Australians go after cause of bulker losses ". Tradewinds, 4 September 1992.

Three years later, a report and accident figures were published for the period 1983 to 1993 for American ships (20) and pollution (21). These showed that more than 80 per cent of all accidents with serious consequences could be attributed directly or indirectly to human error.

• West of England

A survey published in 1992 of 811 compensation claims submitted to the West of England P&I Club between 1987 and 1992 showed that 65 per cent of accidents were due to human error, mainly dangerous practices by the crew, alone responsible for nearly a quarter of insurance claims (22).

• German ISL

In a study carried out in 1994, the Institute of Shipping Economics and Logistics analysed 330 accidents occurring between 1987 and 1991, concerning 481 merchant ships. It emerged that 75 per cent of these accidents were due to two factors: heavy workloads for the crew, particularly in port, and inadequate specialised training (23).

• Canadian TSB

According to the Canadian Transportation Safety Board, 84 to 88 per cent of tanker accidents occurring between 1975 and 1992 were caused by human factors (24).

• UK P&I Club

This P&I Club has for several years been carrying out statistical analyses of the compensation claims submitted to it. The analysis carried out in 1992 (25) showed that 60 per cent of accidents in general were due to human error, and that this was also instrumental in 50 per cent of claims for cargo loss and damage, 65 per cent of bodily lesion claims, 50 per cent of pollution damage claims, and 90 per cent of all claims following collisions.

In a report written in collaboration with the Southampton Institute of Maritime Law (26), the UK Club showed that active crew management policies (AMP) were an increasingly important factor in raising standards and the efficient operation of ships.

C - HUMAN FACTOR ACTION PROGRAMMES

403. - The maritime industry, States and international organisations now include a certain number of measures to do with the human element in their action programmes.

1. Maritime industry

Since 1990, the rules of several classification societies have included human and operational aspects of maritime safety, and no longer solely technical requirements (27). Certain

(20) Department of Transportation. US Coast Guard : " Prevention through people ". Quality action team report, July 15, 1995. Washington DC, appendix G.
(21) IMO. " US casualty and pollution data ". MSC 65/INF 5, 10 Feb. 1995.
(22) West of England. Annual Review 1992. London, 34-35.
(23) " Study highlights human error in accidents ". Lloyd's Ship Manager, March 1993, 11.
(24) Transportation Safety Board. Working paper on tankers involved in shipping accidents 1975-1992. Canada, Dec 1994.
(25) UK Pand I Club : " Analysis of major claims 1993 ". London, 1993.
(26) UK Pand I Club : " The human factor. A report of Manning ". London, 1996, 5-6.
(27) Action on standards as risks take on new dimensions ". Lloyd's List, 9 April 1991.

emphasise the effective enforcement of standards (28), while others consider classification within a total safety approach (29); still others try to understand better the interplay between men and technology (30).

At the 1993 annual IUMI conference, insurers expressed concern about the decline in the quality of crewing, and tried to make shipowners more vigilant in this area (31).

Some have seen the development of quality management methods as a way of improving safety: in theory, a shipping company whose management is organised along quality lines has recognised means of meeting its safety obligations (32).

Problems both of image (33) and of safety (34) in 1989 led ship management companies to adopt a quality procedure.

This movement, initiated by five large management companies (35), culminated in the establishment in 1990 of a Code of ship management standards (36). This Code was published in 1991, and it provided the foundation of the International Ship Manager Association (ISMA), which as soon as it was set up obliged its 35 members to apply a quality assurance system (37).

The quality trend affected other maritime sectors. Shipyards, equipment manufacturers, shipowners and classification societies discovered the virtues of ISO certification (38). More than a passing fashion, the quality trend has brought about profound changes in the managerial ideology of companies, leading them to acknowledge the benefits of self-regulation, and promote an internal safety culture within their organisations (39).

2. National administrations

404. - Maritime administrations now emphasise the human factor in prevention programmes. In a survey carried out in 1992, the MAIB denounced the lack of basic seamanship as the main cause of many accidents (40).

In 1993, the Japan Maritime Research Institute (JAMRI) invited the whole maritime industry to rethink safety around the human element (41).

In 1994, the USCG launched its ambitious "Prevention Through People" programme, and set up a discussion group to study how to improve safety and pollution prevention by applying solutions based on the human factor (42).

An application of the systems theory was carried out by the promoters of this programme, by a human element risk analysis (43).

(28) T.C MATHIESEN : "Implementation of rules and regulations". BIMCO Bulletin, June 1993, 14.
(29) P de LIVOIS : "Total Safety Concept". Bulletin Technique du Bureau Veritas, n° 2, June 1994, 5-11.
(30) "Human error plays major role in accidents". Lloyd's List, 16 Oct. 1995.
(31) "Hull insurers worry about crews". Lloyd's Ship Manager, Nov. 1993, 47.
(32) -"The management of safety in shipping". The Nautical Institute, London 1991.
- A.M. CHAUVEL : "Managing safety and quality in shipping. The key to success. A guide to ISM, ISO 9000, TQM". The Nautical Institute, London, 1997.
(33) J. SPRUYT : "Code of ship management standards of the ISMA". The Nautical Institute on the management of safety in shipping, London 1991, 28-29.
(34) "Managing the managers". Tradewinds, 23 April 1993.
(35) - "Is the Five really dead ?". Lloyd's List, 5 July 1991.
(36) "Group of Five publishes ship management code". Lloyd's List, 28 Dec. 1990.
(37) "ISMA committed to high standard". Lloyd's List, 2 May 1991.
(38) - "Quest for quality". MER, Jan. 1995, 17-20.
- "Long term advantages outweigh short term costs". Lloyd's List, 27 July 1994, 7.
(39) J. HUGHES : "Internal safety management systems controls". BIMCO Bulletin, vol 90, n° 4, 1995, 21-24.
(40) "MAIB criticises seamanship". Loyd's List, 24 Dec 1992.
(41) JAMRI : "Analysis of world/Japan shipping casualties and future prospects thereof". Tokyo, 1993.
(42) "Preparing to tackle the main cause of accidents". Lloyd's List, 5 December 1994.
(43) "Prevention through People". Appendix I, A system approach to human element risk analysis. MSC 65/INF.4, Feb. 1995.

3. IMO

405. - For several years, IMO has focussed its efforts on the human aspects of safety at sea. Apart from the ISM Code and the STCW Convention, which will be examined below, several other initiatives are worth mentioning (44).

• Joint IMO/ILO action

In 1964, IMO and ILO set up a joint committee on training, which led to the first recommendations on seafarers (cf chapter 17 below).

A joint IMO/ILO committee of experts on fatigue met in 1993 and 1994, to draw up the main provisions of the 1995 STCW Convention dealing with this issue.

In 1996, a special IMO/ILO working group was set up to investigate human factors in maritime casualties (45). It was given the brief of drafting guidelines on the subject (46).

• Joint MSC/MEPC actions

In 1992, the principal technical committees of IMO, the MSC and the MEPC, decided to set up a joint working group on the role of the human factors in maritime casualties (47). The work of the group included preparing a draft resolution laying down human element principles and goals for IMO (48), another draft resolution on guidelines on the structure of an integrated planning system for emergency situations on board ships (49), and the preparation of a manual or handbook of IMO requirements for seafarers (50). At present, two MSC/MEPC joint working groups are trying to apply formal safety assessment (FSA) and human element methods to the process of drawing up IMO regulations (51).

• FSI subcommittee

The Flag State Implementation subcommittee has been commissioned to set up an accident database (52). It has also undertaken to classify human elements, combined with a definition of such elements connected with maritime casualties (cf chapter 21 below).

• STW subcommittee

The subcommittee on Standards of Training & Watchkeeping (STW) plays a major role in this area. Its agenda includes use of drugs and abuse of alcohol, simulator training, communication problems on board ship, sensitisation to handling of dangerous cargoes, and arrangement of navigation bridge instruments.

---

(44) W. O'NEIL : " Responsibility to the human element ". Surveyor. Sept. 1996, n° 3, 4-5.
(45) IMO. MSC 66/13/7, 29 March 1996, MSC 66/24, par. 13.18, 18 June 1996.
(46) IMO. HF WG 1, 15 Jan. 1997.
(47) IMO. Report of the Joint MSC/MEPC Working Group. MSC 60/WP.9, 9 April 1992.
(48) IMO. MSC 67/12/3, 12 Sept 1996.
(49) IMO. MSC 66/13/5, 1st March 1996.
(50) IMO. MSC 67/12, 23 July 1996.
(51) IMO. MSC 68/23, 12 June 1997, par. 13.11 - 13.13..
(52) IMO. FSI 4/18, 5.19 and MSC 67/6/2, 12 Sept. 1996.

II - GENERAL HUMAN ELEMENT CONCEPTS

A - DEFINITION

406. - Except in rare cases of *force majeure*, there is nearly always a human action behind every navigational incident or accident.

Human error is not confined to the areas where individuals intervene directly. Many accidents at sea produced by technical or structural failures originate in lack of maintenance of equipment on board, or carelessness in their manufacture. Both can be attributed to human failings. This can occur at any stage in the life of a ship, at the design stage (53), during construction or in operation (54).

Another common idea needs to be corrected. Human error is not necessarily a fault for which a guilty person has to be found. Factors such as fatigue, overwork or economic pressures may colour the judgement of a competent, well-trained individual; and may themselves contribute to the mistake (55).

With the intention of clarifying matters, IMO defines expressions relating to the human element. "Human error", for instance, is " a departure from acceptable or desirable practice on the part of an individual or group of individuals that can result in unacceptable or undesirable results» (56).

For the USCG, the term "human factors" is defined as "the study and analysis of the design of the equipment, the interaction of the equipment and the human operator, and most importantly the procedures the crew and management follow" (57).

In this semantic approach, it is important to have an overall vision of problems. Many systems need to be taken into consideration in order to define the human element: individual qualities, social conditions, regulations, ship condition, health and culture (58).

B - CLASSIFICATION OF HUMAN FAILINGS

407. - Classifications of human failings have been drawn up on the basis of accident inquiry reports. There is no uniform method of collecting shipping data, making it difficult to analyse causes involving the human factor. This diversity of approaches and definitions has led to a wide variety of taxonomies to classify human errors, only the IMO example of which will be discussed here.

In the accident database which IMO is currently engaged in establishing, a major place has been kept for elementary data relating to human factors (59). Current programming defines nine categories of causes and factors relating to persons :
- human error within the organisation to which the ship belongs ;
- human error within the pilot organisation ;
- human error within other organisations ;

(53) Ship Structure Committee : " The role of human error in design, construction, and reliability of marine structures ". Washington, 1er Nov. 1994, SSC-378.
(54) K. MITCHELL : " Minimising the potential for human error in ship operation ". Paper 17, IMAS 1995. The institute of Marine Engineers.
(55) UK Pand I Club : " Analysis of major claims 1993 ". London, 1993, 12.
(56) IMO. Human Element Taxonomy. MSC 67/12/3, 12 Sept. 1996, Annex 3.
(57) OMI. MSC 65/15/1, 10 Feb. 1995, Annex I, par. 4.
(58) D. STRATTON : " Tanker and bulker accidents ". Safety at Sea International, May 1993, 23-24.
(59) IMO. FSI. Report of the Working Group on Casualty Statistics and Investigation. 19 March 1996, Annex 1.

- external bodies liaison factors ;
- company and organisational factors ;
- crew factors ;
- equipment factors ;
- working environment and workplace factors ;
- individual factors such as competence, training, knowledge and skill, health and risk perception.

IMO has also worked out a classification system intended to divide into different categories the human failings and organisational faults that have contributed to an accident.

III - INTERNATIONAL SAFETY MANAGEMENT CODE

408. - The International Safety Management (ISM) Code is undoubtedly one of the major innovations of the end of the 20th century in the area of safety at sea. It illustrates the determination of the international community to learn from major maritime disasters, particularly those that reflect the effects of human factors in navigation.

The importance and originality of the ISM Code justify the scale of the research devoted to it. The following description examines in turn the origin of the Code, its contents, its application and its effects on transport.

A - ORIGIN OF ISM CODE

409. - The ISM Code adopted by IMO in November 1993 is the result of long efforts to introduce consideration of the human factor into maritime safety regulations. Two fatal accidents, to the *Herald of Free Enterprise* and the *Scandinavian Star*, accelerated the standardisation trend that had begun in the late Eighties.

1. Consequences of *Herald of Free Enterprise* and Resolution A.647

Within a few months of the Zeebrugge tragedy, IMO attempted to introduce international standards for ship safety management (61). Resolution A.596 of November 1987 entrusted its main technical committees, MSC and MEPC, to draw up urgent guidelines for shipboard and shore-based management for the safe operation of ships and prevention of marine pollution (62).

The MSC/MEPC working group succeeded quite quickly in drawing up Guidelines on management for the safe operation of ships and for pollution prevention, which were adopted in October 1989 by Resolution A.647. Although these were no more than recommendations, they marked a turning point in the way of controlling safety problems in general (63). For the first time, the basic principles that shipowners should observe in managing their ships were solemnly proclaimed.

(60) An extensive bibliography on the ISM Code has been drawn up by IMO Library. Information Services. Information sheet n° 22, 14 July 1998.

(61) " IMO confronts human element issue in new guidelines ". Lloyd's List, 29 Sept. 1988.

(62) T. FUNDER : " The background of the international safety management code ". BIMCO courses, Copenhagen, April 1996.

(63) J. COWLEY : "The ISM Code - Its development and implementation". Republic of Vanuatu. Maritime Bulletin". August 1995.

2. Consequences of *Scandinavian Star* and Resolution A.680

Six months later, another disaster affecting another passenger ship, the *Scandinavian Star*, led IMO to review its position. The accident inquiry commission recommended that Resolution A.647 should be made mandatory for all passenger ships engaged on international voyages. The suggestion was adopted by five Nordic States, which, at the 55th session of the MSC in May 1991, proposed that the safety management system should be made mandatory, that means of overseeing the system should be devised, and that ISO 9000 standards should be used as the reference (64).

The IMO working group did not manage to integrate these proposals into the revised Resolution A.647. In November 1991, the IMO Assembly adopted Resolution A.680, which unfortunately made only minor amendments in the regulations.

3. Resolution A.741

Three other meetings of the working party were needed between April 192 and May 1993 to produce a text acceptable to all delegations. On 4 November 1993, the IMO Assembly finally adopted Resolution A.741, containing the International Management Code for the Safe Operation of Ships and for Pollution Prevention, to be known as the International Safety Management (ISM) Code (65). The MSC and MEPC were also asked to take urgent action to prepare guidelines for application of the Code. These were adopted by the Assembly in Resolution A.788 of 23 November 1995.

4. SOLAS Conference of May 1994

410. - At the 62nd session of the MSC in May 1993, it was accepted that, given the importance of the issue, a mere recommendation was insufficient to achieve the goals IMO had set itself . The resolution containing the ISM Code would have very little or no effect on poorly run companies operating substandard ships and using inadequate management techniques.

The requirements of the safety management system were made mandatory by the addition of a new chapter IX to the SOLAS Convention. The text was adopted in May 1994 by a diplomatic conference defining its scope of application and a timetable for its implementation (cf table 19).

Table 19 - Implementation of ISM Code according to type of ship

Implementation Date	Type of ship (new and existing)	Lower gross tonnage limit
1st July 1998	Passenger ships Passenger high speed craft	None
1st July 1998	Oil tankers Chemical carriers Gas carriers Bulk carriers Cargo high speed craft	500
1st July 2002	Other cargo ships Mobile offshore drilling units	500

(64) " Norway bids for greater safety at sea ". Lloyd's List, 10 April 1991.

(65) G. PATTOFATTO : " The IMO safety management code ". BIMCO Review 1994, 30-32.

5. EU regulations

411. - The tragedy of the *Estonia* led the European Union to speed up enforcement of the ISM Code. On 8 December 1995, the Council decided to make the Code mandatory for all ro-ro passenger ships not later than 1st July 1996, exactly two years before the date scheduled by IMO, with only two exceptions. An 18-month extension was granted for coastal traffic to the Greek islands, and transport operations performed by small companies in protected zones were exempted until 1st July 1997 (66).

B - ISM CODE RULES

412. - The ISM Code covers organisation and establishes specific procedures for shipping companies, in order to control the safe operation of ships and prevention of pollution (67).

1. Purposes

The Code sets out three main goals for safety management: "provide for safe practices in ship operation and a safe working environment; establish safeguards against all identified risks; and continuously improve safety management skills of personnel ashore and aboard ships, including preparing for emergencies related both to safety and environmental protection" (paragraph 1.2.2).

2. Means of safety management

These goals may be achieved by means of a safety management system (SMS), which the shipping company is responsible for establishing.

Paragraph 1.1.2 defines the company as "the owner of the ship or any other organisation or person such as the manager, or the bareboat charterer, who has assumed the responsibility for operaiton of the ship".

According to paragraph 1.2.3, the SMS should ensure "compliance with mandatory rules and regulations, and that applicable codes, guidelines and standards recommended by the organisation, administrations, classification societies and maritime industry organisations are taken into account".

3. Company obligations

413. - The SMS comprises a number of practical provisions, which may be summarised as follows. The company must :
- Establish and implement a safety and environmental protection policy that will allow the goals of the Code to be achieved.
- Issue instructions and procedures defining responsibilities, powers and mutual relations for all personnel in charge of management, performance and verification of safety-related activities. In particular, it must provide the necessary resources and appropriate support ashore, and ensure that a direct accountable person is designed. Each company should also designate a person or persons ashore having direct access to the highest level of management.

(66) Council Regulation (EC) N° 3051/95 JOCE, n° L320/14, 31 Dec. 1995.
(67) IMO. International Safety Management Code and Guidelines on the Implementation of the ISM Code. 1997 Edition, London.

- Set up an organisation and means of communication allowing shipboard personnel to communicate with one another and with personnel ashore. In the seniority organisation, a special place is reserved for the shipmaster's responsibilities. The company must state in the SMS that the highest authority for safety matters rests with the master of the ship. The Code also deals with other categories of mariners, and emphasises the important of their training.
- Establish plans and instructions for the main operations on board, and define procedures to meet all emergency situations that are likely to arise.
- Collect all the documents used to describe and implement the SMS in a Safety Management Manual, a copy of which must be kept aboard.

4. Practical arrangements

414. - Given the difficulties of understanding and implementing the new systems, several forms of training have been undertaken, to help with application of the ISM Code.

Numerous publications deal with the subject (68). The best-known is a collection of guidelines drawn up by the shipowner associations ICS and ISF (69), which provide useful advice on the important individual elements of an SMS and its introduction by companies.

Another useful source of documentation is the classification societies (70), some of which have also developed software packages to help with implementation of the ISM Code (71).

C - OVERSEEING IMPLEMENTATION OF ISM CODE

415. - The ISM Code lays new obligations, not only on shipping companies, but also on states responsible for overseeing its proper enforcement.

1. Flag State obligations

Three texts define the obligations of flag States: Regulation 4 of the new chapter IX of the SOLAS Convention, paragraph 13 of the ISM Code, and Resolution A.788 of 23 November 1995.

a) Control mechanisms

Enforcement of the ISM Code involves issue of two types of documents a document of compliance (DOC), delivered to any company that meets its requirements (cf paragraph 13.2), and which remains valid for five years, and a ship management certificate (SMC), also valid for five years, to ships certifying that company management and management aboard ship conform to the approved SMS (cf paragraph 13.4).

The controlling authority is usually the administration designated in the Code as "the government of the State whose flag the ship is entitled to fly" (paragraph 1.1.3). The DOC may also be delivered "by an organisation recognised by the administration or by the government of

(68) "New Guides assist compliance with ISM code". Lloyd's List, 3 June 1994.
(69) ICS/ISF Guidelines on the application of the IMO International Safety Management Code - in BIMCO Bulletin, n° 6, Nov./Dec. 1993.
(70)- Bulletin Technique du Bureau Veritas, Special issue on the human element, n° 2, 1995.
- Bureau Veritas. How to implement the ISM Code in your company. Paris, 1995.
(71) "Software on trial. Choose your ISM program with care". Fairplay, 22nd Jan. 1998, 20-23.

the country, acting on behalf of the administration in which the company has chosen to conduct its activities" (paragraph 13.2).

These provisions can raise serious practical difficulties, notably for shipowners that operate ships flying different flags. For example, a company may be registered as a local company in one state, and be operating one ship under flag X and another under flag Y, while two different recognised organisations A and B act respectively for the two flag administrations. This is not an exceptional situation in the maritime sector, and can lead to several problems (72).

IMO has decided not to accept the proposal for automatic recognition by administrations of DOCs issued by another authority. It considers that such recognition is a matter to be settled among sovereign States, by bilateral agreements. Section 13 of the Code stipulates that contracting governments are authorised to issue such a document of compliance only at the request of an administration (73).

b) Guidelines for administrations

416. - Aware of the need to apply the new ISO Code uniformly, IMO has developed Guidelines on implementation of the ISM Code by administrations. Devised by the FSI subcommittee, the draft document was adopted by the Assembly in Resolution A.788 of 23 November 1995 (74).

Although taking the form of simple recommendations, these guidelines contain certain provisions which should be incorporated in the Convention itself. For various reasons, this has not been possible, so that in fact they are regarded by the MSC as binding.

The IMO guidelines cover three main areas :
- Verification of conformity to the requirements of the Code. Establishing the conformity of the SMS relies on assessment criteria. The guidelines recommend limiting their number, and ensuring that assessments are carried out to determine the effectiveness of the system, rather than whether it meets regulatory requirements.
- Administrations must next respect certain rules in delivering documents. Their period of validity has been set at five years. For the SMC, an intermediate verification is needed. The administration may decide to increase this frequency when the SMC is in its initial phase. The same applies in the event of a major non-conformity, indicating absence of proper application of the Code.
- Finally, the guidelines cover the whole process of verification. There are three stages: initial, periodical and renewal verifications. These are carried out at the request of the company, and must include an SMS audit. The guidelines give advice on conducting such audits, writing reports and following up corrective actions. They lay down the obligations of a certification organisation, and of the verification team. They recommend the use of standardised printed forms for all the documents involved.

2. Powers delegated to recognised organisations

417. - According to Regulation IX.1 of the SOLAS Convention, the State may delegate its supervisory powers to an organisation recognised by the administration, provided that it meets the requirements of IMO Resolution A.739. This organisation may be authorised to make regular checks on the functioning of the ship's SMS, and deliver the corresponding

(72) IMO. Comments on the ISM Code submitted by Japan. In MSC 62/14/7, 23 March 1993.
(73) IMO. MSC 66/24, 18 June, par. 13.15 - 13.17.

certificates and statements. In most cases, the organisation will be a classification society (75), the largest of which have the resources needed to perform these tasks properly, such as an international network of surveyors, technical skills in the maritime sector, and proven experience of quality certification.(76)

Delegation is not systematic, however. Some States have reserved the right to keep certain operations under their direct control. In France, for example, safety management documents are issued by the administration (77). The same is true in the United Kingdom during the initial phase (78).

Other States have called in independent experts (79) or non-maritime certification organisations (80).

3. Role of IACS

418. - Aware of their new responsibilities, IACS members have introduced a number of measures to facilitate application of the code worldwide: 8 000 shipowners and operators are concerned. 18 700 ships had to be audited by 1st July 1998, and 20 700 by 1st July 2002 (81). In September 1995, IACS published procedural directives and a unified interpretation of the code, applicable on 1st January 1996 (82). These cover standards of competence and qualification of surveyors (83). Model courses have also been prepared for training of ISM auditors. In 1996, IACS set up a database accessible on the Internet, to provide information on SMCs delivered by its members and certain national administrations (84).

IACS has also always insisted on a clear separation between surveys and audits. It believes that the surveyors supplying advisory and technical assistance services must be independent of those delivering certification. Similarly, any confusion must be avoided between classification and statutory services relating to the safety of life at sea, under the terms of the ISM Code (85).

4. Port State control

419. - As part of its new responsibilities for control of operational standards, the port State must see to proper application of the ISM Code. The control mechanism is set out in Regulation IX/6.2 of the SOLAS Convention, which refers more specifically to the SMC. Control may also relate to the DOC, a copy of which has to be kept aboard ship for verification purposes, and the safety management manual (86).

(74) " Lassoing the cow-boys. The ISM code is coming ! " IMO News, n° 3, 1996, 11-13.
(75) " Classification bodies at the sharp end ". Lloyd's List, 26 May 1997.
(76) " IACS : Auditing the ISM code ". Seaways, August 1995, 4-6.
(77) G. CADET : " L'Administration et la gestion de la sécurité des navires ". Colloque IMTM, Marseille, 21 March 1995.
(78) " All change for safety's sake ". Lloyd Ship Manager, April 1995, 29-31.
(79) M. GREY : " Worrying again about that ISM code ". BIMCO Bulletin, volume 91, n° 1, 96, 4-5.
(80) " Who audits Panama ?". Fairplay 11th Dec. 1997, 36-38.
(81) " ISM code certification ". IACS Briefing, n° 3, Nov. 1996.
(82) - IACS : " Procedural guidelines for ISM Code certification ". 3rd Edition, In OMI FSI, 3/6/1.
- Cf also : " Safety code plan backed by IACS ". Lloyd's List, 8 Sept 1995.
(83) H. PAYER : "The ISM Code : Looking past compliance to its future impact". Connecticut Maritime Associat ion 1998, Stamford..
(84) " IACS data base ". Lloyd's List, 27 Sept. 1996.
(85) " ISM incentive ". Lloyd's Ship Manager, Feb 1997, 61.
(86) R. GRIME : " Legal framework of the code, responsibilities and liabilites ". BIMCO courses, Copenhagen April 1996.

Port authorities have several possibilities of action to reinforce application of the Code: targetting inspections by means of a specific questionnaire, detention in the event of non-conformity, banishing of the ship, pre-arrival ISM status check with arrival information (87).

D - LEGAL EFFECTS OF ISM CODE

420. - The same legal conditions apply to the ISM Code as to other IMO instruments. The flag State is responsible for complete performance and effectiveness of controls, and also assumes full responsibility for the certificate it delivers. In case of faults or negligence during certification operations and delivery of DOCs and SMCs, the administration or organisation recognised by it may by held liable. The same applies to the government of the country acting on behalf of the flag State in which the company has chosen to conduct its business, provided, of course, that it does not claim immunity from jurisdiction.

Following these preliminary remarks, the fact remains that the most important legal consequences affect the shipowner, who bears a general obligation to keep his ship seaworthy (88).

The Code does not make any radical change in the shipowner's legal obligations in this respect (89). It merely gives a new reading of such obligations, within the framework of greater transparency in shipping operations. The effects may be gauged on three levels: civil liability, criminal liability and insurance.

1. Civil liability

421. - Two situations need to be considered : the shipowner's liability during carriage of goods, and liability limitation regimes.

a) *Carriage of goods*

Article 3.1 of the Brussels Convention of 24 August 1924 for the unification of certain rules of law relating to bills of lading stipulates that "the carrier shall be bound before and at the beginning of the voyage to exercise due diligence to make the ship seaworthy ; properly man, equip and supply the ship".

Although the description in article 3 is not properly speaking a preventive safety rule, it tries to prevent any risk of an accident : Seaworthiness, as an essential condition for the performance of the maritime transport contract, becomes the shipowner's prime obligation. The owner bears liability for failure to respect this fundamental obligation (90).

Application of the ISM Code will mean significant changes in the shipping company's obligations concerning human factor aspects of seaworthiness. In case of loss or damage affecting the goods being transported, the shipowner's due diligence will be judged with a two-stage test. First, the content of the SMS is evaluated to ascertain whether it is capable of

(87) " ISM anticlimax ". " Port States take control". Fairplay 6 July 1998.
(88) R. COLINVAUX : "Carver's carriage by sea". Vol. 1, 13th Edition. London. Stevens and Sons, 105 et seq.
(89) E. PAPALEXIS : " The ISM Code - a positive force ". Lloyd's List, 14 Jan. 1997.
(90) S. GIRVIN : "Seaworthiness and the Hague - Visby Rules". IJSL : Part. 4, Dec. 1997, 201-209.

302   *The human element and safety management*

fulfilling its function; second, effective application of the system is examined, in other words practical measures taken to reach this goal. Failure to meet any one of these requirements could create great difficulties in proving that the company has demonstrated due diligence (91).

b) Limitation of liability

422. - The way of preventing the owner of a ship from limiting his liability for a claim is to prove that the event that generated the claim was caused by his "actual fault and privity". This is the meaning of article 1.1 of the Brussels Convention of 10 October 1957 relating to the Limitation of the Liability of Owners of Seagoing Ships, responsible in most cases for a managerial fault in ship maintenance, equipment, training or supplies. The ISM Code provides valuable help to claimants, in defining standards of managerial conduct by which the owner may be judged (92).

Article 4 of the 1976 Convention on Limitation of the Liability for Maritime Claims (LLMC) also defines the conduct that can invalidate such limitation: the damage must result from a personal act or omission, committed with the intent to cause such loss, or recklessly and with knowledge that such loss would probably result. The ISM Code offers new possibilities to anyone trying to remove the limitation, in particular the detailed record of ship operations and company acts or omissions. With the designation of a person onshore responsible for safety (93) and with access to the highest level of management, it will be very difficult for a shipowner to turn a blind eye to non-conformities in the SMS reported to him (94).

The only way for the owner to escape possible liability is to entrust the whole of his fleet to one or more maritime management companies, ensuring each time that the "designated person" communicates with the management and has no contact with his own technical services (95). This will result in a higher legal risk for management companies and for their managers, who could be exposed to unlimited liability (96).

In the particular case of pollution by oil or noxious and hazardous substances, the ISM Code could in the same way invalidate the shipowner's limitation of liability, provided for in the Conventions of 1969 and 1996.

2. Shipowner's criminal liability

423. - Under English criminal law, sections 98 and 100 of the 1993 Merchant Shipping Act, which complete sections 32 and 31 of the 1988 Act (97), treat as a crime the fact of sending an unseaworthy ship to sea, and operating an unsafe ship. A shipping company may be charged with manslaughter in the event of an accident. The House of Lords proceeds in this case with the "gross negligence" test, to define criminal conduct by the company or its mana-

(91) - G. PAMBORIDES : " The ISM Code : Potential legal implications ". International Maritime Law. Vol. 3, Issue 2 Feb. 1996, 56-62.
- R. WHITE : "The human factor in unseaworthiness claim". LMCLR, 1995, 221-239.
(92) D.G HEBDEN, C. SHEEHAN : " The duty of shipowners with regard to safety and pollution prevention ". Paper 4, IMAS 95 1995. The Institute of Marine Engineers.
(93) - G. PAMBORIDES : " Designated person role is key question in ISM Code ". Lloyd's List, 31 July 1996.
- R. SHAW : "The ISM Code and limitation of liability". IJSL, Part. 3, Sept. 1998, 169-172.
(94) I. ORMES : " Major implication of the ISM Code ". Lloyd's List, 29 Nov. 1995.
(95) D. HUGUES : " ISM Code opens shipmanagers to some big claims ". Lloyd's List, 8 May 1997.
(96) " Follow the paper trail. ISM promises windfall for lawyers ". Fairplay, 30 May 1996.
(97) S. HODGES : " Liabilities and penalties for unsafe ships ". The Nautical Institute. Management of safety, London 1991, 64-69.

gers. Could gross negligence by the designated person leave the company open to criminal charges ? English lawyers remain cautious about this interpretation, refusing any presumption of company liability unless it failed to take account of the reports submitted to it (98).

In the American Oil Pollution Act, the shipowner, operator and bareboat charterer are regarded as responsible, and consequently liable to civil and criminal prosecution. Depending on the degree of control exercised, the entity identified on the DOC and SMC as manager could undoubtedly be targetted by this legislation (99).

In French law, the shipowner could be liable, even in the absence of any personal injury or damage, by virtue of the new article 223.1 of the Penal Code concerning the endangering of another person's life (100), if he fails to respect the provisions of the ISM Code.

3. Insurance contracts

424. - According to section 39.5 of the Marine Insurance Act of 1906, an insurer is not liable for any loss attributable to a ship's unseaworthiness, if the ship were in this condition during its voyage, as a result of a fault by the insured person (101). It will be more difficult for the insuree to claim that he did not know whether his ship was unseaworthy once the ISM Code is in force, requiring the establishment of an SMS concerning the status of the ship, its equipment and training of its crew (102).

P&I club rules already include requirements relating directly to the applications of the ISM Code. Any non-conformity may lead the insurer not to provide cover in the event of an accident (103).

CONCLUSION

425. - The entry into force on 1st July 1998 of the ISM Code is without any doubt the most important event in the history of shipping in the last twenty years.

This is because it represents a new and original approach to prevention of accidents, providing a comprehensive response to the problem of safety at sea, to the extent that it deals with both ships and shipping companies, perceived as the whole of their parts.

The Code will also have profound and lasting effects on behaviour, by encouraging the dissemination of a safety culture within the maritime industry (104).

The fundamental question that arises today is how the Code will be perceived by the maritime community during its initial period of application. Drawn up mainly with the help of shipowner associations, the Code reflects the state of good practice in the maritime industry (105). This active participation should therefore facilitate its rapid and uniform implementation (106).

(98) Dr A. MANDARAKA-SHEPPARD : " Maintaining safety standard at sea ". Lloyd's List, 17 April 1996, 11.
(99) L. RAMBUSCH : " The legal Implications of the ISM Code ". Maritime Cyprus 1995. Conference Speeches.
(100) Trib. Corr. Dieppe, 25 juin 1996. Navire Snekkar. DMF 1997, 93 Obs. Le Bihan - Guénolé.
(101) - E. IVAMY : "Chalmer's Marine Insurance Act 1909". Butterworths, London 1983, 9th Edition, 55-60.
- E. IVAMY : "Marine Insurance. Butterworths, 4th Edition, 1985, 296-299.
(102) S. GOODACRE : "Message for insurers : to err is human". Lloyd's List, 24 Sept. 1997 and "ISM and the English marine hull policy". Lloyd's List, 8 Oct. 1997.
(103) " Deadline for radical safety code focuses minds on extent of cover ". Lloyd's List, Insurance Day, 3 April 1996. " ISM raises P and I cover question ". Tradewinds, 27 June 1997.
(104) M. GREY : " Understanding ISM - a culture of safe practice ". BIMCO Bullletin 6/93, Nov/Dec 1993, 78.
(105) E. GOLD : " Lesson in corporate responsability : learning from disaster ? ". BIMCO courses, Copenhagen, 15 April 1996.
(106) " Last chance safety code warning ". Lloyd's List, 30 April 1997.

In addition, there is a broad consensus at present in the maritime world on the strict and effective implementation of the new regulations. A shipowner who fails to respect the Code would have very serious difficulties :

- In finding insurance cover. Many insurance companies (107) and P&I Clubs (108) have announced that compliance with the ISM Code will be regarded as an essential condition of insurance.
- In finding a cargo. Most shipbrokers will make ISM certification a condition of charter (109). For the shipowner, who may feel more comfortable if a specific reference to the ISM Code is incorporated in their charter parties. BIMCO has devised a broad and neutrally worded ISM clause (110).
- In shipping goods. Ships will be detained for any non-conformity to the ISM Code, or even banished from European (111), American (112) and Asian (113) ports. If there is a risk of a two-level system of application of the Code developing (114), it will be limited in time and space with the generalisation of regional agreements on port State control (PSC), which have made compliance with the ISM Code one of their foundations.

By 1st July 1998, about 87 per cent of the 12 500 vessels which required documentation in the first ISM phase had complied (115). This relatively high figure shows the extent to which the new regulations are taken seriously by shipowners. It suggests that the Code will be observed worldwide by 1st July 2002, when all ships covered by the SOLAS Convention will have to possess ISM certification.

(107) - "Active underwriters. Joint Hull Committee takes the initiatives. Fairplay, 25 June 1998.
- "French insurers urge ISM Code". Lloyd's List, 9 July 1998.
(108) - "Turn of the ISM screw". Fairplay, 12 Feb. 1998.
(109) W. PACKARD : "Shipbrokers ISM checklist". Lloyd's List, 19 Jan. 1998.
(110) "BIMCO standard ISM clause for voyage and time charters". BIMCO Bulletin, vol. 93, n° 1, 1998, 36.
(111) "A question of self-interest". Fairplay, 1 Jan. 1998.
(112) "US enforces reports on ISM status". Lloyd's List, 26 Jan. 1998.
(113) "Defaulters to be detained indefinitely". Lloyd's List, 5 May 1998.
(114) "Enforcing the ISM Code - Today's the big day". Lloyd's List, 1 July 1998.
(115) "ISM Code compliance hits 87 % on deadline". Lloyd's List, 2 July 1998.

CHAPTER 17

Ship operation
and manning standards

426. - Operational standards are those legislative, regulatory or professional requirements that apply to ship operations.

Most operations take place when the ship is in port, and include loading and unloading of goods or embarkation of supplies for the next voyage. Failure to respect certain procedures while these operations are taking place can create very serious risk to life and the environment. To prevent such risks, IMO has drawn up advice to be followed during hold and cargo operations. Certain professional organisations like ICS (1), OCIMF, IAPH, and SIGTTO (2) have also provided guidance on observance of safety instructions for cargo movements in ports and terminals.

General operational standards apply to servicing and maintenance of a ship and its equipment, in order to ensure that it is seaworthy. They also cover on-board personnel, shipmaster, officers and members of the crew. The shipowner's obligations towards seafarers include specific requirements concerning working conditions or social security. These arise from maritime labour law, drawn up internationally under ILO auspices. Others are closely related to proper running of a ship and its safety.

This chapter is devoted to such provisions. With the help of international organisations, maritime states have with varying degrees of success drawn up and implemented regulations requiring ships to be manned by competent crews in sufficient numbers. The diversity and multiplicity of current texts reflect three particular areas of concern: shipmasters' status (cf I below), manning regulations (II), and the training and qualification of seafarers (III).

I - SHIPMASTERS' STATUS

427. - No international convention regulates the status of shipmasters. Their rights and obligations are set by various national legislations. In general, the master bears authority for the maritime expedition, and fulfils a number of functions, technical, commercial, legal, public and disciplinary (3).

---

(1) International Chamber of Shipping : "Shipping and the environment : A code of practice". London.
(2) - OCIMF/ICS/IAPH : "International safety guide for oil tankers and terminals". Witherby, London, 4e ed., 1996.
- SIGTTO : "Liquefied gas handling principles on ships and in terminals". Witherby, London, 2 ed., 1996.
(3) R. HERSHEY : "The primacy of the master and its consequences". Maritime Policy and Management. Vol. 15 n° 2 - April/June 1998, 141.

Nowadays, his nautical responsibilities have become the most important. Admittedly, in particular circumstances, certain national laws still authorise him to act commercially, but this remains the exception (4). His prime duty is to sail the ship safety (5).

Certain lawyers have no hesitation in describing this as a "public order duty", because of the very serious human, financial and environmental consequences involved in the loss of a ship. The very importance of the master's safety role explains why his legal protection needs to be assured.

A - IMPORTANCE OF SAFETY ROLE

In general, the master is responsible for ensuring the enforcement of regulations and implementing safety policies on board his ship (7). In this respect, he must ensure that the crew are properly informed, trained and motivated to carry out their duties effectively and efficiently, in accordance with the shipping company's instructions. Section 5.1 of the ISM Code deals with these issues.

Most national legislations provide precise details of the master's safety duties, and grant him a number of prerogatives to enable him to fulfil this fundamental duty. They even provide for severe disciplinary and criminal penalties for any failure to comply with these obligations.

1. Shipmaster's obligations

428. - The SOLAS Convention states the principal safety obligations of a ship-master (8):

- He should ensure that all certificates are up to date and properly posted, and that the condition of the ship and its equipment is maintained in conformity with the requirements of the Convention;

- Regulation I/11 requires the master to report any accident which occurs, or defect discovered, either of which affects the safety of the ship or the efficiency or completeness of its equipment.

- In order to ensure the general seaworthiness of the ship and adequate stability at all stages of the voyage, the master is responsible for ensuring compliance with the various provisions on the carriage of grain and dangerous goods.

- He has the obligation to render assistance to persons in distress at sea, and to ensure that the ship complies with navigation safety rules, such as traffic separation schemes, recommended routes and areas to be avoided.

The 1973-78 MARPOL Convention also contains operational provisions to prevent pollution by ships, for which the master is directly responsible, notably as regards the validity of the International Oil Pollution Prevention (IOPP) certificate (cf MARPOL Annex I), or the Carriage of Noxious Liquid Substances (NLS) certificate (cf Annex II).

---

(4) M. JAYASEKERA : "The rights and duties of masters". Droit européen des transports, vol XXI, n° 5, 1986, 194-396.
(5) P. CHAUVEAU : "Traité du droit maritime". Librairies Techniques, Paris, 1958, 241.
(6) R. RODIERE : "Traité général de droit maritime". Tome I, n° 380, 496 à 499.
(7) C. MAHIDHARA : "Shipmasters' responsibilities for implementing safety policies on board". The Nautical Institute on the Management of Safety in Shipping. Operations and Quality Assurance. London, 1991, 40-43.
(8) W. MORRISON : "The role of the shipmaster in implementing international conventions". Journal of the Honourable Company of Master Mariners. June 1992, 167-176.

Finally, according to the STCW Convention, the shipmaster is under an obligation to ensure that officers and ratings are appropriately trained to use equipment aboard properly.

2. Competencies and prerogatives

429. - A shipmaster, *magister navis*, sole master on board after God, possesses numerous prerogatives, not only disciplinary. The traditional law of the sea recognises his power of decision: he is the sole judge of the action needed for the safety of his ship. For many reasons, this centuries-old principle is in decline, particularly in three areas (9).

a) Loading

First of all, shipmasters are faced with so many rapid turnarounds that they have great difficulty in knowing the exact nature, characteristics and arrangement of the goods loaded on board. The theoretical loading plan of a ro-ro ship, for example, is usually drawn up by the shipping company's agents. Materially, the master has no time to check whether the plan is acceptable, nor whether it has been fully respected by the dock workers.

b) Emergencies

According to the principles of maritime law, the master must not ask the shipowner for nautical instructions. But in practice he usually tries not to spend too much on preventive safety, which could be seen by his employer as superfluous, especially if such measures have been effective (10).

In his report on the *Braer* disaster (11), Lord Donaldson regretted that the master was no longer the only decision taker, something that is extremely dangerous in a crisis, when valuable time may be wasted while a master seeks authority for the necessary action. He further recommended that the master's freedom should not be impeded by the shipowner's attempts to impose a particular route or a certain speed despite the weather.

To help seafarers in dangerous situations or in case of assistance at sea, the ICS and the OCIMF have issued a guide for shipmasters (12). It recommends that all those concerned should establish communication as quickly as possible, and that the request for assistance should not be delayed by contractual negotiations. It also recalls that assistance should have no effect on the master's authority or his overall responsibility.

c) Control of navigation

Certain vessel traffic services (VTS), engaged in active control of navigation, schedule ship movements in such a way as to avoid dangerous situations, and organise traffic in the routeing scheme within the surveillance zone. These systems reduce the master's powers over the conduct of his ship (13).

(9) P. MURPHY : "The master - is he still in command ?" BIMCO Bulletin, vol. 90, n° 6, 1995, 16-21.
(10) M. GREY : "Master's dilemma is key safety issue" Lloyd's List, 29 March 1989.
(11) "Safer ships, cleaner seas". Report of Lord Donaldson's inquiry into the prevention of pollution from merchant shipping. HMSO, London, May 1996, 93 et 299.
(12) ICF/OCIMF : "Peril at sea and salvage - A guide for masters". 4th edition, London, 1992.
(13) Ph. BOISSON : "Le contrôle de la navigation et les pouvoirs du capitaine". AFDM, Journée Ripert 1994, Paris, 1995.

In general, the ISM Code attempts to reestablish the master's authority. The safety management system (SMS) introduced by the company must stipulate the principle that ultimate authority is held by the master, and that he is responsible for taking decisions on safety and prevention of pollution, asking the company for assistance if necessary (cf section 5.2).

3. Master's liability

430. - The master is responsible for conducting the ship safely. He may be held civilly but also criminally liable for non-respect of this fundamental obligation (14).

In the United Kingdom, failure to respect maritime traffic rules, particularly those concerning traffic separation schemes, could lead to criminal prosecution (15).

In France, the Act of 17 December 1926, instituting a disciplinary and penal code for the merchant navy, sets out a list of offences for which the master can be prosecuted in a criminal court (16).

B - LEGAL PROTECTION OF SHIPMASTERS

431. - Whatever means are deployed to oversee, control and intervene at sea, nothing will ever replace the essential role of the master in preventing accidents. To avoid the master's subordination to the shipping company exerting a negative effect on safety (17), a climate of confidence needs to be established within the company. Legally, particular attention should be paid to the conditions under which the master is appointed and dismissed.

1. Appointment of shipmaster

The master is appointed by the shipowner, under State supervision. This principle is applied to varying degrees in maritime countries, and each administration remains free to set the minimum obligatory conditions for the certification of masters and chief mates.

When the maritime administration in certain States exercises inadequate supervision, and legislation is outdated, there can be traffic in false certificates. To combat such practices and harmonise the various national regulations, IMO and ILO have drawn up various international agreements.

The oldest is Convention 53, adopted by ILO in 1936, and which came into force in March 1939 (18). This sets the minimum professional competencies of merchant navy shipmasters and officers,. According to article 3, "no person shall be engaged to perform or shall perform (...) the duties of master (...) unless he holds a certificate of competence to perform such duties, issued or approved by the public authority of the territory where the vessel is registered".

(14) J.P. DECLERCQ : "Le capitaine est-il bien assuré ?" JMM, 18 Oct. 1991, 2535-2537.
(15) C. WARBRICK, R. SULLIVAN : "Ship routeing schemes and the criminal liability of the master". LMCLQ, Feb. 1994, 23-29.
(16) - G. BEYNÉ : "La faute nautique du préposé maritime et aérien". Law thesis, Bordeaux, 1969.
- R. GARRON : "La responsabilité personnelle du capitaine de navire". Law thesis, Aix 1964.
(17) French government memo on the negative effects on safety at sea of certain aspects of the phenomenon of flags of convenience. In JMM, 25 May 1978, 1181.
(18) JMM, 23 Nov. 1978, 2803.

The most important text at present is the Convention on Standards of Training, Certification and Watchkeeping for Seafarers (STCW), adopted by IMO in 1978 and amended in 1995. Chapter II of this Convention ("Master and deck department"), lays down minimum compulsory requirements for the certification of masters and chief mates for ships of least 500 gross tonnage or more (cf Regulation II/2) and of less than 500 gross tonnage (cf Regulation II/3).

2. Protection against unfair dismissal

The master must possess the real means of meeting his responsibilities under all circumstances. Any ambiguity or doubt on this matter must be removed, by providing legislative guarantees or by collective bargaining for officers, or in the form of consultation procedures before the application of disciplinary measures within the company (19).

On 15 November 1978, the IMO Assembly adopted Resolution A.443, which provides for the master to be protected against wrongful dismissal or other measures of constraint or retaliation by the shipowner or charterer, arising from the exercise of his safety responsibilities.

In conclusion, it would appear essential for the master to be given legal protection against interference by the shipowner's agents, particularly when he is performing technical duties relating to safety at sea. The ISM Code goes even further, and asks the company to provide "the necessary support so that the master's duties can be safely performed" (cf 6.1.3) (20).

II - MANNING AND SAFETY AT SEA

433. - Operating conditions for ships have evolved considerably in the last thirty years. The most striking fact is undoubtedly the drastic reduction in manpower. In the Sixties, the crew of an average freighter or tanker numbered 40 or 50. Today, new technologies allow a similar ship to be operated with fewer than 20 people on board (21). This quantitative reduction in manning, made possible by the increasing automation of ships and their equipment, has certain limits, imposed by safety considerations.

A - INTERNATIONAL REGULATIONS ON MANNING

434. - There are utopian ideas of robot ships controlled by computer and satellite communications. Until then, ships will still have to have somebody on board. The question is, how many?

In 1990, the American National Research Council (NRC) published a study of crew size and maritime safety. It was unable to reach any final conclusions, because of the lack of accident data. However, the study helped reveal the effect of crew size in emergencies.

---

(19) Me J.S. ROHART : "Le statut du capitaine face au nouveau défi de la sécurité maritime". In JMM, 31 Jan. 1992, 250.
(20) Cf M. GARRON · French Maritime Law Association Nantes Seminar, May 1979. Le droit de la mer et la sécurité de la terre. In JMM, 17 May 1979, 1151.
(21) IMO. "Better standards, training and certification. IMO's response to human error". World Maritime Day 1994.

The NRC also drew attention to another problem. Most of the maintenance is performed by shipboard personnel, so that a reduction in manning means that different operating procedures have to be introduced (22).

Crew numbers are decided by flag state maritime authorities, depending on national labour laws in force in those countries. International organisations have for long faced difficulties in agreeing on standards.

1 - ILO regulations

The ILO revised two instruments on this issue in 1996:

Article 21 of Convention 109 on wages, hours of work and manning states that "every vessel (...) shall be sufficiently and efficiently manned for the purposes of:

a) ensuring the safety of life at sea;

b) giving effect to the provisions of part III of this Convention" (dealing with hours of work on board);

c) "preventing excessive strain on the crew and avoiding or minimising as far as practicable the working of overtime".

Article 10 of Recommendations 109 on the same subjects states that "a sufficient number of officers and men should be engaged so as to ensure the avoidance of excessive overtime and to satisfy the dictates of safety of life at sea".

2 - IMO regulations

The SOLAS Conventions of 1960 and 1974 introduced no additional requirements on the issue. Regulation 13 of chapter V indicates only that contracting governments must ensure that, "from the point of view of safety of life at sea, all ships shall be sufficiently and efficiently manned".

Since the 1988 Protocol, a document kept on board the ship records the flag State's minimum safe manning requirements. Compulsory since 1st February 1992 on board ships of 500 gross tonnage or more, this document does not question the principle that it is the government that decides on the actual size of the crew.

In Resolution A.481 of 19 November 1981, IMO laid down the main principles to be observed in deciding on safe manning. Nine objectives are set. These include maintaining a safe navigational watch on the bridge and general surveillance of the ship, operating all watertight closing arrangements and maintaining them in effective condition, and deploying a competent damage control party, operating all on-board fire equipment and lifesaving appliances, and carrying out such maintenance as is necessary at sea, maintaining a safe engineering watch at sea of main propulsion or auxiliary machinery, to enable the ship to overcome the foreseeable perils of the voyage.

These guidelines remain recommendations only, and are not applied universally (23). IMO is currently attempting to review them with the idea of giving greater importance to the relationship between actual workload, grades or capabilities of shipboard personnel and their number (24).

(22) National Research Council : "Crew size and maritime safety". Washington, 1990.
(23) A. IRONS : "Unsafe ship manning". Australian Ships and Ports. April 1993, 11.
(24) "IMO warming up to review of safe manning principles". Lloyd's List, 29 Jan. 1998.

B - SHIP AUTOMATION

435. - The increased automation of ships has led to a substantial cut in manning. This rationalisation of work at sea has led to far-reaching legislative changes, to take account of new safety requirements (25).

1. Growth of automation

The late Eighties witnessed a considerable growth in navigational aids and communications. Most of these tools are integrated into systems controlling networks of data and instruction exchanges, in order to draw up detailed information or summaries. They affect every component of navigation: positioning of the ship, automatic routeing, anti-collision system, electronic charts, telecommunications and modern navigation systems have led to One Man Bridge Operation (OMBO) ships.

The automation of ships has affected crewing. Experiments with limited manning have brought about a profound change in working conditions at sea. It is reflected in the removal of distinctions between bridge and engine personnel, replacement of maintenance operations by breakdown and repair work, multiplication of routine and surveillance work (27). These changes have borne on the behaviour of the crew and indirectly on ship safety (28).

2. Automation and manning regulations

At an international level, IMO provisions and classification society rules are among the few regulatory texts to have taken any account of the problems raised by automated ships.

a) IMO regulations

The first mandatory rules were contained in the 1978 STCW Convention, which prohibited OMBO on ship 24 hours a day. Articles 4 and 9 of Regulation II/1 do not permit a single officer to be on watch alone at night.

Article 2.2 of Resolution A.481 of 1981, laying down the principles to be observed in deciding on safe manning, states that the bridge watch has to be provided by at least one officer qualified for this function, and at least one qualified or experienced seaman.

Following the first trials with the officer of the navigational watch acting as the sole lookout, IMO early in 1989 drew up the first provisional guidelines on the question, in MSC circular 566. They amended the requirements of the 1978 Convention. Despite strong reservations among seafarers (29), the provisions came into force on 1st December 1992.

---

(25) J.W. BULL : "Safety and marine automatisation". Nautical Magazine, March 1978, Part. II, vol. 29, n° 3, 137.
(26) A. TROUSSE : "Toward sophisticated and safe navigation, contribution of classification societies". ATMA. Paris, Session 1993.
(27) J.C. LALITTE : "Influence des nouvelles formes de navigation pétrolière sur les conditions de travail et de vie du personnel embarqué". Mémoire DEA, Sciences Economiques, Paris I, 1977.
(28) - P.S. PURKISS : "Automation on the bridge, its avantages and its risks". Safety at Sea, n° 118, Jan. 1979, 42.
- M.D. GRAY : "Unattended machinery spaces. The essential safety features". Institute of Marine Engineers, London, Oct. 1967.
(29) R. CLIPSHAM : "The shipmaster's obsession with safety". Safety at Sea International, June 1994, 28-31.

The 1995 revision of the STCW Convention did not make any fundamental changes in the existing principles. Regulation VIII/2 on the organisation of the watch states that the master of any ship must "ensure that watchkeeping arrangements are adequate for maintaining a safe watch or watches, taking into account the prevailing circumstances and conditions".

Circular 566 is not accepted unanimously within IMO. After asking for an end to trials in which the navigational officer of the watch carried out the visual watch alone during hours of darkness, the MSC went back on its decision in June 1996 (30), and allowed the trials to resume until December 1997 (31).

b) Classification society rules

From the mid-Sixties, the leading classification societies incorporated ship automation into their rules. At the time, they were trying to set standards for climatic tests in engine rooms housing the first electronic equipment, highly sensitive to temperature variations and vibrations.

With automated bridge systems, new classification notations appeared (32), such as Centralised Navigation Control (CNC), introduced by Bureau Veritas in January 1990 (33). The arrival of the first integrated bridge systems and the beginnings of night-time navigation trials with a single officer of the watch encouraged IACS to develop a unified rule. This rule, adopted in December 1992, contains the same rovisions as the IMO guidelines (34).

C - SHIP MANNING AND FATIGUE

436. - Several studies have shown that fatigue could be a cause of accidents at sea. The most important include those of the US Maritime Administration (MarAd) (35), the Japanese Maritime Research Institute (JAMRI) (36), the British officers' union (NUMAST) (37), which considers that about half the accidents at sea are due to fatigue (38), the Seafarers International Research Centre for Safety and Occupational Health (SIRC) at the University of Cardiff (39), and the ITF (40).

In November 1993, IMO adopted Resolution A.772, on fatigue factors in manning and safety, the purpose of which was encourage understanding of the complexity of the phenomenon, and give an incentive to shipowners to make allowance for such factors when taking decisions about operating their ships. The Resolution provides a general description of fatigue, and points out the main causes of the phenomenon, such as inadequate rest, an excessive workload, noise and interpersonal relationships. This is intended not only for companies responsible for management ashore and aboard, but also administrations when they are drawing up legislation on the matter, and designers of marine equipment, to ensure that ergonomic practices intended to avoid the various forms of fatigue are adopted.

(30) IMO, MSC 66/24, 18 June 1996, par 7°31.
(31) "IMO agrees resumption of one man bridge trials". Lloyd"s List, 7 June 1996.
(32) M. RYLE : "One man bridge operation" The Motor Ship, Sept. 1997, 41.
(33) Bureau Veritas - Centralized Navigation Control mark CNC-E and CNC-1, option 1 - Technical conditions for granting and maintenance of the mark - NR 325 RO1E, Paris, May 1993.
(34) UR N1. One man bridge operated ships adopted by the IACS Council in 1992.
(35) "Waking up to problems of fatigue". Lloyd's List, 14 March 1991.
(36) JAMRI : "Analysis of world/Japan shipping casualties and future prospects thereof". Tokyo, 1993.
(37) "Seamen are forced out of work through stress". Lloyd's List, 6 June 1992.
(38) "Waking up to the nightmare of the sleepless ships' officer". Lloyd's List, 15 Feb. 1997.
(39) "Waking up to fatigue at sea". Lloyd's List, 28 Oct. 1996.
(40) ITF : "Seafarer fatigue. Wake up to the danger". London, May 1998.

Until recently, maritime navigation was the only commercial mode of transport that failed to admit the effects of fatigue on the performance of operators, or to have regulations making provisions for such effects (41). Questions concerning hours worked and rest periods were referred back to national legislators (42). Several international instruments now take fatigue factors into consideration and try to prevent them affecting safety adversely (43).

1. STCW Convention and watchkeeping standards

In its very first version, adopted in 1978, the STCW Convention had set a standard of aptitude for the watch. Paragraph 5 of Regulation II/1 states that "the watch system shall be such that the efficiency of watchkeeping officers and watchkeeping ratings is not impaired by fatigue. Duties shall be so organised that the first watch at the commencement of a voyage and the subsequent relieving watches are sufficiently rested and otherwise fit for duty".

This general principle was repeated in detail in the new STCW Convention of 1995. Regulation VIII/1 of the Annex to the Convention requires signatory States to take measures to prevent fatigue among watchkeepers and attend to their application.

Each administration is to "establish and enforce rest periods for watchkeeping personnel and require that watch systems are so arranged that the efficiency of all watchkeeping personnel is not impaired by fatigue".

Section VIII/1 of part A of the Code contains several regulations relating to aptitude for watchkeeping. A minimum of 10 hours' time off duty is to be provided in every 24 hours. Rest periods may not be divided into more than two periods, one of which must last at least 6 hours.

Section VIII/1 of part B of the Code lays down guidelines for the prevention of fatigue and details certain provisions of part A. There is a reference to IMO Resolution A.772, enumerating the fatigue factors that have to be taken into account by those involved in shipping operations. Administrations are also advised to provide regulations on the maintenance of records of working hours and rest periods for seafarers, and their inspection, and to amend regulations on prevention of fatigue on the basis of the findings of accident investigations.

2. Revised Convention on the working hours of seafarers and manning of ships 1996

437. - For lack of the necessary number of ratifications, the 1958 Convention 109 on wages, hours of work and manning never came into force. In October 1996, ILO adopted a new instrument, which sets out several provisions intended to avoid fatigue resulting from an excessive workload (44).

The new Convention 109 sets the daily and weekly limits on working hours or, conversely, the minimum period of daily or weekly rest. The maximum number of working hours is 8 hours, with one rest day per week. The maximum number of working hours must not exceed 14 hours in any 24-hours period and 72 hours in any period of 7 days. Rest periods must not be less than 10 hours per period of 24 hours and 77 hours per period of 7 days.

(41) "Fatigue factors". Lloyd's List, 7 April 1993.
(42) "Time the law lifted pressure off masters". Lloyd's List, 8 Jan. 1992.
(43) D. STEVENSON : "Tanker crew fatigue - Some new solutions to an old problem". JMLC, vol. 27, n° 3, July 1996, 453-468.
(44) "ILO Maritime Conference" in The ISF Year 96-97, London 1997.

The Convention also requires records to be kept of the daily working hours and rest periods of seafarers. The competent authority must check and confirm that regulations are being respected. Otherwise, it must require steps to be taken to avoid breaches recurring.

The new Convention 109 has been included in the 1996 Protocol to Convention 147 laying down minimum standards for the merchant navy. This will allow port States to oversee the enforcement of its provisions (45).

3. SOLAS Convention and ISM Code

438. - The ISM Code encourages ship operators to examine all the elements generating fatigue and to establish their own procedures for countering them, particularly aspects relating to the environment, stress, and psychological and cultural conditions. IMO has stated which measures should be taken in the safety management system (SMS). They include investigations of maritime casualties, to determine the role of fatigue in these events (46).

Significantly, the courts took this factor into account long before the legislators. English case law, for example, contains numerous decisions showing that insufficiency of officers or crew could reveal the unseaworthiness of a ship. In fact, outside the maritime sector, English judges take fatigue factors into consideration whenever they are the cause of an accident involving death or bodily injuries. It may therefore be concluded that a shipowner or ship operator would in theory be held responsible for bodily injury stemming from the tiredness of a ship's crew, injuries to other parties but also to the crew itself (47).

III - TRAINING AND QUALIFICATION OF SEAFARERS

439. - In the late Seventies, economic pressure forced shipowners to make drastic cuts in shipping costs, particular crewing expenses, which represent a significant share of ship operating charges. This economy drive was often to the detriment of the quality of crewing and safety in general. The trend led IMO to pay more attention to the training and qualification of seafarers (48).

A - DECLINE IN CREW QUALITY

The last twenty years have seen a gradual decline in the quality of ships' crews, mainly as a result of the recruitment of mixed crews made up of seamen from different countries. The resulting confusion in training backgrounds, languages, ways of thinking and cultural attitudes has changed navigating conditions.

(45) Ph. PANAYIDES : "Better terms for sea seafarers". Seaways, Feb. 1997, 12-13.
(46) IMO - Report of the joint IMO/ILO Group of Experts on Fatigue. MSC 62/14/6, 16 Mar. 1993.
(47) J. MITCHELL, D. REYNOLDS : "Is fatigue a defense in accidents that stem from human tiredness ?" Lloyd's List, 31 Jan. 1992.
(48) IMO. World Maritime Day 1994. Better standards, training and certification : IMO's response to human error. London, 1994.

1. Characteristics of maritime manpower

The main reasons arise from the cost of labour at sea at a worldwide level. The annual report of the ISF for 1995-96 (49), which shows comparative costs in various countries, reveals considerable wage differences, for both officers and ratings. These economic disparities have had serious consequences on shipping, and explain the success of certain flags, which allow ship operators to choose crew members and officers of any nationality. In certain cases, this can cut personnel costs to a third of the original sum (50).

In 1990, the ISF and BIMCO published a study of worldwide supply of and demand for seamen, forecasting a considerable difference between the availability and need of officers, a shortfall that could reach 400 000 by the start of the next century. The current surplus of about 200 000 ratings could over the same period become a deficit (51). The same report, updated to 1995 (52), estimates that the number of available qualified officers is likely to be 10 per cent short of demand around 2005, if the growth in world shipping is 1.5 per cent. If growth were doubled, the gap between supply of officers and demand would rise to 25 per cent. If this penury is confirmed, there would be a strong temptation for certain shipowners to recruit their personnel in any country. The future looks rosy for mixed crews.

The same report predicts that the geographical origin of officers will shift towards Asia, to the detriment of OECD countries. Nowadays, developed countries account for more than half of all senior officers, and only 23 per cent of seamen. Asia supplies half such seamen, and is catching up on the OECD as regards officers. At present, Asia provides 39 per cent of young officers, compared with 33 per cent from the OECD, and 37 per cent of trainee officers compared with 27 per cent from the OECD.

2. Effect of mixed crews on safety

440. - It is often said that a good crew makes for a good ship. In the past, that was reflected in a homogeneous, usually well trained and practised crew, communicating easily in crew members' mother tongue. This period now appears to have gone, with the spectacular development of mixed crews, multinational and pluricultural (53).

Some commentators have expressed doubt about the quality of their safety performance. The JAMRI study mentioned above showed that Japanese-owned ships sailing under an open registry flag, manned whether by entirely Korean or Filipino crews, or by mixed Japanese and non-Japanese crews, are more often involved in expensive accidents than others. The consequences of accidents, underlines the study, are made worse by problems of communication among members of the crew or with passengers.

Several recent accidents have provided proof of this. In the tragedy of the *Scandinavian Star*, the poor knowledge of English among the Portuguese catering staff contributed to the high number of fatalities. Similarly, the cultural heterogeneity on board the *Braer*, manned by Greek officers and Filipino ratings, was also a contributory factor in the disaster. (54).

(49) International Shipping Federation : "The ISF Year 1995/1996". London 1996, 15.
(50) W. O'NEIL : "A l'heure des bouleversements : le rôle du navigant". JMM, 31 Dec. 1993, 3251-3254.
(51) ISF/BIMCO : "The worldwide demand for and supply of seafarers. Summary and conclusions". University of Warwick. Institute for Employment Research, 1991.
(52) BIMCO/ISF 1995 Manpower update. Summary. The worldwide demand for and supply of seafarers. The University of Warwick. December 1995.
(53) "The challenge facing shipping over multinational crewing". Lloyd's List, 2 March 1993.
(54) "Spills give new edge to training dilemma". Lloyd's List, 9 Feb. 1993.

Language problems are also particularly significant during piloting operations. Not only do the pilot and the master have difficulties in understanding each other, but the same problem exists between officers and crew, further reducing the margin of error when the ship is berthing or during operations in the holds (55).

3. Diversity of training schemes

The flag State is responsible for issuing certificates to seafarers, supervising maritime training institutes and the standards they apply, and approving qualifications granted by other governments.

In practice, flag States vary in the degree of conscientiousness with which they meet these obligations. Industrialised countries have established their own vocational training schemes, which in various ways ensure a satisfactory level of qualification. On the other hand, most Third World countries cannot aspire to this level of quality. For lack of adequate resources, maritime traditions, teaching standards or tools to assess effectiveness, serious disparities exist in the value of certificates issued by public or private training institutions.

It was these disparities that led to the establishment of the STCW Convention, adopted by IMO in 1978.

B - CONVENTION ON STANDARDS OF TRAINING, CERTIFICATION AND WATCHKEEPING FOR SEAFARERS (STCW CONVENTION)

441. - For safety at sea, it is generally accepted that the STCW Convention comes second only to the SOLAS Convention. This importance justifies examination in some detail of its implications (56), from its genesis and content to the revision carried out in 1995.

1. Origin of the Convention

IMO became aware of the acute nature of the safety problems arising from human factors in the mid-Sixties. After concentrating its efforts on improving technical standards, IMO engaged in a rather timid campaign in favour of raising the quality of crews, regarded as the special area of concern of another United Nations agency, the International Labour Office.

However, a Joint ILO/IMO Committee on training succeeded in 1964 in publishing a "Document for guidance", which for the first time formulated recommendations on the training and education of seafarers (57). Even though this document was a great success, IMO decided to go further in 1971, by defining compulsory standards. It took seven years to draw up a draft convention under the auspices of the subcommittee on Standards of Training and Watchkeeping (STW). A diplomatic conference in June and July 1978 in London was attended by representatives of 72 states, a record in the history of IMO. The conference, convened jointly with ILO, adopted the STCW Convention and 23 resolutions laying down additional procedures (58).

---

(55) R. CLIPSHAM : "The shipmaster with mixed nationality crews. Human error and the control of emergencies". The Nautical Institute. Journal of the Honourable Company of Master Mariners, 1995, 647-662.
(56) Cf the important bibliography on the International Convention on Standards of Training, Certification and Watchkeeping (STCW) in IMO Library Information Services. Information sheet n° 23. 1st April 1998.
(57) "Cooperation for maritime training" IMO News, n° 3, 1984, 8-14.
(58) "Training Conference will help to reduce accidents at sea". IMO News, n° 3, 1978, 4-5.

2. 1978 STCW Rules

442. - The STCW Convention was regarded as one of the most important agreements ever reached on safety at sea. It was in fact the first initiative taken to establish global minimum professional standards for seafarers.

The Convention contains 17 articles dealing with legal issues, completed by an annex laying down administrative and technical rules.

The 23 resolutions adopted in London contain more detailed provisions. All the texts accepted in 1978 form a 105-page volume, only 55 of which deal with mandatory standards.

a) Universal application of the STCW Convention

The STCW Convention has been applied worldwide. It came into force on 28 April 1984, and has so far been ratified by 112 States, whose shipping represent 93.5 per cent of world tonnage. Such a success may be explained by the very nature of its provisions. The text is not in itself a model to inspire all nations to draw up their own regulations, for many countries in fact apply more stringent requirements than those in the Convention. It should be seen rather as the expression of a determination to eliminate unsuitable requirements, or complete inadequate ones, wherever necessary, while informing any developing countries keen to build up their own shipping fleet of the "lowest common denominator" for internationally acceptable procedures and standards (59).

b) Convention appropriate to the needs of developing countries

The 1978 Convention first and foremost tried to respond to the concerns of developing countries.

Given the poor level of educational infrastructures in many countries, the Convention gave priority to experience acquired at sea over periods spent in teaching establishments. IMO hoped that this solution would be only provisional, and so it has attempted to set up international cooperation for the training of seafarers (cf Resolution 23). This initiative led to the creation by the Council in November 1979 of a special technical assistance fund for maritime training (60).

c) Need for revision

The absence of constraint that characterises most of the provisions of the STCW Convention has been severely criticised. This is particularly flagrant as regards the arrangements for enforcement which States that have signed the Convention are obliged to apply. The dominant principle is that a certificate issued by one State is generally regarded as a permit to serve on board ships of other States.

In practice, it is impossible to check properly whether the certificate has been issued in accordance with the spirit and the letter of the Convention.

Certain vague expressions, repeated several times in the text of the Convention, have given rise to diverging interpretations, raising doubts about whether the Convention could provide a basis for uniform international regulations (61).

(59) "Doubts creep in on STCW Convention". Lloyd's List, 26 Sept. 1995.
(60) IMO News, n° 1, 1990, 12.
(61) "STCW Convention amended by the IMO". BIMCO Bulletin, vol. 90, n° 4, 1995, 4.

Criticism has also been levelled at the procedures for issuing certificates in certain countries where, apparently, insufficient supervision is exercised over the examination system and delivery of certificates. This even allows the papers needed to become a seaman to be obtained fraudulently without the necessary qualifications (62).

3. 1995 STCW Convention

443. - Drawn up more than 15 years earlier, the STCW Convention was in need of serious amendment. Outdated provisions needed to be replaced, while taking account of future needs of the maritime sector. This was impossible because of the excessively cumbersome amendment process, requiring years to complete. In 1993, aware of these difficulties, the IMO Secretary-General suggested replacing it with more flexible mechanisms (63). This proposal was accepted by the MSC, which decided to convene a diplomatic conference towards the middle of 1995 (64).

The conference was held at IMO headquarters in London from 26 June to 7 July 1995 (65). Another diplomatic meeting, working in parallel, adopted a new Convention on Standards of Training, Certification and Watchkeeping specifically for fishing boats.

a) New structure

The main change lies in the new structure of the Convention, henceforth confined to legal issues. Technical requirements are rearranged in a Code appended to the Convention. This is divided into two parts. Part A describes standards of training, certification and watchkeeping for seafarers, which are rendered mandatory by means of references in the Convention. Part B of the Code contains recommended measures.

IMO has already made use of the method consisting of appending a code to a convention, notably for the SOLAS Convention. The main advantage is that it is far easier and faster to amend a code than a convention. By means of the amendment procedure, it will be possible to update the new STCW Convention without excessive delay, so that its technical relevance can be preserved. It is also intended that certain provisions appearing as recommendations in part B of the Code should be transferred in due course to part A, where they will become mandatory (66).

b) Legal innovations

444. - Fundamentally, the new text contains two major innovations, which represent a major change in traditional mechanisms for enforcing international conventions. First, the functions and responsibilities of the flag State in this area are clarified; second, the first elements of international control under IMO and port State auspices are set out.

• Flag State obligations

Communication, control and investigation are the three new obligations of flag States.

(62) "Plain speaking". Lloyd's List, 17 October 1995.
(63) OMI : "Better standards, training and certification : IMO's response to human error". World Maritime Day 1994, London.
(64) R. KRAMEK : "The human element and the revision of the STCW Convention". BIMCO Review, 1995, 223-226.
(65) C. YOUNG : "Comprehensive revision of the STCW Convention an overview". JMLC, vol. 26, n° 1, Jan. 1995, 1-3.
(66) "The New STCW Convention". Focus on IMO, April 1997.

- First of all, the flag State must supply IMO with information on how it intends to give legal effect to the provisions of the Convention (cf Regulation I/7). Such information covers a general description of training courses provided, examinations and intended assessments for certificates delivered, as well as a list of training institutes and details of these establishments. The signatory State is also requested to supply information on measures taken to prevent fatigue and guarantee that communications on board are not impeded by language problems. It must also give details of the administrative measures introduced, such as the structure of the organisation responsible for maritime matters.

- The flag State must also ensure that all training, assessments and delivery of certificates are subject to monitoring, within the framework of a quality assurance system, to guarantee achievement of the goals defined, including those concerning the qualifications and experience of instructors, and assessments (cf Regulation I/8). An evaluation must be carried out periodically by an outside organisation, whose reports are to be submitted to IMO.

- Finally, the flag State must investigate any reported cases of incompetence, action or omission that could present a direct threat to safety at sea, committed by seafarers certified by that State. It must also apply disciplinary and legal penalties to companies, shipmasters and seamen committing such breaches, and to holders of false documents (cf Regulation I.5).

   • **IMO control**

   The Convention cuts through the Gordian knot of sovereignty, behind which States signing a convention traditionally sheltered when they did not actually want to carry it into effect. It establishes a system for verifying conformity, to be implemented by IMO (68) (cf chapter 24 below).

   • **Port State control**

- A second, more traditional system is provided through the port State. Article X allows it to intervene in the event of deficiencies regarded as presenting a threat to human life, property or the environment (cf chapter 25 below).

   c) Technical innovations

   The amended STCW Convention takes account of technical innovations (69), such as different working practices or use of simulators for training. These have now become compulsory for training in radar and automatic radar plotting aids (ARPA).

   Reference to the ISM Code is also emphasised in Regulation I/14, devoted to company responsibilities. This states their obligations concerning manning, documents and data on all seafarers on board, familiarisation with tasks and ship characteristics, and so on.

   Special attention has been given to the proposal that the Convention should allow other certificates to be delivered. This is provided for in the new chapter VII of the STCW Code, which sets out to eliminate the traditional superiority of bridge personnel over engine room personnel, in determining the various functions to be carried out in operating a ship.

---

(67) IMO News, n° 1, 1995, 10.
(68) M. GREY : "IMO sets seal on major overhaul of STCW rules". Lloyd's List, 10 July 1995.
(69) ISF : "The revised STCW Convention. A guide for the shipping industry on the 1995 amendments to the IMO International convention on Standards of Training, Certification and Watchkeeping for Seafarers". 1st Edition, London, 1995.

d) Implementation of STCW Convention

445. - The amended STCW Convention goes much farther than the version adopted in 1978. This strengthening of standards obviously raises difficulties for developing countries, which traditionally supply cheap and therefore underqualified manpower to the maritime sector (70). The case of the Philippines has been mentioned several times (71). If this country were unable to show that it possesses the required means of management, training and delivery of certificates, its government would face a major political and economic crisis (72).

• Transitional regime

The STCW Convention provides a transitional regime to facilitate implementation of its provisions. Until 1st February 2002, States may continue to issue, recognise and endorse certificates in accordance with the previous formula, if their seafarers have begun seagoing service, an approved training programme or course before 1st August 1998 (cf Regulation I/15).

In order to keep to this timetable, the MSC has asked the STCW subcommittee to draw up a number of measures (73), including recommendations for MSC assessment of information, showing that full effect has been given to the provisions of the Convention, criteria to be applied in deciding whether such information is complete, a method of revising the "white list" of countries approved by the MSC, and provisions on the frequency of such revisions (74).

IMO has also invited parties to the STCW Convention, in circular 1882 of 3 April 1996, to designate "competent persons", to whom the Secretary-General may turn for help in drawing up the report required in Regulation I/7 (75).

• Amendment of the Convention

The new requirements of the STCW Convention do not merely replace outdated provisions adopted in 1978. They are intended to meet the future needs of the maritime sector concerning qualification of crews (76). The introduction of a new amendment procedures meant that technical changes came into effect by 1st February 1997.

IMO has also taken account of information obtained from the *Estonia* disaster, by proposing the amendment of certain provisions of the Convention and the Code (77). Mainly concerned are Regulation V/2 and section A V/2, which set mandatory minimum requirements concerning the training and qualifications of masters, officers, ratings and other members of ro-ro passenger ship personnel.

• IMO technical assistance

To help with implementation of the Convention, IMO has introduced several technical assistance measures for the poorest countries (78). The Secretary-General has created a special section within the Maritime Safety Division, to handle human element issues. A

---

(70) "Labour suppliers face STCW deadline". Lloyd's List, 28 April 1998.
(71) R. DEL ROSARIO : "The Philippines manning industry". International Business Lawyer, Sept. 1996, 358-361.
(72) "Philippines faces economic crisis without white list". Lloyd's List, 2 Dec. 1996.
(73) IMO. MSC 67/22, 19 Dec. 1996, 9.6-9.12.
(74) "Laying down guidelines for STCW Convention". Lloyd's List, 24 Sept. 1996.
(75) Ch. YOUNG : "Monitoring compliance with STCW 95". BIMCO Bulletin, Vol. 93, n° 2, 1998, p 41-43.
(76) Ph. BOISSON : "IMO and the STCW Convention : exemplary revision in response to the needs of shipping fleets in the next century". Bulletin Technique du Bureau Veritas, n° 2, July 1995, 33-41.
(77) "Agreement on implementation of STCW amendments". IMO News n° 4, 1996, 14-16.
(78) "STCW amendments have added teeth". Lloyd's List, 2 Nov. 1995.

series of meetings was scheduled in 1996 to prepare effective implementation of the Convention on 1st February 1997.

A guide to the amended Convention was prepared to facilitate implementation of new provisions. Up to ten regional seminars and workshops were organised in various parts of he world (79). Under the terms of Resolution 12 of the STCW Conference and Resolution A.785 of 23 November 1985, the World Maritime University was brought in, and a pilot course on training and watchkeeping standards was specially devised for the students (80). Finally, IMO experts undertook a series of visits to the countries most concerned by the new regulations, including Panama and the Philippines.

C - EU REGULATIONS

446. - In its Communication of 24 February 1993 on a common maritime safety policy, the European Commission explained clearly that about 50 per cent of accidents occurring at sea were due to the human factor, while the lack of proper communication on board ships, often resulting from language difficulties, was also a major cause of accidents (81).

It noted that neither IMO nor ILO nor member States had so far been able to offer any solution to the problem of multinational crews, their professional qualification and their language abilities. There was no control of effective implementation of the standards laid down by the STCW Convention, and IMO had no power to act in this respect. Only an EU initiative would answer such questions.

On 24 November 1994, the Council adopted Directive 94/58 on the minimum level of training of seafarers (82). The annex to this Directive sets minimum training standards for various maritime occupations, depending on types of ships. It does not lay down higher requirements than those of the STCW Convention (cf article 3), except for adequate language skills. Masters, officers and ratings on board passenger ships, oil tankers, gas and chemical carriers must be able to communicate with one another in a common language (cf article 8).

Since 31 December 1995, all member States must deliver a certificate to seafarers in accordance with the particular provisions of the Directive (cf article 14). They also have to take steps to ensure that the level of qualification of crews consisting of non-nationals of EU countries working on board EU ships operating in Europe meet international requirements on professional training. Finally, ships flying non-EU flags, manned by Third World crews which have not reached an agreement with the EU, will be targetted by port State control authorities (cf article 10).

EU regulations differ significantly from the STCW Convention as regards control. The system introduced by Brussels to check the quality of training institutes outside Europe appears to be more stringent than the IMO scheme. On other points, the Directive remains well within the requirements of the STCW Convention, which could in the future raise a serious problem of law for EU member States (83).

(79) "Seminars will help to implement. STCW changes". IMO News, n° 3, 1996, 2.
(80) D. WATERS : "Implementation of the amended STCW Convention". BIMCO Review 1996, 85-87.
(81) COM (93) final, 24 Feb. 1993, par. 129.
(82) OJEC, 12 Dec. 1994, L. 319, p. 28.
(83) "Safety fears over EC training proposals". Lloyd's List, 4 Dec. 1996.

CHAPTER 18

Aids to navigation

447. - Aids to navigation consist of equipment or services intended to facilitate the conduct of ships, and thereby improve the safety and efficiency of maritime navigation. Such aids may be divided into two specific categories:
- aids to navigation, namely devices and systems not on board ships, usually ashore or along the coast;
- navigational aids, namely shipborne equipment or installations (1).

While both categories of aids have the same end goal, to prevent shipping accidents, their conditions of use and the financial costs involved remain quite different: aids to navigation are the responsibility of coastal States, and sometimes require cooperation among maritime administrations in order to function properly, while shipowners bear responsibility for navigational aids, whenever flag States impose their use.

The last few years have seen the spectacular development of navigational aids, as advances in computer technologies have allowed many processes aboard ships to be automated (2). One of the first applications was the system of automatic radar plotting aids (ARPA), which calculates all the data needed to help detect echoes and plot vectors to enable the officer to avoid risks of collision.

Computers have become a common feature on board ships (3). They no longer operate in isolation, but connected with one another and even, thanks to maritime satellites, with shipping company networks,. The latest development is centralised navigation control (CNC), which comprises a set of instruments that display on several screens all the data and commands needed to oversee and navigate the ship: manoeuvring station, engine and loading monitors, means of communication, and navigational aids such as ARPA, electronic boards and radiopositioning equipment. CNC is intended to allow the ship to be controlled by a single man. This is known as "one man bridge operation" (OMBO), generalisation of which will be one of the major trends as the century ends (4).

Other new features will be the installation on board ships of voyage data recorders (VDR), known as "black boxes". IMO Resolution A.861 defined the performance standards for these in November 1997 by the IMO Resolution A.861 (5). In order to facilitate the work of vessel traffic services (VTS), it is also planned to equip ships in the near future with automatic ship identification systems (transponders) (6).

(1) Commision internationale pour la réception des grands navires. Rapport du groupe de travail II. Coordination et concertation internationales souhaitables dans le domaine des aides à la navigation et en ce qui concerne la compatibilité des équipements de bord et à terre. Annexe du Bulletin n° 31, (vol. VII/1978), AIPCN, 2.
(2) D. ABADIE, A. TROUSSE : "Développement et coordination de l'informatique à bord des navires marchands". Bull. Tech. du Bureau Veritas, Aug.-Sept. 1984, 498-503.
(3) X. LEFEBRE : "Des souris et des marins... pour la sécurité de la navigation". Navigation, vol. 41, n° 164, oct. 1993, 455-491.
(4) A. TROUSSE : "Un seul homme à la passerelle". Navigation n° 157, Jan. 1992.
(5) "IMO safety revisions set to hit target". Lloyd's List, 30 July 1998.
(6) "Transponders and electronic charts take centre stage". Lloyd's List, 20 July 1998.

Navigational aids and aids to navigation are inseparable. Neither in principle can function without the other. They will therefore be presented together here for each category of aids: maritime signals and beacons (cf I below), radio aids (II), meteorological aids (III), hydrographic aids (IV), pilotage (V) and towage (VI).

I - MARITIME SIGNALS AND BEACONS

448. - Beacons are defined as "all fixed or floating signals, possibly equipped with lights or sound signals, established to signal dangers or assist a ship in following a channel"(7). More generally, aids to navigation comprise visual, sound or radio devices helping to ensure the safety of ships and facilitate their movements.

This chapter confines itself to studying traditional systems, such as lights, unlighted aids and sound signals at sea. Because of their extensive development, radio signals will be presented in the next section. According to IALA statistics (8), conventional aids to navigation were divided up as follows in 1993 throughout the world:
- 39 690 lights, including 26 802 on fixed structures (watched, unwatched and remote-controlled);
- 40 263 unlighted aids;
- 2 909 sound signals.

A - INTERNATIONAL OBLIGATIONS ON AIDS TO NAVIGATION

1. Definition of obligations

449. - Recognised by the International Court of Justice in the case of the Straits of Corfu, the obligation to provide aids to navigation was proclaimed officially in the Law of the Sea and SOLAS Conventions.

a) Law of the Sea (LOS) Conventions

The 1982 Law of the Sea Convention explicitly declares the obligation to signal potential hazards. According to article 60.3 concerning artificial islands, installations and structures in the exclusive economic zone (EEZ), "due notice must be given of the construction of such artificial islands, installations or structures, and permanent means for giving warning of their presence must be maintained".

According to article 24.2, a "coastal state shall give appropriate publicity to any danger to navigation of which it has knowledge within its territorial sea".

Finally, article 43 indicates that States using or bordering a strait "should by agreement cooperate in the establishment and maintenance in a strait of necessary navigational and safety aids or other improvements in aid of international navigation".

---

(7) Dictionnaire GRUSS de Marine, EMOM, Paris 1978.
(8) IALA : "The development of aids to navigation during the year 1998. Tables and statistics". France.

b) 1974 SOLAS Convention

According to Regulation V/14 of the SOLAS Convention of 1974, "the contracting governments undertake to arrange for the establishment and maintenance of such aids to navigation (...) as, in their opinion, the volume of traffic justifies and the degree of risk requires".

The Convention lays down an obligation to "arrange for information relating to these aids to be made available to all concerned".

2. Enforcement of the obligation to provide aids to navigation

450. - It is incumbent on every State bordering on a sea to provide aids to navigation. For various reasons, enforcement is sometimes difficult, and international cooperation is needed to remedy certain local shortcomings. This was the case with the establishment of the Cape Spartel lighthouse, set up by the Treaty of 31 May 1865, signed between the Sultan of Morocco and the leading maritime nations of that time. Similarly, the lighthouses of Abu Ail and Djebel Teir in the Red Sea were covered by a convention signed in London in February 1962, concerning maintenance of lights in this region of the world and two IMO resolutions on their maintenance (9). There are currently about 80 national aids to navigation services, all of which belong to IALA (cf chapter 5 above). The most important include the Service des Phares et Balises in France (10), Trinity House in the United Kingdom (11) and the United States Coast Guard (12).

* **The obligation involves three specific areas:**
- Coastal areas and natural access routes.
- Wrecks and other dangers. The extent of the hazard represented by wrecks may be gauged by estimating their number: the United Kingdom alone announces 10 000 wrecks in its territorial waters (13). American experts calculate that over the last 2 000 years a million ships have been wrecked, corresponding to a wreck every 14 square miles of the surface of the world's oceans. IMO launched an international survey of the removal of wrecks in 1974 (14). Since most raising operations prove impossible or economically unfeasible, it is important to signal these hazards with the utmost care.
- Sea routes. The 1972 COLREG Convention introduced new responsibilities for coastal States concerning buoyage (15).

Aids to navigation also have to meet certain conditions to be effective. First, they must be sufficient in number. While this requirement is met on the coasts of North Western Europe (16), the same is not true of all regions of the world. Next, they must be reliable. All users of the sea agree on the importance of proper maintenance of beacons: a badly maintained buoy is probably more dangerous than none at all. On several occasions, the

---

(9) IMO Assembly. Res. A. 47, 18 Oct. 1963 and Res. A. 96, 27 Sept. 1965.
(10) Assemblée Nationale, France. La sécurité maritime : un défi européen et mondial. Rapport d'information N 1482, 5 July 1994.
(11) R. GRIME : "Shipping Law". 2nd ed., Sweet and Maxwell, London, 1991, 210-212.
(12) J. REASON : "Basic coast guard mission : aids to navigation". Surveyor, May 1977, 2.
(13) V.L. OUDET : "Nouveau printemps pour la circulation maritime", JMM, May 1971, 117.
(14) IMO. Legal Committee. LEG 3/5, 18 May 1990. Consideration of possible work on wreck removal and related issues.
(15) M. EYRIES : "Les pollutions marines accidentelles et le code de la mer", Navigation, vol. 27 - Jan. 1979, n° 105, 94.
(16) J.F. LEVY : "La signalisation maritime en France". TSM n° 11, Nov. 1975, 485.

IMO Maritime Safety Committee has drawn attention to the danger of unmarked buoys adrift. In 1975, it published a circular recommending that the large buoys used for offshore installations should be properly marked and lit (17). Finally, beacons must be fully appropriate to the new needs of navigation. The introduction of VLCCs, for instance, has involved the establishment of special light signals (18).

• **Penalties for non-compliance**

In France, the signalling obligation is a fact of positive law. It has been confirmed by the Administrative Supreme Court "Conseil d'Etat", in the Le Borgne decision of 11 December 1885 (19). Generally speaking, if an accident occurs, the administration is liable for inadequate maintenance of public structures.

In the United Kingdom, the relevant authorities have equally broad obligations. They may be held liable in the event of an accident (20).

B - HARMONISATION OF BUOYAGE SYSTEMS

451. - Lack of harmonisation of national legislations on aids to navigation is as much a cause of accidents as the shortcomings of any particular State. For more than a century, maritime nations have been striving to unify buoyage regulations. Despite IALA and IMO efforts, a consensus remains for the present unattainable.

1. Quest for harmonisation

Following the Second World War, there were thirty different buoyage systems in force in the world, many of them conflicting with one another. More than 30 000 lights and beacons had up to 34 different meanings (21). This situation was bound to be of concern to the IALA, which set up a commission in 1965 to examine contradictions among regulations, and propose ways of achieving harmonisation.

The IALA did not manage to bring about complete unification. However, it did succeed in harmonising worldwide buoyage on the basis of two systems:
- System A, which uses the colour red to mark the port side of channels and comprises both cardinal marks and lateral marks;
- System B, lateral only, using the colour red to mark the starboard side of channels.

System A rules were drawn up in 1976, and approved by IMO. Introduction of this system began the next year, and its use was gradually extended throughout Europe, Australia, New Zealand, Africa, the Gulf and a few Asian countries. The rules for system B were drawn up in 1980, and subsequently applied in North and South America, Japan, Korea and the Philippines.

(17) IMO. MSC, 38th session in IMCO News, n° 3, 1978, 3.
(18) L. RIBADEAU-DUMAS : "Les aides à la navigation et le chenalage à Antifer". Revue Tech. du Service des Phares et Balises, n° 39, Sept. 1978, 12.
V. DEGRE, LEFEVRE, BELLO : "Navigation et évolution des navires dans le Golfe de Fos, atterages immédiats". Rev. Tech. du Serv. des Ph. et Bal., n° 36, Dec. 1977, 45-61.
(19) J. GROSDIDIER DE MATONS : "La responsabilité de l'Etat pour le fonctionnement de certains services maritimes". DMF 1968, 73.
(20) 17 QBD 795 (1886), quoted by R. GRIME, op. cit., 212.
(21) JMM, 30 Oct. 1975, 2694.

In November 1980, a special conference on buoyage adopted a draft single system, dividing the world into two regions, A and B, the only difference being the reversal of lateral mark colours.

The agreement on the IALA buoyage system was finally signed in Paris on 15 April 1982. The representatives of 25 buoyage services undertook to implement the IALA system, by stating to which of the two regions, A or B, they wished to belong, and the period needed for them to convert their installations (22).

2. Present maritime buoyage system

452. - This system is described in an IALA publication (23), which lays down the general principles and rules to be following by maritime signalling services.

The system is based on five types of marks, which may be used in combination. These are lateral and cardinal marks, isolated danger marks, safe water marks, special marks, and a mark reserved for new hazards. The seafarer can easily distinguish among these different types of marks, by readily identifiable characteristics. Only lateral marks differ from region A to region B, while all the others are common to both regions.

Rules apply to all fixed and floating marks, other than lighthouses, sector lights, leading lights and marks, lightships and large navigational buoys. They are used to show the lateral limits of navigable channels, natural dangers and other obstructions such as wrecks, other areas or features of importance to mariners, and new dangers.

II - RADIO AIDS

453. - There has been a considerable development of radio navigation aids in the last few years, because of the increase in the number, size and speed of ships. In the past, mariners could rely only on soundings, seamarks and stars to find out their approximate position. Today, radio waves are used as maritime positioning and navigational aids (24).

A - CLASSIFICATION OF POSITION-FIXING SYSTEMS

There are several major radio position-fixing systems, which can be classified on the basis of their degree of precision (25).

Radiobeacons are the least accurate. They give an approximate position for a ship, with margins of error that can reach 4 to 10 nautical miles. Used with the radio direction finder, they are today being replaced by other more efficient systems for merchant shipping, such as radar beacons (racons) and transponders.

Terrestrial hyperbolic radionavigation systems offer an additional degree of precision. However, they have two drawbacks:
- The coverage and precision of such system remain dependent on the positioning and number of onshore stations, and the distance that separates the ships from these stations and the navigation zone, in order to ensure proper crosschecking of the hyperbolae.

---

(22) Ch. VILLE : "AISM, 1957-1990. 33 ans de coopération internationale". AISM, France, 1991, 36-49.
(23) IALA : "Maritime buoyage system". France, 1980.
(24) M. WINGATE : "The future of conventional aids to navigation", Journal of Navigation, Vol. 39, n° 2, May 1998.
(25) IALA : Aids to navigation guide (NAVGUIDE). 2nd Ed., dec. 1993, Annex 3. Technical description of radio aids to navigation.

- The working frequency of nearly all such systems remains subject to electrical wave propagation disturbances.

The commonest systems are Differential Omega, Decca Navigator, Loran C and Chaika.

Satellite radio position-fixing is the most precise system, allowing all-weather positioning and navigation anywhere in the world. However, because of the high cost of the equipment, the use of satellites long remained the preserve of warships. Satellite systems are now becoming commoner in the merchant navy (26), leading international organisations and state to review their policies on this matter.

The Global Positioning System (GPS) is currently the universal positioning system that meets almost all needs. However, it has the serious disadvantage of being under the control of the United States military authorities, who take all decisions about its future. Meanwhile, the Russian Federation has introduced a similar system, Glonass. The European Union is developing its own Global Navigation Satellite System (GNSS), in order to escape dependence on American and Russian positioning policies.

B - INTERNATIONAL REGULATIONS

1. Coastal state obligations

454. - Radio aids are mentioned expressly in Regulation V/14 of the SOLAS Convention, already referred to, asking states on the one hand to attend to the establishment and maintenance of such aids when the volume of traffic justifies and the degree of risk requires, and on the other hand to arrange for information to be made available to all concerned.

Radar beacons and transponders must meet the functional standards laid down in annex 2 to Resolution A.615 of 19 November 1987. IMO provides a definition of the operational specifications of such equipment. For the technical aspects, it refers to either the ITU or the IALA.

2. Shipborne navigational equipment

Navigational equipment on board a ship, which complements shore-based installations, depends on the age of the ship and its gross tonnage. Regulation V/12 of the SOLAS Convention mentions the following equipment: compass (magnetic and gyrocompass), radar (two installations for ships of more than 10 000 gross tonnage), automatic radar plotting aid (ARPA), echo-sounding device, speed and distance indicators, indicators to show the rudder angle, the rate of revolution of each propeller, rate-of-turn indicator and radio direction finder.

(26) R. NIJJER : "Marine navigation in the 21st Century. A shift to precision navigation". Maritime Studies, March-April 1993.

Numerous IMO recommendations have helped define the functional standards for such electronic navigational aids. General requirements are set out in Resolution A.574 of 20 November 1985.

C - WORLDWIDE RADIONAVIGATION SYSTEM

455. - A worldwide radionavigation system has been under examination since 1983, when the Netherlands asked IMO to consider the issue (27). Resolution A.666 of 1989 contained initial general policy considerations, amended by Resolution A.815 of 23 November 1995. This document is intended to provide a basis for amending SOLAS Regulation V/12, by making it mandatory for ships to carry means of receiving transmissions from a suitable radionavigation system throughout their voyage.

The study begins with the principle that it was not feasible for IMO to fund a worldwide radionavigation system. According to paragraph 2.2.1 of the Resolution, it is up to governments and interested organisations to provide and operate such a system. The question of IMO recognition or approval of existing and future systems is then examined.

1. System recognition procedure

It is the role of IMO to recognise radionavigation systems with the consent of the governments and organisations that operate them. This means accepting that a system can supply adequate information on position within the zone which it covers, and that the presence of shipborne receiving equipment intended for use with the system complies with the requirements of the SOLAS Convention.

In addition to the requirement of formal notification of introduction of the system, governments and organisations must provide IMO with information to assist in its consideration of the system, and advise it well in advance of proposed changes in any characteristics or parameters.

2. Shipborne receiving equipment

Navigational equipment on board ship must also possess certain characteristics:
- suitability for function with either a worldwide or a local radionavigation system, in order to avoid the need to duplicate equipment;
- conformity to general requirements for navigational equipment and IMO resolutions;
- availability of automatic selection of stations to determine the ship's position;
- availability of an output to supply other equipment with position information in standard form.

(27) P. GRIFFITHS : "The IMO worldwide navigation study". The Journal of Navigation, vol. 43, n° 1, Jan. 1990, 41.

D - EU DEVELOPMENT POLICY FOR AIDS TO NAVIGATION

456. - In its Communication of 24 February 1993 (28), setting out a common policy on safety at sea, the European Commission outlined its intentions for developing the maritime infrastructure and systems to ensure safety of navigation. The action programme proposed by Brussels assigns an important position to aids to navigation.

1. Imbalances and inequalities in protection

The Commission first notes that the financial efforts made by member states to improve aids to navigation are unbalanced. Certain countries cannot supply the expected services because of the length of their coastlines, while charges to users differ from one state to another. Some, like the United Kingdom, apply the user-payer principle, by charging lighting fees to ships using their ports. In others, like Belgium, Germany, Denmark, France, the Netherlands and Italy, services are paid for out of the public funds.

Coverage of the cost of operating and maintaining infrastructures raises a problem: states provide extensive aids to navigation in European waters, without users, particularly ships in transit, having to bear any of the cost.

These imbalances and lack of coordination result in risks for protection and safety at sea within the EU. While certain parts of Western Europe are fairly well covered by radionavigation systems, the same is not true in the Mediterranean, even though it is more prone to pollution.

2. Proposed remedies

a) Aid to navigational infrastructures

The European Commission suggests that radionavigation infrastructures should be an integral part of trans-European traffic management networks. This would enable them to benefit from various Community sources of funding.

In collaboration with the IALA, it proposes to make a report on an EU radionavigation scheme comparable and compatible with Russian and American systems, with the aim of establishing a civil satellite radionavigation system, completed if necessary by terrestrial systems.

b) Funding

The Commission also emphasises the need to establish some mechanism to harmonise the "rules of the game" for infrastructure investments, and restore competitiveness among the ports of different member States. This mechanism would have to ensure that expenditure corresponds to the actual needs of shipping and of the coastal populations of the EU. It would also have to be based on the user-payer principle.

(28) COM (93) 66 final, Brussels 24 Feb. 1993, paragraphs 31-57 and 101-113.

The first step would be to collect information from member States on the cost of aids to navigation installed outside ports, financing arrangements, length of coastline, number of light buoys and beacons, volume of traffic, and income from fees charged in countries practising this system.

This action could ultimately lead to the introduction of a "Eurocontrol" system in which each State could recover the running costs of the system from a central authority.

3. Actions taken

The policy recommended by the Commission has already begun to be implemented. On 25 February 1992, the Council took a decision concerning LORAN C regional networks (29). Several steps will be needed before the establishment of a proper public civil navigational system under international management. The first step consists of developing a Global Navigation Satellite System (GNSS), providing a European complement to the American and Russian systems and using certain geostationary satellites. On 18 June 1998, the Council took a Decision on the agreement between the European Community, the European Space Agency and the European Organisation for the Safety of Air Navigation on a European contribution to the development of a global navigation satellite system (30).

III - METEOROLOGICAL AIDS

457. - Weather forecasting is of vital importance at sea. Today, however inclement the weather, ships ply their routes back and forth (31). Mariners therefore need maximum information, so that they can avoid or evade weather hazards. Without such information, any form of navigation becomes risk-prone.

An IMO study shows that about a third of all accidents at sea in recent years happened in heavy seas and strong winds. Weather conditions would therefore appear to remain a serious danger, despite the progress made in weather forecasting (32). According to London insurers, bad weather remains the main cause of casualties at sea. Of 620 accidents between 1992 and 1996, 187 (30.2 per cent) were attributable to bad meteorological conditions (33).

A - SOLAS OBLIGATIONS

458. - Chapter V of the 1974 SOLAS Convention contains general obligations concerning meteorological aids to navigation, and more specifically ice patrol services.

1. General obligations

The general obligations enumerated in article 4 of the SOLAS Convention concern both collection and dissemination of meteorological data.

---

(29) OJEC, L 59, 4 March 1992, 17.
(30) OJEC, L 194/15, 10 July 1998.
(31) "A struggle for survival against the forces of nature". Safety at Sea, April 1983, 30.
(32) WMO Bulletin, Jan. 1979 in METMAR, 2nd quarter 1979, n° 103, 1.
(33) Institute of London Underwriters. Casualty statistics 1996, London 1997, 7.

Each State undertakes to encourage ships at sea to collect information and to ensure that it is examined, disseminated and exchanged in the most suitable way to aid navigation (cf Regulation 4a). Arrangements are needed to equip selected ships with tested instruments, and encourage other vessels to take observations on tropical storms or gales, for instance.

Governments also undertake to cooperate on the application of certain meteorological arrangements, including warning ships of gales and storms, daily weather bulletins and daily weather maps (cf Regulation 4b).

This information must be applied in form for transmission, and transmitted in the order of priority prescribed by the Radio Regulations (cf Regulation 4c).

Mutual arrangements may be made among States to transmit forecasts in the best position to serve various zones and areas (cf Regulation 4d).

2. Specific ice patrol obligations

Navigation in the waters round Greenland has been the cause of innumerable disasters, including the loss of the *Titanic* in 1912. The London Convention of 31 May 1929 for the safety of life at sea marked the beginning of ice patrols and a study and research service for ice conditions in the North Atlantic. These were entrusted to the American government. The obligations were repeated in Regulation 5 of the 1974 SOLAS Convention. The American government continues to manage the services mentioned, with the financial participation of the countries concerned (34).

3. Sea routes and climatic conditions

In certain parts of the world, sea routes may be determined by the coastal State, on the basis of particular climatic conditions:
- The Northern sea route, which connects the ports of North West Europe with Japan, is theoretically open only to ships reinforced for navigation in ice, and meeting classification society requirements in this respect.
- Numerous natural obstacles to safe navigation have led Russia to establish a special compulsory pilotage and icebreaker service for ships passing through the Straits of Veljkitskij and Schokaljskij (35).
- South Africa has prohibited fully laden oil tankers from coming within 12 miles of its coasts, and requires them to keep at least 20 miles from the edge of the continental shelf when they meet particular atmospheric conditions between Richard's Bay and Great Fish Point. The possibility of rogue waves more than 18 metres high, which have caused numerous shipwrecks in this area, explains the ban (36).

B - METEOROLOGICAL ASSISTANCE FOR SHIPPING

459. - The World Meteorological Organisation (WMO) published a manual in 1990, to define state obligations on meteorological assistance (37). This contains two types of requirements: standard practices and procedures that states have to apply, informing the

---

(34) "US demands Ice Patrol payments". Lloyd's List, 22 July 1998.
(35) JMM, 27 July 1967, 1682.
(36) J.D. TERRANCE : "Rogue waves of South Africa's wild coast". Lloyd's List, 4 Jan. 1997.
(37) World Meteorological Organisation : Manual of Marine Meteorological Services. Vol. 1. Global Aspects. OMM n° 558. Geneva 1990.

WMO Secretariat of any failure to observe a particular regulation, and recommended practices and procedures, which states are asked to adopt, without notifying the WMO.

Meteorological assistance depends on the maritime zone involved, whether high seas, coastal or offshore waters, large ports or port zones and, for each zone, the type of services supplied: weather bulletins, assistance with search and rescue services, supply of information by radio facsimile, marine climatological summary programme, supply of special climatological information, and information and advice on maritime meteorology.

In legal terms, what value is attached to meteorological information ?

In France, the courts have always considered that a storm is not an act of God or a case of *force majeure* "because ships, by their very nature, must be built to withstand force" (38).

In general, French case law considers that heavy weather and storms are not automatically events that relieve the shipper of a presumption of liability. Judges assess in each individual case whether such events were predictable, and whether their consequences were insurmountable (39).

In the United Kingdom, heavy weather is less and less regarded as an act of God, giving the shipowner a chance to evade his responsibilities. This is because of the arrival of rapid and constant ship-to-shore communications (40).

C - SHIP WEATHER ROUTEING

460. - For several years, the role of the meteorological services of the leading maritime nations has no longer been confined to drawing up and broadcasting weather forecast bulletins. Their activities have been diversified, to meet the demands of all users. Weather routeing is a good example. It consists of recommending optimum routes for ships. This method has proved particularly beneficial for ship operations and safety, and for the protection of their crews and cargoes (41).

IMO Resolution A.528 adopted on 17 November 1983 refers to damage caused by heavy weather and other factors, and recognises that weather routeing can contribute to safety. It recommends governments to advise ships flying their flags of the availability of weather routeing information, particularly from services listed by WHO.

IV - HYDROGRAPHIC SERVICE AIDS

461. - Maritime safety information is of the utmost importance for all ships. It consists of meteorological and navigational warnings, and other urgent safety-related messages (42).

Dedicated State services collect, monitor and publish such information, using all available technical resources and equipment. In many countries, these services are traditionally part of the military navy organisation.

---

(38) DMF, 1954, 46.
(39) R. RODIERE, E. DU PONTAVICE : "Droit maritime". 11e édition, Precis Dalloz, Paris, 1991, 287.
(40) M. GREY : "Why heavy weather is not like Act of God" Lloyd's List, 2 March 1989.
(41) J. SPAANS, P. STOTER : "New developments in ship routing". Navigation vol. 43, n° 169, Jan. 1995, 95-106.
(42) Definition given by IMO Resolution A. 705 adopted by IMO Assembly on 6 November 1991 : "Promulgation of maritime safety information".

In France, this role is performed by the Service Hydrographique et Océanographique de la Marine (SHOM), set up in 1720 (43), and in the United Kingdom by the Royal Naval Hydrographic Service, set up in 1795 (44).

IMO and IHO nautical information takes the form of regulations and recommendations concerning two areas: charts and nautical publications, and maritime safety information.

A - CHARTS AND NAUTICAL PUBLICATIONS

462. - According to SOLAS Regulation V/20, states must ensure that ships flying under their flags "carry adequate and up-to-date charts, sailing directions, lists of lights, notices to mariners, tide tables and all other nautical publications necessary for the intended voyage". Enforcement of this obligation raises a series of technical, legal and financial problems.

1. Promulgation of nautical documents

Hydrographic services in each state are in charge of establishing and revising nautical documents, in standard international form.

a) Establishment of revision of charts

Obligations are defined, not in the SOLAS Convention, but in two IMO resolutions:
- Resolution A.532 of 17 November 1983 refers to the importance to safe navigation of providing accurate and up-to-date hydrographic information, and to the fact that many areas have not been surveyed to modern standards. It invites governments to conduct hydrographic surveys and cooperate with other governments where necessary.
- Resolution A.580 of 20 November 1985 urges IMO members to establish regional hydrographic commissions or charting groups and to support groups already set up by IMO to prepare accurate charts.

In future, these are to become mandatory requirements. In July 1977, the NAV subcommittee on Safety of Navigation outlined government responsibilities in carrying out hydrographic surveying: preparing and issuing official nautical charts and promulgating notices to mariners to keep charts up to date. This draft regulation is part of the revision of Chapter V of the SOLAS Convention, which is due to be completed in 1998. The likely date of entry into force is 2002 (45).

b) Standardisation of nautical documents

In 1984, the IHO issued its Regulations for international charts (46), to be observed by hydrographic services in preparing and revising such documents. These regulations concern international chart schemes, chart specifications, which differ depending on the scale, maintenance of charts, exchange of reproduction material among services, and financial aspects of chart production.

(43) A. GOUGENHEIM : "Le Service hydrographique de la Marine a 250 ans". Revue Maritime, Dec. 1970, 1321.
(44) - S. SHIPMAN : "200 years of the Royal Naval Hydrographic Service". Seaways, Nov. 1995, 10-11.
- N. ESSENHIGH : "Hydrography in a changing world". Seaway, Nov. 1995, 3-5.
(45) IMO - NAV 44/14, 4 Sept. 1998, 14.
(46) International Hydrographic Bureau. "Regulation of the IHO for International (int) charts". Monaco, 1984. Annex B to IHB circular letter 16/1984.

Other documents written in the language of each country are not so far subject to international standardisation, except for the Light Manual, the contents of which may be standardised by means of international symbols (47).

2. Value of charts and hydrographic service responsibilities

463. - Most charts currently available to mariners ensure safe navigation. However, many regions hold hazards not shown on charts. These shortcomings have led to sometime very serious accidents (48), such as when the *Queen Elizabeth II* ran aground twice in shallows in the Vineyard Sound in 1992 (49).

The question is whether hydrographic services bear liability for inaccuracies or imprecisions in the information contained in charts, and which lead to an accident.

In France, the reply appears to be in the negative. The administration is required only to be "diligent", and its liability is never claimed (50). The shipmaster is considered to remain sole master of the route followed by his ship, and carries full responsibility for the results. The fact that certain regional charts are not infallible should simply make him more cautious.

In the United States, cartographic services, whether public, like the Defense Mapping Agency (DMA) and the National Oceanic and Atmospheric Administration (NOAA), or private, may be held liable for shortcomings in their products (51). According to US law (52), charts must be accurate, to ensure safety of navigation.

Two texts provide a basis for legal claims against the administration: the Federal Torts Claims Act (FTCA) and the Suits Admiralty Act (SAA). Charges are based either on the theory of negligence (gross errors in charts) or on product liability. The administration is liable only to claims for negligence, whereas commercial companies are subject to both types of charges.

3. Electronic charts

464. - For many experts, the appearance of the electronic chart is the major navigational event of the 20th century. Electronic charts first appeared in the early Eighties, originally as a simple electronic image of the paper chart. They have now become a comprehensive electronic system for displaying navigation data (53), requiring new resource management on the bridge (54).

The safety benefits are obvious. The electronic chart can be continuously updated, and integrated with other navigational aids and equipment, such as radar or tracing tables (55). It allows the master to monitor the route followed by his ship, by facilitating the display of the data needed for safe navigation, on the desired scale and in real time (56).

(47) G. BESSERO : "Aides à la navigation - Hydrographie". JMM, 26 July 1996, 1831-1833.
(48) J. PASQUAY : "Accidents maritimes en relation avec les documents nautiques et les systèmes de navigation : passé, présent et futur". Navigation, vol. 42, n° 168, Oct. 1994, 380-392.
(49) M. GREY : "QE 2 grounding : charts blamed". Lloyd's List, 8 July 1993.
(50) J. GROSDIDIER DE MATONS : "La responsabilité de l'Etat pour le fonctionnement de certains services maritimes". DMF 1968, 69.
(51) E. OBLOY : "The liability of the United States Government as a producer of electronic charts". 2nd international conference on Maritime Law and the Electronic Chart. Tulane Law School, USA, March 1995.
(52) 10 VSC § 2791-96 et 44 VSC § 1336.
(53) M. GREY : "Electronic navigation - The end of the paper chart". BIMCO Bulletin, vol. 91, n° 6, 1996, 44-45.
(54) L. STOEL : "Integrated bridges and electronic charts". Safety at Sea International, Oct. 1997, 16-18.
(55) W. O'NEIL : "Keynote speech at XVth International Hydrographic Conference. Monaco, 14-25 April 1997.
(56) O. GUNDERSRUD : "Certificats de sécurité nautique de DNV". Contour n° 8, 1996, 24-25.

a) Definitions

IMO Resolution A.817 of 23 November 1995 defined the electronic navigation chart (ENC) and electronic chart display systems (ECDIS).

ECDIS is "a navigation information system which (...), by displaying selected information from a system electronic navigational chart (SENC) with positional information from navigation sensors" assists "the marine in route planning and route monitoring" (paragraph 2.1).

The ENC is a "database standardised as to content, structure and format, issued for use with ECDIS on the authority of government-authorised hydrographic offices". It differs from a system electronic navigation chart (SENC) "resulting from the transformation of the ENC by ECDIS for appropriate use, updates to the ENC and other data added by the mariner" (paragraph 2.3).

In practice, the ECDIS consists of a database containing all the necessary geographical data in numeric form, and data processing equipment to process such data in real time (57). The construction and marketing of on-board information systems are a matter for the private sector, while data issue and updating are the responsibility of the authorities.

b) Standardisation

465. - In order to be able to use ECDIS instead of paper charts, three series of standards have to be observed, namely those of IMO, the IHO and the IEC (58).

• IMO standards

Resolution A.817, already referred to, sets performance standards for ECDIS, which must meet "the general requirements for shipborne radio equipment forming part of the global maritime distress and safety system (GMDSS) and the requirements for electronic navigational aids contained in IMO Resolution A.694" (paragraph 1.3).

Performance standards enable designers and manufacturers to ensure that their equipment meets the level of operational requirements defined by IMO.

• IHO standards

These apply more specifically to the format, content and display of numeric data. By the early Nineties, the IHO had created a worldwide electronic navigation database (WEND), to facilitate the production and issue of information. This general framework stipulates that responsibility is shared between two entities:
- Government hydrographic offices are responsible for establishing and revising national databases;
- Regional electronic chart coordination centres have the task of integrating data from national hydrographic offices, and distributing and selling integrated datafiles for a particular geographical region (59).

(57) I. GONIN : "ECDIS - The story so far". Safety at Sea International. Feb. 1997, 8-12.
(58) L. ALEXANDER : "International Standards for ECDIS : current status". Contour/Maritime Magazine n° 12, 1998, 84.
(59) A. KERR : "Base de données mondiale". Contour n° 7, 1996, 8-10.

• IEC standards

Since 1992, the International Electrotechnical Commission has been trying to lay down requirements for ECDIS performance tests and checks. Once adopted, these standards will provide a reference for specifications for approval of operational testing methods and test results, to be respected by ECDIS in order to comply with IMO regulations.

• IMO/IHO group

This joint Harmonisation Group on ECDIS has been functioning since 1987 (60). Its present role is to examine possible backup measures that could be regarded as satisfactory for an IMO-compliant ECDIS. It is also concerned with preparing guidelines or performance standards for non-compliant electronic chart systems.

c) Legal problems

466. - Despite the development of regulations, standards and specifications for ECDIS, this new technology raises many legal problems, all the more complex because no system yet complies with IMO and IHO requirements, so that no legal precedents exist. Three main questions may be raised, however.

• Definition of electronic chart

Should an electronic chart be regarded as a nautical chart or as an aid to navigation ? The distinction is of substantive importance as regards certain private law provisions contained in international conventions or certain national laws on the environment. An example is article 3.3c of the CLC 1969 Convention on Civil Liability for Oil Pollution Damage, which provides for exemption from liability of the owner of a polluting ship if a State has failed to maintain lights and other aids to navigation.

• Equivalence of electronic charts for the purposes of SOLAS V/20

Does a ship equipped with an ECDIS meet the requirements of Regulation V/20 of the SOLAS Convention concerning the presence of charts on board ? In adhering to the principle that the ECDIS should be regarded as the legal equivalent of a paper chart, the IHO has somewhat distorted the debate, by focussing on form and not on content, in other words the available information in quantity, quality and ease of use (61).

Regulation I/5a of the SOLAS Convention provides for the possibility for administrations to authorise the presence on board of equivalent substitute installations, devices or appliances, if it is established that they are "at least as effective" as those stipulated in the Convention. The Netherlands have drawn attention to this provision, and asked for temporary recognition of scanned electronic charts under certain conditions (62).

In a submission to the IMO NAV Subcommittee in June 1997, the IHO stated that the delivery of authorised electronic navigational charts used in ECDIS had been slower than expected, "thus precluding the use of ECDIS until such data becomes available" (63).

---

(60) P. EHLERS : "International perspectives on electronic charts". 2nd Int. Conf. on Maritime Law and the Electronic Chart. Tulane Law School, March 1995.
(61) "Raster chart, a course for recognition". Lloyd's List, 16 July 1996.
(62) IFN : "Les cartes électroniques". Navigation vol. 38, n° 150, Apr. 1990, 150.
(63) "When politics govern safety. Progress delayed on electronic charts" Fairplay, 18th Sept. 1997, 18-21.

Because of the difficulties encountered by IMO in financing proposed draft performance standards for raster chart display systems, a 23-nation group in the NAV subcommittee has agreed that these systems "with adequate backup arrangements" and "use together with an appropriate portfolio of up-to-date charts", as determined by the national administration, may be accepted as complying with Regulation V/20 of the SOLAS Convention (64). This means that ships using raster charts will continue to be legally obliged to carry paper charts on board (65).

• **Electronic chart maker's liability**

467. - Two types of entities need to be considered:
- Private companies which, without awaiting the production of official ENCs, have already for several years been marketing more or less sophisticated systems, combined with products obtained by simply scanning paper charts. These companies have generally been careful to warn their clients that they disclaim any responsibility for faults or negligence on their part. These clauses will be regarded differently by the courts in each State.
- National hydrographic services producing official ENCs. It may be argued that their responsibility for such charts will not be any different from those applying to paper charts, organisations being subject to the same obligations of care, precision and revision concerning information (66).

The question will then arise as to how the chart maker can escape liability, and simply prove that his obligations have been properly met. Several mechanisms have been considered: production certification or type approval by a classification society (67) or an independent assessor, survey and inspection by port state authorities, who would not only assess hardware and software conformity to regulatory standards, but also the professional ability of the users.

There are two potential areas in all charting arrangements. The first concerns the accuracy of the displayed data and the second concerns the need to keep all working charts up to date with changes such as wrecks, new routeing systems, port layout, pipelines, cables and other relevant data. Electronic charts can be updated much more simply provided if there is a quality system in place.

B - DANGER MESSAGES AND NAVIGATIONAL WARNINGS

468. - Shipmasters and States bear a fundamental obligation to disseminate information on immediate dangers for navigation.

1. Danger messages

According to SOLAS Regulation V/2a, a shipmaster who finds himself in the presence of an immediate danger for navigation is obliged to inform ships in the vicinity and

(64) "IMO delays decision on raster charts". Lloyd's List, 21 July 1997.
(65) "A. DE BIEVRE : "Some problems never seem to go away". Lloyd's List, 5 Nov. 1998.
See also : - "Difficult learning curve". Lloyd's Ship Manager. Sept. 1997.
- "Raster charts : acceptance but not equivalence". Safety at Sea International, August 1997, 3.
(66) D. DION : "The first International Conference on Maritime Law and the Electronic Chart. A look in the near view mirror". 2nd International Conference. Tulane Law School, March 1995.
(67) F. KLEPSIK : "EDCIS and classification. perspectives of Det Norske Veritas Classification A.S.". 2nd International Conference. Tulane Law School, March 1995.

the competent authorities, at the first point on the coast with which he can communicate. No special form of transmission is specified: the information may be issued in plain language, preferably in English, or by means of the International Code of Signals.

Regulation V/3 indicates several types of information that must be included in these messages, such as the presence of ice, derelicts or other immediate dangers to navigation, tropical storms or storm-force winds.

According to Regulation V/2b, every state must take the necessary steps to ensure that any information received about such dangers is brought promptly to the knowledge of those concerned, and communicated to other interested governments. Such information is transmitted free of cost to the ships concerned (cf Regulation V/2c).

2. Worldwide navigational warning service

469. - Several accidents have shown that the international dissemination of information in the maritime sector was far from being as efficient as in the aviation sector. In the Seventies, IMO and the IHO began work on a Worldwide Navigational Warning Service (WWNWS), adopted in 1977 (68).

a) Definition of WWNWS

The plan for the creation of a warning service adopted by Resolution A.381 of 14 November 1977, as amended by Resolution A.419 of 15 November 1979, is intended to ensure the fastest possible dissemination of navigational information.

Under this plan, oceans are divided into 16 navigation areas (NAVAREA). In each area, a state assumes responsibility for transmitting messages via a single station. Within the area, each country designates a national coordinator to collect and issue coastal warnings, and send appropriate information to the area coordinator.

NAVAREA warnings generally refer only to the area concerned, and are transmitted at fixed times, at least twice a day. Steps may also be taken to ensure that warnings are available in harbour offices and presented in printed form if necessary.

In addition, NAVAREA warning bulletins, which give the serial numbers of recent information, must be issued periodically. Coastal warnings covering a region or part of the area may be transmitted by national coordination authorities: the plan also provides for the issue of local warnings in the national language. For area and regional warnings, English is used.

b) Development of WWNWS

Because of its original nature, the WWNWS has been regarded by some as the first step towards the unified organisation of shipping. It was amended by Resolution A.706 of 6 November 1992, to adapt it to the new GMDSS, and introduced on 1st February 1992 (cf chapter 20 below).

It now comprises NAVTEX, an automated service for dissemination of maritime safety information. This system allows ships equipped with a dedicated receiver to obtain printed navigational and meteorological warnings and urgent messages. The establishment and operation of NAVTEX services must comply with the requirements of Resolution A.617 of 19 November 1987.

---

(68) A. FULLER : "Marine safety information". The Journal of Navigation, vol. 41, n° 2, May 1988, 242-248.

The WWNWS forms part of the Marine Safety Information System, which is an internationally coordinated network of radio broadcasts of information essential for safety of navigation, received on board all ships by means of equipment which automatically monitors the proper frequencies, and which prints in simple English only information of concern to the receiving ships. Resolution A.706 of 6 November 1991 sets out the organisation, standards and methods for the transmission and reception of such information (69).

C - DEVELOPMENT POLICIES FOR HYDROGRAPHIC AIDS

470. - Do hydrographic aids currently meet the requirements of safety at sea ? The question is worth asking at a time when so many states are redefining action programmes and policies on the issue.

1. Evolving needs of navigation and hydrographic possibilities

Three factors have weighed upon the evolvement of the role and tasks of hydrographic services in the last twenty years:
- First, there has been a gradual deterioration in the quality of hydrographic information. Apart from coastal regions of States which have well developed services, most surveys were made by means of depth soundings in the 19th and early 20th centuries. The new independence of Third World countries abruptly interrupted survey work in progress in certain areas, such as the West coast of Africa. For other regions, certain charts have had to be updated continuously, because of recurrent changes in navigating conditions, such as the seas around Newfoundland, where so many icebergs are adrift (70).
- Next, the needs of navigation have changed. The increased draught of ships in the Sixties and changes in shipping traffic mean that the state of surveying throughout the world, and the situation of marine cartography, no longer meet the needs of users (71).
- Finally, the workload of hydrographic services has grown considerably, with the introduction of traffic separation schemes and the promulgation of electronic navigational charts, which require high-precision survey data.

Some commentators conclude that modern techniques are incapable of reducing the growing gap between the needs of shipping and the state of hydrography (72). What solutions could be envisaged to remedy this situation on an international scale ?

2. Cost optimisation policy

471. - In addition to strengthening international cooperation on hydrography, there have been proposals for a cost optimisation policy to improve aids to navigation.

Hydrographic services have a long tradition of exchanging data without any charges being made. This principle was called into question at the IHO five-year conference in 1992, at which certain states expressed their wish to introduce a cost optimisation policy.

---

(69) MANNEVY : "Une nouvelle organisation de la diffusion des avertissements radio destinés aux navires". Navigation, vol. 25, n° 98, Apr. 1977, 181.
(70) D.C. KAPPOR : "Coopération internationale en Hydrographie". Revue Hydrographique Internationale LIII, July 1976.
(71) L. OUDET : "Le prix de la circulation maritime". JMM, 12 avril 1971, 2052.
(72) J.N. PASQUAY : "La sécurité du trafic maritime moderne et les besoins en levés hydrographiques et en carto-graphie marine". Navigation, vol. 33, n° 132, Oct. 1985, 425-441.

There are now two differing concepts of hydrographic aids. Some countries, like the United States, are keen to preserve the concept of free exchange of hydrographic data, considering that this is a public service which cannot be subject to legislation on copyright, and is by nature non-commercial. Others are keen to break with that tradition, by making users pay a fair price for hydrographic data (73).

IMO has not really come down on one side or the other of this debate (76). A few States, like the United Kingdom, have asked their hydrographic services to cut costs, by leaving open the possibility of marketing their products. Most IMO members remain at present hostile to excessive optimisation of public expenditure. The solution may be to find a fair balance between these two attitudes.

V - PILOTAGE

472. - Pilots have been used to guide ships since the most ancient times. In the Middle Ages, maritime voyages were so dangerous that shipowners employed on the one hand a shipmaster, to be responsible for safe delivery of the cargo, and a *"grand lomant"*, offshore pilot responsible for the safety of the voyage (as opposed to a *"petit lomant"*, also known as a lodesman, the inshore pilot who took charge of a ship entering and leaving port) (75).

At the present time, the modern pilot no longer confines his role to offering advice. He generally is given the conduct of the ship, a task made increasingly difficult by the increase in the size and technical complexity of modern ships.

A - HARBOUR PILOTAGE

473. - Pilotage in harbour areas is the concern of States, which usually organise it as a public service. This form of organisation has consequences for the rights, obligations and responsibilities of pilots, who provide this service essential to the safety of navigation in harbour approaches.

1. State responsibilities

Article 11 of the 1923 Convention on the Regime of Maritime Ports recognises the right of each State to organise and administer pilotage services as it thinks fit. It is free to impose a compulsory service, providing that it respects the principle of equality in the charges made; it may also exempt its own citizens from mandatory use of a pilot, provided they meet certain technical conditions.

---

(73) "Data sales open fault lines in world of hydrography". Lloyd's List, 9 June 1995.
(74) A. DE BIEVRE : "A sleeping dog which we should waken". Lloyd's List, 21 July 1977.
(75) H. HIGNETT : "Brief history of pilotage". The Nautical Institute on Pilotage and Shiphandling, London, 1990, 16-19.

IMO Resolution A.159 of 27 November 1968 recommends member States to "organise pilotage services in those areas where such services would contribute to the safety of navigation in a more effective way than other possible measures and should, where applicable, define the ships or classes of ships for which employment of a pilot would be mandatory".

This freedom stated in international agreements results in great diversity in organising pilotage services, which may be provided by public, semi-public or private organisations.

In France, pilots are commissioned by the State, and belong to a professional association, under the Act of 28 March 1928, setting conditions for maritime pilotage, completed by the implementing order of 14 December 1929, which contains general pilotage regulations and the enabling order of 19 May 1969; repeating the regulatory part of the 1928 Act (76).

In the United Kingdom, pilotage was originally the responsibility of independent individuals. Later, it was administered by the Corporation of Trinity House in certain districts, and by local pilotage authorities elsewhere. Since the Pilotage Act of 1987, it has been provided by competent harbour authorities (77).

2. Mandatory pilotage

474. - While most national legislations impose mandatory pilotage, there are considerable variations from one State to another, depending on the gross tonnage and type of ship, and the type of cargoes. Certain ships, like fishing boats, carferries or service craft, may be exempted from this requirement, which may also in some cases involve only ships carrying noxious or dangerous goods. Each time, this obligation is justified by the fact that maritime pilots make a significant contribution to safety at sea and protection of the marine environment, particularly in high-risk areas like ports. Because of its mandatory nature, pilotage is regarded in many countries, such as France (78), as a public service, warranting State intervention in its organisation and performance.

In some coastal States, there is the practice of issuing pilotage exemption certificates. These may be given to shipmasters who use a port on a regular basis. Such ship masters usually have to take an examination to satisfy the local pilotage authority that they are competent.

3. Protection and safety of pilots

One of the problems facing pilots is to obtain actual access to a ship, particularly when the weather is bad or the ship is very large (79). International regulations have been drawn up to cope with these difficulties and improve the safety and protection of pilots. They consist of SOLAS Regulation V/17 concerning transfer arrangements, including ladders and pilot hoists. These mandatory provisions have been completed by IMO Resolutions A.275, A.426 and A.667.

---

(76) Fédération Française des Syndicats Professionnels de Pilotes Maritimes : "Le pilotage maritime". Etude du 13 Jan. 1995, Paris.
(77) A. CORBET : "The Law of pilotage. A brief commentary with special reference to the UK Pilotage Act of 1987". The Nautical Institute on Pilotage. London, 1990, 24-26.
(78) R. REZENTHEL : "Le pilotage dans les eaux portuaires". DMF 1988, 658.
(79) R. VOORT : "Accidents relating to pilots whilst embarking and disembarking. Causes and prevention". The Nautical Institute on Pilotage, 1990, London, 113.

4. Pilot obligations and liabitities

a) Obligations

• **General safety obligation**

475. - This obligation is not usually stated in regulations. It arises merely from the very essence and practices of the pilotage contract, namely the assistance given to the shipmaster in conducting the ship when entering or leaving port and within the harbour and pilotage area. Yet this concept of assistance is subject to widely differing interpretation, depending on the country involved:
- In most cases, the pilot is regarded as a mere adviser under the orders of the shipmaster who, as the head of the maritime expedition, retains all his prerogatives. This interpretation concurs with Regulation II/1.10 of the STCW Convention of 1978, which declares that the presence of a pilot on board "does not relieve the master or officer in charge of the watch from their duties and obligations for the safety of the ship".
- Certain national legislations go further than this. The pilot no longer confines his action to giving advice, but is also in charge of conducting the ship, with all the accompanying responsibilities. This situation is set out clearly in section 742 of the British Merchant Shipping Act of 1894, which was not amended by the 1987 Act (80).
- In the particular situation of the Panama Canal, pilots take full and entire responsibility for the ship's navigation (81).

• **Obligation of information**

EU legislation has added another safety obligation for pilots engaged in boarding, weighing anchor or manoeuvring a ship. Directive 93/75 of 13 September 1993 concerning minimum requirements for vessels bound for or leaving Community ports and carrying dangerous or polluting goods requires them to "immediately inform the competent authority whenever they learn that there are deficiencies which may prejudice the safe navigation of the vessels" (article 8.2).

• **Training and qualification**

States developing pilotage services have established more or less precise general rules for access to the profession of pilot. It is generally necessary to be a master mariner, show proof of several years' navigation, and possess specialised knowledge or experience of local conditions. Diversity of practice in this respect, particularly in relations between the pilot and ship's crew, can detract from the effectiveness of the assistance and lead to accidents. This explains why IMO Resolution A.185 of 19 November 1981 lays down recommendations for:
- minimum training and qualification standards for seagoing pilots;
- working methods used.

(80) R. DOUGLAS, G. GEEN : "The Law of Harbours and Pilotage". LLP, London, 1993, 4th Edition, 640-704.
(81) B. McMANUS : "Limit of the pilot's responsibilities". Lloyd's List, 25 Sept. 1992.

b) Liabilities

476. - Does pilotage continue to be one of the most effective guarantees against accidents ? A series of recent mishaps suffered by ships with a pilot on board has created some anxiety within the maritime world(82). They include:
- grounding of the *Queen Elizabeth II* in the Vineyard Sound in 1992 (83);
- grounding of the *Aegean Sea* on 3 December 1992 at the entrance to Corunna (84);
- grounding of the *Sea Empress* on 15 February 1996 near the port of Milford Haven, Wales (85);
- striking of the *Bright Field* against a shopping mall on 14 December 1996 in New Orleans (86).

An analysis by the United Kingdom P&I Club reveals that 6 per cent of claims submitted to it are attributable to pilot error (87). Another study by INTERTANKO in United States ports denounces numerous shortcomings in pilotage (88), and recommends improvements to existing systems (89). Certain pilots have underlined the decline in quality of teams on the navigation bridge (90), and the difficulty of carrying out their work on board substandard ships (91).

Is the pilot liable in the event of error or negligence ? Does he enjoy any limitation of liability ? Can a shipowner claim against a pilot or pilotage service ? Legislation differs depending on the country involved (92).

Most European countries provide for limited liability for the pilot in the event of an accident, even when caused by a deliberate act or gross negligence. As in many countries, this liability has never been the subject of legal appeals, making it difficult to draw the line between negligence and non-negligence.

The amount of compensation for damage caused by a pilot also shows wide variations. Limitation of liability is usually justified by economic considerations. Laying unlimited liability on a pilot would force him to take out very expensive insurance, increasing his pilotage fees accordingly, and thereby the cost of maritime transport. A study of pilotage in Europe was unable to reveal whether the amount of liability had any effect on the quality of services: pilots are not personally liable, but remain open to criminal charges in the event of an accident (93). According to certain commentators, making pilots personally liable for their faults in the event of an accident would have no effect on casualty statistics, and would oblige the shipowner to pay double insurance at higher cost. The answer seems to lie in better education and training of pilots, and in improving navigational aids.

Most major ports have introduced Vessel Traffic Services (VTS) to improve navigational safety by monitoring the position of buoys via radar, monitoring vessel movements (and pleasure craft) controlling traffic with rights to proceed, restrictions on speed and permission

(82) "Pilots never pay". Lloyd's List, 30 Sept. 1991.
(83) "Pilots advice" Lloyd's List, 12 August 1992.
(84) - "Oil disaster pilot probe". Lloyd's List, 5 Dec. 1992.
- "Aegen Sea oil spill controversy deepens". Lloyd's List, 7 Dec. 1992.
(85) "Sea Empress report : approach not agreed". Lloyd's List, 8 March 1996.
- "Milford Haven curb on pilot of Sea Empress". Lloyd's List, 21 June 1996.
- "Pilot error blamed for Sea Empress grounding". MER, August 1977, 4.
(86) "Bright Field pilot's order was ignored". Lloyd's List, 19 Dec. 1996.
(87) UK P and I Club. Analysis of major claims 1993. London, 12-13.
(88) "Pilots voice concern on Intertanko study". Lloyd's List, 7 Oct. 1996.
(89) MSC 67/9/1, 2 Oct. 1996.
(90) H. WILSON : "Pilot relationships on board ship". Seaways, February 1997, 8-10.
(91) S. PELECANOS : "Quality pilotage". Seaways, Feb. 1997, 3-7.
(92) - "Pilotage Law". Gard News 149, March 1998, 5-12.
(93) Commission of the European Communities. DG VII/D3. EU Maritime Pilotage Study. Final Report, July 1995.

to sail. The VTS does not control the navigation of the ship. This is left to those on board, but the VTS does have the power to control port entry and departures to minimise hazardous occurrences (cf chapter 26 on Marine traffic management).

B. DEEP-SEA PILOTAGE

477. - According to Annex 1 to IMO Resolution A.485, a deep-sea pilot (DSP) is "a person, other than a member of the ship's crew, who performs pilotage duties during the ship's passage outside the seaward limits of local pilotage areas".

Although a deep-sea pilot plays a vital role in preventing accidents, there is no legal obligation to use his services, equivalent to the requirement of harbour pilotage, even in European waters regarded as dangerous for shipping.

1. Non-mandatory nature of deep-sea pilotage

a) International regulations

No international convention makes deep-sea pilotage mandatory. There are merely a few IMO recommendations for the use of pilotage services in certain areas and for certain types of ships:
- Sund between Sweden and Denmark for loaded oil tankers with a draught of more than 7 metres and for all gas and chemical carriers (cf Resolution A.339 of 1979, amended by Resolution A.579 of 20 November 1985);
- Baltic (cf Resolution A.480 of 19 November 1981) and in the straits giving access to that sea (cf Resolution A.620 of 19 November 1987);
- North Sea, the English Channel and the Skagerrak (cf Resolution A.486 of 19 November 1981);
- Channels of access to Rotterdam-Europoort and Ijmuider (cf Resolution A.668 of 19 October 1989);
- Regions of the Torres Strait and the Great Barrier Reef off the coast of Australia (cf Resolution A.619 of 1987 amended by Resolution A.710 of 6 November 1991), for all ships more than 70 metres in length and for loaded oil tankers, chemical and gas carriers.

b) EU regulations

Spectacular accidents involving oil tankers in the Channel and the North Sea have credited the idea of recommending pilots for certain ships, in this region with its arduous shipping conditions.

These considerations culminated in the adoption by the European Council of Ministers, on 21 December 1978, of Directive 79/115 on deep-sea pilotage in the North Sea and the Channel (95). This does not make pilotage compulsory in the region, but simply encourages member states to foster the use of ocean pilots on ships registered with them. It does not apply to ships sailing under other flags. These deficiencies led the promoters of the survey of European pilotage to suggest an amendment to the Directive, in order to ensure promotion of the use of deep-sea pilots by all ships under all flags.

(94) D. DAVIES : "Pilotage - a legal view". Seaways, Feb. 1997, 10-11.
(95) 33/32 du 8 Feb. 1979.

c) National regulations

Some States have made it mandatory to use pilots on ships within their territorial waters, such as Chile for passage through the Straits of Magellan, Sweden for ships using channels along its coasts, or Russia for certain parts of the Barents, Karan Laptex, Eastern Siberian, Bering and Okhotsk Seas (96).

Outside territorial waters, pilotage is obligatory in only a very few zones. In the United States, pilotage has been made mandatory in Prince William Sound (cf Section 4116 of the Oil Pollution Act).

2. Professional organisation

478. - Unlike port pilots, deep-sea pilots are subject to no international harmonisation of the conditions of their work. IMO Resolution A.485, setting conditions for training, qualifications and working methods for maritime pilots, do not apply to their deep-sea counterparts.

Deep-sea pilotage, which has existed for many centuries, developed in areas where shipping was exposed to the greatest dangers. Until recently, pilotage was confined to the North Sea through the Flanders Banks, and in the Baltic. It is therefore in this region that the most highly structured organisations are to be found (97).

VI - TOWAGE

479. - As with pilotage, there are two main forms of towage:
- Harbour towage, which permits port access and ship movements in harbour areas, (to be distinguished from simple berthing and unberthing of ships).
- Deep-sea towage, which may concern all types of craft, barges, offshore platforms and fishing boats, and which also applies to ships in distress or difficulty.

All these forms of towage can present serious hazards for shipping and the environment if they are not under proper control. This is why states have regulated, more or less effectively.

A - HARBOUR TOWAGE

Considered, like deep-sea and inshore pilotage, as an auxiliary service for shipping (98), towage is a major factor in port safety. There is no standard worldwide organisation of towage. Depending on local conditions and administrative traditions, every port acts as it sees fit.

In France, the port authority may, in order to ensure the safety of installations and the best possible use of public property, lay down certain conditions for towage. These

---

(96) W.E. BUTLER : "The Soviet Union and the law of the sea". The Johns Hopkins Press Ltd. London 1971, 76-77.

(97) A. BUTCHER : "Deep sea pilotage : North European Waters". The Nautical Institute on Pilotage. London, 1990, 39-43.

(98) M. CARBONES, R. MUNARI : "Port service ancillary to navigation between market and safety requirement". 2nd International Conference Piraeus Bar Association, May 1995.

requirements are defined under an agreement signed between the port and the tug company, which is obliged to comply with certain public service obligations and duties relating to port safety, such as permanent watchkeeping, minimum safety service, firefighting, and assistance in case of pollution (99).

In general, the towage operation requires close association and mutual trust among the pilot, the shipmaster and the tugmaster (100). Tugs are employed under a towing contract. When an accident occurs, the courts always seek to find out who had been in charge of ship movements.

B. DEEP-SEA TOWAGE

480. - Unlike port towage, deep-sea towage has been given less close attention by certain national legislators. With the expansion of offshore operations, towage of platforms, installations, structures and other floating structures has become commonplace. When it is not under proper technical control, it can present serious hazards for shipping. Structures under tow that become detached from the tug will drift off, collide with other installations, or run aground, sometimes causing pollution of the marine environment.

To fill this regulatory hiatus, IMO Resolution A.765 of 4 November 1993 contains a series of guidelines on the safety of towed ships and other floating objects, including installations, structures and platforms at sea. These guidelines concern route planning, careful preparation of the towage operation, towing arrangements and procedures, the actual tow, operating manuals and emergencies.

To facilitate legal relations between deep-sea towage companies and various users, BIMCO, in agreement with the International Salvage Union and the European Tugowners Association (ETA), offers three model contracts, one for the transport of heavy packages ("Heavycon"), and two other specific contracts ("Towcon" and "Towhire") (101).

(99) R. REZENTHEL : "La gestion privative de terminaux dans les ports maritimes". Port autonome de Dunkerque, 1994.
(100) R. HAZEL : "Pilotage and towage". The Nautical Institute on Pilotage, London 1990, 51-55.
(101) CMI Newletter, Autumn 1985, 1-2.

CHAPTER 19

Rules of navigation

481. - Collision is no longer the main risk in maritime navigation. A statistical study carried out in 1984 (1) revealed a very marked decline in this type of accident between 1953 and 1982, affecting both small and large ships. The trend is confirmed by the latest figures from marine insurers, who put collisions and contacts only third among causes of total losses (10.93 per cent), far behind bad weather (32.58 per cent) and fires or explosions (20.7 per cent) (2).

There are several reasons: the greater manoeuvrability of ships, ultrasophisticated on-board equipment for safe navigation day or night, in clear weather or fog, considerable advances in aids to navigation, and the universal application of shipping traffic regulations.

But although collisions happen less often than in the past, they often cause considerable casualties when they do occur, because ships are now built of steel, are larger and faster. This makes any impact far more serious. The financial consequences of a collision should be seen in relative terms, however, as shown by the study of the types of claims on the UK P&I club (3). Those arising from collisions are not the most important, in either number or value. The same analysis shows that this type of accident can happen to any ship, whatever its age or type. Port areas are no longer the commonest location for collisions: only 14 per cent occur there, compared with 19 per cent on the high seas, 32 per cent in coastal waters, and 11 per cent in the dense shipping traffic to be found in traffic separation schemes.

Prevention of collision at sea is an area where all States have felt an urgent need to achieve uniform regulations. These are now contained in the 1972 Convention on the International Regulations for Preventing Collisions at Sea (COLREG).

(1) A. COCKCROFT : "Collision at sea". Safety at Sea, June 1984, 17-19.
(2) ILU Casualty Statistics. IUMI Conference Lisbon 1998. London, Sept. 1998.
(3) UK P and I Club. Analysis of major claims 1993, 5 et 37-40.

I - ORIGIN OF ANTI-COLLISION REGULATIONS

482. - Regulations intended to prevent collisions were first introduced several hundred years ago. They began in England, and were gradually codified during the second half of the 19th century by legislators of the leading maritime nations (4). They were later harmonised at international diplomatic conferences, in Washington in 1889, Brussels in 1910 and particularly in London in 1929, 1948 and 1960 (5) (cf chapter 2 above).

International regulations for preventing collisions at sea were established at these conferences, providing what is now the standard reference for maritime navigation.

As they were amended over the years, these regulations became more and more complex, making them difficult to interpret (6). The version adopted in 1960 proved completely out of date within ten years, because of major changes in navigating conditions, with routine use of radar, the huge increase in the size and specialisation of ships, the disappearance of sailing ships, and the establishment of Traffic Separation Schemes (TSS) (7).

In 1969, IMO drew the obvious conclusions from these far-reaching changes, and decided to call an international conference to revise the 1960 regulations, which at the time were part of the SOLAS Convention. The conference met in London in October 1972, and drew up a new instrument: the Collision Regulations (COLREG) Convention, which came into force on 15 July 1977.

II - CHARACTERISTICS AND ORIGINALITY OF COLREG CONVENTION

483. - The 1972 COLREG Convention differs from other IMO conventions in several original ways, described below.

A - FORM AND STRUCTURE OF COLREG CONVENTION

The COLREG Convention contains nine general articles, accompanied by the International Regulations (8). These consist of 38 rules, seven more than in the 1960 version, but the provisions are more concise, with matters of secondary interest being transferred to four technical annexes. Part A contains general information, while part B considers steering and sailing rules, part C lights and shapes, and part D sound and light signals.

---

(4) "Collision Regulations : a 200-year quest for safety". IMCO News, n° 2, 1977, 4-8.
(5) J. COLOMBOS : "The International Law of the Sea". 6th ed. London, 1967, Chapter IX.
(6) HUGON : "La révision du Règlement international pour éviter les abordages en mer". Académie de Marine, 23 avril 1971, JMM, 29 Apr. 1971, 1053.
(7) Peter PADFIELD : "An agony of collision". Hodder and Stoughton Ltd. London 1966.
(8) IMO. International Conference on revision of the international Regulations for preventing collision of sea, 1972. 1985 Edition. London.

B - UNIVERSAL APPLICATION OF COLREG CONVENTION

The Regulations form an integral part of the COLREG Convention, which is legally mandatory. Under the terms of the first article, laying down general obligations, "the parties to the present Convention undertake to give effect to the Rules and other Annexes constituting the International Regulations for Preventing Collision at Sea, 1972".

Unlike other IMO conventions, the COLREG Convention applies to all ships, regardless of the zone of navigation. This emerges clearly from Rule 1.a: "These Rules shall apply to all vessels upon the high seas and in all waters connected therewith navigable by seagoing vessels". According to Rule 3.a, "the word 'vessel' includes every description of water craft, including non-displacement craft and seaplanes, used or capable to being used as a means of transportation on water".

However, local navigational requirements take precedence over COLREG provisions. Rule 1.b stipulates that "nothing in these Rules shall interfere with the operation of special rules made by an appropriate authority for roadsteads, harbours, rivers, lakes or inland waterways connected with the high seas and navigable by seagoing vessels".

But although the supremacy of local over international regulations is acknowledged, the grounds for this situation remain uncertain. French commentators consider that local regulations make allowance for "the particulars of the locality of which general regulations are unaware" (9). Northern European and North American lawyers regard it as an application of the principle *lex specialis per generalem non derogatur* ("particular law is not superseded by general law" (10).

Rule 1.b applies only to the extent that general and local regulations conflict. If there is no such conflict, and the two sets of regulations correspond, the conditions of Regulation 1.b are superfluous, even though general regulations are added to local ones (11).

C - LEGAL CONSEQUENCES

484. - Legally, local regulations and the International Regulations are mandatory. In nearly all countries, courts consider that those failing to observe their requirements can incur civil and criminal penalties (12).

1. Criminal liability

In France, article 80.1 of the Disciplinary and Penal Code of the Merchant Navy inflicts a fine or prison sentence on "any shipmaster or officer of the watch who is guilty of a breach of the rules stipulated by maritime regulations, concerning lights to be shown at night and signals to be given in conditions of fog, or the route to be followed, or manoeuvres to be performed in the event of meeting a vessel". Criminal liability may arise without any

(9) R. RODIERE : "Traité général de droit maritime. Evénement de mer", 39, n° 31.
(10) Plino MANCA : "International maritime law". European transport law, Vol. III, Antwerp, 1971.
(11) - S. GAULT : "Morden on collisions at sea". British Shipping Laws, 12th Edition. London. Sweet and Maxwell, 1998.
- John Wheller GRIFFIN : "Griffin on collision. The American law of collision". Edward Brothers Inc. 1963.
- A.N. COCKCROFT and LAMEIJER : "A guide to the collision avoidance rules". London. Stanford Maritime Ltd. 1977, 135.
(12) J. LE CLERE : "L'abordage en droit maritime". LGDJ. 1955, 33.

accident necessarily taking place. Mere infringement of the regulations is enough (13). On the other hand, if it causes an accident, the penalties are increased, under the terms of article 81 of the Code.

In the United Kingdom, sections 418 to 424 of the Merchant Shipping Act of 1894 have been amended by Regulations 1 to 5 of the Merchant Shipping (Distress Signals and Prevention of Collisions) Regulations of 1983 and 1989. These clarify criminal liabilities. In the event of a breach of anti-collision rules, the owner of the ship, the master and anyone currently in charge of the ship may be charged with an offence. Any person prosecuted under these regulations may defend himself by showing that he has taken all reasonable precautions to prevent the offence being committed (cf Regulations 5.1 and 5.2). Fines are very high. The penalty may include detention of the ship under Regulation 6 of the 1989 Merchant Shipping Regulations (14).

2. Civil liability

The provisions of the COLREG Convention constitute international requirements for good navigational practice, and civil liability applies to any failure to comply with them. In France, breach of these regulations is regarded as proof of the wilful fault of collision, when courts are examining problems of compensation for damage cased by an accident at sea (15).

D - FLEXIBILITY OF REGULATIONS

485. - COLREG should be seen as a code of good practice, rather than a legal code, because of the great adaptability of its provisions, which leave considerable initiative and responsibility to the users: fourteen times, the text refers to "special conditions" and "existing rules of navigation". The expression "as far as practicable" is also frequently used (16).

Rule 2 on responsibility lays down two elementary safety principles to be observed by ships under all circumstances. These require regard for "any precaution which may be required by the ordinary practice of seamen, or by the special circumstances of the case" and "all dangers of navigation and collision and to any special circumstances, including the limitations of the vessels involved, which may make a departure from these Rules necessary to avoid immediate danger".

Ultimately, anti-collision regulations leave a wide margin of interpretation to courts, which assess offences in relation to circumstances, rather than applying strictly the provisions of the Regulations (17).

---

(13) R. RODIERE op. cit., 76-77.
(14) R. GRIME : "Shipping law". Sweet and Maxwell. London 1991, 180-182.
- "The collision prevention regulations 1983 and the courts". Safety at Sea, June 1984, 23-24.
(15) R. RODIERE, E. DUPONTAVICE : "Droit maritime". Précis Dalloz, 11e édition, Paris, 360.
(16) J. DUMONTIER : "A propos du nouveau Règlement international pour prévenir les abordages en mer". Jeune Marine, n° 20, Nov.-Dec. 1977, 18.
(17) F. BUZEK, H. HOLDERT : "Collision cases judgements and diagrams". LLP, London, 1990.

E - CHANGES IN REGULATIONS

The COLREG Regulations are not fixed. They have been amended by IMO resolutions four times since 1972:
• Resolution A.464 of 19 November 1981, which came into effect on 1st June 1983, to allow ships carrying out various safety operations successfully to use traffic separation schemes;
• Resolution A.626 of 19 November1987, which came into effect on 10 November 1989, amending three provisions: Rule 1c concerning specially constructed ships, Rule 3h concerning the concept of a ship "constrained by her draught", and Rule 10.c concerning the crossing of traffic lanes;
• Resolution A.678 of 19 October 1989, which came into effect on 19 April 1991, to prevent unjustified use of coastal navigation zones;
• Resolution A.736 of 4 November 1993, which came into effect on 4 November1995, concerning the positions of lights.

III - TECHNICAL PROVISIONS

486. - The 38 Regulations of the COLREG Convention fall into two categories: steering and sailing in part B, and lights and signals in parts C and D.

A - SAILING AND STEERING

Part B of the Regulations defines three conditions for the conduct of ships: in any condition of visibility, in sight of one another, and in restricted visibility.

1. General regulations

a) Lookout

Maintenance of a proper lookout has always been required under international regulations, and the 1972 COLREG Convention makes it an absolute obligation. Rule 5 stipulates that "every vessel shall at all times maintain a proper lookout by sight and hearing as well as by all available means appropriate in the prevailing circumstances and conditions". Rule 7 further requires the vessel to determine if there is a risk of collision when two ships are navigating close to each other. Insufficiency or absence of watchkeeping is a punishable offence.

b) Safe speed

Rule 6 requires ships to proceed at all times at a safe speed, that will allow them to take proper and effective steps to avoid collision. Several factors have to be taken into account to decide on this speed: visibility, traffic density, manoeuvrability of the ship, meteorological conditions, state of the sea and the constraints of any radar equipment on board.

c) Action to avoid collision

According to Rule 8.a, any action undertaken to avoid collision must, if circumstances allow, be "positive, made in ample time and with due regard to the observance of good seamanship".

d) Narrow channels

Rule 9a stipulates that ships navigating in a channel or fairway must keep as near as is safe and practicable to the outer limit on its starboard side (cf). Ships less than 20 metres in length and sailing boats must not impede the passage of ships that can navigate safely only within a narrow channel (cf Rule 9b). Except in special circumstances, no ship is to anchor in a narrow channel (Rule 9g). The 1972 COLREG Convention completed these arrangements with a new rule prohibiting ships from crossing a channel if, in so doing, they impede the passage of other vessels.

e) Traffic separation schemes

487. - The recognition of traffic separation schemes is one of the most important new features of the 1972 Rules. These schemes do not remove all margin of manoeuvre for ships. The freedom of the high seas prevails except where technical considerations require its suspension. The shipmaster almost always retains the possibility of passing outside the traffic lanes, provided that he keeps as far away as possible (cf Rule 10h). If he chooses to use such a scheme, he must respect not only the particular requirements of Regulation 10, but also the COLREG Convention as a whole.

In France, an Act of 15 December 1986 makes it possible to take action against breaches of traffic separation schemes committed by French ships, even outside French territorial waters (18).

• Use of traffic separation schemes

According to Rule 10b, ships using a traffic separation scheme must proceed in the appropriate traffic lane in the general direction of traffic flow for that lane, keeping as far as practicable clear of traffic separation lines or separation zones. As far as practicable, ships must avoid crossing traffic lanes, but if obliged to do so should cross at right angles to the general direction of traffic flow (cf Rule 10c).

In general, ships should join or leave a traffic lane at the termination of the lane, but when joining or leaving from either side should do so at as small an angle to the general direction of traffic flow as practicable (cf Rule 10b.iii). As far as practicable, ships should avoid anchoring in a traffic separation scheme or in areas near its terminations (cf Rule 10g).

• Ships with restricted manoeuvrability

Two new paragraphs were added to Rule 10 by Resolution A.464 in 1981. These allow any ship whose manoeuvrability is restricted because it is engaged in operations for the maintenance of safety of navigation, such as dredging or surveying, to perform such functions while within traffic separation schemes.

(18) JO, 16 Dec. 1986 and P. BONASSIES : "Le droit positif français en 1987". DMF 1988, 4.

IMO Resolution A.428 of 15 November 1978, containing general provisions on ship routeing, states three conditions on which such exceptional permission should be granted:
- authorisation by the coastal state responsible for the safety of the scheme;
- provision of information before and at regular intervals during operations;
- performance of such operations in clear weather.

2. Rules of the road

488. - Section II of part B of the COLREG Convention applies to the conduct of ships in view of one another.

a) Basic anti-collision regulations

There are four basic regulations. Rule 12 deals with sailing vessels. Rule 13 requires any ship overtaking another to keep out of its way. Rules 14 concerns head-on situations, in which both ships must alter course to starboard, so that each passes on the port side of the other. Rule 15, better known as the "starboard rule", applies to crossing situations, in which the ship seeing the other on the starboard side is to keep out of its way and , if circumstances permit, avoid crossing ahead of the other.

b) Specific regulations

According to Rule 16, any ship directed to keep out of the way of another must take "early and substantial action to keep well clear". Rule 17, concerning action by the stand-on ship, is the major innovation of the 1972 Convention. The stand-on ship may take preventive action to avoid allowing a critical situation to develop. The give-way ship is obliged to keep out of the way. The highest priority is given to ships which are not "under command" (namely with no control of their actions), those restricted in their ability to manoeuvre, craft engaged in fishing, and sailing ships. Any other vessel must avoid impeding the free passage of a ship constrained by its draught, and displaying signals to this effect.

According to Rule 3g, ships with restricted ability to manoeuvre include "those engaged in laying, servicing or picking up a navigation mark, submarine cable or pipeline; dredging, surveying or underwater operations; replenishment or transferring persons, provisions or cargo while under way; aircraft launching, landing or recovery operations; mine clearance operations; towing operations".

3. Conduct of ships in restricted visibility

489. - The expression "restricted visibility" means "any condition in which visibility is restricted by fog, mist, falling snow, heavy rainstorms, sandstorms or any other similar causes" (Rule 3l). Such conditions increase navigational risks (19), and may cause spectacular accidents. Examples include:
• Collision between the *Emmanuel Delmas* and the oil tanker *Vera Berlingieri* near Rome on 25 June 1979, which caused a conflagration and the deaths of 26 French seamen (20);

---

(19) 38 per cent of collisions occur in poor visibility, in Analysis of major claims. UK, Pand. I Club, 38-39.
(20) JMM, 5 July 1979, 1674-1676.

• Collision between two Liberian tankers, the *Aegean Captain* and the *Atlantic Express*, on 29 July 1979 in the Caribbean, with 26 fatalities (21);
• Collision between the *British Trent* and the bulk carrier *Western Winner* on 3 June 1993 in the North Sea near Ostend, with the death of seven crew members (22).

When visibility is restricted, shipmasters must respect the special rules applying to conduct of their ship, and to use of radar.

a) Conduct of ships

Rule 19 lays down requirements for conducting ships in restricted visibility. They must proceed at a safe speed adapted to the prevailing circumstances. Action to avoid a close-quarters situation must be taken in ample time. Certain actions are to be avoided (cf Rule 10d). When ships are close to each other, they must take all their way off and navigate with extreme caution until danger of collision is over.

b) Use of radar

Even the use of radar for navigational purposes did nothing for twenty years to reduce the number of accidents and fatal collisions in fog. Nowadays, collisions in conditions of restricted visibility still account for nearly 40 per cent of such accidents (23). Several reasons have been suggested to explain the high frequency of accidents occurring despite or because of radar installations:
• Technical failures and omissions: far less information is provided by radar than by the naked eye, making it impracticable to conduct a ship as if at sight (24).
• The human element: radar long gave its users an unjustifiable sense of confidence and false security (25), whereas misinterpretation of data (26), excessive speed (27), negligence by officers or their lack of training in using radar were the main causes of accidents (28).

Early regulations on the use of radar remained purely national. It was not until 1960 that the first international provisions were established, in the form of simple recommendations.

The COLREG Convention replaced these recommendations with proper rules, which no longer apply only in fog as in the past (cf Rule 19d), but under any conditions of visibility (cf Rules 6a, 7b and 8b).

IMO has recommended the use of automatic radar plotting aids (ARPA), as a way of helping interpret radar data and increasing efficiency. These must comply not only with general conditions applying to electronic navigational aids (cf Resolution A.281) but also with IMO functional standards (cf Resolution A.422).

(21) JMM, 6 Dec. 1979, 2970.
(22) M. GREY : "British Trent inquiry seems rule breaking", Lloyd's List, 24 April 1995.
(23) UK P AND I CLUB. Analysis of Major Claims, 38.
(24) L. OUDET : "Les auxiliaires du radar". JMM, 21 Aug. 1958, 1753.
(25) L. OUDET : "Le radar et l'élément humain". NPC, Jan. 1958.
(26) L. OUDET : "Un travail soigné". JMM, 7 Jan. 1960, 5 and letter of Capitaine BONELLI in JMM, 13 Aug. 1956, 1689.
(27) The Nautical Institute. "Accident and loss prevention at sea". Conference London, Nov. 1993. Part III, The human element, 31.
(28) L. OUDET : "Exorcisons le radar". JMM, 25 Apr. 1957, 833.

B - LIGHTS AND SIGNALS

490. - COLREG Convention requirements for lights and signals come under three headings: part C on lights and shapes, part D on sound and light signals, and part E on exemptions.

There are also four technical annexes, dealing with the positioning and technical details of lights and shapes, additional signals for fishing vessels fishing in close proximity, technical details of sound signal appliances, and distress signals. All states must ensure that ships sailing under their flag comply with these requirements.

1. Lights and shapes

Regulations on lights and shapes must be observed in all weathers. Rules on lights apply from sunset to sunrise. During this period, no lights may be exhibited that could be mistaken for the lights specified in the Rules, or could impair their visibility or distinctive character, or interfere with the keeping of a proper look-out. Lights must also be exhibited from sunrise ro sunset in restricted visibility zones or in any other circumstances requiring it (cf Rule 20c). Rules on shapes are to be complied with by day (cf Rule 20d).

For example, Rule 23a requires a power-driven vessel under way to exhibit three types of lights: a white masthead light forward, sidelights, green to starboard and red to port, and a white sternlight.

The range of visibility of these lights is stipulated in Rule 22: 6 miles for masthead lights and 3 miles for sidelights.

Special requirements apply to seaplanes, small craft, tugs and pushed craft, sailing ships under way, vessels under oars, fishing boats, ships not under command or restricted in their ability to manoeuvre, ships constrained by their draught, pilot vessels, and ships at anchor or aground.

These rules do not apply to sunken ships or wrecks, which coastal states are responsible for signalling. In certain cases, the owner may be held responsible for an accident resulting from deficient signalling (29).

2. Sound and light signals

491. - COLREG regulations for sound and light signals cover three aspects: manoeuvring and warning signals. sound signals in restricted visibility, and distress signals.

a) Manoeuvring and warning signals

Rule 34 sets out a series of requirements for the sound signals produced by the ship's whistle and the light signals produced by a white light with a visibility range of at least 5 miles, when the ship is manoeuvring as authorised or required by the Rules. There are signals and replies for overtaking, for ships in sight of one other in a narrow channel, and for ships failing to understand the intentions or actions of another ship.

b) Sound signals in restricted visibility

According to Rule 33, ships 12 metres or more in length must be provided with a whistle and a bell. Ships 100 metres or more in length must also be provided with a gong.

---

(29) MARSDEN, British Shipping Laws, vol 4. "The law of collisions at sea". Kenneth C. Mac GUFFIE, B.L. 1961. Ed. Stevens and Sons Ltd. Londres, 414.

Under the terms of Rule 35, these signals are to be used by day or night in or near an area of restricted visibility. Sound signals vary depending on the type of ships and actions being taken. For instance, a power-driven ship under way is to sound one prolonged blast at intervals of not more than 2 minutes. When it is stopped, it must sound two prolonged blasts in succession, at the same intervals.

Special signals are stipulated for ships in tow, sailing ships, ships engaged in fishing, ships not under command, and pilot vessels.

c) Distress signals

Annex IV of the COLREG Convention describes 15 signals, which are used together or separately to indicate distress and need of assistance. The best known is the Morse code "SOS" signal broadcast by radiotelegraphy. Use of such signals is prohibited for any other purpose than indicating distress.

In general, the shipmaster may be held liable for any breach of lighting and signalling regulations.

CONCLUSION

492. - Two questions are worth raising in conclusion to this chapter: one concerns the efficiency of current regulations, and the other their possible transformation.

Although it is hard to assess with any accuracy the effects of navigational regulations on safety at sea, an improvement in the situation has been recorded: for example, there are far fewer collisions. All the experts acknowledge that the introduction of TSS has considerably reduced the number of accidents at sea. This is because they resolve the ambiguous problem when ships are approaching each other end on or nearly end on. Between 1956 and 1960, 60 collisions occurred in the Straits of Dover and the southern part of the North Sea. Twenty years later, the figure has dropped to 16. Over the same period, maritime regions with no traffic separation schemes have shown a steep rise in the number of such accidents. In parts of the Far East, their number rose from 35 between 1958 and 1965 to 129 between 1974 and 1981 (30). These findings are certainly related to the measures taken by IMO on this issue, and their strict enforcement by coastal States.

On the second question, regulations on safety of navigation in their present form change very little. The COLREG Convention has been amended only once. In July 1996, the subcommittee on Safety of Navigation (NAV) decided not to prepare a mandatory code

---

(30) A. COCKCROFT : "Collision at sea". op. cit., 17.

for safe navigation and watchkeeping (SNW). The draft code, combining all current operational requirements, was finally abandoned by IMO for practical reasons. It was seen as duplicating the provisions of the STCW and SOLAS Conventions, and making it more difficult to implement the ISM Code. Similar codes also exist, such as the ICS Bridge Procedures Guide (31).

Chapter V of the SOLAS Convention, also concerned with safety of navigation, has been under review since 1994. It is generally felt that all its provisions require updating, to introduce a functional approach focussing on the human element, and to take account of recent technological developments, including transponders or automatic data recorders. This work, which for the moment has been postponed in the face of reservations shown by flag states with large shipping fleets (32), should theoretically culminate in 1998, with the new provisions coming into effect in 2002 (33).

(31) "Mandatory SNW code rejected" IMO News, n° 4, 1996, 12.
(32) "IMO urged to delay SOLAS rewrite". Lloyd's List, 23 July 1996.
(33) "IMO faces heavy safety agenda in 1997". Lloyd's List, 27 Dec. 1996.

CHAPTER 20

Communications at sea

493. - Regulations for communications at sea are intended to organise the exchange of maritime information, ship-to-ship and ship-to-shore. The main purpose is to prevent ships at sea being cut off from the rest of the world, and to send help faster when a ship is in distress.

Radio transmissions perform an essential function in rescue operations at sea. At one time, ships in difficulty had no other recourse than to send up flares, with the hope that they could be seen by other ships in the neighbourhood. Radio distress messages, which could be picked up hundreds of miles from the site of an accident, removed this uncertainty:. The first application of radiocommunications for maritime purposes dates from 1899, when the lightship moored on the Goodwin Sands near Dover used it to report that the steamer *Elbe* had run aground. Prompt rescue action saved the crew (1).

Since Marconi invented the wireless by in 1896, two major accidents at sea have demonstrated the importance of radiocommunications in saving human lives at sea (2). In 1909, radio helped speed up the rescue of 1 700 passengers on board the *Republic* and the *Volturno*, which had collided off the East coast of the United States. In 1912, one of the distress messages sent by the *Titanic*, which had hit an iceberg and was sinking near Newfoundland, was picked up by the *Carpathia*, which managed to save 700 survivors among the 2 300 passengers on board (3).

The huge success of the wireless, which in a few years gained international recognition as a means of telecommunication, encouraged the world community to regulate its use, in order to ensure that the new system would perform properly.

This chapter describes the main regulations in force at present (cf I below), and the latest developments in this area, including the global maritime distress and safety system (GMDSS) (II).

I - INTERNATIONAL REGULATIONS

494. - International regulations are contained in the SOLAS Convention of 1974 and various IMO resolutions.

---

(1) W. GOODWIN : "One hundred years of maritime radio". Brown, Son and Ferguson, Glasgow, 1995.
(2) See also the story of the Empress of Ireland. R. MACONACHIE. "An Empress Dies. Disaster in the St Lawrence River". Safely at Sea. July 1982, 23-26.
(3) "IMO and radio at sea". Focus on IMO, Jan. 1985.

A - RADIOTELEGRAPHY AND RADIOTELEPHONY

Chapter IV of the SOLAS Convention deals mainly with installations for distress and safety purposes. It contains no specific provisions for equipment intended for public correspondence. ITU Radio Regulations contain technical specifications for equipment used for this purpose.

1. SOLAS regulations

Chapter IV is divided into four parts.

Part A concerns the types of radio installations which are mandatory on board ships:
• Passenger ships irrespective of size, and cargo ships of 1 600 gross tonnage and upwards, must be fitted with a radiotelegraph station (cf Regulation 3).
• Cargo ships of 300 to 1 600 gross tonnage must be fitted with a radiotelephone station installations (cf Regulation 4).
• Passenger ships irrespective of size, and cargo ships of 300 gross tonnage and upwards, must also be equipped with a VHF radiotelephone installation.

Part B states the operational requirements for radio watches:
• Regulation 6 stipulates the compulsory number of hours' radiotelegraph listening, depending on the number of passengers carried and the length of the voyage. For example, a ship carrying 250 or fewer passengers must provide for at least 8 hours' listening a day, and a radio officer is required to be on board. Beyond 250 passengers, provision must be made for 16 hours' listening a day, and there must be two radio officers. Cargo ships with a radiotelegraph auto-alarm system have to provide at least 8 hours' listening a day on the distress frequency (2182 kHz).
• Regulation 7 stipulates the same radiotelephone listening watch "on the radiotelephone distress frequency in the place on board from which the ship is usually navigated (...) using a loudspeaker, a filtered loudspeaker or radiotelephone auto-alarm".
• Regulation 8 requires ships possessing a VHF radiotelephone installation to maintain a continuous listening watch on channel 16 (156.8 Mhz) and/or other channels, depending on national regulations.

Part C details the technical conditions for this equipment.

Finally, Part D describes the tasks incumbent on the radio officer regarding information to be entered in the logbook.

The regulations in chapter IV have to be supplemented by certain provisions of chapter III concerning the use of radio installations on lifeboats and liferafts. All ships, except those which are equipped on each side with a motor-driven lifeboat fitted with a radiotelegraph station, have to carry a portable radio of an approved model (cf Regulation 13). On board ships carrying more than 199 people, at least one of the lifeboats must be equipped with a radiotelegraph station. If the ship carries more than 1 500 passengers, every motor-driven lifeboat must have such a station.
Since 1st February 1995, GMDSS (cf II below) has replaced this regulation. But many flag authorities have granted exemptions from GMDSS requirements on the grounds of lack of availability of the equipment.

2. Amendments to SOLAS regulations

Since the SOLAS Convention was adopted in 1978, its regulations have been amended several times, in 1981, 1983 and particularly 1988, when the GMDSS was introduced. The most recent major change took place in 1995, following the *Estonia* disaster.

B - INTERNATIONAL CODE OF SIGNALS

495. - The International Code of Signals consists of a volume containing a description and the regulations for all visual, sound, radiotelegraph and radiotelephone signalling systems used for the purposes of communication at sea.

The first international code was created by an agreement among a small number of leading maritime nations in the 19th century. An international conference met in London in 1879 to draw up the regulations, adopted by 19 states and amended in 1896 and 1926. The following year, the Washington International Radiotelegraph Conference recommended the adoption of a new British project, and the code was published in seven languages to facilitate its application.

In January 1959, IMO took charge of amendments to the Code. The MSC embarked on a five-year overhaul of the text, in order to take greater account of the conditions of modern navigation. The draft document, presented for the first time in 1965 (4), was revised in 1967 (5), when the World Administrative Radiocommunication Conference (WARC) met, to make a final examination of parts for which its approval was necessary. The new Code came into force on 1st April 1969 and has been published in nine languages (6).

Methods and procedures for signalling with flags, in Morse and by semaphore have not been amended. However, the word-for-word transmission used in the old system has been abandoned.

C - STANDARDISED MARINE NAVIGATION VOCABULARY (SMNV)

496. - Another problem affecting the vocal transmission system is that the very words may be a hindrance to international understanding of distress messages and information for search and rescue services.

In 1972, IMO Resolution A.380 introduced the Standard Marine Navigation Vocabulary (SMNV) in English. This is intended to remove language difficulties in communications during navigation at sea or manoeuvres, in port approaches and traffic separation schemes (7).

IMO Resolution A. of recommends the use of the SMNV for on-board, ship-to-ship and ship-to-shore communications. The SMNV is due to be replaced shortly by the Standard Marine Communication Phrases (SMCPs), intended to be more comprehensive. Following agreement at the 68th session of the MSC in May-June 1997, the SMCPs were submitted to governments, training institutes and others involved in maritime communications, so that the

(4) IMO : Assembly. 4th session. Res A 80. 27 Sept. 1965.
(5) IMO : Assembly 5th session. Res. A 113, 25 Sept. 1965.
(6) IMO : "International code of signals". London, 1987 edition.
(7) Robin BURTON : "The Standard Marine Vocabulary" Safety at Sea n° 131, Feb. 1980, 29.

new system may be tested and improved before its adoption by the IMO Assembly in 2001 (8).

The SMCPs are phrases developed to cover the most important safety-related fields of verbal communications at sea. They have two purposes: to overcome the language barrier in this area of communications and to avoid misunderstandings that could cause accidents (9).

II - GLOBAL MARITIME DISTRESS AND SAFETY SYSTEM (GMDSS)

497. - In November 1988, IMO adopted a new global distress and safety system at sea (GMDSS). Two purposes lie behind the introduction of this new system:
  • It was originally devised to ensure that search and rescue authorities ashore, as well as shipping in the immediate vicinity of a ship in distress, are alerted quickly, and can assist a coordinated rescue operation with the minimum of delay.
  • It is also used to disseminate a number of essential safety messages, including distress messages, navigational and meteorological warnings, and urgent information for shipping.

There is a major difference between the old system and the new GMDSS : the old one is based on ship-to-ship communication and is manual ; the new one organises ship-to-shore communication and is completely automatic.

A - ORIGINS OF GMDSS

1. Deficiencies in terrestrial transmission techniques

498. - The GMDSS emerged from the realisation that maritime radiocommunications using the Morse code and VHF radio telephony had serious shortcomings for safety at sea. There are four major failings in terrestrial transmission techniques (10).

a) *Limited technical capacity of radio equipment*

Current rules fix the maximum range of telegraphic and telephonic equipment. The system relies on short-range VHF and medium-range MF communications, with a maximum garanteed range of around only 150 miles. A distress message from a ship in mid-ocean has therefore very little chance of being picked up by a station on land. The most hopeful outcome is for it to be received by another ship sailing within this range. These technical limitations make the reception of messages quite uncertain, particularly in parts of the world where the volume of traffic is low. It may sometimes prove impossible to raise the alarm, and sometimes impossible to obtain help when needed.

---

(8) IMO : MSC 68/23, 12 June 1997. Par. 23-25.
(9) "IMO and the safety of navigation". IMO News, Jan. 1998.
(10) "The GMDSS" Focus on IMO, Jan. 1992.

b) Propagation conditions

Some radio waves travel in straight lines. Since the Earth is round, a message does not follow its curvature but eventually heads off into space. Other waves are reflected from the ionosphere and the quality of reception of messages may be affected by climatic and other conditions.

c) Congestion of air space

The number of radio frequencies available for communication at sea is materially limited, and cannot be increased. The expansion of radiocommunications on land may in certain cases result in congestion, which can imperil ships that have no other means of communication.

d) Need to acquire specialist knowledge

Years of training and practice are needed to perfect the use of a Morse code transmitter, on which traditional communications at sea depended. The whole system therefore quickly fails anything happens to the radio operator.

2. New opportunities offered by space technologies

499. - The arrival of satellites has revolutionised communications (11). Placed far above the Earth's surface, they offer a way of overcoming the disadvantages of propagation of radio waves. The message is sent from the Earth to the satellite, which redirects it back to Earth, to the recipient. Quality of reception remains unaffected by the distance between the two operators.

As early as 1966, IMO realised the opportunities offered by satellites for safety at sea. It tried to avoid the growing gap between this public service area and commercial radiocommunications, which have become increasingly efficient in the use of new technologies. Four years after the launch of the first Telstar satellite, IMO decided to take the opportunity to create a new communication system for maritime navigation. In 1987, it received the support of the ITU, responsible for coordinating international radiocommunication regulations.

B - ESTABLISHMENT OF GMDSS

500. - Preparatory work occupied several years. Many exchanges of views and negotiations took place, with all IMO member States and other international organisations participating. A group of experts, which met from 1969 to 1971, set the three main goals to be reached by the new satellite maritime communication system. The first intention was to establish a long-term global distress and maritime safety system, taking advantage of the improvements in radiocommunication techniques and the new possibilities provided by satellites. The second aim was to create a intergovernmental organisation dedicated to the development of satellite communications. Finally, it was hoped to establish a new

---

(11) L. BRÖDJE : "Satellite communication". Sea Trade Tanker Industry Convention. London, Feb. 1995.

worldwide system for search and rescue operations. The use of satellites could henceforth allow these operations to be coordinated from land, and not depend on the initiative of a particular ship happening to pick up an SOS.

The three projects were gradually brought into effect from the mid-Seventies. 1976 saw the creation of the International Maritime Satellite Organisation (INMARSAT) to manage the new system (cf chapter 4 above). In 1979, the Convention on Maritime Search and Rescue (SAR) was signed, its main purpose being to facilitate intergovernmental cooperation on SAR services. Introduction of the GMDSS required more time than expected, because of the complex technologies involved.

The Radiocommunication subcommittee set to work in September 1978. Resolution A.420 of 15 November 1979 created the GMDSS and laid down its basic principles. In November 1988, a diplomatic conference organised by IMO adopted amendments to the SOLAS Convention, in order to incorporate the new system. These amendments began to come into force on 1st February 1992, in such a way that new or existing ships over 300 tons engaged in international voyages would comply with the new requirements by 1st February 1999 at the latest (12).

C - GMDSS OPERATING PRINCIPLES

501. - The GMDSS is a radiocommunication system with worldwide coverage, which uses both satellites and traditional terrestrial radio techniques (13).

1. Division of oceans into areas and its consequences

The GMDSS, with its global role, comprises onshore and onboard means of communication, regardless of time and distance, between ships and land stations. In order to comply with this requirement, seas and oceans have been divided into four areas.

a) Sea and ocean areas

The limits of the four areas depend on the possibilities of radio coverage:
• Area A1 is within range of VHF coastal radio stations and extends from 20 to 30 nautical miles;
• Area A2 extends beyond area A1 up to the range of MF coastal radio stations, i.e. about 100 miles;
• Area A3 extends into the area of coverage of an INMARSAT geostationary satellite, i.e. between approximately 70° North and 70° South;
• Area A4 comprises remaining sea areas, notably close to the North Pole, which remain out of range of geostationary satellites.

b) Obligations for ships

502. - Implementation of the GMDSS lays three kinds of obligations on ships (14).

(12) M. WAKED : "Greatest steps since radio". Lloyd's List, 8 July 1992, 7.
(13) P. SMITH, J. SEATON : "GMDSS for navigators". Butterworth - Heinemann, Ltd, 1994.
(14) R. COOPER : "Global Maritime Distress and Safety System and its impact on ships' radio services and surveys'. Lloyd's Register Technical Association. Paper n° 2, Session 1993-1994.

• Equipment

Onboard radio equipment requirements depend on the area or areas in which the ship will be navigating. Coastal vessels, for instance, need only minimum installations, provided they remain within range of VHF coastal radio stations. Ships moving further away from the coast must carry both VHF and MF equipment. Beyond 200 miles, they must also be equipped with HF or INMARSAT equipment. Finally, in area A4, ships have to have HF, MF and VHF equipment.

Radio equipment for GMDSS in areas A3 and A4 must meet certain maintenance standards laid down in SOLAS Regulation IV/15 and defined in Resolution A.702 of 6 November 1991.

In addition to radio equipment, ships must be equipped with distress installations intended to increase their chances of survival, including:

• Emergency position-indicating radiobeacons (EPIRBs) which emit a signal to alert SAR authorities, and enable rescue craft to head for the spot where the accident has occurred.

• Digital selective calling (DSC) system, one of the most important parts of GMDSS. In effect, it makes a marine radio as easy to use as a mobile telephone. Instead of a telephone number, every ship or shore station has a unique Maritime Mobile Service Identity (MMSI) number, which is programmed into the equipment. DSC can be used to call a specific station using VHF/MF/HF frequencies, where an alarm will sound and then revert to a normal communication channel of frequency for the subsequent conversation. In addition, DSC can be used to alert a rescue coordination centre (RCC) for distress alerting.

• NAVTEX, another system to emit maritime safety information in written form, using a special onboard printer (cf chapter 18 above).

• Survival craft radar transponders (SART), which send messages that are displayed automatically on the radar screen of the searching ship or aircraft. This system helps locate the survival craft easily and inform those on board that help is coming.

• Frequencies

All radiocommunication apparatuses covered by GMDSS must broadcast on certain frequencies assigned by the ITU World Administrative Conferences of 1983 and 1987.

• Qualification and training

GMDSS requirements apply not only to equipment but also to human resources. IMO and the ITU have defined three types of training in preparation for three compulsory certificates. The general operator certificate is required for any ship subject to the SOLAS Convention and likely to navigate in all areas. The special operator certificate concerns ships not covered by the SOLAS Convention but which navigate in all areas. Finally, there is a restricted operator certificate, intended for shipmasters whose ships remain within area A.

GMDSS training of radio personnel must meet certain requirements defined in IMO Resolution A.703 of 6 November 1991.

c) *State obligations concerning terrestrial infrastructures and rescue operations*

503. - In order to provide the radiocommunication services required for GMDSS,

States undertake to provide, either individually or in collaboration with other States, shore-based facilities to cover the maritime areas designated by them.
 • In area A1, for example, coastal states have to provide comprehensive and continuous VHF coverage by DSC.
 • Resolution A.704 of 6 November 1991 gives IMO power to coordinate the distribution of coast earth stations (CES) for space and terrestrial radio services.
 • This Resolution has been replaced by Resolution A.801 of 13 November 1995, which makes recommendations on the provision of radio services for GMDSS, including criteria to be applied when onshore DSC installations are being set up, criteria for establishing sea areas, criteria for the NAVTEX service, and criteria for INMARSAT installations.

SAR operations are carried out within the framework of the system set up by the SOLAS Convention, in accordance with procedures contained in the 1979 SAR Convention, which came into force on 22 June 1985 (15).
 • All such operations are directed from a rescue coordination centre (RCC) informed of the alert by satellite or from coastal radio stations participating in GMDSS.
 • The actual search is conducted in accordance with procedures stipulated in two manuals: the merchant ship search and rescue (MERSAR) manual, providing guidance for masters who may be required to carry out SAR operations at sea; and the IMO search and rescue (IMOSAR) manual, providing guidelines for the introduction of a common SAR policy for all maritime states.
 • GMDSS provides the necessary means of communication, regardless of the area where the ship is navigating.

2. Satellite communications

504. - Satellite communications are likely to be the main means of sending distress messages. The service is provided by two systems, INMARSAT and COSPAS SARSAT.

a) INMARSAT system

The INMARSAT system has three components:
- Geostationary satellites, positioned in such a way as to provide coverage of the Atlantic, Pacific and Indian Oceans. Operational functioning of the whole space sector is provided by an operational control centre (OCC) at the London headquarters of the INMARSAT Organisation.
- About forty coast earth stations (CES) when the system is be fully operational.
- Ship earth stations (SES) consisting of the equipment on ships.

There are several sorts of SES. The INMARSAT-A SES consists of a dish antenna, usually mounted on the ship superstructure. The INMARSAT-C SES, which is less expensive, relays telex and distress messages but does not allow voice communication. The INMARSAT service also allows enhanced group calling (EGC), used to send a message to a particular group of ships, rather than to all ships within receiving range.

---

(15) "Shipping emergencies - search and rescue and the GMDSS". Focus on IMO, Feb. 1998.

b) COSPAS-SARSAT system

This system, established in July 1982 by four countries, France, the United States, Canada and Russia, is designed to monitor for distress transmission from the latest generation of EPIRBS. It is based on the use of polar orbiting satellites.

This system has three components: four satellites, local user terminals (LUT), which receive signals relayed by satellites and processes them to locate racons, mission control centres (MCC), which validate data from LUTs and forward distress messages to SAR authorities, and finally racons, which may be onshore, aeronautical or maritime.

D - IMPLEMENTATION OF GMDSS

505. - GMDSS came officially into force on 1st February 1992. Its introduction was heralded as the most important event occurring in radiocommunications at sea since the invention of the wireless. For financial reasons, it was to come into use in stages, in accordance with a timetable established by the 1988 conference:
   • Regulations on NAVTEX and EPIRBs have applied to all ships since 1st August 1993;
   • From 1st February 1992 to 1st February 1999, existing ships may meet either GMDSS requirements, or the existing provisions of chapter IV of the SOLAS Convention;
   • Ships built after 1st February 1995 must meet all GMDSS requirements;
   • After 1st February 1999, all ships must comply with these rules.

The major problem with GMDSS is now that the equipment specified by SOLAS rules is out of date. Technology has advanced so much in the last ten years that updating is necessary.

Despite early scepticism about the new system (16), it already appears to have become an indispensable part of the modern maritime scene (17). On several occasions it has proved extremely effective in the saving of life at sea. The most spectacular instance was the *Achille Lauro*, an Italian cruise liner which caught fire on 1st December 1994 while rounding the Horn of Africa, en route to the Seychelles. The rescue operation, launched promptly thanks to GMDSS, and coordinated thousands of kilometres away from the accident by the Norwegian maritime rescue centre in Stavanger, allowed all of the thousand passengers from the ship to be saved (18).
   The proven and acknowledged usefulness of GMDSS still failed to silence certain criticisms, and remove lingering doubts about its implementation. The new system raises a dual problem, both human and financial.

1. Human problem

GMDSS uses automatic message transmission techniques, which make it less essential to have a radio officer on board. His role becomes more that of ensuring a listening

---

(16) "Doubts voiced, but GMDSS will come". Special Report on Maritime Communications. Lloyd's List, 24 Jan. 1992.
(17) W. LUSTED : "GMDSS - A catalyst for change". BIMCO Review, 1996, 408-412.
(18) "GMDSS critics silenced". Ocean Voice, January 95, 4-5.

watch, or being able to use certain frequencies manually. His work is confined to maintaining and keeping the equipment available.

Several states have already granted dispensations to shipowners, allowing them to operate ships equipped with GMDSS without a radio officer, in order to cut costs. This issue is being widely discussed, and no international solution has yet been found (19):

• ITU Radio Regulations, amended in 1987 by WARC, requires the presence of a holder of a radioelectrician's certificate on board all ships sailing beyond the range of MF coastal radio stations;

• The IMO Conference of 1988 on GMDSS did not repeat this requirement, leaving States free in this respect.

2. Financial problem

506. - Introduction of the GMDSS will involve significant financial costs for States and ships. The new system requires States to provide adequate onshore facilities. Some countries may not possess the means of meeting their commitments. Technical and financial cooperation and assistance will be needed to ensure global coverage. GMDSS will also weigh on shipowners' budgets. The cost of equipment, which depends on the area in which the ship is to be operated, ranges from US$ 7 000 to 42 000 (20). There is also the cost of training personnel, estimated at US$1 200 per person. These financial considerations have led shipowners and operators to delay initiating a programme of installations and training.

IMO, concerned about the delay in implementing the system, raised the alarm in early 1995. Three problems were pointed out:

• Installation of equipment on ships

Surveys had shown that only a very small proportion of ships had been adapted to use GMDSS. By 1994, for example, only about 15 per cent of European flag ships had been converted. The present rate of replacement of equipment is about 5 per cent a year, which means that theoretically barely 40 per cent of European shipping would have completed conversion by 1999. It seems likely that most shipowners will make the necessary changes only shortly before the final deadline of 1st February 1999. It remains to be seen whether shipbuilders will be able to cope with a rush of late orders.

• Personnel training

Training is of the utmost importance, if the 250 000 bridge officers are to obtain GMDSS certificates. IMO has estimated that an average of 4 000 would have to be trained every month between 1995 and 1999, in order to reach this goal.

• Infrastructures

The latest version of the GMDSS outline plan shows that not many A1 and A2 areas will be available to ships using the system by 1999. The establishment of these areas is essential, to encourage small ships of less than 1 600 gross tonnage to instal GMDSS equipment without delay.

---

(19) J. BREWER : "Save our Sparks". Lloyd's List, 26 Mars 1993.
(20) "Industry unprepared for GMDSS". Lloyd's List, 22 May 1995.
(21) IMO. Implementation of the Global Maritime Distress and Safety System (GMDSS) COM/Circ. 121, 14 Feb. 1995.

3. IMO actions

507. - IMO has taken several initiatives in an attempt to speed up implementation of GMDSS. In June 1996, the MSC published circular 748 (22), which recognises the urgent need to instal GMDSS equipment on board ships, and to train a sufficient number of GMDSS radio operators. It reminds shipowners and operators that administrations would grant absolutely no exemptions from SOLAS requirements after 1st February 1999. It also pointed out that ships could experience considerable delay awaiting the supply of GMDSS equipment, and be unable to trade (23).

IMO also asked the ITU for assistance. The aim is to encourage all ships and coast radio stations to use GMDSS techniques and frequencies as fast as possible, in order to avoid the coexistence of two distress systems for too long a period.

In an effort to complete the global SAR plan, IMO has since 1992 organised a series of regional SAR/GMDSS conferences, seminars and workshops (24).

Political and practical considerations relating to safety finally led IMO to defer the mandatory implementation of the system (25). MSC Resolution 77 of 13 May 1998 (26) states that, in accordance with SOLAS Regulation IV/12.3, all ships taking part in the GMDSS should, when at sea, continue to maintain wherever possible a continuous listening watch on VHF channel 16 until 1st February 2005.

It had emerged that many ships to which the SOLAS Convention did not apply might well not have converted to GMDSS by 1st February 1999 (27) and that, if the listening watch on channel 16 was no longer provided by ships subject to the SOLAS Convention, other ships in distress might not be able to alert those that have converted to GMDSS (28).

(22) OMI. MSC/Circ. 748, 13 June 1996.
(23) L. ARAMSON : "GMDSS : too late to act?" Ocean Voice, July 1996, 24-32.
(24) E. MITROPOULOS : "The GMDSS implementation status and perspectives". 1996 COSPAS- SARSAT Seminar. IMO, London, 23-25 Oct. 1996.
(25) "GMDSS deadline postponed six years", Lloyd's List, 6 March 1998.
(26) IMO. MSC 69/22, 29 May 1998, 10.2-10.3. Resolution MSC. 77 (69) in Annex 21. MSC 69/22/ADD.2.
(27) "The GMDSS deadline. Who is going to be ready ?". Fairplay Solutions, Nov. 1998, 26-28.
(28) A. DE BIEVRE : "Magical clock to GMDSS". Lloyd's List, 30 March 1998.

PART THREE

CONTROL OF SAFETY

508. - To ensure safety at sea, it is not enough to lay down more or less precise and consistent regulations. Consideration also has to be given to ensuring compliance with their requirements. A standard that cannot be enforced remains a dead letter.

Such control cannot be effective unless a number of prerogatives are recognised, and in the first place the power of monitoring and inspection. Inspections are intended to guarantee that the ship itself, its equipment and crew meet current regulatory requirements, whereas monitoring is carried out to detect any breach of navigational codes. The exercise of these powers is in most cases accompanied by the possibility of prohibition, suspension and intervention. Such measures include boarding, arrest, seizure or detention of the ship.

Control procedures have little meaning unless they are backed up by legal powers of repression. In the event of infringements, offenders must be liable to criminal proceedings and, if found guilty, to sentences that will act as a deterrent to others.

Who holds these powers of control ? Under national law, where there is a functional specialisation of legislative and executive authorities, the problem does not seem to arise. In international law, the sovereign equality of all States means that the same legal entities are called upon both to create legal rules and to apply them. The law of the sea is no exception to this logic. According to article 92.1 of the 1982 Law of the Sea (LOS) Convention, which reflects the principle of freedom of the high seas and its corollary, the sole power of the flag State, in stipulating, ships "sail under the flag of one State only and (...) shall be subject to its exclusive jurisdiction on the high sea".

In other parts of the sea, certain aspects of this flag State power have to be shared:
- with port States, as regards the safety of the ship;
- with coastal States, as regards safety of navigation

CHAPTER 21

Flag State control

509. - Traditionally, the law of the sea entrusts control of ships to the flag State. Two theories have been advanced to justify this special prerogative. According to the concept of territoriality, a ship is regarded as a floating portion of the national territory (1), while the concept of jurisdiction is based on the need to keep maritime areas within the rule of law, namely that of the flag state (2). The subjection of a ship to a legal system that can control it helps prevent and allow action to be taken against potential abuse of the principles of freedom of use of the high seas and freedom of navigation.

As already stated in the introduction to this part of the book, the exclusive jurisdiction of the flag State is laid down in article 92.1 of the 1982 LOS Convention. Article 92.2 adds that "a ship which sails under the flags or two or more States, using them according to convenience, may not claim any of the nationalities in question (...) and may be assimilated to a ship without nationality".

This article does not refer to "flags of convenience" (cf chapter 23) but to eitheir the international criminal offence of "masquerade" in which a vessel disguises herself by the unauthorised use of a flag (e.g., a "Q-ship"), or the offence of dual registry, which is effectively prohibited by the terms of the 1986 Convention on the Conditions for Registration of Ships.

Flag law, which expresses a State's sovereignty over its shipping fleet, does not only confer rights. Where safety at sea is concerned, it also imposes duties. This chapter is devoted to analysing these fundamental responsibilities. The principal flag State obligations are contained in United Nations conventions on the law of the sea, and detailed in specialised IMO and ILO instruments on safety at sea. No legal difficulties are raised by such definitions, but their enforcement is another matter.

I - DEFINITION OF OBLIGATIONS

510. - States are invested with very extensive powers to control the safety of ships sailing under their flag. These may be put under three headings; inspection of ships, penalties for failure to observe regulations, and casualty inquiries.

A - ADMINISTRATIVE CONTROL POWERS

1. 1982 Convention on the Law of the Sea (LOS)

According to article 94.1 of the LOS Convention, "every State shall effectively exercise its jurisdiction and control in administrative, technical and social matters over ships flying its flag".

(1) P. GUGGENHEIM : "Traité de droit international public". Librairie de l'Université, Geneva 1953, Tome I, 450.
(2) G. GIDEL : "Le droit international public de la mer". 1932, Sirey, Paris, Tome I, 225.

Article 94.2 adds further provisions:

"In particular, every State shall:

a) maintain a register of ships containing the names and particulars of ships flying its flag, except those which are excluded from generally accepted international regulations on account of their small size; and

b) assume jurisdiction under its internal law over each ship flying its flag and its master, officers and crew in respect of administrative, technical and social matters concerning the ship."

Article 217 describes flag State powers for protection of the marine environment:

• They must ensure compliance by vessels flying their flag or of their registry with applicable international rules and standards, and the effective enforcement of such rules, standards, laws and regulations, irrespective of where a violation occurs (cf article 217.1).

• They must take appropriate measures in order to ensure that ships are prohibited from sailing, until they comply with international rules and standards, including requirements in respect of design, construction, equipment and manning (cf article 217.2).

• They must ensure that ships carry on board certificates required by and issued pursuant to international rules and standards, and that they are periodically inspected in order to verify that such certificates are in conformity with the actual condition of the vessels (cf article 217.3).

2. IMO conventions

511. - IMO conventions lay two types of obligations on flag States: performance of ship surveys and inspections, and issue of the corresponding certificates.

a) Surveys and inspections

Surveys are intended to check that the ship complies with current safety regulations. They are generally carried out by administration officers (cf article 13 of the Loadline Convention), the administration being "the government of the State under whose authority the ship is operating" (MARPOL article 2.5).

Every international convention provides arrangements for survey and inspection and the procedure to be adopted. In any case, according to Regulation 6e of the SOLAS Convention, the administration must "fully guarantee the completeness and efficiency of the inspection and survey" and "undertake to ensure the necessary arrangements to satisfy this obligation".

The MARPOL Convention lays down extremely precise, detailed rules for control of enforcement of regulations, leaving very little freedom to the flag state to exercise any discretionary power to alter them.

b) Issue of certificates

On completion of the survey of the ship, certificates are issued by the maritime administration, or by another government at its request (cf SOLAS Regulation 13 and LL article 17).

They are drawn up in the official language of the issuing country, and in the form of the models laid down by each convention (cf SOLAS Regulation 15 and LL article 18). Some of them have to be posted up in a prominent and accessible place in the ship (cf SOLAS Regulation 16).

Certificates confirm that a ship conforms to regulatory requirements for a limited period, which varies depending on circumstances. Delivered or endorsed by the flag State, they acquire international validity, being "accepted by the other contracting governments and regarded for all purposes (...) as having the same force as certificates issued by them" (LL article 20).

Flag State control prerogatives are recognised officially. According to LL article 16.3, "in every case the administration assumes full responsibility for the certificate".

The flag State is considered internationally as guarantor towards other States that its ships meet current standards. To some extent flag law ensures a dual function, expressing both the sovereign powers accompanied by public prerogatives, and the duties imposed by the international community (3).

3. ILO instruments

512. - The ILO first defined flag State responsibilities on social matters in 1958, when it adopted Recommendation 108 on social conditions and safety for seafarers. The preamble refers to the principles of the 1958 High Seas Convention, regarding exercise of jurisdiction and effective control of ships.

These provisions were repeated and completed in the 1976 Convention on Minimum Standards for Merchant Shipping (Convention 147). Article 2 lays two types of obligations on the registration State:

• It has to exercise its effective jurisdiction or control over ships, particularly as regards safety standards, including standards of competency of the crew, hours of work and manning, in order to ensure the safety of human life at sea (cf article 2b);

• It must also verify by inspection or other appropriate that ships comply with applicable international labour conventions and its own national laws (cf article 2f).

Neither the 1976 Convention nor Recommendation 144, adopted by the ILO the same year, and concerning the improvement of standards, detail the nature of such inspections. The issue is covered by Recommendation 26 of 1926 on Labour Inspection, and particularly the general survey produced by a group of experts in 1989, which explains procedures to be followed for controls, particularly during unannounced ship surveys, examination of documents and ship detentions. In general, these recommendations are respected by ILO members, despite the difficulties inherent in overseeing labour standards on board ships (4).

B - CRIMINAL AND DISCIPLINARY POWERS

513. - Flag States are in control of disciplinary penalties and criminal charges. This principle was for the first time established in Article 1 of the CMI 1952 Brussels Convention for the unification of certain rules relating to penal jurisdiction in matters of collision or other incidents of navigation. It appears also in article 11 of the 1958 High Seas Convention and in article 97 of the 1982 LOS Convention:

"1. In the event of a collision or any other incident of navigation concerning a ship on

---

(3) P. BONASSIES : "La loi du pavillon et les conflits de droit maritime". RCADI 1969, vol. 128, Tome III, 625.
(4) International Labour Conference - 77th session 1990 - Labour standards on merchant ships - General survey by the Committee of Experts on the application of conventions and recommendations, 125-126.

the high seas, involving the penal or disciplinary responsibility of the master or of any other person in the service of the ship, no penal or disciplinary proceedings may be instituted against such person except before the judicial or administrative authorities either of the flag State or of the State of which such person is a national.

2. In disciplinary matters, the State which has issued a master's certificate or a certificate of competence or licence shall alone be competent, after due legal process, to pronounce the withdrawal of such certificates, even if the holder is not a national of the State which issued them.

3. No arrest or detention of the ship, even as a measure of investigation, shall be ordered by any authorities other than those of the flag State."

The powers of the flag State to act against violations of anti-pollution regulations are provided for in article 217 of the LOS Convention. The State must carry out an immediate investigation and where appropriate institute proceedings in relation to the alleged violation (cf 217.4). It must institute proceedings if satisfied that sufficient evidence is available (cf 217.6). It must promptly inform the requesting state and IMO of the action taken and its outcome (cf 217.7). Finally, penalties must be adequate in severity to discourage violations (cf 217.8).

The 1982 LOS Convention simply reproduces the MARPOL provisions on violations of regulations, adopted nine years earlier under IMO auspices (cf article 4).

Voluntary observance of regulations by the shipping industry is the ideal way of preventing accidents. In reality, this is not what happens, and some deterrence is needed, by state control of these activities, and penalties for violation. The moral effect and exemplary value of such deterrence can prove extremely effective, given that human factors play such an important part in the occurrence of accidents at sea.

While it is true that fear of punishment cannot alone prevent disasters, criminal legislation and its enforcement by the flag State remain an important element of the maritime safety system. Its deterrent purpose cannot be achieved properly except by strict penalties, and the promptness and certainty of punishment. Unfortunately, the diversity of national criminal laws against breaches of maritime safety regulations and of case law in their application makes any global deterrent effect rather patchy.

C. CASUALTY INVESTIGATIONS

514. - The investigation carried out after an accident at sea that has caused death, injury, material damage or pollution of the marine environment is one of the duties of flag States for their own ships (5).

An accident inquiry is useful in two ways:

• It provides an excellent means of investigation, by which the flag State can if necessary institute proceedings. It is intended as a preliminary to legal proceedings or an official report. In other words, it sets out to establish precisely how the events occurred, and supply the flag state's administrative or legal authorities with all the information they need to press charges, whether disciplinary or criminal, for any violations of regulations.

• It also plays a fundamental role in preventing accidents (6). It provides maximum information on the circumstances and causes of marine casualties, and thereby helps States to learn from them.

(5) W. CHADWICK : "Marine casualties and how to prevent them". Trans I Mar E (TM), Paper 46, vol. 96 (1984).
(6) M. HERNQVIST : "Bridge resource management preventing accidents". BIMCO Review 1996, 222-224.

International law makes the flag State responsible for accident inquiries, and tries to organise intergovernmental cooperation on the matter.

1. Flag State obligations

515. - These obligations are defined in three types of instruments.

a) LOS Convention

Three articles in the 1982 LOS Convention concern accident investigations.

• Inquiry obligation

Article 94.7 stipulates that each State must "cause an inquiry to be held by or before a suitable qualified person or persons into every marine casualty or incident of navigation on the high seas involving a ship flying its flag and causing loss of life or serious injury to nationals of another state or serious damage to ships or installations of another state or to the marine environment".

• Policing powers

Article 217 concerns violations of regulations for the prevention, reduction and control of pollution of the marine environment, and allows the flag State to exercise policing powers, in particular to investigate certain incidents, in cooperation with other interested parties.

• Penalties

Article 223 concerns actions to facilitate proceedings following such infringements and other breaches mentioned in part XII, on the protection and preservation of the marine environment.

b) IMO conventions

Accident inquiry obligations were laid down for the first time in the SOLAS Convention of 1948. They were repeated in the SOLAS Conventions of 1960 and 1974 (cf article 21), and in the LL Convention (cf article 23):

"a) Each administration undertakes to conduct an investigation of any casualty occurring to any of its ships subject to the provisions of the present Convention when it judges that such an investigation may assist in determining what changes in the present regulations might be desirable.

b) Each contracting government undertakes to supply the Organisation with pertinent information concerning the findings of such investigations."

Article 12 of the MARPOL Convention stipulates this dual obligation, whenever an accident has caused serious harm to the marine environment.

IMO plays a fundamental part on this issue, by encouraging and facilitating the effective use of casualty inquiries by flag States (7). Under the terms of the SOLAS and LL Convention, IMO receives the conclusions and findings of such investigations. It can then use the information to issue reports or recommendations. However, these may not "disclose the identity or nationality of the ships concerned, or in any manner fix or imply responsibility

---

(7) IMO Secretariat : "Work of the International Maritime Organization in relation to the investigation of marine casualties". Seminar on Marine Inquiries and Casualty Investigations - London, 23 Nov. 1982, Nautical Institute.

upon any ship or person" (SOLAS Regulation 21). These reports or recommendations are confined to the purposes of preventing casualties and improving safety at sea.

c) ILO conventions

The 1970 ILO Convention 134 on prevention of accidents to seafarers requires inquiries to be made into casualties affecting them and a report sent to the relevant authority.

A similar provision appears in article 2g of ILO Convention 147, which requires a State "to hold an official inquiry into any serious marine casualty involving ships registered in its territory, particularly those involving injury and/or loss of life, the final report of such inquiry normally to be made public".

It is the requirement that the final reports of casualty investigations normally be published that makes the investigation obligation of ILO 147 the strongest provision in current international law. However, many flag States parties to the Convention simply ignore this clear requirement, and the failure of ILO to enforce the provision has negated its great potential usefulness in casualty prevention.

2. International cooperation on casualty investigations

516. - The 1982 LOS Convention and IMO and ILO instruments recognise the rights of flag States and other States with major interests in an issue. For example, article 2 of the LOS Convention, which grants the coastal State full sovereignty in its territorial waters, implicitly grants it the right to make inquiries after any casualty or incident.

When two ships sailing under different flags collide, and their crews and owners are of yet different nationalities, in the territorial seas of yet another country, the international dimensions of the incident can assume enormous proportions, and raise problems that the principle of the exclusive rights of the flag State is powerless to resolve (8).

In the shipping sector, which is so international in nature, cooperation among States is absolutely vital. IMO has been trying since 1968, with varying degrees of success, to foster such cooperation.

a) Diversity of national inquiries

Different types of inquiries

517. - The approaches that the various states adopt to marine accident investigation vary from the judicial to solely technical investigations. This tends to reflect the division between administrations which fix blame, liability and punishment, and those which have a separate system for apportioning blame and taking punitive action (9).

A large number of States carry out safety investigations, in order to identify the circumstances of an accident at sea, and establish its causes. These inquiries are not intended to assign blame and liabilities, but to avoid any recurrence of a similar accident. Safety inquiries may be carried out on two or more levels, under the terms of current legislation, whether by investigators in the field possessing technical qualifications, or in accordance with a more formal system based on quasi-judicial process and rules. A safety inquiry is usually performed by an administrative body specialising in this type of investigation, and

---

(8) IMO. FSI 4/5/1, 5 Dec. 1995. Annex 2.
(9) IMO. FSI 5/10/2, 23 Sept. 1996. Annex Par. 2.

results in the publication of an official casualty report. Other administrations carry out more structured inquiries, intended to establish who was to blame and inflict punishment. This involves a formal procedure in a courtroom, with rules of evidence and procedures governing the facts submitted to the investigation commission for examination. Hearings are usually public. In certain cases, they may be preceded by a preliminary inquiry (10).

Divergent interests

518. - The main difficulty arises from the fact that too much freedom is left to States. The non-binding nature of international law is reflected in the adoption of instruments having no mandatory legal effects. IMO Resolution A.849 even takes care to recall that national laws take precedence over the procedures recommended by IMO. Paragraph 3 states that "this code applies, as far as national laws allow, to the investigation of marine casualties or incidents where either one or more interested states have a substantial interest in a marine casualty involving a ship under their jurisdiction".

The absence of obligation, leaving states so much latitude, is seen by some commentators as prejudicial to the proper conduct of investigations. The technical difficulties of such inquiries (11) are compounded by the risk of partiality, reflecting nationalistic sentiments, which may be expressed openly or not (12).

Major maritime disasters generally give rise to several parallel inquiries:

• After the grounding of the *Olympic Bravery*, one was carried out by Liberia, as the flag State, and the other by France, as the coastal State (13);

• The wreck of the *Amoco Cadiz* resulted in an inquiry by Liberia as the flag State, as well as several investigations in France, including two parliamentary inquiries (14);

• The explosion of the *Betelgeuse* also gave rise to two inquiries, one on the initiative of the Irish government and the other carried out by France, resulting in two reports that contradicted each other on essential points (15).

The accident to the *Celebration* in February 1989 showed the difficulties for certain States in carrying out their investigations properly. This collision between a small bulk carrier and a Liberian cruise liner with American passengers on board occurred in international waters off Cuba,. Despite issuing subpoenas, the National Transportation Safety Board (NTSB) was unable to question the crew of the Liberian ship (16).

Similar difficulties affected inquiries into the *Zulfikar*, a Cypriot cargo ship which collided in the English Channel in April 1991 with the fishing boat *Wilhelmina J* (17). The accident gave rise to two inquiries, one carried out by the British Marine Accident

---

(10) WILLIAMSON : "Marine inquiries and litigation - The legal dimension". Seminar of the Nautical Institute, 23 Nov. 1982.
(11) C. SINCLAIR : "Marine Enquiries. The technical dimension". Seminar of the Nautical Institute, London 23 Nov. 1982.
(12) Y. ROCQUEMONT : "Les enquêtes sur les accidents de mer sont-elles impartiales". JMM, 27 Jan. 1983. 162-166.
(13) Seaways, June 1977 and JMM, 15 July 1976, 1695.
JO, Débats parl., Assemblée Nationale, 20 Oct. 1976, 6836.
(14) Rapport du Sénat n° 486, Paris June 1978. Rapport de l'Assemblée Nationale n° 665, Paris Nov. 1978. Agence judiciaire du Trésor : "Amoco Cadiz : l'Etat français devant les juridictions américaines". Paris, 1992.
(15) JMM, 13 Sept. 1979, 2238.
JO, Débats parl., Sénat, 6 June 1979, 1691.
(16) M. SOBEY : International cooperation in maritime casualty investigations : an analysis of IMO Resolution A.637 (16). Marit. Pol. Mgmt, 1993, vol. 20, n° 1, 3-29.
(17) Lloyd's List, 24 April 1991.

Investigation Branch (MAIB). The British courts issued an injunction banning publication of its interim report, at the request the owners of the *Zulfikar* (18). The final report, published in September 1992 (19), concluded that a series of regulations had been contravened by the master and second mate of the Cypriot vessel, who very conveniently had been acquitted in November 1991 by a court in Nicosia (20). These malfunctions led the British government to amend its legislation on accident investigations in September 1994 (21).

It is quite common for commercial interests to affect the appearance of witnesses or evidence. In this conflict between the objective quest for the facts and the protection of public or private interests, truth does not always emerge the winner (22). In the case of the *Western Winner*, the triple investigation carried out separately, by Panama on the one hand, and Bermuda and Belgium on the other, showed how relative was the effectiveness of the IMO Resolution. These various procedures were carried into effect following the collision in June 1993 in the North Sea between the oil tanker *British Trent* and the Panamanian bulker *Western Winner*, whose owner, on the advice of his lawyers, refused to allow the crew to be questioned by the MAIB, acting for the flag state, Bermuda (23).

• Legal obstacles

519. - Cooperation among States with different investigative procedures may be limited, if the evidence gathered within the framework of one legal system proves incompatible with the principles of another system. For instance, a voluntary statement during a safety inquiry, made available to a state with a different legal system, may be used against its author or someone else, without any guarantee of legal protection.

Some commentators have regretted IMO's lack of any real powers to require states to carry out an accident inquiry, or to make its own inquiries (24). A voluntary system for communication of inquiry reports on major accidents has been introduced, but with unsatisfactory results. By 1st August 1992, IMO had made 1 477 requests for reports, only 804 of which had been met (25). IMO is still awaiting 600 reports, some of which concern accidents that happened in the Seventies (26). Some states are particularly reluctant to supply this kind of information (27).

• Aviation example

520. - Annex 13 to the 1944 Chicago Convention, dealing with aircraft accident and incident investigation, states the principles to be followed and the goals to be achieved.

Investigation is defined as "a process conducted for the purpose of accident prevention which includes the gathering and analysis of information, the drawing of conclusions, including the determination of causes and, when appropriate, the making of safety recommendations".

(18) Lloyd's List, 4 July 1991.
(19) Lloyd's List, 11 September 1992.
(20) Lloyd's List, 7 October 1992.
(21) Lloyd's List, 3 Sept. 1994.
(22) D. BRUCE : "Marine inquiries. The international issue". Seminar of the Nautical Institute. London, 23 Nov. 1982.
(23) J. LANDELLS : "Money put before safety, claim disaster investigations". Tradewinds, 9 July 1993.
(24) A. HARROLD : "The investigation of marine casualties". Trans. I. Mar. E., vol. 100, 111-133, 1988.
(25) "IMO aims to get tough with rogue states". Lloyd's List, 31 March 1993.
(26) IMO. World Maritime Day 1993. A message from M. W. O'NEIL in IMO News, n° 3, 1993, II.
(27) "Small sinking somewhere : not many dead". Seatrade Review, Oct. 1998, 6-9.

In general, Annex 13 recognises the power of States to obtain evidence and the need to preserve this authority in relation to safety interests within a national and international context.

In addition, the International Civil Aviation Organisation (ICAO) is a driving force for harmonisation of procedures, by publishing a technical investigation manual and improving cooperation among States (28). The state where the accident occurs must send a preliminary report to the ICAO within thirty days (cf Annex 13, chapter 6.6.1-6.6). It must also submit a data report as soon as possible after completion of the inquiry. This system, known as ADREP, has enabled the ICAO to examine and analyse 19 000 reports since it was introduced (29).

b) Code for investigation of marine casualties and incidents

521. - IMO has tried on several occasions to reinforce cooperation among States in investigating accidents. These efforts are illustrated by Resolutions A.173 in 1968, A.322 in 1975, A.440 in 1979 and A.637 in 1989.

Since 1995, IMO has been at work on several projects for collecting and analysing casualty statistics, and improving accident investigation procedures. This is the work of the subcommittee on Flag State Implementation (FSI), which acts through a casualty analysis correspondence group (30). Current projects concern:
- creation of a casualty database containing information on the characteristics of the ship, the circumstances of the accident and the conclusions to be drawn (31);
- merging and harmonisation of the reporting procedures contained in IMO conventions (32);
- development of a Code for investigation of marine casualties and incidents.

This Code, adopted by Resolution A.849 in November 1997, aims to promote a common approach to the conduct of inquiries into casualties and incidents, as well as cooperation among States in order to identify the factors causing these accidents and take corrective steps. The purpose of an inquiry and the guiding principles for its conduct are defined clearly, as well as a framework for consultation and cooperation among states with substantial interests. Rules are laid down for the publication of information, to encourage the free flow of information. Finally, there is a common format for presenting reports, so as to facilitate publication and make it easier to share the lessons to be learned. Guidelines to assist investigators are appended to the Resolution (33).

II - CONDITIONS OF IMPLEMENTATION OF OBLIGATIONS

522. - The bases of flag State control powers are the same as those that justify regulatory powers. The whole system rests on the concept of nationality. This may be

(28) D. FOY : "Marine inquiries and the public interest". Seminar of the Nautical Institute, London, 23 Nov. 1982.
(29) IMO. FSI 4/5/6, 19 Jan. 1996.
(30) IMO. FSI 4/18, 12 April 1996, Annex 2.
(31) IMO FSI 4/5/2, 22 Dec. 1993.
(32) IMO. FSI 4/8, 19 March 1996, Annex 3.
(33) IMO New, n° 4, 1997, 23.

defined as the legal relation established between a ship and a State (34). The availability on the ship of papers, the number and nature of which are set by each State, provides proof of this relationship. The flag, a sign of nationality, is merely a symbol, the mark of State sovereignty over the ship. It does not in principle have any legal bearing (35).

In international maritime conventions, a ship is regarded as belonging to a State if is it registered there. The International Court of Justice, in an opinion handed down on 8 June 1960 on the constitution of the Maritime Safety Committee (36) placed particular emphasis on this criterion in defining the concept of countries with the largest merchant shipping fleets.

Flag states traditionally have the power to set conditions for attribution of the nationality of a ship. The practice, confirmed up to a recent date by international case law, is for every State to exercise complete freedom regarding the right to fly its flag. In its famous decision of 8 August 1905 on the "Muscat dhows", the Hague Court of Permanent Arbitration confirmed the sole competency of the authorities in each State on this question (37). Article 91 of the 1982 LOS Convention returns to this principle, recalling that "every State shall fix the conditions for the grant of its nationality to ships, for the registration of ships in its territory, and for the right to fly its flag".

To limit any abuse of this freedom, the Convention requires there to be a "genuine link" between the ship and the State whose nationality it bears, but it leaves each State to define this concept (38).

A close reading of the text of the Convention shows that the genuine link is not a condition of recognition of nationality, but a simple consequence of such attribution. It consists of the exercise by the flag State of its jurisdiction and control over the ship after registration. The State must not lose all contact with it: "Control must follow the flag" (39).

A - GENUINE LINK IN 1982 CONVENTION

523. - As in the text adopted in 1958, the new LOS Convention recalls the freedom of States to set the conditions for granting their nationality to ships, and the requirement of a "genuine link".

Two differences appear, however: the genuine link becomes a prior condition for registration (cf article 91), and no longer corresponds to effective exercise of jurisdiction (cf article 94).

No agreement could be reached at the LOS Conference on the actual definition of a genuine link. OECD members, as part of their policy against substandard ships, at least came out in favour of a British proposal enumerating flag State obligations. This later became article 94 (40).

(34) F.M. FAY : "La nationalité des navires en temps de paix". RGDIP 1973, vol. 77, Tome II, 1002.
(35) J.M. ROUX : "Les pavillons de complaisance". Thesis, Paris, 1959, LGDJ 1961, 25.
(36) Cf Constitution of the Marine Safety Committee of the Inter-Governmental Maritime Consultative Organization, 1960, ICJ 150, 170.
(37) The Hague Court of Permanent Arbitration : "The Muscat dhows case (France v. Great Britain)". Hague Ct. Rep. 93 (ScoH) (Perm. Ct. Arb. 1916).
(38) B. BOCZEK : "Flag of convenience. An international legal study". Harvard University Press, 1962, 831.
(39) E. DUPONTAVICE, P. CORDIER : "Navires et autres bâtiments de mers". Jurisclasseur commercial. Fascicule 1045, 3, 1984, n° 74.
(40) W. BETTINK : "Open registry, the genuine link and the 1986 convention on registration conditions for ships". Netherlands Yearbook of International Law, 1987, 98.

B - 1986 CONVENTION ON CONDITIONS FOR REGISTRATION OF SHIPS

524. - UNCTAD concerned itself with defining the genuine link, as a means of acting against flags of convenience. Through its efforts, the Convention on conditions of registration for ships was adopted on 7 February 1986. This provided the first definition of the criteria of the link between a ship and a flag State (41).

1. Criteria of a genuine link

In July 1984, a conference of plenipotentiaries in Geneva held the first of four sessions prior to the adoption of a draft convention. The link between ship and flag, a basic factor in harmonisation, and the criteria for defining it, were the main subject of debate. Discussions showed two very different approaches to this concept: developed countries emphasised the administrative aspects of the genuine link, while developing countries and Eastern European nations underlined economic factors.

In February 1986, the Conference succeeded in finding a compromise solution. It managed to define the genuine link that must exist between the ship and the flag state, focussing more on the administrative than on the economic implications, and removing any element of compulsion from economic aspects (42).

a) Administrative aspects of the genuine link

Two factors must exist for there to a genuine link: establishment of a competent maritime administration, and the role to be played by the flag State in controlling shipowners and ships.

Article 5 enumerates the duties of this maritime administration, which must ensure that its ships:
- respect rules on registration, safety and prevention of pollution;
- are surveyed periodically by its authorised surveyors;
- carry documents evidencing its right to fly a particular flag and those required by international conventions.

The flag State also requires all relevant information needed for it to identify and take responsibility for its ships to be supplied. This information about the ship and its owner or owners must be published in a register of ships, available to any person with a legitimate interest (cf article 6). Its contents are stipulated in article 11. The register plays an important role in establishing a genuine link. Before entering a ship on its register, the flag State must ensure that its owner is domiciled on its territory and subject to its jurisdiction. Article 10 provides for a choice among three types of representation on its territory: establishment of a company owning the ship, installation of its principal place of business in the country, or presence of a representative domiciled there or who is a national.

(41) G. MARSTON . "The UN Convention on Registration of Ships" Journal of World Trade Law, 1986, vol. 20, 575-580.
(42) I.M. SINAN : "UNCTAD and Flags of Convenience". Journal of World Trade Law, 1984, vol. 18, 95-109.

b) Economic aspects of the genuine link

The economic definition of the genuine link caused controversy between industrialised and Third World countries, and the Conference achieved a compromise solution, leaving the flag State to choose between participation of its nationals in the ownership or in the manning of ships flying its flag (cf article 7).

According to article 8, the flag State's laws and regulations must set the levels of participation of its nationals in ownership of ships flying its flag. Such participation should be sufficient to enable it to exercise effective jurisdiction and control.

According to article 9, a satisfactory number of officers and crew must be nationals or persons domiciled or in permanent residence in the flag State. A number of factors, however, may modify this requirement, such as the availability of qualified seafarers, binding bilateral or multilateral agreements, and sound and economically viable operation of its ships (cf article 9.2). The Convention grants particular importance to training and education (cf article 9.5) and qualification of seafarers: the state must see to it that the level of competence of seafarers manning its ships is such as to ensure observance of relevant international regulations and standards, more specifically as regards safety at sea.

2. Bareboat charter

525. - Article 12 of the Convention recognises the possibility of registering ships bareboat chartered-in. The technique consists of allowing a ship bareboat chartered-in provisionally to fly the flag of the charterer's State. This allows shipowners in countries where operating costs are high to operate their ships under an economic flag, without removing them from their original register (43). This temporary exemption from flag state rules is meeting with some success. It is authorised by most open registry countries, and certain traditional maritime States (44).

Article 12 of the 1986 Convention authorises registration of ships bareboat chartered-in for the duration of the charter contract, provided that these ships remain fully subject to the jurisdiction and control of the contracting States. However, no details are given of which State is responsible for issuing safety certificates, the State of original registration or the State of temporary registration. The question was raised in March 1992 at the Legal Committee of IMO without any final decision being reached (45). The CMI, which had raised the problem in connection with enforcement of the 1969 CLC Convention, nevertheless expressed its opinion on the issue: "Since the ship acquires, albeit on a temporary basis, the nationality of the bareboat charterer's State and flies the flag of such State, it must necessarily be subject to all regulations of the State of temporary registration as respects safety and all other public law requirements. For example, there cannot be any doubt, in our view, that for the purposes of Regulation 13 of chapter I of SOLAS, the 'country in which the ship is registered' is, in case of bareboat charter registration, that of the temporary registration." (46)

---

(43) E. FONTAINE : "L'affrètement coque nue". Speech delivered at the French MLA Assembly of 20 April 1989.
(44) Joint Intergovernmental Group of Experts on Maritime Liens and Mortgages. 4th session. London, 16-20 May 1988. Item 2. Part. B. Current practices on bareboat charter registration. JIGE (IV)/2. UNCTAD TB/B/C.4/AC.8/12, 25 March 1988.
(45) IMO. LEG 66/9, 22 March 1992.
(46) Document submitted by CMI : "Identification of the state of the ship's registry in case of bareboat chartered ship temporarily registered" in Register of bareboat charter in IMO LEG 66/6/1. 13 February 1992.

Despite so many compromises in the 1986 Convention, it is unlikely to be ratified in the near future, because of the very stringent conditions for it to come into force. It is to take effect twelve months after the date on which at least forty States with a combined tonnage representing at least 25 per cent of world tonnage have become parties to it (47). The Convention was rather badly received by the maritime industry, while shipowners (INTERTANKO) and seamen's unions (ITF) strongly criticised its imprecision, resulting in an unacceptable compromise (48). Doctrine has remained split on the effectiveness of this instrument: certain commentators see it as the officialisation of current registration practices (49) while others consider on the contrary that it would provide a reference for all maritime conventions (50).

III - FLAG STATE LIABILITY

526. - Can a flag State be held liable for failure to comply with its obligations under international conventions on safety at sea, or for inadequate compliance? Are penalties applicable in such cases ? The answer to these two questions needs to considered carefully: theoretical solutions exist, but they come up against the principle of immunity of sovereign States.

A - THEORETICAL SOLUTIONS

The consequences of violating a treaty are covered by two international legal texts.

1. Vienna Convention on the Law of Treaties 1980

Article 18 of the Vienna Convention on the Law of Treaties states that the signatory to a treaty assumes "an obligation of good faith" (51) to refrain from acts calculated to frustrate the object of a treaty.

Article 60 also states that a material breach of a multilateral treaty by one of the parties entitles:

"a) the other parties by unanimous agreement to suspend the operation of the treaty in whole or in part or to terminate it either:

i) in the relation between themselves and the defaulting State; or

ii) as between all parties; and

b) a party specially affected by the breach to invoke it as a ground for suspending the operation of the treaty in whole or in part in the relations between itself and the defaulting State" (52).

(47) S. STURMEY : "The United Nations Conventions on the conditions for Registration of ships". LMCLQ, Reb. 1987, 97-117.
(48) G. KASOULIDES : "The 1986 United Nations Conventions on the conditions for registration of vessels and the question of open registry". Ocean Development and International Law. Vol. 20, 1989, 543-576.
(49) M. McCONNELL : "Business as usual : an evaluation of the 1986 United Nations Conventions on conditions for registration of ships". Journal of Maritime Law and Commerce, vol. 18, n° 3, July 1987, 435-449.
(50) D. MOMTAZ : "La convention des Nations Unies sur les conditions d'immatriculation des navires". AFDI XXXII 1986, 715-735.
(51) R. PINTO : "Le droit des relations internationales". Payot, Paris, 1972, 126.
(52) P. REUTER : "Introduction au droit des traités". PUF, Paris, 1985, 160-162.

However, these measures are bereft of all meaning in the case of multilateral legislative treaties. The fact that a State fails to respect certain provisions of the SOLAS or MARPOL Conventions on board its ships clearly cannot justify other States, on grounds of reciprocity, suspending their own obligations towards their own ships. The penalty would militate against the very purpose of these provisions, which is to improve safety at sea.

2. EU law

527. - Articles 169 to 171 of the Treaty of Rome provide for the possibility of pursuing a member State which fails to meet one of its obligations under the treaty before the European Court of Justice of the European Communities (ECJ) (53).

Such a process is open to the Commission as it is to any member. The Commission is responsible for noting such failure to comply. It then issues a reasoned opinion on the matter, after giving the state concerned the opportunity to submit its observations. If it does not comply within the prescribed period, the Commission may bring the matter before the ECJ (cf article 169).

Any member State may also bring matters before the Court, but it must first refer to the Commission. If, within three months of the application, the Commission has not issued an opinion on the claimed breach of treaty obligations, the matter may be placed before the ECJ (cf article 170).

Under the Treaty of Rome, the decision reached by the ECJ could not be enforced. It did not demand that the state in question put an end to the failure, but merely recorded it (cf article 171). The assertion of the primacy of Community law and the obligation for member States to respect it are not enough to force the defaulting state to take action. Despite the considerable political and moral importance of Court decisions, member states retain a certain freedom of legal manoeuvre even within the integrated Community framework (54). This makes it easier to understand the difficulties faced by IMO in enforcing its conventions worldwide. The absence of a supranational authority prevents any enforcement form of enforcement that would be against the wishes of States.

B - SOVEREIGN IMMUNITY OF FLAG STATE

528. - The immunity granted to a State under international law prevents it from being held liable before the jurisdictions of another State. The basis of this privilege is not a matter of courtesy. It illustrates the equal sovereignty of all States (55) and the wish to protect their functional independence (56).

The immunity rule theoretically applies only to acts of public power (*jure imperii*), and not those of private management (*jure gestionis*). Even if this distinction is not always easy for national jurisdictions to draw, it is clear that the promotion of safety at sea, which

(53) - B. GOLDMAN et A. LYON-CAEN : "Droit commercial européen". Dalloz, Paris 1983, 1-52.
- V. POWER : "EC Shipping Law". LLP, London, 1992, p. 77-82.
(54) G. HODGKINSON : "Flags and quality - dilemma of opportunity. international legal framework". IBC Conference - London, Nov. 1992.
(55) N. SINGH : "Maritime flag and state responsibility". International Law in honour of judge Manfred Lachs. London, Graham and Trotman/Maritinus Nyhoff. 1984, 657-669.
(56) THIERRY, COMBACAU, SUR, VALLEE : "Droit International public". Montchrétien, Paris, 1975.

is one of the essential sovereign prerogatives of flag States, comes under the heading of public power. Performance of inspections and surveys on board ships, or delivery of safety and anti-pollution certificates, by their very nature cannot be commercial activities.

This immunity, which prevents any legal action against a State, is particularly shocking when safety at sea is concerned. Certain authorities have recently called for changes in this privilege: the flag state should not be able to hide behind its sovereign immunity when its failings infringe upon the rights of others (57).

The report of the Donaldson inquiry into pollution from merchant shipping tried to provide an answer to this problem. In theory, flag States that do not respect their obligations under international agreements could be subject to severe penalties, such as cancellation of recognition of their authority. The result of this would be to force ships to be registered under the flags of other more trustworthy States. While acknowledging this possibility, the report emphasises the practical difficulties of implementation, and recommends an attempt to improve safety at sea by other short- and medium-term approaches (58).

(57) "Institute criticises flag states' legal immunity". Lloyd's List, 22 April 1993.
(58) "Safer ship, cleaner seas". Report of Lord Donaldson's inquiry into the prevention of pollution from merchant shipping. HMSO, May 1994, p. XXVI, paragr. 8.

CHAPTER 22

Control procedures and methods

529. - The enforcement of safety standards obliges flag States to apply on increasingly elaborate approaches and methods of control. This involves the performance of various surveys and inspections, to ensure that ships respect current regulations, and check the issue of the corresponding certificates.

The whole system is currently characterised by its extreme complexity (1), the result of several factors, namely the increasing density of international, national and local regulations for the prevention of risks at sea, the variety of the ships, craft and other structures, the diversity of procedures and methods, and finally the overlapping functions of inspection and survey authorities.

This chapter is devoted to all these procedures and methods, including the principal forms, which are surveys (cf I below), and the delegation by flag States to classification societies (II).

I - SURVEY METHODS

530. - The safety of a ship is subject to regular survey by two different bodies, the maritime administration of the State where the ship is registered, and the private organisation responsible for classification. The two systems do not have the same end purpose, even though survey methods and approaches are similar.

A - SHIP CLASSIFICATION

Ships are surveyed so that they can be assigned a class rating, and to allow this to be maintained, and also for the extension or confirmation of their term.

1. Classification surveys

531. - These surveys are performed at the intervals and under the conditions laid down by each classification society's rules. The general survey procedure comprises three aspects: examination of the parts of the ship covered by provisions in the rules, examination of the methods used by the shipowner or shipyard for maintenance and repairs, and more detailed verifications using spot checks and cross checks.

---

(1) Ph. BOISSON : "Why inspection systems must be simplified". Lloyd's List, 11 Oct. 1995, 9.

a) Types of surveys

Bureau Veritas rules stipulate three main types of surveys: special surveys, periodic surveys and occasional surveys.

• Special survey

The main purpose of special surveys is the renewal of class: when the results are satisfactory, a new term is assigned to the ship, and new classification certificates are issued for this period. It consists of a thorough examination of the ship while it is in dry dock. The survey varies considerably in extent, depending on the age and type of the ship. The term is five years for ships awarded the highest rating (I, 3/3), and three years in other cases.

To avoid lengthy technical stoppages, classification societies, aware of the cost of surveys for shipping companies, have proposed adaptations to the traditional procedures. An example is the introduction by Bureau Veritas of continuous special survey and distributed special survey schemes (2).

• Annual survey

Every classed ship must undergo an annual survey. This general survey is carried out afloat, and involves thorough visual examination of the ship and its equipment, and the performance of certain tests to confirm that they are maintained in good condition. The scope of this annual survey is up to the surveyor, as sole judge of the state of the ship and its equipment. If there is any doubt, he is empowered to ask for additional examinations and tests.

• Intermediate survey

Intermediate surveys are stipulated in classification rules. Their requirements depend on the type and age of the ship. The same applies to certain sensitive parts, such as propeller shafts.

• Periodic survey

Periodic surveys apply more specifically to the underwater parts, propeller shaft and boilers. The frequency of such surveys is different for each of these items.

• Occasional survey

Occasional surveys take place in two precise cases: if the ship has run aground or is otherwise damaged, and when it has undergone maintenance work.

b) Conditions of performance of surveys

532. - Several constraining factors affect the technical performance of surveys and inspections.

• Large ship surveys

At a hearing of the British House of Lords Carver Commission of Inquiry, the Salvage Association emphasised the impracticality of any attempt to survey the huge structures of a large ship. Complete survey of a very large crude carrier (VLCC) would involve 50 000

---

(2) Bureau Veritas. Rules and Regulations for the Classification of Ships Part I. Classification - Surveys, Section 2-01, Edition 1st Sept. 1998, Paris, NR 212 DNS R08 E, p. 27-28.

square metres of outside plating, and 100 000 metres of main welds. Ultrasonic testing of all the exterior plate would take 50 000 hours, inspecting the main welds for cracks would require 20 000 hours by means visual examination, or 100 000 hours by magnetic particle inspection. The Salvage Association admitted that large ships were "virtually uninspectable" (3) (cf chapter 13). A 100 per cent survey is therefore clearly out of the question. Indeed, this is not the intention of classification surveys.

• Subjectivity of surveys

Being unable to check everything, the surveyor must necessarily make choices. He does so on the basis of his technical knowledge, and particularly the experience he has acquired over a number of years' practical surveying work. For example; visual examination of the ship may sometimes be usefully completed by a discussion with the crew, in order to find out about particularly sensitive zones.

Inspections do not consist merely of checking plate thickness measurements for acceptable levels of corrosion. They also reflect a subjective assessment of the structural state of a ship. Since every surveyor has a slightly different interpretation of what is acceptable, his decisions could lead to disagreements and arguments, unless he relies on sound professional judgement.

• Surveyor qualification

No international convention or national regulations set any standards of qualification for surveyors. Every organisation has its own criteria for hiring surveyors, who may be shipmasters, naval architects or mechanical engineers, or even simple technicians. Each organisation also has its own internal training arrangements, the standing of which may vary quite considerably. More than 100 000 people are ranked as surveyors throughout the world, and yet there is no official training institute. This further increases the disparities in levels of qualification and the quality of service.

c) Shipowner's obligations

533. - To be effective, classification society services depend on the shipowner complying with certain requirements incumbent on him. The CMI has included a number of fundamental obligations in its draft model contract clauses (4): maintain the ship, machinery and equipment in compliance with classification rules, check that the plans and particulars of any alterations to the hull, machinery and equipment that could affect or invalidate its class status are submitted to the classification society for prior approval, inform the classification society promptly of any collision or grounding, damage, defect, breakdown, incident of navigation or proposed repairs, and of any change in the use of the ship that might affect or invalidate its class status.

The CMI text also states that failure to fulfil these obligations may lead to the suspension or cancellation of classification, or the withholding of the certificates and reports.

Case law also shows that failure to comply with these obligations prevents the classification society from being held responsible by the shipowner or other parties (5) who

(3) House of Lords. Select Committee on Science and Technology. "Safety Aspects of Ship Design and Technology" Report. London, HMSO, 14 Feb. 1992, p. 16, n° 3-17.
(4) CMI. Antwerp I. Document for the Centenary Conference. Joint working group on a study of issues re classification societies. Annex B. Model contractual clause. 338-342. Scandinavian University Press, Stockholm, 1997.
(5) In Re Oil Spill by Amoco Cadiz. 1986, AMC 1945, 1951-52 (N.D. III, 1986).
Affaire du Compass Rose III : Tribunal correctionnel d'Avranche, 12 Jan. 1982. Cour d'appel de Caen, 12 Jan. 1983. Cass. chambre criminelle 8 Oct. 1985 (unpublished decisions).

are victims of an incident at sea. Similarly, in case of sale of the ship, the shipowner must notify the society of any information of which he learns before delivery and which could lead to withdrawal of class or the issue of recommendations (6).

2 - Classification certificates

a) Certificates and recommandations

534. - When a ship has been surveyed satisfactorily, the surveyor delivers the classification certificates and their appendices, or endorses existing documents. There are three main types of certificates, for the hull, the machinery, and the boilers. All these documents must be carried in a safe place on board, and made available to surveyors on request. They are valid for the full term of classification. Various annotations may be made on the classification certificates, either notes, which are simple indications not requiring any repairs to the ship before the expiry of the term, or recommendations, consisting of descriptions of surveys or reservations. Such reservations are entered when repairs are deferred or when their examination is considered necessary; and a deadline is usually included.

b) Legal value of certificates

Does a classification certificate constitute proof of the shipowner's due care in ensuring that his ship is seaworthy ? Legal precedents in various countries reflect fairly similar positions on this question.

Under American law, it is quite clear that classification cannot alone prove a ship's seaworthiness, a concept that encompasses a whole series of items which are not the concern of a classification society, such as the presence aboard of up-to-date charts or navigational equipment (7).

English case law has undergone a remarkable change in this respect. Classification certificates were long seen as proof of a shipowner's due care. Nowadays, courts consider on the contrary that such documents provide a mere presumption of care, which is overthrown by evidence of negligence on the part of the classification society (8).

French courts adopt a fairly similar attitude: classification certificates possess no absolute value, and constitute a simple presumption of seaworthiness (9). They do not relieve a shipowner of the need to cxcrcise surveillance over maintenance of equipment subject to wear, and normally accessible (10). Similarly, technical survey of a ship and its various installations does not relieve the shipowner of his obligation to be vigilant at all times. Finally, the absence of any certificate creates a presumption of unseaworthiness, which is overridden by evidence to the contrary (11).

(6) The Niobe. High Court of Justice. Queens Bench Division Commercial Court. 2 Lloyd's Rep 52 (1993). Court of appeal, 8 February 1994. Lloyd's Rep. Part. 3 (1994) Vol I - 487.
(7) - The Negus Mowinckel et al. v. New York Bermudez Co. May 2, 1923. District Court, S.D. New-York. Cf also the Argo Merchant Case. District Court, S.D. New York February 7, 1980.
(8) Muncaster Castle case. 1.L1. Lloyd's Report 1961, 57 DMF 1963, 246 - Cf also 1.L1. 1 LR 1962, 532.
(9) Paris, 12 Dec. 1972. BT. 1973, 72.
(10) Tribunal Commerce Marseille, 9 Sept. 1975. Scapel 1975, 54.
(11) Rennes, 18 Feb. 1974. DMF 1974, 335.

3 - Classification society liability

535. - There is general agreement that classification societies play a major role in safety at sea. The importance of this role may be explained, in the case of the largest societies, by the extent and density of their international networks of surveyors, which allow them to take action anywhere in the world. This also makes them more vulnerable. With their high profile, they are exposed to the risk of legal proceedings worldwide. A plaintiff will be tempted to choose the legal forum that is most likely to be favourable to him, in order to obtain compensation for alleged damage.

The need for third party insurance against these risks has given added attraction to such charges: insurance has become synonymous with a guarantee of solvency, encouraging claimants to seek compensation in the well-lined pockets of the classification societies.

Their diversified services, extensive geographical coverage and potential solvency have placed classification societies at the heart of a wide-ranging legal debate, involving the scope and nature of their obligations (12). There has been discussion of their contractual undertakings towards shipowners and shipyards, but also their responsibility towards third parties, hull insurers, P&I clubs and charterers, all of which use classification information (13).

(12) - Ch. HOBBS : "Classification societies are put under the microscope again". Lloyd's List, 12 March 1997. "Great strides forward by class societies". Lloyd's List, 19 March 1997.
- P. RODGERS : "Classification societies facing a whole new world of liability". Lloyd's List, 26 May 1997.
(13) On the liability of classification societies, cf :
- E. LANGAVANT et Ph. BOISSON : "L'affaire du naufrage de la drague Cap de la Hague et le problème de la responsabilité des sociétés de classification." DMF, March 1981, 131-145.
- J. GORDON : "The liability of marine surveyors and ship classification societies." JMLC, vol 19, n° 2 April 1988. 301-306.
- B. BECK : "Liability of marine surveyors for loss of surveyed vessels : When someone other than the captain goes down with the ship". Notre Dame Law Review. 1989, 244-270.
- K. HARLIKIG : "The liability of classification societies to cargo owners". LMCLQ, February 1993, 1-8.
- J. LUX : "Classification societies". Published by IBA and LCP, London 1993.
- P. KIELY, A. JANUSZKIEWICZ : "Classification societies : To whom may they owe a duty of case". Journal of the MLAANZ. Vol 9, part 2, 1993, 1-16.
- S. BARTON : "Possible third party liability of the classification society : recent developments". Maritime Cyprus 1993.
- P.F. CANE : "The liability of classification societies". LMCLQ, August 1994, 363-376.
- A. KENNEDY : "The legal position of classification societies". The Royal Institution of Naval Architects. London, 13 Oct. 1994.
CMI : 35th International Conference Sydney. October 1994. Special session on classification societies habilities in CMI. Yearbook 1994, Sydney documents of conference Scandinavian University Press, Stockholm, 1995.
- H. HONKA : "The classification system and its problems with special reference state liability of classification societies". Tulane Maritime Law Journal. Vol 19. 1994, 1-36.
- Ph. BOISSON : "Classification society liability : maritime law principles must be requestioned ?" CMI. Yearbook 1994. Sydney II, 235-252.
- W. FRANCE : "Classification societies : their liability- An American lawyer's point of view in light of recent judgments". The international Journal of shipping law. Part 2. March 1996, 67-77.
- Ch. BAKER : "Claims against classification societies by owner and third parties". 16th New Orleans Maritime Seminar. January. 16-17, 1997.
- M. MILLER : "Liability of classification societies from the perspective of United State Law". Ibid. New Orleans 1997.
- M. HUYBRECHTS : "A touch of class : classification societies held liable by the Antwerp Appeals Court". International Encyclopedia of Laws, 1998.
- H. McCORMACK : "Classification societies, insurance coverage and potential liabilities". 1998 Houston Marine Insurance Seminar.

a) Contractual liability

536. - In the course of performing its various services, a classification society may be sued by its clients, namely shipowners and shipbuilding yards. Conditions of liability vary considerably from one national legal system to another.

• French law

French case law has traditionally considered classification societies as information agencies which have a general *"obligation de moyens"* or duty of care and diligence, with any guarantee of the achievement of a particular result (14).

The classification society may avoid its contractual liability by inserting special clauses in its general conditions or rules. Such clauses are usually accepted by the courts, unless the society has been guilty of gross negligence.

• Common law systems

Under common law, professionals may in certain cases bear an implicit obligation of performance. United States law, for example, allows claims on both the contractual and the tort liability of a contracting party. Three main claims are possible under the terms of contractual liability, namely breach of contract, gross negligence and negligent misrepresentation. Tort claims rely on the theory of implied warranty of workmanlike performance, better known as the Ryan Doctrine (15).

When liability arises in an extra-contractual context, United States case law refuses to apply the Ryan doctrine to classification societies, namely to hold them liable for any implied warranty of workmanlike performance.

The exemption clauses inserted in the classification contract are admitted in the United Kingdom, although the Unfair Contract Term Act confines their effects to purely material damage, and provided that their terms are reasonable.

Certain courts in the United States have expressed doubt about the validity of exemption clauses for reasons of public order (17).

These principles are in conformity with international rules on maritime transport contracts, according to which the shipowner must show "due diligence" in making his ship seaworthy. In English case law, this legal obligation cannot be delegated to a third party: in the case of the Muncaster Castle, the House of Lords considered that negligence by a classification society surveyor in no way released the shipowner from his responsibilities (18).

The case of the *Sundance* in the United States (19) reaffirmed the principle that the shipowner is not entitled to consider the classification certificate as a guarantee of proper construction of his ship.

b) Third party liability

537. - Tort liability continues to be the most controversial subject for classification societies. Tort arises by definition outside any contractual framework, when negligences causing injury to third parties have been committed.

(14) A. TUNC. "La distribution des obligations de résultat et des obligations de diligence". La Semaine Juridique 1945, I, 449 n° 2-6.
(15) Ryan Stevedoring Co v. Pan Atlantic Corp. 350 U.S. 124, 1956. A.M.C. 9 (1956).
(16) Tradeways II case in. Great American Insurance Co. v. Bureau Veritas 338F Supp 999, 1972, AMC 1455 (S.D.N.Y.) 1972 aff'd, 478 F. 2d 235, 1973, AMC 1755 (2d Cir 1973).
(17) In the Oil Spill by the Amoco Cadiz 1986, AMC 1945, 1951-54.
(18) 1.L. 1 LR 1961. 57 DMF 1963, 246 et 1.L.1 LR 1962, 82 Confirmed by House of Lords, 15th September 1963.
(19) - U.S. District Court, Southern District of New York, 31 July 1992. Sundance Cruises Corp and SCI Cruise, Inc. v. The American Bureau of Shipping. U.S. Court of Appeals for Second Circuit. 15th Oct. 1993.

• **French law**

The French legal system is based on article 1382 of the Civil Code, according to which anyone guilty of causing injury must provide reparation. This principle is particularly severe for classification societies when a ship is sold. The purchaser usually considers that he is entitled to rely on the accuracy of information supplied by the society to the vendor as its client. Any fault or negligence in assigning class could be grounds for a claim against the classification society, even if the vendor is guilty of fraud. The society cannot rely on exclusion clauses, which have no value in relation to third parties.

This principle was applied by the Court of Appeal in Versailles in March 1996 in the case of the *Elodie*. The judges recognised the classification society's delict liability to the purchaser of a ship for failing to detect defects that due diligence in making the inspection could have revealed (20).

• **German law**

In the *Mayonami* case of 1990, the Hanseatic Appeal Court in Hamburg decided that a classification society's duty of care towards the purchaser of a ship was not unlimited, because the terms of the contract between the society and the vendor remained valid in relation to the purchaser (21).

• **United States law**

538. - The tort liability of the classification society towards third parties may be claimed under United States law, where negligence is proven, and provided that there is a causal link between the offence and the injury suffered.

It was precisely this absence of a causal link that prevented the District Court of Louisiana finding against Bureau Veritas following the wreck of the *Pensacola*. In his verdict, the judge acknowledged that certain negligences had been committed by the classification society surveyor shortly before the ship's last voyage, but that the insurer, who was the plaintiff, had not been able to show proof that these faults had caused the accident. The presumption of unseaworthiness following an incident at sea cannot be blamed on an organisation that has classed the ship but does not control it.

• **English law**

539. - In the United Kingdom, extra-contractual responsibility is based essentially on the existence of a duty of care, incumbent on certain persons under certain circumstances.

The conditions under which classification societies may be faced with a duty of care were laid down in the case of the *Morning Watch*. This concerned the sale in 1985 of a yacht which subsequently proved to be suffering from major defects that made it unseaworthy, despite the existence of a fully valid classification certificate. In a verdict handed down on 15 February 1990 (23), the High Court refused to give satisfaction to the purchaser of the yacht. According to the verdict, there was not sufficient proximity between his purely economic loss and the role of a classification society.

(20) - Tribunal de commerce de Nanterre, 26 June 1992. Note P. Bonnassies in DMF, Jan. 1994, 19.
- Cour d'appel de Versailles, 21 March 1996. Dalloz 1996, 547, note Ph. Le Tourneau. DMF, 1996. 721, note P.H. Delebecque et DMF 1997, 22 note P. Bonnassies.
(21) The Mayonami. Hanseatic Appeal Court of Hambourg 14 June 1990 in DMF May 1998, 496-507.
Cf also : Luc GRELLET : "Fondement et limites de la responsabilité des sociétés de classification : rigueur de l'analyse outre Rhin". In DMF May 1998, 451-465.
(22) Steamship Mutual Underwriting Association Ltd. v. Bureau Veritas. 1973 AMC 2184.
(23) High Court of Justice. Queens Bench Division. Commercial Court, 15 Feb. 1990.

The problem of classification society liability towards the owners of cargoes was raised in the United Kingdom in the famous case of the *Nicholas H*. En route to Europe, this bulk carrier was forced to cast anchor off Puerto Rico, following the discovery of cracks in the hull. The classification society surveyor examined the damaged structure, and demanded that repairs be done as soon as possible, on pain on suspension of class. Later he went back on his decision, and authorised the ship to continue its voyage. A week later, it sank in the Atlantic, without loss of human life, but with its whole cargo of zinc and lead.

An initial verdict reached on 2 July 1992 by the Commercial Chamber of the Queen's Bench Division considered that the classification society had failed in its safety obligations. In the court's view, there was very close proximity between the owner of the cargo and the surveyor, whose decisive influence on the owner could be regarded as control. On appeal, the judges reversed this decision, declaring that the classification society had no duty of care as regards the interests of the cargo owner. The verdict, given on 3 February 1994, caused much comment, despite the unanimous opinion of the three judges on the issues raised (24).

This precedent, apparently favourable to classification societies, in fact rests on the basic principles of maritime law, universally acknowledged and accepted. One of these is the owner's obligation to make sure that his ship is seaworthy. The owner alone remains responsible for maintenance of his ship, over which he exercises continuous control. He cannot delegate this role, so vital to safety at sea, to a classification society, which has the duty only of certifying that the ship conforms to its rules and the requirements of international conventions.

However, the fact remains that the growing risk of huge damage claims creates an ultimate uncertainty about the survival of classification societies, and is detracting from the effectiveness of their everyday work. As explained in chapter 6 above, the absence of a legal system to protect classification societies raises a serious problem, which threatens their very existence (25). The CMI tried to provide a practical answer by issuing model contract clauses and principles of conduct to define the role and obligations of classification societies, towards their shipowner clients and towards third parties (26).

Because of the growing complexity of the ships to be inspected and the increasingly intricate tasks that surveyors have to perform, a reasonable solution must be found as regards conditions of liability. If classification societies are forced tomorrow to assume responsibility for every measurement or decision taken by their surveyors, legal experts will probably have to take priority over technicians, in order to set up systems of defence that could alter the nature of classification. In such a new system, where the surveyor's subjective judgement and statistical inspection methods would become meaningless, it is by no means certain that safety at sea will emerge with any improvement (27).

B - INSPECTIONS AND STATUTORY CERTIFICATES

540. - In the maritime sector, the word "statutory" applies to anything that conforms

---

(24) - High Court of Justice. Queens Bench Division. Commercial Court. 2 July 1993. (1992) 2 Lloyd's Rep. 481. - Lloyd's Maritime and Commercial Law Quaterly. 1993 Part I, February 1993, 1-8.
- See also C. FEEHAN : "Liability of Classification Societies from the British Perspective : The Nicholas H". Tulane Maritime Law Journal Vol. 22, 1997, 163-190.
(25) F. WISWALL : "Responsibilities and liabilities of classification societies in the 21st century". Annual members' meeting of the Swedish Club. Gothenburg, 8 June 1995.
(26) CMI. Antwerp I. Document for the Centenary Conference. Report of the Joint Working Group on a study of issues reclassification societies. CMI yearbook 1996, 328.
(27) "Taking the blame" Lloyd's List, 5 March 1997.

to a regulation, which in turn means a requirement set out in an international convention or national law concerning safely at sea and prevention of pollution. The texts adopted and implemented by State authorities provide for an enormous number of elaborate control mechanisms. As with classification, the system is based on the performance of ship surveys and the issue of certificates.

1 - Types of surveys

541. - IMO technical regulations provide for seven types of surveys (28):
- Initial survey, involving a thorough and complete examination, and tests when required, of a ship and its equipment. It takes place before the ship is brought into service, to ensure that it is satisfactory for the service for which it is intended.
- Periodical survey, involving examination of parts of a ship at specified regular intervals.
- Renewal survey, namely a periodical survey for the purposes of issue of a new certificate.
- Intermediate survey, involving examination of certain parts of the ship specified in the certificate. It is performed between periodical surveys within specified periods.
- Annual survey, involving a general examination of a ship and its equipment, conducted annually, to confirm that they remain satisfactory.
- Additional survey, conducted after a repair resulting from an inquiry or whenever the ship undergoes major repairs or renovations.
- Unscheduled survey, performed without prior notice to the owner or master, to confirm that the ship and its equipment remain satisfactory.

Theoretically, a report is issued after every survey, summarising the facts recorded during the inspection, together with the resulting comments or requests for action. Whatever its form, the survey is mainly preventive in its purpose: its prime object is not to look for breaches of regulations, but to detect defects, in order to prevent a ship from going to sea without being fit to do so.

2 - Types of certificates

541. - Certificates prove the conformity of ships to the requirements of the very numerous international regulations. In general, every vessel must be in possession of a registry certificate (1965 FAL Convention), a tonnage certificate (1969 TONNAGE Convention), a safe manning document (Resolution A.481), certificates for masters, officers and ratings (1978 STCW Convention), and a cargo handling gear certificate (ILO Convention).

Three instruments provide for specific safety certificates.

• 1966 Loadline Convention
Article 19 of the LL Convention mentions two types of documents: an international loadline certificate valid for 5 years, and an exemption certificate.

---

(28) IMO. Resolution A 413 (XI) adopted on 15 Nov. 1979. Guidelines or Surveys and Inspections under the Protocol of 1978 relating to the SOLAS and MARPOL conventions. Par 1. Definitions.

• SOLAS Convention

Regulation 14 of chapter I states the periods of validity of the five certificates of conformity to SOLAS requirements. The safety certificate for a passenger ship is valid for 12 months. The radiotelegraphy and radiotelephony safety certificates are also valid for 12 months. The safety equipment certificate lasts 24 months, while the construction certificate, which is usually issued on the basis of compliance with classification requirements, is valid for a maximum of 5 years. Finally, the exemption certificate must not exceed the period of validity of the certificate to which it refers.

• MARPOL Convention

This Convention covers the delivery of three types of documents: an international oil pollution prevention certificate (cf Annex II, Regulation 5), a pollution prevention certificate for the carriage of noxious liquid substances in bulk (cf Annex II, Regulation 12), and a sewage pollution prevention certificate (cf Annex IV Regulation 7). The maximum period of validity of these documents is five years.

Some ships receive specific certificates arising from IMO regulations. Chemical carriers, for instance, need a certificate of fitness for the carriage of dangerous chemicals in bulk (cf IBC Code section 1.5). Gas carriers need a certificate of fitness for the carriage of liquefied gases in bulk (cf IGC Code, section 1.5). There are also certificates for special-purpose ships (cf Resolution A.534), diving systems (cf Resolution A.536), mobile drilling units (cf Resolution A.649) and high-speed craft (cf HSC Code).

3 - National administration liability

542. - In controlling safety standards, the flag State administration respects two principles. First, it is the absolute guarantor of complete and effective performance of inspections and surveys. This principle is set out formally in article 16 of the LL Convention, SOLAS Regulation 6e, and MARPOL Annex I Regulation 4.3. It also bears full responsibility for certificates (cf LL article 16.3, SOLAS Regulation 12a.vii and MARPOL Annex I Regulation 5.2). These provide grounds for claims of liability against the flag administration, and against its officials and agents, if faults or negligence are committed during a survey or when a safety certificate is being delivered.

a) Administrative liability

In France, few legal precedents exist for successful claims targeting the liability of officials responsible for carrying out safety checks on board ships. The main decisions are as follows:

- On 26 April 1954 the Council of State decided that there had been no administrative fault in the delivery of a certificate of navigation (29);
- On 13 March 1998 (30), following the loss of the *François Vieljeux* with 23 deaths, the Council of State decided that the State was not liable for overseeing safety standards and seaworthiness;

---

(29) Arrêt veuve Vacher, CE 26 Apr. 1954 cité par GROSDIDIER DE MATONS : "La responsabilité de l'Etat pour le fonctionnement de certains services publics". DMF 1968, 67.

- On 31 December 1996, in the case of the fish factory ship *Snekkar Arctic*, Rouen Administrative Court decided that the State bore 20 per cent liability for the accident (31).

In the United Kingdom, courts also held that a coastguard was not liable for any lack of duty of care (32).

b) Criminal liability

Although not many cases exist, an official's criminal liability may also be claimed after an incident at sea. In France this is based on article 221-6 of the New Penal Code, which provides for punishment of anyone who, through negligence, error or failure to observe regulations has been guilty of manslaughter ("involuntary homicide").

In the case of the *Snekkar Arctic*, lost at sea with 18 fatalities in 1986 off the Shetland Islands, several contradictory decisions were handed down. Finally, the Rennes Court of Appeal decided on 17 September 1998 to annul the case against the Chairman of the Ship Commissioning Committee.

C - CHANGES IN SHIP SURVEY SYSTEMS

What is the current trend of changes in the ship survey system ? Three aspects appear to be emerging. IMO has attempted to simplify and harmonise procedures for surveys carried out in order to enforce international conventions. Under the pressure of accidents at sea, there has been a considerable strengthening of inspection procedures on certain types of ships. Finally, there is a plethora of initiatives taken by various protagonists in the maritime sector, duplicating systems already in place.

1 - Harmonisation of survey procedures

543. - IMO has gradually established a harmonised survey system. First, it adopted two protocols to the SOLAS and LL Conventions, while synchronising their application deadlines. It then made the necessary amendments to the MARPOL Convention.

The harmonised system adopted for the SOLAS and LL Conventions does not involve any fundamental change in traditional methods. It seeks only to simplify practices regarding the frequency of surveys and the period of validity of certificates. Administrations are not obliged to apply these requirements to the letter. They can set up other programmes, provided that the number and maximum frequency of surveys are preserved.

• **Principles of harmonisation**

Six principles have governed the definition of the harmonised system (34). These include a one-year standard interval between surveys; a scheme for providing the necessary flexibility for the execution of each survey, the possibility of the renewal survey being completed within three months before the expiry date of the existing certificate with no loss of its period of validity, a maximum period of validity of five years for all certificates for cargo ships and of 12 months for the passenger ship safety certificate, extension of

(30) CE, 13 Mar. 1998. Navire François Vieljeux, in DMF Sept. 1998, 788-805.
(31) Le Marin, 4 Apr. 1997.
(32) Ph. PARRY : "Coastguard found to be not liable for negligence". Lloyd's List, 9 July 1997.
(33) Le Marin, 25 Sept. 1998.
(34) IMO News, n° 1, 1989, p. 2.

certificates limited to three months to enable a ship to complete its voyage (one month for ships engaged on short voyages), and provision for the period of validity of a newly extended certificate to start from the expiry date of the existing certificate before its extension.

Three IMO Resolutions, A.728 of 6 November 1991, A.745 and A.746 of 4 November 1993 set out guidelines for the early implementation of the system. By 1991, IACS introduced the harmonised system into classification society inspection methods. Significant changes in their rules included extension of the special survey interval from 4 to 5 years, and the introduction of an intermediate survey halfway through the special survey cycle (35).

2 - Strengthening of survey procedures

a) Origin of regulations

544. - The occurrence of major tanker disasters, like that of the *Exxon Valdez*, and the frequent bulker losses in the early Nineties, led to a strengthening of control procedures. Because of the very arduous operating conditions for dry bulk carriers and the relatively advanced age of the world fleet, IMO took a number of initiatives to improve ship inspections.

In November 1991, Resolution A.713 on the safety of ships carrying dry bulk cargoes asked the MSC, among other things, to draw up requirements for an enhanced survey programme (ESP) for bulkers. In March 1992, MEPC Resolution 62 amended Annex I to the MARPOL Convention, in order to bring in similar provisions for oil tankers. The new Regulation 13G requires crude carriers of 20 000 dwt or more, and product carriers of more than 30 000 dwt, to undergo an enhanced survey programme.

b) IACS action

IACS showed the way in 1992 when it issued requirements for structural surveys of oil tankers. This is the purpose of unified rules which comply with MARPOL Annex I Regulation 13G: URZ.10.1 for oil tankers, and URZ.10.2 for bulk carriers. All these proposals were submitted to the various IMO committees for adoption. Without awaiting its conclusions, IACS members decided to apply the new unified rules from 1st July 1993, for all types of oil tankers and bulk carriers, irrespective of tonnage (36).

IMO finally adopted the IACS unified rules, subject to a few amendments, in Resolution A.744 of 4 November 1993, which contains guidelines on ESP for bulker and oil tanker surveys. These provisions were made compulsory through an amendment to the SOLAS Convention, adopted in May 1994. They now appear in Regulation 2 of the new chapter XI of the Convention, stipulating special measures to strengthen safety, and they came into force on 1st January 1997.

c) Enhanced survey programme (ESP).

545. - ESP is intended to ensure that drawings and documents are examined properly, and to guarantee harmonisation in applying Resolution A.744. Enhanced surveys have to be conducted during the periodic, annual and intermediate surveys stipulated in the MARPOL and SOLAS Conventions.

---

(35) "Surveys scrutinize older tonnage". Shiprepair. December 1993, 22-24.
(36) J.A. BURTON : "Enhanced survey of oil tankers and bulk carriers". Maritime Transport International 1993, 42-43.

IMO guidelines in Resolution A.744 give special attention to corrosion. Anticorrosion coatings and systems for tanks must be examined carefully, as well as plate thicknesses. These measurements become more important as the ship grows older. The guidelines provide a wealth of detail to explain the additional checks to be carried out in the course of an enhanced survey. Section 5 deals with preparations for the survey in accordance with a well established specific programme. Section 6 requires the shipowner to supply and maintain on-board documents, readily available for the surveyor. This file must contain structural survey reports, ship condition evaluation report, thickness measurement reports, and various supporting documents (main structural drawings, repair history, cargo and ballast history), and any other information likely to help identify critical structural areas or suspect areas requiring inspection. This introduces a preventive aspect into ship maintenance.

Application of ESP means several significant changes in the work of classification societies (37). In general, one of the keys to success of this programme is careful planning of the operations involved (38).

d) Effectiveness of ESP

When it was launched, ESP was regarded as an essential step towards the improvement of safety (39). A survey carried out in 1995 by IACS among 500 tanker and bulk carrier owners showed that 80 per cent of them were satisfied with the programme. Technically, the survey revealed that ESP had led to the discovery of paintwork defects in 22 per cent of the ships surveyed, and serious corrosion in 18 per cent. Generally speaking, it drew attention to the practical value of enhanced surveys for shipowners and their effects on the safety of large carriers (40).

Three accidents at the beginning of 1997 cast doubt, however, on the real effectiveness of the programme. The oil tanker *Nakhodka* was wrecked, according to the Japanese authorities, because of structural weaknesses caused by the corrosion of certain parts of its hull (41). The bulk carriers *Leros Strength* and *Albion Two* are also thought to have sunk as a result of structural failures (42). In all three cases, these were old ships that several months earlier had undergone an enhanced survey. These events have shown that ESP alone cannot prevent accidents, or be regarded as a panacæa for a safer bulk carrier fleet (43).

3 - Duplication of inspections

546. - The current complexity of safety systems arises largely from a general tendency in the maritime world to multiply the number of controls (44). Originally, surveys and inspections were carried out mainly by flag State officials and classification society surveyors. Today, up to twenty-five people from different inspection services intervene simultaneously on board ships, with different functions (45).

Has this duplication of surveys become a necessary evil, to guarantee greater safety of shipping ? One may well doubt this, as an analysis of the phenomenon will show.

(37) "Enhanced surveys for bulkers/tankers". Safety at Sea International, August 1993, 20.
(38) M. GUYADER : "Hull special surveys for the enhanced survey programme (ESP)". Bull. Tech. du Bureau Veritas. N° 3. Sept. 1994, 9-23.
(39) "ESPs perceived as an essential step for safety". Lloyd's List, 28 September 1996.
(40) "IACS owners endorse ESP". IACS. Press Release 14 November 1995.
(41) "How standard are standards". Seatrade Week Newsfront, 28 March 1997.
(42) "What is being done". MER, April 1997, 24.
(43) "IACS stands ground on safety measures". Tradewinds 14 February 1997.
(44) Ph. RANKING : "The tanker inspection jungle". Seaways. August 1993, 6-10.
(45) F. FRANDSEN : "Effective coordination of vessel surveys". BIMCO Bulletin 1993. N° 17.

a) Causes

There are three main reasons for the multiplication of controls.

In the last few years, there has been growing mistrust towards traditional survey methods. This climate of suspicion has encouraged the development of individual initiatives. Many prefer to protect their own interests outside the system, rather than correct shortcomings at source.

Second, the growing level of supervision involved in ship surveys corresponds to an ever-growing safety need, expressed by public opinion, which does not accept that the perils of the sea should result in shipping disasters.

Finally, a maritime transport undertaking gives rise to the conclusion of a whole series of commercial contracts (financing, insurance, chartering), which require a perfectly seaworthy ship. Everyone involved prefers individually to ensure that the clauses in its contract are respected, in order to prevent any risk of an incident, rather than relying on a third party to exercise this control (46). Because of the growing risks of legal claims, attempts to harmonise or globalise certain control approaches have so far failed. It is difficult to expect anyone to accept an inspection report produced by an inspector he cannot control, or whose standards and working methods differ too much from his own (47).

b) Drawbacks of a fragmented system

The cause of safety is not best furthered in a fragmented system. The wreck of the *Kirki* illustrates the limits of duplication of controls. This oil tanker had been inspected by the flag State, the classification society, the charterer and the oil company, and was in possession of all the corresponding certificates before breaking in two off the coast of Australia in 1991.

Duplication of inspections has not convinced seafarers either. Most consider that the repeated presence of surveyors on board causes a great waste of time and keeps the crew away from their basic duties during loading and discharging operations. Rather than helping them, the plethora of inspectors is felt as a self-defeating nuisance, prejudicial to general safety at sea.

Finally, the repetitious inspections of seaborne transport affects high-quality vessels in exactly the same way as those in poor condition. It does not provide any stimulus or bonus to reward good shipowners. In all cases it generates extra costs which have to be borne by all users indiscriminately (48).

The maritime industry has worked to achieve harmonisation in certain areas. In 1993, five international organisations published a Code of practice for organising and conducting inspections of tankers (49). These praiseworthy efforts lead to a reduction in the total number of inspections required, and need to be extended to other types of shipping.

(46) C.J. PARKER : "Port and Shipping Management : Workshop presentation". Marine Policy- September 1993, 391.
(47) "Shared opinions". - Lloyd's List, 29 September 1993.
(48) M. GREY : "The buck must stop at survey". Lloyd's List, 29 January 1992.
(49) CEFIC, INTERTANKO, ICS, IPTA, SIGTTO : "Code of practices for organizing and conducting inspections of tankers". 1st edition 1993.

II - DELEGATION TO CLASSIFICATION SOCIETIES

547 - A flag State has two ways of meeting its obligations under international safety regulations. It may exercise its own legal inspection functions by entrusting the task to a competent administration. Alternatively, it can delegate all or part of its powers to recognised organisations, such as classification societies.

A - DEVELOMENT OF DELEGATIONS

Delegation of powers to classification societies originated in British legislation on freeboard at the end of the last century. The development of technical regulations and changes in the maritime transport industry in the second half of the 20th century have accelerated the transfer of powers. There are several reasons for this trend.

Having issued the first safety rules, classification societies are best placed to apply regulations: they possess universally acknowledged skills, and an international network of surveyors, so that they can apply regulatory requirements in a uniform way.

Budget restrictions have encouraged flag States to turn to private bodies to carry out inspections. This is the case not only in developing countries, but also in leading seagoing nations (50). In Europe, North America and Australia, the intensification of port controls leaves ever fewer resources to administrations, to carry out proper statutory surveys of the national fleet.

Finally, traditional maritime States have seen their fleet decline steadily over the last twenty years, in favour of open registry States, less expensive, more flexible and which rely widely on classification societies to apply international conventions. SECNAVES, the general directorate for maritime and consular affairs of Panama, has recognised as many as 25 private bodies to carry out surveys and inspections (51). The creation of "second registers" has reinforced a general tendency to privatise inspection services (52).

Today, the leading classification societies are "recognised" by more than one hundred flag States (53). The exceptional nature of this situation cannot be overemphasised. It has no equivalent in any other area of activity. The fact that this state of affairs has existed for more than a century, and that it continues to intensify, shows that classification societies meet specific needs within the maritime world, and particularly that they have succeeded in adapting to changes in these needs.

B - TRADITIONAL DELEGATION PROCEDURES

548. - The statutory services performed by classification societies are important enough to merit a brief account of the procedures by which States turn to them for such services.

(50) J. GUY : "Class distinction". Fairplay, 9 January 1986, 35.
(51) - Seatrade Review, August 1992, p. 37.
- Lloyd's List, 11 September 1992.
- S. WADE : "Inspecting the inspectors". Fairplay, 19 Nov. 1992, 47.
(52) "Luxembourg flag authority deal with BV". Lloyd's List, 18 March 1997.
(53) - Ed. REILLY : "The application and maintenance of survey-related standards by major classification societies. IACS". Marine Surveying Standards and Opportunities. London Conference, 11 April 1994.
- J. SMITH : "IACS and IMO. The essential relationship". Edition 3, 1st July 1998. IACS. London.

1 - IMO conventions

All the main international technical conventions provide expressly for the use of classification societies, in stating that "the administration may (...) entrust the inspections and surveys either to surveyors nominated for the purpose or to organisations recognised by it" (cf LL article 13; SOLAS Regulation 6; MARPOL Annex I Regulation 4.3).

The 1978 Protocol to the SOLAS Convention provides some details of this transfer of powers (cf Regulation 6c and d). An administration designating recognised organisations must delegate minimum powers to them, notably the power to require a ship to undergo repairs and the possibility of being available to port State authorities. It must notify IMO of the specific responsibilities entrusted to the societies, and the conditions of the authority delegated to them. When a society decides that the state of a ship of its equipment fails to comply substantially with the information on the certificate, or that it cannot go to sea safely, it must ensure that corrective action is taken, and inform the administration promptly. When the port State has been informed of such measures, it must provide all necessary assistance to the society.

The final aspect is that delegation of powers results in a transfer of part of the State's inspection functions, but not its responsibility: the administration remains guarantor of these services. IMO international conventions universally recognise this principle.

2 - Recognition agreements

Legal processes for delegating powers used to be very rudimentary, usually involving an administrative formality, empowering the organisation to carry out surveys and inspections for a particular international convention, and to issue the corresponding certificates of conformity.

The first agreements between States and classification societies appeared in the late Seventies. To begin with they were very general. As time passed, their content became more substantial, stipulating the relevant laws, the scope of delegation, conditions of issue of certificates and, above all, conditions of liability and arrangements for settling disputes (54). These agreements gradually gave flag States the power to evaluate the performance of classification societies (55).

3 - Conditions of liability

549. - In exercising its statutory powers under the terms of international and national regulations, the society may be held liable on three levels: administrative, civil and criminal.

a) Administrative liability

When it exists, the agreement signed between the flag State administration and the classification society establishes a comprehensive and consistent legal framework, intended to prevent any misunderstanding or dispute between the State and the society. It lays down the maximum amount of possible repairs, determines whether liability encompasses direct and indirect damage, and provides for legal assistance in order to adopt a common defence.

(54) B. JEGOU : "La responsabilité des sociétés de classification de navires agissant par délégation des pavillons". Bureau Veritas. Paris 1993. Unpublished study.
(55) E. JANSEN : "Government's Responsabilities to ensure that ships meet international convention standards". The National Institute. Management of safety. London 1991, 47.
- "Norway in technical inspection initiative". Lloyd's List, 26 September 1994.
- "Norway cracks down on class inspections". Tradewinds, 19 August 1994.

b) Civil liability

In addition to exemption and liability limitation clauses in contracts, classification societies enjoy certain legal protections guaranteed by the flag State. One of the most important is immunity from jurisdiction. This prevents claims on the liability of the State and its agents before the courts of another State. Two recent cases, involving the *Sundancer* and the *Scandinavian Star*, have shown how effective this protection can be.

In both these cases, American courts considered that the law of the flag State, the Bahamas, applied to any disputes, and that it conferred immunity on a classification society which had acted on behalf of that government.

c) Criminal liability

As regards the penal liability of the classification society surveyor who has acted under powers delegated by a State, the remarks made earlier apply.

The CMI has taken account of the particular features of relations between the administration and the classification society, by including several provisions applying to approval agreements in its model contract clauses. They state in particular that the society whose liability is being claimed will be entitled to the same legal protection as the delegating authority, if it benefits from such protection under national law.

C - HARMONISATION OF DELEGATION PROCEDURES

550. - The early Nineties saw more serious attempts to achieve greater harmonisation among various procedures for the approval, recognition, authorisation or accreditation of classification societies. The initiative came from States and the societies themselves, which had realised that too great a diversity in such authorisations and conditions of liability was a source of legal uncertainty, and ultimately detracted from their development. IACS members therefore tried to align their positions and adopt a common attitude in negotiating agreements with maritime administrations.

States tried to impose minimum standards on the societies acting in their name, in order to guarantee the effectiveness of the delegation procedure. In the past, this practice was confined to a small number of societies with the necessary manpower and skills to carry out inspections and surveys worldwide. The situation has changed radically in the last few decades. The number of classification societies has increased substantially since 1950, to more than fifty today (56). Most of these do not have the qualities traditionally required to act on behalf of States (57). This has led to unacceptable distortions.

Two international organisations, IMO and the European Union, have recently provided a solution to this problem of minimum standards for agents acting for flag States.

---

(56) See the list drawn up by the US Coast Guard in "Report to congress on the Coast Guard's Port-state control initiative targeting substandard ships". Senate Report (103-150) April 1994. Washington.
Cf also the list of non-governmental organisations authorized to carry out surveys and issue certificates on behalf of Administration in IMO FSI 4/8/1. 19 Jan. 1996.
(57) Commission of the European Communities : "A Common Policy on Safe Seas". Communication from the Commission, Brussels, 24 Feb. 1993, COM (93) 66 final, p. 24.

1 - IMO Resolution

a) Authorisation of organisations acting on behalf of the administration

551. - Resolution A.739 of 22 November 1993 for the first time provided guidelines for the authorisation of organisations acting on behalf of the administration. The aim is to help them implement the relevant IMO conventions effectively, by encouraging the adoption of uniform procedures and mechanisms.

National administrations are recommended to respect several requirements, check that the delegated body has adequate technical, management and research resources to carry out the tasks entrusted to it, have a formal written agreement with the organisation, including the main aspects of the delegation operation, provide instructions detailing actions to be followed when the ship is regarded as unfit to go to sea, provide the organisation with all appropriate elements of national law to carry out its assignment, and finally specify that the organisation should maintain records supplying data to assist in interpretation of convention regulations.

The administration should also establish a system to check the adequacy of the work carried out by the classification society. This system should comprise communication procedures, procedures for reporting to the administration, additional ship inspections by the flag State, acceptance or assessment by the administration of certification of the society's quality system by an independent body of auditors, and finally the monitoring and verification of class-related matters as applicable.

Resolution A.739 contains two appendices, one laying down minimum standards applying to delegated organisations, the other stating elements to be included in an agreement.

b) Specifications of functions of recognised organisations

These specifications, contained in Resolution A.789 of 23 November 1995, are divided into four elementary modules relating to surveys and certification. These cover management, technical appraisal of services, surveys, and qualification and training of surveyors.

c) New SOLAS XI/1 Regulation

The SOLAS Conference of May 1994 included a new chapter XI in the Convention, on special measures to enhance maritime safety. Regulation 1 of this chapter makes the provisions of Resolution A.739 mandatory. This came into force on 1st January 1996 (58). Resolution A.739 has also been incorporated in the SOLAS Convention, by including a reference to it in a footnote accompanying Regulation XI.1 (59).

2 - EU Directive

552. - In December 1994, the EU Council adopted Directive 94/57, establishing common rules and standards for ship inspection and survey organisations and for the relevant activities of maritime administrations (60). It is intended to involve national administrations more closely in the process of ship certification and surveying, requiring member States to introduce a recognition procedure.

(58) IMO News N° 4 - 1995, 24.
(59) IMO, FSI 4/18, 12 April 1996, 8-10.
(60) OJEC, 12 Dec. 1994, N° L 319/20.

This obligation comprises two aspects. First, article 3.2 states that statutory duties may be delegated only to recognised organisations. Second, article 14.1 states that each member State must ensure that ships flying its flag are constructed and maintained in accordance with the rules of a recognised classification society.

The EU Directive goes further than the IMO Resolution, by laying down qualitative and quantitative criteria for obtaining recognition, to guarantee the professionalism and reliability of classification societies.

a) Recognition criteria

These criteria come under two headings.

First, there are general qualitative and quantitative criteria.

The first quality criterion concerns the classification society's experience of assessing the design and construction of ships. The second criterion concerns the rules published by the society, and continuously upgraded and improved through research and development programmes. The third relates to the register of shipping, which must be published annually. The final criterion requires the society to be independent of other maritime industries, including shipowners and shipyards.

The Directive lays down two quantitative criteria. The society must class at least a thousand oceangoing ships of more than 100 gross tonnage, representing no less than 5 million gross tonnage. It must also have a technical workforce commensurate with the number of ships classed, and at least a hundred exclusive surveyors. The effect of these quantitative criteria is to exclude small classification societies operating in Europe. In May 1998, the Commission applied these criteria in turning down an application by the Hellenic Register of Shipping to gain EU recognition (61).

Second, particular criteria return to the minimum standards laid down in IMO Resolution A.739, concerning the world network of surveyors, the ethical code, quality policy and approved quality assurance system.

b) Recognition procedure

553. - Recognition is valid only for a period limited to three years (cf article 4.3).

The procedure is initiated by the applicant organisations, which must provide member States with any evidence and information to establish that they meet the criteria (cf article 4.1). Each State then informs the Commission and other EU members of the names of organisations recognised by it.

Recognition may be withdrawn if a society's record is unsatisfactory on matters of safety or pollution. This measure is pronounced by the State, after the Commission has examined the grounds for it (cf article 10).

The State may also withdrawn recognition from organisations that no longer comply with the criteria set by the Commission, in accordance with a procedure described in article 9.2.

c) Obligations arising from recognition

Recognition imposes obligations both on member States and on classification societies.

(61) "HRS fails EU test". Fairplay 28 May 1998.

• **State obligations**

There are two requirements for a State recognising a society to carry out statutory surveys and inspections: it must establish a working relationship between its administration and the organisations acting in its name; and it must monitor the services that have been delegated.

According to article 6, the working relationship is "regulated by a formalised written and non-discriminatory agreement, or equivalent legal arrangements setting out the specific duties and functions assumed by the organisations". Each member State must supply precise information on the relationship to the Commission, which subsequently informs other states.

Article 11 asks each State to exercise regular monitoring of recognised organisations. It may have the organisations monitored twice a year by its competent organisation or by relying on another State, to check that the criteria continue to be satisfied. It must also report to the Commission on the results of monitoring, which consists of assessing the performance of each organisation. All societies are monitored by a special committee, which decides whether to extend recognitions (cf article 4.4).

Unreognised societies are still subject to controls. Their performance is recorded by member States, and this record is updated yearly and submitted to the Commission (cf article 12.2). The certificates they deliver are one of the primary criteria for selecting ships for inspection by port states which are are EU members (cf article 12.1).

• **Recognised classification society obligations**

Article 15 lays down four requirements. First, recognised organisations are to consult one another periodically, with a view to maintaining equivalence of their technical standards. Periodic reports are then sent to the Commission. They must also show willingness to cooperate with port State control administrations when a ship of their class is concerned by a statutory inspection. They must also provide the administration with all relevant information about changes of class or declassing of ships. Finally, they cannot issue certificates to a disclassed ship before consulting the competent administration.

CONCLUSION: towards privatisation of safety inspections ?

554. - The delegation of certain statutory services to classification societies currently raises the general issue of the organisation of State action on safety at sea.

For developing countries, the question arises mainly in economic terms. Not having adequate administrative infrastructures, Third World States rely largely on services offered by private organisations (62).

---

(62) M. MAHMOOD : "Role of classification societies, governments, administrations". IMAS 95. The Institute of Marine Engineers 1995. 67-72.

For traditional maritime States, the debate comprises both political and economic aspects. At a political level, there is the question of whether safety is better assured by delegating survey of ships to private organisations, rather than to a public administration. Partisans of deregulation point to the benefits of free competition on this market: reduction in costs, improvement in services and tax income for governments applying such a policy. Opponents of liberalisation point to the social consequences: excessive concentration on profits leading to loss of employment for surveyors, with in certain cases a decline in the quality of service (63).

For certain developed States, the problem is also economic. Canada, for example, has considered privatising part of its government services because of the increase in its monitoring obligations, arising from its participation in two regional port State control schemes. Budgets remain the same, and so politicians are forced to make choices, entrusting certain flag State obligations to outside organisations, in order to meet their new Port State control commitments (64).

(63) S.B. BUTLER, P. STARR : "Does privatization improve services and lower costs ?". CQ Researcher, 1992, November, 13, 2, 42.
(64) M.R. BROOKS : "The privatization of ship safety". Maritime Policy Management, 1996. Vol 23 - N° 3, 271-288.

CHAPTER 23

Substandard ships

555. - There is a lack of uniformity in international observance of ship inspection procedures. Not all flag States are equally careful and strict in fulfilling their obligations. Much depends on the amount of shipping on a country's register and the administrative resources available to it. Clearly, some countries with a merchant fleet do not have the material capacity to oversee the safety of individual ships. This creates the conditions for the appearance and persistence of substandard shipping.

This chapter examines the concept of substandard ships, by describing the reality behind the term. Accurate knowledge of the phenomenon should make it easier to find ways of combatting the effects on safety at sea.

I - SUBSTANDARD SHIPPING: A MULTI-FACETTED PHENOMENON

The expression "substandard ship" raises several questions. What exactly are minimum standards ? How can a ship that fails to meet these requirements be identified ? Is there is a typology of substandard ships ? Can the scale of the phenomenon worldwide be assessed ?

A - MINIMUM STANDARDS

556. - ILO Convention 147, adopted on 29 October 1976, catalogues the minimum safety rules to be observed by merchant ships. It draws a distinction between technical standards and social protection standards.

1. Minimum technical standards

Article 5 makes reference to three fundamental IMO technical documents: the SOLAS Conventions of 1960 and 1974, the Loadline Convention of 1955, and the COLREG Convention of 1960 and 1972, as well as any convention subsequently revising these instruments.

2. Minimum social standards

These standards are equivalent to those contained in the ILO instruments appended to Convention 147: Minimum Age Convention of 1920, 1936 and 1973, Shipowners' Liability (Sick and Injured Seamen) Convention of 1936 and 1969, Medical Examination (Seafarers) Convention of 1946, Prevention of Accidents (Seafarers) Convention of 1970, Accommodation of Crew Convention of 1949, Food and Catering (Ships' Crews)

Convention of 1946, Officers' Competency Certificates Convention of 1936, Seamen's Articles of Agreement of 1926, Freedom of Association and Protection of the Right to Organise Convention of 1948, and the Right to Organise and Collective Bargaining Convention of 1949.

A recommendation concerning the improvement of standards on board merchant ships, adopted on 29 October 1976, added the Accommodation of Crews Convention of 1970, Workers' Representatives Convention of 1971, Paid Vacations (Seafarers) Convention of 1949 and 1976, Social Security (Seafarers) Convention of 1976, and Recommendation 147 of 1970 on training of seafarers.

B - IDENTIFYING CRITERIA

557. - The work of inspectors in identifying substandard ships was facilitated by IMO Resolution A.787 on port State control of ships, and US Coast Guard regulations on the targetting of substandard ships.

1. Regulatory criteria

Resolution A.787 of 23 November 1995 considers as substandard a ship if its hull, machinery or equipment, such as lifesaving appliances, radio installations and firefighting equipment, are substantially below the standards required by the relevant conventions, owing for example to the absence of the necessary equipment, or if it is not equipped in the way required by regulations, when the equipment or arrangement do not meet regulatory specifications, or the ship or its equipment has suffered substantial deterioration, because of poor maintenance.

The Resolution states that these evident factors, as a whole or individually, make the ship unseaworthy, and would put at risk the life of those on board if it were authorised to set sail.

Section III of the USCG report of 8 April 1994 (1) contains a rather similar definition of a substandard ship. Such shipping comprises vessels whose "hull, crew, machinery, or equipment, such as for lifesaving, firefighting and pollution prevention, are substantially below the standards required by US laws or international standards".

As in the IMO Resolution, several identifying criteria are listed. If such criteria, as a whole or individually, endanger the ship or those on board, or present an unreasonable risk to the marine environment, the ship should be regarded as substandard.

2. Principal defects

558. - The principal defects discovered on board substandard ships by the PSC authorities may be put into three categories.

a) Hull condition

Many substandard ships are old vessels, poorly maintained, presenting major areas of corrosion which detract from their structural strength (2). Some are in an extremely dilapidated condition (3). Others have undergone inadequate repairs, following repeated

---

(1) US Coast Guard. Port State Control initiative boarding Regime to target substandard ships. Washington. 1994.
(2) J. SPIERS : "Kirki corrosion holes deliberately concealed". Lloyd's List, 3 April 1992.
(3) - "Platytera sparks state control row". Tradewinds 5 March 1993.
- "Concern at class role in worst ever ship". Telegraph, 8 April 1993.

damage (4). Yet others try to cover the defects with a few coats of paint, sometimes using painted canvas. A few sail with quite noticeable holes in the hull (5). These ships represent the most visible face of substandard shipping.

b) Ship equipment

Not all substandard ships are immediately detectable, particularly if they give the impression of being properly maintained, with a coat of fresh paint on the deck or in the engine room. Defects may appear in its equipment, items of which are either absent or in poor working order (6).

The commonest failings found by port State inspectors concern lifesaving appliances, firefighting equipment and navigational aids (defective nautical instruments or out-of-date marine charts) (7).

c) Ship operation

Seaborne transport remains a broadly open market, where shipowners have considerable scope in operating their ship. The result is huge disparities in safety management policies (8).

This freedom enjoyed by shipowners results in numerous failures to observe elementary safety rules. The ship is not fully manned, or the crew is manifestly incompetent (9), characterised by a lack of cohesion. This may be the result of systematic recourse to ship management companies, which is reflected in far higher crew turnover. The many nationalities and different languages used by the crew impede communication on board.

C - SIMILAR CONCEPTS

Care must be taken not to compare substandard shipping with other similar material or legal concepts.

1. Older ships

559. - Many commentators consider the age of a ship as the determining factor in rendering it substandard. This idea is based on the fact that older vessels encounter more safety problems than new ones (10). Several studies have shown that accident proneness increases with the age of the ship (11).

A Danish study for the first time quantified the relationship between vessel age and the incidence of major casualties (12). There are three times as many losses among tankers and dry cargo vessels over 11 years old, compared with ships less than 5 years old.

---

(4) - "The old bulk carrier problem" Seatrade Week, 2-8 April 1993.
- " Faulty bulker *Iapetos* allowed to beep trading ". Tradewinds, 8 April 1993.
(5) - I MIDDLETON : "Holes in the system". Seatrade Review January 1994 6-9.
- "San Marco - A shameful, sorry saga". International Bulk Journal - April 1994.
(6) "Too many holes. Why port state control is essential". Fairplay, 4 July 1996.
(7) Paris MOU. Annual Report 1997. Major categories of deficiencies relation to inspections/ship.
(8) OECD. "Competitive advantages obtained by some shipowners as result of non-observance of applicable international rules and standards". Paris 1996. OCDE/GD (96) 4.
(9) "Liberté de couler à pic". Jeune Marine, n° 17 March-Apr. 1997.
(10) "It's the old, old story". Tony Gray's City View. Lloyd's List, 7 January 1993.
(11) "Vessel age a key factor in marine losses". Lloyd's List, 12 September 1992.
(12) "New Danish study shows risk of older vessels". Lloyd's List, 2 August 1993.

According to another study by the UK Club (13), the critical age is between 14 and 20 years. It is during this period that structural problems, lack of maintenance and a decline in crew quality are most frequent.

Ageing of world shipping has become a major source of concern: in 1997, 43.65 per cent of ships of more than 100 gross tonnage had been in service for more than 20 years (14). The threats to safety presented by old ships have led some public authorities and private organisations to consider setting an age limit for commercial navigation. The Oil Pollution Act of 1990 introduced the concept of age limit for tankers not fitted with a double hull. In 1991, the Suez Canal authorities considered charging higher canal dues to older ships (15). Early in 1992, certain shippers refused to have Australian coal carried on bulkers more than 15 years old (16). Insurers had no hesitation in raising premiums for cargoes loaded on to ships more than ten years old (17). In April 1994, the major Saudi tanker charterer Vela gave notice that it would no longer use ships more than 20 years old, except for those that have undergone a condition assessment programme (CAP) offered by a leading classification society (18). All these initiatives have contributed, more or less powerfully, to the success of scrapping policies, to the detriment of schemes to renovate older shipping (19).

Several voices have been raised within the maritime community against such practices (20).

Some commentators have suggested that it would be more appropriate to reduce the capacity of ships in service as they grow older. From a purely technical angle, old ships cannot be equated with substandard ships. At the very most, statistically, a higher proportion of older ships, except those that carry passengers, is found not to meet the requirements of safety regulations.

2. Seaworthiness

560. - Can a substandard ship be equated with an unseaworthy ship ? To begin with, unseaworthiness is a legal concept used in shipping contracts (21) and insurance (22).

Seaworthiness is a broad concept, indicating that a ship is perfectly equipped for an intended voyage. It must not only be in a condition that enables it to cope with the risks it may normally encounter, but must also be able to ensure the transport of its cargo in complete safety. This is a question of fact and not of law (23).

Materially, the concept of seaworthiness covers such varied aspects as the good condition of the hull and deck, means of propulsion and steering, installations and equipment, manning (by a large enough competent crew), the fitness of the ship to carry the

(13) "Warning on common causes of maritime liability claims". Lloyd's List, 9 February 1994.
(14) Lloyd's Register. World Fleet Statistics. 1997.
(15) "Suez Canal plan for older vessels'. Lloyd's List, 11 October 1991.
(16) Age bar set on capesize bulkers". Lloyd's List, 3 Feb.1992.
(17) "Old vessels and falling safety standards : the jury is still out". Lloyd's List, 5 December 1991.
(18) "Age and beauty". Lloyd's List, 8 April 1994.
(19) - "To scrap or not to scrap : the challenge of the nineties". Lloyd's List, 23 October 1992.
- B. BOX : "Broken promise". Seatrade Review, June 1994".
(20) - M. GREY : "Age alone does not answer all the questions". Lloyd's List, 12 Februay 1992.
- "No euthanasia". Lloyd's List, 3 December 1992.
- "Scrapping old fleet is no answer to tanker accidents around the world". Lloyd's List, 4 Feb. 1993.
- "Call to reduce capacities not age limits". Lloyd's List, 5 Feb. 1993.
(21) - S. GIRVIN : "Seaworthiness and the Hague-Visby Rules". Intern. Journal of Shipping Law. Part 4, Dec. 1997, 201-209.
(22) P. LUREAU : "L'innavigabilité est-elle un risque". DMF 1975, 261.
(23) R. COLINVAUX : Carver's. Carriage by sea. Vol 1. London, 1982, 105 - 124.

cargo (loading and unloading gear, good condition of holds), and preservation of merchandise (e.g. ventilation, cargo battens, dunnage, refrigerating installations) (24).

Because of the wide range of case law decisions on the issue, unseaworthiness is not sufficient in itself to prove that a ship is substandard. This remains above all a variable concept: the due care required of the shipowner in a charter contract depends on the voyage to be performed and the goods to be carried. It is governed by professional practice and the normal means available (25). This variability in requirements is incompatible with the need for uniform maritime safety rules and harmonisation of the conditions for enforcing them. On the other hand, a substandard ship is very likely also to be unseaworthy. Some courts have accepted that the absence of a safety or classification certificate created a presumption of unseaworthiness, which could be overridden by evidence to the contrary (26).

3. Dangerously unsafe ships

561. - The concept of a "dangerously unsafe ship" is a criminal definition introduced in the British Merchant Shipping Act of 1988, following the *Herald of Free Enterprise* disaster. This piece of legislation provides for criminal charges against anyone found guilty of sailing such a vessel, whether owner or master.

According to section 30.3 of this Act, four features characterise a dangerously unsafe ship: the condition or the suitability for its purpose of all or part of the ship or its machinery or equipment, undermanning, overloading or unsafe or improper loading, and any other matter relevant to the safety of the ship.

This last criterion allows courts to extend the interpretation of such a ship to include not only unseaworthiness, but also any factor threatening the safety of life at sea (27).

Not all substandard ships come into this category, only the worst, which present a danger for crew or passengers.

D - A DIFFICULT CONCEPT TO GRASP

562. - The disparity in definitions and identifying criteria makes it difficult to grasp the concept of substandard shipping.

Technically, IMO Resolution A.787 accepts that it is "impossible to define a ship as substandard solely by reference to a list of qualifying defects". It all depends on the surveyor's discernment and technical skill. In fact there are no absolute safety standards. They vary depending on time and place, in accordance with several factors, including the service for which the ship is intended, the goods carried, and how the ship is operated (28). This is why some commentators consider that the substandard ship is almost impossible to spot or to anticipate (29).

(24) G. LEFEBVRE : "L'obligation de navigabilité et le transport maritime sous connaissement". Les cahiers du Droit, vol 31, n°1, March 1990, 81 - 123.
(25) M. REMOND-GOUILLOUD : "Droit Maritime". Paris, Pedone 1988, 332.
(26) - Chambre des Requêtes, 2 août 1932, Dor 27, 240. Cour d'Appel de Rennes, 18 Feb. 1974, DMF 1974, 335.
(27) S. HODGES : " Liabilities and penalties for unsafe ships". The Nautical Institute. Management of Safety London 1991, 64 - 69.
(28) - M. ABE : " What should be the standards". BIMCO Review 1994, 53
- Fairplay, 2nd September 1993.
(29) "Keeping mum" Lloyd's List, 26 June 1993.

In social terms, the obstacles are even greater. How can one gauge the degree of compatibility between what is substandard in highly industrialised Western countries and the same phenomenon in developing countries that cannot pay proper wages to their crews ? (30)

The difficulties in identifying the substandard phenomenon explain the highly approximate evaluation of the number of ships coming under this heading, even when the criteria are purely technical. Shell estimated that approximately 20 per cent of the world oil tanker fleet was substandard (31). Figures for bulk carriers range from 10 per cent (32) to 30 per cent (33).

II - CAUSES OF SUBSTANDARD SHIPPING

563. - The emergence of substandard shipping may be attributed to two series of factors; the recession that has devastated the shipping industry, and the shortcomings of certain flag States.

A - CRISIS IN SHIPPING

Nearly the whole shipping industry has been affected by the persistent crisis that began in the mid-Seventies. Over-capacity, responsible for a steady decline in freight rates, led shipowners to use every device to reduce their operating costs. Routine use of old ships, the cutting of maintenance costs to a strict minimum, and the recruitment of cheap manpower were the main aspects in this scramble to save money. The crisis has affected all professions, subjecting their members to commercial pressures that it is hard to reconcile with proper safety management.

1. Shipowners

564. - Shipowners, in an attempt to make up for the decline in freight rates by paring down the costs of providing services, have begun to contract out certain services.

a) Subcontracting

Subcontracting consists of transferring to third parties certain expenses that weigh too heavily on operating costs (34). Shipping company structures have thus been broken up into various separate entities. Most shipowners have retained only the financing responsibility for the ships they own, leaving all other tasks to ship management companies. This applies in particular to crew management, technical management (ship equipment and maintenance, purchases, insurance, dry docking, cost accounting) and commercial management (charter prospection).

(30) A. SELANKER : "Flag changes have major implications for structure of marine employment". Conference Which Register ? Which Flag ? London, 2-3 Sept. 1987. Lloyd's of London Press.
(31) "Shell urges tanker crack down". Lloyd's List, 21 January 1993.
(32) "Vessel's age a major cause of concern". Lloyd's List, 28 Sept. 1991.
(33) F. IAROSSI "Improving safety through enhanced survey" - BIMCO Review 1994, 49.
(34) P. LEONARD : Introduction to the 6th session Conseil Supérieur de la Marine Marchande, Paris, 1993.

b) Consequences for safety

This reliance on externalisation policies has led to a decline in the level of safety at sea. The shipowner's managerial decisions, governed by financial considerations, are more and more short-term, with the object of immediate profitability: maintenance programmes have limited the number of dry dockings and the frequency of surveys by superintendents. Training budgets have been slashed, leading to a drop in the level of crew qualification and skill. Some shipowners have embarked on a policy of buying second-hand or even third-hand ships, near the age limit and often poorly maintained. Changes of ownership have sometimes been accompanied by a transfer of flag or class, whether to get round national safety regulations or to evade the over-stringent requirements of classification societies formulated during special surveys (35).

Such transfers have been regarded as a flagrant example of the use of flags of convenience, and as dangerous for safety (36). Of the 182 ships lost in 1991, 92 had undergone one or more changes of ownership in the previous five years. In 17 cases, the exact number of transfers could not be established (37).

Simultaneously with the appearance of substandard shipping there has emerged an "evasion culture" (38) which, out of a need to survive, confers legitimacy on non-compliance with safety standards, considered too high or incompatible with economic constraints.

c) Competitive advantages

565. - Several studies have drawn attention to the competitive advantages enjoyed by substandard shipping.

• OECD report

In a report published in 1996 (39), the OECD demonstrated that the operation of substandard ships could generate substantial savings. Five different levels of safety maintenance have been identified:

- **Ceiling**, representing the maximum level of expenditure decided by a shipowner, influenced by the revenue-earning potential of the ship on the freight market and his financial costs;
- **Good practice**, representing a high level of expenditure adopted by a minority of shipowners;
- **Common practice**, representing an average level of expenditure adopted by a majority of shipowners;
- **Standard practice**, representing the minimum level of expenditure to ensure an owner's compliance with basic safety standards;
- **Floor**, representing a minimum level of expenditure to keep the ship operational.

Between these last two levels is the substandard operating margin, within the limits of which a shipowner can operate his ship, provided that its shortcomings are not detected by inspection authorities, and that no steps are taken that could narrow this margin.

---

(35) Shell International Marine Limited : "A study of standards in the oil tanker industry". May 1992.
(36) "Societies seek improved standards in class of 92". Lloyd's List, 6 October 1992.
(37) Lloyd's List, 15 September 1992, 4.
(38) D. MOREBY : "Cults and cultures in modern shipping". BIMCO Bulletin. Vol. 91, n° 4, 1996. p. 32.
(39) Op. cit. OECD/GD (96) 4, p. 9-13.

Table 20 illustrates the considerable difference in daily expenses between a shipowner operating a ship to the highest standards and one making do with minimum safety standards. Two cases have been considered:
- 30 000 dwt bulk carrier 20 years old;
- 40 000 dwt product carrier tanker ship built in the Nineties.

Table 20. Financial advantages obtained by running vessels at different operating standards
(Source : OCDE)

BULK CARRIER US $/Day		PRODUCT TANKER US $/Day
7 500	Ceiling	9 500
4 500	Good practice	4 850
3 750	Common practice	4 250
3 250	Standard	3 750
2 750	Floor	3 100

The differences between these various levels vary depending on a number of factors, including the age, flag and type of ship, its nationality, size and manning, the financial costs borne by the shipowner, and the market in which the ship operates.

• Manaus Consultants studies

In a study of risks, regulations and competition in international maritime transport, Manaus Consultants showed that substandard ships almost systematically enjoy an advantage in economic competitiveness (40).

Simulations involving five types of oil tankers and bulkers led to two conclusions. First, the quality premium that the market would theoretically have to allocate to counterbalance the handicap suffered by an operator who respects standards, compared with one who ignores them, would be at least 20 to 30 per cent of the market rate, up to 40 per cent in certain cases. Next, the time of inactivity of a ship which, failing a premium on quality, would cancel out the comparative advantage of a substandard shipowner, would have to be 2 to 3 months a year, or even 6 months in the most extreme cases.

Noting that bad ships drive out good ones, the author of the study concluded that, in the medium and long term, the gap between the two types of operators is likely to widen, perpetuating the downward pressure on freight rates and postponing any renewal of world shipping fleets (41).

(40) M. DESAUTEL JAMOIS : "Les transports maritimes en quête de qualité : Enjeux, obstacles et leviers". MANAUS Consultants, Paris, décembre 1994.
(41) M. DESAUTEL JAMOIS : "Transports maritimes internationaux. Risques, réglementation et compétition". Recherche. Transports Sécurité n° 49, Déc. 1995. Paris.

2. Ship managers

566. - The unbridled competition that has raged among ship management companies in the last few years has led unscrupulous shipowners to "go shopping" for managers that charge extremely low fees. Some are past masters in the art of making do, and keeping the most dilapidated ships in service. Two methods have been used to cut operating costs: a drastic reduction in maintenance, and the recruitment of cheap manpower (42).

The low calibre of crews recruited by specialised agencies, for short periods on a wide variety of ships, has no doubt had the most disastrous effect on safety. The lack of any continuity in these recruitment contracts prevents crews from becoming familiar with any one ship, and explains their lack of motivation for maintenance and servicing. The plethora of ethnic origins, languages and cultures on board has increased difficulties of communication, and this reflects on prompt compliance with orders and instructions when any danger arises (43).

3. Shipyards

567. - The recession that hit this industry in the early Eighties forced shipbuilders to adapt their products to new market demands. In order to obtain fresh orders, shipyards had to cut their costs. The use of high-tensile steel and reduced scantlings helped them achieve this goal, but it made ships more vulnerable, and considerably shortened their useful life (44).

4. Classification societies

568. - The large number of classification societies and the competitive climate in which they operate has not made it easy to eliminate substandard practices (45). The existence of "floating coffins" on the registers of major societies exposed them to several barrages of criticism. It was not so much possible loopholes in classification rules that were questioned, as the way the rules were being applied.

The main criticisms were aimed at the very basis of classification, which generates an "unanswerable conflict of interests" (46): the shipowner, who is the classification society's client, is forced to increase safety on board his ships, and therefore cut his profit margin and the profitability of his business. In a fiercely competitive situation, certain societies have been tempted to be less unbending about current standards, in order to retain certain ships of doubtful quality on their register.

The results of this conflict of interest have been much decried. A shipowner's freedom to change class resulted in a dangerous flexibility in the interpretation and application of rules. Indulgence was shown in granting term extensions. Dry-dock surveys were postponed without real justification (47). Criticism was also made of a certain negligence in establishing procedures for transfer of class, enabling unscrupulous shipowners to go class hopping and obtain a particular advantage offered by such and such a society, or escape a

---

(42) G. MOREL : "La gestion de la qualité dans la gérance des navires". Communication at the 6th session of the Conseil Supérieur de la Marine Marchande. Paris 1993.
(43) A. SE LANDER : "The human element. A critical factor in marine safety". 2nd International Summit Safety at Sea. Oslo 1993.
(44) - B. BOX : "High-tensile steel". Seatrade May 1994.
- "Low-cost ships now pay the price". Lloyd's List, 8 July 1993.
(45) Drewry Shipping Consultant : "Marine pollution and safer ships. Implication for the tanker industry". London, 1992.
(46) J. PRESCOTT : "An unanswerable conflict of interest". Lloyd's List, 15 October 1987.
(47) "Top-Class : how good is good". Seatrade, February 1985, 4-7.

special survey (48). In certain cases, there were allegations of lack of integrity and independence among surveyors, too closely linked to the shipowner's technicians. Finally, there was general concern about the confidential nature of the information in survey reports, and the impossibility of obtaining access to the records of ships suspected of being substandard (49).

5. Insurers and P&I clubs

569. - Hull and cargo insurers, operating in a very tough international climate, have not managed to clean up the market. It has not proved possible to include systematically in all contracts classification clauses that would lift the veil of confidentiality and allow access to the records of classed ships (50). Certain hull insurers have even admitted that they earned far less by insuring good operators than bad ones, for whom competition was less, and premiums higher (51).

In the same way, P&I clubs have been subjected to commercial pressures from shipowners looking for undemanding insurers. The reluctance to exclude bad clients illustrates the contradictions that exist between the political will displayed by shipowners on the boards of such clubs and the standards their employees apply in reality or try to have respected (52).

6. Shippers

570. - The oil crisis of the Eighties led to an extraordinary growth of short-term market transactions, related to the excess of transport capacity over demand. On these markets, mainly involving large oil groups, but also more than two thousand independent trading companies, the cost of seaborne transport is a major factor in any decision (53). This explains why certain charterers do not recognise the quality of ships, or are not ready to give any preference to quality ships (54). Others go so far as to manipulate the market by taking maximum advantage of the benefits arising from available tonnage, in order to force freight rates down (55).

In general, shippers are convinced that one must not pay more than is necessary. There is another general problem of information about the quality of charter tonnage, making any action by shippers against substandard shipping difficult (56).

B - FLAG STATE DEFICIENCIES

571. - Maritime industries do not bear sole responsibility for the development of substandard shipping. It is primarily the task of the authorities to ensure maritime safety; by

(48) - "Class Warfare". Fairplay 6, November 1992.
- "Tracking Troubles". Lloyd's List, 30 November 1992.
- JMM 4 Dec. 1992.
(49) M. GREY : "Full marks for another scheme to help mend cracks in shipping standards". Lloyd's List, 12 May 1993.
(50) G. DANEELS : "Les clauses de classification dans les polices d'assurance maritime". Thèse, Droit, Nantes 1996.
(51) N. HERLOFSON : "The role and contribution of the underwriter in securing safety at sea". 2nd International Summit Safety at Sea, Oslo, 1993.
(52) SHELL Int. Mar. : op. cit. p. 14.
(53) M. de COMBRET : "Les négociants (traders) sont-ils et doivent-ils être intéressés à la qualité des transports maritimes ?". Communication of the 6th session of Conseil Supérieur de la Marine Marchande. Paris 1993.
(54) "Bad ships, good money. Low quality still means high return". Fairplay, 14th Nov. 1996, 37.
(55) B. PAPACHRISTIDIS : "Safety at sea : the human problem at our own doorstep". 2nd International Summit Safety at Sea. Oslo, 1993.
(56) "Lack of fleet data hampers sub-standard ship action". Lloyd's List, 31 Oct. 1996.

laying down rules and overseeing their enforcement. The flag State is first and foremost responsible. In reality, States vary considerably in the degree to which they meet their international obligations. They fail to exercise effective jurisdiction over their ships, or to take action against negligence on the part of shipowners and other parties. This easygoing attitude prevails at several levels.

1. Legislative and regulatory inadequacies

Not all States have ratified IMO and ILO conventions, even though they are regarded as the reference for safety and environmental protection. These shortcomings are not overcome by the adoption of equivalent national legislation. A major part of substandard shipping is to be found among small craft engaged on coastal trade between the ports or islands of one State. Coastal navigation, which comes within the scope of national jurisdiction, has always been responsible for the greatest numbers of fatalities. Certain States, through lack of resources or gross negligence, fail to lay down any regulations whatsoever on this matter. Others hesitate to oversee enforcement of the most elementary safety measures. Because of this state of affairs, the greatest maritime disasters since 1948 have been the result of carferries or simple ferries used to carry passengers over very short distances: 1 000 in 1980 on the *Don Juan*, 4 400 in 1987 on the *Dona Paz*, another 2 000 on the *Neptune* in 1993. A total of 10 500 people have died in ten years in shipwrecks occurring off the coasts of Third World countries (57).

These deficiencies are most glaring in the area of standards for seafarers. In most developing States, laws on the issue of certificates or manning are out of date and inappropriate to modern maritime transport conditions. Regulations on the registration and operation of merchant fleets remain fragmentary and sometimes contradictory. There are not always provisions to protect shipmasters against the arbitrary power of their employers. There is no appeal against unfair dismissal, nor prior consultation before the application of internal disciplinary measures in shipping companies. In the absence of proper social protection, the person responsible for the safety of a ship may therefore be tempted to defer certain decisions necessary for the safety of the voyage (58).

2. Administrative failures

Such failures may be assessed on two levels. First, there are maritime training systems. Many countries do not have their own training schools or institutes. And when they do exist, the quality of teaching is often woefully inadequate.

Then there is the question of control. Certain States do not provide the means of checking that the laws they pass are enforced. Several features typify substandard administrations: ineffectiveness of the officials engaged in inspection, routine use of classification societies which do not belong to IACS, absence of control of delegated services, insufficiency of disciplinary and penal measures against bad operators (59). The lack of efficiency displayed by several national administrations in the application of safety standards has led to criticism aimed at certain flags characterised by a high concentration of maritime risks.

(57) J. MULREMAN : "Will Neptune be remembered ?". Lloyd's List, 20 February 1993.
(58) French government memo on the negative effects on maritime safety of certain aspects of the FOC phenomenon. IMCO. MCS 38/21 Add 1. in JMM, 25 May 1978, 1181.
(59) T. FUNDER : "The role and contribution of the various parties in securing safety at sea. The responsibilities and views of the authorities". 1st International Summit Safety at Sea. Oslo, 1991.

III - FLAGS OF CONVENIENCE (FOC)

572. - Before examining the relationship between flags of convenience and substandard shipping, certain terminological precautions need to be taken.

A - CONVENIENCE : A DIVERSE, ILL-DEFINED PHENOMENON

Many different expression are used to describe the indulgent attitude of some flag States. Several definitions have been drawn up to make it easier to identify the phenomenon. Its shifting and changing nature makes it difficult, however, to adopt a purely conceptual approach. It is usually better to rely on lists to understand the reality behind the concept.

1. Diversity of concepts

573. - The whole flag of convenience phenomenon is based on the fact of a ship being put under a flag that is not the flag of its genuine nationality (60). Transfer occurs either upon delivery of the ship or when it is sold. This is a case of abandonment of the national flag. The transfer may also occur on the expiry of a certain period during which the ship has remained under its national flag. This is a change of flag. Neither form of "flagging out" is possible except in a State that authorises the registration of ships owned and controlled by non-nationals. They will take place if they present benefits for the owner.

a) OECD definition

In 1958, the Maritime Transport Committee of the OECD provided an early definition of a flag of convenience as "the flag of such countries whose laws allow - and indeed make it easy for - ships owned by foreign nationals or companies to fly these flags, in contrast to the practice in the maritime countries where the right to fly the national flag is subject to stringent conditions and involves far-reaching obligations" (61). The American legal expert B.A. Boczek similarly defined a flag of convenience as "the flag of any country allowing the registration of foreign-owned and foreign-controlled vessels under conditions which, for whatever the reasons, are convenient and opportune for the persons who are registering the vessels" (62).

b) UNCTAD definition

UNCTAD uses the concept of "open registry" country or fleet rather than flag of convenience. This category include countries in which there is no clear link between the ships and their State of registration (cf chapter 21 above) (63).

c) OECD and EEC definition

To distinguish flags of convenience from tax havens, the OECD used criteria established by a 1970 British Committee of Inquiry into Shipping, chaired by Lord Rochdale (64).

(60) Economic and Social Committee of the European Communities. EEC Shipping Policy Flags of Convenience. Own-initiative Opinion, Brussels, April 1979, Appendix 1, 131.
(61) OECD, Maritime Transport Committee "Study of the expansion of the flags of convenience and of various aspects thereof". Paris, Jan. 1958, 3.
(62) B.A. BOCZEK : "Flag of convenience. An international legal study. Cambridge, Massachusetts, 1962, 2.
(63) I.M. SINAN : "UNCTAD and flag of convenience". Journal of World Trade Law, vol 18 n° 9, 1989, 99.
(64) Committee of Inquiry into Shipping Report, Chairman Lord Rochdale. London HMSO, May 1970.

There are six such criteria, according to this report: the country of registry allows ownership and/or control of its vessels by non-citizens; access to the registry is easy; taxes on the income from the ships are not levied locally or are low; the country of registry is a small power with no national requirement for all the shipping registered; manning of ships by non-nationals is freely admitted; the country of registry has neither the power nor the administrative machinery effectively to impose any government or international regulations, nor the wish or the power to control the companies themselves.

The same criteria were used by the Economic and Social Council of the EEC to differentiate between "cheap flags" and flags of convenience.

d) Overseas flags

The maritime States most affected by the "ship drain" have proposed the creation of more economical "second registers" to reduce operating costs, while retaining a fleet under their national flag (65).

Since 1985, many traditional maritime nations have turned to a solution that preserves the existence of a genuine link between the ship and the flag state (66). Registration of a ship on an overseas register means that the provisions of domestic legislation regarding traffic and safety at sea are maintained. In return, it offers a chance to operate fleets on conditions closer to those of the market, by allowing, for example, the recruitment of crews with no nationality stipulations.

e) Donaldson Commission definition

In the report issued after the *Braer* disaster, Lord Donaldson defined a flag of convenience as "a register where the State does not have the capability of supervising the safety of its ships or does not do so effectively" (67).

This definition deliberately refrained from making any reference to "free registry", regarded as not being the cause of substandard shipping. According to Donaldson, it is quite possible for a free registry State to maintain high safety standards, perhaps even higher than those of States with a traditional register.

2. Identification and types of flags of convenience

574. - The many different concepts and definitions of flags of convenience makes it difficult to achieve any absolute identification of the phenomenon. One solution is to examine the lists published by various organisations in order to establish a comprehensive picture of free registry countries.

The following initial classification may be offered (68):
- **Independent open registers**, such as those of Liberia, Panama and Cyprus, which have existed for about thirty years, and which alone represent three quarters of the open-registry fleet. Alongside these are more modest registers, such as those of Malta, Sri Lanka, Vanuatu and Singapore.
- **Dependency registers**, such as those of Bermuda, Gibraltar and other British dependent territories, and the Dutch West Indies.

(65) J-P BEURIER : "Les pavillons d'outre-mer : havres ou écueils" in La Communauté Européenne et la Mer - Economica, 1990, 683-692.
(66) G.S. EGIYAN : "Flag of convenience or open legislation of ships". Marine Policy, March 1990, 106-111.
(67) "Safer ships, cleaner seas". Report of Lord Donaldson's Inquiry into the prevention of pollution from merchant shipping, 61-63, Paragraphe 6.22, 6.25.
(68) J. WHITWORTH : "The Registration options. Causes and consequences". Which. Register ? Which Flag ? Conference Lloyd's of London Press 1987.

- **Offshore registers**, deliberately created, unlike the preceding ones, by traditional maritime States to reduce operating costs. They include those of Wallis and Futuna, the Canary Islands, and Danish and Norwegian second registers.

Another way of classifying them draws a distinction among free registry countries (69). These may be captive (Isle of Man, Kerguelen, Nis, Gibraltar), traditional (Panama, Liberia, Cyprus, Honduras) or new, in existence since 1980 (Bahamas, Vanuatu).

3. Scale and extension of flags of convenience

575. - All observers agree that there has been an extension in recourse to flags of convenience in the last twenty years. They also agree on the scale of the phenomenon (70).

Table 21. Top 10 merchant fleets by flag (million grt)
(Source : Lloyd's Register of Shipping)

1965		1975		1985		1995	
United Kingdon	21.7	Liberia	65.7	Liberia	54.4	Panama	62.5
Liberia	18.4	Japan	37.9	Panama	40.4	Liberia	57.4
Norway	15.5	United Kingdom	32.1	Japan	37.4	Greece	29.9
Japan	11.9	Norway	25.8	Greece	29.1	Cyprus	22.8
United States*	11.4	Greece	22.4	USSR	17.2	Bahamas	22.6
Italy	8.2	Panama	13.3	United States	16.7	Japan	20.6
USSR	5.9	USSR	12.3	United Kingdom	11.9	Norway	19.8
Greece	5.7	United States*	11.4	China	10.8	Malta	15.4
Germany	5.4	France	10.3	Norway	10.3	China	14.9
France	5.0	Italy	9.9	Cyprus	9.4	United States	13.2
Total world fleet	**159**	Total world fleet	**325**	Total world fleet	**386**	Total world fleet	**451**

* Excluding US reserve fleet

In 1995, open registry countries totalled 204 million gross tonnage, more than half the world shipping fleet. If one adds semi-open registry countries like Singapore and the Philippines, and second registers, the proportion rises to 63 per cent (71).

B - FLAGS OF CONVENIENCE AND RISKS AT SEA

576. - Open registers have for long been denounced as the cause of most accidents at sea. Several factors explain this accusation. First, there is their relative importance in the shipping trade, in terms of number of ships and tonnage. Another reason is their negative image. For the public, the flag of convenience has often been associated with large-scale maritime disasters (72). These include the *Torrey Canyon* in 1967, the *Ocean Eagle* in 1968, the *Argo Merchant* in 1976; the *Amoco Cadiz* in 1978, the *Exxon Valdez* in 1989, the *Scandinavian Star* in 1990, the *Braer* in 1993 and the *Sea Empress* in 1996 (73).

(69) J. SMITH : "The tradition of open registers. Can they maintain their position ?". Which Register ? Which Flag ? Conference. Lloyd's of London Press 1987.
(70) C. HORROCKS : "Stiffening the resolve of the Flag States". BIMCO Review 1996, 233-235.
(71) C. LYONS : "Raising the flag". Seatrade Review, March 1997, 61-64.
(72) R. CARLISLE : "Sovereignty for sale". Naval Institute Press, Annapolis, Maryland 1981, 191.
(73) "Sea Empress disaster reopens the flag issue". Lloyd's List, 27 March 1996.

1. Statistical studies

Several statistical studies show that the number of substandard ships and casualty rates were higher for flags of convenience than for traditional flags.

The Van Poelgest analysis of oil tanker casualties for the period 1972 to 1976 used the statistics of the Liverpool Insurers Association. The findings were that Liberia accounted for the largest number of casualties (82.3 per cent). Among the four flags representing the highest risk (58 per cent of the total number of incidents) there were three flags of convenience: Cyprus, Liberia and Panama (74).

Another study published in 1976 by R.S. Donagis and B.N. Metaxas (75) showed that casualty rates for flags of convenience as a whole were markedly higher than for traditional fleets. According to these authors, there is an obvious link between casualty rates and the flag of registration. Flags of convenience all show poor casualty figures between 1958 and 1972, compared with the world average, and more particularly with regard to the figures for the main national fleets.

A third analysis, again by B. Metaxas, for the period 1977 to 1980, led him to revise his initial conclusions (76). Casualty rates for small flags of convenience countries such as Lebanon, Somalia, Singapore and Cyprus are far higher than for large registers such as those of Liberia and Panama. Metaxas explains this difference by the fact that small registers contain a far larger number of shipowners with "a high propensity to avoid regulatory standards", and look for the "regime of immunity" benefits of a flag.

A study published in 1989 by S.R. Tolofari consolidated all these findings (77). An analysis of casualties between 1975 and 1983 shows that casualty rates for traditional nations, except for Greece, are low, and well below those for open registers. Greece and Liberia contribute most to world losses in terms of tonnage. As for accidents, fleets sailing under flags of convenience account for 24 per cent of all shipping losses. An analysis over a longer period, from 1970 to 1983, indicates that the casualty rate for the FOC fleet is substantially higher than for regulated fleets and than the world average.

The most recent work carried out in France by Manaus Consultant (78) shows a clear concentration of risks on the new registers of Cyprus, Malta, Saint Vincent and Grenadines, Antigua and Barbados, and the Bahamas.

2. Political debate

577. - The studies mentioned above also contribute to the political debate between supporters and opponents of open registers as regards safety at sea and protection of the environment.

a) Open registers and safety

For certain commentators, the spectacular growth of open registry fleets is directly

(75) R.S. DONAGIS, B.N. METAXAS : "The impact of flags of convenience". Central London Polytechnic, 1976.
(76) B.N. METAXAS : "Flag of convenience. A study of internationalisation". Gower, 1985, 93.
(77) S.R. TOLOFARI : "Open registry shipping. A comparative study of costs and freight rates". Gordon and Breach Science Publishers 1989, 71.
(78) M. DESAUTEL JAMOIS : "Exploitation maritime et populations à risques". Manaus Consultants. Paris. April 1996.

responsible for an increase in risks at sea. In a report published in 1981 (79), UNCTAD identified the ten fundamental reasons for flags of convenience failing more frequently to observe safety rules than traditional registers.

More cautiously, an OECD study of the competitive advantages of substandard shipping does not criticise flags of convenience as such. Noting a strong link between accidents at sea and certain registers, it merely regrets that a number of flag State administrations fail to conform to minimum inspection standards. This situation persists, it believes, because "ship registration remains for these flag states primarily a competitive business and that commercial considerations are often seen to override safety matters" (80).

b) Open registers as a source of risk: a false charge

Several experts agree, however, that criticism of free registers on safety grounds is unfounded. This attitude is based on several arguments.

A few of the most modern ships today sail under flags of convenience. In fact, many registers have taken steps to ban transfers of registration for old ships. The limit is 20 years for Liberia, Panama and Vanuatu, between 17 and 23 for Cyprus, and 23 for the Bahamas (81).

The leading open registry countries are parties to the main international conventions on safety at sea (82).

Contrary to the UNCTAD argument, certain political, economic and social ties may exist between the governments of open registry States and the shipowners using their registers. The aim of a country that decides to create an open flag is to reap economic benefits, but also to exert political influence internationally (83). To this effect, open registry States and shipowners from industrialised countries have forged very close political and economic links (84).

Such trends suggests that it is unfair to condemn flags of convenience out of hand.

CONCLUSIONS: TWO SIDES

578. - The political debate about open registers could be settled once and for all by quoting a French Senatorial report which admits that "a laxist attitude in applying safety rules is not, it seems most likely, the sole responsibility of States which have an open registry flag" (85). This report, published in May 1994, puts open registry flags into three categories: those with the worst casualty rates (St Vincent and Grenadine, Cyprus, Malta and Vanuatu), those with rates fairly close to the world average (Panama, the Bahamas), and those that have the safest fleets in the world (Liberia and Bermuda).

(79) UNCTAD. Report of the Secretariat. Actions on the question of open registries. Geneva. TD/B/C. 4/200, 3rd March 1981.
(80) Op. cit. OECD/GD (96) 4, p. 18.
(81) LARS LINDFELT : "Insurer's view flag and quality - Dilemma or opportunity". Conference/BC London. Nov. 1992.
(82) ISF : "Guide to International Ship Register".
(83) Cf Professor BARSTON, in Lloyd's List, 23 Nov. 1996.
- "Distinctions becomming more blurred". Lloyd's List, 11 Feb. 1997.
(84) E. ANDERSON : "The nationality of ships and flags of convenience : economics, politics, and alternatives". Tulane Maritime Law Journal, Vol. 21, 1996, 139-170.
(85) Sénat : "Transport maritime : Plus de sécurité pour une mer et un littoral plus propre". Rapport d'information n° 500, 1993, 75.

However, fresh controversy has sprung up with the new policies adopted by port States, aimed at identifying bad flags and publicising the findings of port inspections. It must be admitted that certain flags of convenience do not have a good reputation. In 1994, the US Coast Guard branded six open registers as the worst, those of St Vincent, Honduras, Malta, Vanuatu, Cyprus and the Bahamas (86). In Europe, on the other hand, only two open registers, those of Honduras and Belize, appear among the ten worst flags (87).

Ultimately, any assessment of actions in the last few years by flags of convenience to improve safety needs to be looked at critically: although some have made real progress, most efforts remain largely insufficient to eradicate substandard tonnage. Only a general mobilisation of the maritime community to combat this dangerous phenomenon might in the end prove effective.

(86) Lloyd's List, 15 July 1994.
(87) "EU Shipping initiative starting to bear fruit". Lloyd's List, 7 Oct. 1998.

CHAPTER 24

Action against substandard shipping

579. - There are two attitudes to the form that action against substandard shipping should take.

One argument is that the phenomenon is universal, and is spreading regardless of the flag state involved. In this case, efforts focus on the actual ships, regarded as failing to conform to international regulations on safety at sea. Corrective action, however, quickly comes up its own limitations, with the difficulty of tracking down, and acting against, the owners of substandard ships (1).

On the other hand, preference may be given to more general measures, aimed at substandard practices, and the failings of certain protagonists in the shipping sector. This broader approach does not meet with unanimous approval. Some commentators warn of the risks of equating flags of convenience with substandard shipping. Others point out that there is very little substandard shipping actually in existence.

Strenuous efforts have been made since 1990 to eradicate substandard vessels. These efforts come from private bodies (cf I below), individual states (II) and international organisations (III). The results have been more or less successful.

I - SHIPPING INDUSTRY ACTION

580. - In the early Eighties, IMF Chairman J. Davis warned the shipping sector against the danger of the spread of substandard ships, pointing out that if the maritime industry failed to self-regulate, governments would intervene and, if governments intervened, they could be more heavy-handed than might be wished (2).

It was at this time that most of the measures against the threats raised by substandard practices for safety at sea were introduced.

A - MARINE INSURERS AND P&I CLUBS

Some observers see underwriters as in a privileged position to eliminate substandard shipping: without insurance, a ship cannot set sail, nor enter port, and its owner cannot raise

---

(1) E. ARGIROFFO : "L'OIT face au problème des pavillons de complaisance". Revue Internationale du Travail, vol. 110, 486.
(2) JMM, 29 Nov. 1981, 241.

a loan if his ship is uninsured. Unfortunately, these opportunities for action are not taken in all cases, whenever short-term commercial considerations prevail over long-term strategies aimed at improving the quality and safety of shipping fleets (3).

1. Action by P&I clubs

a) Premium policy

P&I clubs, which cover the shipowner's third party liability, practise a premium policy based on the number of casualties attributable in the past to the ship operator. If this "loss record" shows frequent claims for compensation, the club may conclude that the claimant is operating substandard ships, and may decide that the higher level of risk justifies raising premiums and apply higher "deductibles" (4). Three other methods of acting against negligent shipowner have been added to these traditional procedures.

b) Inspection programme

In the last twenty years, the largest clubs have set up their own inspection system, in order to establish the real level of quality of the ships they are to insure. In 1974, the West of England P&I Club introduced an inspection programme, to assess the condition of ships (5). These surveys are compulsory for all ships more than ten years old (6). They are carried out by the club's own inspectors, and focus mainly on points not covered by classification (7).

These programmes have been considerably reinforced over the years. From 1990 to 1995, the UK Club inspected more than 2 000 ships (8). The quality of these "condition surveys" also improved, and many of them now include operational aspects and the human factor (9). Shipowners applying unacceptable operational standards had the renewal of their insurance policies refused. In 1993, the Standard Club expelled twenty such owners (10). In 1994, the UK Mutual Steamship Association applied the same treatment to nine shipping fleets totalling 800 000 gross tonnage (11). Clubs are engaged in prevention as much as in cure. Programmes include both condition surveys and overall safety appraisals (12).

c) Classification clauses

Another arm increasingly used by clubs is the insertion of classification clauses in insurance policies. These contractual provisions allow them direct access to the records of the society that classes a particular ship (13). Certain clubs go so far as to accept only ships classed by societies belonging to IACS (14).

(3) N.B. HERLOFSON : "The roles and contribution of the underwriters in securing safety at sea". International Summit Safety at Sea, Oslo, April 1991.
(4) E. NORDSTRÖM : "Maritime Safety. The role of cargo owners/shippers and marine insurers". Swedish Maritime Administration. Feb. 1998.
(5) Ph. SPORIE : "Clubs keep an eye on ship standards". Lloyd's List, 2 March 1982.
(6) "Ship shape". Lloyd's Ship Manager, Nov. 1997, 71.
(7) K. NORMAN : "P and I surveys promote shipboard safety". Safety at Sea, December 1982, 34.
(8) "UK Club inspectors pass 91 % of vessels". Lloyd's List, 2 Sept. 1995.
(9) "Condition surveys". The Swedish Club News. N° 2, Nov. 1993.
(10) Lloyd's List, 25 August 1993.
(11) Lloyd's List, 5 Sept. 1994.
(12) "West of England develops safety appraisals". Lloyd Ship Manager, May 1993, 47.
(13) "Gard tightens its rules on record access". Lloyd's List, 8 Jan. 1994.
(14) "Standard tightens rules for members". Lloyd's List, 12 Sept. 1994.

2. Action by hull and cargo insurers

a) Premium differentials

581. - Some underwriters attempt to differentiate premiums on the basis of an overall quality assessment of a shipowner's fleet. The Norwegian Central Union of Marine Insurers CEFOR takes into account not only a company's casualty statistics and the frequency of claims, but also its quality assurance system, fleet maintenance policy, choice of flag and classification society, as well as its financial position and operational policy (15).

b) Classification clauses

London underwriters first introduced classification clauses in August 1988 (16). The Joint Hull Committee recommended the introduction of new warranties in hull policies, giving insurers access to a ship's classification, maintenance and servicing records (17).

At the IUMI Congress in Antwerp in 1989, French and Norwegian insurers gave their backing to these classification clauses (18), which have since been applied almost everywhere (19).

The new "Institute Time Clauses-Hulls" put forward by the United Kingdom Joint Hull Committee in 1995 (20) introduce nothing really new compared with P&I club clauses. Some commentators even see them as less stringent (21).

c) Reinforcement of surveys and inspections

In December 1991, the Joint Hull Committee decided to include a "Structural Condition Warranty" (JH 722) in British hull policies (22). This guarantee required compliance with a system of surveys intended to gauge the structural integrity of a ship. These surveys were entrusted to the Salvage Association, which provides technical advice to the London insurance world, (23).

In March 1993, this system was completed by the insertion of two other clauses, JH 115 concerning hull condition surveys and JH 115A, which forces shipowner to have their ships inspected by the Salvage Association, and to disclose the reports and recommendations to the insurance company. The survey consisted of a preliminary inspection of the ship which, if it was unsatisfactory, could be followed up by a full structural condition survey (24).

These measures appear to have had some effect. Nearly 80 per cent of Salvage Association surveys led to major repairs (25).

(15) "Insurers to set premiums based on ship owner quality". Tradewinds, 2 Sept. 1994.
(16) "Insurance moves to push ship safety". Lloyd's List, 26 August 1988.
(17) "Classification warranties relaunched". Lloyd's List, 1 July 1987.
- "Class clause critics ignored". Lloyd's List, 20 Aug. 1989.
(18) "Support for classing warranties". Lloyd's List, 15 Sept. 1989.
(19) G. DANEELS : "Les clauses de classification dans les polices d'assurance maritime". Law thesis, Nantes, oct. 1996.
(20) - "Revision of ITC-Hulls clauses brings changes to world of marine safety". Lloyd's List, 29 Nov. 1995.
- L. HOWLETT : " The new institute time clauses : a lost opportunity ?". The Baltic, Jan. 1996, 79-80.
- R. HEWARD : " Amended form not very popular". Insurance Day, 6 Feb. 1996.
(21) N. CHAPMAN, P. JAFFE : "The new institute time clauses - Hulls 1/11/95". The International Journal of Shipping Law, Part. 4, Sept. 1996, 202-210.
(22) "Shipowners face hangovers with Heineken style surveys". Lloyd's List, 28 Jan. 1992.
(23) Jeff ALLEN : "The hull cassification clause JH131 and the structural condition warranty JH 722". International Seminar on Marine Insurance and Average. Genova, 29 June 1992.
(24) "Underwriters to see condition surveys". Fairplay, 24 March 1994.
- "Prevention not cure". Fairplay, 14 July 1994.
(25) "Association reports increase in condition surveys". Lloyd's List, 12 Oct. 1994.

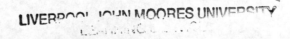

B - CLASSIFICATION SOCIETIES

582. - Sometimes accused of being negligent and over-lenient in enforcing standards, classification societies have tried to regain the trust of the maritime world since the early Nineties, by introducing a series of individual and collective measures to improve the safety of world shipping.

1. Individual measures

The political determination to improve the quality of classed ships led classification societies to take action on two aspects of safety.

a) Reinforcement of criteria for acceptance for classification

Some societies began by tightening the conditions for inclusion on their register. For example, the NK refused to class certain old vessels (26). Meanwhile, Bureau Veritas required a preliminary survey of any ship that was to be classified, to show whether it was in acceptable condition. For disclassed ships, or those classed by societies not belonging to IACS, Bureau Veritas asked the owner for a complete set of drawings and an admission survey to be carried out in dry dock (27).

b) Increase in class withdrawals

Many factors encouraged classification societies to withdraw class from many ships, particularly older large ships which failed to conform to their rules. Also struck off from the register were ships displaying flagrant defects, as well as any not presented for the regular inspections required by classification societies.

In 1991, ABS dropped 428 ships from its register (28), DNV 239 (29) and LR 138 (30). In 1992, these three societies disclassed more than a thousand ships (31). In 1993, the number of withdrawals was 377 for ABS, 184 for LR and 90 for DNV (32). For its part, Bureau Veritas withdrew class from more than a thousand ships between 1995 and 1997 (33).

2. IACS and class transfers

583. - Classification societies also took a whole series of collective steps to improve the quality of world shipping. From 1992, IACS set up a permanent secretariat to help implement this policy (cf chapter 6 above). The most spectacular measures were rules on class transfers (34), and the publication of "black lists" of substandard ships.

(26) "Classification societies". Shipping World and Shipbuilder, September 1994, 16.
(27) "Fighting bad image". Tradewinds, 22 Feb. 1991.
(28) Tradewinds, 4 Sept. 1992.
(29) Journal of Commerce, 12 Nov. 1992.
(30) Lloyd's List, 29 Sept. 1992.
(31) Lloyd's List, 9 Oct. 1992.
(32) "Restoring Faith". Lloyd's List Maritime Asia, Feb. 1993.
(33) "BV sets itself standards". Fairplay, 28th August 1997, 23.
(34) "IACS makes its mark". Lloyd's List, 27 June 1994.

a) Problem of class transfers

Class transfers are nothing new in the world of shipping. In most cases, they correspond to a transfer of ownership or change of flag. The principle has always been accepted that a shipowner was free to choose a classification society when having his ship built or operated.

The limitations of this liberal regime emerged when certain transfers were used as a way of evading the strict approach of some societies. "Class hopping" or "class shopping" increased from 1990, with the start of the economic crisis, pushing shipowners to cut costs and look for societies with the most lenient attitude to safety. At the end of 1992, sharp criticism began to be aimed at certain IACS members, accused of accepting ships deleted from other registers (35). IACS reacted promptly and revised transfer procedures (36).

b) Transfer of Class Agreement

The Transfer of Class Agreement (TOCA) is intended to remove the possibility for a shipowner to avoid necessary repairs by swapping classification societies (37). The latest version of the text, which came into force on 1st July 1995, allows transfer only when the shipowner has complied with all the conditions and recommendations formulated by the society losing the ship. This information is also sent to the IACS Secretariat, which thus oversees the conditions of transfer, and makes investigations in certain cases (38).

Non-compliance with TOCA can result in suspension of IACS membership. Such a decision was taken by the IACS Council in 1997 in the case of the Polish Register (39). Introduction of the new system led to a large exodus of ships towards more tractable non-members of IACS: 1 128 in 1993 (40), 1 578 in 1994 (41), 2 500 in 1995 (42), and about the same number in 1996. These huge departures are to be explained mainly by failure to meet the requirements of classification rules.

c) Publication of lists of disclassed ships

IACS issues regular figures on class transfers among its members, and on ships that have left its sphere of control. In December 1998, the IACS Council agreed to make available on the Internet the names of ships which left members' classification each year and explore the possibility of developing a database to track these ships (43). Additionally, a central database would be created in 1999, which would include all known port State control detentions, accompanied, where necessary, by IACS comments on the accuracy of specific entries. This would be made available on its website (44). Two problems arise here: the responsibility of a society that issues false information, and the contractual obligation of confidentiality between classification societies and their shipowner clients (45).

(35) "Class warfare". Fairplay, 6th Nov. 1992.
(36) "IACS may tighten notification system". Lloyd's List, 16 Nov. 1992.
(37) "1995 Review". IACS Briefing, n° 1 March 1996.
- J. BELL : "Current development in classification". BIMCO review 1996, 121-123.
(38) "IACS may probe Leros Strength class transfer". Lloyd's List, 7 March 1997.
(39) "IACS suspends Polish Register". Lloyd's List, 20 May 1997.
(40) "Thrown out of class !". MER, Sept. 1994.
(41) "Exodus from IACS" Safety at Sea Internat, Feb. 1996.
(42) "IACS, London and maritime safety". The Baltic, Sept. 1996, 62-63.
(43) "IACS moves on transparency". Lloyd's List, 10 Dec. 1998.
(44) "IACS contribution to Quality Shipping". IACS Press Release, 9 Dec. 1998. London.
(45) Ph. BOISSON : "The challenges facing classification societies : transparency and liability". Shipping in the new Millenium. BIMCO, Brisbane, March 1999.

C - CHARTERERS

584. - Several voices have been raised against the irresponsible practices of certain shippers using old (46) or substandard (47) ships in order to boost their profits. This criticism needs to be moderated (48), given the action taken by charterers to eliminate poor-quality vessels.

1. Revision of charter-parties

Most charter-parties involving oil transport contain environmental protection clauses (49). Large oil companies and leading charterers impose certain requirements on shipowners, regarding the age of ships and their safety management. Mobil, for example, includes an inspection clause under which the charterer is entitled to inspect the ship at any time, to ensure that it is being operated in line with the agreed conditions. Exxon demands that a ship should "be in full compliance with all applicable international conventions, all applicable laws, regulations and/or other requirements of the country of vessel registry and of the countries of the port(s) and/or place(s) (...) where vessel shall load or discharge". The shipowner must also guarantee that all certificates, files and other documents required by regulations are carried on board. Certain contracts go so far as to stipulate maintenance of the ship or most of its equipment "in perfect operating condition".

2. Vetting

The fear of having to face a major crisis following an oil spill has also encouraged companies to introduce ship vetting programmes. In addition to environmental concerns, there is the matter of image and the financial risks inherent in accidents (50).

Shell was one of the very first oil companies to reinforce its vetting system in 1978, following the wreck of the *Amoco Cadiz*. All companies in this group are now required to ensure that chartered ships are approved in accordance with an inspection programme. Surveys are carried out by 120 inspectors worldwide (51). Inspections cover the condition of the ship, but also the quality of the owner's management (52).

Following an explosion on board the *Meta Borg* in 1990, off the coast of the United States, Elf reviewed its procedures for selecting charter ships. Several procedures have been introduced, including a risk analysis method, physical inspection of ships, and shipping company audits. Elf inspects 800 to 1 000 ships every year (53).

Exxon (54), Mobil (55), Statoil (56) and BP (57) have also brought in vetting systems when selecting ships.

(46) "Oldie chartering saves millions for majors". Tradewinds, 13 June 1997.
(47) "Swedish Club boss calls for safety responsibility". Tradewinds, 9 Feb. 1996.
(48) J. SPRUYT : "Blaming charterers is too easy a way out". Lloyd's List, 23 Jan. 1995.
(49) H. WILLIAMS : "Tanker charters and the law". BIMCO Review, 1996, 49-54.
(50) B. de COMBRET : "Les négociants (traders) sont-ils et doivent-ils être intéressés à la qualité des transports maritimes ?". Conseil Supérieur de la Marine Marchande, Paris, juillet 1993.
(51) "Pressure grows for quality associations". Lloyd's List, 8 Dec. 1992.
(52) Communication of P.B. OWEN : IBC Conference : "Flags and quality". London, 1992.
(53) "Sécurité de pétroliers : un courtier suédois rend hommage à Elf". JMM, 14 May 1993, 1143.
(54) - J. MICHALSKI : "The responsibility and views of the cargo owner". International Summit Safety at Sea, Oslo, April 1991.
- S. HOLLIDAY : "Port and shipping management practice : role of the oil industry and charterers". Marine Policy. Sept. 1993, 387-390.
(55) - "Safety more than lip service for Gerhard Kurz". Tradewinds, 5 March 1993.
- "Information big bang set to blow away shipping's veil". Lloyd's List, 11 April 1995.
(56) "Statoil inspectors reject more than 50 % of ships". Lloyd's List, 1 Feb. 1995.
(57) "Reducing an inspector's calls". Lloyd's List, 28 March 1995.

3. Development of databases

a) OCIMF action

585. - The Oil Companies International Maritime Forum has set up procedures to reduce the disparities found in the quality of inspections carried out by its members (58).

• Regulation of vetting procedures

Following the accident to the *Argo Merchant* in 1977, the OCIMF prepared standard questionnaires for ship charters. It also issued guidelines for ship inspections in 1989, in order to encourage a common approach.

• SIRE programme

The most important action was the establishment in September 1993 of a databank, the Ship Inspection Report Exchange programme (SIRE), which centralises information collected separately by each company (59). The system has a dual purpose: first, to limit duplication of inspections and improve the objectivity of the 3 000 survey reports issued every year by the oil companies, and second to make oil tankers safer by tracking down substandard ships (60). The survey report must be as impartial as possible, containing no rating or assessment of the ship. The owner has two weeks to make comments on the report, before it is entered in the computerised database (61).

Access to the database is reserved strictly for OCIMF members, and organisations sharing with the oil industry a direct interest in the safety of oil tankers (62). SIRE is now supported and acknowledged by the whole profession (63). Since it was introduced, the system has received more than 17 000 inspection reports (64).

b) Action by Chemical Distribution Institute (CDI).

The chemical industry has also tried to combine efforts to improve the safety of ships carrying noxious or dangerous products (65). In August 1993, CEFIC, in liaison with independent gas and chemical carrier shipowners (IGCC) created a discussion forum, which a year later became the Chemical Distribution Institute. It has been given the task of administering an inspection system (66).

The CDI, based in Rotterdam, had 28 inspectors in 1997, located in European and American ports (67). Their work consists of making technical surveys of ships and auditing the operational management of shipowners (68). All their operations are standardised, based on a thousand-point questionnaire and a physical inspection of the ship (69). Findings are consolidated in a database available to CDI participants and associate members.

(58) See the Lloyd's List special issue on OCIMF, 17 Nov. 1995.
(59) "Leading oil firms launch safety drive". Lloyd's List, 29 Sept. 1993.
(60) "Oil chartered ship info pool". Seatrade Week, 14-20 May 1993.
(61) "Owners back tanker safety database". Lloyd's List, 13 August 1994.
(62) "Tanker quality data pooling under fire". Lloyd's List, 4 October 1993.
(63) "SIRE tackles oil pollution". Lloyd's List, 28 July 1998.
(64) OCIMF. Revised Ship Inspection Report Programme SIRE. London, Rev/3000/4.97.
(65) J. SPRUYT : "A new chemical compound". Lloyd's List, 9 Dec. 1991.
(66) Ian WALKER : "CDI Ship Inspection scheme". Paper presented at Marichem, Dec. 1995, Cologne.
(67) "Boost for ship inspection programme". Lloyd's List, 24 Feb. 1997.
(68) "CDI : all systems go". Hazardous Cargo Bulletin, July 1995, 46.
(69) "Charters move to standardise inspections". Fairplay, 29 Sept. 1994.

4. Towards greater responsibility for shippers

586. - Some observers consider that the most effective way of combatting flags of convenience is to increase the responsibility of shippers, on the grounds that, behind substandard ships, there may well be unscrupulous shippers knowingly using them to carry their goods.

The European Union seems to be moving in this direction: it is currently considering more draconian legislation laying greater liability on shippers (70).

So far, shippers' associations have opposed any move to involve the profession in policing substandard ships. French shippers in the Association des Utilisateurs de Transport de Fret (AUTF) have argued that it is impossible for them to obtain objective information on the condition of ships, despite access to existing ship databases (72).

It is difficult in the present legal situation and with current information technologies to consider increasing shipper liability, but it would be possible to establish some standardisation of professional chartering practices (73). In June 1998, the European Shippers Council issued a code of practice for shippers, designed specially for the dry bulk trade, and which stipulates minimum operational and safety standards (74). Some have considered going further, proposing an international code for shippers, that would require them to prove the existence of good safety management practices when they charter ships (75).

D - ITF AND TRADE UNIONS

587. - Historically, seamen's unions, and particularly the International Transport Federation (ITF), were the first to lead the fight against flags of convenience. Their main weapon was a boycott, which kept a ship blocked at its berth. A dockers' strike made it impossible to load or discharge cargo, and the ship could not sail because of a strike by the seamen on board or the refusal of tugs to provide assistance (76).

A boycott was not primarily seen as a measure to improve safety by trying to eliminate substandard ships. It was aimed solely at flags of convenience. The ITF justified its action by emphasising the very close causal link between flags of convenience and levels of safety, as shown in casualty statistics and port State detentions (77). A boycott is first and foremost an expression of trade union militancy. It allows unions to force a shipowner to sign agreements on wages and working conditions. When such collective agreements are reached, the owner is issued with a "blue certificate" (78).

(70) "Brussels to drive out unsafe ships". Lloyd's List, 12 June 1997.
(71) "Ship policing not a charterer problem". Lloyd's List, 1 Sept. 1994.
(72) Assemblée Nationale : "La sécurité maritime : un défi européen et mondial". Rapport d'information n° 1482, Paris, 1994, 55-56.
(73) J. WEALE : "The ethics of chartering". The International Journal of Shipping Law. 1996, 78-85.
(74) "Code of practice for shippers". Lloyd's List, 4 June 1998.
(75) - "Shippers urged to bear more liability for cargo". Lloyd's List, 14 June 1996.
- "Look first". Lloyd's List, 17 June 1996.
(76) International Transport Workers' Federation: "Reports 1950-51 and Proceedings of the Stockholm Congress 1952, London, p.74.
(77) "Flag system facing a bumpy ride ahead". Lloyd's List, 31 March 1993, 11.
(78) H. NORTHRUP, R. ROWAND: "The International Transport Workers' Federation and Flag of Convenience Shipping". University of Pennsylvania, 1983, 129-135.

The first ITF action against flags of convenience was decided in 1948. General boycotts lasting several days were organised in 1958, 1965, 1976 and 1977.

The end of the Seventies was marked by a radical shift in ITF policy, with reliance on less militant action based on contractual bargaining with shipowners and flags of convenience (79). The ITF also tried to increase its influence by appointing its own flag of convenience (FOC) inspectors in the world's leading ports, with the task of advising seafarers, negotiating wage agreements and informing the relevant outside authorities (80).

Since 1993, the ITF has changed tack again, toughening its stance on certain registers (81), by blacklisting bad shipping firms (82) and manning agents (83). The results of this policy have been variously appraised. Some (84) consider that this action has done nothing to remove substandard ships, but has enriched the ITF as its promoter.

E - SHIPOWNERS AND OPERATORS

588. - Several associations of shipowners have for some time been campaigning against substandard shipping, both to make seaborne transport safer, and to improve their image or credibility within the international community. INTERTANKO has drawn up quality guidelines, to be observed by its members on pain of expulsion (85). These new requirements include a requirement to have ships classed by an IACS member, and to be affiliated to a P&I club (86). INTERCARGO has also introduced vetting procedures for its members, and requires them to class their ships through an IACS member (87).

The International Chamber of Shipping is planning to draw up a league table which would attempt to rank national shipping registers in terms of effectiveness (87).

Finally, ISMA has drawn up quality standards for ship management companies (88). ISMA membership requires companies to prove the existence of a quality management system that complies with the Code of Shipmanagement Standards. This reference, which covers all aspects of the profession, is based on ISO 9002 and the IMO rules contained in Resolution A.680. Its effective enforcement is checked by external audits carried out by classification societies specially authorised for the purpose (89). Application of this Code has helped raise the level of quality of ship management services (90).

(79) "Malta pledges safety crackdown". Tradewinds, 28 May 1993.
(80) "ITF free-flag fight wins fresh backing". Lloyd's List, 15 Sept. 1994.
(81) - "ITF toughens stance on second registers". Lloyd's List, 21 Jan. 1993.
- "ITF blacks GIS-flag vessels". Lloyd's List, 13 March 1995.
(82) "ITF lists worst shipping firms". Lloyd's List, 2 July 1998.
(83) "ITF black list sharpens drive against flags of convenience". Lloyd's List, 31 Jan. 1995.
(84) H. NORTHRUP, P. SCRASE : "The international transport workers' Federation Flag of Convenience Shipping Campaign : 1983-1995". Transportation Law Journal, Vol. 23, Nb 3, Spring 1996, 369-423.
(85) Cf Adriatic Tanker in "New MD at Intertanko". Seatrade Week Newsfront, 4-10 August 1995.
(86) "Intertanko image on an upward curve". Lloyd's List, 17 Oct. 1997.
(87) - "Intercargo acts to boost dry bulker safety record". Lloyd's List, 11 Nov. 1994.
- "Owners plan to draw up league table". Lloyd's List, 28 Jan. 1998.
(88) "How goes it with ISMA ? It's all in the book". Lloyd's List, 19 Sept. 1994.
(89) "The way to ISMA certification". International Shipping Review. Autumn Winter 1994.
(90) H. GILBERT : "Shipmanagement 10 years on". BIMCO Review 1998, 279-280.

II - INDIVIDUAL STATE ACTION

589. - Port States are at present responsible for most public action against flags of convenience (cf chapter 25 below). But certain initiatives are also taken by flag States, whether to combat open registry or, on the contrary, to defend or promote the system.

A - REACTIONS TO SPREAD OF FLAGS OF CONVENIENCE

Reactions consist mainly of incentives or disincentives, intended to discourage owners from changing and abandoning flags, and encourage the return of ships operated abroad by a state's citizens to the national register.

1. Incentives

Most such incentives are financial and fiscal. They are aimed at national shipping companies, and consist of equipment grants, subsidies, interest payments (91), bonuses for scrapping old tonnage (92). A European Commission report has suggested authorising subsidies for the employment of seamen who are citizens of EU States. Some authorities have also mentioned the possibility of total tax exemption for payments to crews sailing under EU flags (93).

Tax disincentives can also be used to impose higher charges on shipowners operating their fleets under flags of convenience, by taxing their profits, charging surtax on ships in ports, or raising landing charges. There has even been talk of introducing an EU tax on goods carried under certain flags (94).

2. Regulatory measures

Some States have introduced draconian transport legislation, preventing decommissioned old ships from starting a fresh career under another flag, to the detriment of safety (95). Systems such as regional bilateral cargo reservation agreements have also been devised to prevent open registry fleets competing unfairly with other international traders (96). Whatever means are considered, it seems easier to halt class transfers than to persuade shipowners to return to their national flags.

B - ACTION BY OPEN REGISTRY STATES

590. - Some flags of convenience have reacted to the growing phenomenon of substandard ships.

---

(91) E. DU PONTAVICE : "Les pavillons de complaisance". DMF 1977, 569.
(92) Economic and Social Committee of the European Communities. op. cit. 9.
(93) Rapport d'information n° 1482. Assemblée Nationale : "La sécurité maritime : un défi européen et mondial". 78.
(94) JO, Débats parlementaires, Sénat, 31 May 1979, p. 1580.
(95) J.M. ROUX : "Les pavillons de complaisance, Paris, LGDJ, 1961, 147.
(96) Sénat, Rapport de la commission d'enquête sur le naufrage de l'Amoco Cadiz, Paris, June 1978, 162.

1. Panama

The largest merchant fleet in the world is administered by the Panamanian Directorate General of Consular and Maritime Affairs (SECNAVES). Its New York office, SEGUMAR, attends to technical and administrative matters.

Several actions have been taken since 1993 to improve the quality of the Panamanian fleet (97). These include selection of organisations acting on behalf of the administration (98), even certain classification societies belonging to IACS (99), elimination of substandard ships (100), better training of seafarers, introduction of an inspection programme and a network of 328 inspectors, authorised to survey Panamanian ships in 300 ports worldwide (101).

2. Liberia

The second largest merchant fleet in the world is administered by a private organisation based in Reston, Virginia, the International Registry Inc (IRI) (102). It has a team of 160 inspectors in all the major ports in the world. The IRI delegates IACS members to carry out ship surveys on behalf of the Liberian government. It carries out all its own accident investigations concerning Liberian ships. Out of 75 IRI reports requested by IMO since 1978, only eight have not been submitted (103). The IRI, which also manages the Marshall Islands flag, was the first register to obtain ISO 9002 certification in 1995 (104).

3. Malta

Malta has reinforced its control over ships sailing under its flag, through the Malta Maritime Authority, which employs about thirty surveyors throughout the world. Its target is to inspect 25 per cent of the Maltese-registered fleet each year (105).

4. Cyprus

A candidate, like Malta, for European Union membership, Cyprus has taken drastic steps since 1995 to improve the safety of its merchant fleet (106). Department of Merchant Shipping measures include a new inspection programme to ensure that ships are surveyed at least once a year (107), the removal of bad classification societies (108), withdrawal from the register of ships showing serious deficiencies (109), sanctions against ships breaching flag law (110), and an increase in the number of inspections (111) through a network of 36 surveyors worldwide (112).

(97) Fairplay, 25 March 1993.
(98) "Register benefits from Law 36". Lloyd's Ship Manager, Oct. 1996.
(99) "Panama rejects 8 classification societies". Lloyd'd List, 19 May 1994.
(100) "Panama acts on safety". Fairplay, 10 Feb. 1998.
(101) "Panneau putting the accent on quality". Lloyd's List, 27 March 1996.
(102) "The flag question". Seatrade Review, Sept. 1998, 5-9.
(103) J. SMITH : "Shipowners and their association's preference in choosing a flag".
Flags and quality. Dilemma or opportunity, IBC Conference, London, Nov. 1992.
(104) "Liberia bids for competitive edge". Lloyd's List, 27 March 1996.
(105) "Maltese flag takes world's fifty slot". Lloyd's List, 19 Nov. 1998.
(106) "Rebuilding the flag's reputation". Lloyd's List, Cyprus, Oct. 1997.
(107) "Keeping a class act". The Motor ship, April 1995, 3.
(108) "Cyprus Minister raps classification societies". Tradewinds, 16 June 1995.
(109) - "Substandard tonnage to be weeded out". Lloyd's List, 3 Sept. 1996.
- "Cyprus action on substandard vessels". Lloyd's List, 23 Janv. 1997
(110) "Cyprus acts over flag rules". Lloyd's List, 21 March 1995.
(111) "Cyprus aims for better standards in shipping". Lloyd's Ship Manager, May 1997, 25.
(112) "Island's maritime administration on the long march to quality". Lloyd's List, 6 Oct. 1998.

5. Bahamas

The London-based Bahamas Maritime Authority (BMA) also practises strict selection of ships applying for inclusion on its register (113). They must be classed by one of the seven leading members of IACS, and undergo a condition survey if they are more than twelve years old (114).

III - ACTION BY INTERGOVERNMENTAL ORGANISATIONS

591. - Three intergovernmental organisations have taken clear action against substandard shipping: IMO and ILO at a global level, and the EU within its more limited boundaries.

A - IMO ACTION

Chapter 3 above explained the fundamental role played by IMO in drawing up international regulations on safety at sea. But it has not shown any lack of concern for the problems of enforcing such standards, the theme of the World Maritime Day in 1993 (114). Its efforts focus on three aspects: assistance to flag States in implementing their obligations under international conventions, reinforcement of inspections by port States (cf chapter 25 below), and action against substandard ships, by establishing methods of identifying them.

1. Action towards flags

IMO has often been criticised for its excessive caution in combatting flags of convenience or the safety shortcomings of certain flags. In fact, the organisation is handicapped by two major legal obstacles. The principle of sole jurisdiction of the flag State has always prevailed in the law of the sea. This does much to impede the powers of intervention of any other authority on the international stage. The constituent charter of IMO is another obstacle. The 1948 Convention permits only very limited means of action: IMO can oversee enforcement of conventions by its members, but it has no powers to penalise failures to comply (115).

These constraints are accepted and even supported by most member States, reluctant to abandon any part of their sovereignty to IMO. This largely explains the slowness of any attempt to confer powers of coercion on IMO. In recent years, however, a system of control has begun to emerge, with the increased obligations of notification, and the action of the new Flag State Implementation (FSI) subcommittee.

a) Notification obligations

The right of certain international organisations to obtain information makes it possible for them to monitor the enforcement of conventions. The obligation to notify IMO is included in all the instruments adopted under its auspices.

(113) "Region is working its way to the top of the list". Lloyd's List, 30 March 1998.
(114) - "Bahamas. Fledgling flag matures". Fairplay, 5 Dec. 1996, 26-27.
- World Maritime Day 1993. A message from Mr William O'Neil. In IMO New, n° 3, 1993.
(115) "IMO to avoid flag sanctions". Lloyd's List, 1 Sept. 1998.

States signing a convention usually have to supply IMO with certain documents (116). These include the texts of laws, decrees, orders and regulations promulgated on the various issues covered by the instrument (cf 1974 SOLAS Convention article IIIb), a sufficient number of specimens of certificates (cf 1966 LL Convention article 26.1a), a list of inspectors or non-governmental organisations authorised to act on behalf of the flag State (cf SOLAS article IIIa), exemptions granted for certain convention provisions (cf SOLAS chapter 1 Regulation 4b), and inquiry reports following an incident at sea (cf SOLAS chapter I Regulation 21b).

In practice, these obligations are respected to varying extents. In 1993, the IMO Secretary-General noted that, of the 79 parties to the MARPOL Convention, only 30 had sent reports on measures taken to implement it. For the STCW Convention, 46 documents containing copies of certificates in force in signatory countries had been sent to IMO by 1997 - which meant that only one in every three States was meeting its obligations. As regards accident inquiries, IMO is still awaiting more than 600 reports, some of which concern events that occurred in the Seventies.

b) Revised STCW Convention and new control procedure

The STCW Convention, revised in 1995, shows an advance in controlling enforcement of standards. According to section A-I/7 of the STCW Code, each signatory is to "report on the steps it has taken to give the Convention full and complete effect". This includes "a concise explanation of the legal and administrative measures provided and taken to ensure compliance" and "a clear statement of the education, training, examination, competency assessment and certification policies adopted" (117).

All the documents submitted by member states have to be analysed by a group appointed by the Secretary-General and approved by the MSC. Following such examination, the group issues a report stating which States have or have not been capable of showing that they are strictly applying the whole of the convention. The MSC then decides on the inclusion of States that have met their obligations on a "white list". The importance of being on this list is that it governs recognition of a State's certificates by other parties to the STCW Convention. This procedure for assessing States is a major innovation in the international community. For some observers, it is the kernel of a supranational police force.

c) Guidelines for flag States

592. - Adopted for the first time in an interim form in 1993, these guidelines are the result of the work of the FSI subcommittee. They were revised in November 1997.

• Origin of guidelines: FSI subcommittee
In response to various observations by the Secretary-General of IMO, the MSC and the MEPC decided in 1991 to include the problem of enforcing convention in their working programmes. In April 1992, a joint working group was set up, to put forward solutions. The group met for the first time in London in December 1992, and it led to the formation of a new subcommittee to handle flag state implementation of IMO instruments.

---

(116) IMO List of reporting requirements and obligations undertaken by Governments by ratifying SOLAS 74, MARPOL 73/78, LL66, STCW 78 and Protocols relating thereto. Note by the Secretariat. FSI 3/3, 25 Nov. 1994.
(117) "Cooperation make it happen". Seatrade Review, March 1997, 65.

This Flag State Implementation (FSI) subcommittee set to work in April 1993 (119). Its essential remit was to identify the measures needed to ensure effective and comprehensive implementation of IMO instruments by flag states. The subcommittee acted along three lines: approval of organisations acting on behalf of administrations, port State control of ships, and measures to help flag states (120). These points were covered by resolutions adopted by the Assembly in November 1993.

• Guidelines to help flag States implement IMO instruments
Resolution A.847, adopted on 27 November 1997, establishes guidelines to assist flag States in the effective application and enforcement of IMO convention, including SOLAS 74, MARPOL 73/78, LL 66 and STCW 78.

These guidelines note that some States have encountered difficulties in giving full and complete effect to the provisions of IMO instruments and ensuring that prompt and timely surveys are conducted. Reasons for these problems include finances, personnel and technical experts, delegation of authority, division of responsibilities and inadequate supervision of bodies acting on behalf of the flag state. The Resolution stipulates that technical assistance for flag States experiencing difficulties in meeting their international responsibilities is available through IMO.

• The guidelines include different sections:
- **Implementation:** flag States should seek to establish a support infrastructure capable of administering a safety and environmental protection programme;
- **Delegation of authority:** flag States should control the delegation of responsibility to organisations for surveys and inspections;
- **Enforcement:** flag States should take all necessary measures to establish and maintain effective control over ships flying their flag;
- **Surveyors:** flag States should see to professional qualifications for its own surveyors;
- **Investigations:** flag States should also provide qualified investigators to carry out official inquiries in the event of an accident (121).

• Flag State self-assessment
At the 6th session of the FSI subcommittee in June 1998, Canada, Australia and the United Kingdom proposed that IMO should undertake an independent assessment of flag State performance (122). Detailed criteria have been developed for this purpose:
- **Internal criteria** concern the organisational and operational effectiveness of the flag State as a maritime administration;
- **External criteria** concern outside indicators such as casualty data and port state control reports.

(118) A. BLANCO-BAZAN : "Implementation of IMO convention by flag and port States". 25th Annual Conference. The Law of the Sea Institute. Malmö, August 1991.
(119) IMO. Sub-Committee on Flag State Implementation. 1st session Report to MSC and MEPC. FSI 1/21, 18 May 1993.
(120)) "Flag-state system refuses to wave the banner of surrender". Lloyd's List, 28 April 1993.
- "Much talking, little enforcing". LSM, June 1993.
(121) IMO News, n° 4, 1997, P. 22-23.
(122) "IMO in hot seat on flag state standards'. Lloyd's List, 22 June 1998.

A self-assessment form based on these criteria has been drawn up, for adoption by the MSC and MEPC in the near future (123).

2. Action against substandard ships

593. - IMO has also developed methods of tracking down substandard ships, and ensuring greater transparency within the maritime world.

The first step consisted of devising a universal numbering scheme, contained in Resolution A.600, adopted on 19 November 1987. Under this scheme, every ship is assigned a permanent identity number, which appears on all certificates concerning it and which remains the same, even if the ship is transferred to another flag. Originally a simple recommendation, this fraud-prevention measure was made binding at the SOLAS Conference in 1994. A new Regulation XI/3 requires an identity number for all passenger ships of 100 gross tonnage and above, and for cargo ships of more than 300 gross tonnage (124).

The second step taken by IMO is an attempt to set up an international ship condition database.

a) Development of ship databases

Numerous databases now supply detailed and relevant information on the condition of ships and the level of safety of world shipping. They were established by classification societies, certain private organisations like Fairplay Information System (FISYS) or Lloyd's Maritime Information Services (LMIS), shippers (SIRE) and port states (MSIS, SIRENAC, APCIS).

b) IMO database projects

The idea of setting up an international database on ships is relatively recent (125). The feasibility of such a scheme is currently under consideration at IMO (126), for the task raises many technical (127), financial (128) and legal problems. If it were to be adopted, the scheme for an International Ship Information Database (ISID) could have far-ranging repercussions on the maritime world (129).

While awaiting a solution to these problems, IMO has given priority to building an accident database. Its aims are to offer a general overview of trends in incidents at sea, provide a statistical basis for assessing IMO regulations, identify problem areas from the types of accidents, their causes and consequences, and finally to facilitate flow of information on events to all IMO committees.

Difficulties arise in deciding which items to include under the heading "Causes of the accident and contributory factors". Many countries consider that the complexity of these proposals goes well beyond what is appropriate for the IMO database (130).

---

(123) IMO. FSI 6/12, 20 July 1998, 3.11-3.34.
(124) IMO. Note by the Secretariat on Shipnumber scheme. MCS/64/12/2, 20 Sept. 1994.
(125) - "Compulsory sharing of survey results mooted". Lloyd's List, 8 Feb. 1993.
- "The task of rating quality". Tradewinds, 19 Feb. 1993.
(126) JP. DOBLER : "IMO marine casualty statistics and ship deficiencies information systems". 14 May 1994. See also "Confused data". Lloyd's List, 25 April 1994.
(127) "IMO moving full steam ahead for international database". Lloyd's List, 31 December 1994.
(128) IMO. MEPC 37/21/3, 6 juin 1995.
(129) "A secret shared". Lloyd's List, 6 October 1993.
- "Seeing through shipping". Tradewinds, 8 Oct. 1993.
- "Opening up". Fairplay, 2 Dec. 1993.
(130) IMO. FSI 5/10/4 and FSI 5/10/6, 15 Nov. 1996.

B - ILO ACTION

594. - Historically, the ILO was the first international organisation to denounce flag switching. Its efforts subsequently focussed mainly on flags of convenience, then on substandard ships

The ILO began by criticising certain flags of convenience (131). In 1958, it adopted two recommendations, one recalling flag State obligations on safety and social standards, and the other aimed at discouraging the recruitment of seafarers on board foreign ships (132). Three years later, two further instruments were adopted: Convention 147 of 29 October 1976 on minimum regulations, and Recommendation 155 of the same date, concerning improvement of standards on board merchant ships. In order to obtain the broadest possible consensus, neither of these texts referred to flags of convenience (133).

C - UNCTAD ACTION

595. - The subject of open registry took priority in the work of the fifth United Nations Conference on Trade and Development, held in Manila in 1979, and on the agenda for a meeting of its Maritime Transport Commission (133). Discussions culminated in 1986 in the adoption of the United Nations Convention on Conditions for Registration of Ships. It has been ratified by so few States (7 by 1991) that it has never come into force (cf chapter 21).

D - OECD ACTION

596. - In the early Seventies, OECD members decided to examine, within the Maritime Transport Commission, the problem of "open registers". Several studies were undertaken, to assess the general application of this policy, and try to identify its causes (134).

From 1986, the phenomenon of open registry flags continued on an unprecedented scale. This new situation forced the OECD to revise its attitude to the problem (135).

Taking up an economic standpoint, the OECD, in a report published in 1996 (136), denounced the competitive advantages obtained by certain shipowners as a result of non-observance of applicable international rules and standards. The report criticised the lack of control over the seaborne transport industry by the main responsible organisations. It considered that, within the current legal framework, penalties applied to substandard ships, even where they exist, are relatively light compared with the cost advantages obtained by not observing international regulations. Lasting solutions to the problem of flags of convenience can come only from coordinated cooperation of all participants in international shipping operations.

(131) E. ARGIROFFO : "L'OIT face au problème des pavillons de complaisance et des navires ne répondant pas aux normes acceptées". Revue internationale du travail, Nov. 1974.
(132) E. OSIERE : "The International Labour Organisation and the control of substandard merchant vessels". JCLQ, July 1981.
(133) I.M. SINAN : "UNCTAD and flags of convenience". Journal of World Trade Law, vol. 18, n° 9, 1989, 95-109.
(134) OECD. Maritime Transport Committee. 12 Sept. 1975.
(135) OECD. Maritime Transport Committee. DSTI/SI/MTC (91) 20, 28 Oct. 1991.
(136) OECD/GD (96) 4, Paris, 1996.

In 1998, the OECD organised a round table with industry representatives on safety and environment protection (137). Its purpose was to involve more directly those in the maritime industry, other than shipowners, in action against substandard shipping. This concerns financial institutions, marine underwriters, hull and machinery insurers, cargo insurers, P&I clubs, classification societies, cargo generators, shipbrokers and other players. The most important propositions concern greater transparency of information (138).

E - EUROPEAN UNION ACTION

597. - Europe has not remained aloof from the fight against flags of convenience. The earliest initiatives were taken at the end of the Seventies, following the *Amoco Cadiz* disaster. In April 1979, the Economic and Social Council adopted a very important Opinion on Community maritime policy and flags of convenience (139). Since the adoption by the Commission of a new common policy on safety at sea in February 1993 (140), actions against substandard practices were considerably reinforced.

1. Political goal

The goal set by the Commission is to ban substandard companies, ships and crews from EU waters, irrespective of the flag under which they operate. According to the Commission, "the Community, thanks to its political and legislative machinery, is uniquely placed both to ensure that member States apply standards to ships flying their flags in a more uniform and rigorous manner and to enforce, with common methods and rigour, respect of the same standards on vessels of all flags when operating in EC waters".

2. EU quality shipping campaign

598. - At a conference in London in November 1997, the United Kingdom and the European Commission launched a quality shipping campaign, intended mainly to reduce the amount of substandard shipping by ensuring that the existing framework of regulation was fully implemented by all flag States. The intention was also to develop a dialogue with the shipping industry, to ascertain what they might do to help improve operational standards.

An international conference organised by the European Commission in Lisbon in June 1998 decided to develop usable mechanisms for the interchange of information between the maritime industry and administrations, and within various sectors of industry. Another commitment was, wherever possible, to ensure the transparency and immediacy of the information available (141).

(137) "Safety and Environment Protection. Discussion paper on to combat substandard shipping by involving players other than the shipowner in the shipping market". DSTI/DOT/MTC (98) 10/Final, 8 July 1998.
(139) Economic and Social Committee of the European Communities. "EEC shipping policy. Flag of convenience". Opinion. Brussels, April 1979.
(140) Commission of the European Communities. "A common policy on safe seas". Communication from the Commission. Brussels, 24 Feb. 1993. COM (93) 66, final.
(141) "Pinpointing the substandard scandal". Lloyd's List, 10 June 1998.

At an international seminar on substandard and quality shipping, in London in December 1998 (142), EU Transport Commissioner Neil Kinnock presented draft proposals for a charter to "foster industry self-regulation and link quality with the economic benefit".

This charter, which might be adopted at Mare Forum in Amsterdam in June 1999, is designed to open up new areas of self-regulation. Five basic principles have been laid down:

"1. Each link in the maritime responsibility chain shall make safety considerations an integral part of its business transactions.

2. Industry participants shall take reasonable care to ensure that the ships with which they are dealing are of good standards of quality, and, accordingly shall avoid using, servicing, supplying or otherwise doing business with ships which do not meet internationally applicable requirements.

3. Industry associations shall reflect the principles stated herein in their respective charters and/or codes of conduct. They shall make their membership conditional upon the observance of those principles and shall take measures to ensure that such observance is maintained by their members at all times.

4. Each industry association shall endeavour to share with public authorities and the other associations all information related to the observance by its members of the internationally applicable requirements that is permissible under relevant laws and regulations.

5. Industry associations shall monitor the effect of measures adopted under this charter and shall evaluate progress at regular intervals."

Transparency was an important issue at the London seminar. The European Quality Shipping Information System (EQUASIS) developed by DG7 was presented. This computer system, designed to allow users to obtain real-time information using the name of the ship as a keyword, will provide links among existing databases. This will offer more ready access to data on the quality of ships.

CONCLUSION: Towards the elimination of substandard flags

599 - Almost universal and unreserved condemnation of any over-lenient attitudes to safety has come from the maritime community. However, it has been unable to find any effective remedy to the problem of substandard shipping. It is no longer enough today to put flags of convenience in the dock. The phenomenon is far more complex, involving as it does so many often conflicting economic, social and political interests (143).

Solutions to such shifting and many-sided phenomena are not easy to find, whether such solutions are individual or at the level of a profession or State. OECD points out that the effectiveness of any campaign depends on proper cooperation among all those involved in shipping operations. Unless there is clear international solidarity against substandard ships, any measures taken nationally or internationally, publicly or privately, are bound to fail.

(142) "On the campaign trail again". Lloyd's List, 16 Dec. 1998.
(143) D. MATLIN : "Re-evaluating the status of flags of convenience under international law". Vanderbilt Journal of Transnational Law". Vol. 23, 1991, 1017-1055.

All observers agree on the lack of uniformity in the application of safety measures by flag States (144). There is no way at present of ensuring that parties to conventions meet their obligations. The Geneva Convention setting up IMO does not contain any procedural requirements for States to submit reports on the matter (145), much less provide for penalties if obligations are not met (146). International public law remains a matter of consensus: no obligations can be imposed on a State without its consent.

But despite these difficulties, several solutions to the scandal of substandard ships have been considered. All of them converge towards the flag State, regarded as exercising competency and inspection powers in this area, the framework within which laws and safety regulations are enforced.

There has been a host of suggestions, for the establishment of minimum standards for free registers (147), a code of conduct for flag States (148), a checklist of good registration practice (149), a quality certification scheme for administrations (150), and an audit system to be introduced by IMO (151).

Some of these ideas have reemerged at IMO. On the FSI subcommittee, several approaches have been suggested to compel flag States to fulfil their obligations under international conventions (152).

For the moment, in the absence of consensus, IMO has been unable to recommend a precise line of action. Many States remain fiercely opposed to any new instrument that would be binding on them. They argue that there are at present no objective criteria by which to assess the extent of fulfilment by administrations of their responsibilities. IMO is currently directing its efforts towards the establishment of such criteria, which would be used to target technical assistance and even, in the future, matching penalties (153).

(144) IMO. FSI 3/3/5, 30 Dec. 1994.
(145) IMO. FSI 2/14, 21 July 1993.
(146) "The effective flag". Lloyd's List, 16 Dec. 1992.
(147) John A. GAUCI-MAISTRE : "International standards for ship registers". BIMCO Bulletin 1/92, January/February 1992, 17-20.
(148) R. SPEEDIE : "Ship managers flag selection criteria". Flag and Quality IBC conference, London, Dec. 1992.
(149) J. SPRUYT : "Flying with flag of convenience". Lloyd's List, 21 Jan. 1992.
(150) I. MANUM : "Goals for the effective functioning of the complete global safety system - The flag State". 2nd Internat. Summit Safety at Sea, Oslo, June 1993.
(151) - "USCG calls for IMO checks on flag states". Lloyd's List, 20 April 1994.
- "No compromise". Lloyd's List, 21 April 1994.
(152) - IMO. FSI 4/3/3, 19 Jan. 1996.
(153) IMO. FSI 4/WP 2/Rev. 1, 21 Mar. 1996.

CHAPTER 25

Port State Control

600. - There has been a spectacular growth in port State control and inspection of ships since the early Eighties. Some 16 000 inspections are carried out every year in Europe (1). In Australia, the number rose from 1 720 in 1992 to 2 901 in 1996 (2). The prime reason for this trend is the determination of coastal States to play an active part in improving safety at sea and protecting the marine environment. Negligence by flag States has led some coastal States to act against the excessive leniency and substandard ships by severe policing of shipping in their own ports.

Port State Control (PSC) is not a new concept in international law: it already existed in an embryonic form in the early 20th century. Now governed by the Law of the Sea Convention and IMO conventions, it is developing mainly on a regional basis.

I - LEGAL CONDITIONS OF PORT STATE CONTROL

The grounds for PSC are to be found in the traditional principles of international law. Legal doctrine is unanimous in recognising that in internal waters, and ever more so in ports, foreign merchant ships are subject to the jurisdiction of the coastal State (3). Two arguments are commonly put forward to justify the exercise of control prerogatives:
- **Right of self-protection:** In taking coercive measures against substandard ships, the port State protects its own citizens and environment against the dangers presented by such ships.
- **International policing of navigation:** The port State has a duty to see to the application of international conventions on safety at sea, and prevent a ship in poor condition from leaving its territory. This complements the function of the flag State, which is to ensure that its ships conform to international regulations. Under no circumstances should the port State take over these obligations (4). It provides the final safety net to ensure effective enforcement of safety standards (5).

A - PROVISIONS OF THE LAW OF THE SEA

601. - Port inspection and detention of ships have a serious impact on trade and freedom of navigation. This is why the LOS Convention has tried to limit the extent of port

---

(1) Paris MOU. 1996. Annual Report, p. 17
(2) AMSA 1996. Port State Control Report Summary of detentions and inspections. Australia 1997.
(3) - R. CHURCHILL and A. LOWE : "The law of the sea". Manchester University Press, 54-57.
- V. DEGAN : "Internal Waters". Netherlands Yearbook of International Law", vol 17, 1986, 22-23.
(4) E. MITROPOULOS : "Statement of IMO broad general policy in relation to port state control". Port State Control Conference. London. December 1993.
(5) F. PLAZA : "Port State control : towards global standardisation". IMO New n° 1 - 1994, 13-16.

State powers towards foreign ships, and to set down very precise procedures for exercising such powers (6).

1. Definition of powers

Article 219 of the LOS Convention indicates "measures relating to seaworthiness of vessel to avoid pollution" to be taken by port States :

- in case of violation of applicable international rules and threat of damage to the marine environment, they shall take "administrative measures to prevent the vessel from sailing".

- "They may permit the vessel to proceed only to the nearest appropriate repair yard".

- "Upon removal of the causes of the violation, they shall permit the vessel to continue immediately".

The powers conferred on port States concern only protection of the marine environment, not general safety rules. Some commentators have given an extensive interpretation of port State powers, considering that pollution prevention involves respect for safety of navigation (7). Some commentators (8) remain hostile to this broader application. Others refuse to consider such provisions as part of international customary law (9). Port State jurisdiction is based solely on a convention, which is binding only on those states that have ratified it (10). On the other hand, there is general agreement to admit the strengthening of the territorial competency of port States towards foreign ships and the usefulness of combining this extension of powers with clear guarantees.

2. Conditions of exercise of right of control

Several guarantees are stipulated in section 7 of part XII of the 1982 LOS Convention.

a) Nature of controls

According to article 226.1a of the LOS Convention, any physical inspection of a foreign vessel is limited to an examination of such certificates, records or other documents as the vessel is required to carry by generally accepted international rules and standards.

Further physical inspection may be undertaken only after such an examination, and then only in three cases defined in the Convention:

- There are clear grounds for believing that the condition of the vessel or its equipment does not correspond substantially with the particulars of those documents;
- The contents of such documents are not sufficient to confirm or verify a suspected violation;
- The vessel is not carrying valid certificates and records.

In no case may the port State exercise any discrimination "in form or in fact" (article 227).

---

(6) B. OXMAN : "Observations on Vessel Release under the United Nations Convention on the Law of the Sea". The International Journal of Marine and Coastal Law. Vol 11, n° 2, 1996, 201-215.
(7) C. DOUAY : "La Communauté, Etat du port". RMC 1981 n° 244, 60.
(8) Y. VAN DER MENSBRUGGHE : "Les navires inférieurs aux normes, le memorandum d'entente de Paris du 26 janvier 1982 sur le contrôle des navires par l'Etat du Port ". in La Communauté européenne et la mer. Economica, Paris, 1990, 471.
(9) A. SHEARER : "Problems of jurisdiction and law enforcement against delinquent vessels ". ILCQ. Vol 35, April 1986, 340.
(10) Cf contradictory opinion of M. VALENZUELA : "International Maritime Transportation : selected issues of the Law of the Sea". 23rd Conference of the Law of the Sea Institute, 1989, University of Hawai, 205.

b) Ship detention

602. - Again according to article 226.1, the port State may not delay a foreign vessel longer than is essential. After investigations, the ship is to be released promptly, subject to reasonable procedures such as bonding or other appropriate financial security. Release may be refused "whenever it would present an unreasonable threat of damage to the marine environment", or "made conditional upon proceeding to the nearest appropriate repair yard".

c) Institution of proceedings

According to article 228.1, proceedings to impose penalties are suspended if the flag State begins proceedings on corresponding charges. There are two exceptions, however: when major damage has been suffered by the coastal State, or when the flag State "has repeatedly disregarded its obligations to enforce effectively the applicable international rules and standards in respect of violations committed by its vessels". Article 228.2 prohibits duplication of proceedings, or their institution after the expiry of three years from the date on which the violation was committed.

Only monetary penalties may be imposed (cf article 230). Port States are liable for damage or loss attributable to them when the measures they take are unlawful or excessive (cf article 232).

d) Settlement of disputes

If the release of a ship from detention a ship has been refused or made conditional, the flag State may request its release under the terms of part XV of the Convention, which deals with the system for settlement of disputes (11).

According to article 292, proceedings are to be instituted before a court or tribunal agreed upon by the parties. Failing agreement within ten days from the time of detention of the ship or arrest of the crew, the question of release may be submitted, whether to a court accepted by the detaining State, or to the International Tribunal for the Law of the Sea (12). Decisions reached by this tribunal, which sits in Hamburg, are final. They are binding on all parties to the dispute (13).

The available remedies for shipowners whose vessels were unjustifiably or unlawfully detained are not fixed by international law but by the domestic legislation of the port State. These remedies vary from country to country and port to port (14).

B - EXTENSION OF PSC POWERS

603. - Closely regulated in the 1982 LOS Convention, port State powers of intervention are substantially extended by international conventions on safety at sea and by IMO and ILO resolutions.

---

(11) D. ANDERSON : "Investigation, detention and release of foreign vessels under the UN Convention on the Law of the Sea of 1982 and other international agreements". IJHCL. Vol. 11, n° 2, 1996, 165-177.
(12) T. TREVES : "The proceedings concerning prompt release of vessels and crews before the International Tribunal for the Law of the Sea". IJMCL. Vol. 11, n° 2, 1996, 179-200.
- Cf Saïga Case, International Tribunal for the Law of the Sea, Dec. 4, 1997 in the International Journal of International Law, Vol. 92, 1998, 278-282.
(13) R. LAGONI : "The prompt release of vessels and crews before the International Tribunal for the Law of the Sea : a preparatory report". IJMCL. Vol. 11, n° 2, 1996, 147-164.
(14) P. RODGERS in Fairplay : 5th March 1998 : "Controlling port State. Legal aspects of detention".

1. Reinforcement of procedures

As regards safety at sea, the idea of inspection by the port State is nothing new. The SOLAS Conventions of 1914 and 1929 already recognised the principle of mutual control, by giving the officials of contracting states the right to demand to see SOLAS certificates issued to ships. Today, port State powers go well beyond a mere check on documents.

a) Control mechanisms

All IMO instruments offer inspection powers to port States, in order to ensure that safety standards are being respected.

Article 5.2 of the MARPOL Convention, for example, indicates that an "inspection shall be limited to verifying that there is on board a valid certificate, unless there are clear grounds for believing that the condition of the ship or its equipment fail to correspond substantially with the particulars of that certificate". The port State may therefore take the necessary steps to prevent a ship from going to sea until it can do so without an unreasonable threat of harm to the marine environment.

Exercise of control powers is regulated strictly, because they contravene the principle of sole flag State jurisdiction. Conditions are laid down in the IMO conventions mentioned above and in Resolution A.787 of 23 November 1995 on ship inspection procedures.

The port State can act in any of three different ways: on its own initiative, at the request of the flag State, or following an outside complaint.

Resolution A.787 incorporates part of the text of ILO Convention 147, defining a complaint as involving "information submitted by a member of the crew, a professional body, an association, a trade union or, generally, any person with an interest in the safety of the ship, including an interest in safety or health hazards to its crew" (chapter 2.2.1.3).

The same Resolution asks for such information to be submitted as soon as possible after the ship's arrival, so that the authorities have time to make the necessary arrangements (cf chapter 4.2). The authorities must "immediately investigate the matter and take the action required". Such action includes inspection, detention or conditional permission to go to sea.

b) Procedural guidelines

604. - Resolution A.787 gives basic information on action to be taken, with the aim of guaranteeing a certain degree of uniformity in surveys (15). In particular, it sets out ten points concerning "clear grounds to conduct a more detailed inspection". These include the inspector's general impressions and observations that serious hull or structural deterioration could affect equipment, information or evidence that the master or crew is not familiar with essential shipboard operations relating to the safety of ships, or that such operations have not been carried out, and indications that key crew members may not be able to communicate with each another or with other persons on board.

Chapter 3 sets out guidelines for more detailed ship structural and equipment inspections, discharge requirements, and control of operational standards.

Because of the practical importance of procedural guidelines, the FSI subcommittee asked for the text to be issued as an IMO publication and for all PSC officers to have a copy to hand while they are on duty.

---

(15) J. WONHAM : "Some recent regulatory developments in IMO for which there are corresponding requirements in the United Convention on the Law of the Sea". Marine Policy, Vol. 20, n° 5, 1996, 377-388.

c) Quality of inspectors

605. - Only "officers duly authorised" by the port State may perform inspections on board ships. They must meet a number of requirements, defined in Resolution A.787. In theory, they are government inspectors, not classification society surveyors

This provision does not mean, however, that classification societies in any way refrain from helping port inspectors. In fact, IACS tries to foster active cooperation with port States. In 1995, it drew up a procedure to this effect (16). This allowed a constructive dialogue to be established between port authorities and classification societies, for the purpose of tracking down substandard ships and hastening the process of corrective action for any deficiencies affecting the ship's class status (17).

d) Inspector qualification and training

Paragraph 2.5 of Resolution A.787 lays down several requirements for the training and qualification of PSC officers. In particular, they should be capable of communicating in English with the crew, receive training to give them sufficient knowledge of relevant conventions, and attend regular training seminars to update their knowledge.

PSC officers carrying out inspections of operational requirements should be qualified as a master or chief engineer, have appropriate seagoing experience or qualifications from a recognised establishment, and have received specialised training in this type of inspection.

e) Reporting requirements

606. - When it exercises powers of control, the port State has to respect a whole series of reporting requirements. The basic principle, specified in Regulation 19 of the SOLAS Convention, is that "the officer carrying out the control shall forthwith inform, in writing, the Consul or, in his absence, the nearest diplomatic representative of the State whose flag the ship is entitled to fly of all the circumstances in which intervention was deemed necessary".

These requirements are explained in chapter 5 of Resolution A.787. When an inspection results in detention of a ship, a report on the defects observed must be sent to IMO, using a standard format.

The IMO Secretariat is responsible for summarising all such reports, six months before each session of the MSC, for examination there. These summaries also contain the observations of the flag State and the appropriate recognised organisation.

2. Broadening the scope of intervention

In the last twenty years, the port State has considerably extended its sphere of action regarding safety inspections. Initially, inspections concerned only ship particulars, whereas today they also cover observance of technical regulations, as well as operational requirements aboard.

a) Ship condition and maintenance

607. - Under the terms of SOLAS and Load Line Convention regulations, the port State is entitled to inspect:
- Condition of the ship and its equipment. For the hull, the examination may apply to the general condition of the deck, the extent of corroded areas, and the presence of unrepaired damage.

(16) "Port State Control". IACS Briefing n° 2, July 1996.
(17) Ph. BOISSON : "Classification society cooperation with Port State Control : a move towards the end of substandard practices". International Business Lawyer, Sept. 1996, 351-354 (18).

- Conditions of assignment of freeboard: closing devices, means of evacuating water accumulating on deck, devices to protect the crew.

b) Prevention of accidental pollution

Port State prerogatives provided for in the MARPOL Convention are exercised in accordance with procedures laid down in Resolution A.787 appendix 2, containing guidelines for investigations and inspections performed under the terms of annex I, and appendix 3 concerning annex II to MARPOL 73/78.

c) Operating requirements

608. - Procedures for inspecting operating requirements were set out for the first time in 1991 in IMO Resolution A.681. They were made compulsory by an amendment to the SOLAS Convention, in which Regulation 4 of a new chapter XI is devoted to this type of inspection. Similar provisions have been included in the MARPOL Convention since November 1994.

Resolution A.787 provides an exhaustive list of these inspections. In general, the port State must be careful not to impede normal shipboard operations for which the master is responsible, nor demand a demonstration of certain operational aspects, if this would cause unnecessary delay for the ships concerned.

Inspection of enforcement of the ISM Code is provided for in new SOLAS Regulations IX/6.3 and IX/14.2. It covers the safety management certificate (SMC), document of compliance (DOC) and safety management manual (SMS). To facilitate this type of control, IMO issued new guidelines for PSC officers in 1998 (18). Deficiencies include the impossibility of producing the necessary documents, or an inability to implement ISM provisions properly. While the absence of documents is quite easy to verify, failure to observe the ISM Code requires the inspector to possess a certain amount of experience in order to assess the crew's lack of knowledge or the value of management (19). One thing seems certain: it is not up to the port State to act as a shipboard auditor, but to consider the final result, in other words the safety of the actual ship, from a technical and operational viewpoint (20).

d) Qualification of seafarers and manning

609. - Article 10 of the 1978 STCW Convention allows the port State to control standards of qualification of seafarers, according to procedures set out in Regulation 1.4 of chapter I. Inspection aboard is confined to checking the validity of certificates and documents. Every certificate must be accepted, unless there are serious grounds for thinking that it has been obtained fraudulently, or that the holder is not the person to whom the certificate was originally issued (cf article 10.1).

A new factor is that the inspector can take into account the effective behaviour of the shipmaster and officers. He is empowered to assess the abilities of crews to observe watchkeeping requirements, if he has grounds for thinking that they have not been applied, because of any event occurring while the ship is in a port or its approaches. Detention of the ship is possible in very serious cases, listed in Regulation I/4.2 and 3: absence or invalidity

---

(18) - "IMO Guidelines on part checks". Lloyd's List, 30 June 1998.
- IMO. MSC 70/WP. 14/Add 2, 10 Dec. 1998 on Port State control and MSC Circ. 890, June 1998, per 9.19.
(19) R. GRIME : "Legal Framework of the code : Responsibilities and liabilities". BIMCO Courses, Copenhagen, April 1996.
(20) J. RASMUSSEN : "Implementation of the ISM Code. Responsibility of Administration". BIMCO courses, Copenhagen, April 1996.

of the certificates of the shipmaster, chief engineer, officers in charge of navigational and engineering watches, and radio officer.

As regards manning, the port State may exercise certain controls provided for in paragraph 2 of IMO Resolution A.481. These are confined to checking the existence of a document issued by the flag State and indicating the minimum manning needed to guarantee the ship's safety, and also to ensuring that the number of crew on the inspected ship complies with the details on this document.

3. Broadening the scope of competence

610. - In early IMO conventions, the port State could exercise control only over ships flying the flag of a State that had signed the convention. This limitation, justified in international law by application of the principle of the relative effect of treaties, is today being questioned, from the viewpoint of safety at sea.

The MARPOL Convention of 1973 was the first IMO instrument to introduce a "no more favourable treatment" clause. Article 5.4 stipulates that, "with respect to the ships of non-parties to the Convention, parties shall apply the requirements of the present Convention as may be necessary to ensure that no more favourable treatment is given to such ships" (article 5.4).

A second exception to the *pacta sunt servanda* principle was provided by article 4 of ILO Convention 147. Introduced at the request of France, this provision was considered by most authorities (21) as initiating the development of port State jurisdiction.

Since then, the "no more favourable treatment" clause has been inserted in most IMO instruments, namely article 11.3 of the 1978 Protocol to the SOLAS Convention, article X/5 of the 1978 STCW Convention, and Resolutions A.321 of 15 November 1975 and A.787 of 29 November 1995.

II - PORT STATE CONTROL POLICIES

611. - Despite relatively uniform international regulations, port State control is not exercised in the same way in all parts of the world. Everything depends on the importance attached to this type of inspection, and the resources made available In practice, control is exercised in two ways: unilaterally, by a single State which is a party to the conventions, or on a multilateral basis, by means of agreements concluded within a regional framework.

A - UNILATERAL APPROACH: UNITED STATES EXAMPLE

612. - Inspection of ships in American ports was introduced in 1838 by a Federal law designed to make steamships safer. The inspection programme has been considerably reinforced since 1968, although its purpose remains the same: to reduce human and material

---

(21) - G. KASOULIDES : "Port State Control and jurisdiction". Martinus Nijhoff Publishers, 1993, Dordrecht, 93-104.
- E. OSIEKE : "The International Labour Organisation and the control of substandard merchant vessels". ICLQ, Vol. 30, July 1981, 501-510.
- H. BETTINK : "Open Registry. The genuine link and the 1986 Convention on Registration Conditions for Ships". Netherlands Yearbook on International Law, 1987, 94-95.

losses and damage to the environment. Fourteen out of every fifteen ships entering American waters sail under foreign flags.

The inspection programme stipulated in titles 14, 33 and 46 of the United States Code applies to all ships, regardless of nationality. It is applied by the US Coast Guard, using a particular procedure. Owners of certain ships over 1 600 gross tonnage are obliged to provide 24 hours' advance notice of arrival, and to report any deficiencies affecting navigation equipment and cargoes prior to port entry. Ships with defects are allowed to enter port only with the express permission of the harbourmaster, after careful consideration of the risks involved (23).

1. Reinforcement of port inspections

The inspection system has been reinforced in several stages. By ratifying ILO Convention 147 in 1988, the United States finally joined the port State camp. In 1990, following a survey of the safety of passenger ships, the National Transportation Safety Board (NTSB) recommended an increase in powers of control and sanction with regard to cruise ships (24). In 1992, several accidents caused by substandard ships in American waters led Congress to show greater severity towards unseaworthy vessels. On 1st May 1994, the USCG introduced a new PSC programme, intended to eliminate substandard shipping from American waters (25).

The United States took up the fight against substandard shipping on its own account. It was considered fruitless to take part in a regional grouping on PSC, on the grounds of the particular geographical configuration of United States territory and the length of its coastlines (26). This does not mean that the USCG acted completely on its own: cooperation with the authorities of the Paris Memorandum of Understanding was established in 1986, and this continues with other regional bodies.

2. 1994 PSC initiative

613. - The programme introduced by the USCG in 1994 makes use of a computerised database concerning ship inspections in American ports This is the Port State Information Exchange System (PSIX) (27).

a) Targetting substandard ships

The prime goal of the USCG programme is to identify and eradicate substandard shipping from American waters. A targetting technique has accordingly been established, to concentrate boarding operations on ships believed to present the greatest danger to safety and

(22) G. WILLIAMS : "Flag State compliance and Port State control". Euro Shipping 1994. Istambul, 13 Oct. 1994.
(23) D. BRYANT : "Port State Control as practiced by the US Coast Guard". International Maritime Law, Vol. 4, Issue 10, Dec. 1997, 303-309.
(24) M. SOBEY : "International cooperation in marine casualty investigation : an analysis of IMO Resolution A. 637/16". Marit. Pol. Mgmt, 1993, Vol. 20, n° 1, 3-29.
(25) J. CARD : "Port State Control means business". Proceeding of the Marine Safety Council. Special Issue on Port State Control. March, April 1995, 1-2.
(26) - A. HENN : "US Coast Guard policy on ship inspection". SASMEX 92 - London, April 1992.
- J. KIME : "The port state - the shipping aspect". International Summit Safety at Sea. Oslo, April 1991.
- J. KIME : "The maritime safety Network - A port state's perspective. International. Summit Safety at Sea. Oslo, June 1993.
(27) J. CLINE : "Information sharing identifies weak safety nets". Proceedings of the Marine Safety Council - May/June 1994, 25-26.
- B. BUTLER : "Sharing Coast Guard information via the Port State Information Exchange System (PSIX)". Proceedings. July/Sept.1996, 26.

the environment. Apart from the fees imposed on shipowner for inspecting their ships (28), the programme provides for financial penalties for any deficiencies, and a ban on access to American ports until action has been taken to correct them (29).

Shipowners, classification societies and flag States that fail to observe international safety requirements are specially targetted by the programme:
- Ships in which the hull, crew, machinery or equipment are substantially below the standards required by United States laws or international conventions;
- Shipowners or operators of any ships subject to USCG port State intervention;
- Classification societies not recognised by the USCG as complying with the requirements of IMO Resolution A.739 and/or which show an above-average USCG intervention ratio,
- Flag States identified by comparing intervention ratios for various flag States.

A cumulative points system based on five criteria (shipowner, flag, classification society, boarding history and type of ships) is used to set priorities for inspections. The number of points for each ship determines the type of priority: III for possible boarding, II for recommended boarding, and I for systematic boarding before admission to the port.

b) Publication of PSC findings

614. - Publication of the findings of inspections is the second innovation in the American programme. This measure publicises the levels of performance of flag States, shipowners and classification societies, regarded as fundamental to safety at sea.

Since 1994 (30), the USCG has published an annual list of flag States (31), owners (32) and classification societies (33) targetted by the port authorities. This appears in the press and on its Internet site.

Despite its imperfections (34), fiercely criticised by the flag States concerned (35), and by the maritime industry (36), the American system has nevertheless raised awareness of the problems of maintenance on board ships. Training and information efforts directed at crews have been established by shipowners (37), P&I Clubs (38) and classification societies (39).

The unilateral American approach to port State control remains an isolated example among maritime safety policies currently being applied in the world.

(28) "USCG set to charge for vessel checks". Lloyd's List, 16 March 1995.
(29) US Coast Guard : "Port State Control initiative boarding regime to target substandard ships". Washington, 8 April 1994.
(30) "USCG names 15 safety target registers". Lloyd's List, 14 May 1994.
(31) "Eleven registers added to 1996 USCG black list". Lloyd's List, 16 April 1996.
(32) "USCG list 78 firms over ship detention". Lloyd's List, 14 May 1997.
(33) "USCG outlines 12-points guide for vessel inspections". Lloyd's List, 20 May 1996.
(34) - "USCG hit list angers shipping companies". Lloyd's List, 2 June 1994.
- "Don't go it alone on substandard ships". Lloyd's List, 4 June 1994.
- "Intercargo calls on USCG to amend hit list". Lloyd's List, 22 June 1994.
(35) "Cyprus fury at USCG targeting ". Lloyd's List, 22 June 1994.
(36) -"Controller code". Lloyd's List, 4 April 1996.
- M. GREY : "Just why the policeman must be fair". Lloyd's List, 10 April 1996.
- "Rating game". Lloyd's List, 7 May 1996.
- "Germanischer Lloyd to act on USCG detention findings". Lloyd's List, 4 June 1996.
- "Naming names". Lloyd's List, 20 June 1996.
(37) A. DE BIEVRE : "The lingering unpredictability of PSC", BIMCO Bulletin, Vol. 93, n° 2, 1998, 28-30.
(38) P. PARRY : "UK Club members to get route map". Lloyd's List, 26 Feb. 1998.
(39) Fairplay Solutions, Feb. 1997, 6-7.

It is an example that would be difficult to transpose to other countries, because of its many drawbacks. The lack of cooperation with other port State systems reduces its effectiveness. Shortcomings include the lack of pertinent information, absence of continuity in the surveillance of ships leaving territorial waters, and the impossibility of checking that corrective actions are actually taken. It is more expensive, because the whole financial burden of inspections is borne by the State practising such a policy. Proliferation of unilaterally operated systems would result in disparities in the application of rules and procedures. Finally, a unilateral approach could distort competition among ports in the same region (40).

B - REGIONAL APPROACH: PARIS MEMORANDUM OF UNDERSTANDING

615. - International cooperation on PSC was given effect for the first time in Europe in the late Seventies. It became important mainly after the signing in Paris on 28 January 1982 of a Memorandum of Understanding (MOU) on port State control among a number of European countries anxious to eradicate substandard shipping.

Several stages preceded the conclusion of the Paris MOU. It had started with a 1978 agreement, the Hague Memorandum, and a special contribution came from France, victim at the time of two major oil pollution disasters, the *Amoco Cadiz* in March 1978 and the *Tanio* in March 1980 (41).

Geographically, the Paris MOU region covers European coastal States and those of the North Atlantic basin from North America to Europe.

Current Paris MOU members are Belgium, Canada, Denmark, Finland, France, Germany, Greece, Ireland, Italy, Netherlands, Norway, Poland, Portugal, Russian Federation, Spain, Sweden, United Kingdom. Croatia joined in 1997, the eighteenth member.

1. Content of Paris MOU

616. - Like the Hague Memorandum, the Paris MOU sets up "regional cooperation". To this effect, it harmonises control of foreign ships in ports, to prevent any deviation of traffic and consequent distortion of competition. The Paris MOU differs from the earlier Memorandum, however, on four essential points.

a) Maritime authority commitments

Under the terms of section 1 of the MOU, each authority maintains an effective PSC system, to ensure that foreign ships visiting its ports comply with relevant international conventions and all current amendments. There is no discrimination among different flags. Each authority is to achieve an annual total of inspections corresponding to 25 per cent of the estimated number of individual foreign ships that have entered that State's ports during a representative 12-month period. Finally, each authority consults, cooperates and exchanges information with its partners, in order to further the aims of the Memorandum.

b) Scope of the MOU

According to section 2, the Paris MOU is more extensive in scope than the Hague Memorandum, containing reference to both ILO Convention 147 and the main IMO

(40) H. HUIBERS : "Port State view-Europe". International Conference on Flags and Quality London, December 1992
(41) R. SCHIFERLI : "Port State Control at work... a global Future". London, 6 Dec. 1993 in PSC Conference, New Solution or New Problem ? IBC Legal Studies and Services Limited.

instruments. As regards small ships, the safety of which is not regulated by international conventions, the authority must take account of certificates and documents issued by the flag State. If necessary, it will take steps to ensure that these ships are not obviously hazardous to safety, health and the environment.

c) Inspection, rectification and detention procedures

Section 3 of the MOU describes ship inspection and detention procedures, which are much the same as those defined in IMO resolutions. The MOU, however, has taken steps to target inspections at certain types of ships: those which could present a special hazard (oil tankers, gas carriers or chemical tankers), and those for which several recent deficiencies have been recorded. As a general rule, port authorities avoid inspecting ships which have already been inspected by another MOU authority during the previous six months.

d) Organisation

Section 6 of the MOU provides for the establishment of a compact institutional structure, consisting of a committee, a secretariat and a computer centre (cf table 22).

**Table 22 - Organisational structure under
the Paris Memorandum of Understanding on Port State Control**
(Source : Port State Control at work". Paris MOU Secretariat)

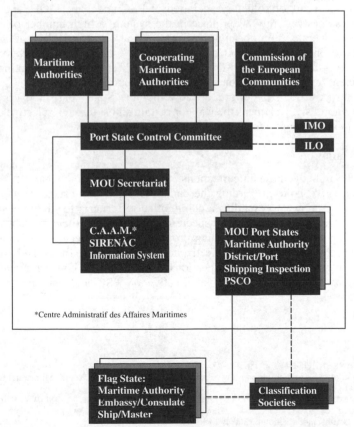

2. Legal nature of Paris MOU

617. - The Paris MOU is not an international convention but an administrative agreement. It does not introduce any new technical requirements, but marks the common will of its signatories to have relevant conventions enforced strictly, while providing the means of doing so.

There are several advantages to this form of commitment: promptness of application as a result of the absence of lengthy ratification periods, flexibility because of the ease with which the text may be amended, and the shared determination not to act against IMO and the ILO by creating an additional legal system superimposed on existing ones.

The major drawback to the formula is its absence of binding force. States bear no liability as a result of its existence and, in the event of failure to observe its provisions, no legal claims are possible (42).

3. Value of Paris MOU

618. - The 4th Regional Ministerial Conference on Port State Control, which met in Paris in March 1991, issued a satisfactory assessment: the goal of 25 per cent of foreign ships inspected in a year was almost achieved by all countries in the region. In other words, 80 per cent of ships stopping in European ports were inspected at least once every twelve months (43).

For the European Commission, this assessment still aroused reservations. Brussels noted that, after ten years of voluntary operation of PSC under the MOU, and although a degree of progress has certainly taken place in the system, a high number of substandard ships continues to operate in European waters. There is also a striking lack of uniformity in inspection criteria, including different choices of ships to be boarded, differences in the importance given to deficiencies and their follow-up, different decision-making processes leading to different levels of inspection and different resource allocations.

This in turn frustrates the efforts of those member States and surveyors who try to apply the rules rigorously, and opens the way for certain ships, through selective use of ports of destination, to slip through the net of proper control (44).

4. EU regulation

619. - To remedy these imperfections, the European Union has defined a more coherent and effective policy regarding the campaign against substandard shipping (45). This policy has five aims: to establish a common set of criteria for the intensification of inspections of certain ships, harmonise inspection and detention criteria, establish adequate national inspection structures and a training programme for inspectors, set up an effective mechanism to control and evaluate the effectiveness of the PSC measures, and finally ensure greater transparency for the results of inspections throughout the Union. Implementation of this policy has resulted in adoption of a directive on PSC and various accompanying measures to improve safety.

(42) Y. Van den MENSBRUGGHE : op. cit. 472-473.
(43) "Safe Operation of ships and pollution prevention". Main conclusions of the fourth Ministerial Conference on Port State Control. 14 March 1991. Paris.
(44) Commission of the European Communities : "A common policy on safe seas". COM (93) 66, final, Brussels, 24 Feb. 1993, p. 45, n° 69-70.
(45) "Brussels raises substandard shipping stakes". Lloyd's List, 14 April 1994.

a) *Directive 95/21*

Adopted by the Council on 18 June 1995, this Directive came into force on 1st July 1996 (46). It concerns "enforcement in respect of shipping using Community ports and sailing in the waters under the jurisdiction of member States, of international standards for ship safety, pollution prevention and shipboard living and working conditions". It is intended to improve the operation of the MOU within the Community framework, by making its provisions uniform and mandatory for the fifteen member states.

• Content of Directive

There are a score of differences between the two texts. Its promoters have no doubt about the additional value of the Directive (47).

Article 5.1 requires each member State to inspect at least 25 per cent of the number of ships entering its ports. To reach this goals, States must "maintain appropriate national maritime administrations", and "take whatever measures are appropriate to ensure that their competent authorities perform their duties" (article 4). According to article 12, inspections are to be carried out only by inspectors who fulfil the criteria specified in Annex VII.

Article 5.2 requires the authority, in selecting ships for inspection, to give priority to the ships referred to in Annex I.

Article 6 provides for a precise inspection procedure, involving first a check on the certificates and documents, and then a more detailed inspection if there are clear grounds for believing that the condition of a ship, equipment or crew does not meet international standards.

If the ship is detained, article 10.1 acknowledges the right of the owner or his representative to appeal against the detention decision by the port authorities. However, such an appeal does not cause the detention to be suspended.

The authority may refuse entry to ships failing to proceed to the appropriate ship repair yard. However, access may be permitted "in the event of *force majeure* or overriding safety considerations or to reduce or minimise the risk of pollution or to have deficiencies rectified.

According to article 13.1, pilots are now required to inform the port authorities of deficiencies noted by them that could prejudice safe navigation of the ship.

Each member State is to publish information at least quarterly on ships detained more than once during the previous 24 months.

Finally, if a ship is detained, all costs relating to inspections are borne by the shipowner. Detention is not lifted until full payment has been made or a sufficient guarantee has been given for the reimbursement of costs (cf article 16.1).

Directive 95/21 CE was amended twice in 1998: the first time to deal with cases where there is no ISM certificate on board (48), and the second time to improve ship targetting methods (49).

---

(46) OJEC, L 157-1, 7 July 1995.
(47) R. SALVARANI : "The EC Directive on Port State Control : A policy statement". IJMCL. Vol. 11, n° 2, 1996, 225-231.
(48) OJEC, 7 May 1998, Council Directive 98/25/CE, L 133/19.
(49) OJEC, 27 June 1998, Commission Directive 98/42/CE, L 184/40.

• Value of Directive

The PSC Directive is of interest on two counts. It gives mandatory force to the provisions of the Paris MOU within the EU. Member States are required to apply its provisions properly and, if they fail to comply, may be penalised by the Commission.(50). It also exerts influence on the operational behaviour of shipowners, confronted with a new definition of unseaworthiness, and of shippers, who may be refused the right to claim compensation for loss or damage caused by "undue detention and delay" of a ship (51).

Despite the benefits it has brought regarding action against substandard ships, the Directive has been subject to criticism. By increasing port State powers well beyond the limits set by international conventions, it increases the risk of unilateral measures, and militates against worldwide harmonisation of PSC practices, currently the aim of IMO. In addition to these two drawbacks, there is the complexity of the system, superimposed in Europe on the Paris MOU, which it deprives of all substance and credibility (52).

b) Accompanying measures

Following a survey carried out in November 1996 by the Commission on application of the Directive by member States (53), drastic action was announced against substandard practices in the maritime industry (54). Brussels raised the threat of prosecution before the European Court of Justice of states failing to respect the Directive requirements. Additional financial means have been provided to train port State inspectors in detailed inspections, particularly of oil tankers and bulk carriers. The Commission is also examining the possibility of imposing financial penalties on shippers, when a chartered ship has been detained because of serious deficiencies.

5. Evolvement of Paris MOU

620. - The Paris MOU is not a fixed, immutable agreement. It can be amended by ministerial conferences, and by the MOU Committee. In May 1996, the Committee adopted a series of detailed amendments, to bring the MOU into line with the Directive. The most important changes made since its creation include targetting of inspections and the publication of "black lists".

a) Improvement in targetting

In 1994, the Committee proposed to improve targetting of ships for which inspection is a priority (55). In addition to the type of ship, various other factors have been considered: the flag, the classification society, age of the ship, and its technical and operational record. To facilitate the work of inspectors, a simplified targetting method has been recommended.

(50) R. SALVARANI, S. LINDSTROM : "Looking behind the Directive on Port State Control". The International Journal of Shipping Law. Part I, March 1997, 49-52.
(51) C. MAGUIRE : "Port State Control - Brussels Style". The International Journal of Shipping Law, 1996, 118-112.
(52) Fairplay, 24 Feb. 1994 and 4 July 1996.
(53) "Brussels monitors port state checks". Lloyd's List, 15 Nov. 1996.
(54) JMM, 20 June 1997, 1421-1442.
(55) "Targeting Ships for priority inspections". The Memorandum of Understanding on Port State Control. PSCC/4/09 B. 16 March 1994.

b) Black lists

At a meeting in Dublin in May 1994, the MOU Committee decided to publish a black list of ships detained at least twice in the previous two years (56).

A first list of 155 ships was issued to the press in July of that year. In addition to the name of the ship, this list contained the IMO number, the flag of registry, the classification society, the total number of detentions with their reasons, port and date of inspection (57).

In April 1998, the Committee agreed to release monthly lists of detained and banned vessels and post these lists on the Paris MOU website.

c) Concentrated inspection programme

Since 1997, the Paris MOU authorities have been applying a "concentrated inspection programme". These programmes, which last three months, focus inspectors' attention on certain aspects of regulations: seafarers' living and working conditions in 1997, the ISM Code in 1998 (58) and bulk carriers in 1999 (59).

d) How effective are these new measures ?

Has the Paris MOU actually increased safety at sea ? The answer to such a question is complicated by several factors (60). Shipping in European ports varies from year to year, as changes of flag, owner and classification society alter the overall reference data. Little is known or can be known about the influence of the MOU on the condition of this shipping. It can be gauged only partly, on the basis of detention figures, but even here the high number of uninspected ships from one year to another makes any firm conclusions hazardous. There are so many interacting aspects that any simple deduction is impossible. If the number of detentions rises, should it be concluded that the quality of the fleet is declining, or that the severity of inspections has increased ? Finally, if targetted ships are subject to more frequent inspection, it may reasonably be assumed that the number of deficiencies and detentions will rise.

C - SPREAD OF REGIONAL PSC INITIATIVES

621. - IMO has fostered the development of regional cooperation in enforcing standards, for several reasons. The region is seen as the most suitable framework for the development of joint political action on safety and protection of the environment. Cooperation among States makes it more difficult to operate substandard ships within their region. Exchange of information is easier among a small number of partners. Finally, regional coordination of PSC procedures reduces superfluous constraints on maritime navigation, while making it easier for participating States to find sufficient resources (62).

---

(56) "European ports to target danger ships". Lloyd's List, 10 May 1994.
(57) "Dispute looms over new list of shame". Tradewinds, 8 July 1994.
(58) "Inspection stance vindicated. Paris MOU encouraged over ISM". Fairplay, 12 Nov. 1998.
(59) Marine Safety Report, 25 May 1998.
(60) Ph. MARCHAND : "SIRENAC. Système d'information du Mémorandum de Paris sur le contrôle des navires de commerce par l'Etat du Port". Navigation. Vol. 44, n° 176. Oct. 1996, 468-477.
(61) T. MENSAH : "The Paris Memorandum of Understanding on Port State Control and Maritime Safety. An IMO Perspective". Conference of the Seamens Church Institute Centre for Seafarer's Right". Unpublished address, 1987.
(62) F. PLAZA : "Port State Control : towards global standardization". IMO News, n° 1, 1992, 13-16.

In November 1991, aware that Europe cannot eliminate substandard ships on its own, IMO adopted Resolution A.682, asking maritime authorities in each region to work together to adopt agreements similar to the Paris MOU. It subsequently tried to provide technical assistance to States keen to set up such a structure. It remains very attentive to how this regional cooperation is evolving. At each session of the FSI subcommittee, the Secretariat presents a report on PSC agreements (63).

1. Latin America Agreement

622. - The Latin American Agreement on PSC was signed in Viña del Mar in Chile on 5 November 1992 by the maritime authorities of ten South American countries (Argentina, Brazil, Chile, Colombia, Ecuador, Mexico, Panama, Peru, Uruguay and Venezuela), at the 6th meeting of the Operative Regional Cooperation Network of Maritime Authorities of South America, Mexico and Panama (ROCRAM). The secretariat and computer centre (CIALA) are provided by the Prefectura Naval Argentina, in Buenos Aires (64).

The Viña del Mar Agreement differs in several ways from the Paris MOU. To begin with, its aims are more modest. Each signatory intends to inspect at least 15 per cent of foreign ships visiting its ports (cf section 3.1) Ultimately, it is not 80 but barely 50 per cent of the total number of such ships that will be inspected, and this is conditional on every country achieving its 15 per cent target. The scope of the Agreement is more limited: ILO Convention 147 has been removed from the list of relevant instruments (cf section 2). The opposition of a number of Latin American countries to ratification of the agreement explains this removal.

On the other hand, the Latin American Agreement contains several new and innovative features. The list of ships requiring special attention has been extended to passenger ships, ro-ro ships and bulkers. For high-risk ships, the minimum interval of six months between inspections need not be respected. The existence of "clear grounds" is not required, leaving the port authorities greater latitude. Finally, the Agreement defines the qualifications required for PSC inspectors (cf appendix 5).

Consideration is at present being given to the introduction of a new computerised system for the PSC database, possible use of the Internet to distribute information, and the introduction of a priority system to target ships for inspection.

2. Asia-Pacific MOU

624. - On 3 December 1993, at the end of the preparatory meeting of maritime authorities in the Asia-Pacific region, a Memorandum of Understanding on PSC was signed in Tokyo, by fifteen countries (Australia, Canada, China, Fiji, Indonesia, Japan, Malaysia, New Zealand, Papua New Guinea, the Philippines, Russia, Singapore, South Korea, Thailand, Vanuatu and Vietnam).

(63) FSI 4/7/2, 19 Jan. 1996 and FSI 5/11, 22 Oct. 1996.
(64) Text in FSI 1/16/1, 26 Jan. 1993.

This Tokyo MOU, which came into effect on 1st April 1994, sets its sights high: it aims to reach an annual inspection rate for foreign vessels of 50 per cent by the year 2000 (cf section 1.4). This will certainly raise problems for maritime authorities in the region, which concentrates 40 per cent of world container traffic, and 33 per cent of bulk cargo imports and 16 per cent of exports (65). Early statistics for 1995 showed that the goal was achievable, since 8 834 inspections had been performed on the 22 786 foreign ships visiting ports in the region, namely 39 per cent (66).

The text of the Tokyo MOU (67) differs only in detail from the Paris MOU. Two countries play a driving role, however: Canada and Australia. Canada gave its Coast Guard the task of operating the Asia-Pacific MOU information centre. Through its participation in the Paris MOU, it can therefore act as a bridge between the two regions. Canada also publishes regular lists of ships detained in its ports, with the name of the shipowner, flag and classification society (68).

Spearheading the campaign against substandard ships in the Pacific basin, Australia was the prime mover of the Tokyo MOU. In 1992, it was the first State in the region to set up a Parliamentary Committee on "ships of shame" (69). Since that date, the number of inspections has continued to rise in Australian ports. In 1996-97, 3 050 foreign ships were inspected and 241 were detained (70). Inspections are carried out by 45 inspectors of the Australian Maritime Safety Authority (AMSA), operating from fifteen centres (71). The list of detained ships is published every month in the press, and may be consulted on the Internet (72).

3. Caribbean MOU

624. - A Memorandum of Understanding on PSC for the Caribbean Region was signed in Barbados on 9 February 1996 by nine countries of the region (73). In August 1996, this MOU was also signed by the British High Commissioner on behalf of five United Kingdom dependencies. Barbados provides the secretariat, and there are plans to set up an information centre in Curaçao (74).

A particular feature of the Caribbean MOU is that its signatories undertake to ensure observance of a code for the safety of cargo ships operating in the zone. This is a comprehensive series of rules applying to small ships not covered by international conventions, and which form the bulk of Caribbean shipping (75).

(65) M. PICKTHORNE : "Port State Control in the Asia Pacific Region". Seaways. February 1994, 10-12.
(66) "524 Vessels held under Tokyo port state memo". Lloyd's List, 8 Oct. 1996.
(67) "Report on Port State Control in the Asia-Pacific Region 1994-1995". Published by Tokyo MOU Secretariat OMI. FSI 5/INF.3, October 1996.
(68) "Cyprus tops list of Canada detentions". Lloyd's List, 4 June 1996.
(69) Parliament of the Commonwealth of Australia : "Ships of Shame". Dec. 1992. Canberra, Australian Government Publishing Service.
(70) Parliament of the Commonwealth of Australia "Ship Safe". 10 August 1998, p. 29.
(71) "Fine-mesh port net". Hazardous Cargo Bulletin. Sept. 1995, 11.
(72) "Ships of Shame". Australian Ships and Port. March, 1997, 8-9.
(73) IMO News, n° 2, 1996, 11.
(74) BIMCO Bulletin, Vol. 91, n° 1, 1996, 47.
(75) L. KIMBALL : "Memorandum of Understanding on Port State Control in the Caribbean Region". International Legal Material Vol. XXXVI, n° 2, March 1997, 231-234.

4. Mediterranean MOU

625. - Another regional initiative is the MOU on PSC for the Mediterranean Region, signed on 11 July 1997 in Malta by eight countries (Algeria, Cyprus, Egypt, Israel, Malta, Morocco, Tunisia and Turkey) (76). The secretariat is in Alexandria and the information centre in Casablanca. With financial backing from the European Commission, this MOU will be fully operational by the year 2000 (77). Like the Viña del Mar MOU, it provides for the obligation to inspect 15 per cent of foreign ships visiting the ports of each signatory State.

5. Indian Ocean MOU

Fifteen Maritime Authorities (South Africa, Djibouti, Eritrea, Ethiopia, Indian, Iran, Kenya, Maldives, Mauritius, Mozambique, Seychelles, Sri Lanka, Sudan, Tanzania and Yemen) signed the Memorandum of Understanding on PSC for the Indian Ocean Region on 5 June 1998.

This MOU allows for an interim period of two years prior to its full functioning and implementation. The interim Secretariat will be based in Goa (India) and the interim Information Centre for the Region will be set up in Pretoria (South Africa).

Like the other agreements, the Indian Ocean MOU requires each maritime authority to establish and maintain an affective system of PSC and sets an annual required total of inspections of at least 10 % of the estimated total number of foreign ships entering the ports during the year.

CONCLUSION: Globalisation and institutionalisation of PSC

626. - The development of regional PSC agreements tends to prove that these prerogatives cannot be exercised in isolation from other States. There is a whole series of arguments in favour of cooperation on PSC (78). The effectiveness of inspection rests largely on the motivation of the maritime authorities, their awareness of safety problems and their determination to remove substandard ships. At present, there is clearly no international organisation capable of supervising or regulating port state control, and setting up a coherent legal regime (79).

PSC can increase the risk of unilateral measures, as certain authorities are tempted to give preference to application of their own national standards, rather than those contained in international conventions. This absence of uniformity is prejudicial to ships subjected to a host of different jurisdictions and control systems (80). In its policing role, the port authority may suffer from a lack of skill or integrity. It may be subject to local political pressures, or look to an improvement in its tax revenues rather than in safety (81). Finally, the port State

---

(76) IMO News, n° 2 and 3, 1997, 2.
(77) "Mediterranean MOU. Moving in on the Med". Fairplay, 2 May 1996, 12.
(78) G. KASOULIDES : "Port State Control and Jurisdiction". Martinus Nijhoff Publishers. Dordrecht, 1993, 126-129.
(79) C. HORROCKS : "Port State Control. Does it stand up to inspection ?". Port State Control, New Solution or New Problem ? IBC Conference, London, Dec. 1993.
(80) J.F. JOINT : "Port State Control in developing countries". Port State Control, New Solution or New Problem ? IBC Conference, London, Dec. 1993.
(81) P. DONNELLAN : "Port State Control - A P&I perspective on Port State Control". New Solution or New Problem ? IBC Conference, London, Dec. 1993.
- See also "Port detentions criticised". Lloyd's List, 7 Nov. 1996.
- IMO. FSI 5/11/3, 15 Nov. 1996.

is faced with a conflict of interests: it is to its financial benefit not to impede its clients or future clients, which means that both port and flag may show a degree of flexibility in applying regulations.

Cooperation, recognised as vital among port States, exists not only in a regional framework but also at an interregional level. In March 1998, countries that had signed the Paris and Tokyo MOUs signed a joint declaration on interregional action to eliminate substandard shipping, at the first joint ministerial meeting of the two groups, held in Vancouver (82). This declaration also notes that harmonisation of PSC and administration and inspection procedures can be achieved on an interregional basis (83).

Is it possible to go further in globalisation of the system ? Certain observers think so, and propose the establishment of an international convention on the issue (84).

The idea offers initial attractions: port State performance in supervising substandard ships could be guaranteed worldwide, maximum information would be available to combat negligence, and the running costs of a global system would be kept to a strict minimum.

In practice, the introduction of such a system raises numerous political and legal problems. It is to be feared that States would be less committed to a universal structure than a regional one, where geographical and economic affinities matter. The adoption of a new convention implies the amendment of all IMO and ILO instruments on PSC. Who would sign the convention: states, international organisations, maritime authorities ? Finally, a convention inevitably means a lengthy period of implementation, rigid amendment procedures, and compromises prejudicial to a high degree of commitment.

An international convention on PSC could in the end compromise the present system, which was originally intended to be voluntary and temporary. Inspection and detention of ships must remain a right for port authorities, not an obligation (85). On the pretext of the constantly increasing imperative of globalisation, it would be dangerous for PSC to be institutionalised, relieving others with responsibility for safety at sea, primarily shipowners and flag States, of any need for commitment.

This is not the direction currently taken by IMO, which continues working towards harmonisation of basic procedures, and of qualification and experience criteria for inspectors. The FSI subcommittee has agreed on a global strategy for PSC and has developed an accompanying code of conduct for PSC officers.

(82) "Canada pushes Port State". Fairplay, 19 Mars 1998.
(83) IMO News n° 2, 1998, 31.
(84) Port and Harbours, Feb. 1975, 19-22.
(85) - R. LANTEIGNE : "Port State Control in Canada, Europe and the Pacific Rim : future enforcement objectives". Marine Log Conference. Washington DC, 24 April 1995.
- "It's your problem". Fairplay, 4 May 1995 4-5.
(86) F. PLAZA : "Port State Control. An update". IMO News, n° 4, 1997, 30-34.

CHAPTER 26

Maritime traffic management

627. - Maritime traffic is managed by means of Vessel Traffic Services (VTS). Such services have been introduced by port authorities and coastal States over the last fifty years, as a way of helping improve the safety of shipping, increase traffic throughput, and reduce pollution risks (1).

It was in the post-Second World War period that the first local initiatives were taken to try and manage navigation in European waters. Liverpool was the first port in the world, in 1948, to be equipped with a monitoring station and radio equipment. The example was followed a few years later by Southampton and the Medway ports.

At present, more than 250 VTS ensure regular control of navigation. There are several reasons for this massive expansion. To begin with, dangers have multiplied with the increased size and speed of ships, but also because of the concentration of traffic in certain zones, such as the approaches to large ports, straits, and narrow or shallow shipping lanes. In addition, growth in transport of dangerous goods by sea has stepped up the risk of accidents, and this has led to anxiety among coastal populations and an emphasis on the need to protect the environment.

I - TECHNICAL AND OPERATIONAL ASPECTS

628. - According to Annex 1 to IMO Resolution A.857 adopted on 3 December 1997, a VTS is "a service implemented by a competent authority, designed to improve the safety and efficiency of vessel traffic and to protect the environment. They should have the capability to interact with the traffic and to respond to traffic situations developing in the VTS area".

(1) - Ch. KOBURGER : "Vessel traffic systems". Cornell Maritime Press, 1986, Maryland.
- A.N. COCKCROFT : "Routing and the environment". Journal of Navigation, vol. 39, n° 2, May 1996, 213.
- G. KOP : "General principles of VTS and the IMO Guidelines". The Nautical Institute, London, 1990, 205-208.
- P. BELL : "Vessel traffic services". Marine Communication and Control Seminar, London, 21-23 Nov. 1990. BIMCO Bulletin, Vol. 90, n° 1, 1995, 17-19.
- J. PRUNIERAS : "La surveillance du trafic maritime". Navigation, vol. 39 n° 154, April 1991, 211-225.
- R. PELICANT : "Philosophie du VTS ou règle de conduite pour l'établissement d'un VTS". Navigation, vol. 39, n° 154, Apr. 1991, 227-237.
- J.L. GUIBERT : "Organisation et contrôle des flux de trafic maritimes, aériens et terrestres. Cas du Maritime". Navigation, vol. 42, n° 105, Jan. 1994, 15-20.
- T. HUGHE : "VTS - what progress". Safety at Sea International, March 1997, 11-12.

The VTS authority is "the authority with responsibility for the management, operation and coordination of the VTS, interaction with participating vessels and the safe and effective provision of the service". In practice, the way maritime administrations are organised in different countries determines who controls the VTS (2). Despite this diversity, however, it is possible to identify certain common factors, and define the fundamental purposes of a VTS.

A - COMPONENTS OF A VTS

629. - A VTS has three components: an onshore centre, user ships, and a communication system between centre and ships.

Onshore installations comprising one or more VTS centres are usually equipped with efficient means of communication, a radar system and equipment to regulate shipping traffic where necessary. This equipment is used by specially trained personnel, known as VTS operators.

Ships taking part in a VTS are also expected to be equipped with navigational appliances and means of communication, so that they can receive information or follow the instructions of onshore operators, and report their passage.

The communication system between the VTS centre and the ship consists of VHF radio links, in some cases supplemented by visual signals.

A VTS very often covers a surveillance area within which a traffic separation scheme (TSS) or other ship routeing system has been set up (3). The other way of making traffic management more efficient is to require close cooperation by each ship, which has to be fitted with radio equipment to broadcast its own position and identity. Several systems have been recommended (4). The best appears to be a universal automatic identification system (AIS) operating in the VHF band. This is the solution towards which IMO is turning, and which could shortly become mandatory (5).

B - FUNDAMENTAL FUNCTIONS OF VTS

630. - A VTS has many different functions. IMO Resolution A.857 lists three main ones:
- Information service which ensures "that essential information becomes available in time for on-board navigation decision-making",
- Navigational service, which assists on-board navigational decision-making and monitors its effects;
- Traffic organisation service, which prevents the development of dangerous traffic situations and provides for the safe and efficient movement of vessel traffic within the VTS area.

Starting with these fundamental functions, VTS can be classified in two categories, active and passive, depending on the nature of the relations between onshore centres and ships. In a passive system, shipmasters and pilots retain most of the powers of decision about ship navigation, whereas their responsibilities are more limited in an active system.

(2) C.J. PARKER : "VTS : The politics of Ship Control". Seaways, August 1984, 3-6.
(3) D. WILLIAMS : "Sea traffic management". Ian Allan, Shepperton, Surrey, 1988, 4-9.
(4) - Report of Lord Donaldson : "Safer ship, cleaner seas". HMSO, London, May 1994, chp. 15, 15-20 et seq., 228.
- A.G. CORBET : "Navigation management : post Donaldson". Marine Policy 1995, vol. 19, n° 6, 477-486.
- I. MCGEOCH : "Transponders. A response to Donaldson". Seaways, March 1997, 21.
(5) IMO. MSC/67, 19 Dec. 1996, par. 7.64. - IMO News, n° 2-3, 1997, 21-22.

1. Information services

Sometimes known as "organisation service", or "navigational assistance service", a passive VTS leaves the shipmaster, whether or not assisted by a pilot, complete freedom in conducting his ship.

The main purpose of such a system is to broadcast information about ship movements, visibility conditions, the traffic situation, as well as meteorological and hydrological information, advice to navigators, details of navigational obstacles, disabled ships, fishing fleets and small craft.

The onshore operators can sometimes offer assistance to navigation by providing help to ships in difficult nautical or meteorological conditions (6), or which have suffered defects or damage. The system established in the Straits of Dover offers a typical example of this type of VTS (7).

2. Active VTS

An active VTS is not confined to providing information and advice. Its function is to plan ship movements in order to avoid dangerous situations and ensure safe and effective organisation of vessel traffic within the surveillance area, using routeing plans.

The onshore operator's tasks are therefore considerably expanded. He establishes and operates a system of navigating authorisations and records. For example, he programmes ship movements through special areas like one-way traffic lanes. He stipulates the routes to be taken, and speed limits to be observed. He indicates mooring sites, and finally coordinates ship movements by means of appropriate instructions and procedures.

Such a system functions successfully in the United States, Canada, Japan and a few European ports. It implies the existence of immediate, continuous communication between the onshore operator and the master of the controlled ship. The operator must be aware of a ship's manoeuvrability, while the master must realise the limits of observation on a radar screen.

C - COMPARISON WITH AIR TRAFFIC CONTROL

631. - One of the most elaborate forms of traffic control is in the air traffic sector.

Remote guidance or piloting consists of assigning predetermined routes and altitudes to aircraft captains, in order to ensure adequate distances between aircraft. It employs two techniques, which complement each other:
- **procedure control,** in which each pilot files a preflight plan which he updates continuously, on the basis of position and altitude reports above radiobeacons; and
- **radar control,** in which the air space is divided into sectors under the surveillance of a controller who identifies every aircraft and sees to observance of its flight plan.

Could such a system be applied at sea ?

Even if the technologies and procedures used to control air and sea traffic are quite similar (8), the fact remains that the particular features of these two types of navigation show

(6) "The needs for meteorological information in VTS areas". IALA Bulletin 1996/2, 11-13.
(7) H. NEILL : "The Channel Navigation Information Service for the Dover Strait". The Journal of Navigation, Vol. 43, n° 3, Sept. 1990, 331-341.
(8) R. BOOTSHA and K. POLDERMAN : "ATS and VTS - Some observations towards a synthesis". Journal of Navigation, vol. 40 n° 1, January 1987, 42-51.

many differences (9). Unlike an aircraft, a ship is handicapped by its size. It has to move inside confined spaces, and remains exposed to the effects of wind and current. Guidance systems require very thorough training of onshore operators and seafarers, and sources of errors and confusion always remain possible, particularly those resulting from the language barrier. While some international standardisation of operational procedures exists, in the form of IMO Resolution A.857, which provides a set of non-compulsory guidelines for VTS. The same applies to the equipment of each onshore centre, the function of which depends on local circumstances.

Equally important legal differences exist between air and sea traffic control services. Organisation of ship guidance involves a far-reaching revision of public international law and centuries-old maritime customs. In public law, the main difficulty lies in the implementation of requirements concerning notification and reporting. This raises one of the fundamental principles of the law of the sea: freedom of navigation. In private law, another principle governs the conduct of ships: decisions on navigation are the responsibility of the shipmaster, sole authority on board. Even in the cause of greater safety and better protection of the environment, it will always be difficult for a seafarer to admit that his conduct at sea can be dictated to him, and accept decisions, taken in his place or imposed on him, that impinge on his rights and responsibilities.

II - VTS CREATION AND FUNCTIONING

632. - What are the powers of the coastal State regarding control of navigation ? The answer is simple when the ships to be monitored fly the flag of the coastal State itself, or when the monitoring system is applied voluntarily. It becomes infinitely harder when compulsory schemes are imposed on foreign ships. There are two possible sources where solutions may be sought: the general provisions of the law of the sea defining the extent of coastal State jurisdiction, and the stipulations of IMO instruments concerning vessel traffic services.

A - LAW OF THE SEA

633. - The 1982 LOS Convention offers coastal States extensive powers to improve safety of navigation and protection of the marine environment. There is a general requirement for coastal States, in areas over which they have jurisdiction, to exercise their prerogatives in ways compatible with the provisions of the Convention, with full allowance made for the rights and obligations of other States. It is therefore incumbent on coastal States not to create conditions that would impede activities arising from the exercise of such rights and obligations (10). The LOS Convention neither provides for nor excludes the establishment of VTS for each maritime area. It is therefore important to proceed by deduction and analogy with other provisions on safety at sea.

---

(9) D. WILLIAMS : op. cit., 5.
(10) IMO. Legal issues regarding mandatory ship reporting systems and VTS. LE6. 67/8/1, 12 August 1992.

1. Ports and internal waters

The coastal State exercises full sovereignty over this part of its maritime territory. According to article 25.2 of the Convention, it has "the right to take the necessary steps to prevent any breach of the conditions to which admission of those ships to internal waters or such a call "(at its ports)" is subject". It is therefore free to introduce a compulsory VTS.

2. Territorial seas

634. - Article 21.1a and 1f of the Convention allows the coastal State complete freedom to adopt laws and regulations on safety of navigation and regulation of maritime traffic in its territorial sea, preservation of the environment, and prevention, reduction and control of pollution.

The coastal State is also under an obligation to "give appropriate publicity to any danger to navigation within its territorial sea" (article 24.2).

It may therefore be concluded that the coastal State has the power to establish compulsory VTS in this zone, although it must not deny the right of innocent passage or discriminate against any ships (cf article 24.1).

Can a VTS impede the right of innocent passage of foreign ships ? The question is worth examining in the light of provisions on compulsory sea routes.

Under certain circumstances, when a VTS includes routeing measures, the coastal State may lay certain obligations on ships exercising the right of innocent passage in its territorial seas. Specifically, compulsory ship reporting may be imposed. However, a major restriction is stipulated in article 21.2 on the exercise of such powers. It may not require ships to be equipped with special equipment needed to use the VTS. Its jurisdiction over VTS, like any maritime safety measure, must be exercised in a reasonable and non-discriminatory manner.

The same principles apply in part XII of the LOS Convention, concerned with protection and preservation of the marine environment (11). The coastal State may regulate pollution from ships and if necessary adopt VTS intended to minimise the threat of accidents which might cause pollution of the marine environment (cf article 211.1).

3. Archipelagic waters

635. - Although an innovation in the LOS Convention, archipelagic waters enjoy the same status as territorial seas in respect of safety of navigation. Article 52 recognises the right of innocent passage for foreign ships, although they may be required to take designated sea lanes (cf article 53). Criteria for VTS in territorial seas apply, *mutatis mutandis*, to archipelagic waters.

4. Exclusive Economic Zone

636. - Freedom of navigation applies in the EEZ, which extends up to 200 miles from the coast (cf article 58.1). Theoretically, this precludes the establishment of compulsory VTS. Ships in transit are at the most required to "have due regard for" the laws and regulations of the coastal State (cf article 58.3), and specifically traffic separation schemes established in accordance with the procedures laid down in article 211.1 mentioned above. Compulsory measures applying to foreign ships may, however, be adopted under certain circumstances.

(11) Brian SMITH : "Innocent passage as a rule of decision : navigation v. environmental protection". Columbia Journal of Transnational Law, vol. 21, n° 1, 1982, 49-102.

a) Ships intending to enter a coastal State port

There is no convention that expressly confers the right on the coastal State to require reports from foreign ships inside its EEZ. However, reference to article 211.3 on territorial seas may provide a basis for extending the coastal State's powers to require information to be furnished to include foreign ships navigating inside the EEZ and coming from or heading for one of its ports. Article 211.1 in fact makes no distinction between the two zones.

b) Reporting obligation in case of infringement of anti-pollution rules

Article 230.3 of the Convention requires ships within a coastal State's EEZ or territorial sea to furnish information, if the State has "clear grounds for believing" that they have committed a violation of its anti-pollution laws and regulations. A ship in this position is required to report its port of registry, its last and next ports of call, and other relevant information to establish whether a violation has occurred. If such a breach has led to substantial discharges causing or threatening significant pollution of the marine environment, article 220.5 and 6 entitles the coastal State to take proceedings, including boarding and detention of the ship.

c) Particular areas

The coastal State also retains the right, after consultation and with the agreement of the competent international organisation, to adopt mandatory measures in certain "particular, clearly defined areas" of its EEZ. It would accordingly be possible to conceive the establishment of compulsory VTS, provided that coastal State regulations do not require foreign ships to observe other than generally accepted international standards (cf article 211.6c).

5. Straits used for international navigation

637. - The establishment of VTS proves particularly effective in straits where narrow traffic lanes are used by high volumes of traffic. However, for strategic and military reasons, the law of the sea makes provision for a special regime in certain such straits, according to which all ships enjoy the right of transit passage (cf article 38.1).

May compulsory VTS be established in straits ? Doctrine is divided on the point. Certain American commentators (12) are convinced of that such VTS are justified, provided that there is no discrimination against foreign ships, and that they do not deny, restrict or impede the right of transit passage. English commentators are more reserved, particularly for VTS designed specifically to prevent pollution (13).

One thing is clear: as recalled in article 43, States using a strait and coastal States should cooperate by agreement "in the establishment and maintenance in a strait of necessary navigational and safety aids or other improvements in aid of international navigation". This provision seems clearly to imply the possibility of VTS.

6. High seas

638. - Any State with coasts adjacent to part of the high seas may set up a VTS to improve the safety of traffic or reduce pollution hazards, provided that it respects the freedom

---

(12) - ANDERSON : "National and international efforts to prevent traumatic vessel source oil pollution". 30 U. Miami Law Review 985, 1028 (1976).

- B. BOLAND - "Vessel Traffic Services and liability for oil spills and other maritime accidents". Columbia Journal of Transnational Law, vol. 18, 1979, p. 482-524.

(13) G. PLANT : "International legal aspects of vessel traffic services". Marine Policy 1990, 71-81.

under international law to navigate, fish, engage in scientific research, lay submarine cables and pipelines. The VTS therefore has to operate on a voluntary basis, or be confined to passive surveillance of navigation, without any ship reporting obligations or traffic control. Three measures in the LOS Convention place restrictions on this principle, however.

a) Safety zones round artificial islands

Coastal States exercise sole jurisdiction over artificial islands, installations and structures built on the high seas for the purpose of exploring or exploiting resources on the Continental Shelf.

If necessary, a coastal State can set up safety zones round such structures, to a distance of 500 metres (more in certain cases), where they exercise regulatory powers to ensure the safety of navigation and installations. All ships must respect these safety zones and comply with generally accepted international standards on navigation (cf article 60.4, 5 and 6 on artificial islands in the EEZ, which applies *mutatis mutandis* to those situated on the Continental Shelf and governed by article 80 of the Convention). The establishment of mandatory VTS is not only possible from a legal standpoint, but is even common practice (14).

b) Accident reporting obligation

This flag State obligation is not confined to the high seas. It also applies inside territorial seas and the EEZ. According to article 211.7, foreign ships are responsible for "prompt notification to coastal States whose coastline or related interests may be affected by incidents, including maritime casualties, which involve discharges or probability of discharges".

c) Measures to prevent pollution following accidents

According to article 221, coastal States may intervene on the high seas, if a shipping accident causes or threatens damage to their coastline or related interests, including fishing. This provision could certainly include the establishment of mandatory VTS in an appropriate position to regulate navigation and thereby help limit environmental damage (15).

B. IMO RULES

639. - The first IMO rules were adopted on 20 November 1985 in the form of guidelines contained in Resolution A.578. They described "operational procedures and planning for vessel traffic services". IMO was careful to express certain reservations: the guidelines did not address issues of liability or responsibility, nor create any new rights empowering coastal States to introduce binding legislation. They are recommendations with no mandatory legal force, asking authorities operating or intending to operate a VTS to comply with a uniform body of rules, in order to achieve international harmonisation. The situation has changed considerably since 1985: alongside non-compulsory IMO provisions, the SOLAS Convention contains compulsory VTS requirements.

(14) G. PLANT : op. cit., 78.
(15) Aline de BIEVRE : "Responsibility of the VTS authority and possible implication for legal liability". 97.

1. New SOLAS rules

640. - These new rules were adopted at the 68th session of MSC in June 1997, and came into effect on 1st January 1999 (16). The regulations are contained in SOLAS chapter V on safety of navigation, which is currently undergoing complete revision.

Regulation 8.2.1 recalls that "vessel traffic services contribute to the safety of life at sea, safety and efficiency of navigation and the protection of the marine environment, adjacent shore areas, work sites and offshore installations from possible adverse effects of maritime traffic".

There are two requirements for States wishing to set up VTS. They must first of all be justified by the volume of traffic or degree of risk presented by navigation in a particular zone. They also have to follow IMO guidelines wherever possible.

Article 8.2 has been drafted in such a way as to strike a balance between the traditional principle of freedom of navigation and coastal State interests (17). Article 8.2.3 indicates that use of a VTS may be made mandatory only within territorial seas. According to article 8.2.4, contracting States must endeavour to secure the participation in any VTS of ships flying their flag, and their compliance with its provisions; Finally, Article 8.2.5 indicates that "nothing in this regulation or the guidelines adopted by the Organisation shall prejudice the rights and duties of governments under international law or the legal regimes of straits used for international navigation and archipelagic sea lanes".

2. IMO Resolutions

641. - SOLAS regulations refer to IMO guidelines contained in Resolution A.857 of 3 December 1997, which revokes Resolution A.578. This new text defines the principles and general operational provisions applying to VTS. It comprises two annexes, one containing guidelines and criteria for VTS, and the other containing guidelines on recruitment, qualifications and training of VTS operators.

These regulations are far more precise than Resolution A.578, introducing new definitions and concepts, such as interaction, responsibility and the possible participation of pilots as users and providers of information. There are plans in the fairly near future to give this Resolution mandatory force, by incorporating it in a new Regulation 12 of SOLAS chapter V.

a) Establishment of VTS

A State intending to establish a VTS is bound by several constraints. First, it needs to carry out broad-based consultations, in particular among seafarers, in order to find out their opinion about the need for such a system and its operation. This prior cooperation contributes to effective implementation of the VTS, and ensures the commitment of all those involved, and their full participation in the procedures to be followed.

A dozen criteria have to be applied before any decision is taken. It is important to assess the general risk of accidents, the volume of traffic in the area to be covered, the need to protect the environment against discharge of dangerous substances, the effects of the VTS and its economic impact on users and the maritime community, the configuration of the existing or expected traffic and traffic organisation system, and existing or intended means of communication and aids to navigation in the area.

---

(16) Resolution MSC.65 (68) adopted on 4 June 1997 and IMO. MSC 68/23, 12 June 1997, par. 3.10.
(17) "New safety rules on vessel traffic services come into force in 1999". Lloyd's List, 3 June 1997.

These precautions are not intended to discourage States from setting up VTS, but to ensure the best conditions for their implementation. The State may divide a VTS into sectors, if possible indicating their boundaries on nautical documents.

b) VTS operation

642. - When a VTS comes into operation, a number of rules and procedures must be observed.

• Authority's obligations
There are four obligations for an authority introducing a VTS. It must define the geographical scope, and declare it formally as a VTS coverage area. At the same time, it must indicate the categories of ships whose participation is required, and the centres in charge of VTS functions. The authority must then ensure that operators possess the necessary qualifications and have received specialised training to perform their tasks, in particular that they are able to communicate properly in English, commonly regarded as the working language throughout the maritime world. The VTS authority must also see to it that all aids to navigation, pilotage and traffic organisation are consistent. Finally, information is vital to the proper functioning of the system. It is issued in the form of publications for seafarers, which must contain all details concerning the VTS, the limits of the VTS area, ships concerned, services provided and procedures to be followed.

• Operational procedures
These apply to both onshore centres and ships.

The ship is responsible for entering into contact with the VTS centre. This link provides identification of the ship, and an exchange of basic information about its destination and the type of cargo it is carrying. Once it has entered the VTS area, the ship must provide a permanent radio watch on the onshore centre frequency. In some cases it may need to report its passage at certain points and certain times, in accordance with precise instructions.

Meanwhile, the VTS centre also has certain obligations. Any message sent to a ship must indicate clearly whether it contains information, advice or instructions. If it simply providing information, bulletins in a standard format must contain only details essential to safe navigation. If the VTS includes reporting obligations, there must be a clear and straightforward procedure for their submission. Reports must be concise and limited in number, so as not to raise difficulties for ship personnel. The ship and VTS centre may in certain circumstances agree on a routeing plan that provides for the time of arrival in the VTS area or departure from a mooring place within this area. The ship must try to comply with the plan, which may be amended in accordance with a standardised procedure.

In general, care should be taken that VTS operations do not impinge on the powers traditionally exercised by the shipmaster to ensure the safety of his ship, or do not detract from relations between master and pilot.

C - OTHER PROVISIONS

643. - IMO regulations are completed and detailed in two other publications.

The IALA VTS Manual, issued for the first time in 1993 and revised in 1998, offers valuable information to all authorities providing or intending to establish a VTS. It is also of interest to teaching establishments and VTS users (18).

(18) IALA : "Vessel Traffic Services Manual", St Germain en Laye, France. June 1998.

The IALA/IAPH /IMPA World VTS Guide provides clear, accurate information to shipmasters, seafarers and other interested parties, in the form of charts and texts about VTS centre navigation requirements throughout the world. It was approved by IMO in circular MSC 586 of 29 April 1992 (19) and is available from the Internet Website (http://www.worldvtsguide.org/).

III - SHIP REPORTING OBLIGATIONS

644. - The effectiveness of a VTS depends very much on ship reporting requirements. There are three types of reports involving safety at sea:
- Reports facilitating organisation of maritime traffic within a VTS area: sailing plan, position or deviation reports, final report;
- Reports on an incident at sea: loss at sea of packages containing hazardous goods, or discharge of oil, harmful substances or marine pollutants;
- Finally, special reports on defects or deficiencies in hull, machinery or equipment, insufficiencies in manning, or any other factors that could affect safety at sea.

To prevent shipmasters being confused, IMO has adopted various recommendations, laying down general principles for ship reporting systems and requirements (20). These provisions offer standard reporting formats and implementation procedures.   Essential requirements include the need for reports to be concise and simple, to use English wherever possible, the Standard Marine Navigation Vocabulary and International Code of Signals, and finally to be written and submitted as quickly as possible, particularly when safety and pollution issues are involved.

A - IMO CONVENTIONS

1. COLREG Convention

The COLREG Convention of 1972 stipulates several obligations for ships intentionally entering a traffic separation scheme adopted by IMO (cf Regulation 10). Provisions could include ship reports upon entering or leaving the TSS.

2. SOLAS Convention

645. - Regulation V/2 of the SOLAS Convention of 1974 concerns danger messages. The master of any ship finding itself in the presence of direct dangers to navigation is to "communicate the information by all the means at his disposal to ships in the vicinity, and also to the competent authorities at the first point on the coast with which he can communicate".

A new Regulation 7.1 in chapter VII, which came into force on 1st January 1994, requires incidents involving dangerous goods to be reported. If any incident occurs that could lead to the loss overboard of such goods, the shipmaster or any other person in charge of the ship must report the particulars without delay and to the fullest extent possible to the nearest coastal State.

(19) F. WEEKS : "World Vessel Traffic Service Guide". Safety at Sea International, March 1996, 23.
(20) Resolution A. 648 adopted on 19 Oct. 1989 entitled "General principles for ship reporting systems and ship reporting requirements, including Guidelines for reporting incidents involving dangerous goods, harmful substances and/or marine pollutants.
Cf also Resolution MSC.43 (64), "Guidelines and criteria for ship reporting systems". adopted on 9 Dec. 1994.

Finally, a new Regulation 8.1 in chapter V, adopted in May 1994 (21) allows ship reporting systems to be made mandatory.

a) Regulation 8.1

According to Regulation 8.1.a, a ship reporting system is to be applied by all ships, certain categories of ships or ships carrying certain dangerous cargoes, in accordance with the provisions of each system, when adopted and implemented in accordance with IMO guidelines and criteria. For certain commentators (22), this provision appears to conflict with article 22 of the LOS Convention, according to which IMO's chief role is to provide simple advice on the implementation of a "ships' routeing system".

Regulation 8.1.d stipulates that the initiation of action to implement a ship reporting system is the responsibility of the governments concerned. Any such system must be capable of facilitating traffic and helping ships by providing them with the information they need.

By giving mandatory force to IMO-adopted ship reporting systems, the SOLAS amendments of May 1994 require ships entering a VTS area or using such services to give their position, identity and other information. This measure allows the progress of their route inside the VTS area to be monitored.

Regulation 8.1.i requires all reporting systems to be consistent with international law, including the relevant provisions of the LOS Convention. Participation is to be free of charge for all ships concerned (cf Regulation 8.1.k).

Article 8.1 asks States to refer to the guidelines and criteria adopted by IMO for the implementation of ship reporting systems, including those contained in Resolutions MSC 43 of 9 December 1994 and A.648 of 19 October 1989.

b) Implementation of Regulation 8.1

646. - France and Australia were the firs two countries to implement the new SOLAS regulation. Their proposals were discussed in September 1995 by the NAV subcommittee (23) and adopted by IMO on 30 May 1996 in the form of an MSC Resolution (24).

• Protection of the Australian Great Barrier Reef

Regarded as an ecologically sensitive zone, the Torres Strait and the inner route of the Great Barrier Reef present a specific risk for navigation. There are clear grounds for a maritime traffic management scheme.

The reporting system, which came into force on 1st January 1997, applies to all ships 50 metres or more in length, and to all ships carrying dangerous cargoes. Three types of information have to be sent by VHF voice communication to the Hay Point centre: reports on entry into and departure from the VTS area, intermediate position reports for ships in

(21) - IMO, MSC 59/33,
- NAV 37/25 Section 14,
- LEG 67/8,
- LEG 68/5 and
- MSC 63/3 Add. 1. 17 Sept. 1993.
Cf also Ch. YOUNG : "Mandatory Ship Reporting Systems and the International Maritime Organization". 23rd Conference of IALA - Traffic Management and VTS, Feb. 19 - March 1, 1994. Honolulu Hawai.
(22) G. PLANT : "IMO moves follow uncertain course". Lloyd's List, 18 Dec. 1996.
(23) IMO NAV 41/23, 19 Oct. 1995, 5-7. Cf also "Traffic Control". Lloyd's List, 2 Sept. 1995.
(24) Resolution MSC.52 (66). "Mandatory Ship Reporting Systems", in MSC/66/24/Add 1.

transit, giving their identity, position and any variation from the previous speed notified, deficiency reports for disabled ships or those suffering from a failure or breakdown affecting safety (25).

• Ushant VTS

More than 115 ships every day sail through the waters around the island of Ushant, off the Breton coast of France. This area also presents navigational difficulties because of its fierce currents and strong winds. The reporting system covers a circular area 33 miles in radius, centred on Ushant radar tower, and it applies to all ships of more than 300 gross tonnage.

Information to be sent by VHF voice communication to the VTS comprises the ship's name, its IMO identity number, position and speed, in addition to details of deficiencies, damage, failings or restrictions (26). The system, which came into force on 30 November 1996, can follow ships on radar. In 1995, the French authorities were able to identify only 24 000 out of 42 000 vessels.

3. SAR Convention of 1979

647. - Chapter 6 of this Convention contains recommendations on implementing ship reporting systems in any search and rescue regions, and the operational requirements to be satisfied by such systems. States which have signed the SAR Convention are asked to take joint steps to establish mandatory provisions.

4. MARPOL Convention of 1973

648. - Article 8 of this Convention contains provisions concerning reports on incidents involving harmful substances.

Each signatory must make "all arrangements necessary for an appropriate officer or agency to receive and process all reports on incidents" (article 8.2). It must also "notify the organisation with complete details of such arrangements for circulation to other parties and member States". A State receiving a report under these provisions is to "relay the report without delay to the administration of the ship involved, and any other State which may be affected" (article 8.3).

These procedural rules apply to flag States which have signed the Convention and whose ships are on the high seas, or in the EEZ or territorial seas of a coastal State. Indirectly, they involve the shipmaster, who retains considerable latitude in gauging the seriousness of an incident. In practice, reports have tended to be sent only when major problems arise, and there could also be delays in forwarding information.

Drawing a lesson from the *Braer* disaster in January 1993, the Donaldson report recommended amending MARPOL, specifying the situations in which reporting should be made mandatory (27).

---

(25) "Ship reporting schemes set for approvals". Lloyd's List, 14 Sept. 1995.
(26) G. PLANT : "Why curbs on navigation get a green light". Lloyd's List, 11 Dec. 1996.
(27) Report of Lord Donaldson's Inquiry into the prevention of pollution from merchant shipping. "Safer ships, cleaner seas". HMSO, London, May 1994, 240-242.

B - MAREP

649. - Other international instruments also refer to ship reporting systems. One of the best known is the Maritime Reporting (MAREP) scheme, established under a Franco-British agreement on safety of navigation in the English Channel. This agreement, which came into force on 1st January 1979, and was promulgated by IMO, targets ships of at least 1 600 gross tonnage carrying dangerous goods and oil. Such ships must give their position, speed and direction at the entrance to the Dover and Casquets traffic separation schemes. Shipmasters must report any damage that has occurred, and the type of cargo carried.

Based on voluntary participation by ships sailing through the Channel, the MAREP procedure has had worthwhile effects on safety. Such effects are limited, however, by the non-compulsory nature of traffic management arrangements. A survey carried out by British Coastguards in October 1993 showed that only 10 per cent of ships going through the Straits of Dover actually contacted coastal stations (28).

In November 1993, the MAREP system was extended on the British side to include all ships of more than 300 gross tonnage, irrespective of their cargoes. At the same time, IMO recommended extension of the system to other maritime zones off the coasts of the United Kingdom. Loaded oil tankers have to report to an onshore station at least an hour before entering any of the zones to be avoided, and upon leaving it.

C - EU DIRECTIVE

650. - The most comprehensive regulations are undoubtedly contained in EU Directive 93/75, adopted by the Council of Ministers on 13 September 1993. This Directive contains a series of reporting requirements for ships carrying dangerous or polluting goods from or to EU ports.

1. Origin of the 1993 Directive

Adopted barely eight months after the *Braer* disaster off the Shetland Islands, the 1993 Directive did not spring into existence *ex nihilo*. It is based on a precedent, a technical study and a common policy.

a) Precedent: Council Directive 79/116

This Directive, adopted by the Council of Ministers in 1978, (29), required tanker ships of more than 1 600 gross tonnage entering Community ports to give notice to the competent port state authorities, complete an inspection form, use radio and radar station services, and report any incident posing a threat to safety at sea.

b) Study: COST 301

The COST 301 Project (30), launched in January 1983, was intended to examine the technical and financial possibilities of improving VTS networks in European ports, their approaches, and coastal waters up to 200 miles from the shore. The work, which ended in

---

(28) DONALDSON Report . op. cit., 232, Par. 15.30.
(29) Directive 79/116 concerning the minimum requirements for certain tankers entering or leaving Community Ports. OJEC, 8 Feb. 1979, n° L 33/33.
(30) COST stands for "Communittee on Science and Technology". 301 is the number of the project.

July 1986, resulted in the formulation of a set of conclusions and recommendations for the attention of Community bodies (31). Legal issues were dealt with in a separate study, which was subsequently examined by the European Commission's Legal Service (32).

c) Common Policy on Safe Seas

The European Commission outlined an action programme to improve the safety of maritime transport in a White Paper, adopted in December 1992, and in a Communication published on 24 February 1993 (33).

Several of these measures related to the safety of navigation, improvement of which was to be achieved mainly through the establishment of mandatory ship reporting systems and development of VTS networks within the Community.

This action culminated in the adoption on 13 September 1993 of Directive 93/75 specifying minimum requirements for vessels carrying dangerous or polluting goods. It came into force on 13 September 1995 (34).

2. Content of 1993 Directive

651. - The scope of application of this new Directive is much wider than the 1978 Directive on tanker ships. It covers oil tankers, gas and chemical tankers, cargo ships and passenger ships carrying dangerous or polluting products.

a) Dissemination of information on cargoes

The new European Directive acknowledges the need for the broadest dissemination of information on cargoes, in order to prevent or minimise accidents. Member States are accordingly to designate a competent authority, to which shipmasters and operators are to report.

b) Use of VTS and pilotage

Ships entering or leaving a Community port must use VTS and, where appropriate, pilotage services. This provision is intended primarily to avoid repetition of the accident to the *Aegean Sea*, which sank in 1993 off La Corunna, in the absence of a pilot on board.

(31) Cf : KOBURGER : op. cit., chap IV, 57-75.
- GLANSDORP, KEMP, GOODWIN, TREFSON : "Quantification of navigational risk in European waters". Journal of Navigation Vol. 39, N° 1 January 1986, 90.
- A. de BIEVRE, J.F. KEMP : "The environment, COST 301 and coastal State policy". Journal of Navigation Vol. 39, N° 3 September 1986, 310.
- "Safety of shipping in European Waters - The COST 301 Project". RIN/NI Seminar, 12 December 1984. 1985, The Nautical Institute, London.
(32) A. de BIEVRE : "Vessel Traffic Services and the law on responsibility and liability". Cf S. MANKABADY : op. cit., 119 note 5.
(33) Commission of the European Communities. COM (93) 66 final, 23 Feb. 1993.
(34) Council Directive 93/75 EEC of 13 Sept. 1993 concerning minimum requirement for vessels bound for or leaving Community ports and carrying dangerous or polluting goods. OJEC, 22 Oct. 1993, n° 247/19.
See also - Gillian SPROUL : "Dangerous or polluting goods. Towards safer seas". Lloyd's List, 22 October 1993.
- Hazardous Cargo Bulletin, August 1995, 12.

c) *Reporting requirements*

In the case of any incident or event occurring at sea and threatening the coasts and related interests of a member State, the master of the ship concerned must provide a full report, supplying the competent authority promptly with information on the cargoes being carried and the incident itself.

The threatened State may then place restrictions on the ship's movements, or require it to take a particular direction. It may also require the shipmaster to supply information on the ship, its equipment and crew, and confirm the presence on board of a cargo loading plan. The competent authority then communicates details of the incident and ship particulars to the authorities of other States under threat.

d) *Commission role*

The European Commission has the task of presenting a more comprehensive reporting system, for all ships in transit along the coasts of Community members, including electronic data-exchange systems between ships and onshore stations.

D - CURRENT EUROPEAN PRIORITIES

652. - The 8th International Symposium on VTS, held in Rotterdam in April 1996; emphasised the growing importance of organising traffic and intensifying control of navigation over the coming years (35).

Europe will be a driving force in this development. An agreement on safety at sea and prevention of marine pollution was signed in Paris on 26 January 1994, confirming this trend. The five signatories, all Channel or North Sea coastal States (France, United Kingdom, Belgium, Netherlands and Germany), decided to make reporting mandatory for all ships entering this zone on and from 1st January 1996, under the terms of the new SOLAS Regulation 8.1. Two European projects worth discussing are EUROREP and VTMIS.

1. EUROREP

653. - There is a proposal for a Council Directive on the setting-up of a European Vessel Reporting (EUROREP) system in the maritime zones of Community member States. This would require any ship carrying dangerous or polluting goods towards a Community port or in transit through European waters to make itself known, report the nature of its cargo and give notice of its intended route.

Given the technical, legal and financial difficulties of implementing such a project, the Commission intends to proceed in two stages. First, the reporting obligation would apply only to ships flying the flag of a Community State and foreign ships bound for or leaving a Community port, and only subsequently to all foreign ships carrying dangerous or polluting

(35) P. KENT : "VTS 96. The 8th International Symposium on Vessel Traffic Services. IALA Bulletin 1996/2, 4.

goods in transit in the zone (36). The Donaldson report (37) is particularly critical of the EUROREP project. It argues that the scope of the reporting requirement is too wide to be respected. The measure will very soon prove inoperative, given the impossibility of identifying ships violating its provisions, and therefore of exercising any deterrent policing powers. The system is also considered expensive and premature, having been devised before the first lessons could be drawn from the Directive 93/75.

2. VTMIS

654. - Several projects have been examined since 1993 in Europe. The aim in each case is to improve the quality and availability of information of use to various parties involved in the maritime sector; with the intention of increasing the safety and effectiveness of maritime traffic and environmental protection.

Leading current EU projects comprise:
- Information Services in the Atlantic - DGXIII (ATLANTIS), aimed at defining the need and feasibility of an information system along the Atlantic Arc (38);
- European Permanent Traffic Observatory - DGVII (EPTO), a pilot study of ways of systematic observation of traffic flows, to provide a framework for the processing of radar data, in order to identify and classify symptomatic events occurring in a radar coverage zone, and analyse and assess VTS radar performances (39).

The aim of these projects is to find out whether the service rendered by VTS as they are currently defined needs to be simplified by extending their scope or coverage area. Following these investigations, the EU has undertaken a clarification of the Vessel Traffic Management Information System (VTMIS), incorporating services provided by VTS with those proposed under the Trans-European Transport Network programme (40).

IV - LIABILITY

655. - Issues of liability arise, following an incident at sea in which a VTS user or authority is at fault, and causing harm to third parties.

Such accidents are more common that might appear. Several cases of collision or grounding have occurred within a VTS coverage area. The most serious include collisions between the *European Gateway* and the *Speedling Vanguard* in December 1982 near Harwich, between the *Bovenkerk* and the *Antonio Carlos* on the Elba, or between the *Arizona Standard* and the *Oregon Standard* near San Francisco, and the groundings of the *Christos Bitas* and the *Bridgewater* on rocks off Milford Haven.

(36) Commission proposal presented on 17 Dec. 1993, COM (93) 647 final SYN 93 491. OJEC 22, 22 Jan. 1994.
(37) Donaldson Report, op. cit., 239, Par. 15.67 à 15.69.
(38) European Union. Directorate of Regional Policy. Atlantis Program. General Specifications for an Atlantic Arc vessel traffic service. Final Report, version 3.4, July 1995.
(39) - G. BEDGOT : "Le projet EPTO". Navigation, vol. 42, n° 166, avril 1994, 166-176.
- J. PRUNIERAS : "The European Permanent Traffic Observatory (EPTO) Project". Navigation, vol. 42, n° 168, Oct. 1994, 444-457.
(40) J. PRUNIERAS : "Réflexions sur le concept de VTMIS". Navigation, vol. 44, n° 176, Oct. 1996, 409-424.

One of the difficulties comes from the fact that there is no international maritime legislation laying down rules on the matter. IMO Resolution A.857, which contains VTS guidelines, does not deal with the question of liability. The liability aspect of an accident following compliance with VTS guidance is an important consideration, which can be decided only on a case-by-case basis in accordance with national law.

This reference to the laws of each individual State has encouraged the emergence of a wide variety of legal regimes, hardly likely to bring about harmonious development of VTS worldwide, and a source of confusion for shipmasters using such services.

A - PRINCIPLE OF STATE LIABILITY

656. - Many national legal systems allow for the liability of public authorities in the establishment or operation of a VTS, if an accident occurs. In principle, a State is liable for activities over which it has control. Its liability may be involved if damage results from errors or negligence in the performance of a public service or the exercise of control over such a service (42).

Three examples in international law illustrate the link between powers of control and the liability of a State exercising such powers: the Brussels Convention of 29 November 1969 relating to Intervention on the High Seas in Cases of Oil Pollution Casualties (INTERVENTION), the Convention on Civil Liability for Oil Pollution Damage (CLC), signed on the same date, and the UN Law of the Sea Convention.

1. INTERVENTION 69 Convention

Article 6 of this Convention recognises the direct responsibility of a State taking steps that go beyond what is "reasonably necessary" to prevent, minimise or eliminate threats of pollution following an accident at sea. If such measures cause injury to a third party, it is entitled to demand compensation from the State. Article 8 and Annex d provide detailed conciliation and arbitration procedures for settling disputes. The criteria for assessing the reasonable and urgent nature of measures are set out in article 5. They include "the extent and probability of imminent damage (...), and the likelihood of those measures being effective, and the extent of damage which may be caused by such measures" (43).

2. CLC 69 Convention

657. - This Convention does not recognise the direct liability of a coastal State regarding navigation. It contains a mechanism for objective liability channelled on the shipowner in the event of an accident. According to article 3.2.c, the owner may be exonerated if he can show that pollution damage "was wholly caused by the negligence or other wrongful act of any government or other authority responsible for the maintenance of

(41) T. HUGHES : "VTS - are we ready for the new millennium?" BIMCO Bulletin. Vol. 93, n° 1, 1998, 52-27.
(42) Aline de BIEVRE : "Responsibility of the VTS authority and possible implications for legal liability". The Nautical Institute, London, 1985.
(43) A. de ROUW : "Emergency response to maritime pollution incidents, legal aspects". The Law of the Sea Institute, 25th Annual Conference. University of Hawai. 1991.

lights or other navigational aids in the exercise of that function". The expression "other navigational aids" remains general enough to comprise VTS established by the coastal State. The State could be held liable for malfunctioning of such services , either exclusively or jointly with the ship whose error has caused the pollution (44).

3. LOS 82 Convention

658. - Article 192 of this Convention lays a general obligation on all States to "protect and preserve the marine environment". Article 194 defines the steps to be taken for "preventing accidents and dealing with emergencies, ensuring the safety of operations at sea, preventing intentional and unintentional discharges, and regulating the design, construction, equipment, operation and manning of such installations or devices". VTS and the personnel or equipment needed for their operation are part of the "measures taken". Some commentators consider that failure to comply with these obligations constitutes a breach of the Convention, which could involve the liability of parties responsible for such failure (45).

Irrespective of the obligations laid on it by international law, the State remains responsible for defining conditions of liability for its VTS under its domestic law,. It may decide to accept only limited liability, even if gross negligence is committed by VTS operators. This would be similar to the regime that applies, for example, to defective functioning of lights or other navigational aids. In general, a State acts as its own insurer, and will be reluctant to accept more liability for VTS than it is prepared to for similar activities. It may also expect to have a claim on the shipowner, who benefits from limitation of liability, regardless of which party is initially found guilty (46).

In conclusion, as long as maritime law continues to assign a shipmaster full legal and financial responsibility for the conduct of his ship, except in the event of serious negligence or error by the public authorities, the coastal State will have no incentive to improve the system for organising shipping, in case there is a change in the legal framework of its actions and its liability.

B - VTS OPERATOR LIABILITY

659. - Conditions of liability of VTS operators vary substantially in different parts of the world. However, behind this diversity of professional status and the services supplied, a few general principles may be drawn from the systems established in France, the United Kingdom and the United States.

1. Civil liability and professional status of VTS operators

A VTS operator depends legally on the authority employing him. The first part of this chapter showed that this authority could be a governmental maritime administration, public or private port authority, pilotage organisation or any combination of such entities. Two extreme situations will be examined here: where the operator is a government officer, and where he is employed by a private organisation.

(44) M. REMOND-GOUILLOUD : "Droit Maritime" Pedone 1988, 92, n° 167.
(45) E. GOLD : "Marine hazards and casualties : the need for Vessel Traffic Management". Proceedings of the 19th International Law of the Sea Conference. Cardiff, 1985. University of Hawai, 480.
(46) E. GOLD : "Vessel Traffic regulation : The interface of maritime safety and operational freedom". Journal of Maritime Law and Commerce, Vol. 14, n° 1, Jan. 1983, 17.

a) Government-employed VTS operator

This situation is comparable to the international system of air traffic control. In most States that signed the 1944 Chicago Convention, the air traffic controller is a public employee (47). His employer bears civil liability for errors committed in performance of the service.

States may evade their responsibilities by applying the theory of sovereign immunity. However, most have set up procedures for the submission of civil compensation claims, if their officers or the organisations employing them commit faults.

In France, in the event of an accident, the administration may be liable for malfunctioning of certain maritime services (48). Coastal or port VTS are not excluded, as shown by a decision handed down by the French supreme administrative court (*Conseil d'Etat*) on 28 May 1982, criticising the port authority for inadequate surveillance of ship movements. This verdict institutes a real liability for risks and an obligation of results, in respect to safety at sea (49).

b) Privately employed VTS operator

A VTS operator may be employed by a private organisation, as is the case in United Kingdom ports. According to the principles of common law, the port authority has to show reasonable diligence in order to ensure that ships can use the port in complete safety, in the performance of authorised activities. In general, it is civilly liable for faults committed by marine traffic controllers or port officials. Under certain circumstances, it may restrict its liability with regard to ships outside its geographical area of competence.

A port VTS operator may also face charges in a personal capacity. Unlike a pilot, he cannot escape from the civil liability that results from his faults by providing surety. Theoretically, his liability is unlimited. The port authority may dismiss any of its employees provided that due process is respected. This threat is not without a certain influence on the behaviour of port VTS operators in performing their duties (50).

2. Liability for services provided by operator

660. - VTS operators may provide ships with information, advice or instructions. In the first two cases, the shipmaster remains free to decide on his actions. In the third case, he is no longer free. Within the VTS coverage area, he may also be required to submit reports. These obligations raise the problem of relations between ship and shore, and bear on one of the fundamental principles of traditional maritime law, according to which decisions on navigation remain the sole prerogative of the shipmaster (51).

---

(47) See R. BOOTSMA and K. POLDERMAN : "ATS and VTS - Some observations towards a synthesis". Journal of Navigation, vol. 40, n° 1, January 1987.
(48) J. GROSDIDIER DE MATONS : "La responsabilité de l'Etat pour le fonctionnement de certains services maritimes". DMF, 1968.
(49) R. REZENTHEL, A. CAUBERT : "Le Conseil d'Etat et la sécurité maritime". Revue MER, Jan. 1983, 58. Cf also, Revue MER, June 1983, 44.
(50) A.G. CORBET : "Development of vessel traffic services : Legal considerations". Marit. Pol. Mgmt., 1989, vol. 16, n° 4, 277-292.
(51) E. GOLD : "Legal liability aspects of VTS systems - Who is to blame when things go wrong". The Nautical Institute, Pilotage, London, 1990, 216-221.

a) VTS operator's liability for information or advice

When a State voluntarily sets up a VTS including provision of information or advice for ships, it is subject to the same obligations as for aids to navigation.

Ships entering a VTS coverage area are entitled to be able to rely on information about prevailing conditions of navigation to be of proper quality. If accidents occur as a result of the supply of incorrect information or failure to indicate a hazard, the onshore operator may be considered not to have displayed due diligence, and the authority operating the VTS therefore bears liability.

In common law, the degree of diligence increases with the level of danger, to be assessed reasonably in each particular situation. This requirement of vigilance is combined with the duty of watchkeeping and warning in an emergency (52).

b) VTS operator's liability for instructions

When a VTS provides a traffic organisation service, the shipmaster forfeits part of his prerogatives in conducting his ship. He is under a dual obligation: first, to inform the operator by reporting the movements of his ship, immediately on entering the VTS control zone; second, to follow the operator's instructions.

Under English law, these obligations have to be carried out in a reasonable and intelligent way. The master retains a degree of freedom in applying the instructions given by the onshore operator. In other words, VTS instructions are no excuse for not observing anti-collision rules. They are additional, and cannot replace good seamanship. In practice, port VTS operators are very cautious about giving instructions to ships, for fear of laying themselves more easily open to claims for civil liability. This has to a large extent prevented the development of maritime traffic organisation services in the United Kingdom (53).

The opposite phenomenon is to be found in the United States, where the Port and Tanker Safety Act of 1978 gives the Coast Guard the right to organise shipping movements in reputedly dangerous areas. Some have compared the situation of VTS operators to that of pilots. Unlike their French or British counterparts, American pilots are not onboard advisors: they issue instructions to shipmasters, which must be obeyed. However, clear legal precedents require the master to take steps to prevent any damage to the ship and its cargo. Whether there is a pilot on board or whether he receives instructions from land, the master is always responsible for much of the safe conduct of his ship. His duty of vigilance will therefore need to be even greater if instructions come from a VTS operator who, unlike a pilot, is not on board and cannot so effectively estimate the consequences of instructions sent to the ship (54).

Ultimately, the master cannot completely escape liability unless he proves that the accident was caused directly by an incorrect instruction from the onshore operator, and that it was not reasonable in the circumstances to take any initiative to avoid the accident.

(52) A.G. CORBET : op. cit., 282.
(53) S. MANKABADY : op. cit., 127.
(54) B. BOLAND : op. cit., 493.

C - QUEST FOR UNIFORM LEGAL REGIME

661. - The problem of VTS liabilities reveals a wide diversity of situations. There is no uniform legal regime to define the operator's and shipmaster's obligations, the interdependent relations that must exist between them, and their respective liabilities.

Is it possible to imagine a harmonised international approach ? This is the question which the COST 301 project has attempted to answer at a European level. Three alternatives have been considered: direct proportionate civil liability of the shipowner and VTS authority, automatic channelling of liability on the shipowner, in other words making him civilly liable for the onshore operator, and automatic channelling of liability on the VTS authority.

Despite the advantages of this third option, which has the benefit of clarity, the COST 301 task force finally came out in favour of the *status quo*, because of the reluctance of port authorities to accept new responsibilities (55).

CONCLUSION: Towards reinforcement of maritime traffic management

662. - Several recent accidents, including the collision between the *Nassia* and the *Shipbroker* in the Bosphorus in March 1994 (56), led to fresh discussion of the control and regulation of shipping traffic. The Donaldson report also emphasised the importance of increased surveillance in areas with high volumes of traffic.

The current trend is clearly towards reinforcement of VTS powers over ships.

Numerous observers acknowledge that the law of the sea now offers new opportunities to States to reinforce control of navigation in their coastal waters. This realignment of international liabilities in the area of safety at sea and preservation of the marine environment should, in their view, foster the development of active VTS, exercising a certain power of decision over the conduct of ships, at least taking the form of mandatory ship reporting in national legislation and regional agreements.

However, this doctrinal shift cannot remove all the obstacles standing in the way of the development of VTS throughout the world.

To begin with, there are the legal difficulties. However apparently innovative the 1993 Directive may seem, its provisions pay scrupulous attention to the principles of international customary law, by imposing reporting obligations only on ships coming from or bound for EU ports (58). States most favourable to compulsory VTS, like the United States, are careful not to regulate the passage of ships in transit outside territorial seas (59).

Has international law on control of maritime navigation now become adequate, or is further progress necessary ? Certain commentators are of this opinion, considering that the LOS Convention does not provide sufficient legal basis for the establishment of compulsory VTS. Problems also arise in connection with performance and jurisdiction in the event of breaches: are they the concern of the flag State or of the coastal State ?

---

(55) Seaways - March 1987, 17. Cf also A.G. CORBET : op. cit., 288-289.
(56) Lloyd's List, 15 March 1994, 3.
On the *Braer* : Cf Georges SUTHERLAND : "Management and control of shipping around Shetland". Marine Policy. September 1993, 371-379.
(57) Edgard GOLD : "Vessel Traffic Services". Journal of Navigation, Vol. 38, N° 1, January, 1985, 71-76.
- Aline de BIEVRE :
• "Navigational safety in European waters". The Journal of Navigation, vol. 36, May 1983, n° 2, 169-182.
• "International legal strategies to control pollution from ships". The Irish Sea : a resource at Risk. Joh, C. Sweeney, 1989, chp 17, 174-192.
(58) IMO. LEG 67/8/1. Add. 1, 22 July 1992. Annex 1.
(59) IMO. LEG 67/8/1. Add 3, 1 Sept. 1992.

The problem of reporting obligations will be finally resolved when the installation of transponders and radar equipment becomes mandatory on board ships, particularly if such equipment can be programmed with specific information for each voyage, such as type of cargo and destination). Human intervention will be needed only when the ship enters the area covered by a VTS or when the transponder breaks down.

Questions relating to the VTS operator's liability will remain to be settled. Absence of a uniform legal regime is cruelly lacking, and explains the reluctance of VTS authorities to give instructions to ships, for fear of being liable if an accident occurs (61).

In addition, the establishment and operation of VTS represent a substantial financial outlay, which has to be borne by coastal States. In the Straits of Dover, for example, the whole surveillance system is financed by the United Kingdom and France, whereas many neighbouring States obtain substantial benefits from the improvement in safety. The United Kingdom has proposed that IMO should consider establishing a set of principles for charging users the cost of maritime infrastructure (62). This could include VTS.

Legal and financial difficulties should not obscure the psychological factors that ultimately remain the most important. VTS generally suffer from being regarded with suspicion by nearly all users: shipmasters see them as a threat to their authority, while pilots fear loss of employment. Does the improvement in safety at sea not require, first and foremost, shared motivations among all those with the difficult task of getting ships safely to their destination ? Even compulsory VTS do not remove the need for acceptance and cooperation on board the ships using them.

(60) J. KEMP, A. DE BIEVRE : "Mandatory routeing and mandatory reporting, an environmental view". 8th Internat. Symposium on VTS, Rotterdam, April 15-20, 1996.
(61) P. BARBER : "Vessel Traffic Service Training" Marine Management (Holding). Seminar on Maritime Communication and Control. London, Nov. 1990.
- M. GREY : "Clarifying the role of VTS". BIMCO Bulletin, vol. 89, n° 6, 1994, 30-31.
(62) IMO. LEG 76/INF. 2, 12 Sept. 1997.

CHAPTER 27

Right of intervention

663. - The increasingly dangerous situations that arise at sea have led to the emergence of a new balance, reflected in a shift in the law of the sea, from a maritime conception to a coastal conception. Safety at sea in the broad sense has become a key component of public order, bringing about far-reaching changes in the traditional distribution of powers, to the advantage of coastal States. On the grounds of their legitimate right to self-protection, these States can intervene on the high seas if their territorial integrity is under threat. The arguments are that a coastal state is the most exposed to the risk of pollution, and also that it is best placed to combat such risks, both in its own individual interest and in the general interest of the international community.

This chapter examines the extension of the right of intervention by a coastal state on the high seas. This right is now exercised in three situations: pollution (cf I below), compulsory salvage (II) and the removal of wrecks which constitute a navigational hazard (III).

I - RIGHT OF INTERVENTION IN CASE OF POLLUTION

664. - Given the urgency of preserving the marine environment, international law has come to acknowledge the right of a coastal State to intervene and, under certain circumstances, impose constraints on a ship on the high seas. This power, which overturns the traditional principles of freedom of the high seas, is set down in several international conventions (1). In the view of some commentators, this right already existed in customary form, well before the adoption of these provisions. Whatever its form and origin, the right of intervention is interpreted very extensively by all States anxious to protect their environment.

A - 1958 BRUSSELS CONVENTION AND 1973 LONDON PROTOCOL

Two international instruments have recognised the power of a State to combat accidental pollution outside its territorial waters : the Brussels Convention of 29 November 1969 relating to Intervention on the High Seas in Cases of Oil Pollution Casualties, and a Protocol adopted on 2 November 1973 by the London Conference, extending the provisions of the Brussels Convention to cases of pollution by harmful substances other than oil.

1. Origin

The Brussels Convention was adopted under IMO auspices, shortly after the *Torrey Canyon* disaster. It conferred retroactive legitimacy on the decision taken by the British

(1) R. CHURCHILL, A. LOWE : "The law of the sea". Manchester University Press, 1991, 261.

authorities to bomb the ship on the high seas, in an attempt to set fire to its cargo. This legally dubious move had aroused no international protests when it was carried out (2).

2. Nature and characteristics of the right of intervention

665. - According to article I of the Convention, the parties "may take such measures on the high seas as may be necessary to prevent, mitigate or eliminate grave and imminent danger to their coastline or related interests from pollution or threat of pollution of the sea by oil, following upon a maritime casualty or acts related to such a casualty, hich may reasonably be expected to result in major harmful consequences".

Article II designates as "related interests" any threats to coastal and port maritime activities, fishing activities and the conservation of living marine resources, as well as public health and regional tourist attractions (3).

The London Protocol makes the same provisions for dangers caused by other polluting substances, on a list drawn up by IMO. The State may also exercise the right of intervention in case of pollution by other products not appearing on this list, but it must prove that the substance in question could, under the circumstances prevailing at the time of intervention, constitute a grave and imminent danger, similar to that presented by the listed substances (4).

These two instruments mark a profound change in international law in two ways. First, they create a kind of "state of necessity" which overrides the rule of non-interference on the high seas (5). Second, they depart from the principle of the relative effect of treaties,, since their application is no longer confined to ships sailing under the flags of signatory States, but to any merchant ship, whatever its nationality, carrying dangerous or polluting goods (6).

3. Limitations on the right of intervention

When the INTERVENTION Convention was being drafted, the fear that the exorbitant prerogatives held by coastal States might lead to abuses resulted in the inclusion of numerous limitations on the right of intervention (7). There has to be the probability of grave and imminent danger. There must be a likelihood of danger of catastrophic consequences for the marine environment. The origin of the pollution must be a maritime casualty, defined restrictively by article II "as a collision of ships, stranding or other incident of navigation, or other occurrence on board a ship or external to it resulting in material damage or imminent threat of material damage to a ship or cargo". Warships or other vessels belonging to or operated by the State and used solely for non-commercial government services are excluded from the terms of the Convention.

State powers are not discretionary, either. The Convention lays down very precise conditions of intervention. Before starting, the State must consult "other States affected by the maritime casualty, particularly with the flag State or States" (article III), except in an emergency. Before taking action it must also notify the physical and corporate persons concerned of the

(2) J.P QUENEUDEC : "Les incidences de l'affaire du Torrey Canyon sur le droit de la mer". AFDI, 1968, 712.
(3) P. BIRNIE : "Protection of the marine environment : the public international law approach". CMI. Seminar on Liability for Oil Pollution Damage ; 21-25th Sept. 1992, Genoa.
(4) Cl. DOUAY : "Le droit de la mer et la préservation du milieu marin". RGDIP, 1980, Tome 84, 178-215.
(5) Pr JENNING in "Prevention de la pollution des milieux maritimes", AIDI, 1969, Tome II, 264.
- L.F.E. GOLDIE : "A general view of international environment law. A survey of capabilities, trends and limits". RCADI, 1973, 48-50.
(6) R. RODIERE : "Les tendances contemporaines du droit privé maritime international". RCADI, 1972, II, Vol. 135, 371.
(7) R. M'GONIGLE, M. ZACHER : "Pollution, politics, and international law. Tanker at sea". University of California Press, Berkeley, 1979, 147-167.

proposed measures. It must take account of "any views they may submit", although in an emergency it need not carry out these consultations. Finally, to avoid any arbitrary exercise of the right of intervention, the measures taken must be proportionate to the actual or threatened damage. They must not go beyond what is "reasonably necessary" (cf article V.2).

B - LOS CONVENTION AND EXTENSION OF RIGHT OF INTERVENTION

666. - Following the *Amoco Cadiz* disaster, several States called for an extension of the right of intervention (8).

The *Amoco Cadiz* had shown that the French authorities were unable to intervene effectively because they had not been informed in time of the situation of the ship. So it was important to adapt the right of intervention in order to allow action to be taken as promptly as possible.

Article 221 of the LOS Convention introduced the "right of States, pursuant to international law, both customary and conventional, to take and enforce measures beyond the territorial sea proportionate to the actual or threatened damage to protect their coastline or related interests, including fishing, from pollution or threat of pollution following upon a maritime casualty or acts relating to such a casualty, which may reasonably be expected to result in major harmful consequences".

Compared with INTERVENTION 69, the LOS Convention gives a coastal State greater capacity to take action (9), by removing the condition of grave and imminent danger. On the other hand, it restricts freedom of action by providing a strict definition of an accident at sea, including the requirement of "material damage or imminent threat of material damage to a vessel or cargo".

C - CUSTOMARY RIGHT OF INTERVENTION

667. - As suggested in article 221 of the LOS Convention, international customary law acknowledges the coastal State's exceptional powers on the high seas under certain circumstances.

Several arguments have been advanced to justify this departure from the principle of sole jurisdiction of the flag State. First, there is the existence of "an irreducible right to self-protection in the presence of a grave and imminent danger, where any other resource is absent" (10). Next, there is the principle of freedom of the seas, according to which "freedoms conferred on States on the high seas must be exercised while taking reasonable account of the interest of freedom of the high seas for other States" (11). Finally, there is the state of necessity, which gives the State a fundamental right to see to its own preservation (12).

Whatever the basis for this customary law, an extensive interpretation could confer legitimacy on many departures from the principle of freedom of the seas (13).

(8) JP. BEURIER et CADENAT : "Les 6ème et 7ème sessions de la 3ème conférence sur le droit de la mer". DMF 1978, 652.
(9)A. BOYLE : "Marine Pollution under the Law of the Sea". 79 AJIL 1985, 347-72.
(10) Ch. De VISSCHER : "Travaux préparatoires de l'AIDI sur la prévention de la pollution des milieux marins". AIDI 1969, T. I, vol. 53, 652.
(11) J.Y. MORIN : "La pollution des mers au regard du droit international". RCADI. 1973, 294.
(12) J. BALLENEGGER : "La pollution en droit international". Genève, Droz, 1975, 93-94.
(13) A.C.J. DE ROUW : "Emergency response to maritime pollution incidents : Legal aspects". In the Maritime Environment and Sustainable Development : Law, Policy and Science". 25th Annual Conference of the Law of the Sea Institute. Malmö, 1991, 339-341.

D - NATIONAL LEGISLATIONS

668. - Certain States did not await enforcement of INTERVENTION 69 on 6 May 1975 to start exercising the right of intervention on the high seas in their domestic legal system (14).

In the United States, the Federal Water Pollution Control Act Amendment of 1972 authorises the Coast Guard to remove or sink a damaged ship up to 50 miles from its coasts (15).

A Canadian Act of 26 June 1970 recognises the power of intervention of the maritime authorities when a ship is in distress and threatens to cause pollution of Arctic waters (16).

The grounding of the Liberian tanker *Panther* off the British coast decided the United Kingdom to promulgate legislation on 8 April 1971, allowing the Royal Navy to take action, even on the high seas, to arrest or destroy any ship likely to pollute its coasts (17).

In France, two items of legislative give the authorities the right to intervene beyond territorial waters : the Ministerial Instruction of 23 December 1970 (18) on action against accidental coastal oil pollution (19), and article 16 of Act 76-599 of 7 July 1976 on marine pollution caused by dumping operations by ships and aircraft, and action against accidental marine pollution (20).

Intended to remove certain legal and administrative obstacles that stood in the way of the French authorities in the case of the *Olympic Bravery*, this article repeats the terms of INTERVENTION 69 in order to define the conditions of the right of intervention. The ship-owner may be summoned to take all measures needed to remove potential threats to the French coastline. If such measures are not taken, or fail to produce the expected results by the deadline set, the State may have the necessary steps carried out, or make the owner bear the cost (21).

II - COMPULSORY SALVAGE

669. - The *Amoco Cadiz* disaster was also one of the reasons for changes in international legislation on salvage, traditionally governed by the 1910 Brussels Convention on Assistance and Salvage at sea. This ecological disaster revealed the inadequacies of an international instrument restricted to regulating purely private relations between the ships involved, the salvor and the salvaged, and totally ignoring protection of the coastal State. In the aftermath of the accident, the IMO Council was called upon to draw the necessary legal consequences. The main impetus came from France, which described how the master of the *Amoco Cadiz* had hesitated before having recourse to the services of a salvage company. It believed that the only answer was to adopt a compulsory salvage regime.

---

(14) E. GOLD : "Handbook on Marine Pollution". Gard, Arendal, 1985, 91-111.

(15) Yannis SOULIOSTIS : "Les Etats-Unis et la protection du milieu marin". CERDEM, CNEXO, Rapport n° 6, 1997, 220.

(16) R.S. LEFEBVRE, A. LÉONETTI : "Etude comparative des législations nord-américaines et européennes relatives à la pollution par les hydrocarbures." Le pétrole et la mer. CERDEM, PUB 1976, Paris, 164.

(17) In International Legal Materials, 1971, 584. Comments in ICLQ, 1971, 579-581. See also A. SAMUELS : "Oil pollution". The British Yearbook of International Law, 1971, vol. XLV, 385-391.

(18) Called plan POLMAR. V.J.O. 12 Jan. 1971 and BOMM 1970, 1103 replaced by a Prime Ministerial Circular of Oct. 1978 (J.O. 14 October, 3570).

(19) LANGAVANT and BEURIER : "La lutte contre les pollutions accidentelles". DMF 1976, 520.

(20) JORF, 8 July 1976, 4107.

(21) E. LANGAVANT : "Droit de la mer. Le droit des communications maritimes". Cujas, Paris, 1981, 144.

A - 1989 CONVENTION ON SALVAGE

When the Legal Committee of IMO decided in 1982 to amend the 1910 Convention on Salvage, French efforts were directed towards obtaining international acceptance of the idea of ships in difficulty being forced to accept assistance.

In 1985, after lengthy discussion, the Legal Committee refused to accept this concept (22).

The Convention was signed in London on 28 April 1989, and came into force on 1st July 1996. It seeks mainly to rely on the salvor to protect the marine environment, by giving it the right to "special compensation" when it has carried out operations to prevent or limit environmental damage (cf article 14) (23). It also recognises coastal State rights regarding salvage. According to article 9, the Convention does not affect any measures taken by a State under international law to protect its coastline or related interests against the threat of pollution, and specifically to issue instructions on salvage operations. Article 11 also clearly invites signatories to offer aid to private salvors (24).

B - FRENCH COMPULSORY SALVAGE PRACTICE

670. - Certain States assumed the right of intervention in salvage operations well before the 1989 Convention came into force. Immediately after the *Amoco Cadiz* disaster, France adopted a series of measures to impose assistance on ships in danger near its coasts. While the legal implications of such assistance operations are still not clearly defined, the procedure has already proved its practical effectiveness on several occasions (25).

In material terms, assistance is provided by two deep-sea tugs specially chartered by the French Navy, and stationed in Brest and Cherbourg. Reliance on the services of a private company has been justified by the fact that the French authorities had no vessels capable of towing large ships in distress in bad weather (26).

Intervention by the French Navy is facilitated by the existence of a compulsory reporting system. Under the terms of the Decree of 24 March 1978 on action against accidental pollution (27), the competent body must be given notice of the date and time of entry into territorial waters of a ship carrying petroleum products, its position, route and speed and the nature of its cargo (cf article 1). Any accident at sea to an oil tanker sailing within 50 miles of the French coast must also be reported (cf article 2). Article 63 of the Merchant Navy Disciplinary and Penal Code lays down severe penalties for any shipmaster failing to observe these reporting requirements. The 1978 Decree requires salvors to inform the maritime authority of any operations they undertake, and to warn it of the type of damage suffered by a ship in difficulty (cf article 3).

Compulsory assistance is based on article 16 of the Act of 7 July 1976, amended by the Act of 10 May 1983 (28), which recognises the legitimacy of intervention by the coastal

(22) C. DOUAY : "Le régime juridique de l'assistance en mer selon la convention de Londres du 28 avril 1989". DMF 1990, 212 à 214.
(23) P. BONASSIES : "La convention de 1989 sur l'assistance". IMTM, Annales 1996, 117-127.
(24) M. GOURIOU : "L'assistance maritime et la protection de l'environnement : l'assistance imposée". Mémoire DESS, Brest, 1992.
(25) R. RODIERE, E. DUPONTAVICE : "Droit maritime". Précis Dalloz, Paris, 11e édition, 1991, 385 n° 471-1.
(26) Senat : "Transport maritime : plus de sécurité pour une mer et un littoral plus propres". Rapport n° 500, 1994, 58-59.
(27) JO, 26 Mar. 1978, 1338 et JMM, 30 Mar. 1978, 706.
(28) JO, 11 May 1983, 1454.

State as soon as an incident occurs. Such intervention is subject to conditions of content and form. As regards content, French legislation sets the same conditions as INTERVENTION 69, namely the existence of a grave threat of harm to the coastline or related interests. As regards form, the method is to summon the shipowner to "take all necessary measures to end the danger". In practical terms, the maritime authority sends a formal demand by telex, accompanied by a threat of penalties for the shipmaster if the ship refuses all assistance while in territorial waters,. This summons sets a deadline, beyond which, except in an emergency, the authorities are entitled to take action. The allotted deadline varies depending on the maritime authority's knowledge of the circumstances when informed of the accident.

The Decree of 9 March 178 and the Instruction of 8 January 1981 (29) give the maritime authority wide powers. It may use public force against property or individuals, for ships in French territorial waters. Beyond those waters, except in an emergency, the authority may take coercive measures against any ship refusing compulsory salvage. These measures include forced escort by French Navy vessels or towage by a salvor ship sent for the purpose (30).

III -WRECK REMOVAL

671. - Wrecks can present very serious dangers for navigation at sea, so much so that they need to be carefully located, properly marked and, in certain cases, removed or destroyed. Despite the importance of this issue for the safety of life and property at sea, no international convention exists on removal of wrecks. Except for article 303, concerning archaeological and historical objects discovered at sea, the 1982 LOS Convention does not deal with wrecks. The only possibility for removing them would appear to be under a coastal State's right to intervene if there is any risk of pollution. Some national legislators have moved to fill this gap, by providing for certain forms of intervention where wrecks lie outside territorial waters.

A - NATIONAL LEGISLATIONS

Many States limit the application of their laws and regulations to their own territorial waters. In certain countries, national law makes allowance for a geographical extension, if wrecks or similar objects on the high seas may subsequently move or be moved into territorial seas. This is the case in France, Poland, Madagascar and Trinidad and Tobago. Only two States, Denmark and the United States, have introduced more general measures concerning the geographical scope of their legislation (31).

1. United Kingdom

672. - The United Kingdom was very early in introducing legislation on wrecks, first laid down in the Merchant Shipping Act of 1894. Article 530 gives a restrictive definition of a wreck, as "any vessel which is sunk, stranded or abandoned". The administrative

(29) JO, 11 Jan. 1981, 419.
(30) M. GOURIOU : op. cit., 38 and seq.
(31) IMO. LEG 63/5, 18 May 1990, Annex 2.

authorities may intervene at "any place on or near the coasts of the United Kingdom" (articles 511 and 546). These authorities are the Harbour and Conservancy Authorities for seaports and their approaches, and the General Lighthouse Authority outside harbour areas and rivers.

The administration possesses very broad powers. It can require the wreck to be removed, sold and even destroyed. It can act on its own account, and force the owner to pay all the costs of removal (cf article 531). If it sells the wreck, it is entitled to deduct from the proceeds of the sale all the expenses of removal and sale (32).

2. United States

673. - American legislation on wrecks was also laid down a long time ago, in the 1899 Rivers and Harbours Appropriation Act (33). This was amended in 1974 (34), to give the Federal authorities the right to intervene, not only in all navigable waters belonging to the United States, but also in the sea above the Continental Shelf.

The US Coast Guard is empowered to mark and remove any sunken ship or other obstacle that constitutes a threat to navigation. Its owner is held responsible for the cost of marking, until the wreck has been removed, or it legal abandonment decided. When the USCG asks the owner to remove the wreck, it also sets a deadline for action. If the owner fails to comply, the wreck is regarded as abandoned, and may thereupon be removed by the authorities. If the USCG carries out the removal operation itself, no one may interfere with operations (35).

The owner's responsibility for an abandoned wreck is theoretically confined to liability in rem, namely arising from the ship itself. However, if a ship is wrecked through the fault of its owner, he may not simply abandon the wreck and thereby escape his obligation to remove it.

3. France

674. - The Act of 24 November 1961, amended by the Act of 23 November 1982, and the Decree of 26 December 1961, amended by the Decree of 3 August 1978 and the Decree of 21 June 1985 (36) govern French policy on wrecks.

French legislation defines wrecks in the broadest terms, as including:
- Seagoing ships or aircraft abandoned in an unnavigable condition, together with their cargo (from this viewpoint, the wreck should be distinguished from an "abandoned ship" which retains its navigability, and to which the Act of 3 July 1985 applies) (37);
- Boats, engines, rigging, anchors, anchor chains and fishing gear which have been abandoned, as well as the remains of ships or aircraft;
- Cargo jettisoned or fallen into the sea, but not including cargo or objects voluntarily abandoned or thrown into the sea or on shore in order to avoid customs formalities

---

(32) R. GRIME : "Shipping Law". London, Sweet and Maxwell, 1991, 316.
(33) United States Code, title 14, article 86. (Rivers and Harbours Appropriation Act).
(34) USC, titre 33, article 409 et 411. Code of Federal Regulation, title 33, par. 64.01-1-a) and 209. 190 c) 1).
(35) A. BLANK : "Wreck removal ; statutory restrictions Rivers and Harbors Act". Tulane Law Review, vol. 53 n° 4, June 1979.
(36) JP. BEURIER : "Les épaves maritimes". DESS Droit des activités maritimes, Brest 1985 (Recueil des textes).
(37) Y. TASSEL : "Des navires et engins flottants abandonnés dans les eaux territoriales et les eaux intérieures. Loi du 3 juillet 1985". Annuaire de Droit maritime et aérospatial, University of Nantes, Tome X, 1989, 189-208.

Anyone discovering a wreck must report it promptly to the maritime administration, which holds extensive powers to intervene when there is a threat to navigation.

The Decree of 3 August 1978 defines a procedures for the recovery, removal, destruction or other treatment of any type of dangerous wreck, whether causing pollution or not. There are two steps in this procedure. To begin with, the owner is summoned to remove the wreck. If this injunction is not obeyed, the administration may take the second step of carrying out the removal itself, at the owner's expense and risk. If there is a grave and imminent danger to navigation, fishing or the environment, the owner may be required to take immediate action.

The Act of 24 November 1982 reinforced the maritime administration's legal powers. It may intervene without notice if the owner fails to act, or strip him of his rights if the wreck has been in existence for more than five years. When it has not been claimed within the allotted period, the State may sell the ship and its cargo for its own benefit, without prejudice to a claim by the shipper against the carrier or the charterer. The Decree of 21 June 1985 provides the authorities with more effective means of action against dangerous wrecks, and contains special provisions for container wrecks (38).

B - INTERNATIONAL LAW

675. - International law, as expressed in the 1982 LOS Convention, and in other international instruments, is oddly silent on the matter of removal of wrecks presenting a danger for navigation outside a coastal State's territorial waters. This has encouraged IMO to draft a new convention governing State law on the matter, and notably the possibility of requiring shipowners to bear the cost of removing wrecks and the threats they represent (39).

1. Provisions and shortcomings of existing law

The LOS Convention, which does not define wrecks, and indeed makes no direct reference to them, and leaves the scope of State powers of removal in doubt. These loopholes have been partly remedied by certain international instruments covering three main areas.

a) *Removal of abandoned platforms*

676. - Removal of artificial structures installed in the high seas for the purpose of gas and oil production has become a crucial problem for the offshore industry. The gradual depletion of ocean energy reserves in certain parts of the world has led to an increase in the number of abandoned or disused offshore platforms, creating dangerous conditions for navigation (40). The 1958 Geneva Convention on the Continental Shelf was the first instrument to introduce an obligation of complete removal of offshore installations (cf article 5.5). These provisions have since been completed by the LOS Convention and other international instruments.

• Article 60 of the LOS Convention
677. - According to article 60, which refers to the requirements of the Geneva Convention, "any installations or structures which are abandoned or disused shall be removed to ensure safety of navigation, taking into account any generally accepted standards established in this regard by the competent international organisation". Other concepts may

(38) M. REMOND GOUILLOUD : "Droit maritime". Pedone, Paris, 1988, 215-216.
(39) IMO. LEG 75/5/2/Add. I, 5 Sept. 1996.
(40) J. REDDEN : "Platform removal becomes international issue". Offshore, Vol. XLVIII, n° 11, 1987, 27-32.

be taken into account, such as fishing interests and protection of the marine environment. A coastal State carrying out removal operations must take the rights and obligations of other States into account, and give due warning of the position, size and depth of the parts remaining of an installation or structure that has not been completely removed.

• IMO guidelines and standards

678. - IMO, considering that the matter was of concern to it (41), adopted Resolution A.672 on 19 October 1989. This contains a series of standards and guidelines on the removal of offshore installations and structures on the Continental Shelf and in the EEZ. This Resolution lays a general obligation on coastal States to remove any installations as soon as they are no longer used for the purpose for which they were specifically designed and established, . The removal operation must be carried out "as soon as reasonably practical after abandonment or permanent disuse" (par. 1.2). Only in exceptional cases is all or any part of such installations left on the seabed, and IMO guidelines must be observed.

The guidelines are intended to be pragmatic, and any decision to keep a structure in place is taken by the State on a case-by-case basis. Paragraph 2.1 lists six factors to be taken into account, such as the rate of deterioration or the potential effect on the safety of navigation or the marine environment. When the coastal State decides to remove the installations, it must take account of the standards set out in the Resolution. In principle, removal requirements apply to installations standing in less than 75 metres of water and weighing less than 4 000 tonnes in air, excluding the deck and superstructure, and those installed on or after 1st January 1998 if they are standing in less than 100 metres of water.

The State may decide to leave certain installations entirely or partly in position, including those reassigned for another use, not interfering with other users of the sea (cf par. 3.4), whose removal would prove technically impracticable, or could involve extreme cost or unacceptable risk to persons or the marine environment (cf par. 35). Generally speaking, removal should be compulsory in high-risk zones, such as straits, sea routes in archipelagic waters, deep-draught shipping lanes and traffic management systems (cf par. 3.7).

If the State fails to remove the installation, it must comply with certain requirements, such as marking the obstacle on marine charts (cf par. 3.8), identifying the individual or body responsible for aids to navigation, and ensuring that periodic monitoring is provided (cf par. 3.10), and finally seeing that there is no ambiguity as to ownership of the installations, maintenance obligations, and the financial ability to assume liability for future damage (cf par. 3.11).

• Conventions on dumping

679. - The Oslo Convention of 15 February 1972, signed by North Atlantic coastal States, and the London Convention of 29 December 1972, on dumping of industrial waste at sea, also apply to partial removal of installations at sea.

Annex II to the Oslo Convention, which stipulates that "bulky wastes which may present a serious obstacle to fishing and navigation" may be disposed of only in water at least 2 000 metres deep, and at a distance of at least 150 nautical miles from the nearest land. The Oslo Commission, at its 17th session in 1991, completed the provisions of the Conventions with guidelines for the disposal of offshore installations at sea. In 1992, the Ministerial meeting of the Oslo and Paris Commissions adopted the Convention for the Protection of the Marine Environment of the North-East Atlantic, to be known as the Paris Convention. Articles 5, 6, 7 and 8 apply directly to the abandonment of installations at sea.

---

(41) V.I. ANDRIANOV : "The role of the International Maritime Organisation in implementing the 1982 UNCLOS". Marine Policy, March 1990, 120-124.

Finally, the 1972 Convention on the Prevention of Marine Pollution by Dumping of Wastes and Other Matter, known as the London Convention, contains certain rules on the deliberate disposal at sea of platforms. It bans the dumping of certain dangerous substances and requires "special care" for others (42).

b) Intervention on the high seas

680. - Article 221.2 of the LOS Convention makes no explicit reference to wrecks in its definition of a maritime casualty as "a collision of vessels, stranding or other incident of navigation, or other occurrences on board a vessel or external to it resulting in material damage or imminent threat of material damage to a vessel or cargo". However, the definition seems broad enough to include the intervention of a coastal State to prevent pollution of the marine environment by wrecks (43).

c) Reporting wrecks

681. - Article 211 of the LOS Convention calls for "international rules and standards to prevent, reduce and control pollution of the marine environment from vessels". According to article 211.7, such rules and standards "should include *inter alia* those relating to prompt notification to coastal States, whose coastline or related interests may be affected by incidents, including maritime casualties, which involve discharges or probability of discharges". These requirements were implemented in article 8 and Protocol I of MARPOL 73-78.

2. IMO draft Convention on Wreck Removal

682. - For more than twenty-five years, IMO has been trying to fill some of loopholes in international law on the removal of wrecks located outside the territorial waters of a coastal State, and which create dangers for safety of navigation and the marine environment.

In 1995, the question came again to the fore. This was when Germany, the Netherlands and the United Kingdom presented a new draft convention on wreck removal, in order to increase the uniformity and clarity of international law on the matter (44).

In Spring 1996, the CMI also decided to examine the issue (45), and it was raised at its Centenary Conference in Antwerp in June 1997 (46).

This draft convention would be mandatory beyond territorial seas and optional within them, leaving States free to choose. The types of risks concerned are existing or threatened "danger or impediment to surface navigation, or substantial physical damage to the marine environment, or damage to the coastline or related interests". Two types of objects are concerned: ships of any type : hydrofoil boats, air-cushion vehicles, submersibles, floating craft, and fixed or floating platforms or mobile offshore units, and wrecks in the meaning used in MARPOL ("a sunken or stranded ship, or any part thereof, including anything that is on board such a ship or which is stranded, sunken or in danger at sea lost from a ship").

(42) J. SIDE, M. BAINE, K. HAYES : "Current controls for abandonment and disposal of offshore installations at sea". Marine Policy, September 1993.
(43) IMO. LEG. 7415/2 Add 1, 5 Sept. 1996. Document submitted by the CMI.
(44) LEG 73/11, 8 August 1995.
(45) CMI. Yearbook 1996. Antwerp I, Documents for the Centenary Conference, 173-224.
(46) CMI. Yearbook 1997. Antwerp II. Documents of the Centenary Conference. 193-203.

A provision has been inserted to avoid overlapping with the 1969 Convention and the 1975 Protocol on coastal State intervention on the high seas.

According to article IV, shipowners would be obliged to submit without delay a report on accidents involving their ships. Any State learning of the existence of a wreck would be required to inform navigators and other coastal States. If it has clear grounds for assuming that there is a dangerous wreck in the vicinity of its coastline, it would be expected to take all reasonable steps to locate the wreck. According to article V, it would be the responsibility of the State whose interests are the most directly threatened by the wreck to decide whether a hazard exists. Dangerous wrecks would have to be marked (cf article VI). Their removal would be the primary responsibility of shipowners, with the possibility for the coastal State, if the shipowner fails to comply, of carrying out the removal itself within a reasonable deadline set by the State (cf article VII). Shipowners would automatically have to bear the cost of locating, marking and removing dangerous wrecks, except under certain circumstances (cf article VIII). Finally, they would be required to take out insurance to cover their liabilities under the Convention.

The IMO draft Convention leaves many questions unanswered. One of the most difficult issues concerns the relationship between the provisions of public law and private law. Should they be incorporated in a single convention, or dealt with in separate instruments ? Several years will be needed to establish a text acceptable to IMO member States, particularly since some of them (48) are not always convinced that an international convention can solve the practical problems of wreck removal.

(47) IMO. LEG 78/4/2, 14 August 1998. Report of the correspondence group on wreck removal.
(48) IMO. LEG 74/5/3, 13 Sept. 1996. Document submitted by ICS.

CHAPTER 28

The quest for safer shipping

683. - Has there been a deterioration in the safety of seaborne transport ? Are the steps that have been taken and the mechanisms introduced adequate and appropriate ? Can they prevent accidents and disasters at sea ? As this study of safety at sea comes to a conclusion, I would like to contribute to the cause of safer shipping by making an assessment of the current safety system, and discussing prospects for its evolvement as the third millennium approaches.

I - ASSESSMENT OF SAFETY AT SEA

There are so many contradictory opinions about the effectiveness of the current system of prevention that it is hard to reach any overall assessment of the issue. Those in favour of the present system, which means most of the shipping industry, can point to the objective reality of a fairly satisfactory statistical picture, to justify the grounds for actions taken so far. However, a far more negative view of safety at sea is prevalent in the media and among the general public, and this is reinforced by recurrent shipping accidents.

A - STATISTICAL REALITY

Several statistical studies carried out over lengthy periods show a marked improvement in safety at sea. The conclusions drawn from these quantitative analyses are not unanimous, however: while acknowledging the efforts that have been made, some commentators feel that much remains to be done.

1. Positive trend

684. - Three main statistical criteria are used to evaluate improvements in safety at sea. These are the number of ships lost, loss of life, and accidental oil pollution.
• **Ship casualties**
The last thirty years have seen a marked drop in the number of accidents at sea. Marine insurers estimate that total losses, as a percentage of tonnage and of the number of ships

afloat, have decreased in the last ten years (cf diagram 23). This reflects the arrival of new ships on the market, and the scrapping of the oldest vessels in the late Eighties and early Nineties (1).

23 - Total losses as a percentage of shipping afloat (ships over 500 grt) 1987-1997
(Sources : ILU/IUMI 1998 Chart 5)

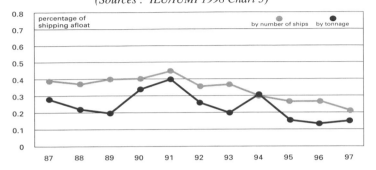

24 - Lives lost at sea in accidents involving ships over 500 grt (1990-1997)
(Sources : ILU/IUMI 1998 Chart 4)

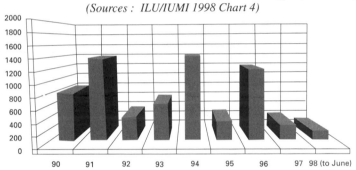

25 - Quantities of oil spills (1970-1997)
(Source : ITOPF. Statistics on website)

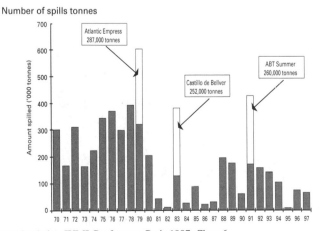

(1) ILU. Hull Casualty Statistics. IUMI Conference, Paris 1997, Chart 6.

• **Loss of life at sea**

Figures for lives lost at sea show no significant variation since 1989 (cf diagram 24). Some years are better than others, such as 1992 and 1995. Others show very poor results, because of serious shipping accidents: 1994 with the loss of the *Estonia*, and 1996 with the sinking of the *Bukoba* ferry on Lake Victoria.

These figures need to be put into perspective.. At the end of the last century, there was an average of 650 deaths every year in the British merchant navy alone (2).

A recent survey shows that a current average of 140 people die in shipping accidents in European waters every year. This is three hundred times fewer fatalities than on EU roads and nine times fewer than in train accidents. On the basis of accidental deaths per passenger-kilometre, however, ships prove to be twenty-five times more dangerous than aircraft (3).

• **Accidental oil pollution**

Several indicators show a positive trend here :

- A GESAMP study published in 1993 noted that accidental pollution had decreased over the last three decades, and that tanker accidents contributed only 5 per cent of total oil pollution of the marine environment (4).
- According to the International Tanker Owners Pollution Federation (ITOPF), oil spills by tankers reached a record low in 1995, at only five thousand tonnes, and the number of serious accidents has fallen markedly over the last twenty-five years (cf diagram 25) (5).
- The United States Academy of Sciences has made more detailed calculations, showing that the quantity of oil spillage at sea as a result of navigational operations has dropped by about 60 per cent since the early eighties (6).

685. - In general, safety statistics appear quite positive, proving that the rapid expansion in maritime trade since the end of the Second World War did not bring about a corresponding increase in the number of accidents. Prevention of risks at sea has progressed overall (7). IMO notes with satisfaction the decrease in the serious casualty rate, despite generally poor economic conditions and the ageing fleet.

Professor Edgar Gold considers that maritime accident statistics need to be seen in the context of overall shipping figures (8). "About 1.9 billion tonnes of oil is moved annually at sea by some three thousand tankers over an average of 4 700 nautical miles. Only a very small amount of this cargo is spilt, as 99.9995 per cent of all oil cargoes is delivered safely. In addition, over 2.4 billion tonnes of dry cargo, including a billion tonnes of bulk commodities, are also carried at sea annually. This means that over 4.4 billion tonnes of goods is carried at sea annually by over 28 000 vessels" (9).

---

(2) JMM, 16 sept. 1955, 2005.

(3) Estimating that each year around 100 million passengers embark in European ports, it can be calculated that the rate is 1.4 deaths (including crew) per 100 million passengers kilometres. This figure is 25 times higher than in civil aviation (0.05 deaths per 100 million passenger/km). European Transport Safety Council. "Priority measures for maritime accident reduction". Brussels, August 1997, 14.

(4) GESAMP : "Impact of oil and related chemicals and wastes on the maritime environment". Reports and Studies n° 50. IMO, London, 1993, 5.

(5) "Oil spills by tankers fall to a record low". Lloyd's List, 15 July 1996.

(6) IMO. World Maritime Day 1995. 50th anniversary of the United Nations. IMO's achievement and challenges. J/ 6068, 14-15.

(7) Les entretiens de l'Assurance. Colloque Paris, 13 Dec. 1994.

(8) E. GOLD : "Corporate responsibility : learning from disaster ?" BIMCO Bulletin, vol. 91 n° 3, 1996, 10.

(9) UNCTAD : "Review of maritime transport 1994". Geneva 1995, Tables 1 and 10.

Finally, one can argue in terms of probability of occurrence of an event. It has been calculated that "the chances of being killed as a passenger on a British ship are such that you would need to cross the Channel from Dover to Calais and back again one million times before finding a place in the mortality statistics (...) equivalent to about 150 round trips to the Moon" (10).

2. Figures to be treated with caution

686. - Two comments need to be made about safety statistics. First of all, it is accepted that figures can be interpreted in all sorts of ways, and accident statistics do not escape this rule. They are used by the various participants to suit their case, defend sector interests, promote a positive image of an activity, increase a client portfolio, and so on (11). They can be massaged to make them say anything, and the contrary of everything. For example, there is the classic distinction between active and passive safety. For some people, casualty figures illustrate the persistent failure of maritime safety systems, while for others, they serve to show the remarkable efficiency of the very same systems. To salvage the negative image of the maritime industry after an oil spill, emphasis is placed on the fact that 99.98 per cent of the oil carried by sea leaves no trace of pollution (12).

The second reservation is that accident information is incomplete, and on the whole inadequate. Events at sea continue to be shrouded in secrecy, because of the legal consequences they involve, in particular the possible civil or criminal liability of those concerned. The decision taken by- the Salvage Association in 1994 to stop supplying the press with any details of accidents is a clear example of the cautiousness that can lead to a scarcity of hard news (13).

Lord Donaldson's report on the *Braer* disaster recommended greater transparency on the issue (14). The need for a universal, impartial and univerally accessible accident database is increasingly felt (15). Only such a tool could provide both accurate and global information on risks at sea.

3. Differing opinions

687. - a) Despite these reservations, experts in risk prevention rely on the statistical trend in shipping losses to present a positive picture of the safety issue. In his report on safety aspects of ship design and technology, Lord Carver states, "Statistically, the sea would seem to be becoming a safer place. The rate of serious failures of ships in generally has been steadily improving and the number of lives lost at sea is decreasing. (16)

As the Chairman of a leading classification society puts it, "Very generally speaking, maritime safety has progressed uninterruptedly over the last thirty years. Rates of losses have

(10) P. LE CHEMINANT : "Maritime safety - perception and reality". BIMCO Bulletin n° 4, July-August 1992, 27-29.
(11) "On the other hand...". Tradewinds, 12 March 1993.
(12) "INTERTANKO : Oil disasters spur industry to improve image". Lloyd's List, 6 May 1994.
(13) M. GREY : "Secrecy no way to salvage an industry image". Lloyd's List, 6 April 1994.
(14) "Safer ship, cleaner seas". Report of Lord Donaldson's inquiry into the prevention of pollution from merchant shipping. HMSO, London, 1994, 164 et suivant.
(15) "Lies, damn lies...". Safety at Sea, July 1994.
(16) Select Committee on Science and Technology : Safety aspects of ship design and technology. 2nd report House of Lords. Session 1991-1192, 14 feb. 1992. London HMSO, chp. 1, 1.11, 7.

been halved over this period. And if the number of ships lost every year (between two and three hundred) still seems high, let us not forget that in 1821 two thousand ships vanished at sea, causing the deaths of twenty thousand sailors." (17)

The same optimism is to be found in the remarks of a senior French civil servant. "Over the last twenty-five yeas, useful information has been obtained from the accidents that have occurred, and although the number of ships has increased 60 per cent, the number of casualties has fallen by a quarter." As for loss of life during transport by sea, overall figures show a favourable picture of the maritime sector: EU statistics for the five years from 1989 to 1993 show that an annual average of 50 860 people were killed on the roads, 222 on the railways, 196 in aeroplanes, and 68 at sea (18).

b) This confidence in increasing safety at sea is not shared by everyone, however. Highly sensitive to public opinion and particularly attentive to the concerns of their electors, politicians are usually more reserved about the issue. In the introduction to his report on safety at sea, the French parliamentarian Charles Josselin writes : "The present situation is too unsatisfactory for the *status quo* to be acceptable. In any case, the populations concerned are less and less ready to accept accidents with increasingly serious consequences, and the economic situation of the shipping industry remains a source of concern, while observance of regulations is inadequate, and international action, so vital in this area, is moving forward only very slowly." (19)

The French Senator Le Grand, in a report on the prevention of coastal pollution risks, also emphasises "a seriously deteriorating situation" in maritime transportation, and draws the following conclusion from his analysis of total shipping losses in all categories from 1983 to 1990: "On average, then, for these eight years, one ship was lost every two days throughout the world. (...) The improvement recorded since the War remains vulnerable, as is shown by figure for 1991. During that year, 258 ships were lost, while there were 1 204 dead or missing, compared with 389 in 1990, 688 in 1989, and 763 in 1988" (20).

These differences of opinion are worth noticing, revealing as they do the growing gap between image and reality. For the general public, maritime transport is regarded as a high-risk activity, whereas in reality the industry has become relatively safe. This involves a problem of image and communication, which the whole profession has difficulty in handling.

B - PERSISTENT DANGER AND THE IMAGE OF SAFETY

688. - There is no need for elaborate surveys to study the negative image of maritime transportation. The man in the street, if asked about an industry which uses nearly eighty thousand ships, carries 4 billion tonnes of goods every year, and represents 97 per cent of world trade, will quote a number of preconceptions (21). Oil tankers pollute the sea. Car ferries are dangerous and kill people. Substandard ships that can turn into floating coffins are universally known to shelter behind flags of convenience. Constantly hunting the highest

(17) H. LAURIN : "Sécurité maritime et classification. Vers une approche globale ". Académie de Marine. Paris, 15 Feb. 1995.
(18) G. CADET : "La sécurité maritime". JMM, 16 Dec. 1994, 30.
(19) France - Assemblée Nationale. Rapport d'information n° 1482, sur la sécurité maritime : un défi européen et mondial, 5 July 1994, 11.
(20) France - Sénat. Rapport d'information n° 500 sur les conditions de sécurité du transport maritime, les risques de pollution du littoral et les propositions de nature à prévenir ces pollutions. 13 June 1994, 12.
(21) M. GREY : "Ethics in shipping and its public image". INTERCARGO Seminar, Oslo, 12 June 1995. in Maritime Monitor, 1st Aug. 1995, 7.

profit, shipowners are champions at tax evasion, and exploit their underpaid and poorly qualified Third World crews. In the maritime world, "where colossal sums pass from hand to hand, where boats can change their name and flag on the high seas, where swindlers enjoy the support of corrupt officials; the law of silence and the cult of confidentiality reign" (22).

Various conferences and seminars have drawn attention to the poor image of maritime transport today. Even if simple, immediate and lasting solutions are not available, it is possible to discern the causes of this image problem, and explain the reasons for the industry's bad reputation outside its sphere of activity.

Some of these causes arise within the press itself, which forms public opinion and imposes a certain perception of reality Unfortunately, the mass media have no shipping correspondents, who are restricted to the specialist press with professional readerships.

Another very obvious factor is that the media, by their very nature, are on the lookout for what is out of the ordinary. They pay little attention to the routine and monotony of daily life. They focus far more on bad news rather than good, because their readers are interested mainly in others' misfortunes. Accidents clearly offer an opportunity to satisfy the insatiable curiosity about other people's problems. This is why the media revel in any kind of disaster, especially those, like oil slicks, that provide material for spectacular footage and repeated bulletins. The *Amoco Cadiz*, the *Exxon Valdez* and the *Braer* have given television companies throughout the world a chance to broadcast striking pictures of oily birds floundering on polluted beaches (23).

Information reassures people, but it can also move and disturb them. The maritime industry has signally failed to measure the extent of this growing public feeling created by the media, whereas this has been the main reason for its deteriorating image. There are several reasons for this worrying situation. Few shipping companies in the world have implemented a real communication policy. Most of them do not realise what journalists are interested in, and how they work. On the contrary, they foster an atmosphere of distrust and suspicion, convinced that anything they say will be distorted. Forgetting that the views of the general public are moulded by the press, the industry has not made the effort to explain the realities of sea transport, and the risks that go with it.

Another difficulty is that very few managers have been trained in crisis communication, leaving their companies extremely vulnerable if an accident happens. Many take refuge in a suspicious silence, practising a "no comment" policy, and leaving it to others to comment on events. As long as the shipping world persists in its secretiveness, it will remain the target of criticism and controversy. It is not possible to change one's image if one is not prepared to admit reality (24).

A coordinated approach to communication is cruelly lacking in the shipping sector. Each association of shipowners tends to act without any consistency, or real collaboration with other members of the maritime world. The shipping industry has no easily identifiable spokesman, no major figure, no leading personality who could defend and explain the whole business of shipping in all its complexities (25).

(21) M. GREY : "Ethics in shipping and its public image". Séminaire INTERCARGO, Oslo, 12 juin 1995. Texte dans Maritime Monitor, 1er août 1995, 7.
(22) Marketing presentation of the book of P. BENQUET et Th. LAURENCEAU : "Les pétroliers de la honte". Edition n° 1, Paris, 1994.
(23) D. GILBERTSON : "The reputation of the shipping industry". 2rd Summit Safety at Sea. 24/25 June 1993, Oslo.
(24) "Public perceptions". Fairplay, 12 Oct. 1995.
(25) "A call for coordinated action on the shipping industry's image". Lloyd's List, 16 Jan. 1997.

Those involved with safety at sea no longer have to cope only with situations that are technically and economically difficult, but also with the pressure and volatility of public opinion, which, when something happens, can turn hostile. In a world where the media have taken on extraordinary importance, public opinion exerts powerful leverage for change. Since 1990, noone can any longer ignore the importance of this factor. By interfering radically with the maritime oil trade and the conditions under which it operates, the American Oil Pollution Act will remain the cruellest example of expensive, exaggerated, sometimes inappropriate legislation, adopted hastily under popular pressure.

II - SAFETY AT SEA IN THE 21st CENTURY

689. - The Nineties have produced a far greyer picture of maritime safety. In particular, it appears that the present system has run out of steam, its malfunctions arising as much from political and legal shortcomings as from economic factors. Damaged by the recession, maritime transport at the end of the century offers the spectacle of ruthless competition, in which the weapons are labour costs, ship condition and maintenance, and observance of regulations. The Nineties have also drawn attention to new features: under the influence of powerful forces which tend to privilege profit over prevention, safety provisions are undergoing profound changes, affecting players, decision processes, the regulations they generate, and the values on which these are based.

It is not enough merely to assess the system. In order to understand the ways in which it is being recast, the main trends over the next ten years need to be identified. Readers will understand that, given the massive amount of information to be processed, I have had to adopt a clear position in order to complete this task of forecasting. I believe that ten fundamental trends will have the most far-reaching influence on the maritime safety regime, as the next century dawns.

A - EMERGENCE OF INTERNATIONAL CONTROL

690. - IMO, which celebrated its fiftieth anniversary in 1998, can point to what it has achieved : since it came into existence, more than forty international conventions and more than eight hundred codes and resolutions have been adopted through its efforts. Most of these relate to safety at sea and protection of the marine environment.

The persistent recurrence of major disasters in recent years, however, has spoiled its image and reputation. It is true that IMO is in a weak position in relation to its hundred and fifty member States: it facilitates the establishment of international instruments, but plays a small part in their effective implementation. This lack of control has resulted in very unequal levels of ship safety and unacceptable differences from one country to another.

Legally blinkered by its constituent charter, IMO has tried to correct this situation by sponsoring the first steps towards international control. Since 1993, two approaches have been adopted. First, conventions contain stronger notification stipulations, requiring States signing an instrument to inform IMO of the stages of its implementation. Certain conventions go very far along this path: STCW 95, for example, provides for the issue of a "white list" of countries that are regarded as having complied with their obligations. Second, IMO has also set up a dedicated structure to help flag States apply its instruments : this is the Flag State Implementation (FSI) subcommittee.

Is it possible to go further with control procedures ? Since the *Torrey Canyon* disaster, proposals have proliferated (26), suggesting the establishment of a body of international officials to check ship safety (27), setting-up of an international sea management fund, with the task of organising surveillance of shipping (28), development of an international registration scheme administered by IMO (29), creation of an international maritime court to prosecute flag States defaulting on their obligations (30).

Such projects, although they reflect an admirable ideal, cannot apply in the present situation, for several reasons. In practice, the creation of a new surveillance organisation would be far too costly for the international community, with the need to recruit hundreds or even thousands of officials for any effective control of world shipping. Second, international law does not give international organisations any access to the legitimate constraints available to States for internal law and order : no coercion can be put on a defaulting State for safety failings, without its consent. Finally, from the political viewpoint, few States would be prepared to surrender any part of their sovereignty to a supranational authority that could penalise negligence or failure to observe the rules.

In the present state of law and the international community, IMO cannot behave as the world's policeman. However, it could influence attitudes, and provide more guidance to flag states in applying international standards. The first step has been to issue "guidelines". The second will be to make these compulsory, issuing criteria for drafting and using a shipping register, and to set up the necessary administration. It will not be long before flag states, in order to be members of IMO, will have to observe a certain level of performance, and obtain quality certification of their national administration.

B - RENAISSANCE OF CLASSIFICATION SOCIETIES

691. - Use of the word "renaissance" should not be taken to mean that classification societies are just emerging from the Middle Ages, but in the ordinary sense of regeneration, new energy, renewed activity.

As they reach the end of the century, classification societies are not, as certain critics claim (31), an anachronism. Because of their multidisciplinary skills in relation to ship safety, and their international networks of surveyors, they play, and will long continue to play, a fundamental role in preventing accidents.

Four major challenges that these societies have had to face since the end of the Eighties will have a decisive influence on their future (32).

(26) P. BONASSIES : "La loi du pavillon et les conflits de droit maritime". RCADI, 1969, III, 625.

See the different projets presented since1918 in "Le principe de la liberté en mer". A. CAPPE. Thesis, Paris II, 1979, 675 to 678.

(27) IMCO : LEG/II/Add 1, quoted by BONASSIES.

(28) Ignacy SACHS : "Des péages pour les tankers". Le Monde, 8 Apr. 1978, 37.

(29) Ph. G. CARR : "Time for one international flag". Lloyd's List, 5 March 1993.

(30) O. SKAARUP : "Safety at sea of paramount importance". BIMCO Bulletin, June 1993, 19-23.

(31) A. SPYROV : "Class lesson : are the societies an anachronism ?" Tradewinds, 1 May 1997.

(32) Ph. BOISSON : Conclusions de la journée d'étude de l'IETM sur la classification des navires. Paris, 1997. In JMM, 28 Nov. 1997, 2726.

The first challenge is technological. Facing increasingly tough commercial competition, the leading classification societies are being forced to make huge investments in order to offer new services to their clients. The aim is to make classed ships safer, more efficient and cheaper. The introduction of information technologies into working methods will soon make continuous surveillance of ships and very fast transmission of data possible.

The second challenge is quality. The quality of the ships classed by these societies is what confers legitimacy on their safety role, and determines their credibility in maritime circles. Quality of services is equally important, guaranteed by very detailed regulation of their operations. The regulations that issue from IACS, IMO, the EU and individual governments are bound to increase in coming years, laying down increasingly stringent quality criteria and requiring ever-improving levels of performance, which very few will be able to achieve.

The third challenge, the most complicated, will be to solve the legal problems arising from the growing tendency to sue classification societies. The CMI showed the way by seeking to harmonise levels of liability for classification societies worldwide. The fact remains that only recognition of a limitation on legal liability will make it possible to protect these organisations when they are involved in a major accident.

Finally, classification societies need to find a stable attitude towards prevention. The tendency is to adopt the idea of total services, a total class concept that takes account of the traditional technical aspects of safety (structural strength), and also human factors (certification of shipping company management, crew, etc). No radical medium-term change is likely to occur in the work of classification societies. One day, of course, classification societies may well carry out an assessment of the permance of shipping companies (33) and grant differentiated ratings to ships, thus returning to their original role as information agencies (34). But this implies a change of clientele, abandoning shipowners and shipyards in order to serve the interests of insurers, charterers and bankers. Market circumstances, unfortunately, make such a possibility unlikely.

One thing seems certain: the new requirements stipulated by safety players are going to bring about far-reaching changes in the classification picture. A major reduction in the number of organisations supplying classification services will come about through certain regroupings and alliances. There will be mergers between smaller-sized societies, anxious to keep a foothold on the international market.

C - REGIONALISM AND UNILATERALISM : THE END OF UNIVERSAL RULES

692. - International trade, global standards : the recent proliferation of unilateral measures and regional safety regulations are making this motto for the maritime industry ring increasingly hollow. The trend began in the early Eighties, with the introduction of the first mechanisms to guarantee effective application of standards on a regional level. Its scope was widened in 1990, with the adoption of the US Oil Pollution Act, the requirements of which go far beyond internationally accepted standards. It gathered pace a few years later with the establishment of a European Union maritime safety policy and regulations to supplement IMO conventions.

---

(33) "Le Conseil Supérieur de la Marine Marchande favorable à la notation des armements". JMM, 8 Feb. 1991, 309.
(34) Ph. BOISSON : "Classification societies and safety at sea. Back to basics to prepare for the future ". Marine Policy 1994, 18, 363-377.

Since the Stockholm conference in February 1996, specific rules have applied to the stability of car ferries in the North Sea and the Baltic. This is no longer an instance of "derived regionalism" (35), arising from local initiatives under world treaties or rules, but proper regional requirements, stricter than those of the SOLAS Convention, and applying to a geographically limited maritime area.

Regionalism and unilateralism have marked a turning point in the development of maritime safety law : by lending credence to the possibility of creating standards outside international conventions and major international bodies, they are hastening the fragmentation of the traditional regulatory system, which was intended to be universal. Reflecting the growing difficulties of obtaining a worldwide consensus, unilateralism threatens the maritime transport industry in several ways. There is the risk of legal uncertainty and arbitrariness for ships operating on international markets. And above all, shipowners could be caught between the contradictory requirements of increasingly piecemeal regulations.

There are fears that this fragmentation may gather pace as the 21st century dawns, under the influence of several factors: the inability of international organisations to halt repeated shipping disasters, the growing frustration of coastal States about the inertia of the institutional system, the growing pressure of public opinion and the media after a serious accident, and the presence of the European Union, which is increasingly flexing its political muscle on the international stage.

Only a strong and united IMO can prevent the maritime world from being confronted with "a confused overlapping of divergent national and regional requirements, which it would be a nightmare to observe and which would be extremely costly and almost impossible to implement and enforce" (36). IMO will have to introduce new working methods, in order to foster a global consensus on the establishment and application of safety standards, and also find new sources of funding, in order to help the poorest countries.

D - NEW APPROACHES TO REGULATION

For more than a hundred and fifty years, safety at sea has relied on a deterministic philosophy, based on the postulate that every event has a cause and that, all other things being equal, the same causes produce the same effects. Those trying to promote safety tended to devise regulations and preventive measures based on malfunctions in the maritime transport system, namely accidents and incidents at sea. This attitude is now being called into question, criticised for being permanently out of date, always failing to keep up with technological innovations, being reactive, and therefore necessarily inadequate to meet the overall challenge of safety at sea.

New methods have been devised, in an attempt to remedy these shortcomings. They are meant to be more forward-looking, less reactive; in particular, they all try to assign responsibility to the person taking the risk, encouraging him to attain certain safety goals. Formal Safety Assessment (FSA) is an acknowledged safety management method, based on risk-assessment techniques. It was worked out about thirty years ago in the nuclear industry, and is now applied in many sectors regarded as risk-prone, such as aviation and the chemical and offshore industries.

(35) D. FREESTONE et T. IJLSTRA : "The North Sea : Basic Legal Documents on Regional Environmental Cooperation. Graham and Trotman /Martinus Nijhoff, London 1991, XVIII.
(36) W. O'NEIL : "IMO: seeking excellence through cooperation". Secretary-General's message. World Maritime Day 1996.

Oddly enough, maritime transport, which remains prone to large-scale disasters, has so far escaped this trend. The United Kingdom first submitted comments on FSA to IMO in 1993 (37), following the recommendations of a House of Lords Select Committee on Ship Design and Technology (38). Since then, the same country has increased its efforts to have FSA incorporated into maritime regulations. Other states have followed suit, trying to apply risk-assessment techniques to the standardisation process (39). To achieve progress on the subject, the Maritime Safety Committee (MSC) decided in December 1993 to set up a working group, responsible among other things for defining a procedural approach and drafting guidelines for the use of FSA in the process of establishing IMO regulations.

Even though certain IMO delegations show reluctance to accept FSA, the idea of drawing up regulations on the basis of a comprehensive analysis of maritime risks is making headway. Interim directives, to be applied on an experimental basis by administrations and organisations, were submitted to the MSC in July 1996. (40) FSA has been seen as a valuable tool for regulation, but which could be used only to the detriment of other factors in the standardisation process, such as politicisation, public interest and common sense (41).

For the moment, FSA is being applied experimentally to high-speed craft (42), and new propulsion and emergency steering devices for oil tankers (43). These practical applications should build up the experience needed to allow FSA guidelines to be drawn up and a decision taken on the feasibility of applying them to the IMO decision-making process.

Introduction of FSA in the maritime sector raises a whole series of problems (44), principally the low level of standardisation of ship design, construction and operation, and the lack of any globally available database on shipping accidents and failures. These difficulties are not insurmountable, and new ideas are already emerging, such as the concept of the "generic ship", allowing the use of a formal safety assessment by attributing common characteristics to certain types of vessels operated under similar conditions.

One thing is clear : new approaches to safety will have many serious consequences for the whole maritime sector. In future, for example, IMO will have to review its strategies, so as to devise rules for performance standards, rather than just technical requirements, as is the case today (45). The shipowner or operator will also assume greater responsibility, bearing the particular burden of proof that their ships offer a minimum level of safety, or the level recommended by the maritime community.

Classification societies, as both standardisation and survey organisations, cannot stand back from this movement. The new methods will force them to revise their rules to take account of risk analysis requirements. They will also need to integrate continuous survey of installations into inspection procedures (46).

(37) IMO. MSC 62/24/3, 2 Mar. 1993.
(38) House of Lords. Select Committee on Science and Technology. "Safety aspects of ship design and technology". Report, 14 Feb. 1992. London, HSMO.
(39) IMO. MSC 64/21/1, 14 Oct. 1994.
(40) IMO. MSC 67/13, 24 July 1996.
(41) IMO. MSC 68/WP. 11 add.1, par 14.3.
(42) "IMO backs safety case approach". Safety at Sea International, June 1995, 12-15.
(43) Cf also American developments in Proceedings, vol. 53, n° 2, April-June 1996.
(44) Ch. KUO : "Demystifying safety jargon". Lloyd's List, 15 Nov. 1996.
(45) D. BELL : "Toward rationality in regulations". Seaways, September 1996, 12-16.
(46) Ph. BOISSON : "New approaches to safety". Bulletin Technique du Bureau Veritas n° 3, 1996, 3-5.

E - INFORMATION TECHNOLOGY AGE

694. - Advances in information technologies and telecommunications have finally dragged the shipping industry kicking and screaming into the information age (47) New applications are constantly appearing, and their day-to-day effects are still difficult to discern. The maritime world is quite welcoming towards this technological revolution, which is expected to improve safety and environmental protection, while making maritime transport cheaper and more efficient.

Above all, information technologies are altering the way work is organised and conceived. The new decision-making tools are revolutionising operating methods : the computer provides unequalled help with ship design, construction, classification and operation. Navigation has not been left out of these technological breakthroughs: electronic system and integrated bridges have been designed to facilitate centralised navigational control (CNC) and the practice of one-man bridge operation (OMBO) (48).

Among the most prominent examples of the new information society are interactive multimedia tools, which are making daily inroads into our lives. Regulations, technical standards, class status and statutory status are now available for certain groups on CD-ROM or the Internet, making searches and consultation easier and more user-friendly (49).

The latest important development is the availability of databases, offering online access to any type of information. Shipping quality and safety are given plenty of space, with the mechanisms introduced by port States, insurers, oil companies, the European chemical industry and classification societies. This may well be the most significant change, introducing as it does the concept of information-sharing, in a community that for centuries has tended to give priority to secrecy and confidentiality (50).

What is to be expected from this technological explosion ? How will the maritime world integrate the information revolution ? One thing is obvious : new communication methods will change how business is conducted, and its organisation (51). The need to work in a network should lead to a redistribution of tasks and responsibilities.

The new rule of transparency, which is gaining ground within the shipping world, could also upset certain habits inherited from the past. Information on the condition of a ship and its operational status cannot remain indefinitely in the sole possession of the shipowner (52). The need for free flow of information will bring about a redefinition of relationships and responsibilities among shipowners, insurers, charterers and classification societies (53).

It is likely that the emergence and generalised application of information technologies in the various sectors of maritime trade will be increasingly subordinated to an organised array of new, complex internationally applicable standards. A worldwide environment of confrontations and alliances involving Europe, the United States and Asia has already seen

(47) P. de LIVOIS, A. SERIDJI, S. MELLO : "Classification societies in the information age". Bulletin Technique du Bureau Veritas, n° 2, 1996, 5-18.
(48) R. ROSS : "How technology is affecting the maritime world". Proceedings, July-Sept. 1996, 4-5.
(49) L. MONNET : "Veristar Info. A new system of communication between Bureau Veritas and its clients". Bulletin Technique du Bureau Veritas, n° 2, 1996, 35-39.
(50) P. SLATER : "Time for a change - and it can't come too soon". Lloyd's List, 20 Jan. 1995.
(51) G. KURZ : "The information explosion : safety boom or bureaucratic bonanza ?". BIMCO Review 1996, 397-399.
(52) "Secrecy blights the market. Time for free flow of information". Fairplay, 2 January 1997.
(53) A.S. NUNN : "Maritime information : getting the answer". Insurance Day, 26 Sept. 1996.

the inception of the European Marine STEP Association (EMSA), the Integrated Shipboard Information Technology project (ISIT) and the Maritime Information Society (MARIS), intended to promote research projects in the information technology sector (54).

F - PRIMACY OF HUMAN AND CULTURAL FACTORS

The fact remains that the most important safety breakthroughs in the 21st century will depend less on technological progress than on recognition of the primacy of human factors. Given the increasing complexity of systems, the presence of a human being is both a source of risk and a unique guarantee of the capacity to react to an unforeseen situation. It also helps avoid an exaggerated belief in the infallibility of technology.

This is why all those concerned with safety now put man at the very centre of the prevention system. IMO, which has encouraged adoption of the ISM Code and revision of the STCW Convention, is now concentrating on the establishment of a total approach focussing on the human element. Classification societies developing a total safety approach are increasingly interested in the ergonomics of a ship and its equipment, the subtle relationships between man and machine. Certain countries are financing ambitious research projects into human factors: in 1998, Australia will complete its FASTOH study of fatigue, stress and health on board ships; the United States is banking on its Prevention Through People (PTP) programme to reduce accidents and pollution.

The greatest difficulty may be for the maritime world to go through a cultural revolution, abandoning the cults of evasion and compliance in favour of a genuine safety culture (55). The attitude of avoidance that typified the behaviour of certain operators in the Eighties and Nineties developed against an extremely competitive background, in which business took precedence over ethics: the costs of conforming to regulations were so high that it was to a company's ultimate advantage to evade them (56).

The conformity culture, sometimes known as the "fault culture", dominates the shipping transport industry at the end of this century, leading to an attitude of submissiveness towards regulatory constraints. In an environment characterised by the extension of civil and criminal liability, and the growing demand for compensation and the temptation to seek a scapegoat (57), the operator is concerned mainly with observing the rules as cheaply as possible, rather than the quest for more efficient ways of improving safety (58). The driving force is the fear of blame and punishment (59).

In the maritime world of the very late 20th century, few companies yet argue for reliance on a safety culture (60). This consists of creating an environment in which nothing is done and no measure taken without first assessing the likely consequences for safety (61). This ideal, in which safety becomes a daily concern, rather than a factor to be taken into account after something has happened, involves not just the shipowner but all those with an interest in

(54) A. SERIDJI : "Information technology : challenges and commitment for Bureau Veritas in the XXIst Century". Bureau Veritas, Paris, 19 June 1997.
(55) D. MOREBY : "Cults and cultures in modern shipping". BIMCO Bulletin, vol. 91, n° 4, 1996, 32-35.
(56) "Operators still evade rules". Lloyd's List, 31 March 1997.
(57) D. SALAS : "Du déclin de la faute à la tentation du bouc émissaire". Revue Droit et Culture n° 31, 1996/1, 7-18.
(58) M. NEUMEISTER : "Sécurité maritime. Un déficit culturel". JMM, 5 May 1995, 1097-1098.
(59) A. DE BIEVRE : "Too much talk on liability is misguided". Lloyd's List, 16 Sept. 1996.
(60) Cf case of Shell in "Safety culture proves a life saver". Insurance Day, 12 July 1995.
(61) W. O'NEIL. Speech at Annual Meeting of NUMAST, May 1995.

the issue. It cannot be imposed by regulations, but demands strong involvement by company management (62).

In adopting Resolution A.792 in 1995, calling upon governments and international organisations to make efforts aimed at establishing a safety culture, IMO threw down one of its most ambitious challenges to the maritime world: to behave in such a way that everyone involved with ships will feel responsible for safety. Patience and determination will be essential: a few years may be needed to amend regulations, but it will take decades to bring about a thorough change in the dominant culture of shipping.

G - END OF TRADITIONAL IDEOLOGIES AND EMERGENCE OF NEW CONCEPTS

696. - The change is so profound that it will require a radical transformation of ways of thinking, and the reexamination of many traditions and customs. The principle of freedom of the seas is particularly under fire. Given the perils of maritime navigation, it is becoming less and less tolerable for an operator to retain the inalienable right to run substandard ships or for a flag State to misuse its sovereignty by facilitating their registration.

New values are gaining on the traditional dogmas of freedom. Take the safety principle expressed in the maxim "cleaner seas and safer ships". In the name of prevention and protection, increasingly stringent constraints are being imposed on navigation (63) (such as compulsory reporting, required for shipping traffic management), and on application of conventions (such as compulsory notification of implementation of regulations, required under IMO's new control and audit powers).

The principle of precaution is another response to the criticisms raised by the occurrence of major disasters at sea. Already implemented for environmental protection, this approach consists of "taking appropriate preventive measures when there is reason to think that substances or energy introduced into the marine environment could cause damage, even in the absence of conclusive proof of the existence of a causal link between the items inroduced and their effects". As Principle 15 of the Rio Declaration puts it, in the event of risk of serious or irreversible damage, the absence of absolute scientific certainty should not be used as a pretext for inaction (64).

This principle of precaution is beginning to be applied in safety regulations. Signatories to the 1996 Stockholm Agreement have not awaited completion of investigations into the *Estonia* disaster before strengthening rules on the stability of carferries plying the North Sea or the Baltic. This new approach will probably lead organisations to review the process of safety decision-making and management, study the cost-efficiency ratio of measures to be taken, examine whether pursuit of the activity in question meets an essential need of the community, create economic incentives to encourage a responsible attitude to safety. Application of the "polluter pays" or "user pays" concept (65) could in future lead certain coastal States to collect taxes, fines or dues from potential polluters, such as owners of substandard vessels, and use the proceeds to fund new prevention schemes.

The principle of precaution is intended to find cost-effective ways of achieving the goal of preventing accidents. If existing provisions fail to meet this purpose, they will have to

---

(62) G. KURZ : "Developing a safety culture : Teamwork makes talk reality". Surveyor, Sept.1996, 8-9.

(63) E. GOLD : "International Shipping and the New Law of the Sea: New Directions for a traditional Use". Ocean Development and International Law, Vol. 20, 1990, 433-444.

(64) Guidelines on the application of the precautionary approach in the context of specific IMO activities. MEPC 37/10/5, 16 June 1995, Annex.

(65) "The user pays". Lloyd's List, 29 July 1996.

be amended to make them cost-effective ; otherwise, new provisions will have to be sought out and developed.

H - OVER-REGULATION AND FRAGMENTATION

This law on safety, so difficult to understand and interpret, so complicated to implement and enforce, raises a new set of problems for those concerned with safety. These arise from the fact that the very standards that are intended to introduce some order into the international community are in fact becoming a source of confusion and uncertainty, paralysing the development of international trade or affecting its efficiency. This situation is disturbing the shipping industry, and several of its representatives have denounced the harmful effects of over-regulation (66), and the fragmentation of rules in an internationally highly competitive sector (67). It is also worrying for lawyers, faced with the "aberrant proliferation of so-called technical law" and its "esoteric aspects", which mean that it is reserved for experts, alone capable of understanding and explaining it (68).

Difficulties arise from the fact that the international standards governing safety at sea are heterogeneous, many in number and incomplete. It is hard to see how this trend towards growing complexity can be turned around after the Millennium.

Lack of uniformity will persist as long as the public regulations issued by States exist alongside private standards drawn up by the shipping industry (69). But even if only public regulations remained, they would still be extremely dense, with the same instruments containing legal provisions and technical requirements, mandatory requirements and mere recommendations.

All those concerned with safety express their disquiet at the prolixity of international organisations and the textual density of the resulting documents. For example, it has been calculated at IMO that each State has to produce more than thirty-two thousand pages of documents in order to amend a standard (70). IMO has admitted that it was publishing some fifteen million pages of documents annually (71). The technical nature of the problems raised cannot alone explain this regulatory frenzy, which in fact arises from two phenomena: increasing competition among legislators who tend to try to outbid one another, and the growing pace of the lawmaking process.

Another source of anxiety is the increasing speed at which the law changes. Technical standards also become obsolete far more quickly, forcing IMO member States to keep a close watch on technological innovations, so that they can draw the necessary regulatory conclusions. These endless changes place an ever-increasing workload on IMO (72). The thirst for improvement can detract from what is already very positive. The strenuous efforts to make international regulations so rich, so precise, so detailed, makes them far too complicated to be translated easily and effectively into national legislation. Effects may even be perverse, such as the creation of a two-speed system, in which legislative and regulatory differences among States reflect their level of economic development.

(66) Speech by G. KURZ, Chairman of OCIMF. Tanker Legislation Conference. Washington, Oct. 1995. Cf also "New Age Shipping". Lloyd's List, 6 Oct. 1995.
(67) P.N. TSAKOS : "Shipping beyond 2000 - Views of an independent owner". BIMCO Bulletin, vol. 91 n° 3, 1996, 27-32.
(68) M. REMOND-GOUILLOUD : "Entre Science et Droit, le mirage de l'exactitude". Le Jaune et le Rouge. Revue de la Société amicale des anciens élèves de l'Ecole Polytechnique. N° 513, March 1996, 25-27.
(69) A. DE BIEVRE : "Techno-management emerges as business concept". Lloyd's List, 9 Dec. 1996.
(70) "Atlantic death toll is highest since war". Sunday Times, 13 Feb. 1994.
(71) "Secretary General calls for mandatory training". Lloyd's List, 24 Sept. 1987.
(72) Ph. BOISSON : "La problématique des normes". Colloque de Nantes. Droit maritime 13 and 14 May 1997.

Despite the proliferation of regulatory organisations, certain loopholes persist in the law. Overlapping and duplication of efforts to promote maritime safety continue, in the absence of global coordination. Even more serious is the absence of any solution for certain issues involving the attributions of more than one organisation, such as the problem of ship/port interfaces (73). On 23 November 1995, IMO took the first step towards ending this situation: Resolution A.798, which indicates a strategy for this interface, suggests that the London-based organisation will provide a global platform on the issue. Other initiatives will have to taken in the near future to strengthen coordination and cover all aspects of safety.

I - RISK OF TWO-TIER SAFETY REGIME : INTERNATIONAL SOLIDARITY AND PREVENTION

698. - Accidents at sea cost money (74) ; but their prevention by improving safety standards also has its cost. A study has shown that the increase in regulations has significant effects on the price of seaborne transport (75). Introduction of the ISM Code will result in expenditure put at between Usd 50 000 and 400 000 for each company in its initial phase, plus Usd 10 000 annual costs. The annual cost of providing crew training under the terms of the STCW Convention amounts to more than Usd 15 000. The extra costs to be borne by shipping companies for environmental protection will double, from about 2.5 to 5 per cent of their pretax revenues.

Who will pay for greater safety ? Ultimately, the shipowner or the charterer are mere intermediaries, and the cost will have to be passed on to the end consumer, namely passengers and purchasers of the goods carried (76).

Another consequence will be the increasing difficulty for developing countries with few financial resources or little experience in the matter to implement regulatory stipulations. Without greater North-South solidarity, the new century could see the emergence of the spectre of two-tier safety : regulations with the sternest requirements reserved for rich countries, able to offer international transport services, and more limited regulations, more or less adhered to by Third World shipping, which would be confined to domestic traffic.

The worst may never happen, of course. But the experience of recent years has shown that, with few exceptions, the most tragic shipping accidents have occurred in the seas around developing countries.

Aware of what is at stake, IMO has introduced a cooperation programme, unfortunately handicapped by lack of funds. The only way of guaranteeing a durable future for this programme will be to find fresh sources of financial backing. Some will probably come from the United Nations, as in the past, but the whole of the maritime community will also have to take on a growing share of the burden in the years to come (77).

J - THE AIR SAFETY MODEL

699. - The air transport industry shows many similarities with maritime transport. Both are cyclical activities which in recent years have suffered a severe crisis. Airlines have been

---

(73) H.J. ROSS : "Correlation of ship and port safety". 3rd International Conference on Safety in Port Environment, Bremen, 10-12 Oct. 1994.
(74) About USD 10 billion per year in IMO : "Optimum maritime safety demands a focus on people". World Maritime Day, 1997.
(75) DREWRY : "Safer cleaner ships. What are the financial implications ?" London, Sept. 1996.
(76) R. GOSS : "The future of maritime safety". 8th Chua Chor Teck Annual Memorial Lecture. Singapore 12 Jan. 1994. Department of Maritime Studies and International Transport. University of Wales Cardiff.
(77) "IMO seaking excellence through cooperation. World Maritime Day, 1996.

faced with over-capacity on an increasingly deregulated market, particularly in the United States, which has led to a price war, damaging profitability.

Despite the crisis, the aeronautical sector can feel some satisfaction about its safety record. The 1996 report of the International Civil Aviation Organisation shows that, in relation to the volume of traffic, the number of passengers killed per 100 million passenger-kilometres fell from 0.07 in 1977 to 0.04 in 1997. Over the same period, the number of fatal aircraft accidents per 100 million aircraft-kilometres decreased from 0.18 to 0.12, while the number of fatal aircraft accidents per 100 000 landings also dropped from 0.24 to 0.14 (78).

There are obvious difficulties in comparing air transport with sea transport (79): aircraft are engaged mainly in passenger transport, while ships carry far more freight. One thing is clear, however: the air safety system has the undeniable advantage over marine safety that it can create and enforce application and maintenance of high safety standards on an international scale, regardless of the economic circumstances of players on the market. I feel it appropriate, therefore, to conclude this book by considering the lessons that the maritime community can draw from the aviation model.

700. - Unlike maritime navigation, where the principle of freedom of the high seas has ruled supreme for centuries, air transport was from the beginning based on the concept of safety, regarded as a vital condition for its worldwide expansion. This historical antinomy has led to profound differences between the two systems that have been set up. The maritime model encouraged the emergence of many different sets of regulations, with wide disparities in their application, encouraged by the splitting of responsibility for surveys among different authorities. The aviation model has resulted in the introduction of fixed legislation, implemented uniformly by a single regulator, the State of registration (80). This has created conditions under which fair competition can take place among the various operators on the aviation market.

One could find many other differences between safety at sea and in the air, including deeply rooted disparities between the two industries from the technical, economic and legal standpoints (81). At the dawn of the third millennium, the question remains whether the maritime world should remain a prisoner of its history and traditions, or whether it should follow the air safety model, with the risks of additional regulations and constraints that this would imply (82).

The maritime safety system could draw at least five lessons from aviation:

1. Establish regulations based on fundamental safety goals, laying down performance standards on the basis of quantified assessment of risks, and analysis of the costs and benefits of new standards. These regulations should also be based on an international agreement establishing an acceptable level of risks for transport by sea.

---

(78) Annual Report of the Council. 1996. Appendix 12, table II A-49.
(79) IMO. Sub-committee on Standards of Training and Watchkeeping : "The International Civil Aviation Organization (ICAO) and the regulation of the competence of personnel in the aviation industry". STW 25/INF.3, 7 Sept. 1993.
(80) C. HODG : "Outline of International Legal Framework", in Flag and Quality - Dilemma or opportunities. Seminar IBC London, 30 Nov. 1992.
(81) "Disparate industries". Lloyd's Ship Manager, June 1993, 17.
(82) "Ideas out of thin air". Tradewinds.

2. Improve enforcement of standards on a global scale, introducing greater uniformity into the mechanisms of State control (83). Some go as far as to suggest the creation of a single authority in each State to be responsible for maritime safety, in line with aviation organisations such as the CAA or FAA (84). These bodies would be independent of administrations whose role it is to support the regulated activity (85).

3. Reduce the huge number of inspections and standards required for the construction and operation of ships. This kind of rationalisation would require greater uniformity of types of surveys and survey procedures, and an extension of the role of classification societies. A limited number of these societies would be duly authorised by states for any action relating to safety, and they would enjoy the confidence of all maritime industries.)

4. Bring about greater transparency in the publication of safety information. This implies better cooperation among states in technical investigations after accidents, the establishment of maritime accident and incident databanks, and closer involvement of shipbuilders in the control of failures occurring on ships in operation (86).

5. Establish procedures to improve the selection and training of seafarers, ensure observance of working hours and rest periods, check regularly the skills and physical condition of seamen, and in general learn to discipline the profession (87) in controlling the human element on a day-to-day basis.

Faced with the new challenges of safety, the maritime world is undergoing far-reaching changes, with the appearance of new players on the international stage leading to the development of new ways of functioning, and the disappearance of certain values and ideologies that are incompatible with the prevention of accidents.

The safety system has begun the process of mutation, tending to bring it closer to the air safety model. Technical advances in shipbuilding and navigation are encouraging certain parallels. For example, control of speed is bringing about radical changes in the conditions of transport by sea. Regulations affecting highspeed craft (HSC) will soon be based on a formal safety assessment, ships' bridges will have the most sophisticated computer tools, in no way inferior to aircraft pilots' cabins, ships will be equipped with voyage data recorders, the equivalent of aeronautical black boxes. Tomorrow will also see the generalised use of transponders, those automatic data transmission systems that will enable the authorities to regulate maritime traffic.

Highspeed craft offer some idea of the shipping of the future, in which new safety requirements will impose the same constraints on operators as those in the aviation sector.

(83) R. SUNDERLAND : "Port State Control: a flag State view point". IBC Conference Documentation on Port State Control. New solution or new problem ? London, 7 Dec. 1993.

(84) Ian McGRATH : "Oil transportation in an in creasingly regulated environment". Shipping World and Shipbuilder, Oct. 1994, 15-19.

(85) Lord CARVER : "An independent view of ship safety". Flag and quality conference. IBC Seminar, London, 30 Nov. 1992.

(86) M. MEEK, W R. BROWN, K.G. FULFORD : "A shipbuilder's view of safety". Marine Policy and Management, vol. 12, n° 4, Oct./Dec. 1985, 251-262.
D.J. MACKENZIE : "Response to the question raised at the 1990 Conference of the IUMI". London, 19 Sept. 1990. The Nautical Institute, Loss Prevention.

(87) J. SPRUYT : "Learning discipline from the world of aviation". Lloyd's List, 24 July 1995.

INDEX